Table of Contents

Math Manipulatives

Below are suggested materials to support the activities in this book and help you create a stimulating math environment in your home. Most of these can be purchased at a teacher store.

- paper
- two-pocket folders
- Unifix cubes
- pattern blocks
- number line
- hundred chart
- place value mat
- base-ten blocks
- geoboard and rubber bands
- calendar
- analog clock
- digital clock
- "play" clock
- pencils
- resealable plastic bags
- envelopes
- play money (or real)
- money chart
- ice-cream sticks
- buttons
- sea shells
- marbles
- uncooked pasta
- beans
- paper clips
- collections of other small objects
- markers
- crayons
- playground chalk
- double-sided counters
- flash cards
- attribute blocks
- tangrams
- calculator
- game pieces
- dice
- spinners

Place Value

Name 

Outstanding Elephant Math

Connect the dots in order from least to greatest.

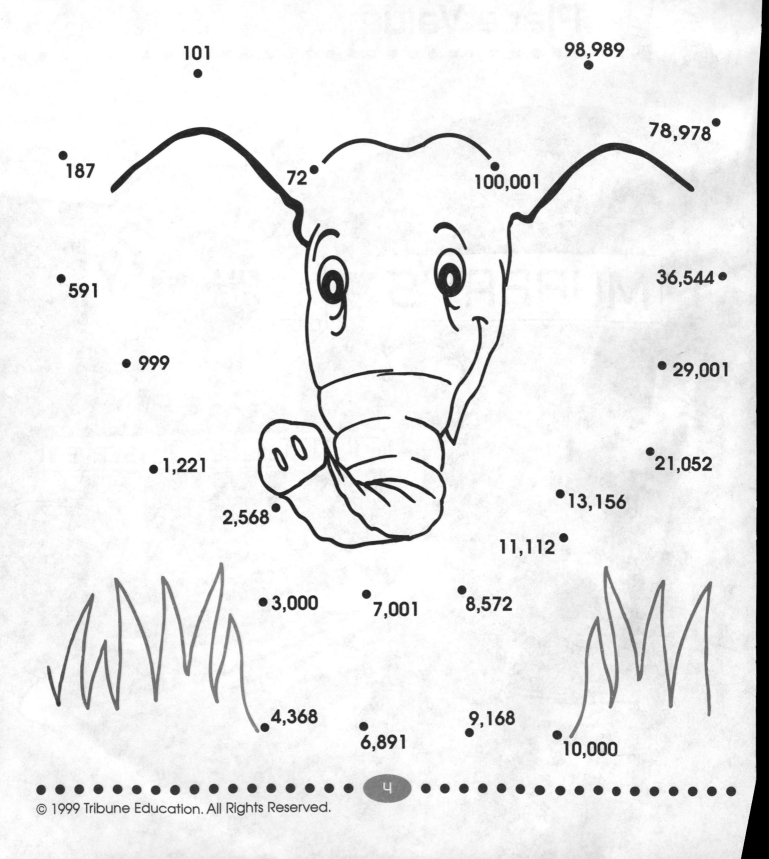

Name ______________________________

Place Value Riddles

Using the clues below, choose the number each riddle describes. As you read, draw an **X** on all the numbers that do not fit the clue. After you have read all the clues for each riddle, there should be only one number left.

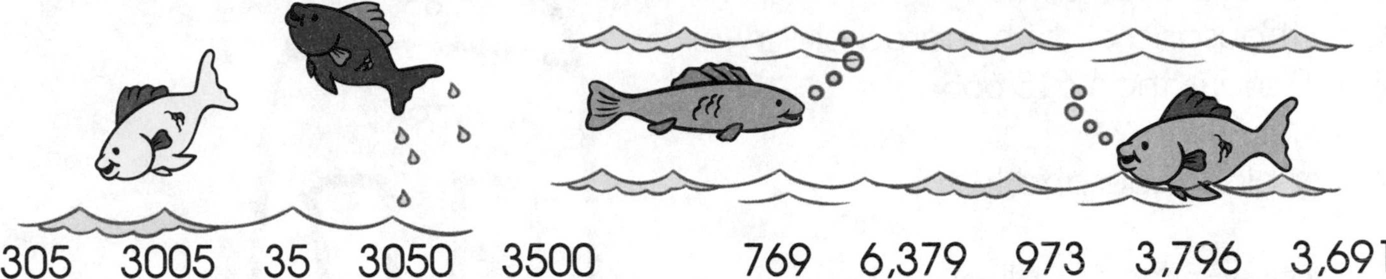

305 3005 35 3050 3500

1. I am greater than 300.
2. I have a 5 in the ones place.
3. I have a zero in the hundreds place.
4. Circle the number.

769 6,379 973 3,796 3,691

1. I have a number greater than 6 in the tens place.
2. I am between 3,000 and 4,000.
3. I have a 6 in the hundreds place.
4. Circle the number.

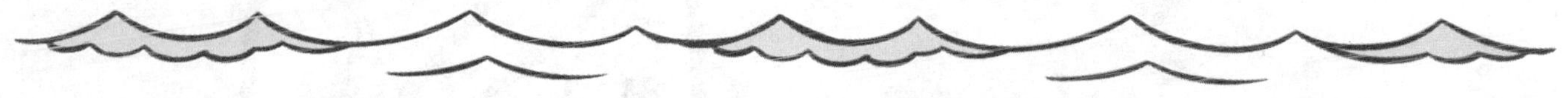

423 4023 324 3,412 2,143

1. I have a 2 in the tens place.
2. I am less than 1,000.
3. I have a 4 in the ones place.
4. Circle the number.

4058 584 845 5048 8540

1. I have a 4 in the tens place.
2. I am greater than 5,000.
3. I have a 0 in the hundreds place.
4. Circle the number.

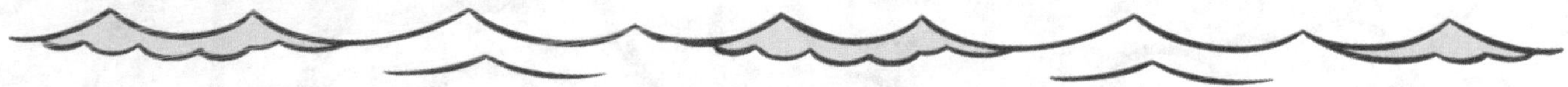

Now, fold a blank sheet of paper in half three times to create eight boxes. Create eight of these place value riddles. You may want to use words like these when writing your clues:

ones, tens, hundreds, thousands place
greater than
less than
have a ___ somewhere

Name ______________________________

4–3–2–1–Blast Off!

Color these spaces red:

- three thousand five
- 1,000 less than 3,128
- six thousand eight hundred eighty-nine
- 100 more than 618,665
- 10 less than 2,981
- fifty-nine thousand two

Color these spaces blue:

- 10 less than 4,786
- eight thousand six hundred two
- 1,000 less than 638,961
- two thousand four hundred fifty-one
- 100 more than 81,136
- 10,000 less than 48,472

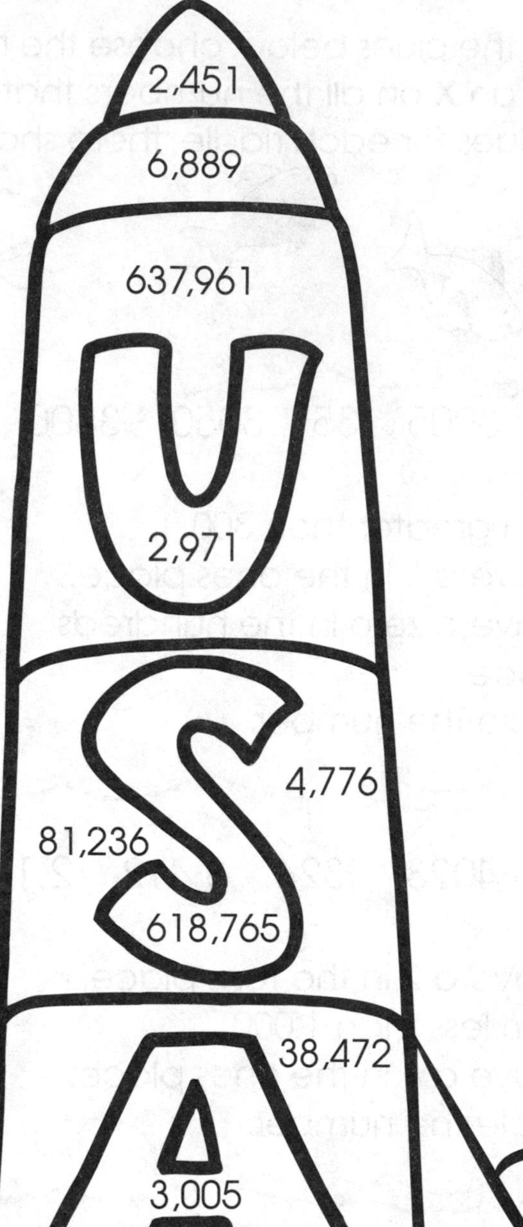

Name ____________________________

Place Value Puzzles

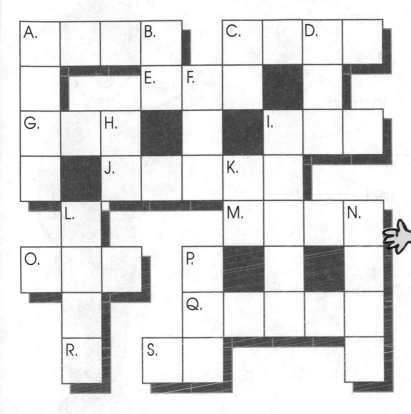

Complete the puzzle.

ACROSS

A. 3 thousand 5 hundred 9
C. 100 less than 8,754
E. one hundred sixty-two
G. seven hundred eighty-two
I. 100, 150, 200, ___
J. 1, 2, 3, 4, 5 mixed up
L. two
M. 100 less than 9,704
O. three zeros
P. eight
Q. 10,000 more than 56,480
R. one
S. 1 ten, 1 one

DOWN

A. 10 more than 3,769
B. ninety-one
C. 28 backwards
D. 5 hundreds, 8 tens, 5 ones
F. 100 less than 773
H. 5, 10, 15, 20, ___
I. ten less than 24,684
K. 2 tens, 9 ones
L. two thousand one
N. 1000, 2000, 3000, _____
P. eight hundreds, 6 tens, 1 one

Name ______________________

Write That Number

Write the numeral form for each number.

Example: three hundred forty-two = 342

1. six hundred fifty thousand, two hundred twenty-five ______________

2. nine hundred ninety-nine thousand, nine hundred ninety-nine ______________

3. one hundred six thousand, four hundred thirty-seven ______________

4. three hundred fifty-six thousand, two hundred two ______________

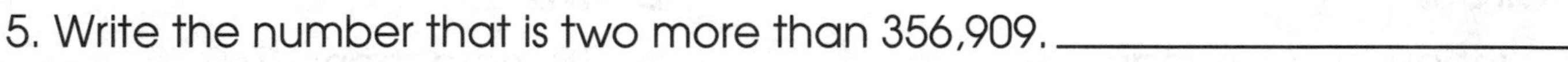

5. Write the number that is two more than 356,909. ______________

6. Write the number that is five less than 448,394. ______________

7. Write the number that is ten more than 285,634. ______________

8. Write the number that is ten less than 395,025. ______________

Write the following numbers in word form.

9. 3,208 ______________

10. 13,656 ______________

Name ______________________________

Place Value

1 , 2 3 4 , 5 6 7

millions | hundred thousands | ten thousands | thousands | hundreds | tens | ones

Write each numeral in its correct place.

1. The number 8,672,019 has:

_____ thousands _____ ten _____ hundred thousands

_____ millions _____ ones _____ ten thousands

_____ hundreds

2. What number has:

6 ones 3 millions 9 tens

7 hundreds 4 ten thousands 8 thousands

5 hundred thousands

The number is ______________________ .

3. The number 6,792,510 has:

_____ ten thousands _____ millions _____ hundreds

_____ ones _____ thousands _____ ten

_____ hundred thousands

4. What number has:

5 millions 3 tens 6 thousands

1 hundred 8 ten thousands 4 ones

0 hundred thousands

The number is ______________________ .

Name ____________________________

Big Numbers Game

Preparation: Cut out the spinners, number cards and gameboard pattern on the next page. Glue the spinners and gameboard onto cardboard and let them dry. Cut them out. Attach a large paper clip or safety pin to the spinner base with a brad or paper fastener. The paper clip (or safety pin) should spin freely.

Give each player one set of ten cards. Also, each player will need a marker and a copy of the gameboard.

Rules: This game involves 2–6 players. The first player is the one who has the most letters in his/her last name. Play goes in a clockwise direction.

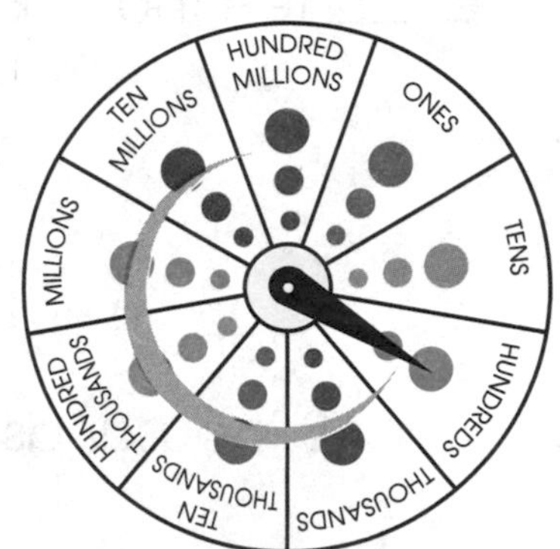

Directions: Player One spins the place value spinner first. Then, he/she spins the numerical spinner. Player One then puts the number marker on the place indicated by the spinner. (For example, if Player One spins hundreds on the place value spinner and 8 on the numerical spinner, he/she should put an 8 number marker in the hundreds place on the gameboard.) If the number shown on either spinner is already filled on the board, Player One loses his/her turn. The first player who fills all the spaces on his/her board and is able to read the number aloud is the winner.

HUNDRED MILLIONS	TEN MILLIONS	MILLIONS	HUNDRED THOUSANDS	TEN THOUSANDS	THOUSANDS	HUNDREDS	TENS	ONES
						8		

Name ________________________________

Game Parts for Big Numbers Game

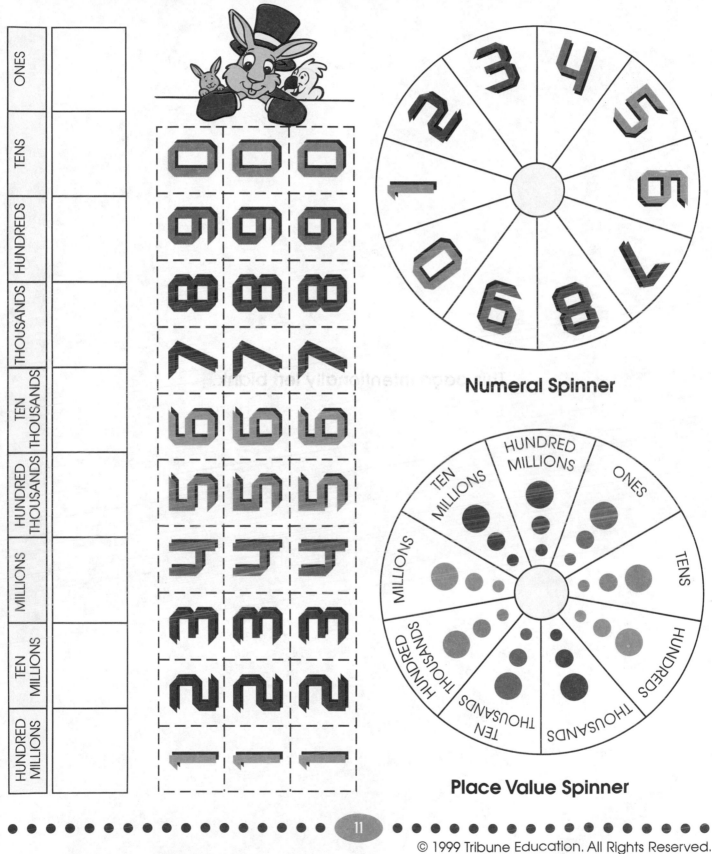

HUNDRED MILLIONS	TEN MILLIONS	MILLIONS	HUNDRED THOUSANDS	TEN THOUSANDS	THOUSANDS	HUNDREDS	TENS	ONES

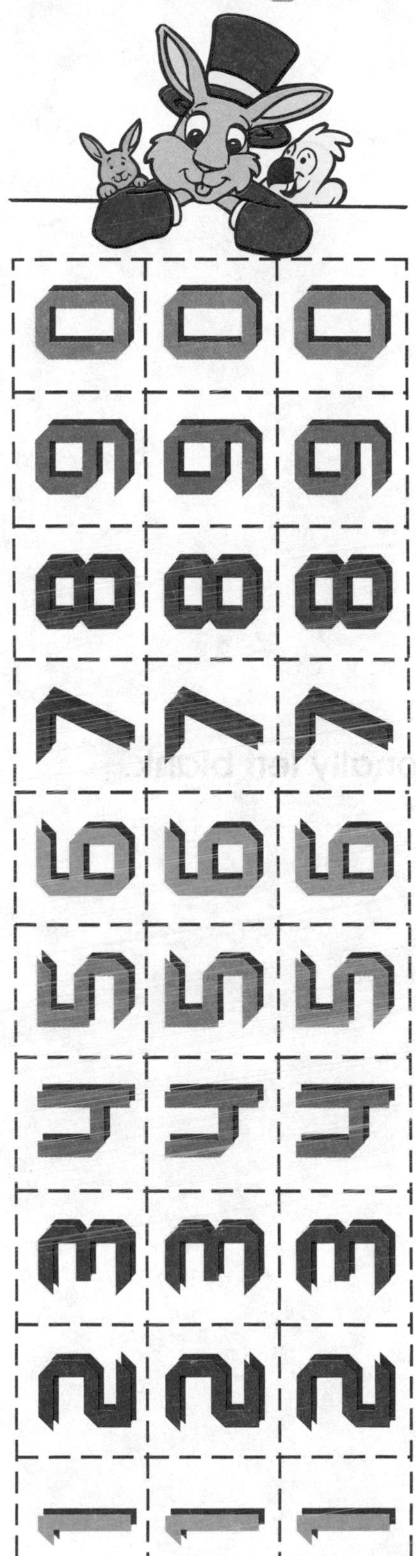

Numeral Spinner

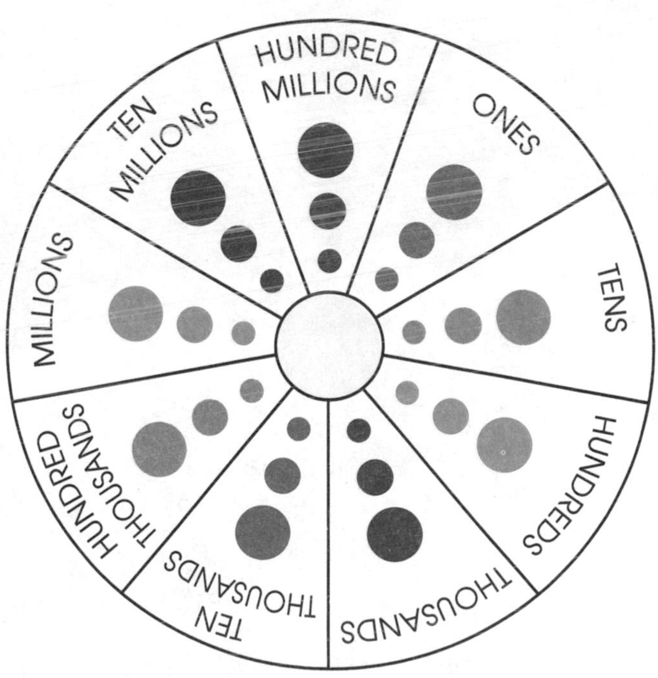

Place Value Spinner

This page intentionally left blank.

Name ___________________________

Estimate by Rounding Numbers

Estimate by rounding numbers to different place values. Use these rules.

Example: Round 283 to the nearest hundred.

- Find the digit in the place to be rounded. (2)83
- Now, look at the digit to its right. (2)83
- If the digit to the right is less than 5, the digit being rounded remains the same.
- If the digit to the right is 5 or more, the digit being rounded is increased by 1.

- Digits to the right of the place to be rounded become 0's. Digits to the left remain the same.

Examples: Round 4,385 . . .

to the nearest thousand	to the nearest hundred	to the nearest ten
4,385	4,385	4,385
3 is less than 5.	8 is more than 5.	5 = 5.
The 4 stays the same.	The 3 is rounded up to 4.	The 8 is rounded up to 9.
4,000	4,400	4,390

Complete the table.

NUMBERS TO BE ROUNDED	ROUND TO THE NEAREST THOUSAND	NEAREST HUNDRED	NEAREST TEN
2,725			
10,942			
6,816			
2,309			
7,237			
959			

Name ______________________

Round, Round, Round You Go

Round each number to the nearest ten.

45 ________ 72 ________ 61 ________ 255 ________

27 ________ 184 ________ 43 ________ 97 ________

Round each number to the nearest hundred.

562 ________ 1,246 ________ 761 ________ 4,593 ________

347 ________ 859 ________ 238 ________ 76 ________

Round each number to the nearest thousand.

6,543 ________ 83,246 ________ 3,741 ________ 66,357 ________

7,219 ________ 9,814 ________ 2,166 ________ 8,344 ________

Round each number to the nearest ten thousand.

32,467 ________ 871,362 ________ 334,212 ________

57,891 ________ 45,621 ________ 79,356 ________

Round each number to the nearest hundred thousand.

116,349 ________ 946,477 ________ 732,166 ________

762,887 ________ 365,851 ________ 225,631 ________

Round each number to the nearest million.

2,765,437 ________ 7,762,997 ________

1,469,876 ________ 5,564,783 ________

14,537,123 ________ 4,117,655 ________

Name ______________________________

The First State

What state is known as the first state? Follow the directions below to find out.

1. If 31,842 rounded to the nearest thousand is 31,000, put an **A** above number 2.
2. If 62 rounded to the nearest ten is 60, put an **E** above number 2 .
3. If 4,234 rounded to the nearest hundred is 4,200, put an **R** above number 7.
4. If 677 rounded to the nearest hundred is 600, put an **L** above number 3.
5. If 344 rounded to the nearest ten is 350, put an **E** above number 5.
6. If 5,599 rounded to the nearest thousand is 6,000, put an **A** above number 4.
7. If 1,549 rounded to the nearest hundred is 1,500, put an **A** above number 6.
8. If 885 rounded to the nearest hundred is 800, put a **W** above number 2.
9. If 521 rounded to the nearest ten is 520, put an **E** above number 8.
10. If 74 rounded to the nearest ten is 80, put an **R** above number 6.
11. If 3,291 rounded to the nearest thousand is 3,000, put an **L** above number 3.
12. If 248 rounded to the nearest hundred is 300, put an **R** above number 4.
13. If 615 rounded to the nearest ten is 620, put a **D** above number 1.
14. If 188 rounded to the nearest ten is 200, put a **W** above number 1.
15. If 6,817 rounded to the nearest thousand is 7,000, put a **W** above number 5.

Peach Blossom
State Flower

Blue Hen Chicken
State Bird

Fort Christina—site of the first state's first permanent settlement. Built by the Swedes and Finns.

____	____	____	____	____	____	____	____
1	2	3	4	5	6	7	8

Addition

Name ______________________________

Dial-A-Word

Use the phone pad to calculate the "value" of the words.

Example: PHONE = 74663
PHONE = 7 + 4 + 6 + 6 + 3 = 26

(your name) = ________________________ = ________

CALCULATOR = ________________________ = ________

DICTIONARY = ________________________ = ________

PET TRICKS = ________________________ = ________

BASEBALL GAME = ________________________ = ________

COMPUTERS = ________________________ = ________

TENNIS SHOES = ________________________ = ________

ADDITION = ________________________ = ________

MENTAL MATH = ________________________ = ________

1 | ABC 2 | DEF 3
GHI 4 | JKL 5 | MNO 6
PQRS 7 | TUV 8 | WXYZ 9
* | 0 | #
CLR | SEND | MUTE

Name ______________________________

Using Number Concepts 2 7 5 4 8

Cut out the set of cards on the next page. Use them to form number sentences that answer the questions below.

1. Use only two cards to list all the ways you can make the sum of 10.

____

____

2. Use only two cards to list all the ways you can make the sum of 13.

____

____

3. Use only two cards to list all the ways you can make the sum of 16.

____

____

4. Use only two cards to list all the ways you can make the sum of 12.

____

____

5. Use only two cards to list all the ways you can make the sum of 15.

____

____

6. Use only two cards to list all the ways you can make the sum of 17.

____

____

7. How did you know you found all the ways?

____

____

Extension: Repeat this exercise using three cards to make each sum.

Name ______________________

Using Number Concepts

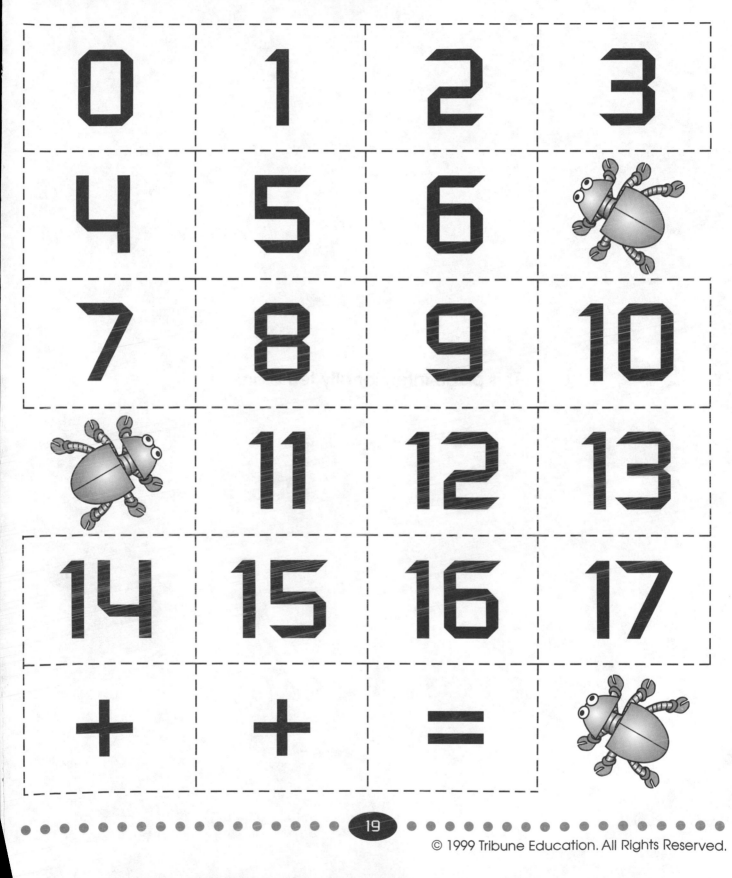

0	1	2	3
4	5	6	
7	8	9	10
	11	12	13
14	15	16	17
+	+	=	

This page intentionally left blank.

Name ______________________________

Mushrooming Addition

Follow the arrows to **add**.

Example: 52 + 28 = 80
28 + 91 = 119
119 + 80 = ?

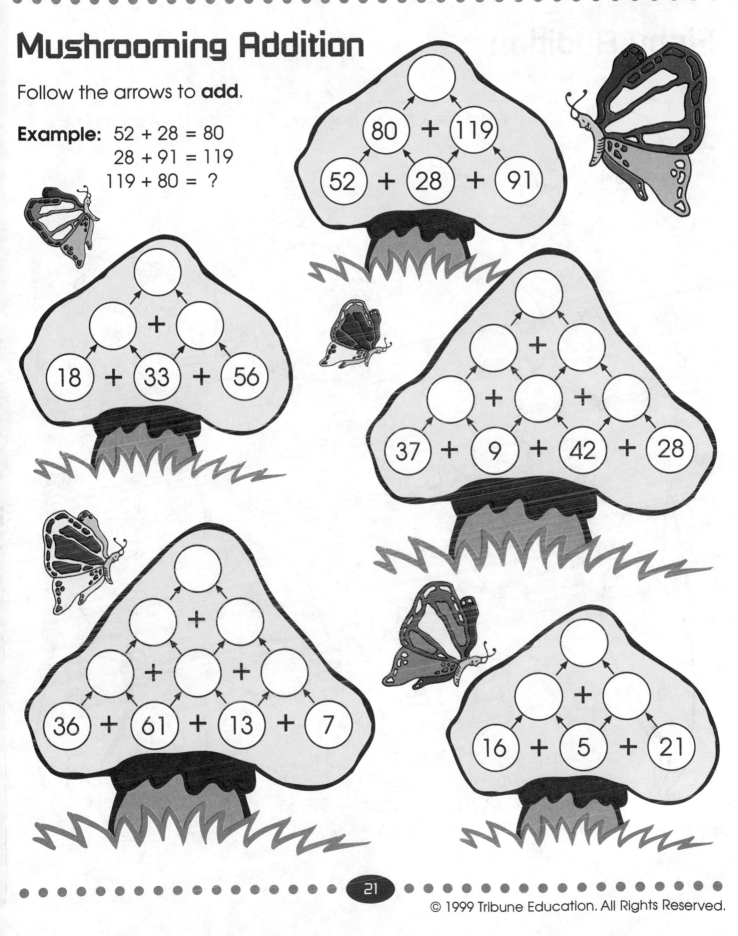

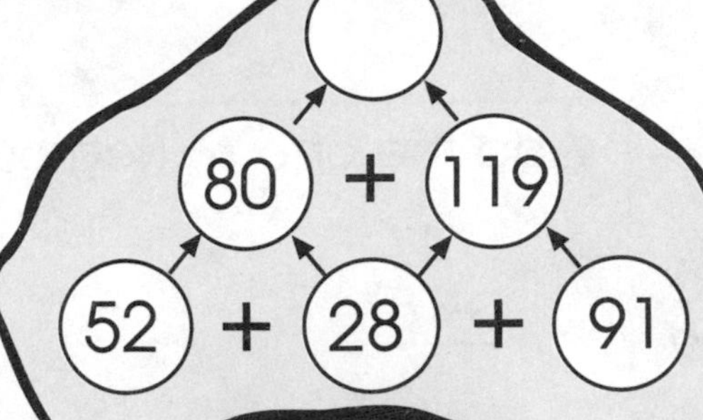

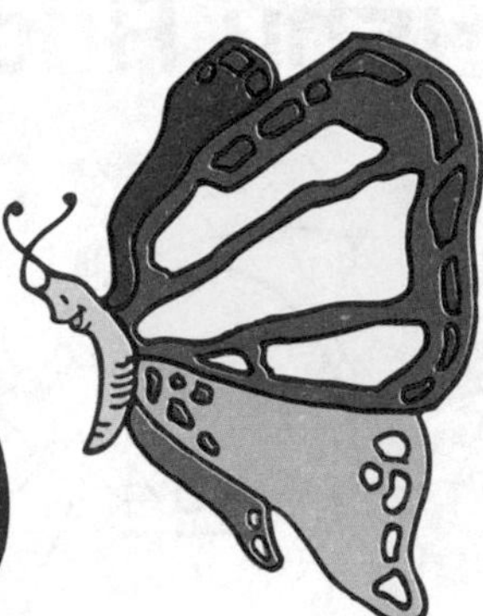

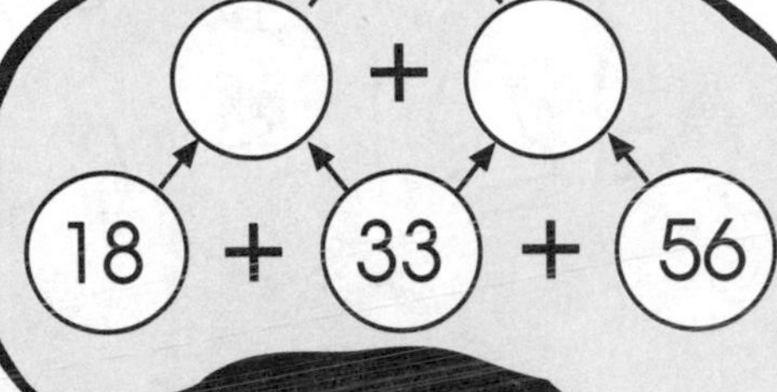

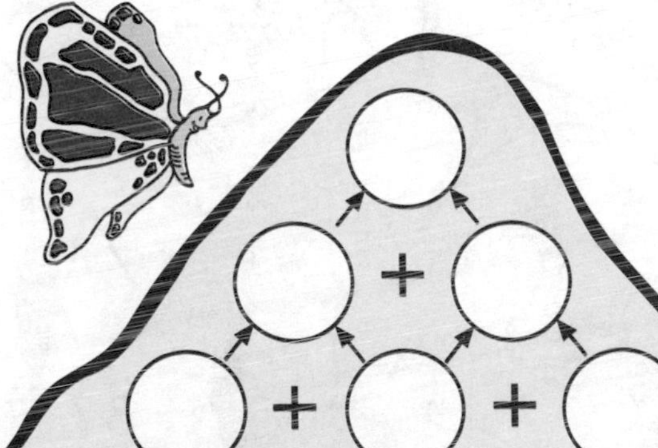

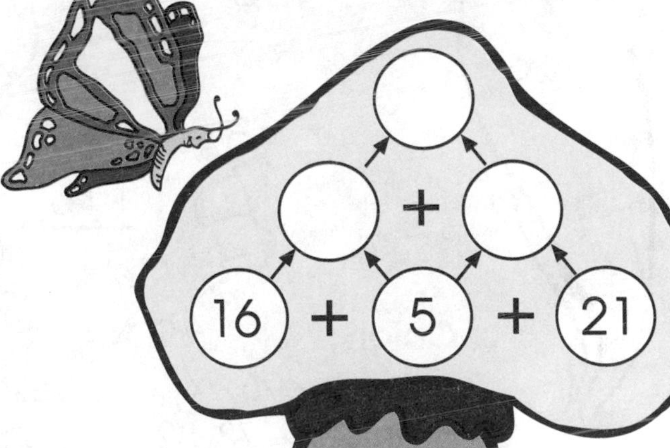

+

16 + 5 + 21

Name ______________________________

Fishy Addition

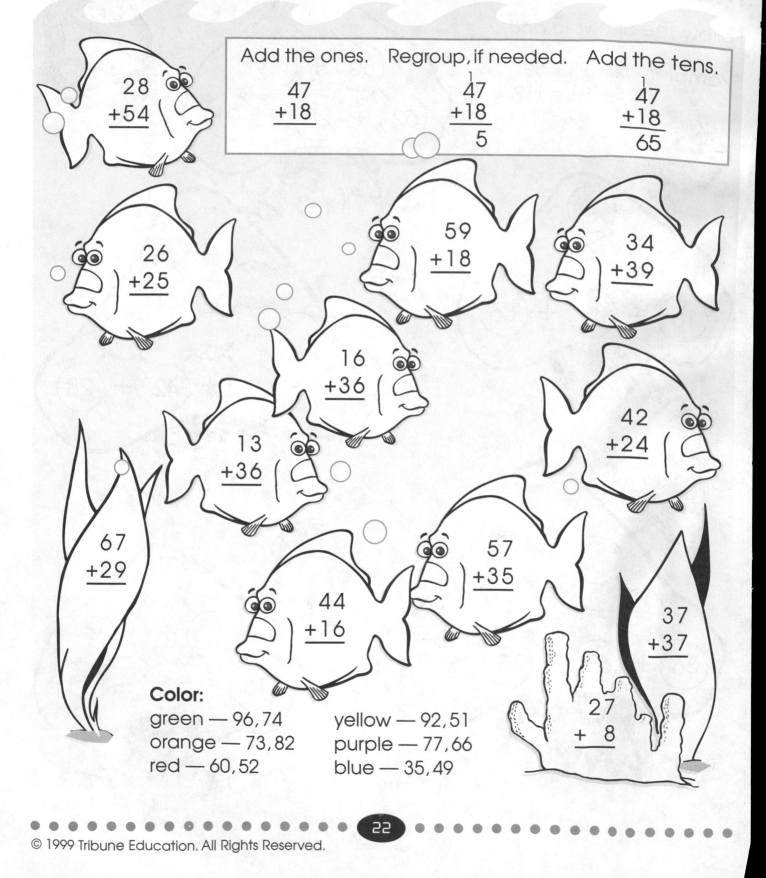

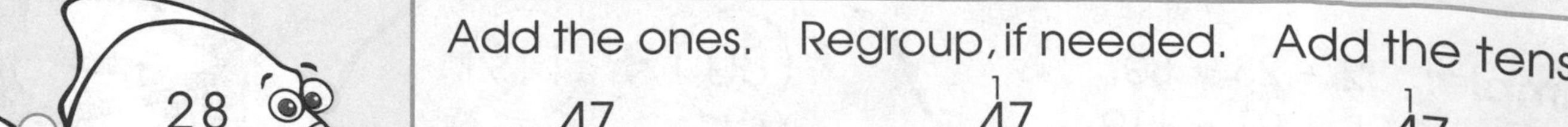

Add the ones.	Regroup, if needed.	Add the tens.
47 +18	1 47 +18 5	1 47 +18 65

28 + 54 =

26 + 25 =

59 + 18 =

34 + 39 =

16 + 36 =

13 + 36 =

42 + 24 =

67 + 29 =

57 + 35 =

44 + 16 =

37 + 37 =

27 + 8 =

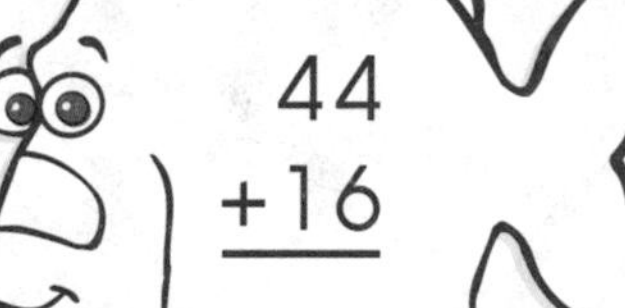

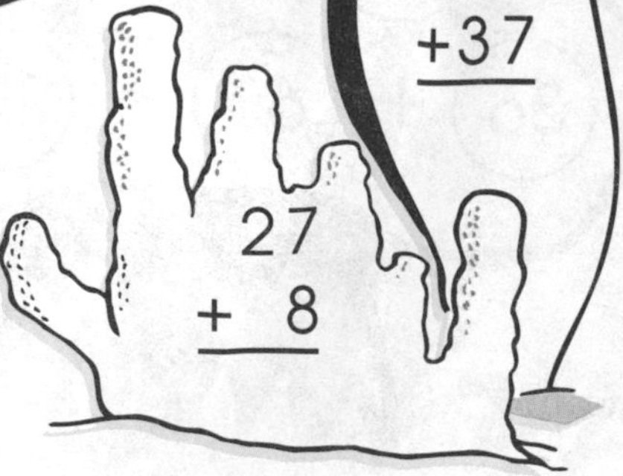

Color:

green — 96, 74
orange — 73, 82
red — 60, 52
yellow — 92, 51
purple — 77, 66
blue — 35, 49

Name ____________________________

Make the Windows Shine!

Add.

476 +319	248 +629	327 +544	
572 +318	815 +177	527 +144	
429 +343	462 +319	462 +529	648 +238
756 +127	563 +208	646 +248	924 + 66
628 +259	526 +347	927 + 46	765 +218

Name ______________________

Addition Ace

Add. Color the ribbon according to the code below.

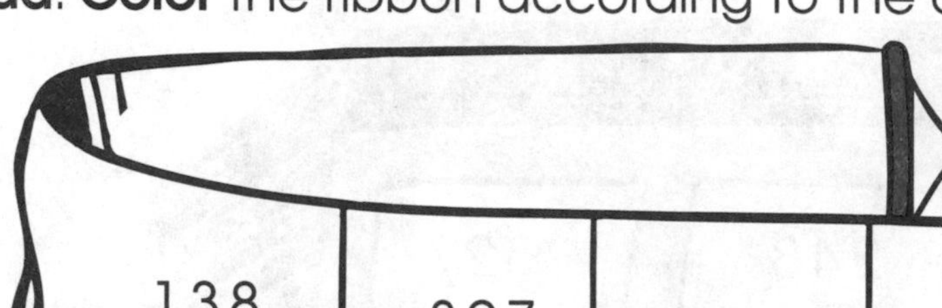

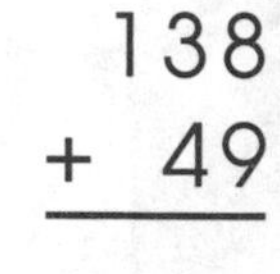

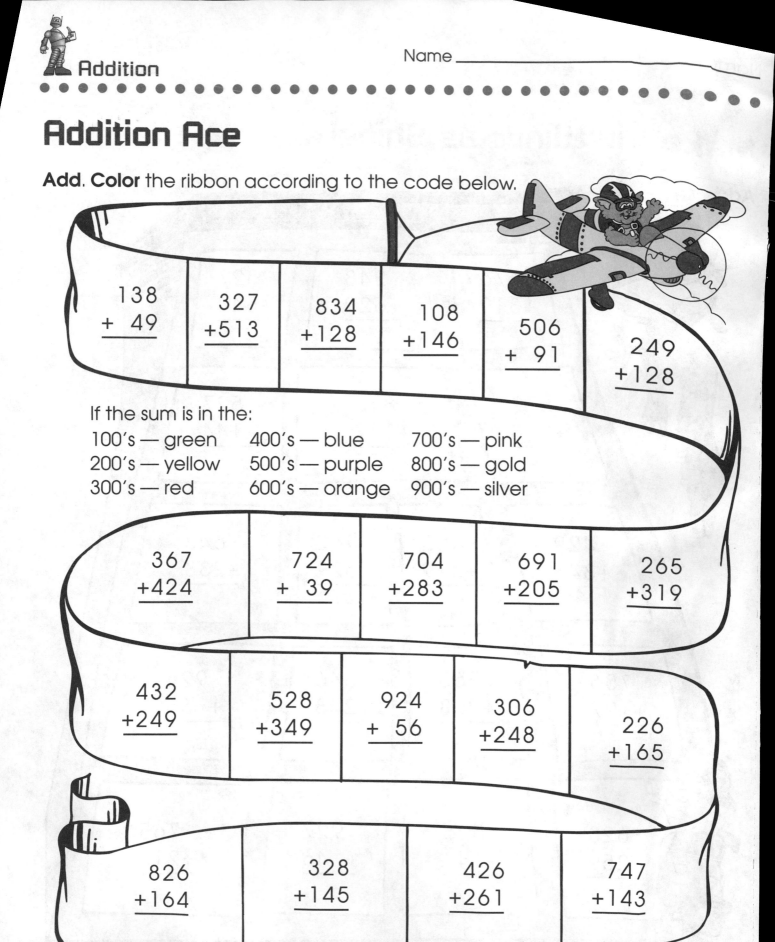

138 + 49	327 +513	834 +128	108 +146	506 + 91	249 +128

If the sum is in the:

100's — green	400's — blue	700's — pink
200's — yellow	500's — purple	800's — gold
300's — red	600's — orange	900's — silver

367 +424	724 + 39	704 +283	691 +205	265 +319

432 +249	528 +349	924 + 56	306 +248	226 +165

826 +164	328 +145	426 +261	747 +143

Name ______________________________

Space Shuttle Addition

Add the ones.	Regroup.	Add the tens and regroup.	Add the hundreds.
362 +439	1 362 +439 1	1 1 362 +439 01	1 1 362 +439 801

Add.

371 +439	629 +184	146 +587	264 +483	438 +290
347 +328	362 +459	528 +391	382 +249	327 +649
283 +346	409 +292		465 +193	566 +283
			283 +519	423 +392
			625 +246	498 +123

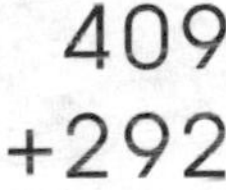

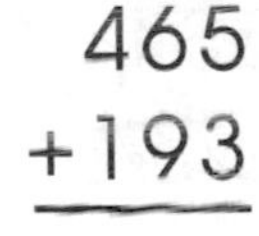

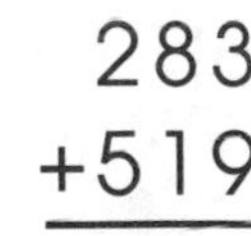

Name ____________________

Underwater Addition

Add.

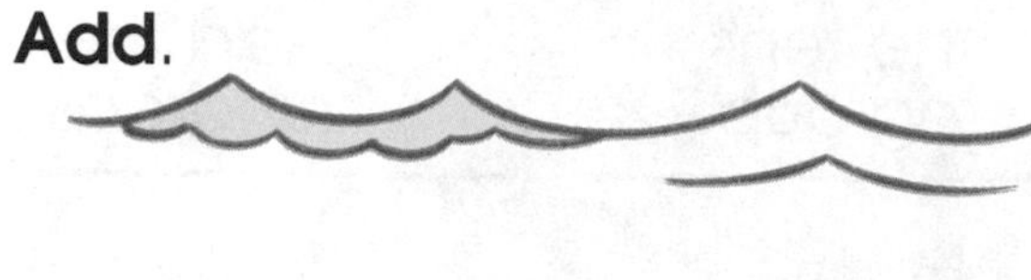

446 +489	476 +527	509 +375	251 +368	
		708 +507	438 +419	334 +278
464 +456	589 +322	288 +377	811 +386	609 +475
	531 +249	810 +428		
831 +438	445 +476	211 +396	230 +284	319 +287
	714 +185	767 +246	911 +427	

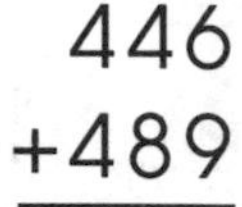

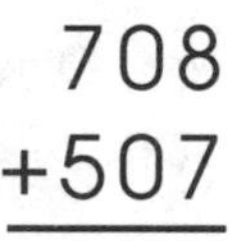

Name ____________________

Let's Climb to the Top!

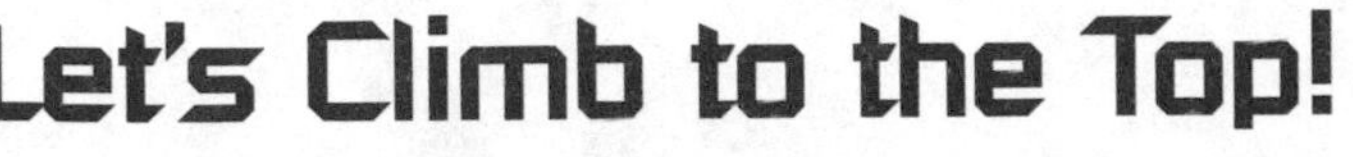

Add.

328 +449	246 +492	462 +781	621 +489	429 +636
	409 +736	921 + 87	562 +614	824 +597
	982 +220	207 +913		826 + 95
	547 +782	284 +493		506 +214
200 +489	684 +519	425 +594	536 +184	623 +192

Name ______________________________

Picnic Problems

Help the ant find a path to the picnic. **Solve** the problems. **Shade** the box if an answer has a 9 in it.

836 + 90	536 +248	952 + 8	362 + 47	486 +293	368 +529
789 526 +214	2,846 +6,478	932 +365	374 +299	835 +552	956 874 + 65
4,768 +2,894	38 456 +3,894	4,507 +2,743	404 +289	1,843 +6,752	4,367 +3,574
639 + 77	587 342 +679	5,379 1,865 +2,348	450 +145	594 +278	459 +367
29 875 +2,341	387 29 +5,614	462 379 +248			

Name ______________________________

Grand Prix Addition

Solve each problem. Beginning at 7,000, run through this racetrack to find the path the race car took. When you reach 7,023, you're ready to exit and gas up for the next race.

3,536 +3,482	1,792 +5,225	3,838 +3,178	3,767 +3,248	1,874 +5,140	4,809 +2,204
3,561 +3,458	4,162 +2,858	3,771 +4,213	4,123 +2,887	5,879 +1,132	1,725 +5,287
3,544 +3,478	1,273 +5,748	2,435 +5,214	4,853 +2,156	3,589 +3,419	5,218 +1,789
5,997 +1,026	5,289 +1,713	3,698 +3,305	4,756 +2,248	4,248 +2,757	4,658 +2,348
4,853 +2,147	2,216 +4,785	1,157 +6,412	3,720 +3,698	3,612 +3,552	1,687 +5,662

Name ____________________

Gearing Up

Add the ones. Regroup.	Add the tens. Regroup.	Add the hundreds. Regroup.	Add the thousands. Regroup.
1	11	1 11	1 11
7,465	7,465	7,465	7,465
+4,978	+4,978	+4,978	+4,978
3	43	443	12,443

Solve the problems. **Color** each answer containing a **3**—blue, **4**—red and **5**—yellow.

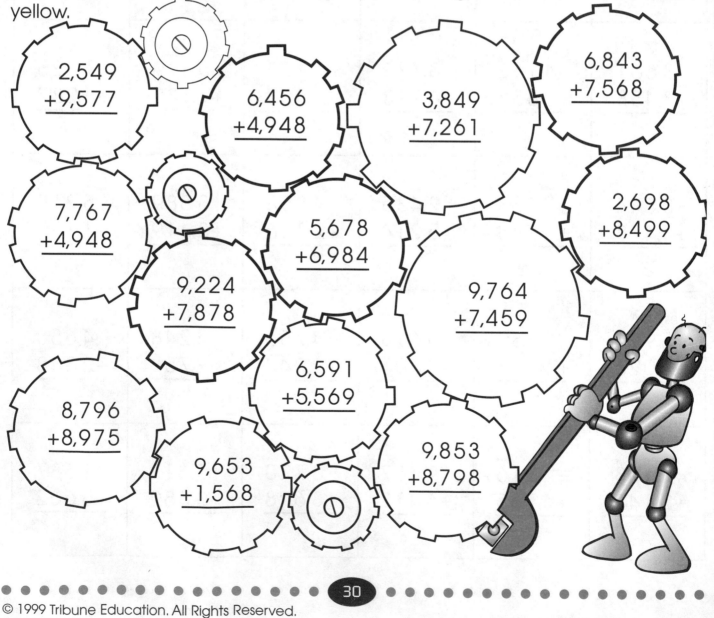

2,549 +9,577	6,456 +4,948
3,849 +7,261	6,843 +7,568
7,767 +4,948	5,678 +6,984
2,698 +8,499	9,224 +7,878
9,764 +7,459	6,591 +5,569
8,796 +8,975	9,653 +1,568
9,853 +8,798	

Name ______________________________

Bubble Math

Add to solve the problems.

- 2,647 + 3,281
- 3,426 + 2,841
- 5,642 + 1,819
- 4,629 + 1,258
- 3,690 + 2,434
- 5,942 + 1,829
- 6,241 + 2,363
- 6,843 + 2,391
- 4,826 + 2,098
- 4,625 + 1,817
- 2,648 + 1,923
- 8,465 + 1,386
- 2,641 + 6,259
- 5,642 + 2,919
- 3,142 + 2,639
- 9,124 + 1,348
- 7,205 + 1,839
- 2,643 + 7,427

Name ____________________

Cotton Pickin' Math

Solve the problems.

7,215	4,621	6,117	2,481	3,204
62	35	24	2,514	182
141	1,318	315	2	23
+2,015	+ 9	+2,136	+ 43	+ 5

8,143	35	7,006	521	496
60	242	242	3,134	8,172
235	6	9	64	83
+1,423	+1,203	+ 31	+ 243	+ 199

6,201	5,242	4,162	6,425
325	342	328	41
41	8	41	324
+2,136	+ 51	+ 503	+ 3

4,205	2,516	5,426
81	310	310
3	82	512
+ 414	+ 3	+ 4

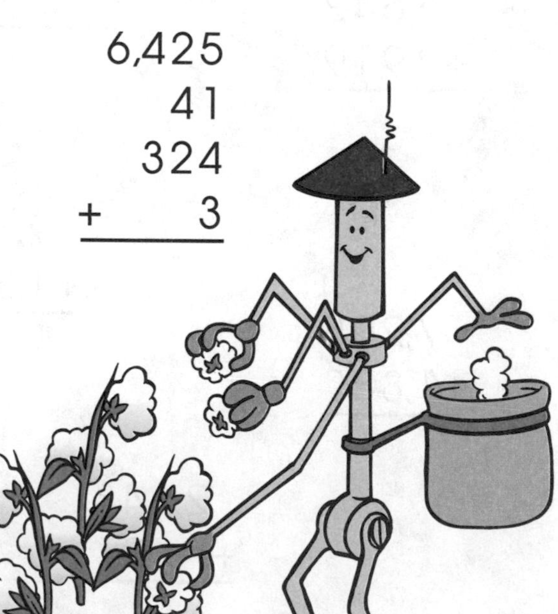

Name ______________________

Palindrome Sums

A **number palindrome** is similar to a word palindrome in that it reads the same backward or forward.

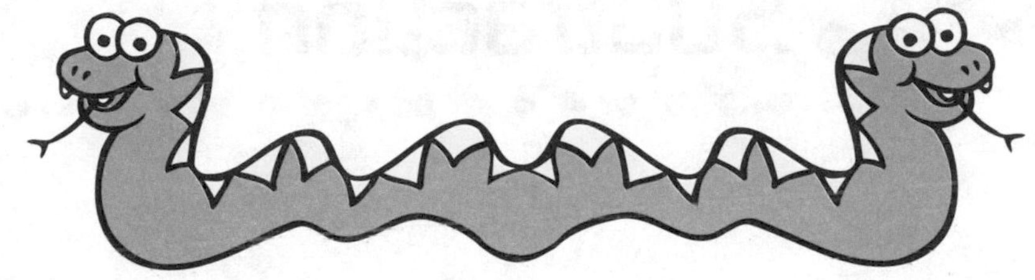

Examples:
75,457
1,689,861

Create number palindromes using addition. **Your Number**

To do this, choose any number: ______________________

652

Then, **reverse** that number's digits: ______________________

256

and **add** the two numbers together: ______________________

652 + 256 = 908

If the sum is not a palindrome, **reverse** the digits in that sum and add as you did in the first step: ______________________

908 + 809 = 1717

Continue in this manner until the sum is a palindrome. ______________________

1717 + 7171 = 8888

____

____

____

The example required three steps to produce a palindrome.
How many steps did it take for you to create a number palindrome? ________

Subtraction

Name ______________________________

Mountaintop Getaway

Solve the problems. **Find** a path to the cabin by shading in all answers that have a 3 in them.

			98 −52	46 −12	68 −17
		79 −53	65 −23	63 −31	86 −32
	59 −45	75 −64	67 −24	87 −54	55 −43
87 −65	44 −32	57 −24	88 −25	75 −61	48 −26
69 −25	95 −24	48 −13	58 −16	35 −13	39 −17

SECRET PATHS

Name ____________________

Stay on Track

Add or **subtract**. **Write** each answer in the puzzle.

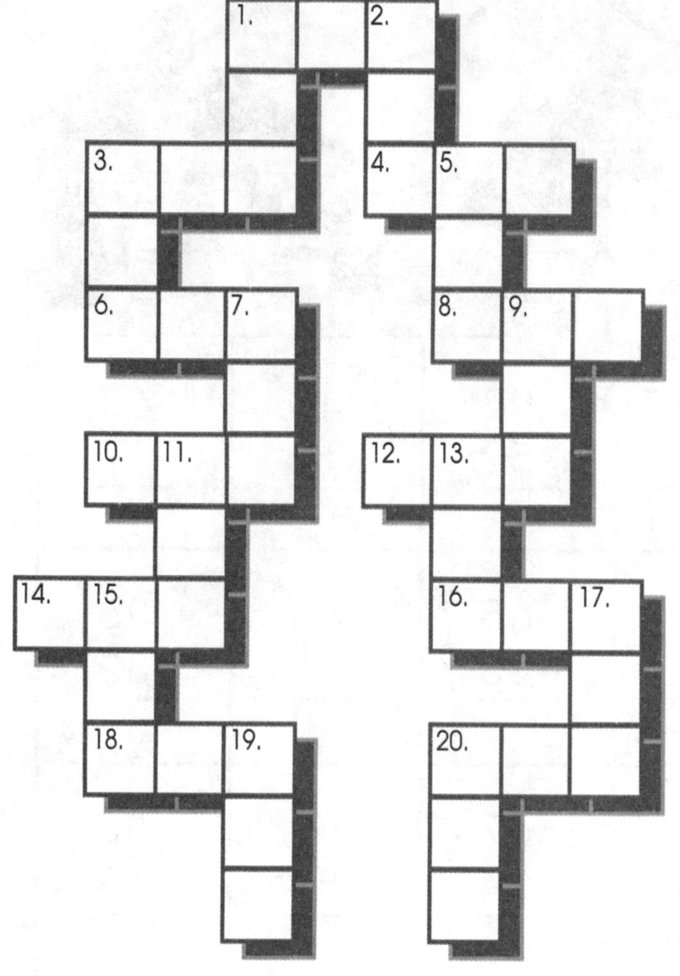

Across

1. 413 + 312 = ____
3. 102 + 415 = ____
4. 223 + 103 = ____
6. 131 + 253 = ____
8. 324 + 321 = ____
10. 207 + 222 = ____
12. 105 + 214 = ____
14. 315 + 400 = ____
16. 121 + 503 = ____
18. 451 + 421 = ____
20. 312 + 281 = ____

Down

1. 859 − 112 = ____
2. 985 − 402 = ____
3. 887 − 344 = ____
5. 789 − 583 = ____
7. 699 − 240 = ____
9. 589 − 100 = ____
11. 767 − 512 = ____
13. 497 − 321 = ____
15. 259 − 151 = ____
17. 974 − 511 = ____
19. 689 − 450 = ____
20. 797 − 236 = ____

Name ____________________

Subtracting Two-Digit Numbers
With Regrouping

Step 1: Decide whether to regroup. In the ones column, 3 is less than 9 so, regroup 4 tens 3 ones to 3 tens 13 ones.

$$\begin{array}{r} \overset{3}{\cancel{4}}\,{}^{1}3 \\ -\,1\;9 \\ \hline \end{array}$$

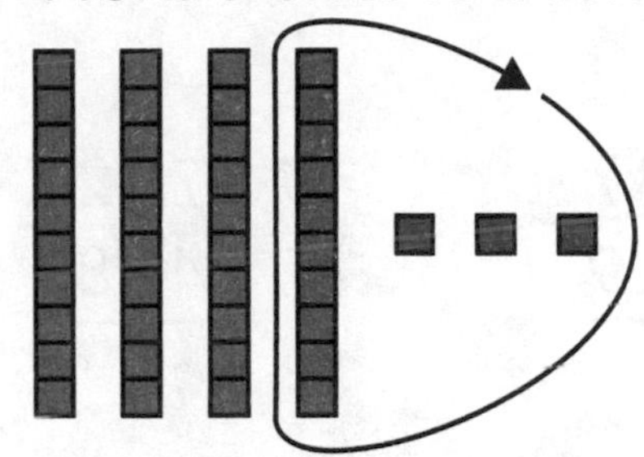

Step 2: Subtract the ones.

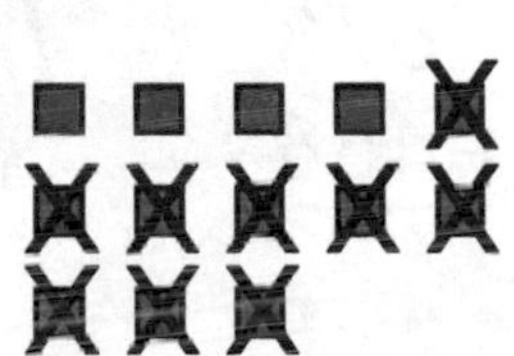

Step 3: Subtract the tens.

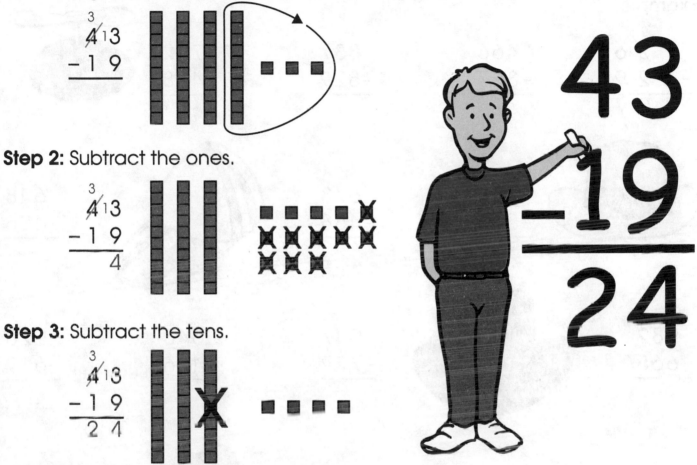

Subtract to find the difference. **Regroup**, if needed.

67	85	86	91	44	61
−34	−12	−47	−48	−27	−34

32	97	60	52	71	83
−14	−36	−45	−22	−19	−15

Name ______________________________

Hats, Hats, Hats

Subtract to find the difference. If the bottom number is larger than the top number in a column, you will need to regroup from the column to the left.

Example:

$$\begin{array}{r} 7\,\overset{2}{\cancel{3}}\,{}^{1}6 \\ -\,6\;2\;9 \\ \hline 1\;0\;7 \end{array}$$

$$\begin{array}{r} 466 \\ -327 \\ \hline \end{array} \qquad \begin{array}{r} 837 \\ -529 \\ \hline \end{array} \qquad \begin{array}{r} 742 \\ -428 \\ \hline \end{array}$$

$$\begin{array}{r} 784 \\ -565 \\ \hline \end{array} \qquad \begin{array}{r} 673 \\ -458 \\ \hline \end{array}$$

$$\begin{array}{r} 648 \\ -426 \\ \hline \end{array}$$

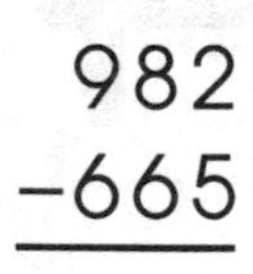

$$\begin{array}{r} 982 \\ -665 \\ \hline \end{array}$$

$$\begin{array}{r} 947 \\ -729 \\ \hline \end{array} \qquad \begin{array}{r} 543 \\ -426 \\ \hline \end{array} \qquad \begin{array}{r} 928 \\ -619 \\ \hline \end{array}$$

$$\begin{array}{r} 847 \\ -628 \\ \hline \end{array} \qquad \begin{array}{r} 427 \\ -318 \\ \hline \end{array} \qquad \begin{array}{r} 524 \\ -318 \\ \hline \end{array} \qquad \begin{array}{r} 245 \\ -126 \\ \hline \end{array}$$

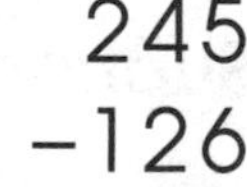

$$\begin{array}{r} 852 \\ -328 \\ \hline \end{array} \qquad \begin{array}{r} 545 \\ -221 \\ \hline \end{array}$$

Name ______________________________

Soaring to the Stars

Connect the dots in order and form two stars. Begin one star with the subtraction problem whose difference is 100 and end with the problem whose difference is 109. Begin the other star with 110 and end with 120. Then, **color** the pictures.

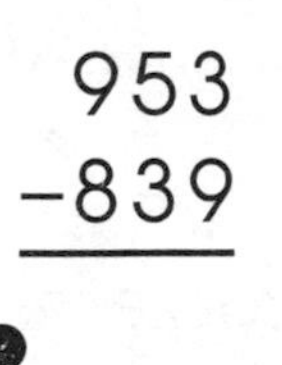

953 − 839

774 − 658

493 − 378

364 − 247

751 − 638

844 − 726

839 − 728

570 − 458

446 − 327

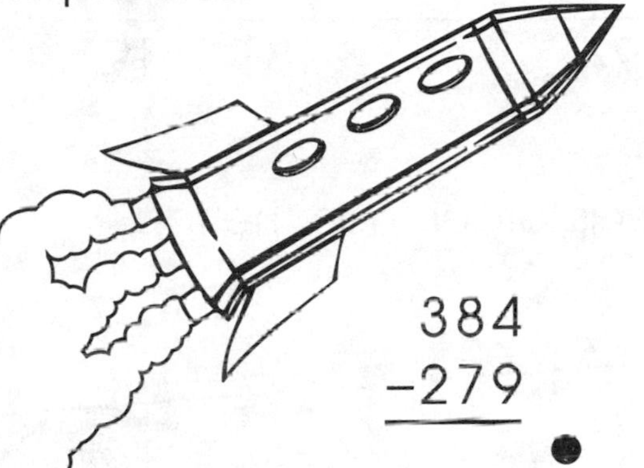

384 − 279

383 − 273

696 − 576

653 − 547

590 − 487

575 − 471

493 − 386

862 − 754

359 − 257

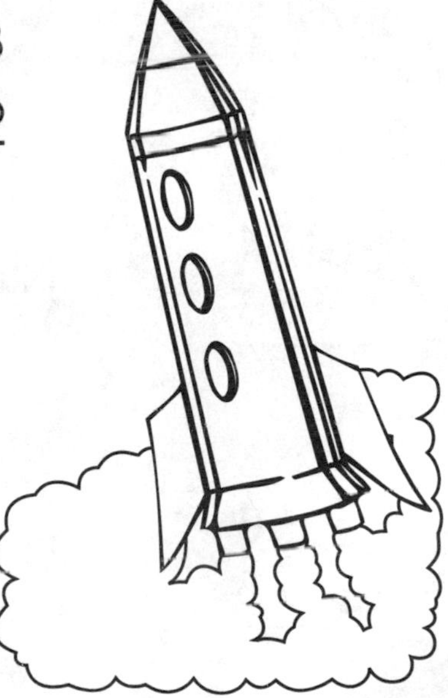

190 − 89

359 − 259

585 − 476

Name ______________________

Dino-Code

How is a T-Rex like an explosion?
To find out, **solve** the following problems and **write** the matching letter above each answer on the blanks.

He's . . . ___ ___ ___ ___   ___ ___
195 185 92 92   171 195

___ ___ ___ ___ – ___ ___ ___ ___ ___!
265 74 183 171   93 74 45 181 191

Remember to regroup when the bottom number is larger than the top number in a column.

F = 348 − 153 = ____

L = 765 − 673 = ____

G = 427 − 382 = ____

T = 637 − 446 = ____

H = 878 − 697 = ____

U = 548 − 363 = ____

O = 824 − 653 = ____

N = 439 − 256 = ____

I = 447 − 373 = ____

M = 568 − 475 = ____

D = 748 − 483 = ____

Name ______________________________

Paint by Number

Solve each problem. **Color** each shape according to the key below.

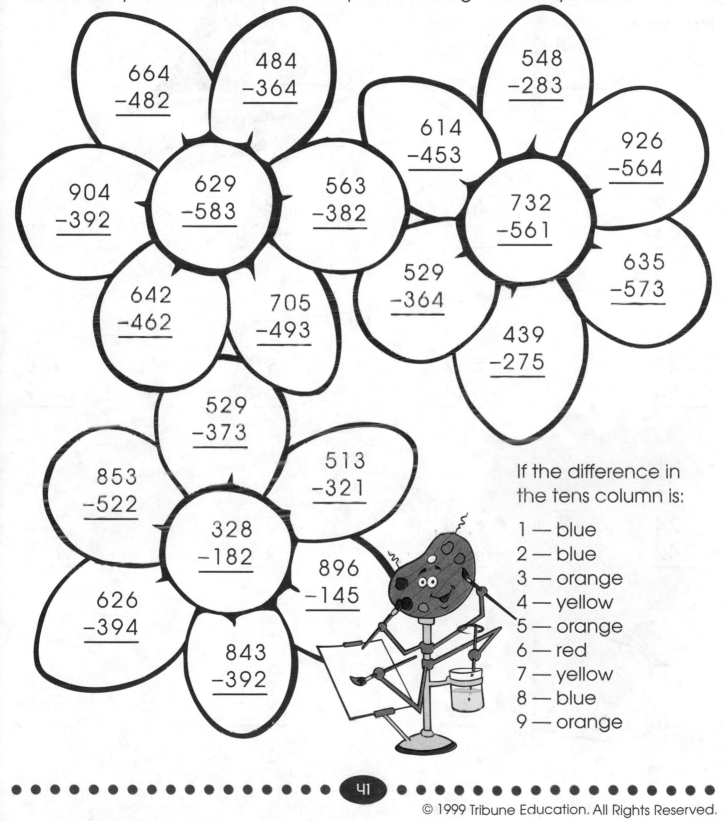

664 −482

484 −364

904 −392

629 −583

563 −382

642 −462

705 −493

548 −283

614 −453

926 −564

732 −561

529 −364

635 −573

439 −275

529 −373

853 −522

513 −321

328 −182

896 −145

626 −394

843 −392

If the difference in the tens column is:

1 — blue
2 — blue
3 — orange
4 — yellow
5 — orange
6 — red
7 — yellow
8 — blue
9 — orange

Name ____________________

Sailing Through Subtraction

Subtract, regrouping when needed.

Example:

$$\begin{array}{r} \overset{7}{\cancel{8}}\,\overset{14}{\cancel{5}}\,{}^{1}2 \\ -\,4\,6\,4 \\ \hline 3\,8\,8 \end{array}$$

$\begin{array}{r} 542 \\ -383 \\ \hline \end{array}$ $\begin{array}{r} 638 \\ -453 \\ \hline \end{array}$ $\begin{array}{r} 836 \\ -478 \\ \hline \end{array}$ $\begin{array}{r} 737 \\ -448 \\ \hline \end{array}$

$\begin{array}{r} 243 \\ -154 \\ \hline \end{array}$ $\begin{array}{r} 567 \\ -384 \\ \hline \end{array}$ $\begin{array}{r} 984 \\ -643 \\ \hline \end{array}$ $\begin{array}{r} 468 \\ -399 \\ \hline \end{array}$

$\begin{array}{r} 524 \\ -342 \\ \hline \end{array}$ $\begin{array}{r} 674 \\ -495 \\ \hline \end{array}$ $\begin{array}{r} 374 \\ -185 \\ \hline \end{array}$ $\begin{array}{r} 246 \\ -158 \\ \hline \end{array}$

$\begin{array}{r} 736 \\ -557 \\ \hline \end{array}$ $\begin{array}{r} 642 \\ -557 \\ \hline \end{array}$ $\begin{array}{r} 435 \\ -286 \\ \hline \end{array}$

Name ____________________

Gobble, Gobble

Solve each problem. **Color** the picture according to the key below. If the answer has a **3** in it, color it orange, **4**—red, **5**—purple, **6**—brown, **7**—yellow, **8**—blue and **9**—green. Remember to regroup when needed.

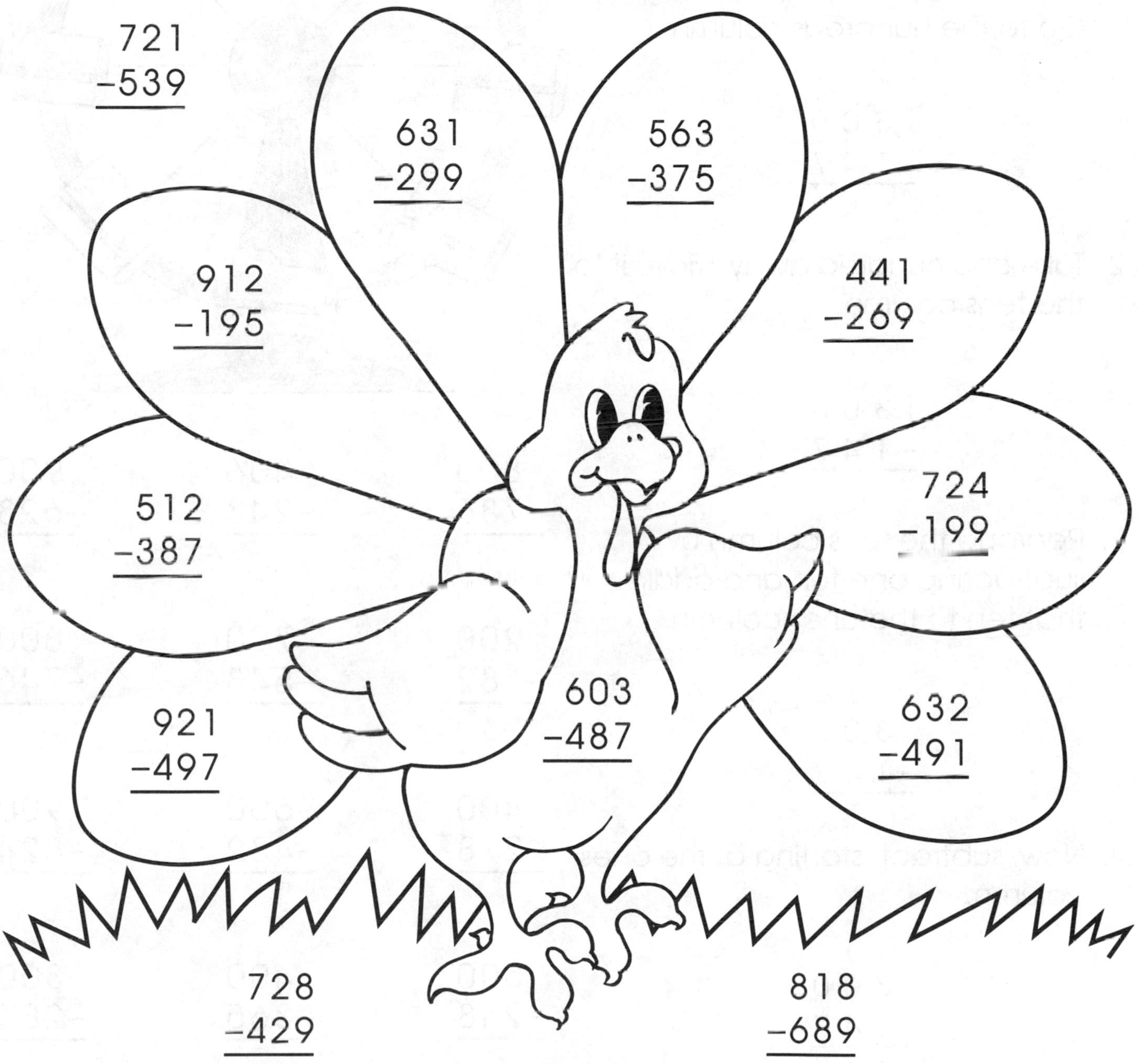

721
−539

631
−299

563
−375

912
−195

441
−269

512
−387

724
−199

603
−487

921
−497

632
−491

728
−429

818
−689

Name ____________________________

Round and Round She Goes

When regrouping with zeros follow these steps:

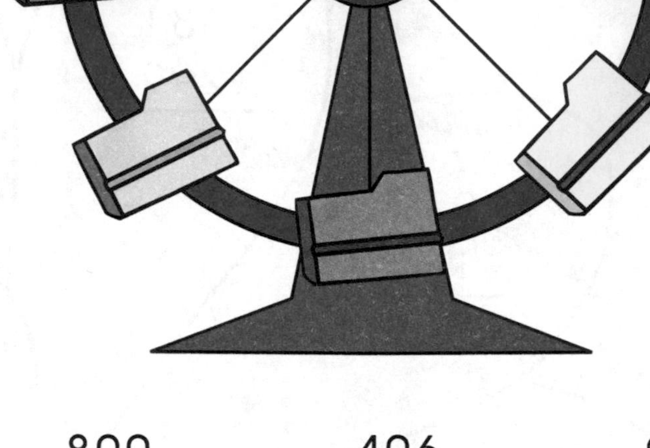

1. 7 is larger than 0. Go to the tens column to regroup. Since there is a 0 in that column, you can't regroup. Go to the hundreds column.

$$\begin{array}{r} {\overset{2}{\cancel{3}}}\,0\,0 \\ -\,1\,4\,7 \\ \hline \end{array}$$

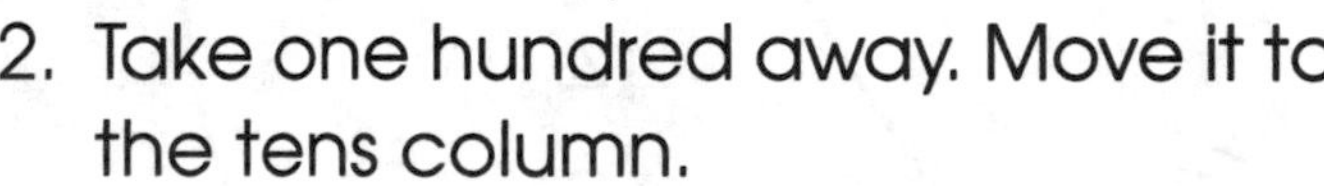

2. Take one hundred away. Move it to the tens column.

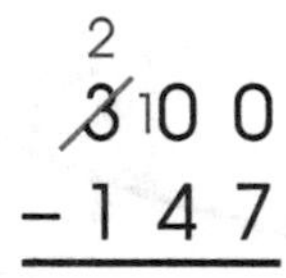

$$\begin{array}{r} {\overset{2}{\cancel{3}}}\,10\,0 \\ -\,1\,4\,7 \\ \hline \end{array}$$

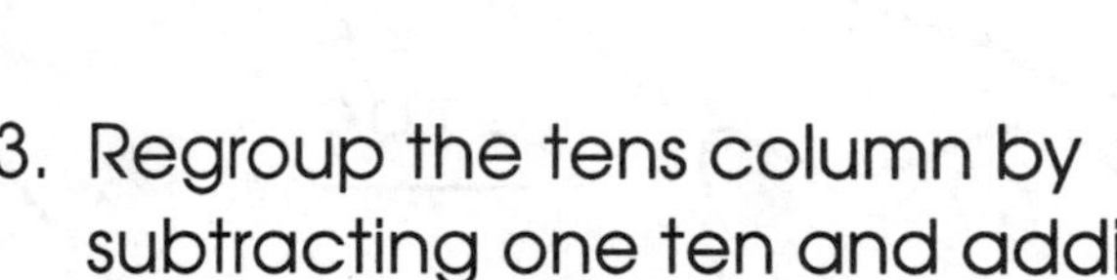

3. Regroup the tens column by subtracting one ten and adding that ten to the ones column.

$$\begin{array}{r} {\overset{2}{\cancel{3}}}\,{\overset{9}{\cancel{10}}}\,10 \\ -\,1\,4\,7 \\ \hline \end{array}$$

4. Now, subtract, starting at the ones column.

$$\begin{array}{r} {\overset{2}{\cancel{3}}}\,{\overset{9}{\cancel{10}}}\,10 \\ -\,1\,4\,7 \\ \hline 1\,5\,3 \end{array}$$

$$\begin{array}{r} 800 \\ -736 \\ \hline \end{array} \qquad \begin{array}{r} 406 \\ -243 \\ \hline \end{array} \qquad \begin{array}{r} 900 \\ -623 \\ \hline \end{array}$$

$$\begin{array}{r} 200 \\ -\ \ 82 \\ \hline \end{array} \qquad \begin{array}{r} 700 \\ -543 \\ \hline \end{array} \qquad \begin{array}{r} 800 \\ -746 \\ \hline \end{array}$$

$$\begin{array}{r} 400 \\ -278 \\ \hline \end{array} \qquad \begin{array}{r} 600 \\ -432 \\ \hline \end{array} \qquad \begin{array}{r} 900 \\ -824 \\ \hline \end{array}$$

$$\begin{array}{r} 500 \\ -248 \\ \hline \end{array} \qquad \begin{array}{r} 400 \\ -365 \\ \hline \end{array} \qquad \begin{array}{r} 300 \\ -284 \\ \hline \end{array}$$

Name ____________________

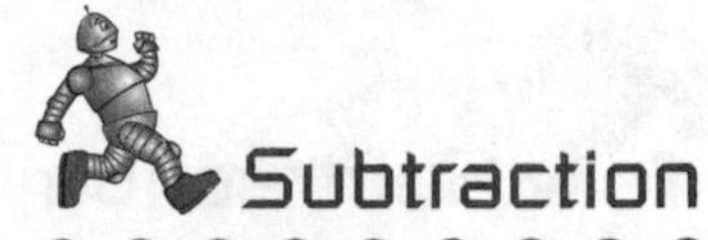

Jungle Math

Solve these problems.

Across

2. 517 − 228

7. 535 − 248

9. 561 − 247

3. 428 − 249

8. 857 − 389

4. 562 − 274

5. 924 − 340

6. 923 − 346

5. 824 − 247

Down

1. 421 − 342

6. 921 − 346

2. 627 − 348

7. 926 − 718

3. 362 − 194

8. 721 − 240

4. 582 − 346

10. 768 − 292

Name ______________________

Timely Zeros

Subtract.

300 −189	803 −324	504 −362		
900 −648	800 −724	702 −561		
200 −149	600 −476	500 −362	807 −298	406 −328
300 −243	600 −421	700 −348	308 −189	500 −384
		302 −195	600 −247	400 −108
			205 −148	308 −189

Name ________________________________

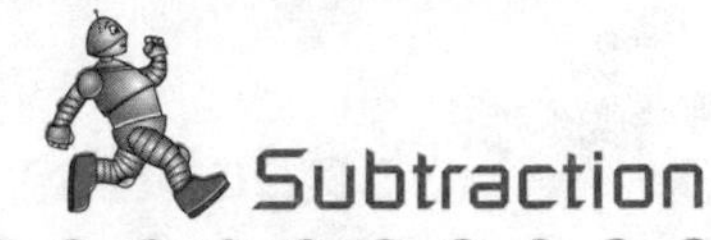

Subtraction Maze

Solve the problems. Remember to regroup, when needed.

4,172 −1,536	6,723 −2,586	547 −259	834 −463	562 −325	7,146 −3,498
9,427 −6,648	8,149 −5,372	5,389 −1,652	421 −275	7,456 −3,724	818 −639
772 −586	6,529 −4,538	5,379 −2,835	6,275 −3,761	5,612 −1,505	8,355 −5,366

Shade in the answers from above to find the path.

	2,514	288	186	3,732	2,989
	2,779	156	1,901	2,414	4,137
3,748	3,337	2,777	371	179	1,991
3,048	3,737	146	2,717 →		
679	237	374	4,107 →		
886	2,636	2,544	3,648		

KITTY

Name ____________________

High Class Math

Solve these problems.

		3,270 −1,529	8,248 −1,513	
7,648 −3,291	4,321 −1,809	8,241 −3,516	3,002 −1,231	9,200 −3,146
5,017 −2,408	8,254 −3,187	7,265 −2,134	3,846 −1,359	8,006 −3,084
3,084 −1,926	6,265 −4,189	4,824 −1,913	6,205 −1,054	5,253 −4,428
	9,205 −3,187	5,809 −3,913	5,642 −2,408	

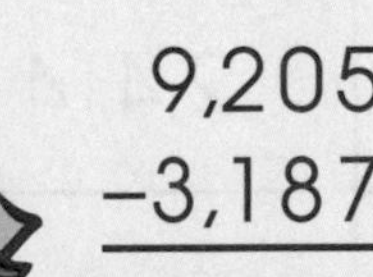

Name ______________________________

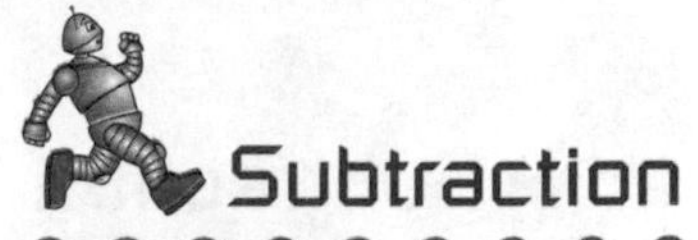

Kite Craze!

Subtract.

8,794 −6,428	9,643 −8,825		
8,825 −7,436	5,648 −3,929		
7,005 −6,223	8,416 −3,509	4,162 −2,840	6,514 −3,282
5,436 −2,924	9,246 −8,518	4,862 −3,946	9,486 −6,294
		9,085 −6,241	8,462 −6,391
		7,643 −6,521	6,430 −4,252

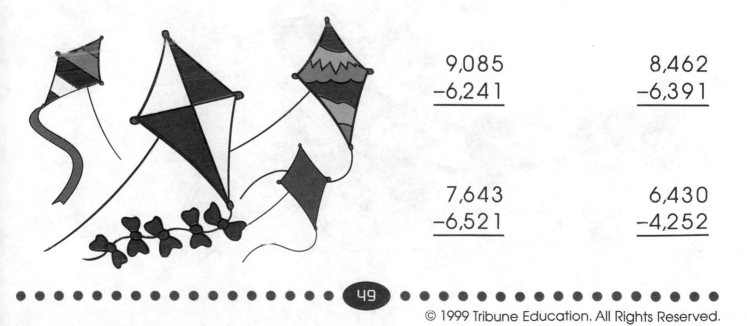

Name ____________________

Subtraction on Stage!

Subtract.

5,648 −2,425	2,148 − 825		
7,641 −5,246	7,648 −3,289	5,408 −1,291	8,209 −4,182
8,419 −2,182	6,249 −1,526	6,428 −4,159	4,287 −2,492
7,645 −2,826	2,016 −1,021	8,247 −6,459	9,047 −6,152
			5,231 −1,642
			7,689 −2,845

Name ______________________________

Subtraction Search

Solve each problem. **Find** the answer in the chart and **circle** it. The answers may go in any direction.

2	1	6	3	2	7	5
6	3	3	2	1	0	8
2	2	1	6	3	3	4
0	2	2	6	5	0	6
8	5	4	2	0	8	7
8	9	0	6	1	5	6
3	2	8	4	4	2	1
8	3	4	8	8	5	0
8	1	9	8	7	2	9
3	4	5	8	5	6	7
8	1	3	7	0	4	2
9	3	2	1	7	0	2

6,003
−2,737

5,040
−3,338

9,000
−5,725

7,200
−4,356

3,406
−1,298

5,602
−3,138

7,006
−5,429

3,006
−2,798

3,605
−2,718

5,904
−3,917

5,039
−1,954

8,704
−2,496

4,081
−3,594

6,508
− 399

5,039
−2,467

9,006
− 575

5,001
−2,351

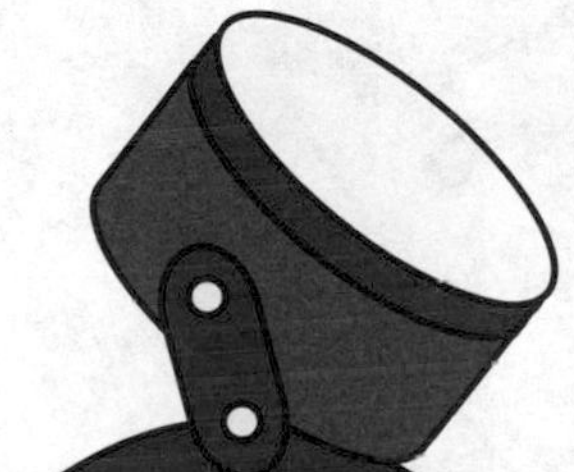

8,002
−5,686

6,058
−2,175

9,504
−7,368

7,290
−1,801

Multiplication

Name ______________________________

Skipping Through the Tens

Skip count by tens. Begin with the number on the first line. **Write** each number that follows.

0, ______, ______, ______, ______, ______, ______, ______, ______, ______, 100

3, ______, ______, ______, ______, 53, ______, ______, ______, ______, 103

1, ______, ______, ______, ______, ______, ______, ______, 81, ______, ______

8, ______, ______, ______, ______, ______, 68, ______, ______, ______, ______

6, ______, ______, ______, ______, ______, ______, ______, ______, ______, ______

4, ______, ______, ______, ______, ______, ______, ______, ______, ______, 104

2, ______, ______, ______, ______, ______, ______, ______, ______, 92, ______

5, ______, ______, ______, 45, ______, ______, ______, ______, ______, ______

7, ______, ______, ______, ______, ______, ______, 77, ______, ______, ______

9, ______, ______, ______, ______, ______, ______, ______, ______, ______, ______

What is ten more than . . . ?

26 ______ 29 ______

44 ______ 77 ______

53 ______ 91 ______

24 ______ 49 ______

66 ______ 35 ______

54 ______ 82 ______

Name ____________________

Counting to 100

Skip count to 100.

By twos:

		6	8				16			22			
30							44						56
				66						78			
							100						

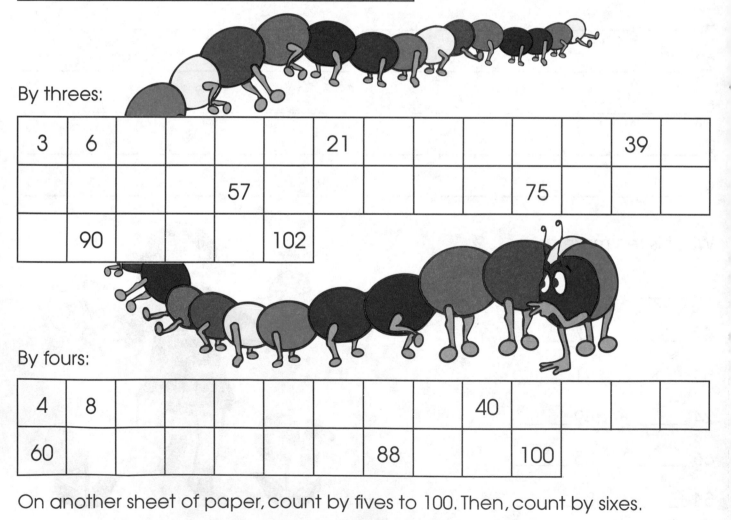

By threes:

3	6					21						39	
				57						75			
	90				102								

By fours:

4	8								40				
60							88			100			

On another sheet of paper, count by fives to 100. Then, count by sixes.

Name ____________________

Count the Legs!

Multiplication is a quick way to add. For example, count the legs of the horses below. They each have 4 legs. You could add 4 + 4 + 4. But it is quicker to say that there are 3 groups of 4 legs. In multiplication, that is 3 x 4.

Multiply to find the number of legs. **Write** each problem twice.

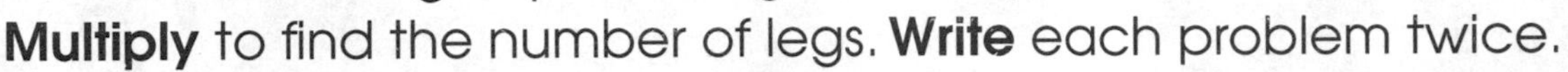

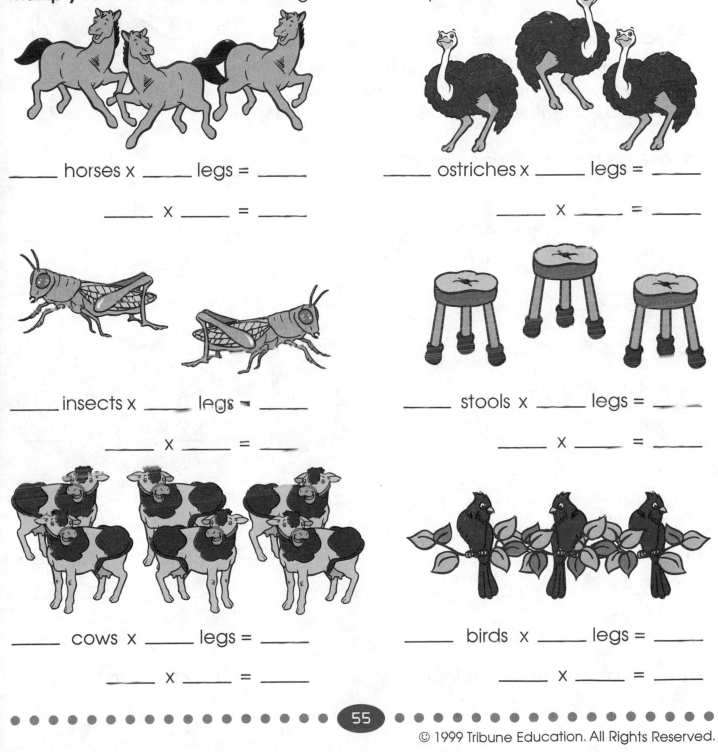

____ horses x ____ legs = ____

____ x ____ = ____

____ ostriches x ____ legs = ____

____ x ____ = ____

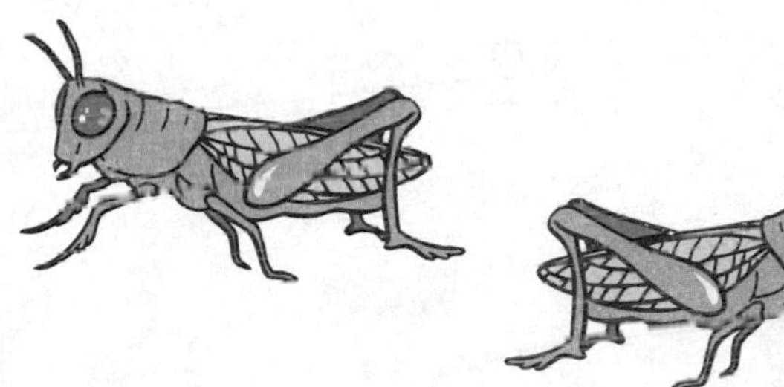

____ insects x ____ legs = ____

____ x ____ = ____

____ stools x ____ legs = ____

____ x ____ = ____

____ cows x ____ legs = ____

____ x ____ = ____

____ birds x ____ legs = ____

____ x ____ = ____

Name ______________________

Fact Snacks

Directions: Ask an adult for a paper plate and a couple of snacks, such as popcorn, pretzels, candy corn or chocolate-covered candies. Arrange the snacks into sets, such as five sets of 5 or nine sets of 3.

Now, **add** the sets together. **Write** the related fact. Use the snack manipulatives to **answer** the following multiplication problems. Group the snacks into sets with the number shown in each set.

4 x 2 = 4 sets with 2 in each set = 8

1. 3 x2

2. 5 x3

3. 1 x7

4. 2 x9

5. 6 x6

6. 7 x4

7. 8 x5

8. 3 x4

9. 6 x7

10. 10 x 2

11. 1 x3

12. 4 x8

13. 9 x2

14. 3 x3

15. 5 x7

After you **answer** and **check** the problems, enjoy the tasty fact snacks.

Name ______________________________

Multiplying

Numbers to be multiplied together are called **factors**. The answer is the **product**.
Example: 3 x 6

1. The first factor tells how many groups there are. There are 3 groups.
2. The second factor tells how many are in each group. There are 6 in each group.

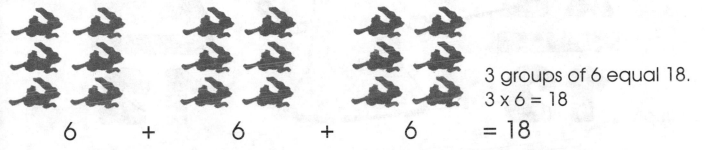

  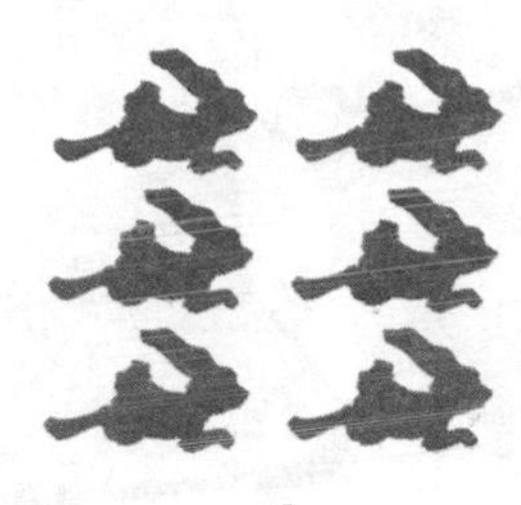

3 groups of 6 equal 18.
3 x 6 = 18

6 + 6 + 6 = 18

Some helpful hints to remember when multiplying:

- When you multiply by 0, the product is always 0. **Example:** 0 x 7 = 0
- When you multiply by 1, the product is always the factor being multiplied. **Example:** 1 x 12 = 12
- When multiplying by 2, double the factor other than 2. **Example:** 2 x 4 = 8
- The order doesn't matter when multiplying. **Example:** 5 x 3 = 15, 3 x 5 = 15
- When you multiply by 9, the digits in the product add up to 9 (until 9 x 11). **Example:** 7 x 9 = 63, 6 + 3 = 9
- When you multiply by 10, multiply by 1 and add 0 to the product. **Example:** 10 x 3 = 30
- When you multiply by 11, write the factor you are multiplying by twice (until 10). **Example:** 11 x 8 = 88

Multiply.

2	3	4	2	5	10	7	11	9
x9	x8	x9	x11	x9	x 5	x6	x 4	x7

8	7	8	10	4	5	8	3	7
x6	x12	x5	x10	x8	x5	x8	x6	x8

Name ______________________________

Factor Fun

When you change the order of the factors, you have the same product.

Multiply.

7 x 3	3 x 7	6 x 5	5 x 6	2 x 3	3 x 2
4 x 6	6 x 4	2 x 9	9 x 2	8 x 4	4 x 8
7 x 2	2 x 7	3 x 6	6 x 3	9 x 4	4 x 9
8 x 3	3 x 8	5 x 2	2 x 5	9 x 3	3 x 9

Name ____________________

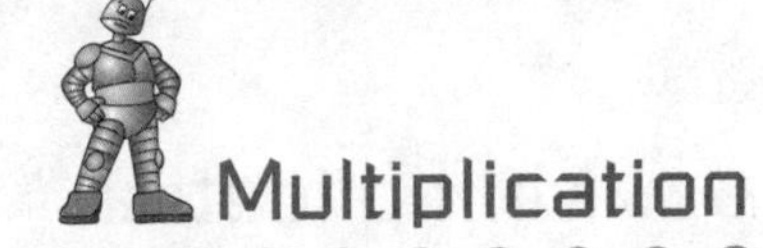

Racing to the Finish

Multiply.

5 x 3	2 x 8	4 x 6	9 x 3	7 x 5	3 x 9
4 x 2	6 x 2	4 x 4	0 x 6	3 x 2	7 x 2
6 x 5	3 x 4	8 x 3	4 x 5	5 x 2	7 x 4
6 x 3	4 x 8	2 x 2	8 x 5	3 x 7	5 x 5
5 x 9	9 x 2	4 x 6	9 x 4		

Name ______________________________

Climbing Granite Boulders!

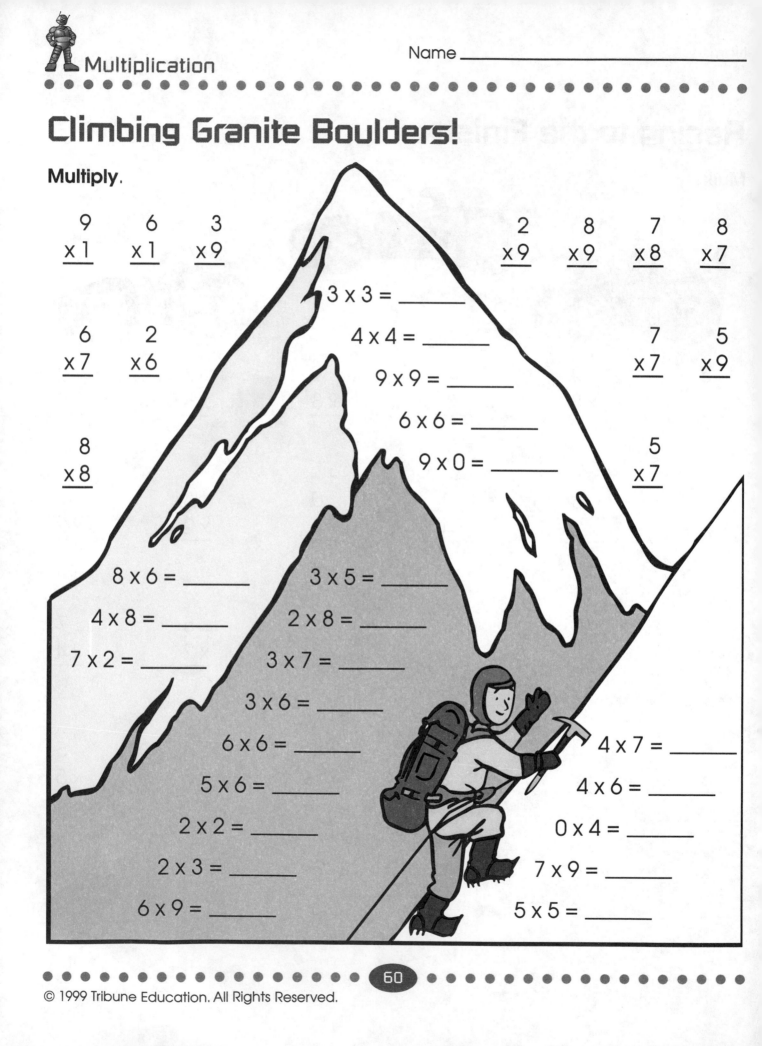

Multiply.

$\begin{array}{r} 9 \\ \times 1 \\ \hline \end{array}$ $\begin{array}{r} 6 \\ \times 1 \\ \hline \end{array}$ $\begin{array}{r} 3 \\ \times 9 \\ \hline \end{array}$ $\begin{array}{r} 2 \\ \times 9 \\ \hline \end{array}$ $\begin{array}{r} 8 \\ \times 9 \\ \hline \end{array}$ $\begin{array}{r} 7 \\ \times 8 \\ \hline \end{array}$ $\begin{array}{r} 8 \\ \times 7 \\ \hline \end{array}$

$3 \times 3 =$ ______

$4 \times 4 =$ ______

$\begin{array}{r} 6 \\ \times 7 \\ \hline \end{array}$ $\begin{array}{r} 2 \\ \times 6 \\ \hline \end{array}$ $\begin{array}{r} 7 \\ \times 7 \\ \hline \end{array}$ $\begin{array}{r} 5 \\ \times 9 \\ \hline \end{array}$

$9 \times 9 =$ ______

$6 \times 6 =$ ______

$\begin{array}{r} 8 \\ \times 8 \\ \hline \end{array}$ $\begin{array}{r} 5 \\ \times 7 \\ \hline \end{array}$

$9 \times 0 =$ ______

$8 \times 6 =$ ______

$4 \times 8 =$ ______

$7 \times 2 =$ ______

$3 \times 5 =$ ______

$2 \times 8 =$ ______

$3 \times 7 =$ ______

$3 \times 6 =$ ______

$6 \times 6 =$ ______

$5 \times 6 =$ ______

$2 \times 2 =$ ______

$2 \times 3 =$ ______

$6 \times 9 =$ ______

$4 \times 7 =$ ______

$4 \times 6 =$ ______

$0 \times 4 =$ ______

$7 \times 9 =$ ______

$5 \times 5 =$ ______

Name ____________________

On the Right Track

Preparation: Glue the gameboard on page 63 onto poster board. Make a spinner, using the pattern below. Use a brass fastener to attach a paper clip to the center of the spinner so the clip spins freely.

Directions: This game involves two players. Players spin the spinner. The player with the highest number goes first. Players start at the station. Player One spins and moves his/her marker to the first space on the track that has a multiple of the number he/she spun. A multiple is the product or answer you would get when you multiply the number on the spinner by another number. If no multiple remains, Player One loses his/her turn. If a player puts his/her marker on a wrong multiple or skips a multiple, he/she must go back to the station. The first player to reach the end of the line is the winner.

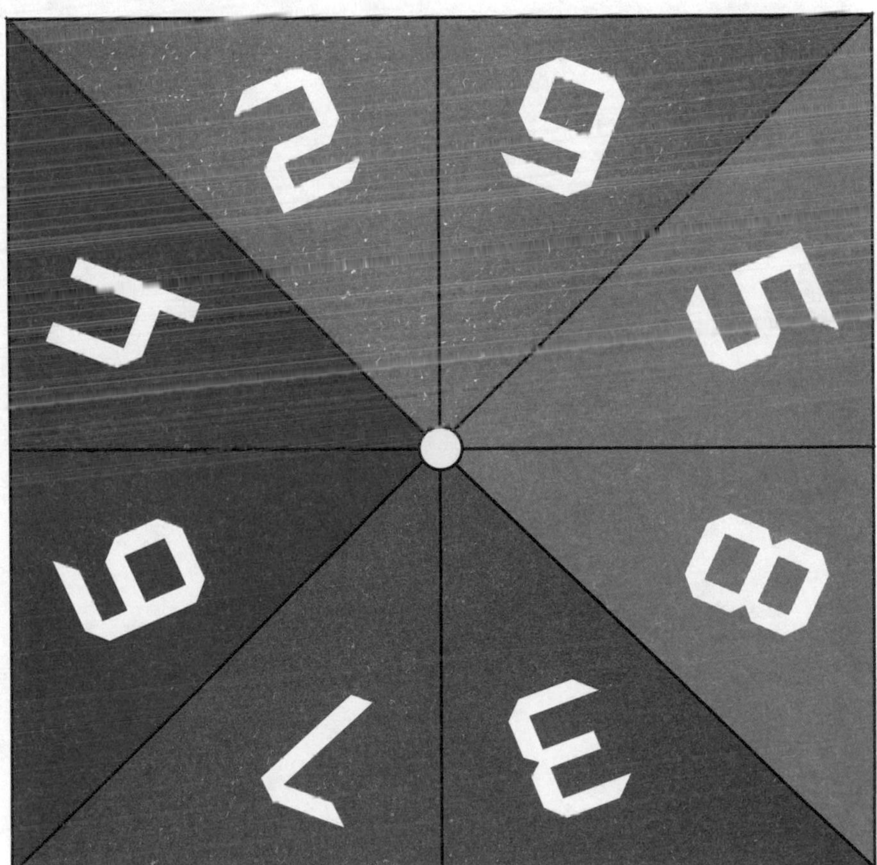

This page intentionally left blank.

Name ____________________________

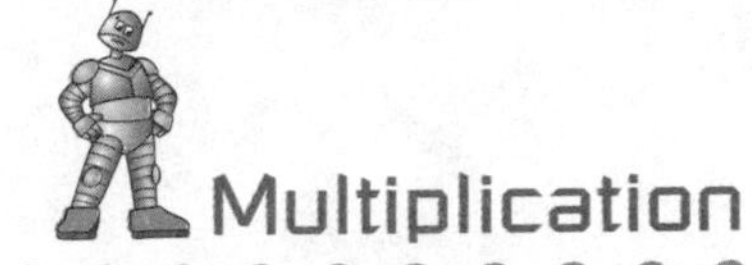

On the Right Track Gameboard

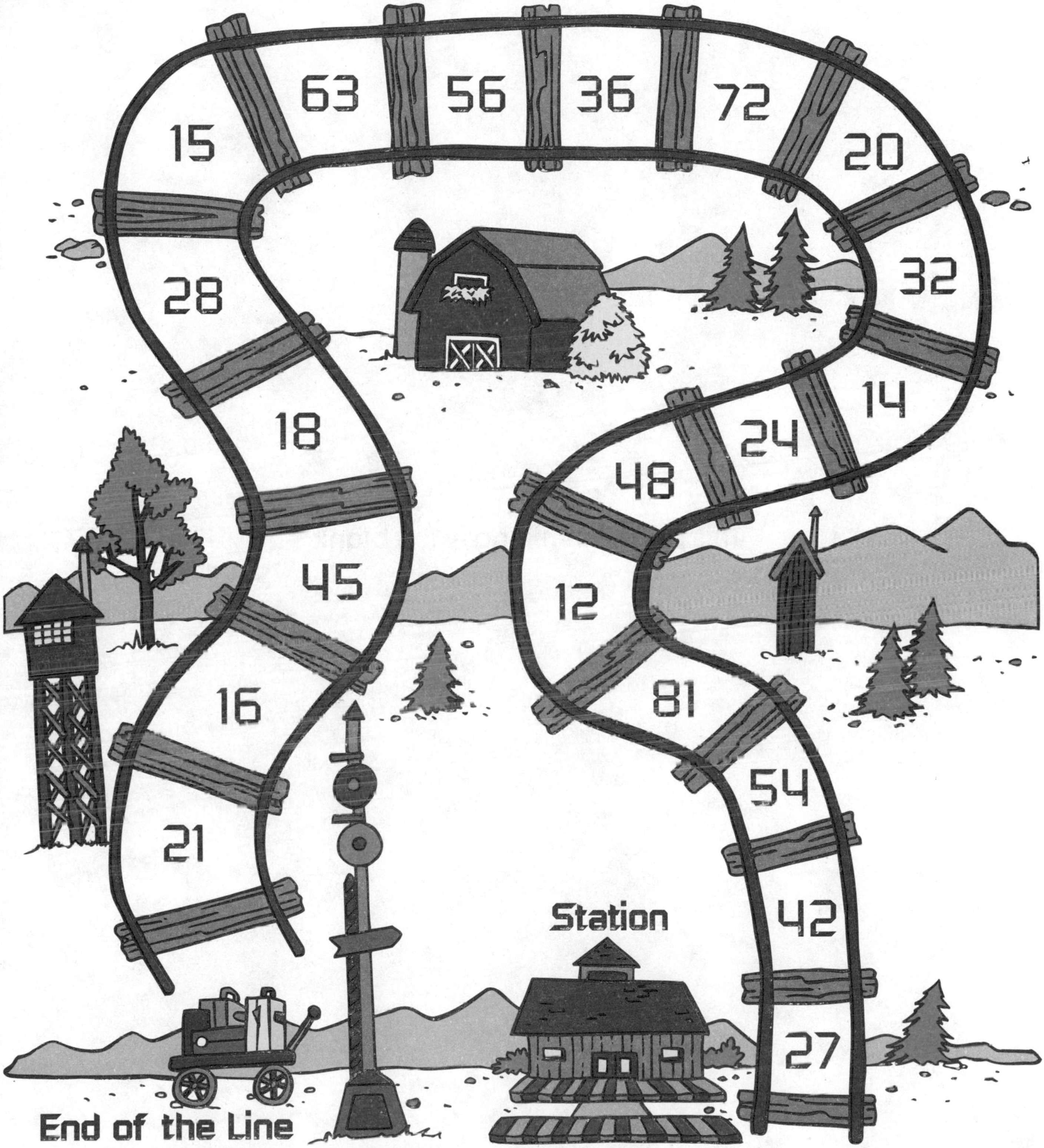

Station

27

42

54

81

12

48

24

14

32

20

72

36

56

63

15

28

18

45

16

21

End of the Line

This page intentionally left blank.

Name ______________________________

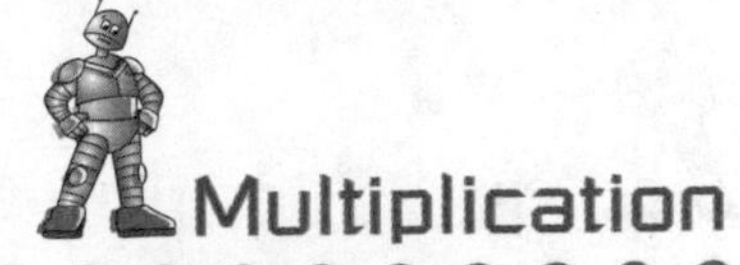

Time To Multiply

Complete the table. Try to do it in less than 3 minutes.

X	0	1	2	3	4	5	6	7	8	9
0	0									
1										
2			4							
3										
4										
5						25				
6										
7										
8										
9										

Name ______________________________

Double Trouble

Solve each multiplication problem. Below each answer, **write** the letter from the code that matches the answer. **Read** the coded question and **write** the answer in the space provided.

1	4	9	16	25	36	49	64	81	100	121	144
E	G	H	I	N	O	S	T	U	W	X	Y

10 x10	3 x3	6 x6

4 x4	7 x7

7 x7	4 x4	8 x8	8 x8	4 x4	5 x5	2 x2

5 x5	1 x1	11 x11	8 x8

8 x8	6 x6

12 x12	6 x6	9 x9

?

Answer: ______________________________

Name ______________________

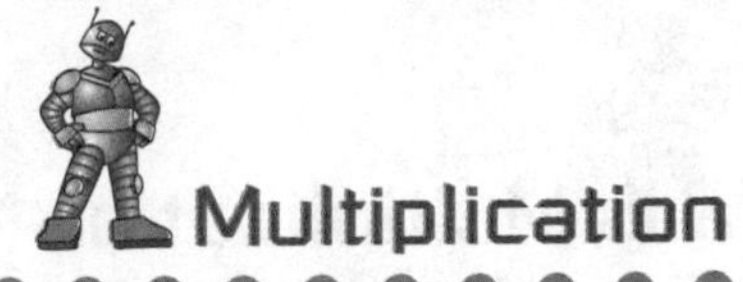

Crossnumber Fun

Write the word form of each product in the puzzle.

Across

3. 9 x 4 = ______
8. 10 x 5 = ______
9. 2 x 9 = ______
10. 3 x 12 = ______
12. 7 x 11= ______
14. 4 x 10 = ______
15. 6 x 5 = ______
16. 0 x 7 = ______

Down

1. 7 x 8 = ______
2. 6 x 1 = ______
4. 2 x 5 = ______
5. 11 x 3 = ______
6. 5 x 1 = ______
7. 5 x 4 = ______
11. 12 x 8 = ______
13. 3 x 8 = ______

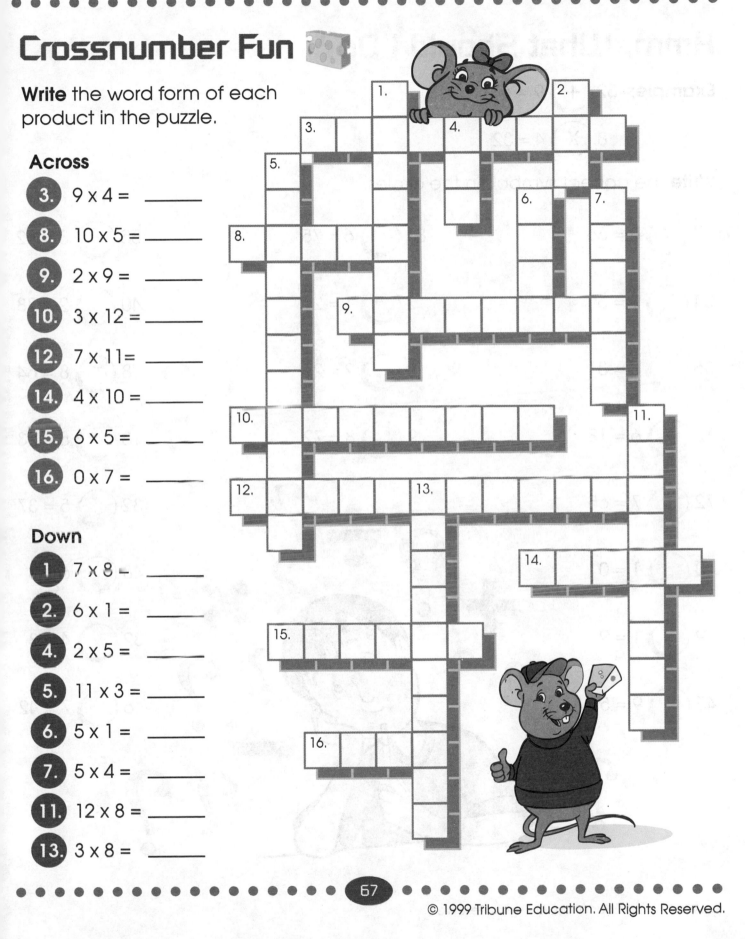

1. 2. 3. 4. 5. 6. 7. 8. 9. 10. 11. 12. 13. 14. 15. 16.

Name ____________________

Hmm, What Should I Do?

Example: 52 (+) 9 = 61

8 (X) 4 = 32

Write the correct symbols in the circles.

7 ◯ 8 = 56

54 ◯ 9 = 6

36 ◯ 5 = 31

12 ◯ 6 = 18

72 ◯ 7 = 65

0 ◯ 1 = 0

9 ◯ 1 = 9

45 ◯ 9 = 5

81 ◯ 6 = 75

2 ◯ 1 = 2

0 ◯ 2 = 2

9 ◯ 8 = 72

55 ◯ 3 = 52

40 ◯ 2 = 38

8 ◯ 8 = 64

18 ◯ 5 = 23

32 ◯ 5 = 37

48 ◯ 6 = 8

32 ◯ 4 = 8

6 ◯ 7 = 42

Name ______________________________

Wacky Waldo's Snow Show

Wacky Waldo's Snow Show is an exciting and fantastic sight. Waldo has trained whales and bears to skate together on the ice. There is a hockey game between a team of sharks and a pack of wolves. Elephants ride sleds down steep hills. Horses and buffaloes ski swiftly down mountains.

Write each problem and its answer.

1. Wacky Waldo has 4 ice-skating whales. He has 4 times as many bears who ice skate. How many bears can ice skate?

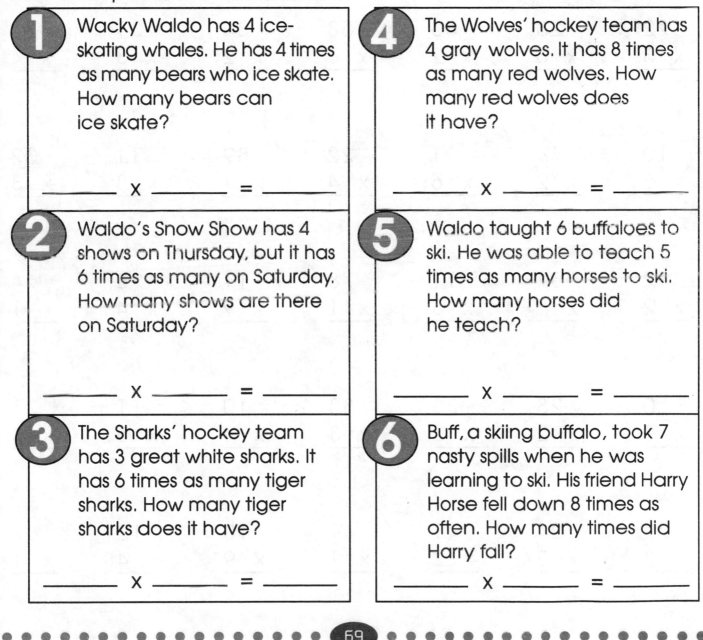

_______ x _______ = _______

2. Waldo's Snow Show has 4 shows on Thursday, but it has 6 times as many on Saturday. How many shows are there on Saturday?

_______ x _______ = _______

3. The Sharks' hockey team has 3 great white sharks. It has 6 times as many tiger sharks. How many tiger sharks does it have?

_______ x _______ = _______

4. The Wolves' hockey team has 4 gray wolves. It has 8 times as many red wolves. How many red wolves does it have?

_______ x _______ = _______

5. Waldo taught 6 buffaloes to ski. He was able to teach 5 times as many horses to ski. How many horses did he teach?

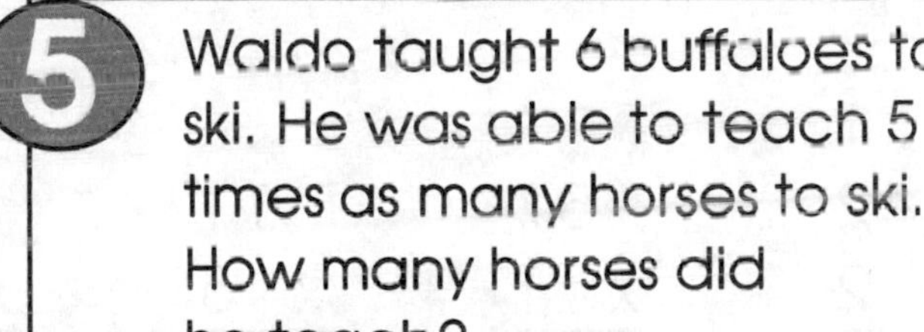

_______ x _______ = _______

6. Buff, a skiing buffalo, took 7 nasty spills when he was learning to ski. His friend Harry Horse fell down 8 times as often. How many times did Harry fall?

_______ x _______ = _______

Name ____________________

Space Race

Complete the products. Begin by multiplying the ones place first, then the tens place. See the shading in the examples.

Example:

11 × 4	11 × 4
4	44

22 x 3	23 x 3	43 x 2	58 x 1	34 x 2	31 x 3	21 x 4
10 x 5	44 x 2	11 x 6	22 x 4	89 x 1	11 x 8	32 x 3
42 x 2	57 x 1	11 x 5	78 x 1	11 x 9	22 x 4	64 x 1
10 x 7	23 x 2	33 x 2	33 x 3	10 x 4	11 x 5	21 x 3
22 x 3	24 x 2	41 x 2	49 x 1	10 x 9	12 x 4	87 x 1

Multiplying and Regrouping

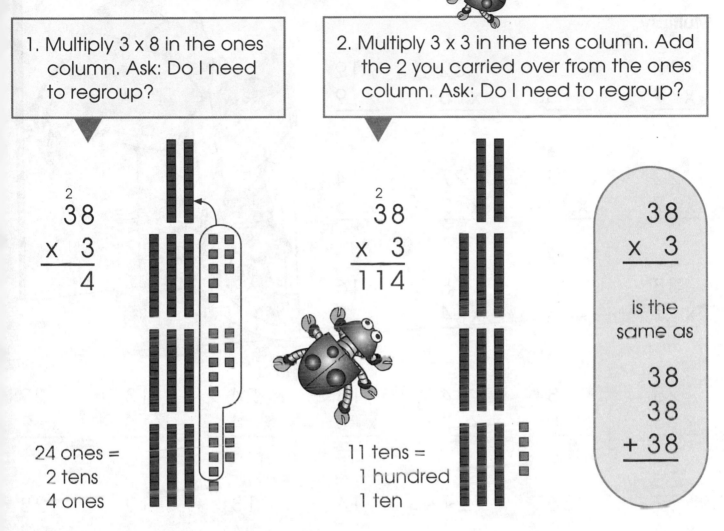

1. Multiply 3 x 8 in the ones column. Ask: Do I need to regroup?

2. Multiply 3 x 3 in the tens column. Add the 2 you carried over from the ones column. Ask: Do I need to regroup?

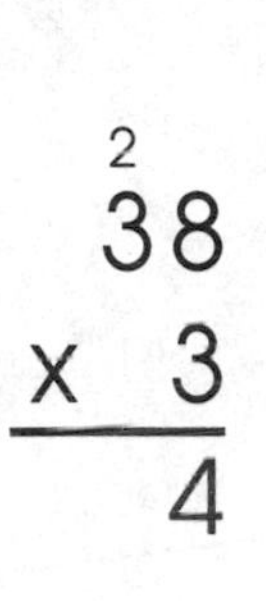

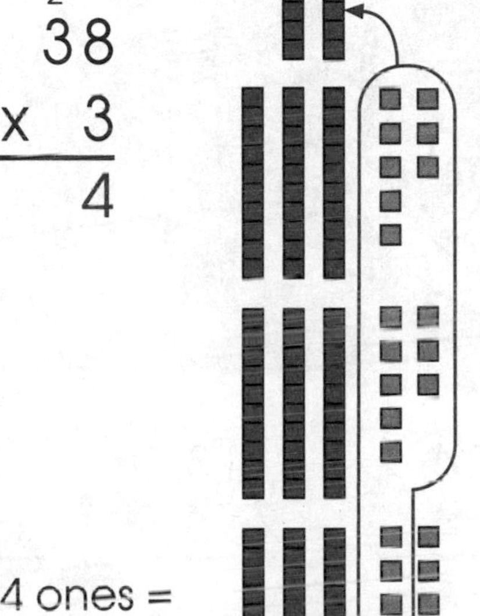

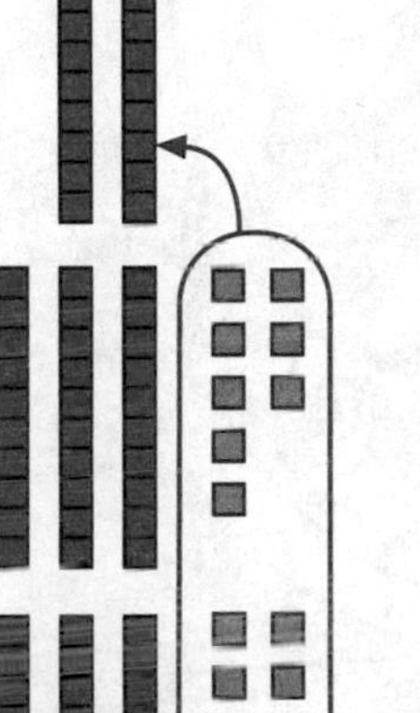

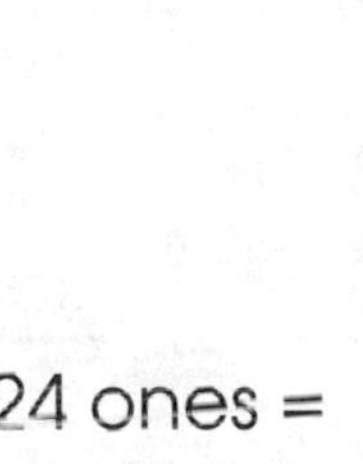

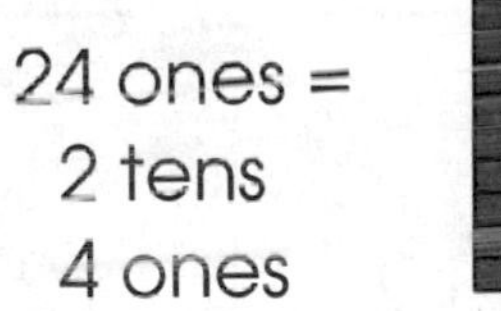

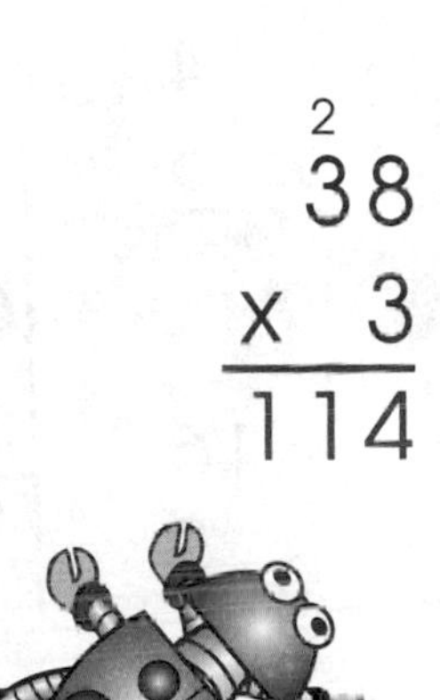

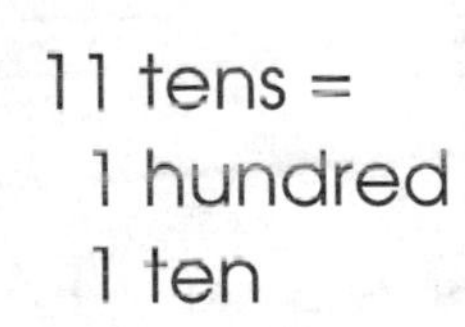

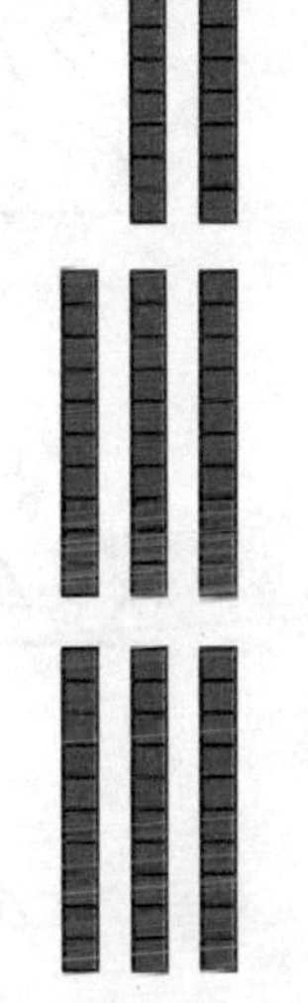

38 x 3
is the same as
38 38 + 38

Multiply.

29 x 3	62 x 4	39 x 4	86 x 7	43 x 6
28 x 6	48 x 2	31 x 9	25 x 5	55 x 5

Name ____________________

Multiplying Points

Multiply.

12 x 9	22 x 8	32 x 5	19 x 9			
22 x 7	33 x 4	27 x 2	14 x 6			
38 x 2	25 x 3	15 x 4	16 x 5			
28 x 3	18 x 5	14 x 7	13 x 5	24 x 4	13 x 6	29 x 2
17 x 4	36 x 2	29 x 3	14 x 5	18 x 4	19 x 3	28 x 2
17 x 5	19 x 4	37 x 2	27 x 3	12 x 8	26 x 3	35 x 5
48 x 2						27 x 4

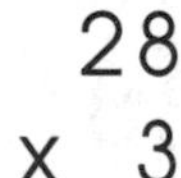

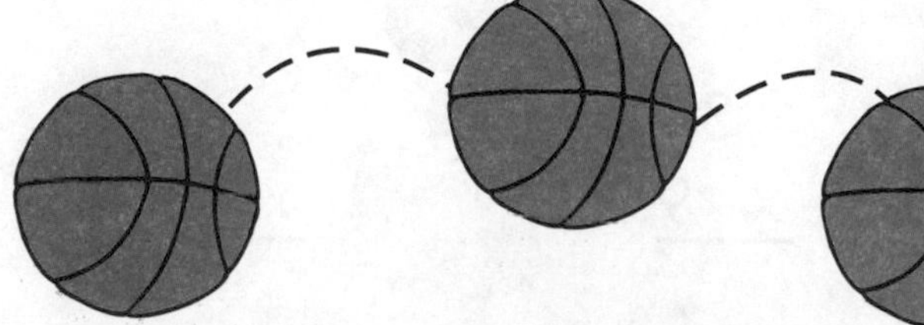

Name ______________________________

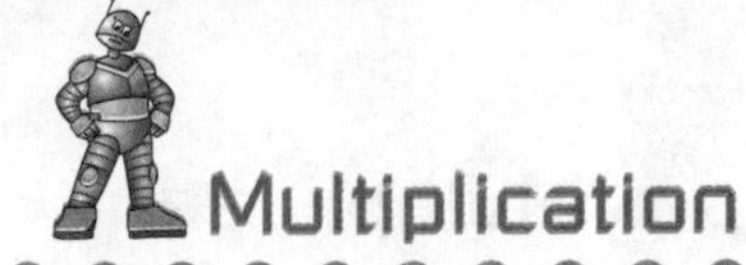

Under the Big Top!

Complete this crossnumber puzzle.

43	x	4	=	
x				
2	x	58	=	
=		x		
	x	7	=	
		=		

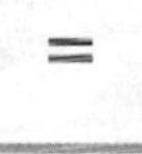

65	x	4	=	
x		x		
5	x	77	=	
=		=		

Name ________________________________

Wacky Ones

Directions: In card games, aces are often considered as ones. Tear out the gameboard on page 75. Have it laminated, if possible. Use a deck of cards with the face cards and the tens removed. Any number of people can play.

Player One chooses a random card from the deck and places that card in any one of the boxes. Repeat this two or more times. After a number is placed, it may not be changed. Then, he/she will solve the problem. Check the product using a calculator and award points. The next player continues play the same way.

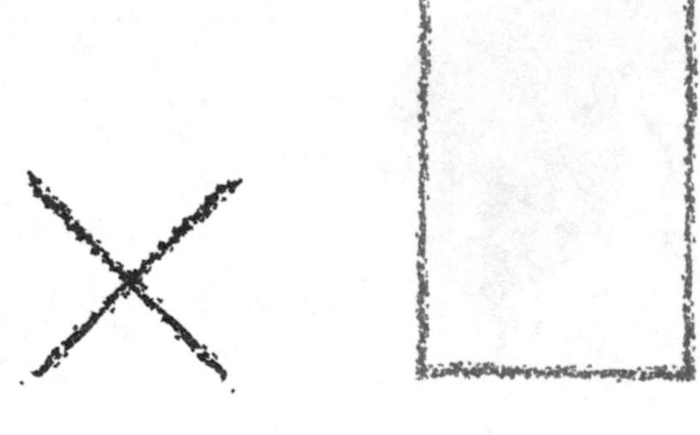

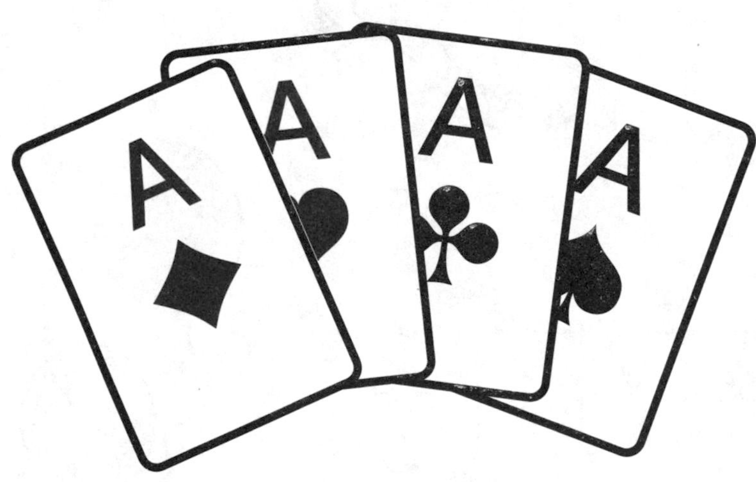

Award points using the following rules:

1. If the product is incorrect, the score is zero.
2. If the product is correct, the score is five points.
3. Bonus—If the product contains a wacky one, the following bonus points are scored: 1 point—ones place, 2 points—tens place, 3 points—hundreds place.

Wacky Ones Gameboard

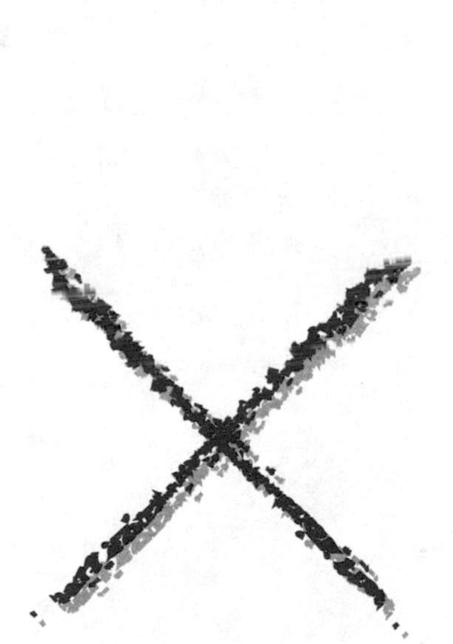

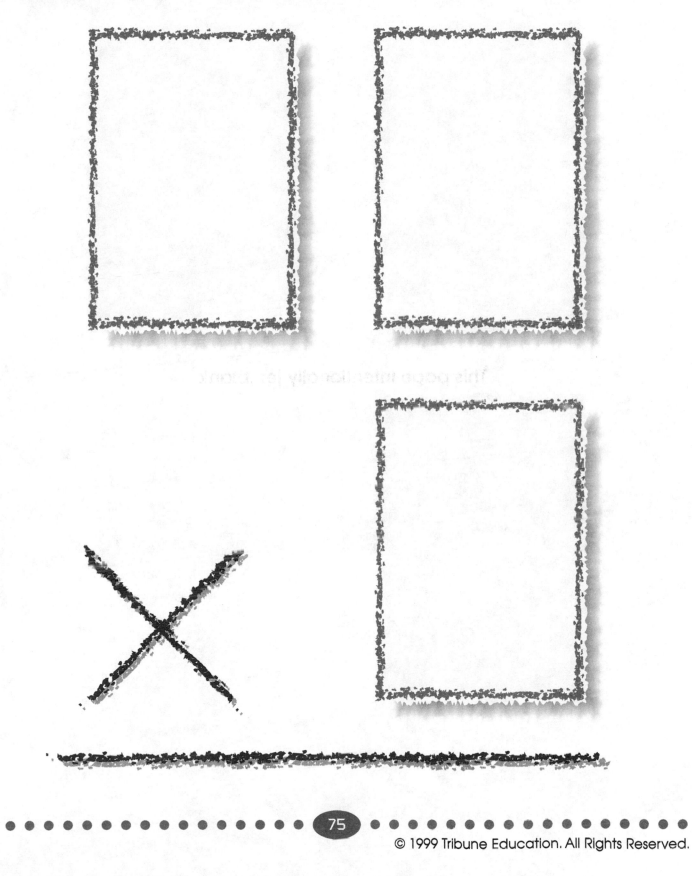

This page intentionally left blank.

More Multiplication

Write the numbers given in the correct boxes to get the given answer.

4 7 5	7 7 9	8 7 9	4 8 7	7 6 3
[5] [4]	[ ] [ ]	[ ] [ ]	[ ] [ ]	[ ] [ ]
x [7]	x [ ]	x [ ]	x [ ]	x [ ]
3 7 8	6 7 9	6 3 2	5 8 8	4 3 8

6 9 4	7 3 9	5 2 9	9 5 6	2 7 5
[ ] [ ]	[ ] [ ]	[ ] [ ]	[ ] [ ]	[ ] [ ]
x [ ]	x [ ]	x [ ]	x [ ]	x [ ]
5 6 4	3 3 3	4 6 0	3 4 5	1 7 5

4 5 6	5 7 6	3 6 9	4 8 7	6 6 7
[ ] [ ]	[ ] [ ]	[ ] [ ]	[ ] [ ]	[ ] [ ]
x [ ]	x [ ]	x [ ]	x [ ]	x [ ]
2 2 4	3 8 0	2 3 4	3 3 6	4 0 2

5 5 4	2 3 3	7 8 4	6 5 7	9 4 2
[ ] [ ]	[ ] [ ]	[ ] [ ]	[ ] [ ]	[ ] [ ]
x [ ]	x [ ]	x [ ]	x [ ]	x [ ]
2 7 0	9 6	5 9 2	3 8 0	9 8

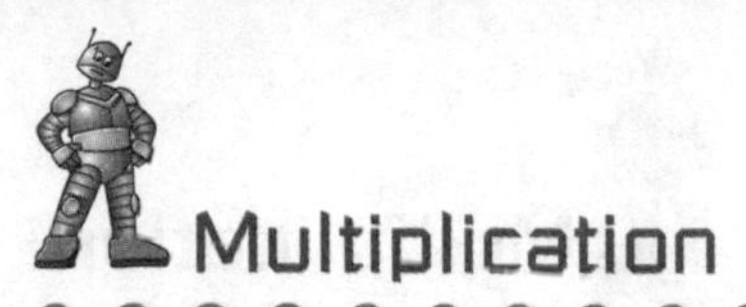

Name ______________________________

Multiplying With Molly

Write the problem and the answer for each question.

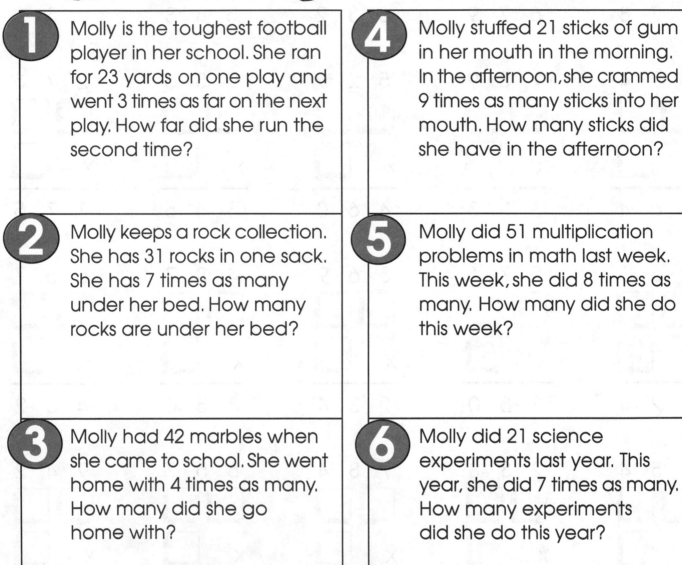

1. Molly is the toughest football player in her school. She ran for 23 yards on one play and went 3 times as far on the next play. How far did she run the second time?

2. Molly keeps a rock collection. She has 31 rocks in one sack. She has 7 times as many under her bed. How many rocks are under her bed?

3. Molly had 42 marbles when she came to school. She went home with 4 times as many. How many did she go home with?

4. Molly stuffed 21 sticks of gum in her mouth in the morning. In the afternoon, she crammed 9 times as many sticks into her mouth. How many sticks did she have in the afternoon?

5. Molly did 51 multiplication problems in math last week. This week, she did 8 times as many. How many did she do this week?

6. Molly did 21 science experiments last year. This year, she did 7 times as many. How many experiments did she do this year?

Name ______________________

Three-Digit Regrouping

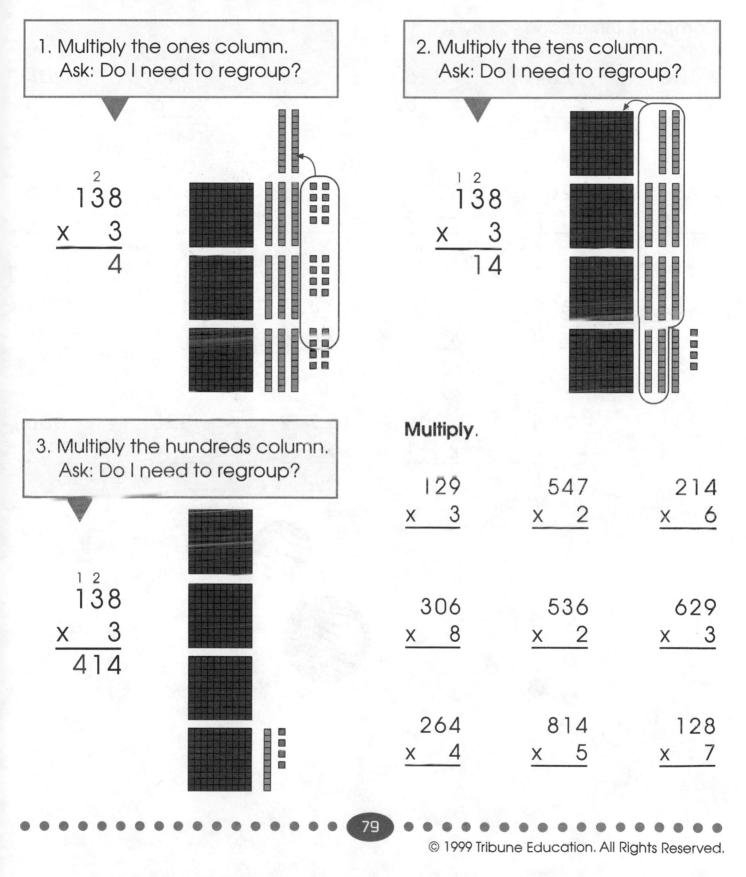

1. Multiply the ones column.
Ask: Do I need to regroup?

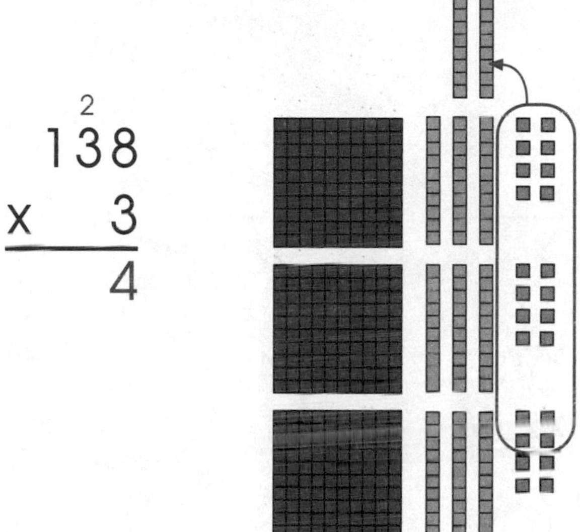

2. Multiply the tens column.
Ask: Do I need to regroup?

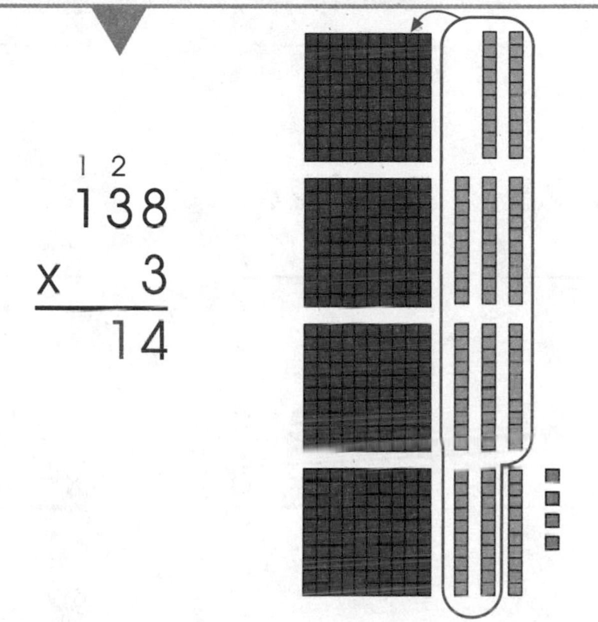

3. Multiply the hundreds column.
Ask: Do I need to regroup?

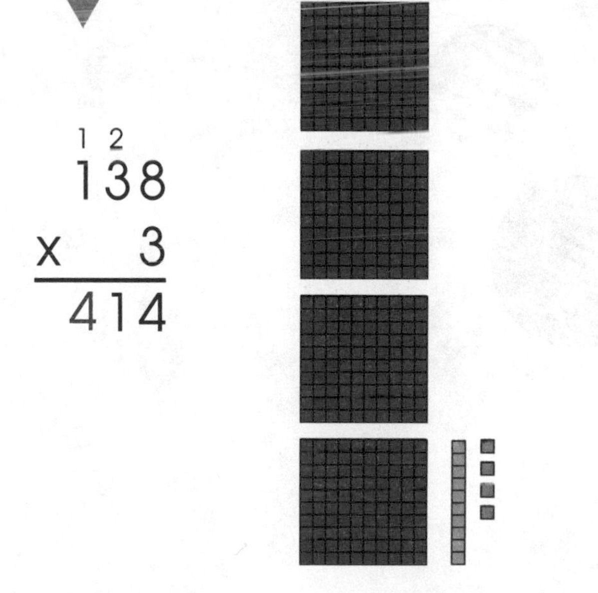

Multiply.

129 x 3	547 x 2	214 x 6
306 x 8	536 x 2	629 x 3
264 x 4	814 x 5	128 x 7

Name ____________________

Space Math

Complete this mission.

406 x 3	281 x 4	326 x 5	923 x 2	817 x 6	204 x 8
231 x 6	262 x 7	214 x 2	218 x 5	126 x 9	306 x 7
241 x 8	329 x 6	310 x 5	421 x 6	431 x 3	814 x 9
231 x 4	624 x 7	896 x 1	742 x 8	525 x 4	606 x 7

Solve It!

What set of ridges and loops are different on every person?
To find out, **solve** the following problems and **write** the matching letter above each answer at the bottom of the page.

I. 303 x 3 = 9 → 09 → 909 (worked example)

R. 214 x 2

N. 413 x 2

N. 142 x 2

R. 211 x 4

F. 104 x 2

T. 131 x 2

P. 232 x 3

E. 301 x 2

I. 134 x 1

G. 244 x 2

S. 334 x 2

___	___	___	___	___	___	___	___	___	___	___	___
208	909	826	488	602	844	696	428	134	284	262	668

Name ______________________

Four-Digit Regrouping

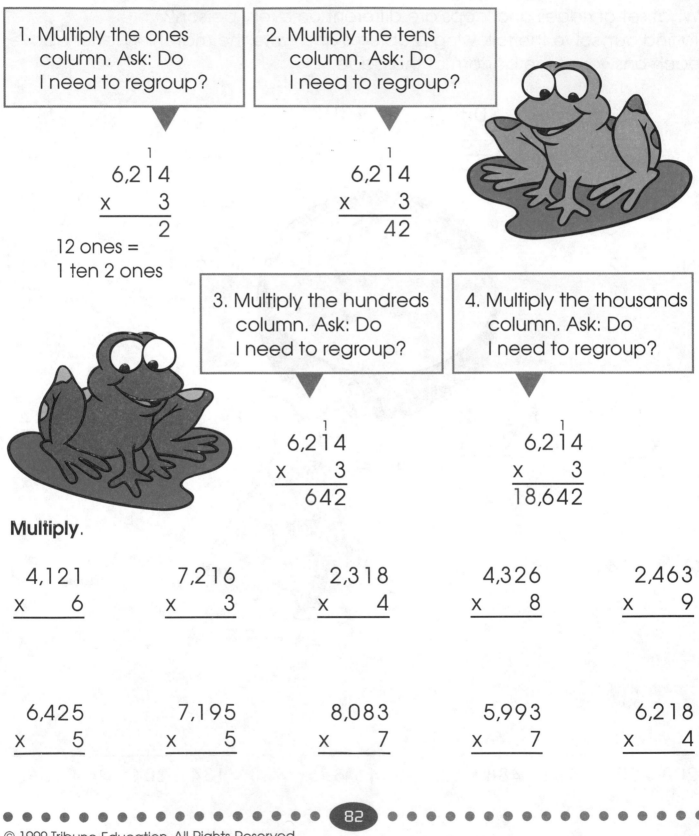

1. Multiply the ones column. Ask: Do I need to regroup?

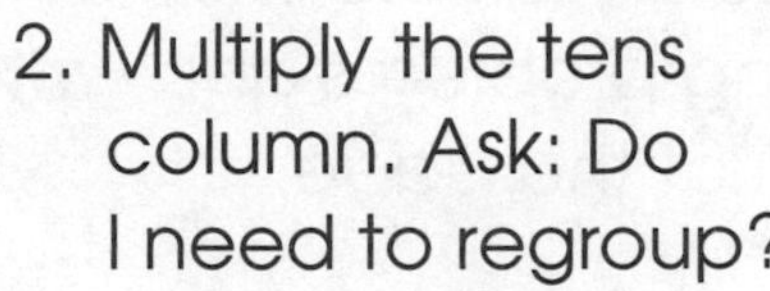
2. Multiply the tens column. Ask: Do I need to regroup?

```
     1
  6,214
x     3
-------
      2
```

12 ones = 1 ten 2 ones

```
     1
  6,214
x     3
-------
     42
```

3. Multiply the hundreds column. Ask: Do I need to regroup?

4. Multiply the thousands column. Ask: Do I need to regroup?

```
     1
  6,214
x     3
-------
    642
```

```
     1
  6,214
x     3
-------
 18,642
```

Multiply.

4,121	7,216	2,318	4,326	2,463
x 6	x 3	x 4	x 8	x 9

6,425	7,195	8,083	5,993	6,218
x 5	x 5	x 7	x 7	x 4

Name ______________________________

Amazing Arms

What will happen to a starfish that loses an arm? To find out, **solve** the following problems and **write** the matching letter above the answer at the bottom of the page.

O. 2,893 x 4

W. 1,763 x 3

W. 7,665 x 5

A. 1,935 x 6

W. 3,097 x 3

E. 2,929 x 4

G. 6,366 x 5

T. 7,821 x 8

L. 6,283 x 7

I. 5,257 x 3

R. 3,019 x 6

N. 2,908 x 7

I. 6,507 x 8

N. 5,527 x 2

L. 6,626 x 3

O. 7,219 x 9

E. 3,406 x 6

___ ___
52,056 62,568

___ ___ ___ ___ ___ ___ ___ ___
5,289 15,771 43,981 19,878 31,830 18,114 64,971 9,291

___ ___ ___ ___ ___ ___ ___ !
11,610 20,356 20,436 38,325 11,572 11,054 11,716

Name ____________________

Multiplying by a Two-Digit Number

1. Multiply by the ones place.
   3 x 2 = 6
   Ignore the 1 in the tens place.

$$\begin{array}{r} 43 \\ \times 12 \\ \hline 6 \end{array}$$

2. Multiply by the ones place.
   4 x 2 = 8

$$\begin{array}{r} 43 \\ \times 12 \\ \hline 86 \end{array}$$

3. Multiply by the tens. Place a zero in the ones column.
   3 x 1 = 3

$$\begin{array}{r} 43 \\ \times 12 \\ \hline 86 \\ 30 \end{array}$$

4. Multiply by the tens place.
   4 x 1 = 4

$$\begin{array}{r} 43 \\ \times 12 \\ \hline 86 \\ 430 \\ \hline \end{array}$$

5. Add.
   86 + 430 = 516

$$\begin{array}{r} 43 \\ \times 12 \\ \hline 86 \\ +430 \\ \hline 516 \end{array}$$

Multiply.

$$\begin{array}{r} 19 \\ \times 11 \\ \hline \end{array} \qquad \begin{array}{r} 32 \\ \times 31 \\ \hline \end{array}$$

$$\begin{array}{r} 54 \\ \times 20 \\ \hline \end{array} \qquad \begin{array}{r} 68 \\ \times 10 \\ \hline \end{array}$$

$$\begin{array}{r} 83 \\ \times 32 \\ \hline \end{array} \qquad \begin{array}{r} 42 \\ \times 24 \\ \hline \end{array}$$

$$\begin{array}{r} 73 \\ \times 23 \\ \hline \end{array} \qquad \begin{array}{r} 62 \\ \times 43 \\ \hline \end{array}$$

Now, **check** your answers with a calculator.

Name ______________________

Multiplying by a Two-Digit Number

With Regrouping

Multiply.

1. Multiply by the ones.
   8 x 7 = 56 (Carry the 5.)

```
  5
  67
 x38
   6
```

2. Multiply by the ones.
   8 x 6 = 48 + 5 = 53
   (When they are completed, cross out all carried digits.)

```
  5̸
  67
 x38
 536
```

3. Multiply by the tens. Place a zero in the ones column.
   3 x 7 = 21 (Carry the 2.)

```
 2 5̸
  67
 x38
 536
  10
```

4. Multiply by the tens.
   3 x 6 = 18 + 2 = 20

```
 2̸ 5̸
   67
  x38
  536
 2010
```

5. Add.
   536 + 2010 = 2,546

```
  2̸ 5̸
    67
   x38
   536
 +2010
 2,546
```

37	77
x24	x21

23	54
x45	x38

48	67
x62	x29

Now, **check** your answers with a calculator.

Name ______________________________

Multiplying by a Two-Digit Number

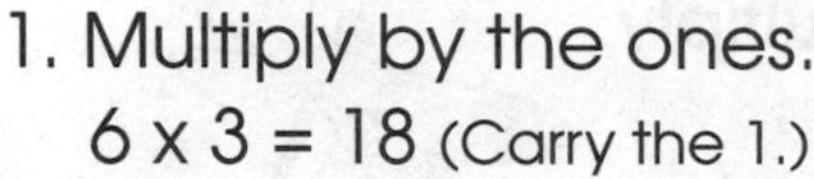

1. Multiply by the ones.
   6 x 3 = 18 (Carry the 1.)

```
  1
  43
 x26
   8
```

2. Multiply by the ones.
   6 x 4 = 24 + 1 = 25
   (When they are completed, cross out all carried digits.)

```
  X
  43
 x26
 258
```

3. Multiply by the tens. Place a zero in the ones column.
   2 x 3 = 6

```
  X
  43
 x26
 258
  60
```

4. Multiply by the tens.
   2 x 4 = 8

```
  X
  43
 x26
 258
 860
```

5. Add.
   258 + 860 = 1,118

```
   X
   43
  x26
  258
 +860
1,118
```

Multiply.

```
 21      52
x54     x34

 56      24
x14     x60

 23      69
x32     x19
```

Now, **check** your answers with a calculator.

Name ____________________

Elephant Escapades

Multiply.

56 x43	13 x24	24 x56	20 x93			
23 x54	28 x43	21 x64	25 x34			
13 x64	13 x82	34 x21	32 x55	42 x23	62 x31	51 x43
21 x64	10 x84	35 x24	24 x30	24 x53	81 x46	32 x27

Name ______________________________

Multiplication Drill

Multiply. **Color** the picture below by matching each number with its paint brush.

134	48	876	432
x 22	x66	x 13	x 64

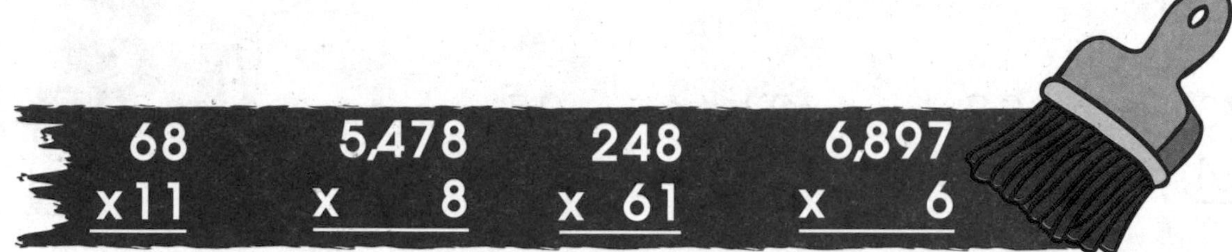

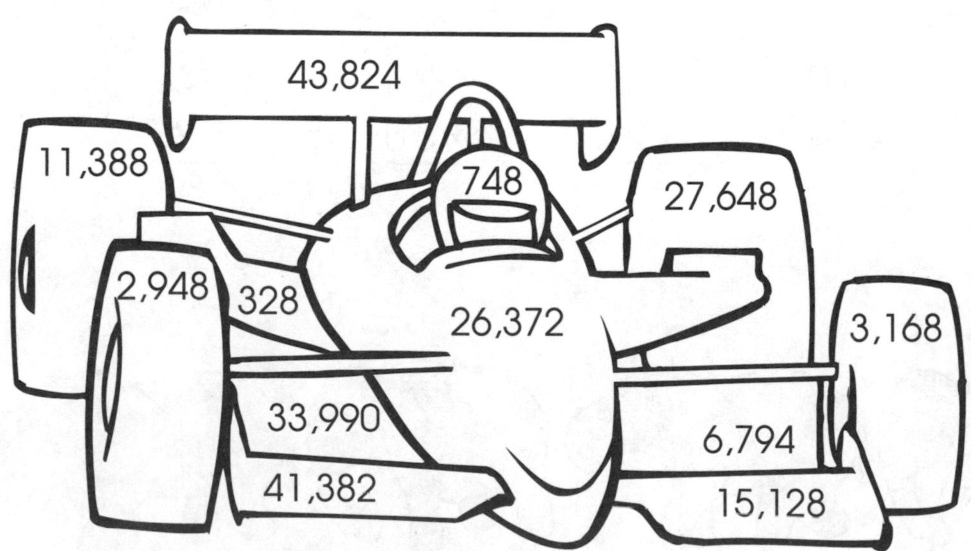

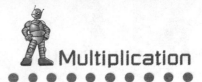

Step by Step

Read the problems below. **Write** each answer in the space provided.

1. One battalion of ants marches with 25 ants in a row. There are 35 rows of ants in each battalion. How many ants are in one battalion?

   ____

2. The Ant Army finds a picnic! Now, they need to figure out how many ants should carry each piece of food. A team of 137 ants moves a celery stick. They need 150 ants to carry a carrot stick. A troop of 121 ants carries a very large radish. How many ants in all are needed to move the vegetables?

   ____

3. Now, the real work begins—the big pieces of food that would feed their whole colony. It takes 1,259 ants to haul a peanut butter and jelly sandwich. It takes a whole battalion of 2,067 ants to lug the lemonade back, and it takes 1,099 ants to steal the pickle jar. How many soldiers carry these big items?

   ____

4. Look-outs are posted all around the picnic blanket. It takes 53 soldiers to watch in front of the picnic basket. Another group of 69 ants watch out by the grill. Three groups of 77 watch the different trails in the park. How many ant-soldiers are on the look-out?

   ____

Work space

Name ______________________________

Equally Alike

Label six shoe boxes with one of these numbers: 12, 18, 20, 24, 36 and 48. **Fill** each box with the number of objects on its label. For example, 12 game pieces may be in one box and 18 marbles in another.

Directions:

1. **Count** the number of objects in each box.
2. **Divide** the number of objects into different sets of equal numbers. **Write** all possible multiplication sentences for each one. Try to **write** the related division sentences as well.
3. **Complete** the activity chart below.

Box #	Number in set	Multiplication problem	Related division problem
12			
18			
20			
24			
36			
48			

Division

Name ____________________

Backward Multiplication

Division problems are like multiplication problems—just turned around. As you solve 8 ÷ 4, think, "how many groups of 4 make 8?" or "what number 'times' 4 is eight?"

2 x 4 = 8, so 8 ÷ 4 = **2**.

Use the pictures to help you **solve** these division problems.

9 ÷ 3 =

6 ÷ 2 =

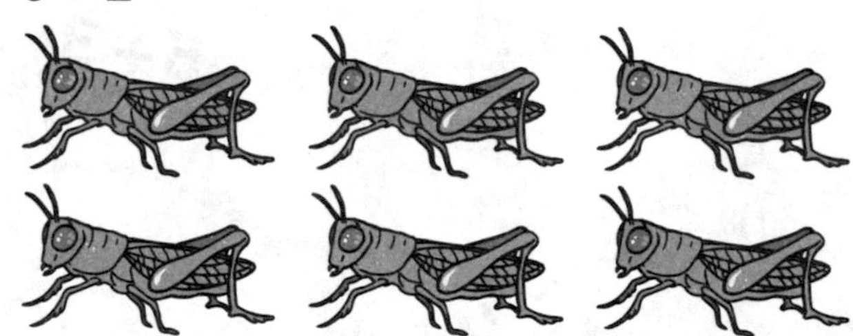

16 ÷ 4 =

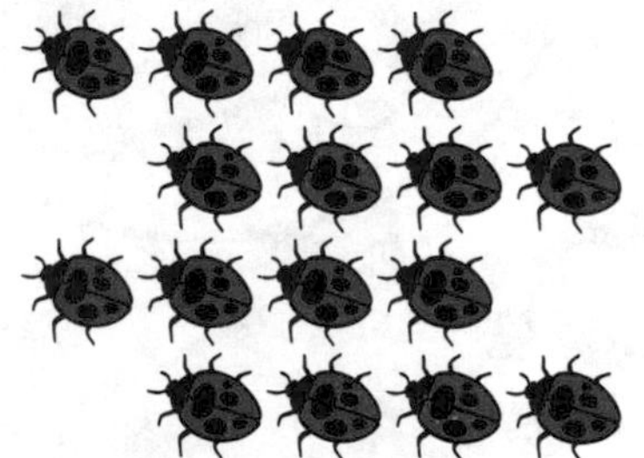

10 ÷ 5 =

20 ÷ 1 =

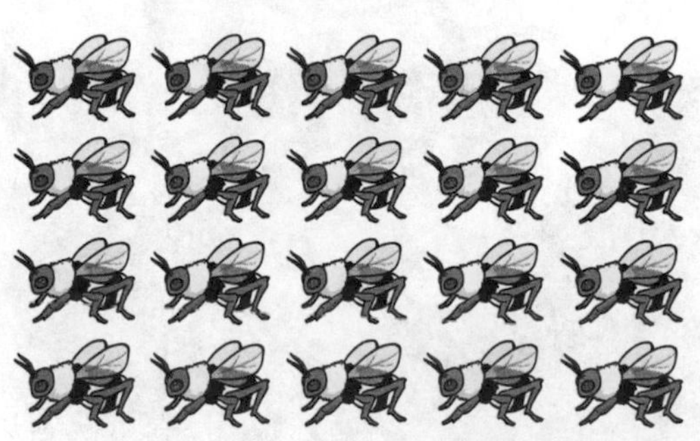

18 ÷ 3 =

Name ______________________________

What Exactly Is Division?

In division, you begin with an amount of something (the dividend), separate it into small groups (the divisor), then find out how many groups are created (the quotient).

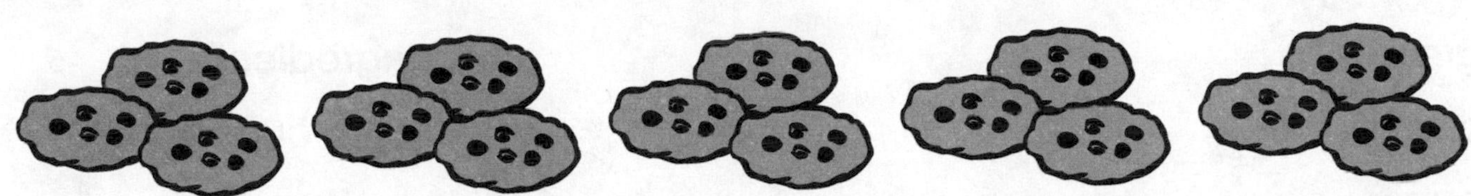

Dividend		Divisor		Quotient
15	÷	3	=	5 sets
in all		in each set		

$$3\overline{)15}$$ 5 sets above; 15 in all; 3 in each set

Solve these division problems.

21 ÷ 3 = ______ $3\overline{)21}$

18 ÷ 3 = ______ $3\overline{)18}$

20 ÷ 5 = ______ $5\overline{)20}$

16 ÷ 4 = ______ $4\overline{)16}$

14 ÷ 7 = ______ $7\overline{)14}$

12 ÷ 2 = ______ $2\overline{)12}$

18 ÷ 2 = ______ $2\overline{)18}$

24 ÷ 6 = ______ $6\overline{)24}$

Name ______________________________

Sandwich Cookie

Oops! This recipe below makes 24 dozen or 288 cookies.
Reduce the ingredients to make four dozen or 48 cookies. Then, follow the directions to bake the cookies. (We divided 24 dozen by 6 to get 4 dozen. Divide the rest of the ingredients by 6 also.)

Ingredients:

6 cups butter

6 eggs

3 teaspoons salt (think 6 half teaspoonsfull)

6 cups sugar

18 cups flour, sifted

strawberry jam

powdered sugar

Ingredients:

____ cups butter

____ eggs

____ teaspoons salt

____ cups sugar

____ cups flour, sifted

strawberry jam

powdered sugar

Directions: In a mixing bowl, cream the butter with the sugar until they are light and fluffy. Beat in the eggs. Sift the flour and salt into the butter/egg mixture. Mix until well blended. Refrigerate for 1 hour. Divide the dough in half and keep one-half in the refrigerator until needed. Preheat oven to 375˚.

Bottom Cookie: Roll out the first half of the dough to 1/8" thickness on a lightly floured surface. Cut out the dough using a 2"–3" round cookie cutter. Place the dough shapes on a cookie sheet. Bake for 10 to 12 minutes.

Top Cookie: Roll out the other half of the dough. Cut the dough using the same cookie cutter, but after it is cut, use a very small cookie cutter or a small bottle cap, floured, to cut a hole in the center of each dough shape. Place the shapes on a cookie sheet and bake them for 10 to 12 minutes. While they are cooling, sprinkle them lightly with powdered sugar.

When both sets of cookies are cool, spread jam on the bottom cookie. Cover it with the top cookie.

Name ______________________________

Make It Fair

While your cookies are baking, practice fair sharing by completing these problems. **Circle** the objects and **write** two division problems to go with each picture.

There are six children. **Circle** the number of cookies each child will get if the cookies are divided equally.

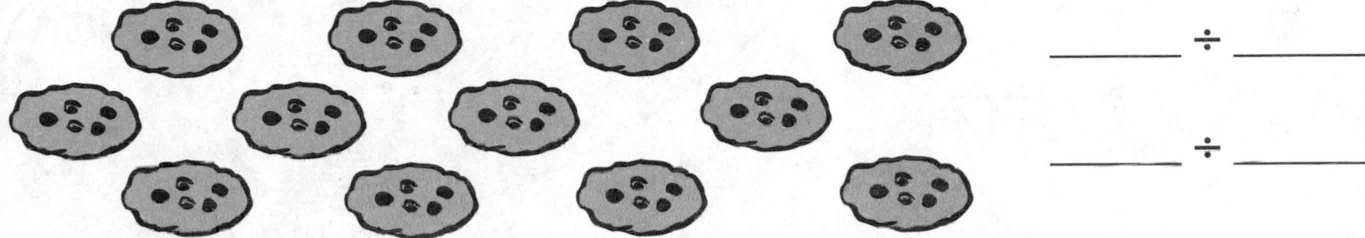

_____ ÷ _____

_____ ÷ _____

There are four dogs. **Circle** the dog bones each dog will get if the dog bones are divided equally.

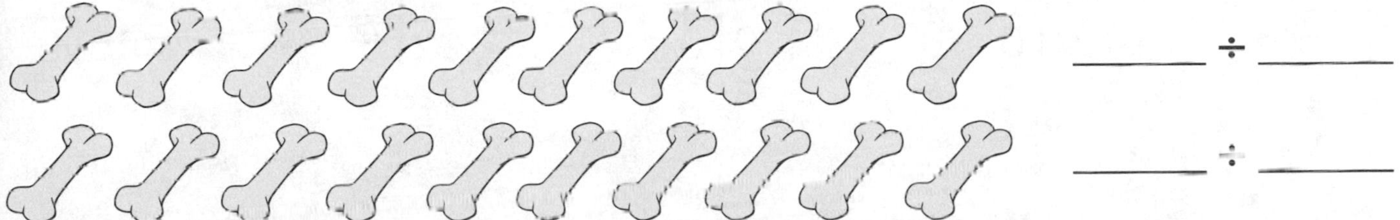

_____ ÷ _____

_____ ÷ _____

Divide the pepperoni so that five pizzas will have the same amount.

_____ ÷ _____

_____ ÷ _____

Divide the books so that there will be the same number of books on three shelves.

_____ ÷ _____

_____ ÷ _____

Name ____________________

Blastoff!

Divide.

$1\overline{)6}$ $20\overline{)0}$

$2\overline{)12}$ $2\overline{)14}$

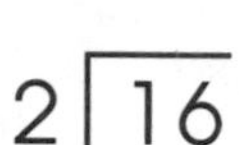

$2\overline{)16}$ $9\overline{)0}$ $9\overline{)0}$ $2\overline{)8}$ $15\overline{)0}$

$1\overline{)19}$ $2\overline{)18}$ $7\overline{)0}$ $2\overline{)10}$ $1\overline{)35}$

$1\overline{)23}$ $1\overline{)17}$ $1\overline{)7}$ $2\overline{)4}$ $12\overline{)0}$

$2\overline{)6}$ $1\overline{)11}$ $1\overline{)5}$

Carrier Math Messengers

Divide.

$3\overline{)12}$ $8\overline{)48}$ $2\overline{)18}$

$5\overline{)25}$ $9\overline{)72}$ $4\overline{)24}$

$6\overline{)42}$ $8\overline{)40}$ $2\overline{)4}$ $7\overline{)56}$ $9\overline{)63}$

$9\overline{)45}$ $7\overline{)7}$ $3\overline{)15}$ $2\overline{)8}$ $7\overline{)63}$

$3\overline{)24}$ $6\overline{)30}$ $9\overline{)54}$

$9\overline{)81}$ $7\overline{)28}$ $4\overline{)32}$

Name ______________________

Bath Math!

Divide.

$8\overline{)32}$ $6\overline{)36}$ $7\overline{)7}$

$7\overline{)56}$ $8\overline{)40}$ $9\overline{)72}$

$6\overline{)12}$ $9\overline{)36}$ $6\overline{)42}$ $6\overline{)48}$ $7\overline{)21}$

$7\overline{)28}$ $8\overline{)24}$

$8\overline{)16}$ $9\overline{)81}$ $6\overline{)54}$ $6\overline{)18}$

$8\overline{)8}$ $6\overline{)24}$ $7\overline{)35}$ $9\overline{)18}$ $8\overline{)48}$

$9\overline{)45}$

$9\overline{)63}$ $9\overline{)27}$

Name ________________________________

Division Tic–Tac–Toe

Solve the problems. **Draw** an **X** on the odd (9, 7, 5, 3) answers. **Draw** an **O** on the even (8, 6, 4, 2) answers.

$4\overline{)36}$	$4\overline{)24}$	$10 \div 5$
$5\overline{)40}$	$32 \div 4$	$25 \div 5$
$35 \div 5$	$20 \div 4$	$12 \div 4$

$4\overline{)32}$	$12 \div 4$	$5\overline{)30}$
$4\overline{)28}$	$4\overline{)20}$	$20 \div 4$
$20 \div 5$	$10 \div 5$	$15 \div 5$

$24 \div 4$	$5\overline{)45}$	$28 \div 4$
$5\overline{)45}$	$5\overline{)20}$	$8 \div 4$
$4\overline{)16}$	$5\overline{)15}$	$30 \div 5$

$25 \div 5$	$4\overline{)8}$	$16 \div 4$
$32 \div 4$	$5\overline{)20}$	$5\overline{)35}$
$40 \div 5$	$4\overline{)12}$	$15 \div 5$

$5\overline{)10}$	$4\overline{)8}$	$24 \div 4$
$4\overline{)36}$	$5\overline{)35}$	$4\overline{)32}$
$45 \div 5$	$5\overline{)30}$	$4\overline{)12}$

$8 \div 4$	$45 \div 5$	$4\overline{)16}$
$5\overline{)25}$	$36 \div 4$	$4\overline{)24}$
$5\overline{)10}$	$25 \div 5$	$4\overline{)36}$

$4\overline{)12}$	$5\overline{)10}$	$5\overline{)45}$
$30 \div 5$	$5\overline{)25}$	$35 \div 5$
$4\overline{)32}$	$8 \div 4$	$5\overline{)20}$

$36 \div 4$	$4\overline{)28}$	$16 \div 4$
$24 \div 4$	$5\overline{)35}$	$5\overline{)40}$
$5\overline{)25}$	$8 \div 4$	$36 \div 4$

$28 \div 4$	$5\overline{)30}$	$45 \div 5$
$16 \div 4$	$32 \div 4$	$15 \div 5$
$4\overline{)20}$	$4\overline{)12}$	$4\overline{)8}$

Name ______________________________

Jersey Division

Write the numbers in the correct footballs to get the given answer.

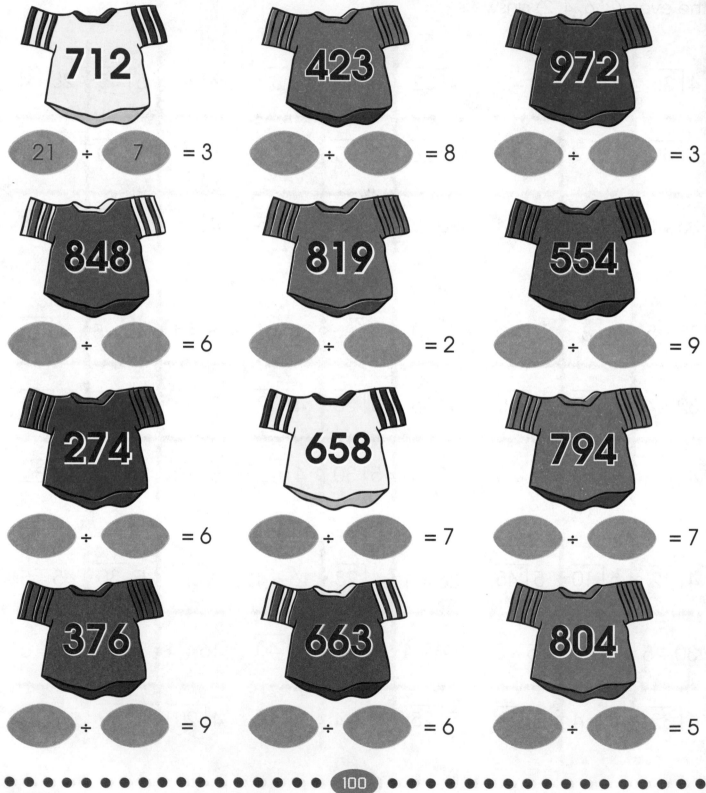

21 ÷ 7 = 3

÷ = 8

÷ = 3

÷ = 6

÷ = 2

÷ = 9

÷ = 6

÷ = 7

÷ = 7

÷ = 9

÷ = 6

÷ = 5

Name ______________________

Lizzy the Lizard Bags Her Bugs

Lizzy the Lizard separates her bugs into separate bags so that her lunch is ready for the week. Help her decide how to divide the bugs.

1 Lizzy caught 45 cockroaches. She put 5 into each bag. How many bags did she use?

_______ ÷ _______ = _______

2 Lizzy found 32 termites. She put 4 into each bag. How many bags did she need?

_______ ÷ _______ = _______

3 Lizzy captured 49 stinkbugs. She put them into 7 bags. How many stinkbugs were in each bag?

_______ ÷ _______ = _______

4 Lizzy bagged 27 horn beetles. She used 3 bags. How many beetles went into each bag?

_______ ÷ _______ = _______

5 Lizzy lassoed 36 butterflies. She put 9 into each bag. How many bags did she need?

_______ ÷ _______ = _______

6 Lizzy went fishing and caught 48 water beetles. She used 6 bags for her catch. How many beetles went into each bag?

_______ ÷ _______ = _______

Name ______________________________

Two-Digit Quotients

Steps:

1. Ask: Is the tens digit large enough to divide into? (Yes.) Divide. Multiply the partial quotient (2) by the divisor (4) and subtract from the partial dividend (8).

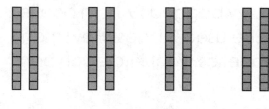

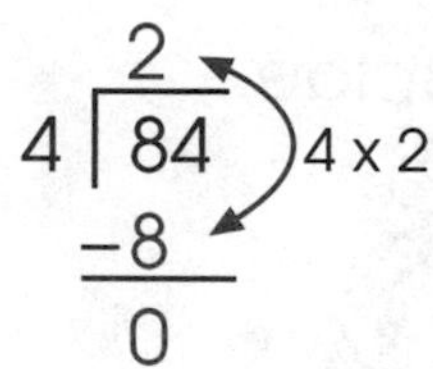

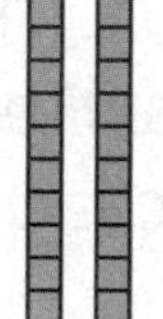

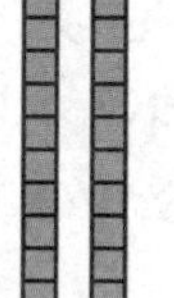

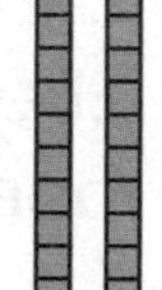

8 tens divided into 4 groups. How many are in each group? (2)

2. Carry down the 4 in the ones column. Ask: How many groups of 4 are there in 4? (1) Divide. Multiply the partial quotient (1) by the divisor (4) and subtract from the partial dividend (4).

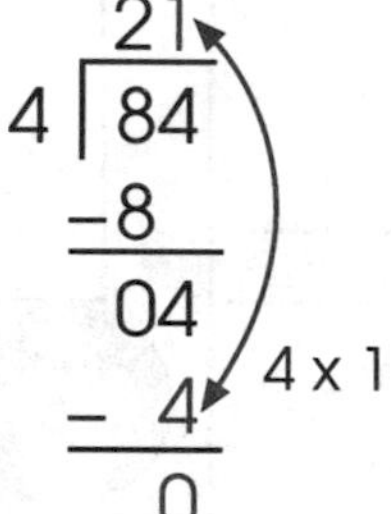

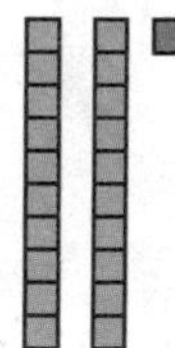

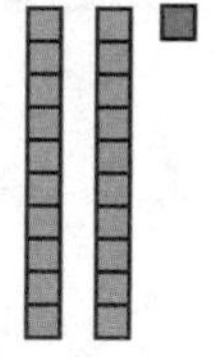

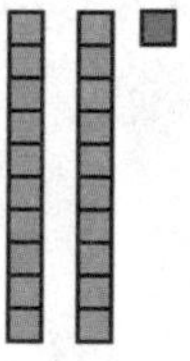

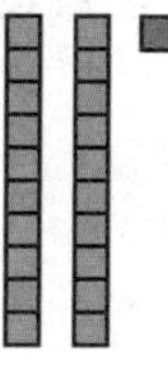

3. When 84 things are divided into 4 groups, there will be 21 in each group.

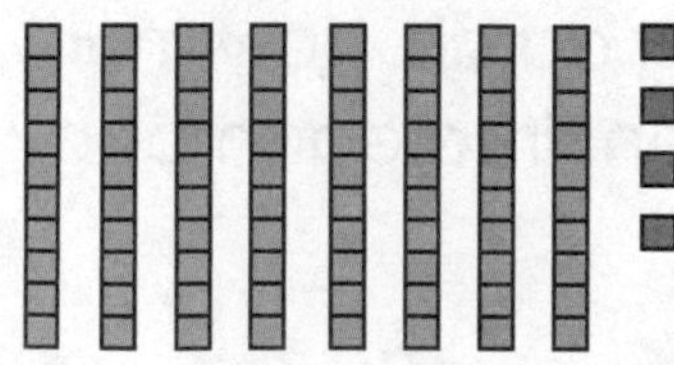

=

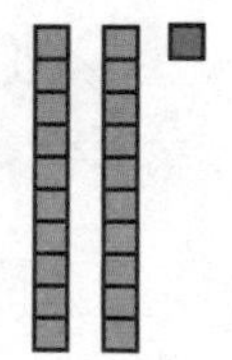

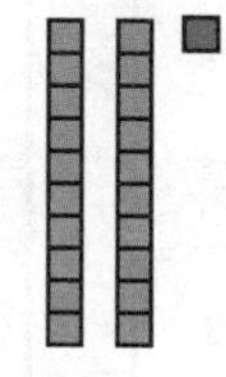

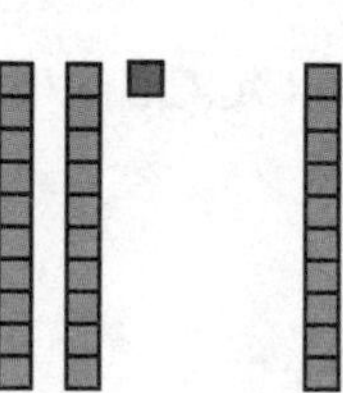

84 ÷ 4 = 21 + 21 + 21 + 21

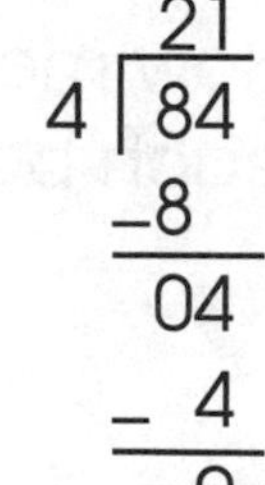

Divide.

3 | 63　　　2 | 72

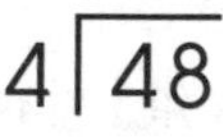

4 | 48　　　2 | 56

3 | 96　　　2 | 82

Name ______________________________

Snowball Bash

Divide this mound of giant snowballs!

$7\overline{)84}$

$5\overline{)75}$

$3\overline{)45}$

$9\overline{)99}$

$4\overline{)88}$

$5\overline{)80}$

$4\overline{)64}$ $3\overline{)57}$

$3\overline{)78}$

$3\overline{)72}$

$8\overline{)96}$

$2\overline{)86}$

$2\overline{)38}$ $6\overline{)66}$

$5\overline{)65}$

$4\overline{)52}$

$4\overline{)68}$

$6\overline{)78}$

$7\overline{)91}$

$2\overline{)42}$ $6\overline{)72}$

Name ______________________

Three-Digit Quotients

Steps:

1. Ask: Is the hundreds digit large enough to divide into? (Yes.) Divide. Multiply the partial quotient by the divisor and subtract from the partial dividend.

$$\begin{array}{r} 1 \\ 7\overline{)938} \\ -7 \\ \hline 2 \end{array}$$

2. Ask: Can I divide the remaining 2 by 7? (No.) Bring down the 3 tens.

$$\begin{array}{r} 1 \\ 7\overline{)938} \\ -7 \\ \hline 23 \end{array}$$

2 hundreds
+ 3 tens
= 23 tens

3. Divide the 23 tens by 7. Multiply the partial quotient by the divisor and subtract.

$$\begin{array}{r} 13 \\ 7\overline{)938} \\ -7 \\ \hline 23 \\ -21 \\ \hline 2 \end{array}$$

4. Ask: Can I divide the remaining 2 by 7? (No.) Bring down 8 ones.

$$\begin{array}{r} 13 \\ 7\overline{)938} \\ -7 \\ \hline 23 \\ -21 \\ \hline 28 \end{array}$$

2 tens
+ 8 ones
= 28 ones

5. Divide the 28 ones by 7. Multiply the partial quotient by the divisor and subtract.

$$\begin{array}{r} 134 \\ 7\overline{)938} \\ -7 \\ \hline 23 \\ -21 \\ \hline 28 \\ -28 \\ \hline 0 \end{array}$$

Divide.

$6\overline{)888}$ $2\overline{)542}$

$3\overline{)693}$ $4\overline{)544}$

$7\overline{)896}$ $5\overline{)635}$

Name ______________________________

On-Stage Division

Divide.

$6\overline{)888}$	$2\overline{)956}$	$2\overline{)712}$	$4\overline{)860}$		$5\overline{)845}$
$6\overline{)750}$	$9\overline{)999}$	$8\overline{)968}$	$3\overline{)774}$	$5\overline{)735}$	$8\overline{)920}$
		$8\overline{)984}$	$4\overline{)500}$	$2\overline{)846}$	$4\overline{)712}$

Name ______________________

Bargain Bonanza at Pat's Pet Place

Pat is having a gigantic sale. Help him divide his animals into groups for the sale.

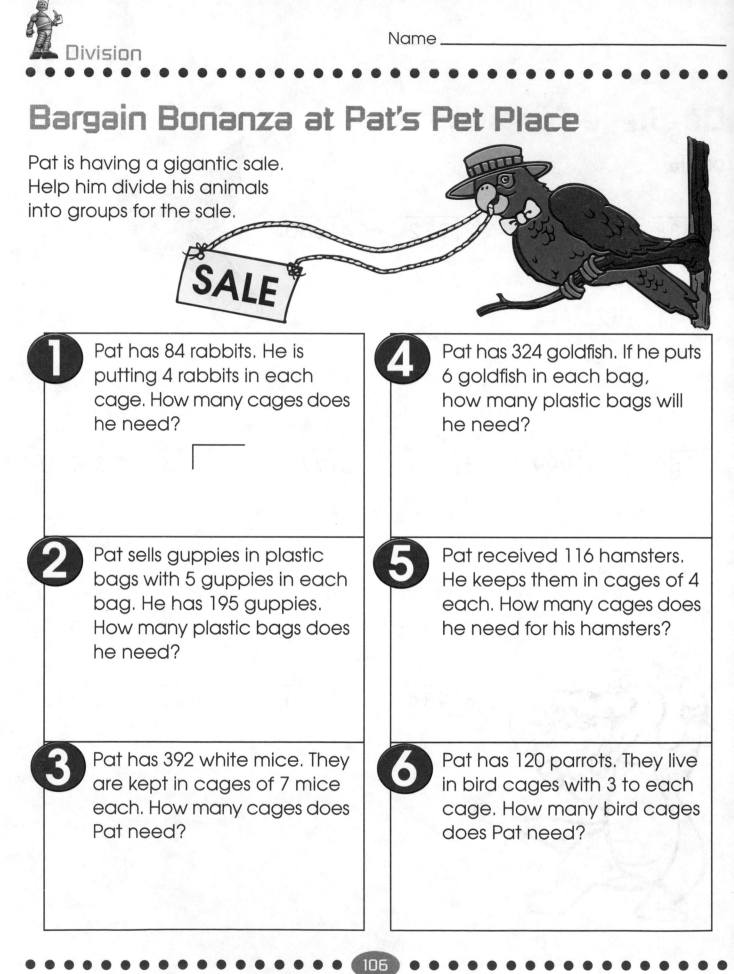

1. Pat has 84 rabbits. He is putting 4 rabbits in each cage. How many cages does he need?

2. Pat sells guppies in plastic bags with 5 guppies in each bag. He has 195 guppies. How many plastic bags does he need?

3. Pat has 392 white mice. They are kept in cages of 7 mice each. How many cages does Pat need?

4. Pat has 324 goldfish. If he puts 6 goldfish in each bag, how many plastic bags will he need?

5. Pat received 116 hamsters. He keeps them in cages of 4 each. How many cages does he need for his hamsters?

6. Pat has 120 parrots. They live in bird cages with 3 to each cage. How many bird cages does Pat need?

Name ______________________________

Zeros in the Quotient

Steps:

1. Decide where to place the first digit in the quotient. — 480 ÷ 3
   - 3 can go into 4.
2. Divide. Then, multiply. — $3\overline{)480}$
   - 4 ÷ 3 = 1
   - 3 x 1 = 3
3. Subtract and compare.
   - 4 − 3 = 1
   - Is 1 less than 3? (Yes.)

```
    1
3 ) 480
   -3
    1
```

4. Bring down. Repeat the steps.
   - Bring down 8.
   - 18 ÷ 3 = 6
   - 6 x 3 = 18
   - 18 − 18 = 0
   - Bring down 0.
   - 3 cannot go into 0.
   - 0 x 3 = 0

```
    160
3 ) 480
   -3
    18
   -18
     00
   -  0
      0
```

Steps:

1. Decide where to place the first digit in the quotient. — 327 ÷ 3
   - 3 can go into 3.
2. Divide. Then, multiply. — $3\overline{)327}$
   - 3 ÷ 3 = 1
   - 3 x 1 = 3
3. Subtract and compare.
   - 3 − 3 = 0
   - Is 0 less than 3? (Yes.)

```
    1
3 ) 327
   -3
    0
```

4. Bring down. Repeat the steps.
   - Bring down the 2.
   - 3 cannot go into 2.
   - 0 x 3 = 0
   - 2 − 0 = 2
   - Bring down the 7.
   - 27 ÷ 3 = 9
   - 9 x 3 = 27
   - 27 − 27 = 0

```
    109
3 ) 327
   -3
    02
   - 0
     27
   - 27
      0
```

Divide.

$3\overline{)624}$ $4\overline{)680}$ $2\overline{)722}$ $6\overline{)648}$ $2\overline{)814}$ $3\overline{)912}$

Name ____________________

Marty's Mania

Help Marty Mouse eat all the cheese by traveling the route.

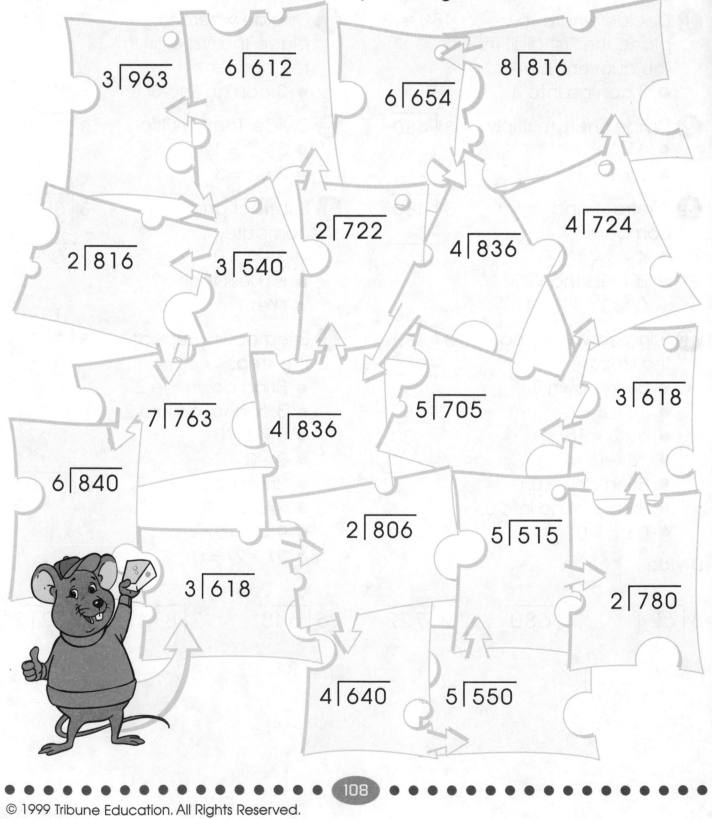

3 | 963   6 | 612   6 | 654   8 | 816

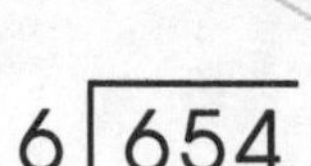

2 | 816   3 | 540   2 | 722   4 | 836   4 | 724

7 | 763   4 | 836   5 | 705   3 | 618

6 | 840   2 | 806   5 | 515

3 | 618   2 | 780

4 | 640   5 | 550

Name ________________________________

Yum! Yum!

What edible fungus is occasionally found on pizzas or in omelets? To find out, **solve** the following problems and **write** the matching letter above the answer at the bottom of the page.

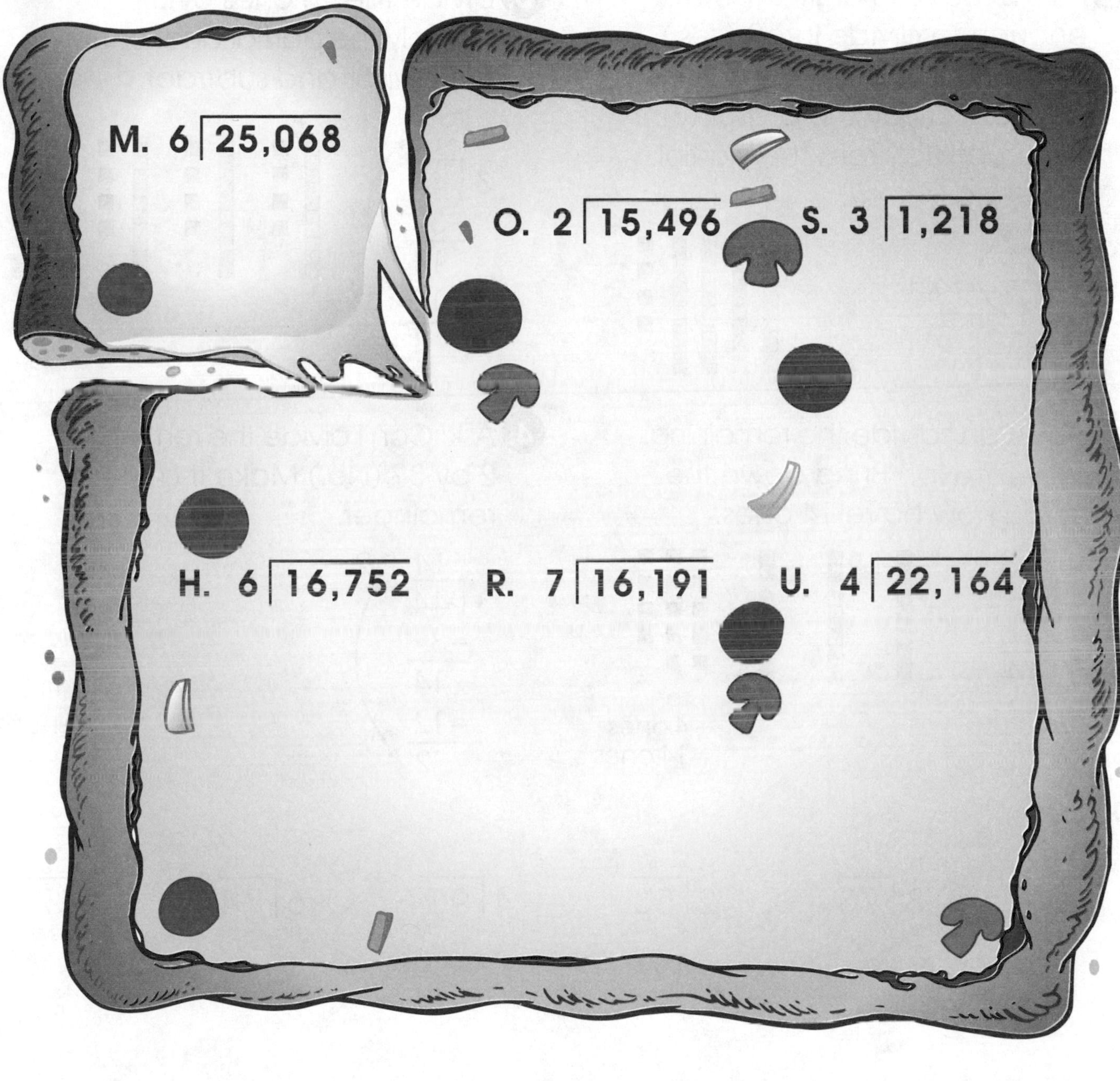

M. $6\overline{)25,068}$

O. $2\overline{)15,496}$

S. $3\overline{)1,218}$

H. $6\overline{)16,752}$

R. $7\overline{)16,191}$

U. $4\overline{)22,164}$

____	____	____	____	____	____	____	____	____
4,178	5,541	406	2,792	2,313	7,748	7,748	4,178	406

Name ______________________________

Two-Digit Quotients
With Remainders

Steps:

1. Ask: Is the tens digit large enough to divide into? (Yes.) Divide. Multiply the partial quotient (1) by the divisor (3) and subtract from the partial dividend (4)

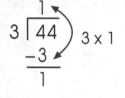

$$\begin{array}{r} 1 \\ 3\overline{)44} \\ -3 \\ \hline 1 \end{array} \quad 3 \times 1$$

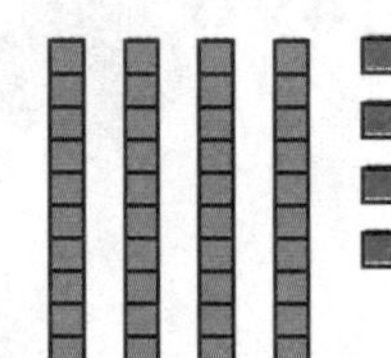

2. Ask: Can I divide the remaining 1 by 3? (No.) Bring down the 4. You now have 14 ones.

$$\begin{array}{r} 1 \\ 3\overline{)44} \\ -3 \\ \hline 14 \end{array}$$

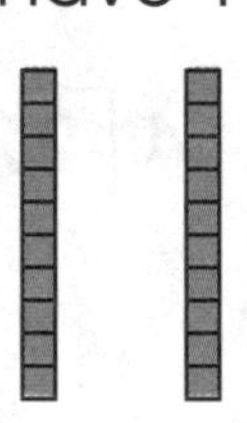
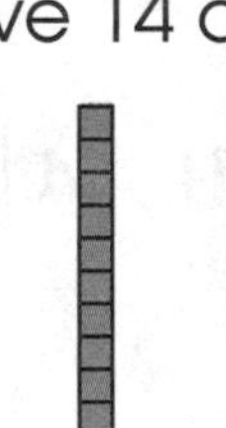
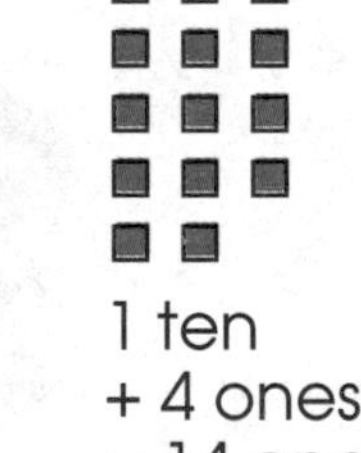

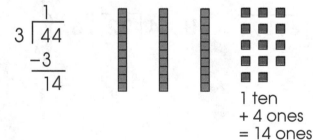

1 ten
\+ 4 ones
= 14 ones

3. Divide the 14 ones by 3. Multiply the partial quotient by the divisor and subtract.

$$\begin{array}{r} 14 \\ 3\overline{)44} \\ -3 \\ \hline 14 \\ -12 \\ \hline 2 \end{array} \quad 3 \times 4$$

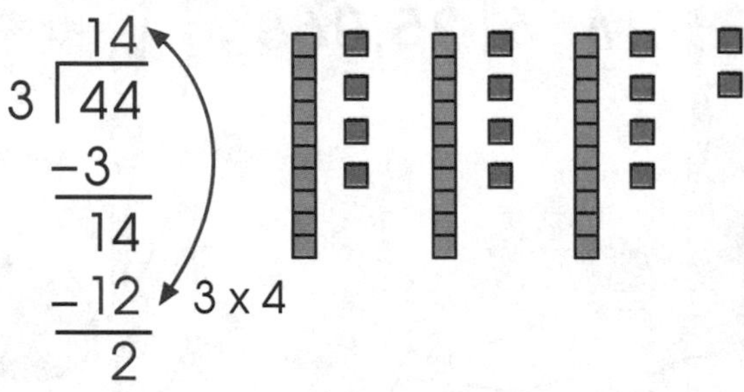

4. Ask: Can I divide the remaining 2 by 3? (No.) Make it a remainder.

$$\begin{array}{r} 14 \text{ R } 2 \\ 3\overline{)44} \\ -3 \\ \hline 14 \\ -12 \\ \hline 2 \end{array}$$

Divide.

$5\overline{)64}$ $3\overline{)73}$ $2\overline{)53}$ $4\overline{)91}$ $6\overline{)74}$ $3\overline{)76}$

Name ____________________________

Mr. R Means Business

Solve the division problems below. **Write** the quotient and the remainder.

Use me when a
problem doesn't
come out even.

No Remainder	Remainder
6	5 R 2
4 ⟌ 22	4 ⟌ 22
−24	−20
	2

5 R 3 5 ⟌ 28 −25 3	4 R 4 ⟌ 19	3 R 8 ⟌ 26	6 R 7 ⟌ 45
R 3 ⟌ 26	R 2 ⟌ 19	R 6 ⟌ 51	R 9 ⟌ 65
R 8 ⟌ 43	R 9 ⟌ 59	R 7 ⟌ 33	R 4 ⟌ 27

Name ______________________________

Division Checklist

How to check division:

Quotient
x Divisor
+ Remainder
Dividend

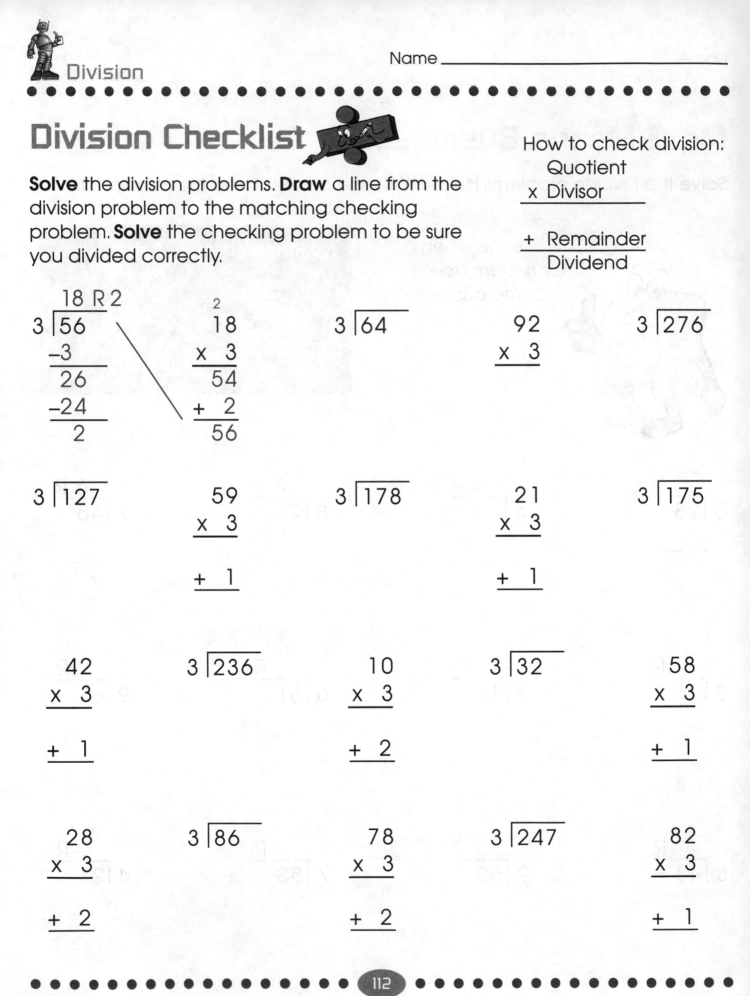

Solve the division problems. **Draw** a line from the division problem to the matching checking problem. **Solve** the checking problem to be sure you divided correctly.

18 R2 3)56 −3 26 −24 2	18 (carried 2) x 3 54 + 2 56	3)64	92 x 3	3)276
3)127	59 x 3 + 1	3)178	21 x 3 + 1	3)175
42 x 3 + 1	3)236	10 x 3 + 2	3)32	58 x 3 + 1
28 x 3 + 2	3)86	78 x 3 + 2	3)247	82 x 3 + 1

Name ____________________

Looking to the Stars

Solve the problems. To find the path to the top, your answers should match the problem number. **Color** the path.

	27. 3)63	28. 3)84	29. 4)97	30. 6)74		
	22. 4)74	23. 2)46	24. 2)48	25. 3)75	26. 6)96	
15. 5)92	16. 3)41	17. 3)57	18. 4)84	19. 4)76	20. 7)86	21. 5)72
8. 5)57	9. 3)65	10. 2)87	11. 5)55	12. 7)84	13. 3)87	14. 7)93
1. 3)96	2. 6)94	3. 5)93	4. 9)36	5. 2)97	6. 6)84	7. 3)68

Name ____________________

Three-Digit Quotients
With Remainders

Steps:

1. Ask: Is the hundreds digit large enough to divide into? (Yes.) Divide. Multiply the partial quotient by the divisor and subtract from the partial dividend.

```
   2
4 |854
  -8
   0
```

2. Bring down the 5 tens. Ask: Can I divide 5 by 4? (Yes.) Multiply the partial quotient by the divisor and subtract.

```
   21
4 |854
  -8
   05
  - 4
    1
```

3. Ask: Is the difference of 1 less than the divisor 4? (Yes.) Bring down the 4 ones.
   1 ten + 4 ones = 14 ones

```
   21
4 |854
  -8
   05
  - 4
   14
```

4. Divide the 14 ones by 4. Multiply the partial quotient by the divisor and subtract.

```
   213
4 |854
  -8
   05
  - 4
    14
  - 12
     2
```

5. Ask: Is the remaining difference of 2 less than the divisor? (Yes.) Make 2 a remainder.

```
   213 R2
4 |854
  -8
   05
  - 4
    14
  - 12
     2
```

Divide.

$2\overline{)631}$ $6\overline{)945}$ $3\overline{)860}$ $5\overline{)914}$ $4\overline{)927}$ $8\overline{)972}$

Name ____________________________

Puzzling Problems

Solve the following problems. **Write** the answers in the puzzle.

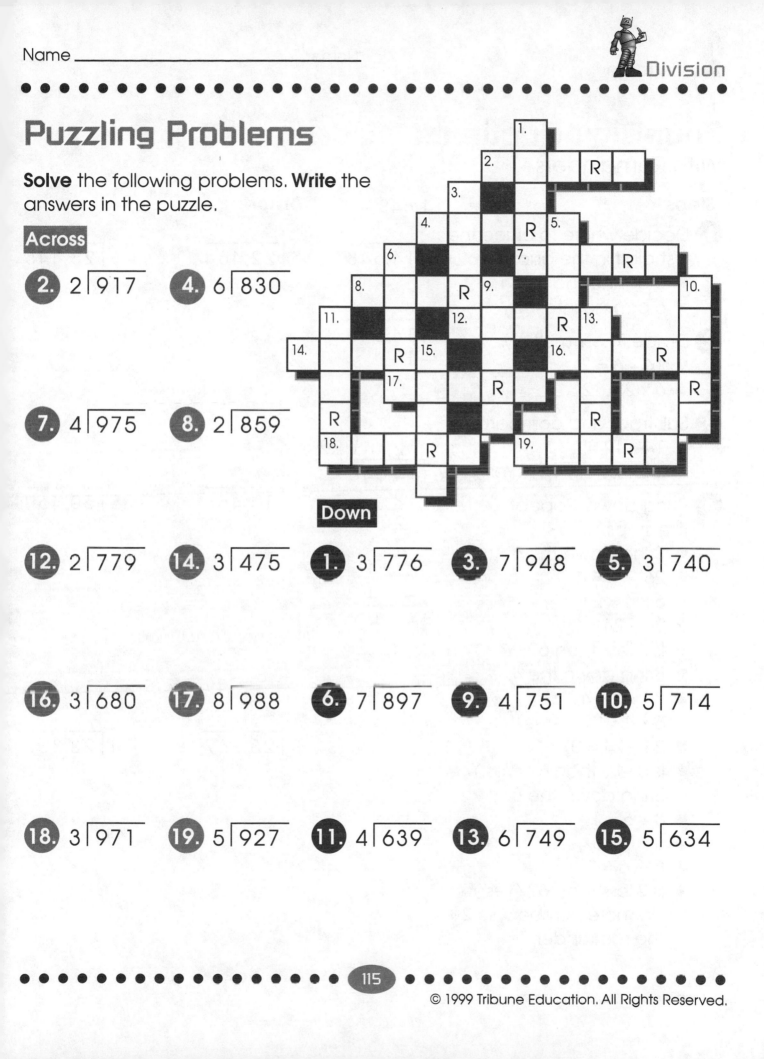

Across

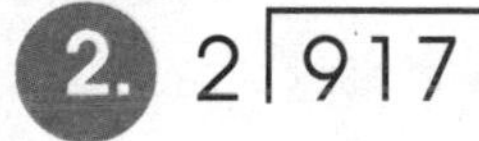

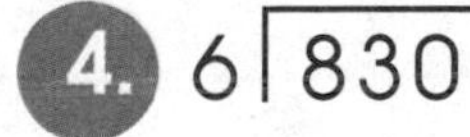

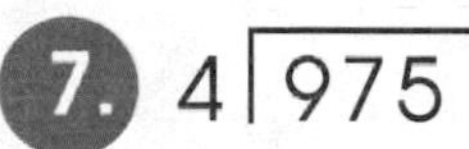

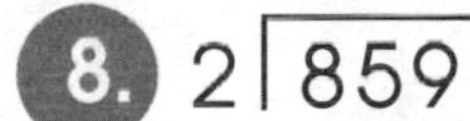

12. 2)779

14. 3)475

16. 3)680

17. 8)988

18. 3)971

19. 5)927

Down

1. 3)776

3. 7)948

5. 3)740

6. 7)897

9. 4)751

10. 5)714

11. 4)639

13. 6)749

15. 5)634

Name ____________________

Four-Digit Quotients

With Remainders

Steps:

1. Decide where to place the first digit in the quotient.
- 6 cannot go into 1.
- 6 can go into 14.

2. Divide. Then, multiply.
- 14 ÷ 6 = 2
- 6 x 2 = 12

3. Subtract and compare.
- 14 – 12 = 2
- Is 2 less than 6? (Yes.)

4. Bring down. Repeat the steps.
- Bring down the 6.
- 26 ÷ 6 = 4
- 6 x 4 = 24
- 26 – 24 = 2
- Is 2 less than 6? (Yes.)
- Bring down the 4.
- 24 ÷ 6 = 4
- 6 x 4 = 24
- 24 – 24 = 0
- Is 0 less than 6? (Yes.)
- Bring down the 8.
- 8 ÷ 6 = 1
- 6 x 1 = 6
- 8 – 6 = 2
- Is 2 less than 6? (Yes.)
- No more numbers, so 2 is the remainder.

14,648 ÷ 6

6 ⟌ 14,648

```
     2
6 ⟌ 14,648
   -12
     2
```

```
     2,441 R2
6 ⟌ 14,648
   -12
     26
   - 24
      24
    - 24
       08
     -  6
        2
```

Divide.

5 ⟌ 22,464

6 ⟌ 23,445

3 ⟌ 14,458

8 ⟌ 50,469

3 ⟌ 23,767

4 ⟌ 23,303

Name ___________________________

To Catch a Butterfly

Solve the problems. **Draw** a line to connect each net to the butterfly with the correct answer.

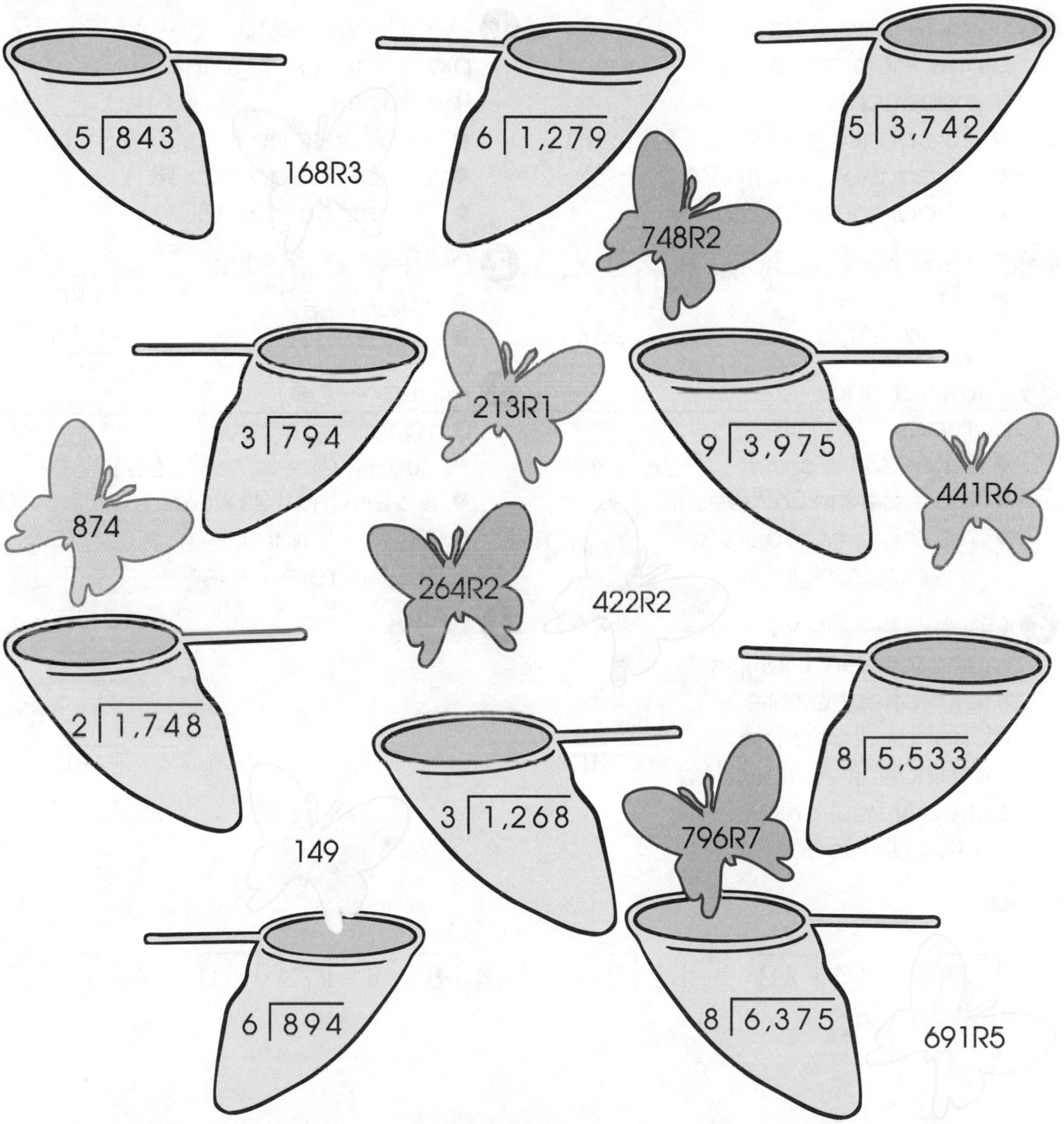

5 ⟌ 843

168R3

6 ⟌ 1,279

5 ⟌ 3,742

748R2

3 ⟌ 794

213R1

9 ⟌ 3,975

441R6

874

264R2

422R2

2 ⟌ 1,748

3 ⟌ 1,268

8 ⟌ 5,533

796R7

149

6 ⟌ 894

8 ⟌ 6,375

691R5

Name ________________________________

Two-Digit Divisors

With Remainders

Steps:

1. Decide where to place the first digit in the quotient. $240 \div 26$

- 26 cannot go into 2.
- 26 cannot go into 24.
- 26 can go into 240.

$26\overline{)240}$

2. Divide. Then, multiply.

- $240 \div 26 = 9$
- $9 \times 26 = 234$

$$\begin{array}{r} 9 \\ 26\overline{)240} \\ -234 \end{array}$$

3. Subtract and compare.

- $240 - 234 = 6$
- Is 6 less than 26? (Yes.)
- No more numbers, so 6 is the remainder.

$$\begin{array}{r} 9\ R6 \\ 26\overline{)240} \\ -234 \\ \hline 6 \end{array}$$

4. Check division with multiplication. Multiply the quotient by the divisor and add the remainder. If you divided correctly, your answer will be the dividend!

$$\begin{array}{r} 26 \\ \times\ 9 \\ \hline 234 \\ +\ 6 \\ \hline 240 \end{array}$$

Steps:

1. Decide where to place the first digit in the quotient. $180 \div 25$

- 25 cannot go into 1.
- 25 cannot go into 18.
- 25 can go into 180.

$25\overline{)180}$

2. Divide. Then, multiply.

- $180 \div 25 = 7$
- $7 \times 25 = 175$

$$\begin{array}{r} 7 \\ 25\overline{)180} \\ -175 \end{array}$$

3. Subtract and compare.

- $180 - 175 = 5$
- Is 5 less than 25? (Yes.)
- No more numbers, so 5 is the remainder.

$$\begin{array}{r} 7\ R5 \\ 25\overline{)180} \\ -175 \\ \hline 5 \end{array}$$

4. Check.

$$\begin{array}{r} 25 \\ \times\ 7 \\ \hline 175 \\ +\ 5 \\ \hline 180 \end{array}$$

Divide.

$14\overline{)77}$ $34\overline{)70}$ $13\overline{)80}$ $24\overline{)82}$ $17\overline{)140}$ $47\overline{)290}$

Name ______________________________

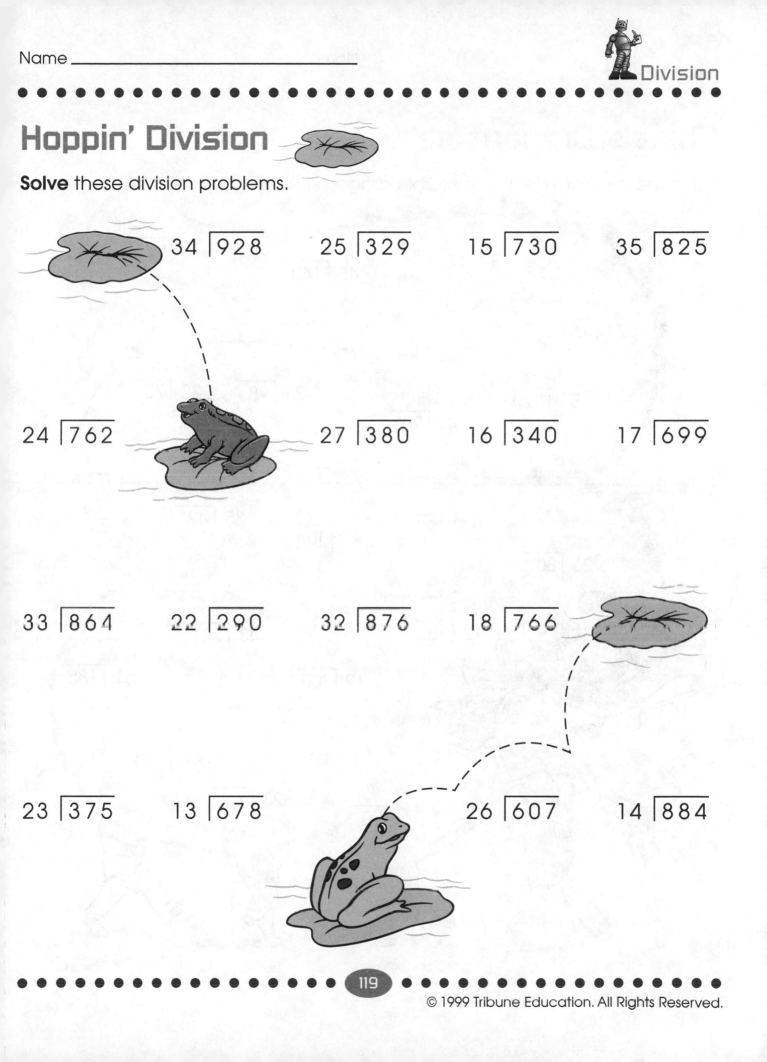

Hoppin' Division

Solve these division problems.

$34\overline{)928}$ $25\overline{)329}$ $15\overline{)730}$ $35\overline{)825}$

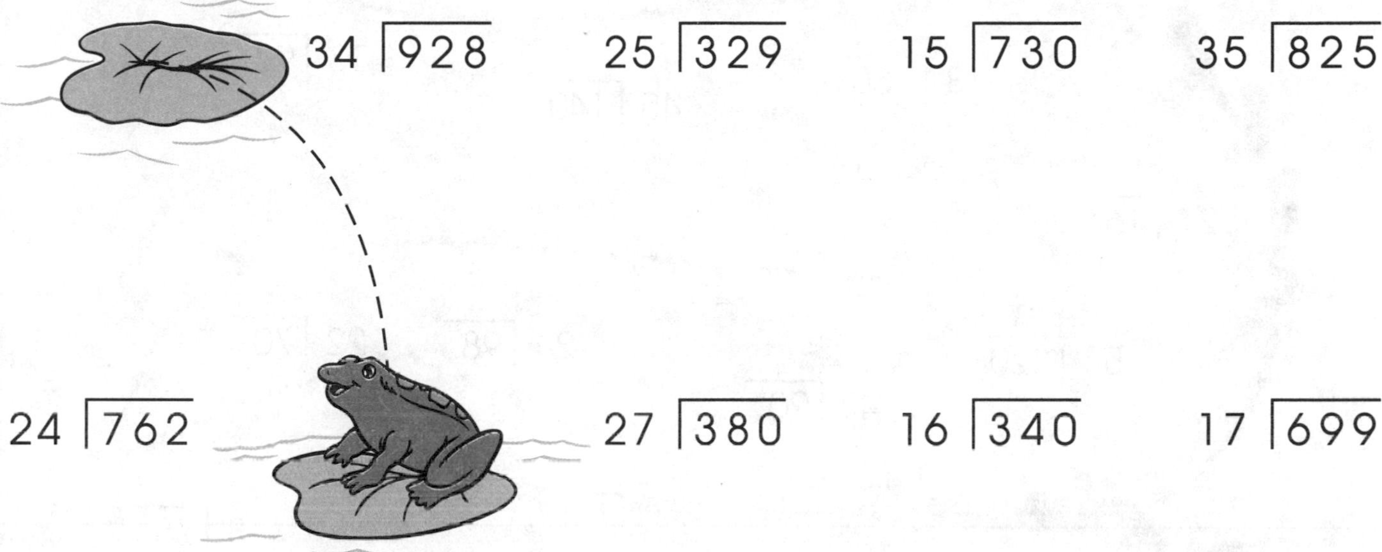

$24\overline{)762}$ $27\overline{)380}$ $16\overline{)340}$ $17\overline{)699}$

$33\overline{)864}$ $22\overline{)290}$ $32\overline{)876}$ $18\overline{)766}$

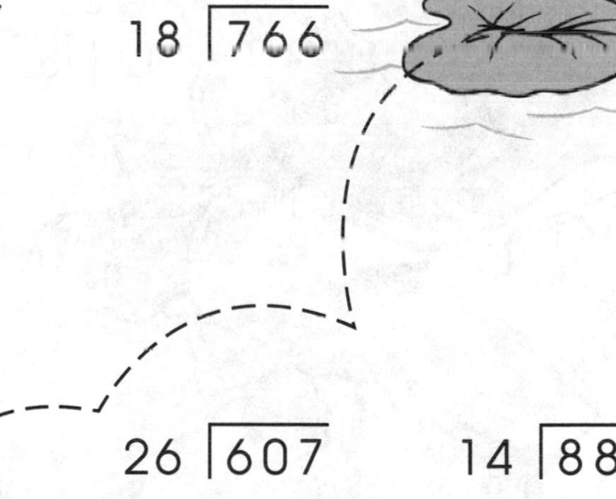

$23\overline{)375}$ $13\overline{)678}$ $26\overline{)607}$ $14\overline{)884}$

Name ____________________

China's Dragon Kite

Solve the problems in this incredible dragon kite!

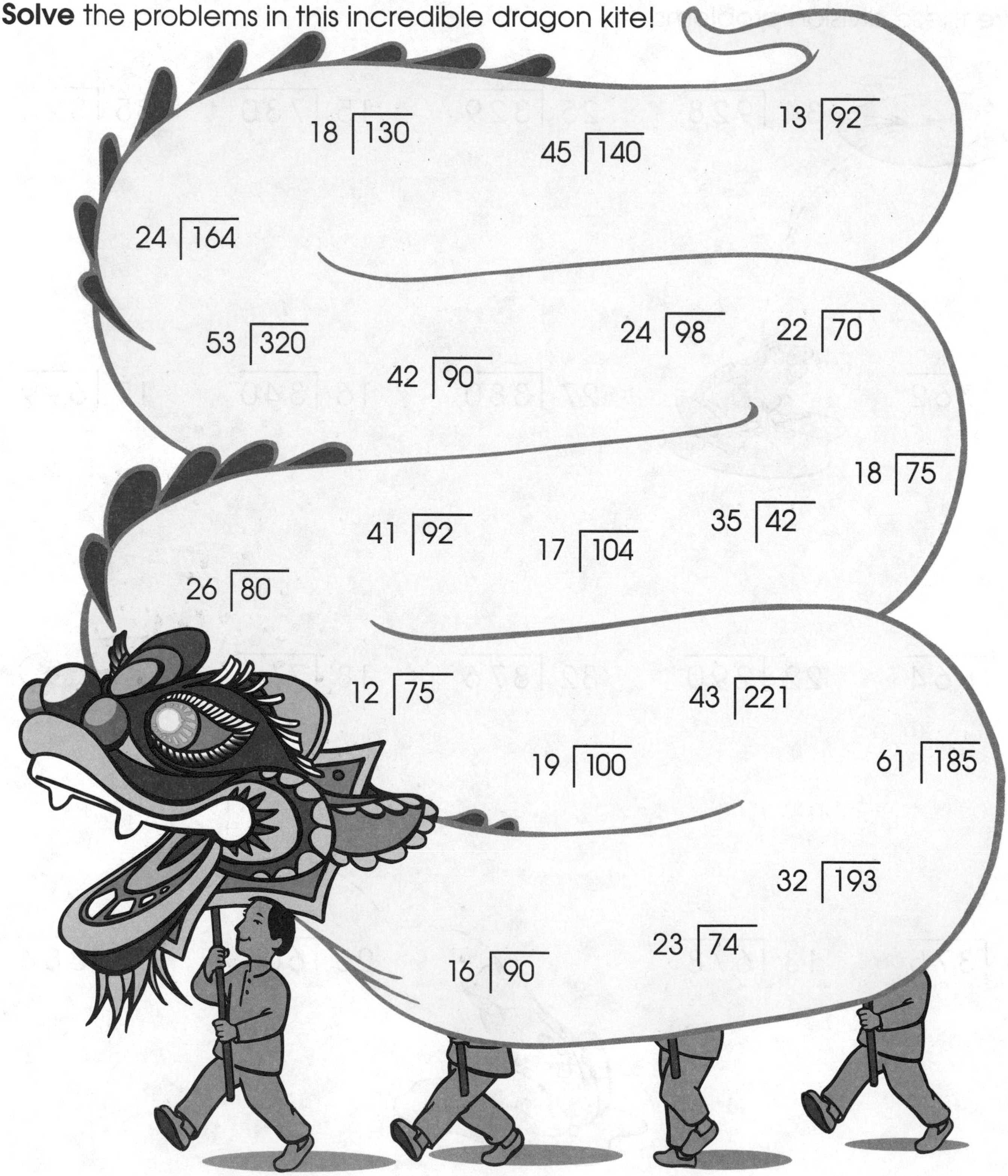

$18\overline{)130}$ $45\overline{)140}$ $13\overline{)92}$

$24\overline{)164}$

$53\overline{)320}$ $42\overline{)90}$ $24\overline{)98}$ $22\overline{)70}$

$18\overline{)75}$

$41\overline{)92}$ $17\overline{)104}$ $35\overline{)42}$

$26\overline{)80}$

$12\overline{)75}$ $43\overline{)221}$

$19\overline{)100}$ $61\overline{)185}$

$32\overline{)193}$

$23\overline{)74}$

$16\overline{)90}$

Name ______________________

Number Puzzles

Solve these number puzzles.

1

Write your age. ________

Multiply it by 3. ________

Add 18. ________

Multiply by 2. ________

Subtract 36. ________

Divide by 6. (your age) ________

2

Write any number. ________

Double that number. ________

Add 15. ________

Double again. ________

Subtract 30. ________

Divide by 2. ________

Divide by 2 again. ________

3

Write any 2-digit number. ________

Double that number. ________

Add 43. ________

Subtract 18. ________

Add 11. ________

Divide by 2. ________

Subtract 18. ________

4

Write the number of children in your neighborhood. ________

Double that number. ________

Add 15. ________

Double it again. ________

Subtract 30. ________

Divide by 4. ________

Name ____________________

Identifying Operations

Write the correct sign in each circle.

5 ◯ 5 = 10

9 ◯ 9 = 81

56 ◯ 8 = 48

91 ◯ 16 = 75

54 ◯ 6 = 9

28 ◯ 17 = 11

25 ◯ 5 = 5

72 ◯ 9 = 63

64 ◯ 8 = 56

36 ◯ 4 = 9

45 ◯ 5 = 40

14 ◯ 59 = 73

56 ◯ 17 = 73

40 ◯ 5 = 8

9 ◯ 3 = 27

29 ◯ 37 = 66

6 ◯ 5 = 30

36 ◯ 5 = 31

56 ◯ 8 = 7

7 ◯ 1 = 7

57 ◯ 9 = 48

7 ◯ 6 = 42

21 ◯ 9 = 30

64 ◯ 8 = 8

7 ◯ 8 = 56

76 ◯ 19 = 57

43 ◯ 7 = 50

4 ◯ 9 = 36

48 ◯ 8 = 6

9 ◯ 1 = 9

45 ◯ 5 = 9

36 ◯ 27 = 63

48 ◯ 6 = 42

9 ◯ 8 = 72

8 ◯ 8 = 64

82 ◯ 9 = 91

36 ◯ 63 = 99

6 ◯ 9 = 54

33 ◯ 57 = 90

27 ◯ 3 = 9

63 ◯ 9 = 54

8 ◯ 38 = 46

2 ◯ 9 = 18

55 ◯ 37 = 92

81 ◯ 9 = 9

80 ◯ 17 = 63

32 ◯ 4 = 8

71 ◯ 15 = 86

Name ______________________________

Which Problem Is Correct?

Circle the equation on the left you should use to solve the problem. Then, **solve** the problem. Remember the decimal point in money questions.

1. $\begin{array}{r} 56 \\ +17 \\ \hline \end{array}$ $\begin{array}{r} 56 \\ -17 \\ \hline \end{array}$

   Bill and his friends collect baseball cards. Bill has 17 fewer cards than Mack. Bill has 56 cards. How many baseball cards does Mack have?

2. $\begin{array}{r} 54 \\ \times\ 3 \\ \hline \end{array}$ $3\overline{)54}$

   Amos bought 54 baseball cards. He already had 3 times as many. How many baseball cards did Amos have before his latest purchase?

3. $\begin{array}{r} 3.80 \\ +3.50 \\ \hline \end{array}$ $\begin{array}{r} 3.80 \\ -3.50 \\ \hline \end{array}$

   Joe paid \$3.50 for a Mickey Mantle baseball card. Ted Williams cost him \$3.80. How much more did he pay for Ted Williams than for Mickey Mantle?

4. $\begin{array}{r} 3.60 \\ \times\ \ \ 9 \\ \hline \end{array}$ $9\overline{)3.60}$

   Will bought 9 baseball cards for \$3.60. How much did he pay per (for each) card?

5. $\begin{array}{r} 8.00 \\ +\ .50 \\ \hline \end{array}$ $\begin{array}{r} 8.00 \\ -\ .50 \\ \hline \end{array}$

   Babe Ruth baseball cards were selling for \$8.00. Herb Score baseball cards sold for 50 cents. Herb Score cards sold for how much less than Babe Ruth cards?

6. $\begin{array}{r} 0.75 \\ \times\ \ \ 8 \\ \hline \end{array}$ $8\overline{)0.75}$

   Andy bought 8 baseball cards at 75 cents each. How much did Andy pay in all?

Name ____________________

Emery Prepares for His Party

Read each story problem carefully. What is the question? What information is given that will help with the answer? Will drawing a picture help? Remember that solving story problems takes time.

Write each problem and its answer.

1. If Emery needed 329 knives, 329 forks and 329 spoons, how many pieces of silverware did Emery need altogether?

   ____

2. Emery cooked 329 eggs for his guests. How many dozen eggs did he need to buy?

   ____

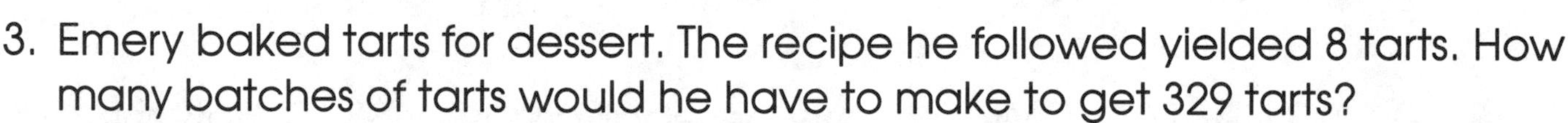

3. Emery baked tarts for dessert. The recipe he followed yielded 8 tarts. How many batches of tarts would he have to make to get 329 tarts?

   ____

4. If each recipe called for 2 eggs, how many eggs would Emery need to make the tarts? To solve this problem, you will need the information from problem 3.

   ____

5. The guests sat at 54 tables. Each table had 2 vases. Emery put 5 flowers in each vase. How many flowers did he have to pick?

   ____

Name ______________________________

The Lion Dance

The Lion Dance, which started in China, became a Japanese folk dance. In this dance, many people line up under a long piece of colorful cloth. The person in front wears a mask of a lion's head. As a group, the line of people dances in the streets around the town.

In this Lion Dance, the children lined up in this order: 2 boys, 2 girls, 2 boys, 2 girls. The order remained the same through the entire line.

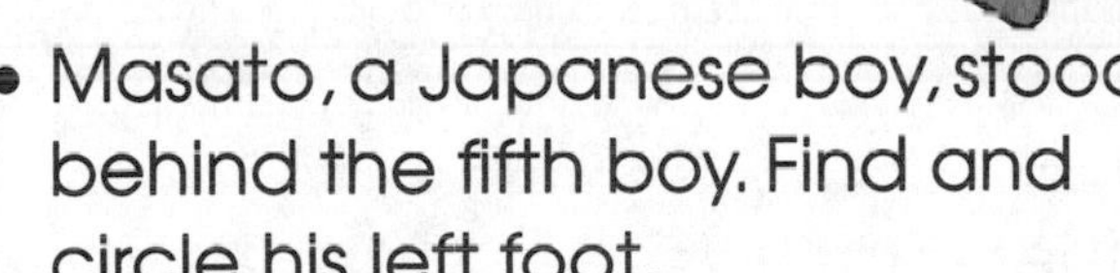

- Masato, a Japanese boy, stood behind the fifth boy. Find and circle his left foot.
- Koko, a Japanese girl, stood in front of the seventh boy. Put a box around her left foot.
- If every two children needed a 4-foot section of the cloth and the lion's head was 4 feet long, how many feet long is the entire costume?

________ feet

Challenge!
How many yards long is the entire lion costume?

________ yards

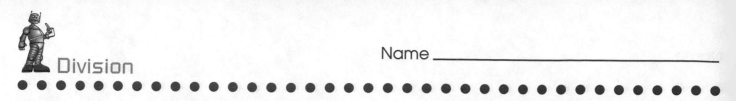

Name ______________________________

On the Average . . .

Division is good for finding averages. An **average** is a number that tells about how something is normally.

The children on the 6-on-6 basketball team made the following number of baskets:

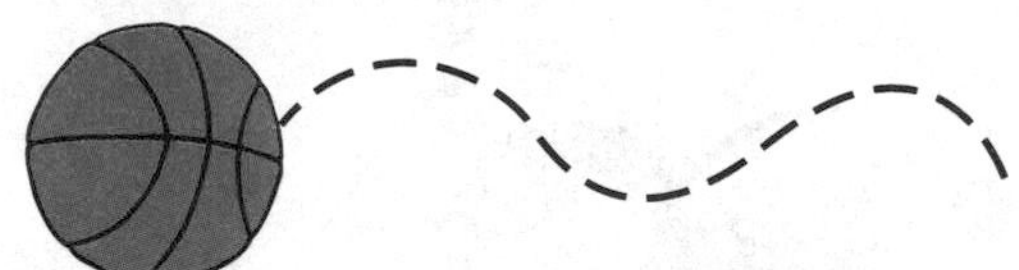

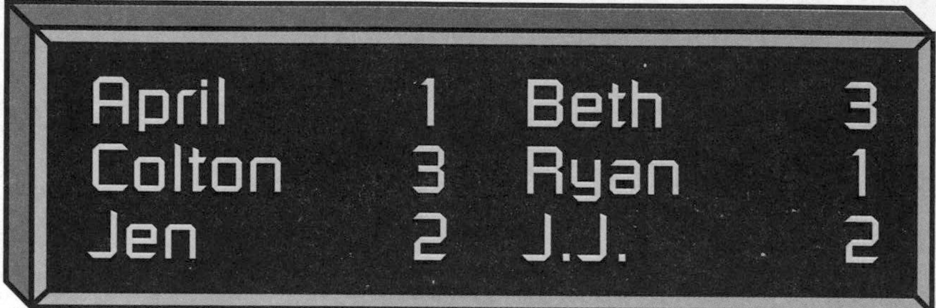

April	1	Beth	3
Colton	3	Ryan	1
Jen	2	J.J.	2

The school paper wants to write about the game, but they don't have room for such a long list. Instead the reporter will find the average by following the steps below.

Steps:

1. **Add** all the team members' baskets together.

_____ + _____ + _____ + _____ + _____ + _____ = _____

2. **Count** to find out how many team members there were.

_____

3. **Divide** your answer for step 1 by the number in step 2.

_____ ÷ _____ = _____

The paper will report that each team member normally makes an average of 2 baskets each. Remember—add, count, divide.

Find the average for the following problem:
In their last 3 games, the Longlegs scored 24 points, 16 points and 20 points.

1) Add. 2) Count. 3) Divide.

What was their average? _______________

Name ____________________

Work It Out

The **average** is the result of dividing the **sum** of addends by the **number** of addends. **Match** the problem with its answer.

Add. 62 + 79 + 87 = 228 } **Count.** **Divide.** 228 ÷ 3 = 76

1. 80 + 100 + 90 + 95 + 100	◯	A. 53
2. 52 + 56 + 51	◯	B. 190
3. 85 + 80 + 95 + 95 + 100	◯	C. 410
4. 782 + 276 + 172	◯	D. 91
5. 125 + 248 + 214 + 173	◯	E. 93
6. 81 + 82 + 91 + 78	◯	F. 55
7. 40 + 60 + 75 + 45	◯	G. 83
8. 278 + 246	◯	H. 33
9. 75 + 100 + 100 + 70 + 100	◯	I. 3
10. 0 + 0 + 0 + 0 + 15	◯	J. 262
11. 21 + 34 + 44	◯	K. 89
12. 437 + 509 + 864 + 274	◯	L. 94
13. 80 + 80 + 100 + 95 + 95	◯	M. 8
14. 4 + 6 + 7 + 12 + 11	◯	N. 90
15. 75 + 100 + 100 + 100 + 95	◯	O. 521

Name ____________________

Story Problems

Solve the following problems.

Work Space

1. The daily temperatures for one week in May were 49°F, 51°F, 52°F, 69°F, 76°F, 77°F and 81°F. What was the average daily temperature for the entire week?

   ____

2. Over a 5-day period, 255 cold lunches were brought to school. What was the average daily number of cold lunches brought to school over the 5-day period?

   ____

3. Kayla scored 86%, 96%, 92%, 98%, 86% and 100% on her last six spelling tests. Based on these percentages, what is her average score?

   ____

4. Jonah practices basketball every night, and his goal is to practice an average of 60 minutes a night. He practiced 50 minutes on Monday, 68 minutes on Tuesday, 40 minutes on Wednesday, 40 minutes on Thursday and 72 minutes on Friday. What is the average amount of minutes per day Jonah practiced this past week? ________

   Did Jonah reach his goal? ________

5. During the past soccer season, the Newhall Rovers had an average of 5 goals per game. If they play 25 games this coming season and score a total of 150 goals, will they achieve the same average number of goals?

   ____

Geometry

Name ____________________

Geometry Match-Ups

A **polygon** is a closed shape with straight sides.

Directions: Cut out each polygon on the next page. To make them more durable, glue them onto cardboard or oaktag. Use the shapes to fill out the table below. (Keep the shapes for other activities as well.)

Game: Play this game with a partner. Put the shapes in a bag or cover them with a sheet of paper. Player One pulls out a shape and tells how many sides and angles it has. Without showing the shape, he/she puts the polygon back. Player Two should name the shape. Then, Player Two puts his/her hand in the bag and, without looking, tries to find the polygon from the description. Then, switch roles. Continue the game until all the polygons have been identified.

When you finish playing, **complete** the chart below.

Drawing of the shape (or polygon)	Shape name	Number of sides	Number of angles (or corners)
	triangle		
	square		
	pentagon		
	rectangle		
	hexagon		

Name ____________________________________

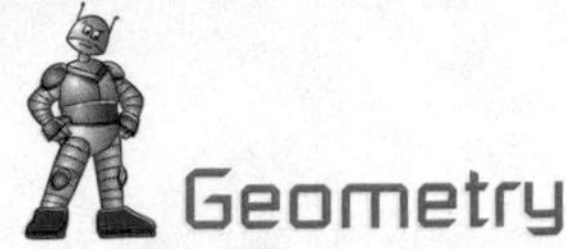

Shapes

hexagon

pentagon

square

triangle

rectangle

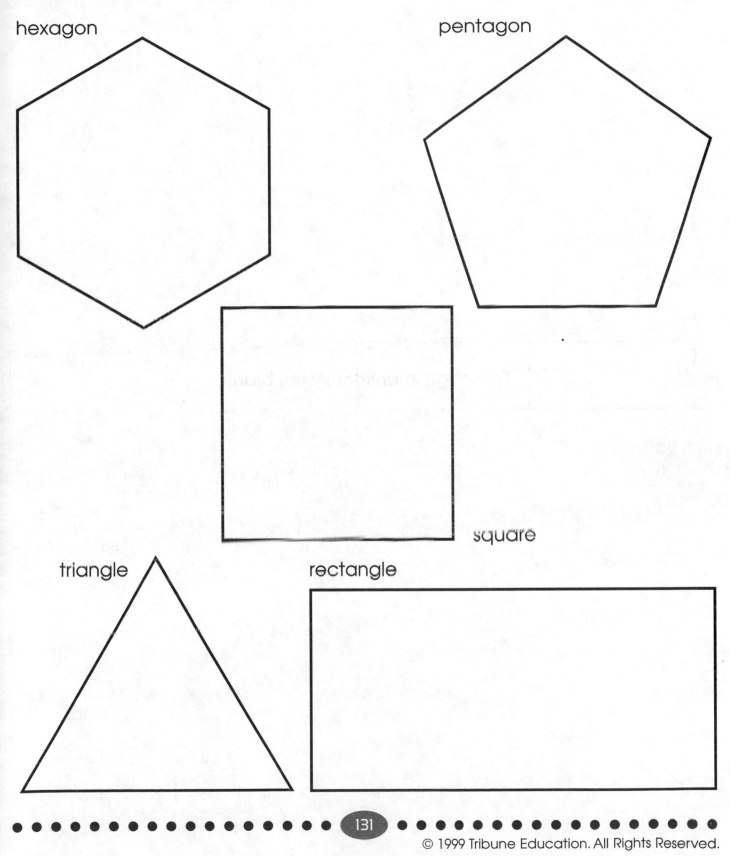

This page intentionally left blank.

Name ____________________

Triangle Puzzle

Directions: Using the triangle pattern below, cut out 37 triangles using the same color of construction paper. If you want, glue the gameboards and the triangles to tagboard for added strength. Next, arrange the triangles to make the shapes on the gameboards on pages 135 and 137. You have the exact number of triangles needed to complete all the shapes. The triangles may not be folded or cut in any way. To make this a game, you could have someone time you to see how long it takes. Keep the puzzle pieces in an envelope to use alone or with someone.

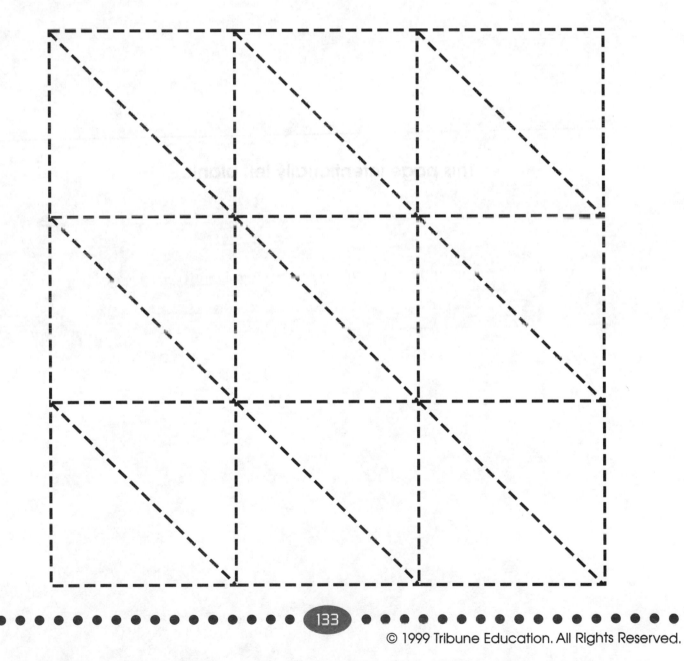

This page intentionally left blank.

Name ______________________________

Triangle Puzzle

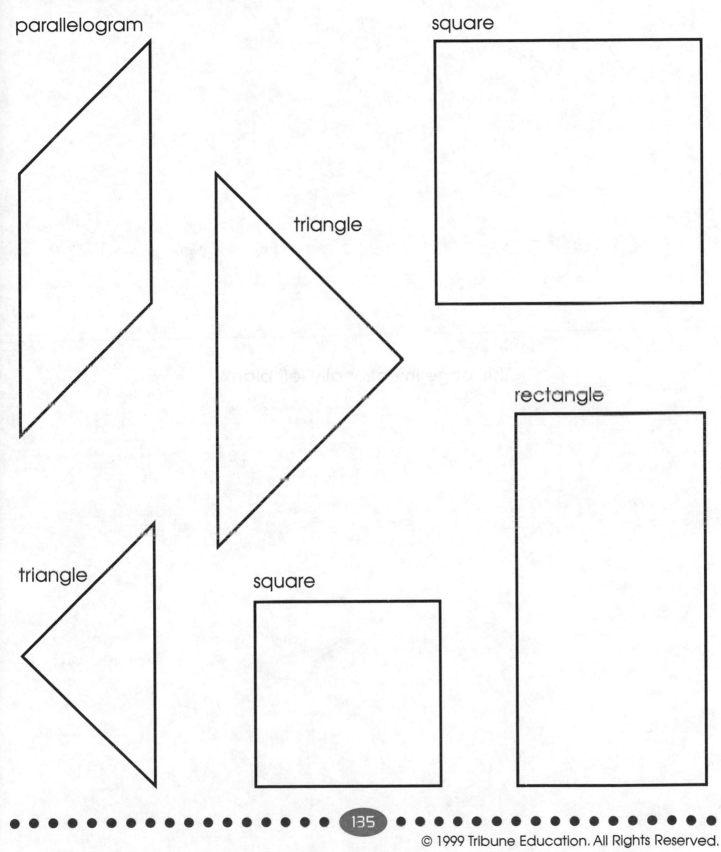

parallelogram

square

triangle

rectangle

triangle

square

This page intentionally left blank.

Name ____________________________

Triangle Puzzle

square

trapezoid

parallelogram

quadrilateral

triangle

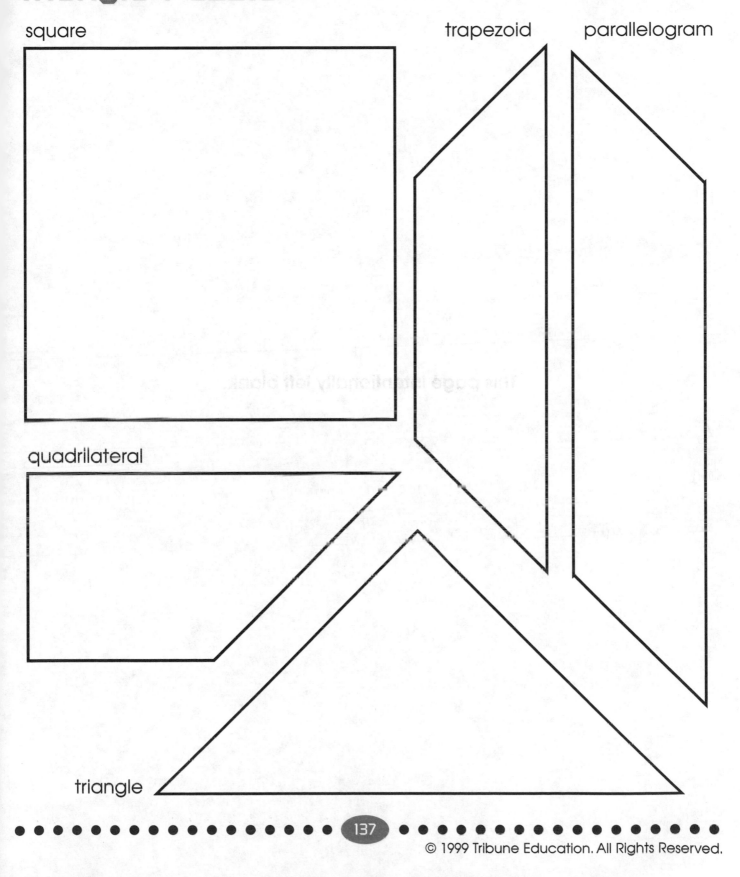

This page intentionally left blank.

Name ____________________________

A Native American Wall Hanging

Congruent figures have the same size and shape. They do not have to be the same color or in the same position.

Congruent figures

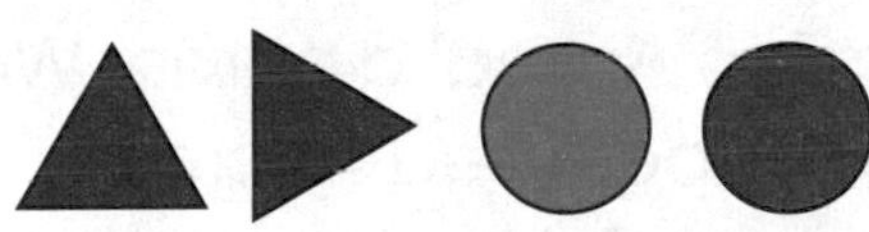

Not congruent figures

Directions: Draw two congruent figures to create a new shape. You can use triangles, squares, rectangles, pentagons, hexagons, octagons, semicircles, quarter-circles or trapezoids to make the shape. Use the new shape to create a wall hanging design. Connect the two congruent figures at one side. Color each part of the congruent pairs. Display your hanging on a wall of your house.

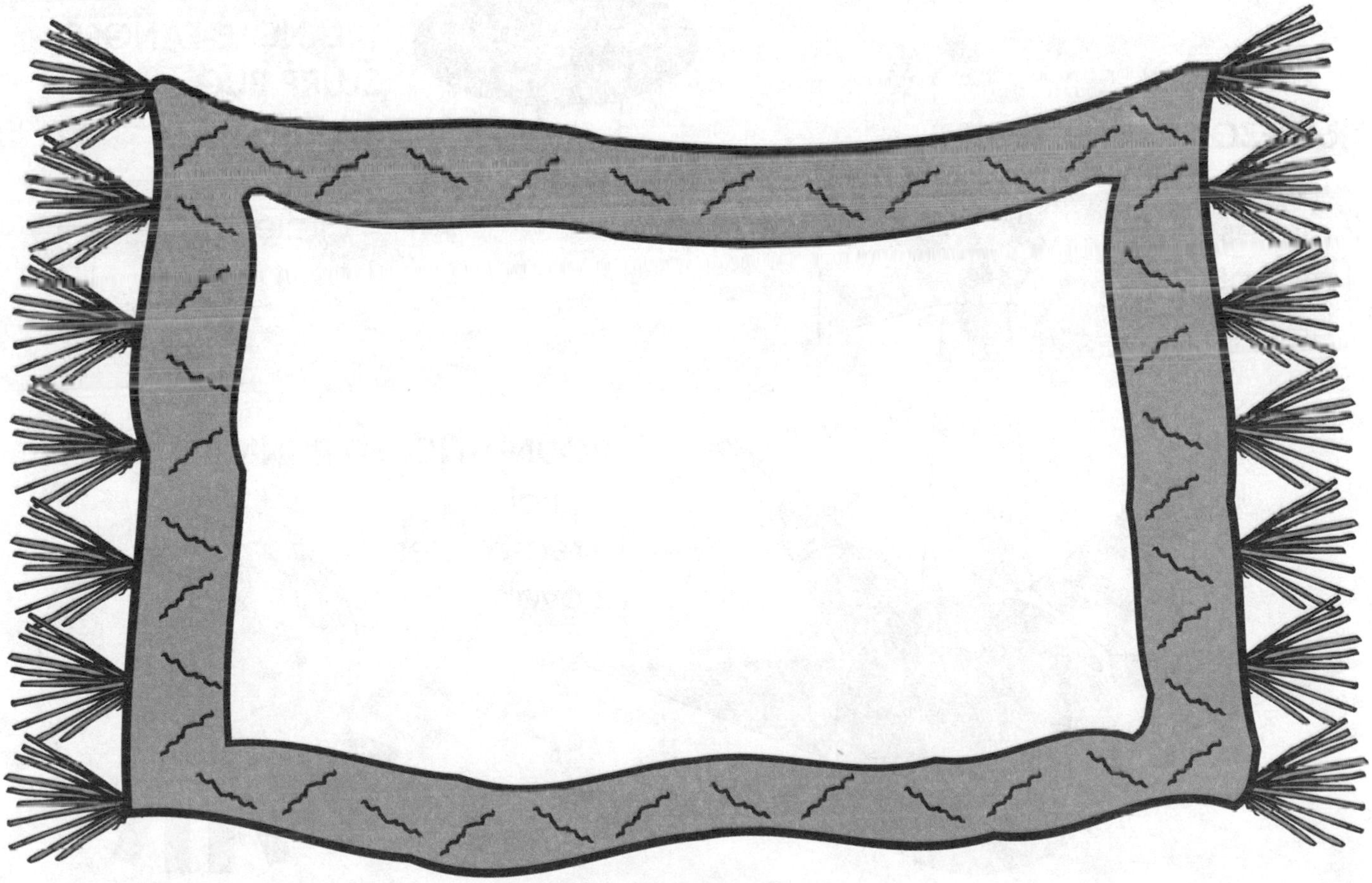

Name ____________________

Who's New in the Zoo?

You are going to create a New Zoo by creating and naming all new animals. You may use the shapes from page 131 or use those as a pattern to make different-colored shapes.

Directions: Glue the shapes together to form the animals. Then, glue the animals onto a sheet of construction paper. Give your New Zoo Animal a name. Write the name on an index card along with a list of the shapes used to create the animal. The animal name should indicate some special feature, such as triangle toad, round-nosed runners, rectangle-tailed tootsie, etc. Try making the animals below.

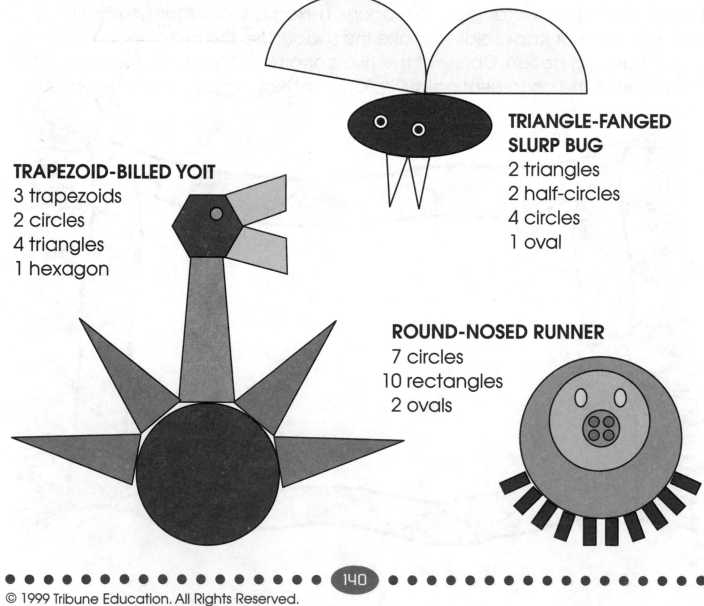

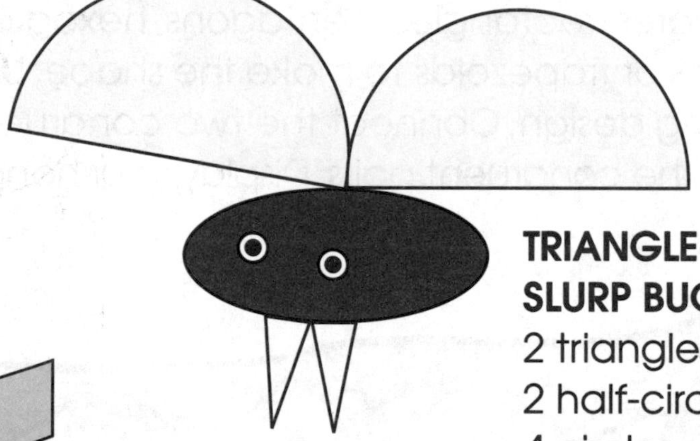

TRIANGLE-FANGED SLURP BUG
2 triangles
2 half-circles
4 circles
1 oval

TRAPEZOID-BILLED YOIT
3 trapezoids
2 circles
4 triangles
1 hexagon

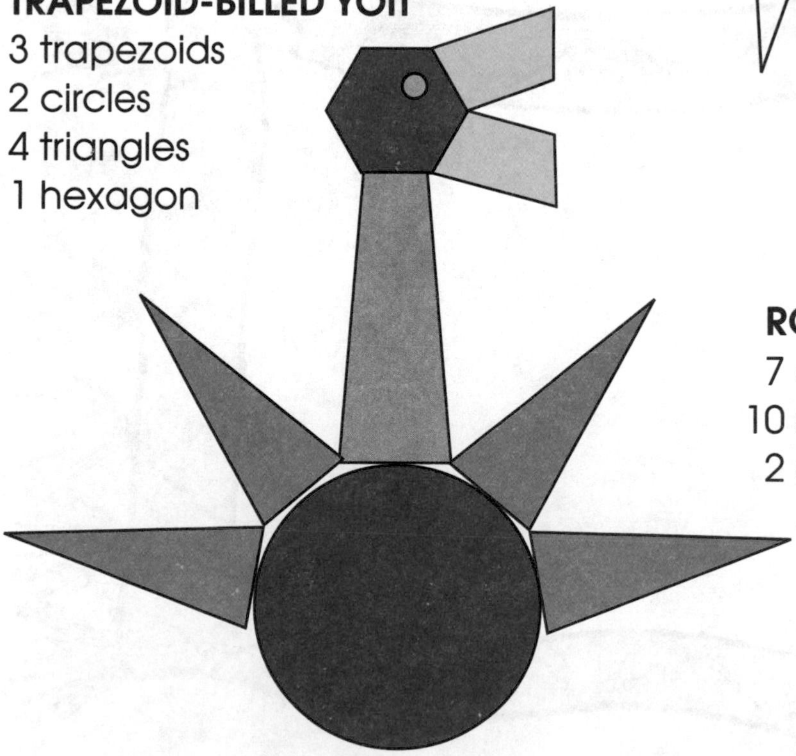

ROUND-NOSED RUNNER
7 circles
10 rectangles
2 ovals

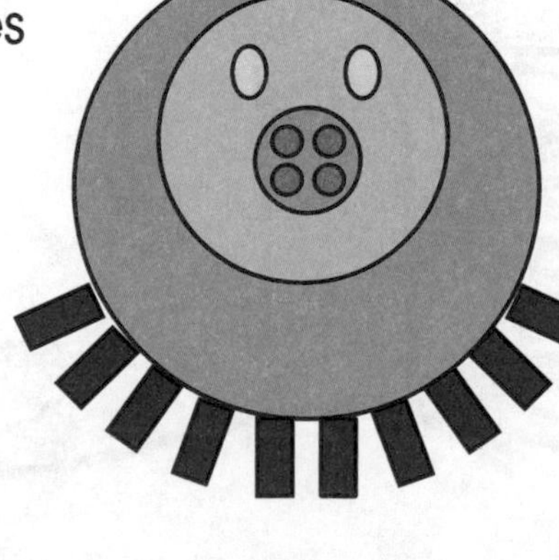

Name ______________________________

Shape Up

Geometric Drop Art

You will need: a set of geometric shapes, an eraser, one sheet of 11" x 18" construction paper.

Directions: Hold one of the shapes above the paper and gently drop it on the paper. Trace the shape exactly where it lands. Repeat this process and erase the lines, if any, that the second shape covered on the first shape. For example, if the second shape, a rectangle, landed on the corner of a hexagon, then that hexagonal corner should be erased so that the rectangle actually appears to be "on top." (See illustration.) For a challenge, color the visible parts of each shape one color.

Once upon a time, Sarah went to a toy store with her mom to buy a present for her brother Tom's birthday. She reached up to get a ball that she wanted to give him. Just as she got the ball to the cash register, it jumped out of her hand and . . .

Shapely Stories

Directions: Make a geometric shape on white paper using a ruler and/or compass and cut it out. The shape should be nearly as large as the paper. Then, write a "shapely" story or poem by following around the inside perimeter of the shape. As the story continues, the center of the shape fills up. You can make an entire shape book by using additional pages and stapling them together.

Name ____________________

Perimeter Problems

The **perimeter** is the distance around the outside of a shape. **Find** the perimeters for the figures below by adding the lengths of all the sides.

Example:

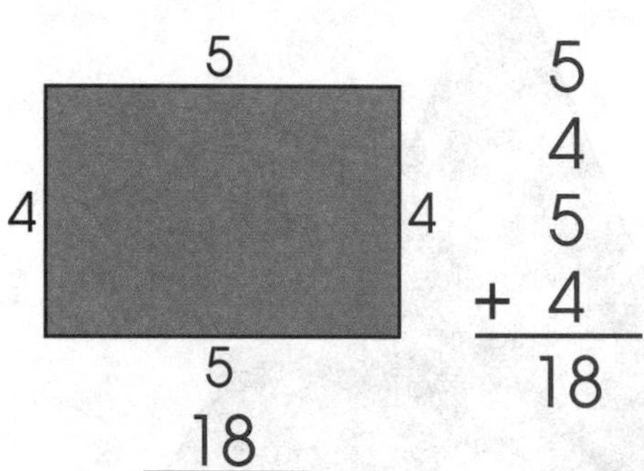

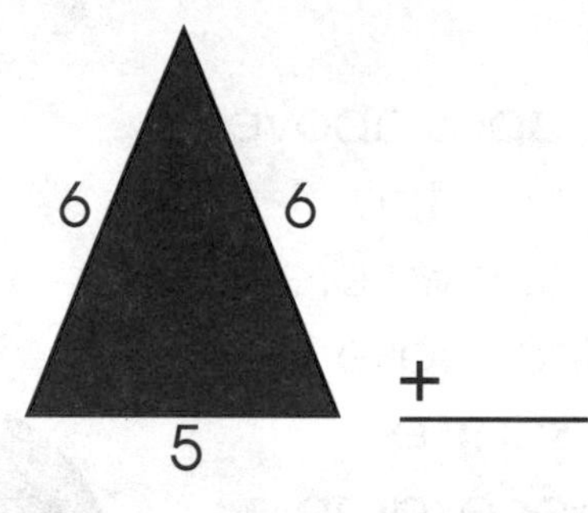

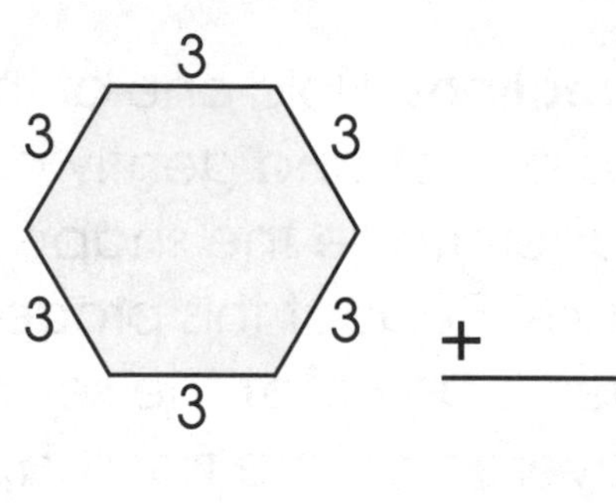

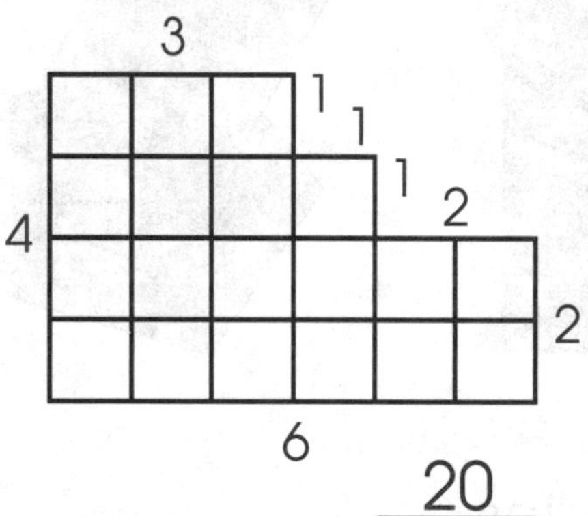

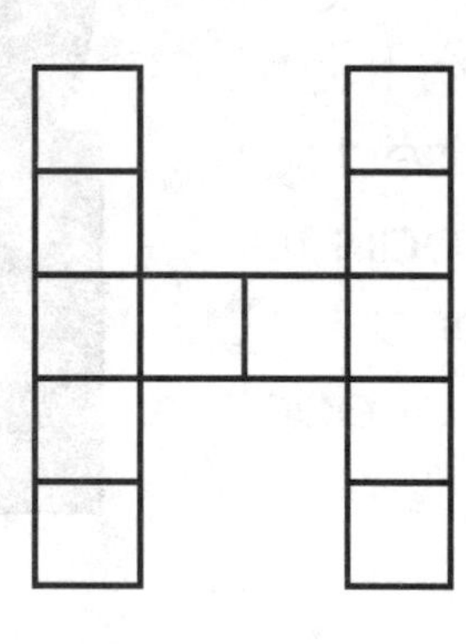

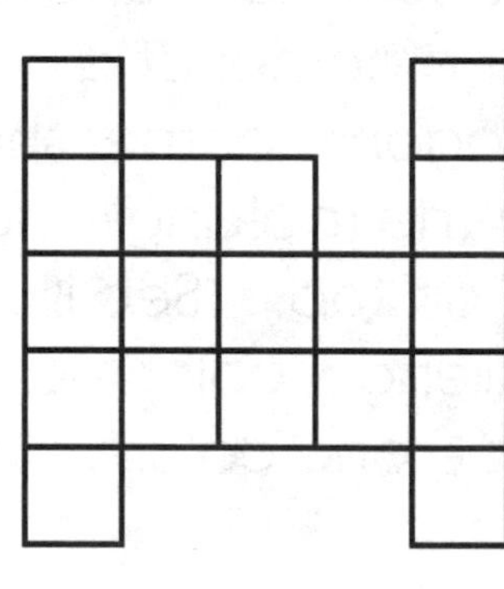

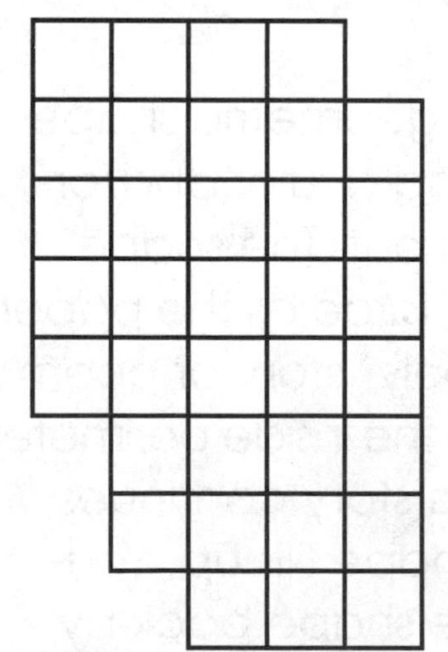

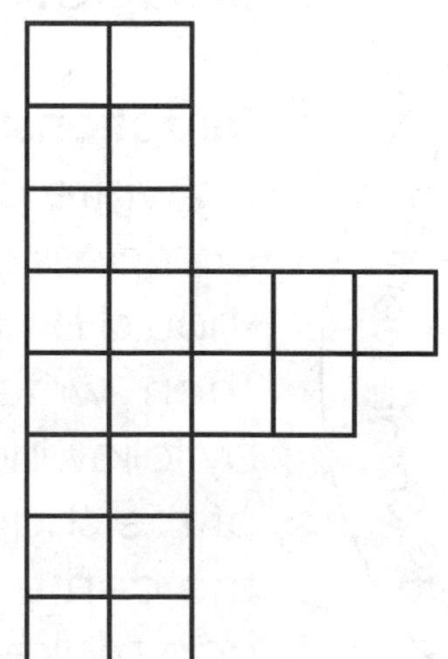

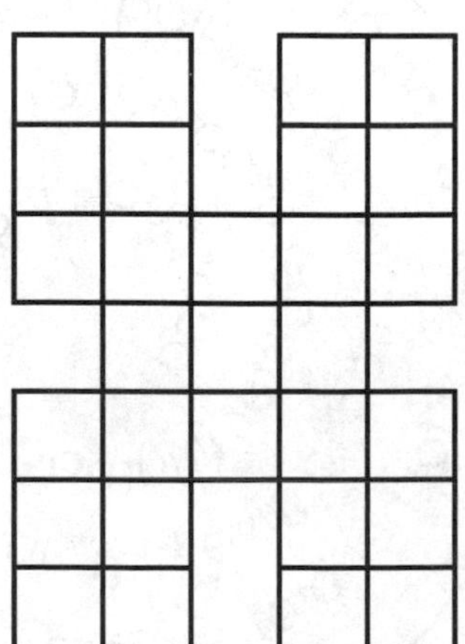

Figuring Distance

Find the perimeter of each figure.

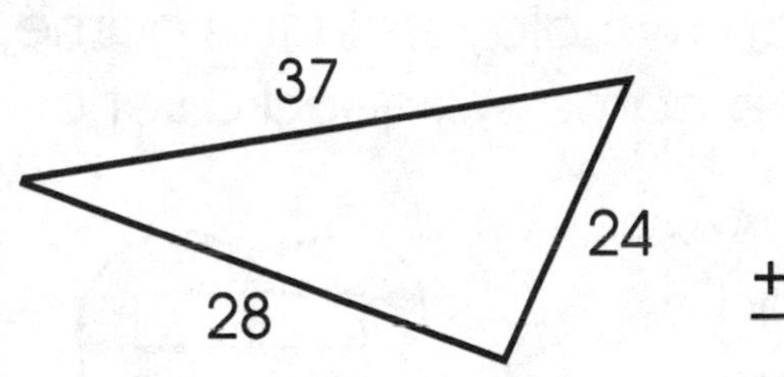

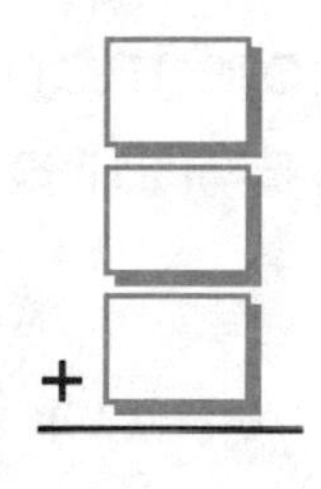

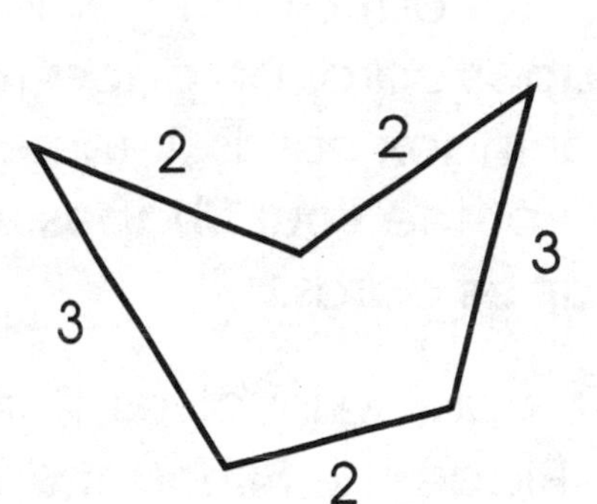

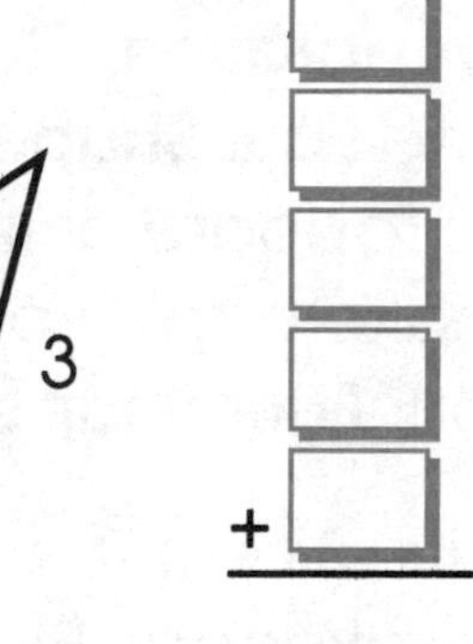

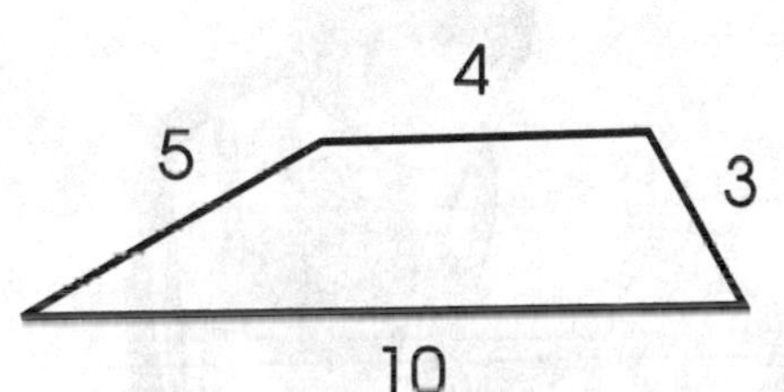

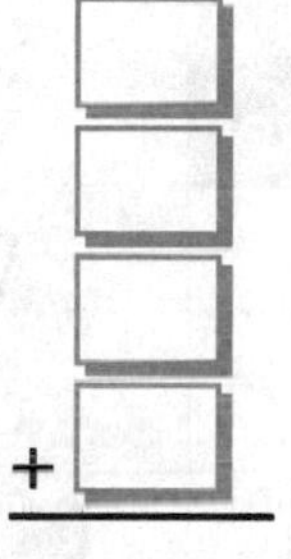

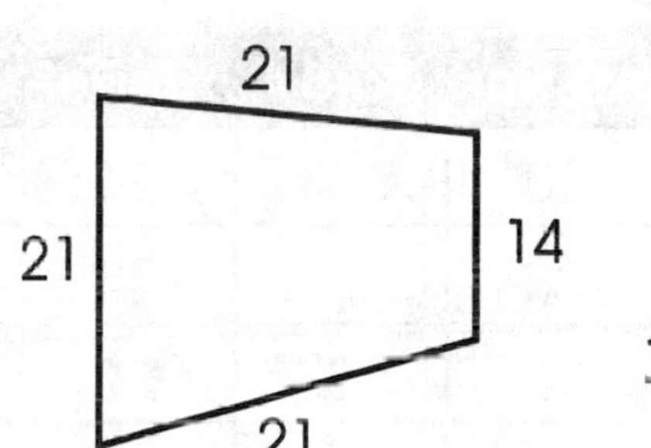

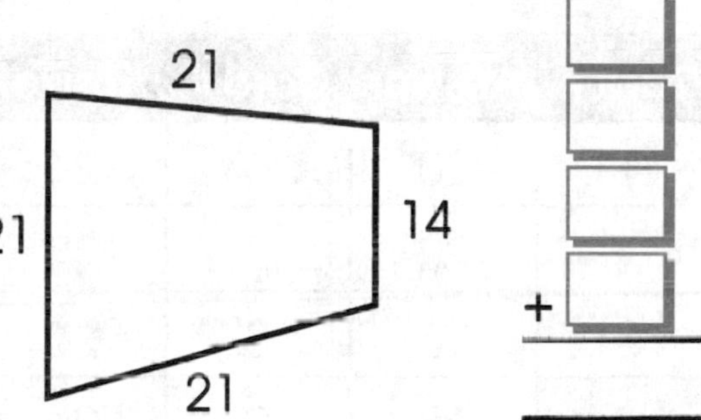

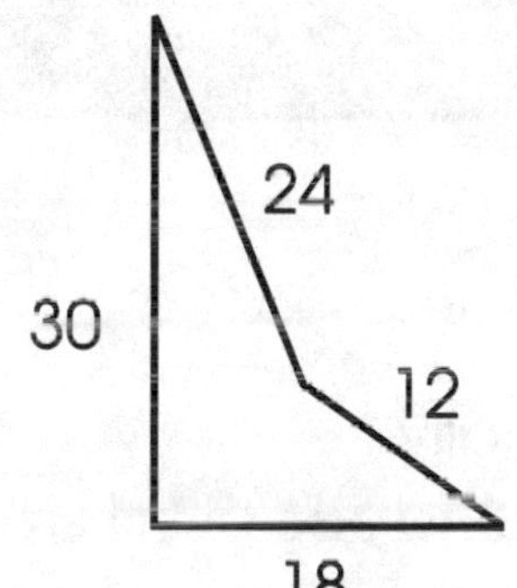

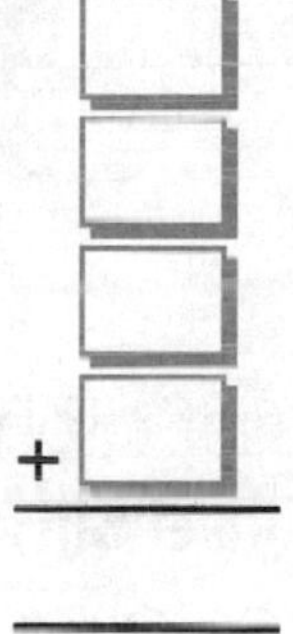

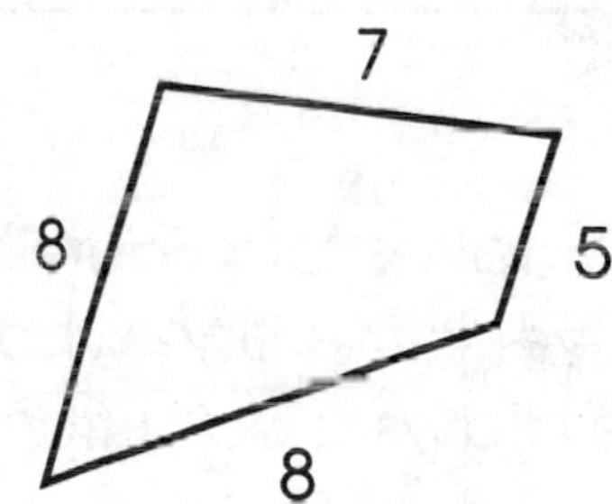

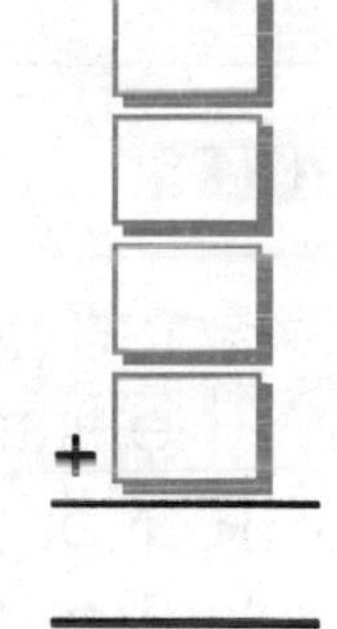

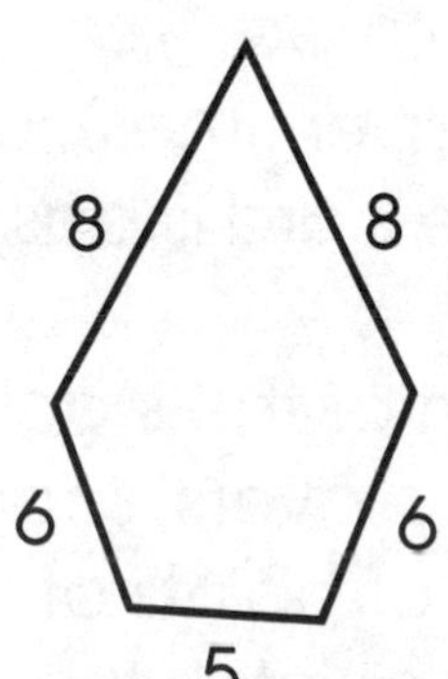

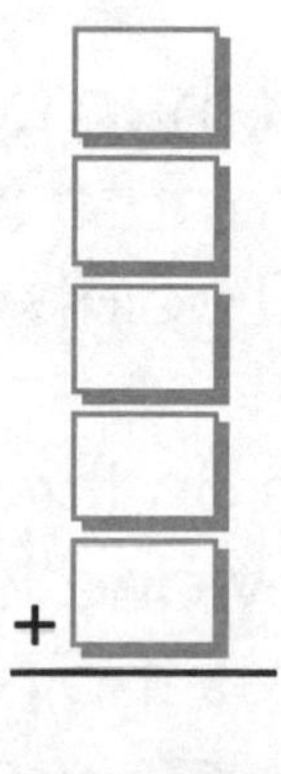

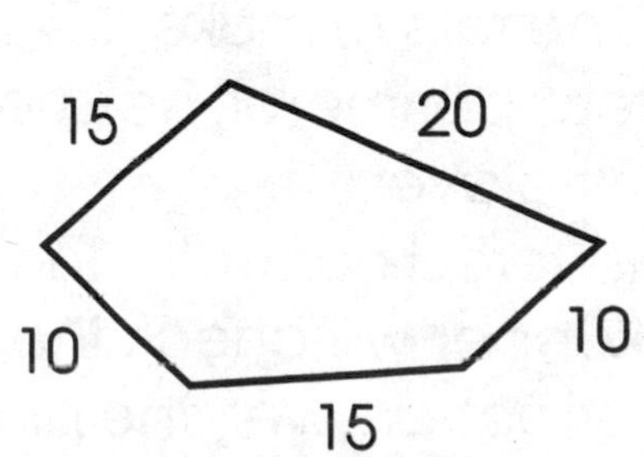

Name ______________________________

Four Shapes Make One Game

Preparation: Cut out all the game cards—the **Silhouette Shapes** on page 145 and **Four Shapes** cards on page 147. To make them last longer, glue them onto cardboard or index cards. If there will be more than two players in this game, make copies of the **Four Shapes**. Each player in the game will need a set of four **Four Shapes** cards.

Directions: This game involves 1 or more players and a timekeeper. Place the **Silhouette Shapes** cards face down in the center of the playing area.

Card #	Answer	Card #	Answer	Card #	Answer
1	20	6	24	11	28
2	22	7	22	12	22
3	26	8	26	13	22
4	28	9	24	14	28
5	22	10	22	15	24

RULES:

1. Each player takes four **Four Shapes** cards.
2. The first player is the one whose name is first alphabetically.
3. Player One draws a card from the top of the **Silhouette Shapes** card stack.
4. In 1 minute, Player One must use all his/her four cards to make the shape depicted on the card he/she drew.
5. The perimeter of the shape made should then be calculated.
6. If Player One fails to make the shape in 1 minute (timekeeper times), or gives an incorrect perimeter, he/she receives 0 points and the card is passed on to the next player.
7. When answered correctly, the card goes on the bottom of the stack.
8. The timekeeper will check the Answer Key and keep all players' scores.
9. For the correct answer, the player receives the number of points of the perimeter he/she calculated. The first player to reach 100 points is the winner.

Name ______________________________

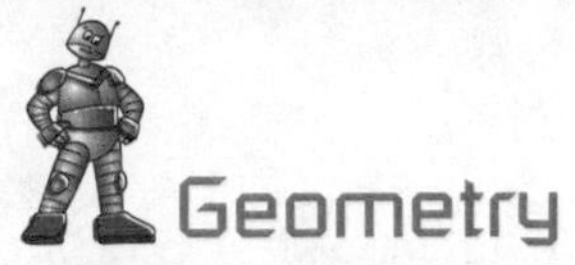

Silhouette Shapes

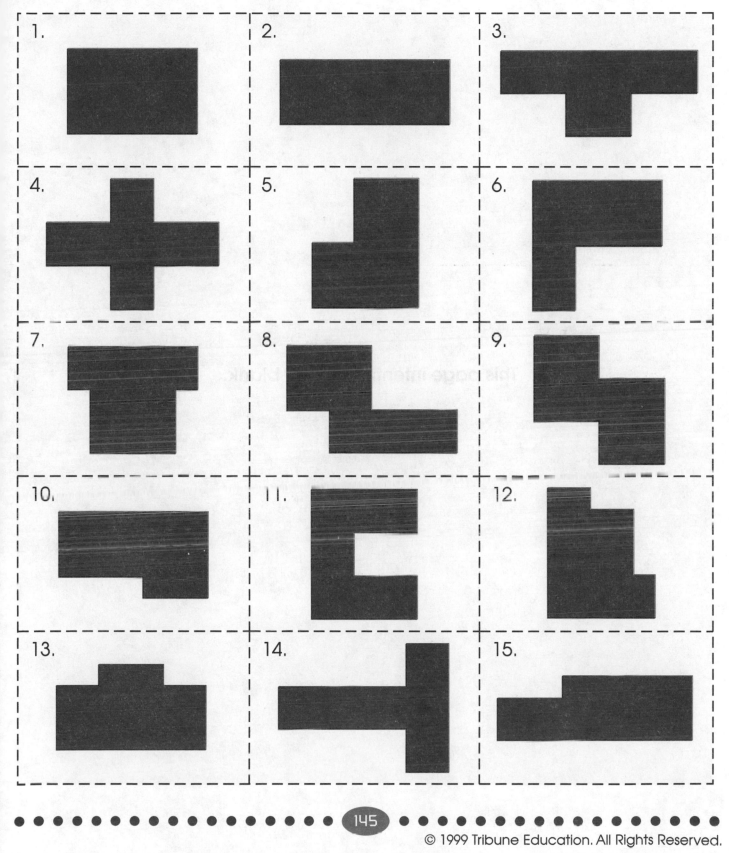

1.	2.	3.
4.	5.	6.
7.	8.	9.
10.	11.	12.
13.	14.	15.

This page intentionally left blank.

Name ______________________________

Four Shapes Cards

This page intentionally left blank.

Name ______________________________

A Square Activity

The **area** is the number of square units covering a flat surface. **Find** the area by counting the square units.

Example: 2 squares x 5 squares = 10 squares

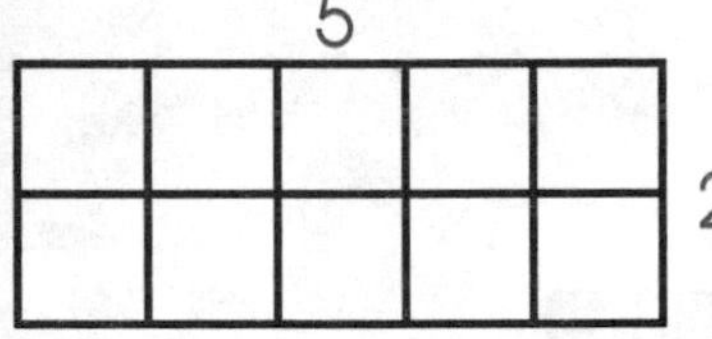

10

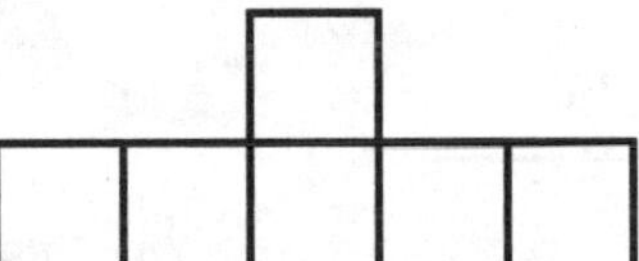

______

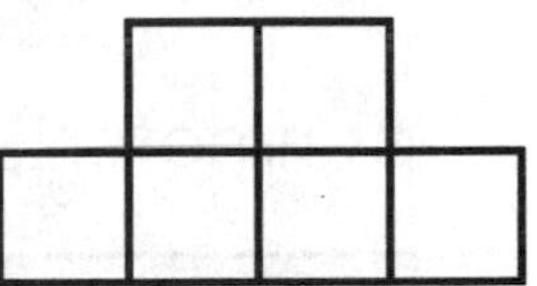

______

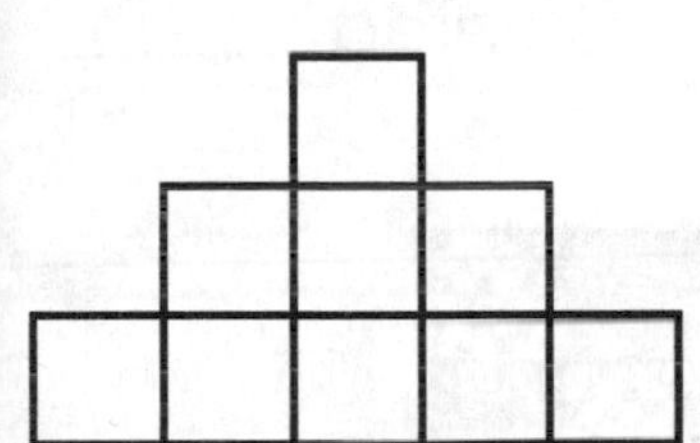

______

______

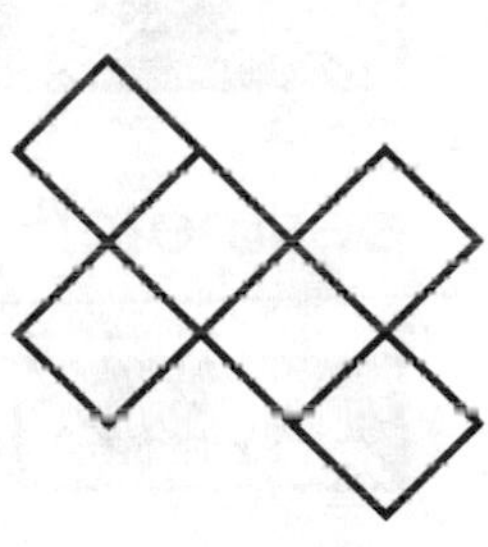

______

______

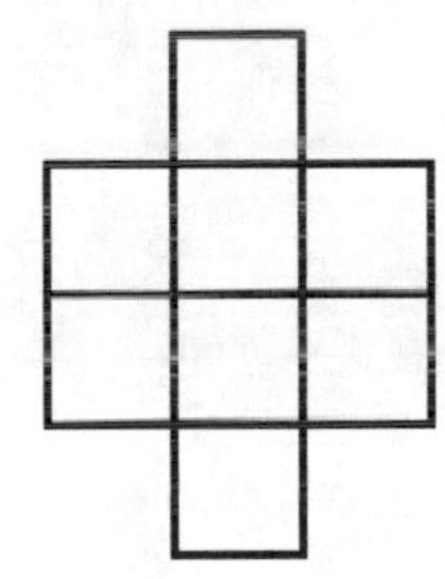

______

______

______

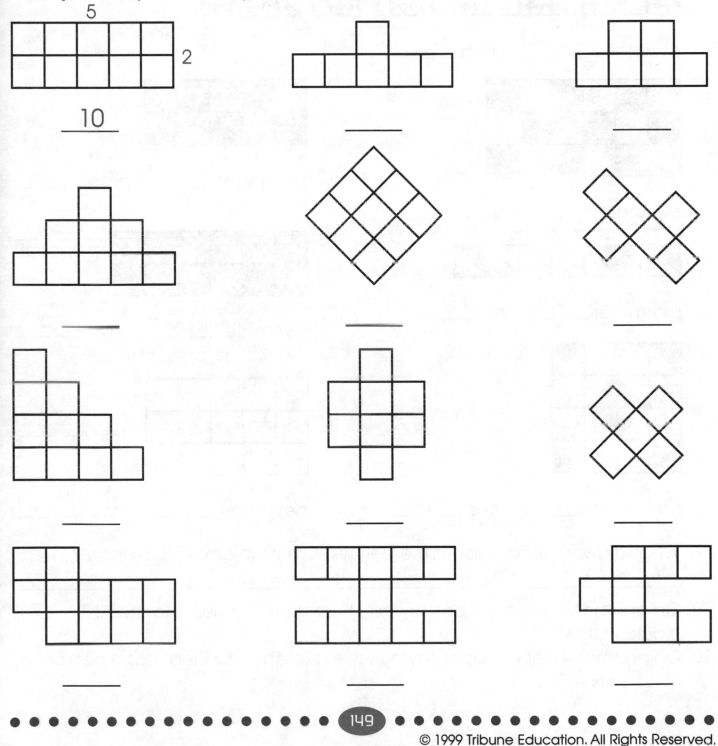

______

______

Name ____________________________

Quilt Math

The area of a rectangle is calculated by multiplying the length of one side by the width of another side. **Find** the perimeter and area of each quilt.

1.

perimeter ______ area ______

2.

perimeter ______ area ______

3.

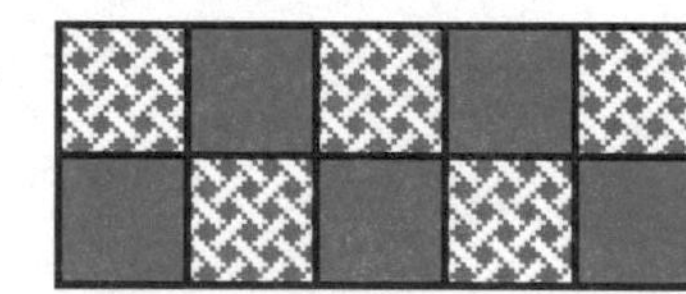

perimeter ______ area ______

4.

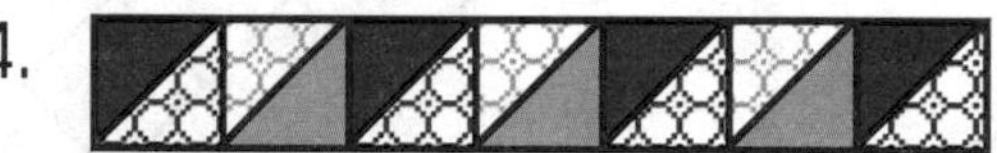

perimeter ______ area ______

5.

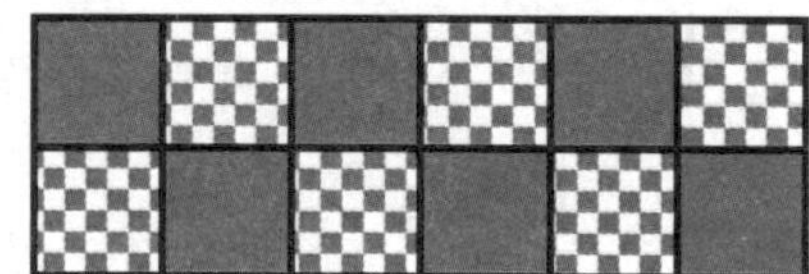

perimeter ______ area ______

6.

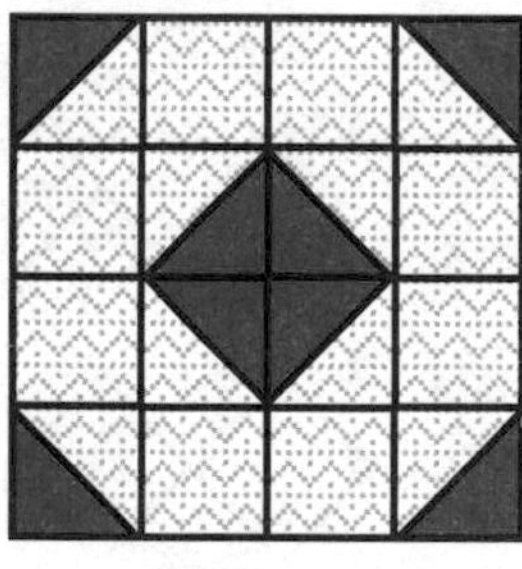

perimeter ______ area ______

7.

perimeter ______ area ______

8. What did you notice about the perimeter in problems 4, 5, 6 and 7?

____

9. On another sheet of paper, lay out, then sketch a quilt that has 30 blocks in it.
10. On another sheet of paper, lay out, then sketch a quilt that has a perimeter of 14 units.

Name ______________________________

The Way Around Polygons

Use the cut-out shapes from pages 131–137. **Write** the name of each shape in the shape column. **Measure** the sides of each polygon and **record** its measurements. Then, **calculate** the perimeter of the polygon in the perimeter column. **Find** the area of every square and rectangle.

Shape	Each Side's Measurement	Perimeter side + side + side + side	Area 1 side x 1 side

Name ______________________________

Suzy Spider, Interior Decorator

Suzy Spider is decorating her house. She is a very clever decorator, but she needs your help **calculating** the area and perimeter. **Draw** a picture to help.

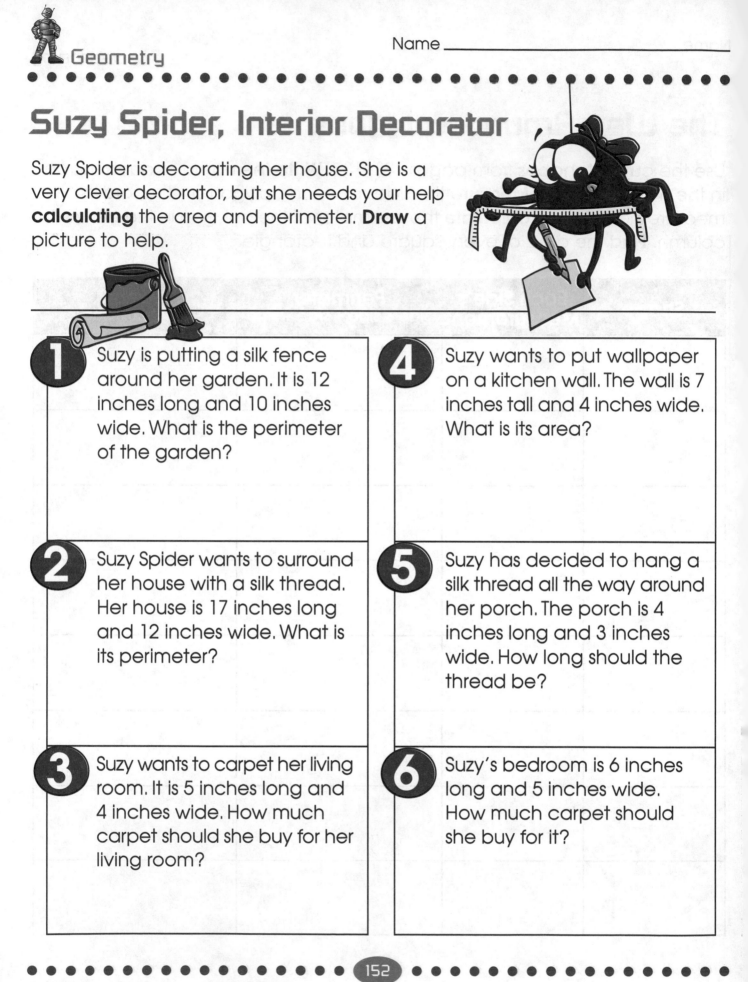

1 Suzy is putting a silk fence around her garden. It is 12 inches long and 10 inches wide. What is the perimeter of the garden?

2 Suzy Spider wants to surround her house with a silk thread. Her house is 17 inches long and 12 inches wide. What is its perimeter?

3 Suzy wants to carpet her living room. It is 5 inches long and 4 inches wide. How much carpet should she buy for her living room?

4 Suzy wants to put wallpaper on a kitchen wall. The wall is 7 inches tall and 4 inches wide. What is its area?

5 Suzy has decided to hang a silk thread all the way around her porch. The porch is 4 inches long and 3 inches wide. How long should the thread be?

6 Suzy's bedroom is 6 inches long and 5 inches wide. How much carpet should she buy for it?

Name ______________________________

"State"istics

Choose ten states. Then, **research** their "lengths" and "heights" and **multiply** them to find their areas.

State Name	Approximate Miles E-W	Approximate Miles N-S	Area in Square Miles

Name ______________________

Turn Up the Volume

The **volume** is the measure of the inside of a shape. **Find** the volume of these shapes by counting the boxes. You might not be able to see all the boxes, but you can tell that they are there.

Example:

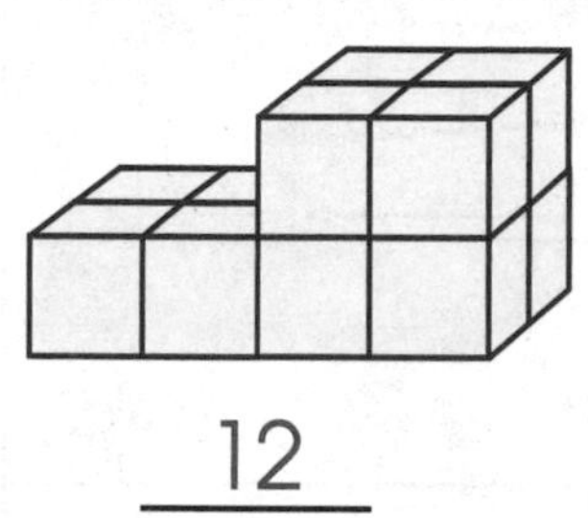

12

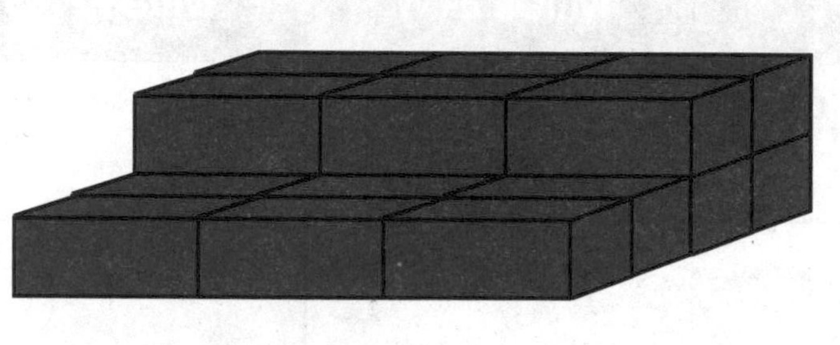

______

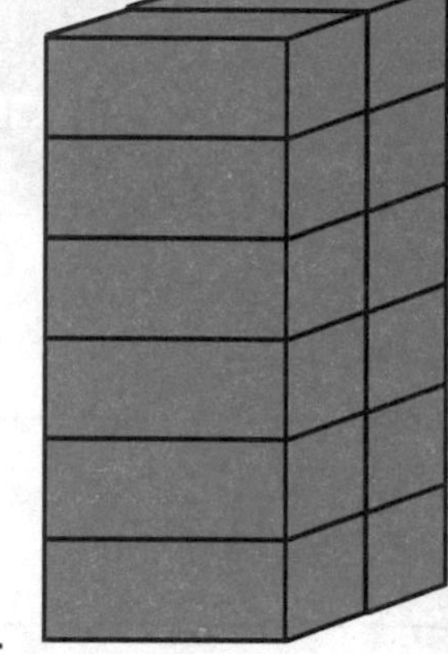

______

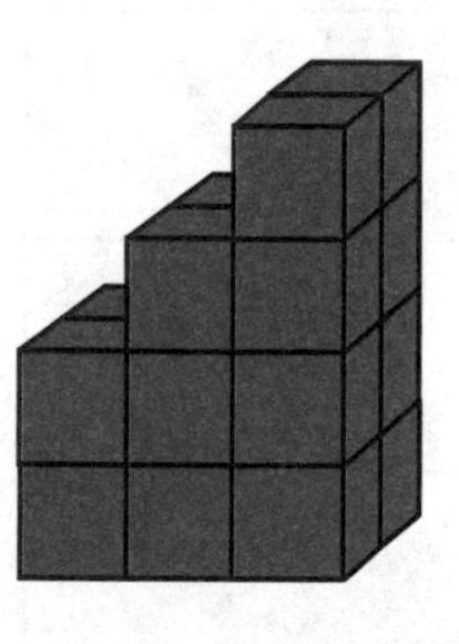

______

______

______

______

______

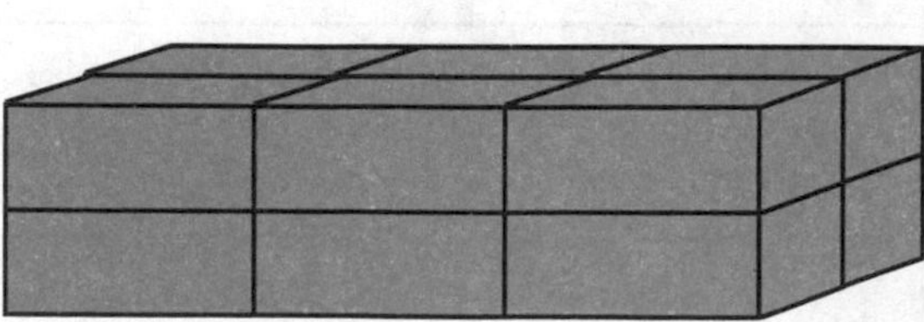

______

Name ________________________________

How Much Can a Container Contain?

To find volume: Multiply length x width x height

1. Select four food boxes and draw and color one in each box below.
2. Measure the width, length and height (the sides) of each box and record it next to its picture.
3. Find the volume of each box and record it next to its picture.

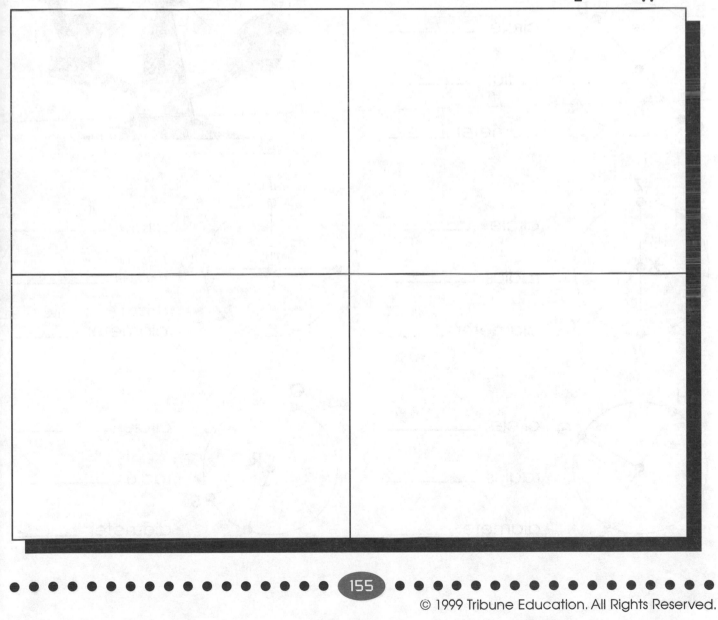

H = ______
W = ______
L = ______

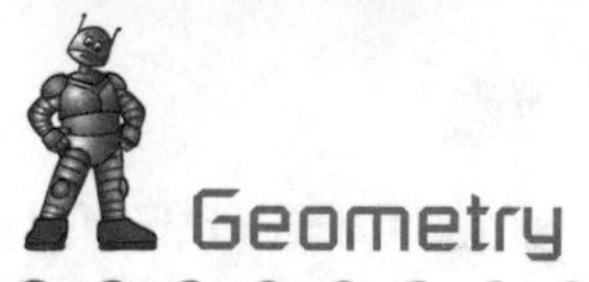

Name ______________________

Going in Circles

A **circle** is a round, closed figure. It is named by its center. A **radius** is a line segment from the center to any point on the circle.
A **diameter** is a line segment with both points on the circle. The diameter always passes through the center of the circle.

Name the radius, diameter and circle.

Example:

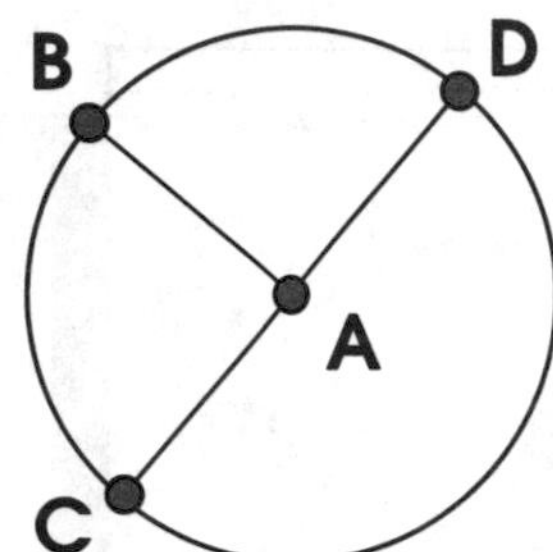

circle A

radius AB

diameter CD

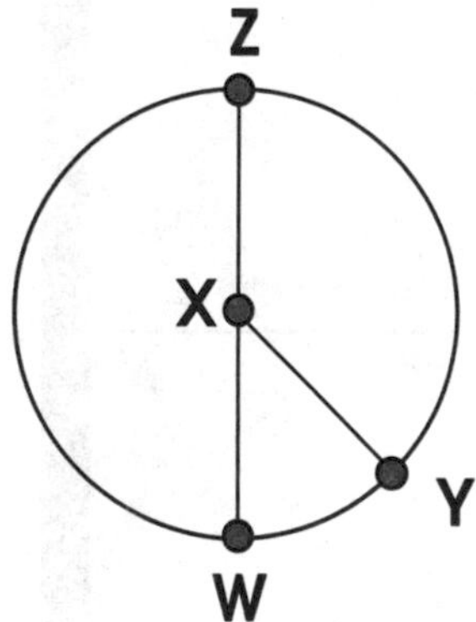

circle ________

radius ________

diameter ________

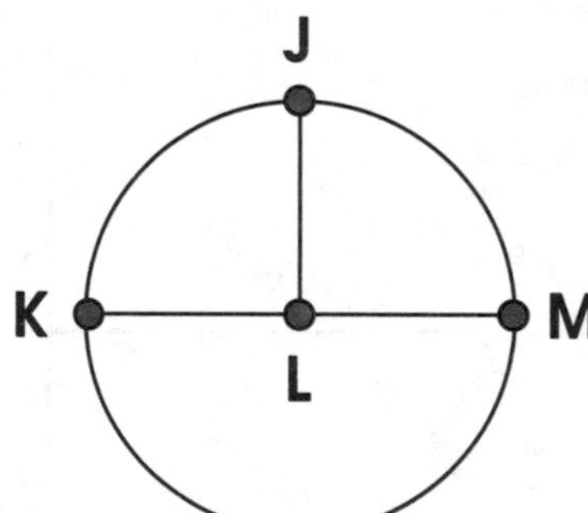

circle ________

radius ________

diameter ________

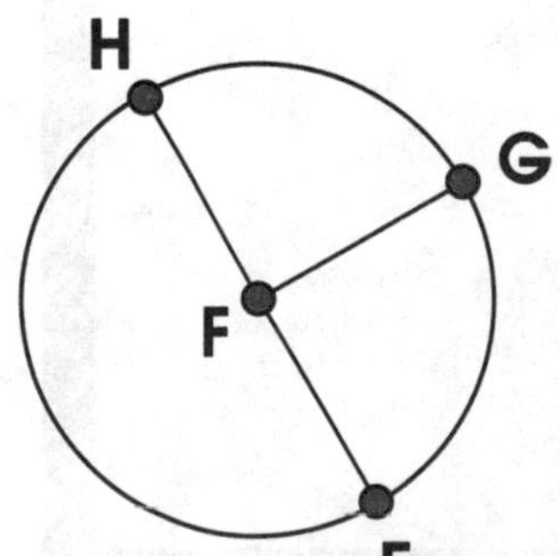

circle ________

radius ________

diameter ________

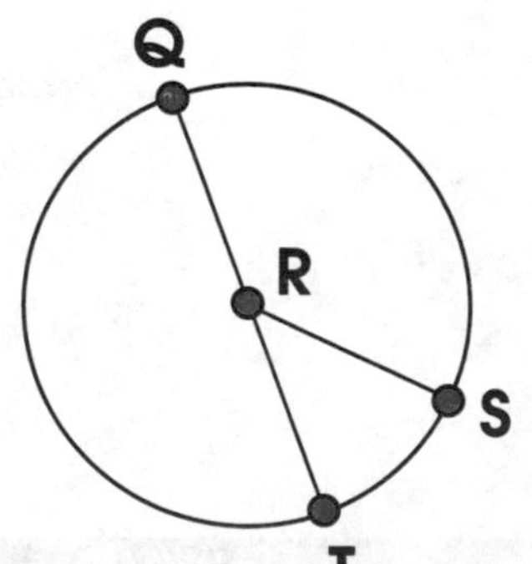

circle ________

radius ________

diameter ________

Name ___________________________

Perfect Symmetry

A figure that can be separated into two matching parts is **symmetric**. The **line of symmetry** is the line that divides the shape in half.

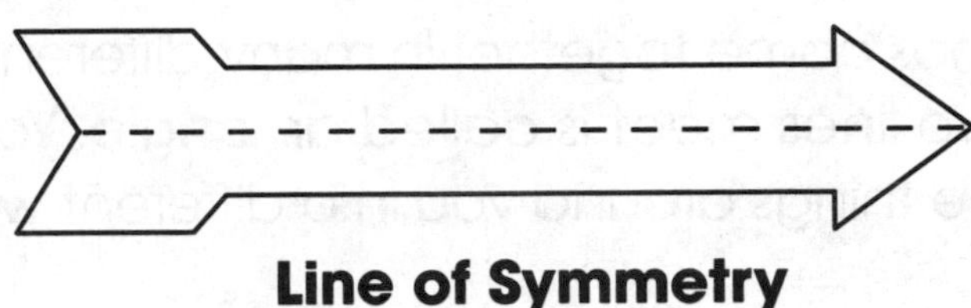

Is the dotted line shown a line of symmetry?

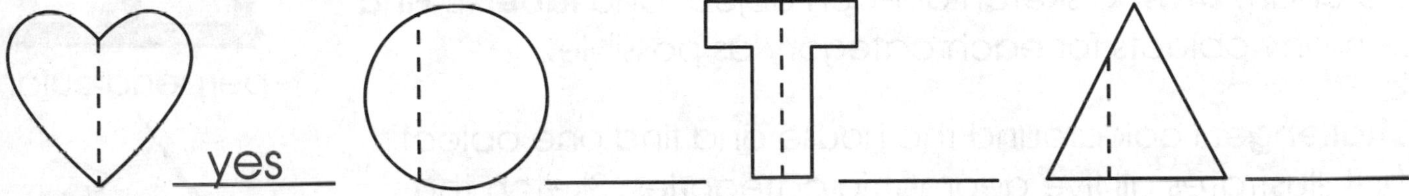

Draw each matching part.

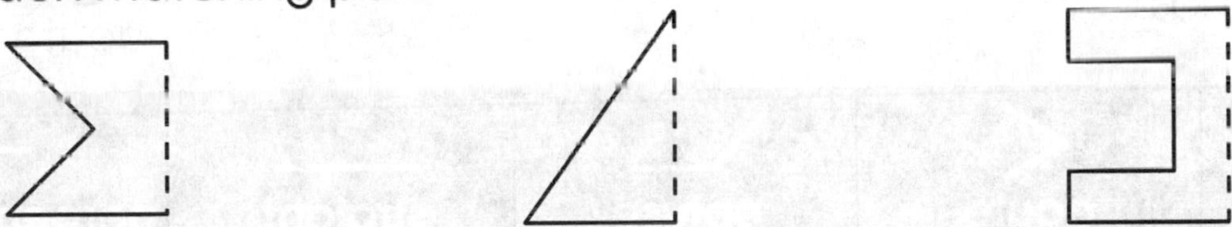

Complete the letters to make symmetric words.

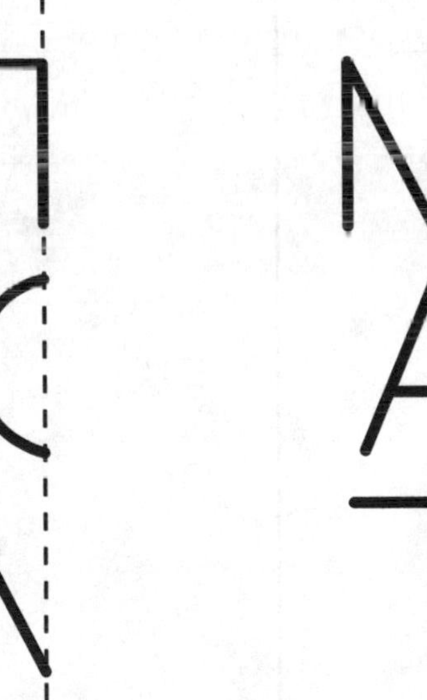

Make two symmetric words of your own.

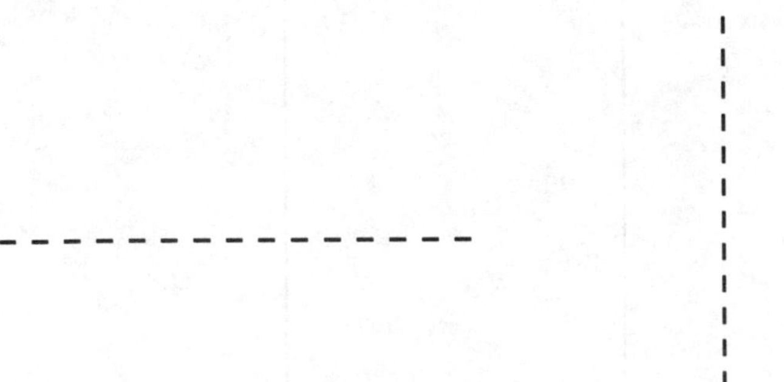

Name ______________________

Look at the World From a Different Angle

perpendicular

acute

Lines come together in many different ways. The point where two lines meet is called an **angle**. You may have to look at the things around you in a different way to find these angles.

Use the table below to **record** your observations from around the house. Look for objects that illustrate each category on the chart. **Draw** a sketch of each object and **label** it. **Find** as many objects for each category as possible.

Challenge: Look around the house and find one object that illustrates all five geometric categories. Sketch the object and label the various types of angles, lines or shapes that it has.

right	acute	obtuse	straight	perpendicular

Fractions

Name ______________________________

Graham Cracker Denominator

Find a cracker. If possible, use one that has four pieces. Break your crackers into as many or as few pieces as desired but make each piece the same size.

With fractions, the number of pieces into which an object is broken is how the bottom number, the **denominator**, obtains its numerical value. Remember that you started with one cracker that is in pieces now. **Write** the number of pieces as a denominator.

$\frac{\square}{\square}$ ← numerator

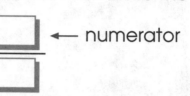

denominator →

To determine the top number, the **numerator**, eat part of the cracker. In the diagram at the right, cross out the part you ate. This is the numerator.

Write two fractions—a fraction to show what is left and a fraction to show what was eaten.

numerator / demoninator $\frac{\square}{\square}$ of the cracker is left. numerator / denominator $\frac{\square}{\square}$ of the cracker is gone.

Eat another piece of the cracker. **Cross out** the part you ate in the diagram. Now, **write** how much is left.

numerator / denominator $\frac{\square}{\square}$ of the cracker is left. numerator / denominator $\frac{\square}{\square}$ of the cracker is gone.

Eat another piece of the cracker. **Cross out** the part you ate in the diagram. Now, **write** how much is left.

numerator / denominator $\frac{\square}{\square}$ of the cracker is left. numerator / denominator $\frac{\square}{\square}$ of the cracker is gone.

Which part changes, the numerator or the denominator?

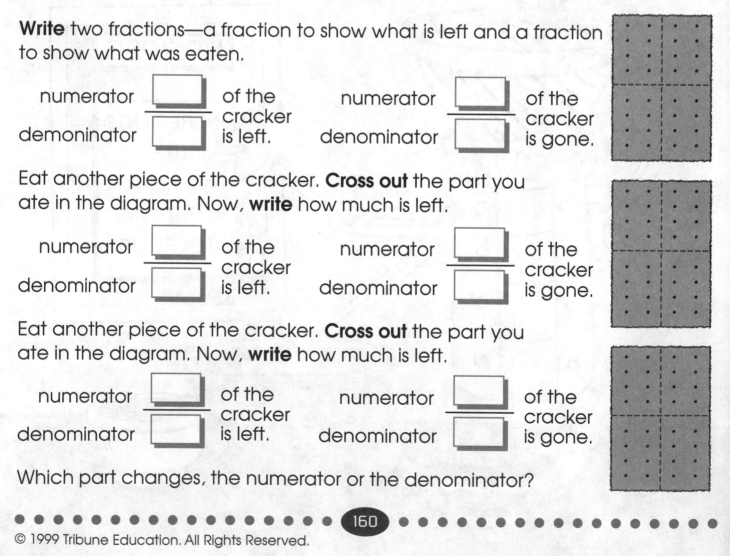

Name ____________________

Fraction Fun

4 gloves are shaded. 9 gloves in all.

 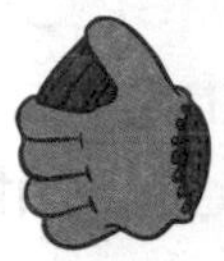 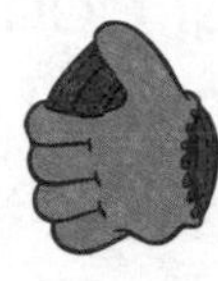      

$\frac{4}{9}$ of the gloves are shaded.

TOYS

What fraction of the balls is shaded? ____________

cars? ____________

trains? ____________

dolls? ____________

airplanes? ____________

teddy bears? ____________

rabbits? ____________

hats? ____________

boats? ____________

Name ____________________

Button Collection

Preparation: Use the boxes from **Equally Alike Boxes** on page 90 or co
of buttons. Count the number of buttons in each box or container. C
response sheet like the one on the bottom of this page. You can ch
to group each of your objects. Those become the categories you w
top of the response sheet.

Remember: A fraction has two numbers with a horizontal line drawn between them. The bottom number is called the **denominator**. The denominator tells how many equal parts or total pieces are in the whole. The top number is called the **numerator**. The numerator tells how many parts of the whole there are.

Example:    

$\frac{2}{5}$ — 2: the part of the total buttons with 2 holes; 5: total number of buttons in the set

What is the fraction of buttons in this set with 2 holes?

Response Sheet							
Box #	# of buttons in box	Fractions showing: Buttons with 2 holes	Buttons with 4 holes	White buttons	Gold buttons	Black buttons	Brown buttons

Name ______________________________

The Mystery of the Missing Sweets

Some mysterious person is sneaking away with pieces of desserts from Sam Sillicook's Diner. Help him figure out how much is missing.

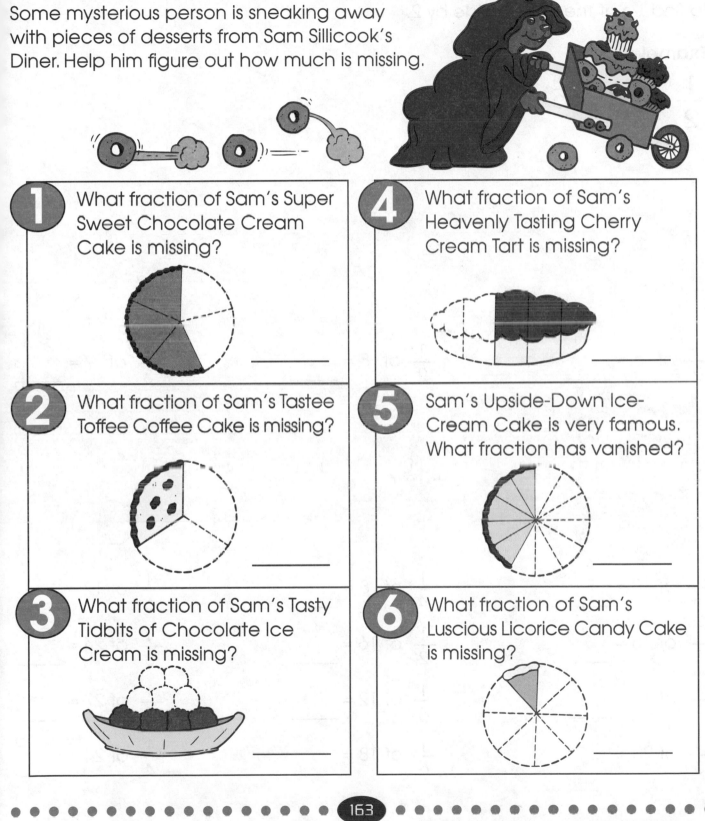

1 What fraction of Sam's Super Sweet Chocolate Cream Cake is missing?

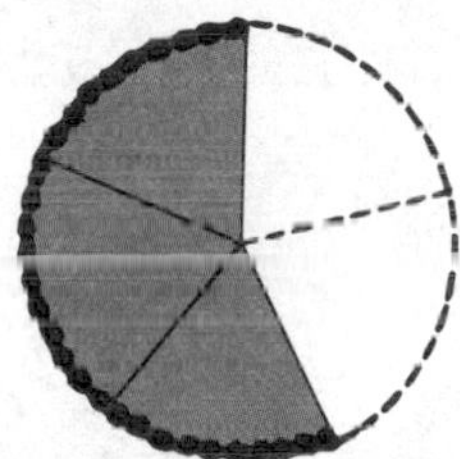

____

2 What fraction of Sam's Tastee Toffee Coffee Cake is missing?

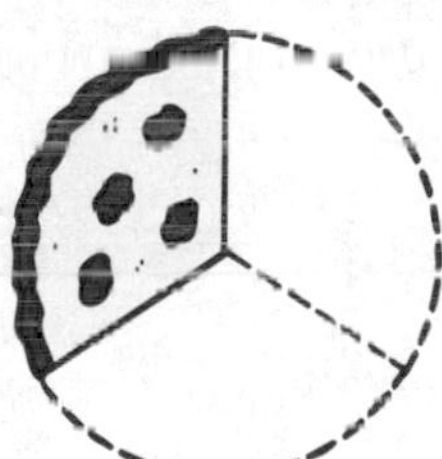

____

3 What fraction of Sam's Tasty Tidbits of Chocolate Ice Cream is missing?

____

4 What fraction of Sam's Heavenly Tasting Cherry Cream Tart is missing?

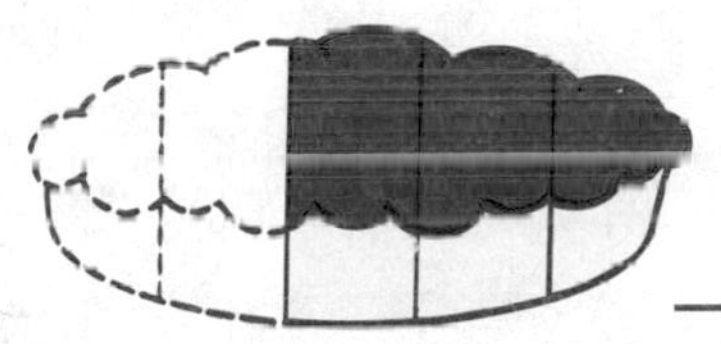

____

5 Sam's Upside-Down Ice-Cream Cake is very famous. What fraction has vanished?

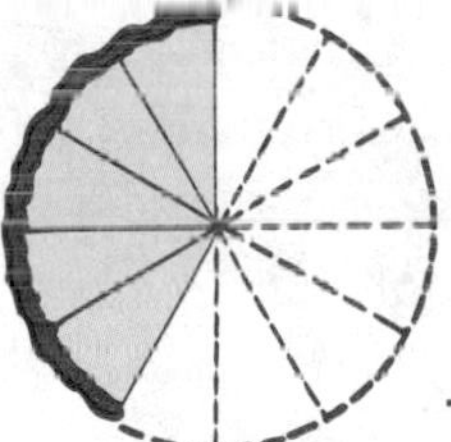

____

6 What fraction of Sam's Luscious Licorice Candy Cake is missing?

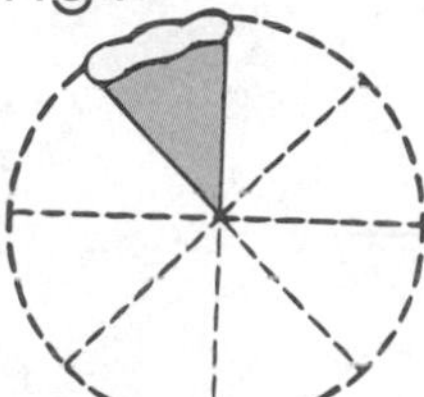

____

Name ______________________________

Star Gazing

To find 1/2 of the stars, **divide** by 2.

Example:

$\frac{1}{2}$ of 10 = 5

$\frac{1}{2}$ of 6 = _____

$\frac{1}{2}$ of 8 = _____

$\frac{1}{3}$ of 9 = _____

$\frac{1}{5}$ of 10 = _____

$\frac{1}{4}$ of 8 = _____

$\frac{1}{6}$ of 12 = _____

$\frac{1}{3}$ of 15 = _____

$\frac{1}{6}$ of 18 = _____

$\frac{1}{5}$ of 20 = _____

$\frac{1}{2}$ of 16 = _____

$\frac{1}{4}$ of 12 = _____

$\frac{1}{6}$ of 18 = _____

$\frac{1}{3}$ of 24 = _____

$\frac{1}{3}$ of 27 = _____

$\frac{1}{4}$ of 24 = _____

Name ______________________

What Fraction Am I?

Identify the fraction for each shaded section.

Example: There are 5 sections on this figure. 2 sections are shaded. 2/5 of the sections are shaded. 3 sections are not shaded. 3/5 of the sections are not shaded.

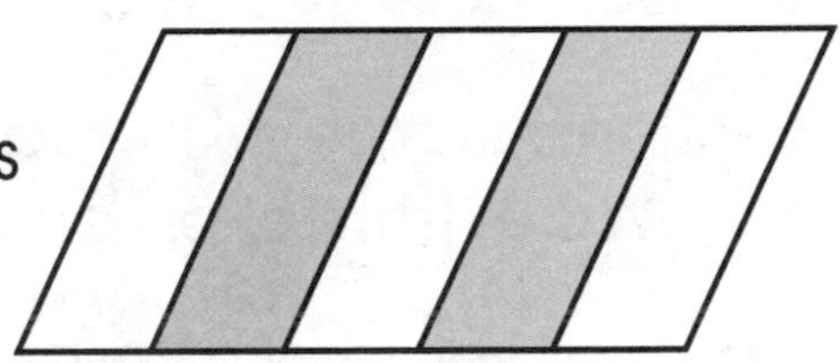

A. ________

B. ________

C. ________

D. ________

E. ________

F. ________

G. ________

H. ________

I. ________

A.

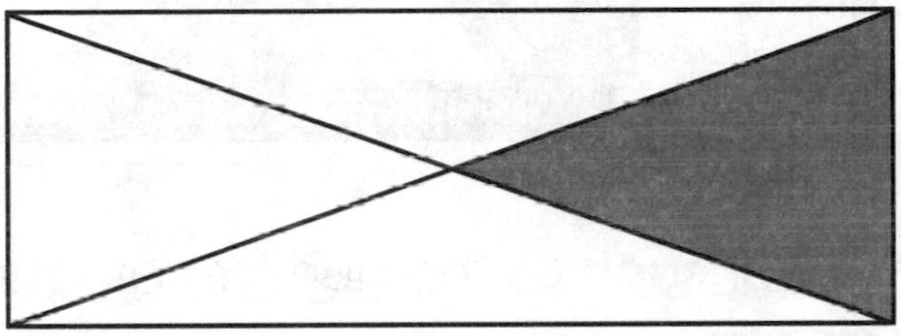

B.

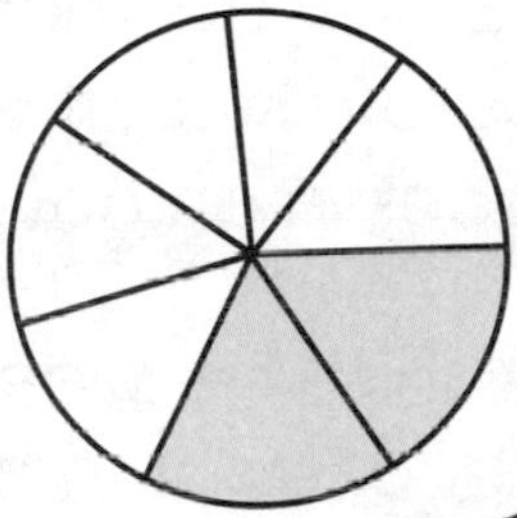

C.

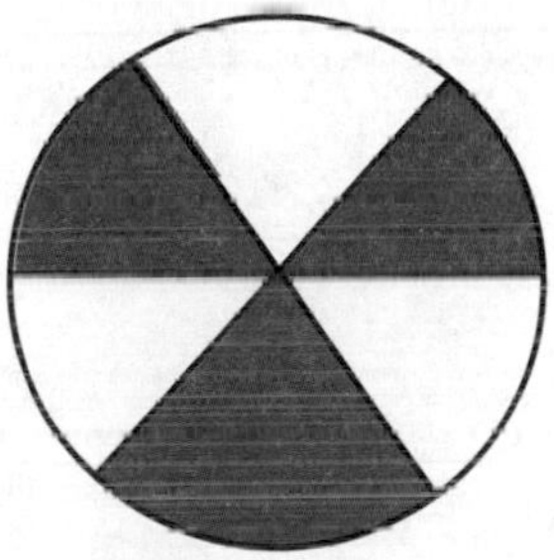

D.

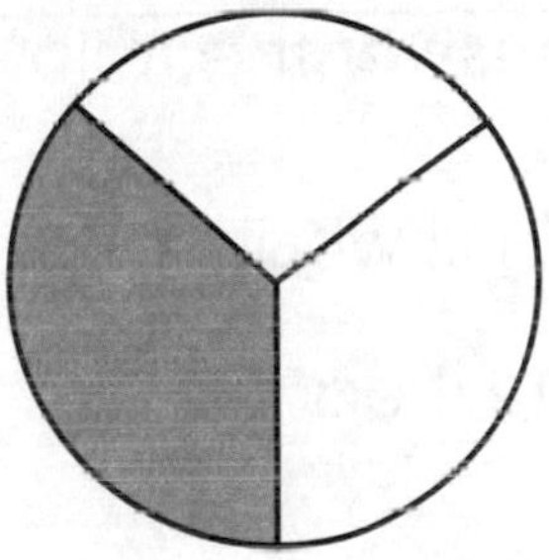

E.

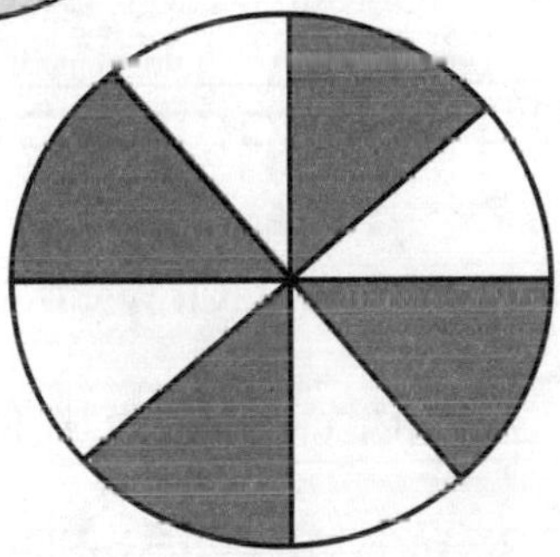

F.

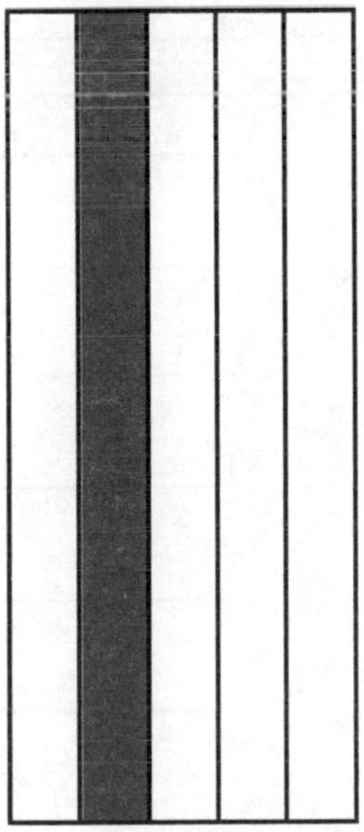

G.

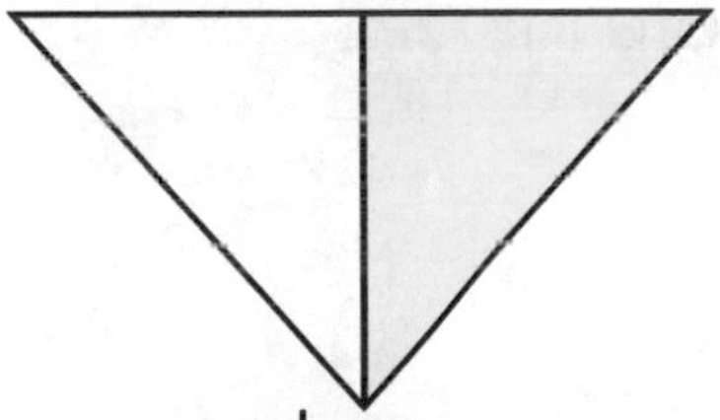

H.

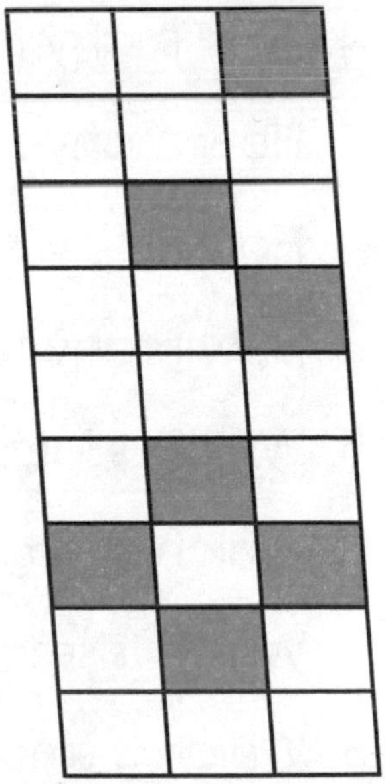

I.

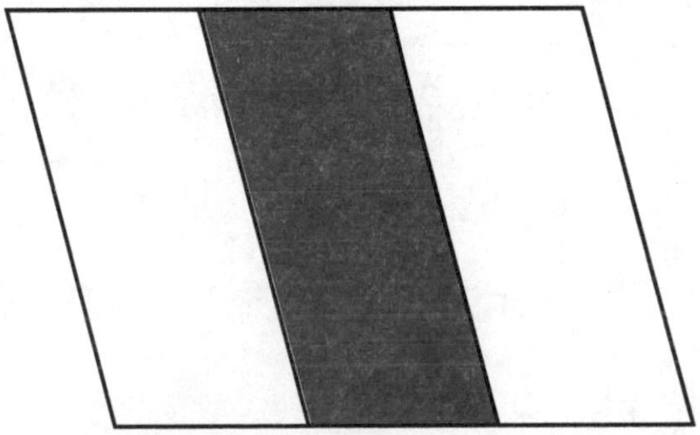

Name ______________________

The Parts Equal the Whole

The one long **Fraction Bar** on page 167 is a whole. Each bar thereafter is broken up into equal parts.

Directions: Name what part of the whole each bar is. **Write** its fraction on it.

Color the whole bar yellow, the halves blue, the thirds green, the fourths red and the sixths orange. Then, **cut** the bars apart carefully on the lines. Store the pieces in an envelope.

Show relationships between the bar, such as the number of fourths in a whole or the number of sixths in a third, etc.

Use the fraction bars to **answer** the following questions:

1. How many sixths are in a whole? ____________
2. Name four fractions that equal 1/2. ____________
3. What fractions equal 1/3? ____________
4. How many fourths are in 1/2? ____________

   How many sixths? ____________

   How many eighths? ____________

   How many tenths? ____________
5. Which is larger, 3/4 or 4/6? ____________
6. Which is larger, 1/3 or 1/2? ____________
7. Which is smaller, 2/3 or 4/4? ____________
8. Which is smaller, 1/2 or 3/4? ____________

Name ________________________________

Fraction Bars

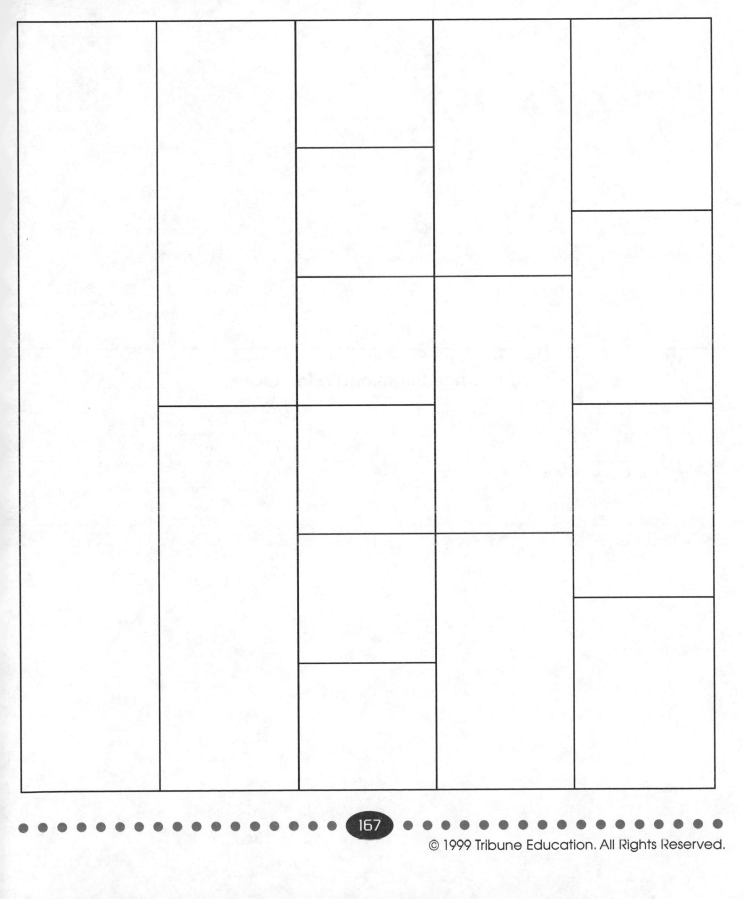

This page intentionally left blank.

Name ______________________________

The Whole Thing

Preparation: Cut 14 index cards in half. Write three copies of the following fractions on them (one per card): $-\frac{1}{3}$, $+\frac{1}{3}$, $-\frac{1}{6}$, $+\frac{1}{6}$, $-\frac{1}{2}$, $+\frac{1}{2}$, $-\frac{1}{4}$, $+\frac{1}{4}$.

On four more cards, write $+\frac{1}{3}$, $+\frac{1}{6}$, $+\frac{1}{2}$, $+\frac{1}{4}$.

Rules: This game involves 2–4 players. Put the stack of fraction cards upside down in the middle of the playing area. Use the **Fraction Bars** on page 167. Each player puts a whole bar in front of him/her and the fraction bars to the side. Fraction cards are always returned to the bottom of the stack after use.

The object of this game is to build a whole bar using a set of fractions. Players may build as many as four sets at a time.

Directions: Player One draws a fraction card. If a minus card is drawn and Player One has no bar, then Player One loses his/her turn. If an addition card is drawn, the fraction bar representing the fraction named on the card is placed on the whole bar. When a subtraction fraction card is drawn, the bar representing the fraction is taken away. If no fraction bar representing the fraction on the minus card is placed above the bar, the player simply loses his/her turn. The first player to build a whole bar is the winner.

Name ______________________________

Working With Fractions

Use the fraction bars to help you **find** the smallest fraction in each row. **Circle** it.

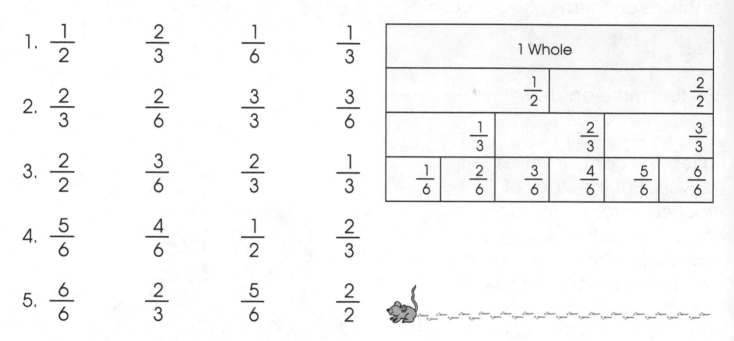

1. $\frac{1}{2}$ $\frac{2}{3}$ $\frac{1}{6}$ $\frac{1}{3}$
2. $\frac{2}{3}$ $\frac{2}{6}$ $\frac{3}{3}$ $\frac{3}{6}$
3. $\frac{2}{2}$ $\frac{3}{6}$ $\frac{2}{3}$ $\frac{1}{3}$
4. $\frac{5}{6}$ $\frac{4}{6}$ $\frac{1}{2}$ $\frac{2}{3}$
5. $\frac{6}{6}$ $\frac{2}{3}$ $\frac{5}{6}$ $\frac{2}{2}$

1 Whole					
$\frac{1}{2}$			$\frac{2}{2}$		
$\frac{1}{3}$		$\frac{2}{3}$		$\frac{3}{3}$	
$\frac{1}{6}$	$\frac{2}{6}$	$\frac{3}{6}$	$\frac{4}{6}$	$\frac{5}{6}$	$\frac{6}{6}$

Use the fraction bars to help you **find** the greatest fraction in each row. **Circle** it.

1 Whole							
$\frac{1}{2}$				$\frac{2}{2}$			
$\frac{1}{4}$		$\frac{2}{4}$		$\frac{3}{4}$		$\frac{4}{4}$	
$\frac{1}{8}$	$\frac{2}{8}$	$\frac{3}{8}$	$\frac{4}{8}$	$\frac{5}{8}$	$\frac{6}{8}$	$\frac{7}{8}$	$\frac{8}{8}$

1. $\frac{1}{2}$ $\frac{3}{4}$ $\frac{6}{8}$ $\frac{8}{8}$
2. $\frac{1}{4}$ $\frac{1}{8}$ $\frac{7}{8}$ $\frac{1}{2}$
3. $\frac{1}{8}$ $\frac{1}{2}$ $\frac{1}{4}$ $\frac{2}{8}$
4. $\frac{1}{4}$ $\frac{3}{8}$ $\frac{5}{8}$ $\frac{3}{4}$
5. $\frac{2}{8}$ $\frac{1}{8}$ $\frac{1}{4}$ $\frac{6}{8}$

More Fractions

Compare the fractions below. **Write** < or > in each box.

Examples:

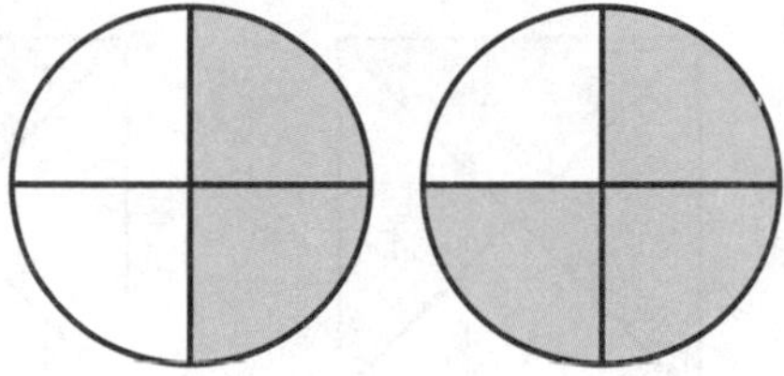

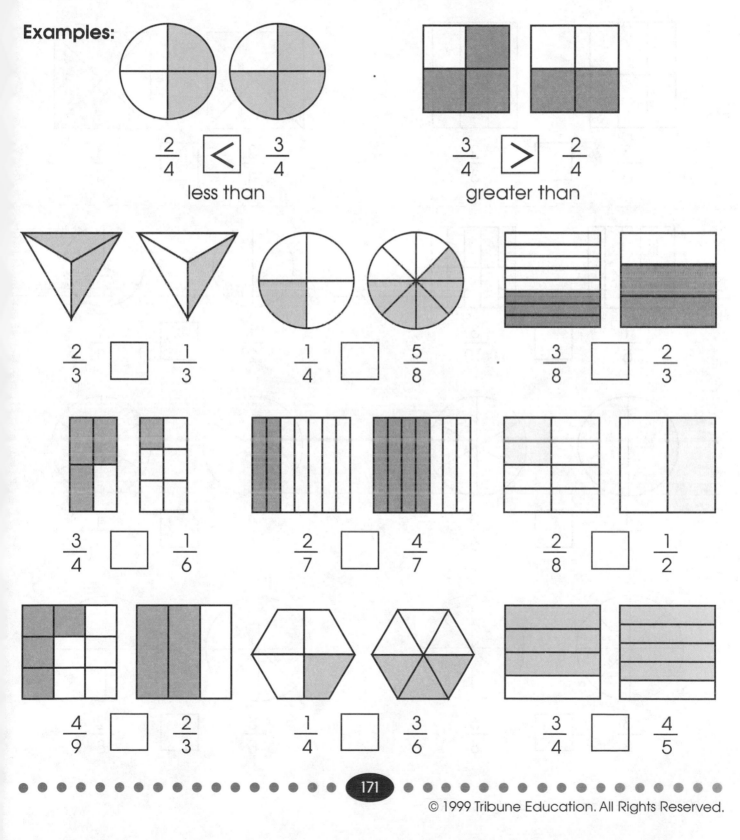

$\frac{2}{4}$ $\boxed{<}$ $\frac{3}{4}$

less than

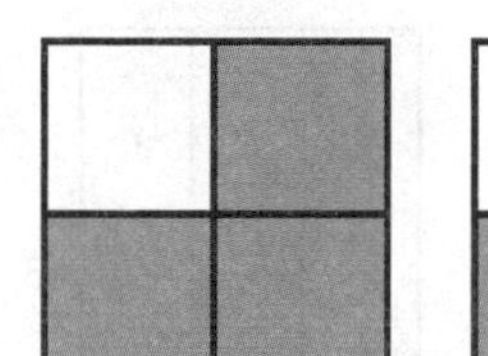

$\frac{3}{4}$ $\boxed{>}$ $\frac{2}{4}$

greater than

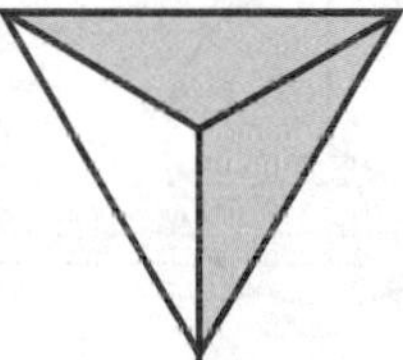

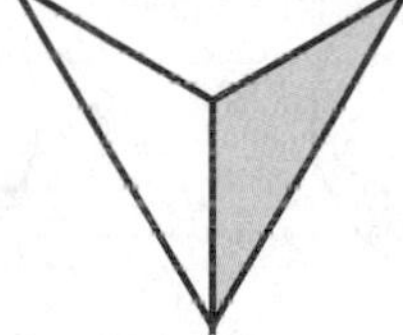

$\frac{2}{3}$ □ $\frac{1}{3}$

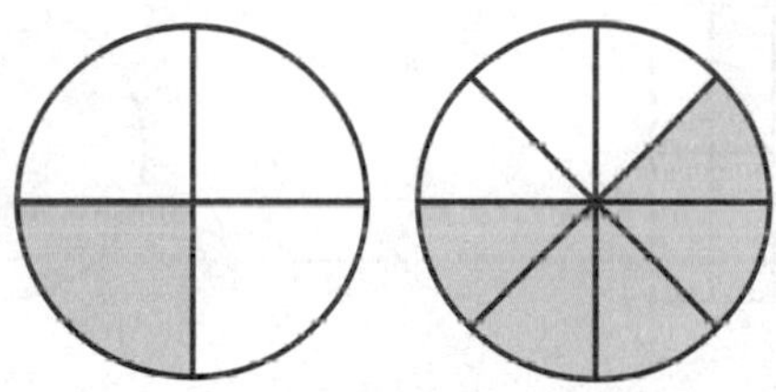

$\frac{1}{4}$ □ $\frac{5}{8}$

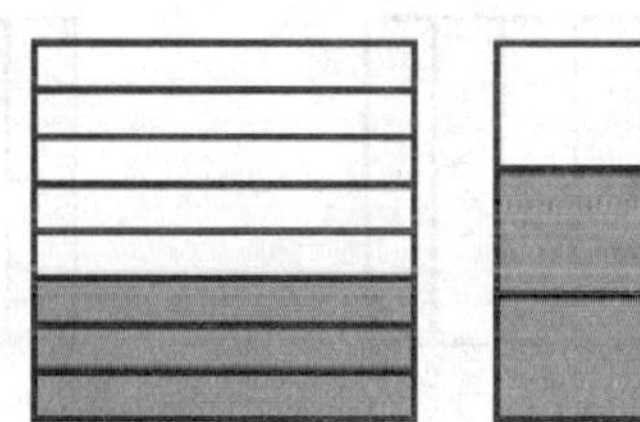

$\frac{3}{8}$ □ $\frac{2}{3}$

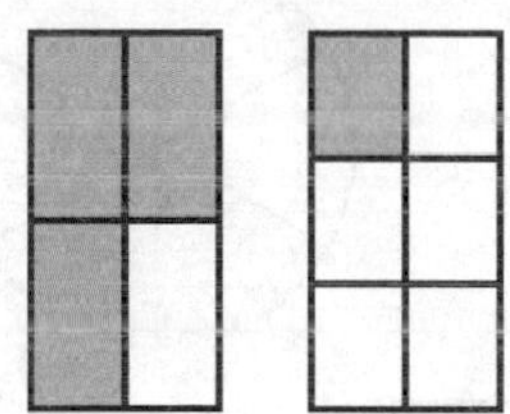

$\frac{3}{4}$ □ $\frac{1}{6}$

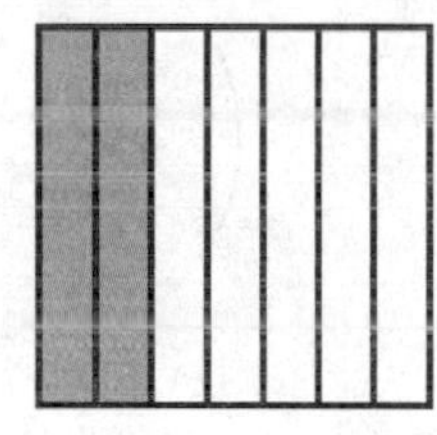

$\frac{2}{7}$ □ $\frac{4}{7}$

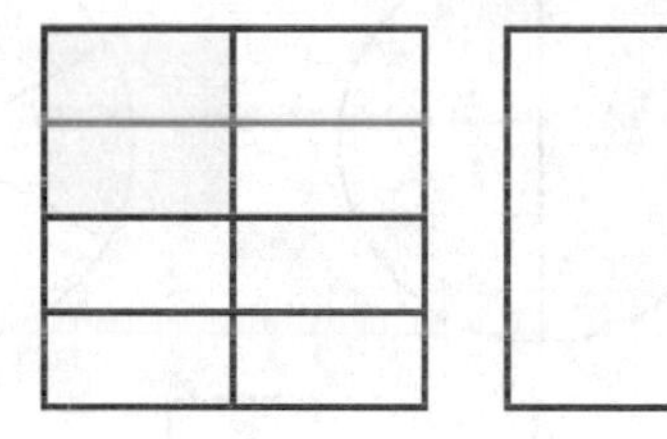

$\frac{2}{8}$ □ $\frac{1}{2}$

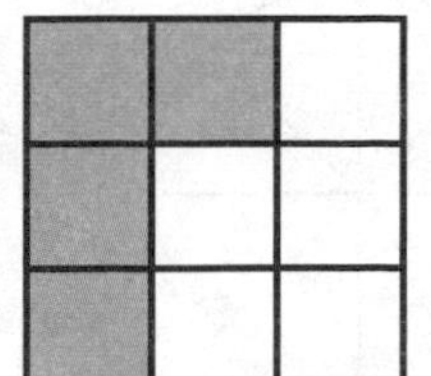

$\frac{4}{9}$ □ $\frac{2}{3}$

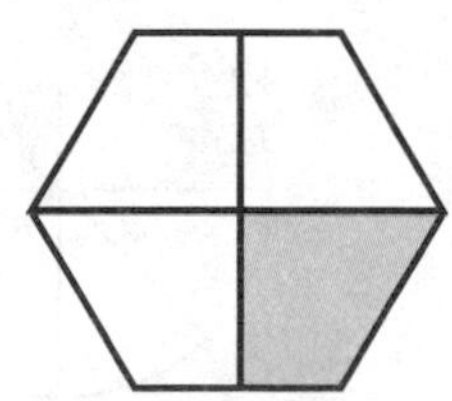

$\frac{1}{4}$ □ $\frac{3}{6}$

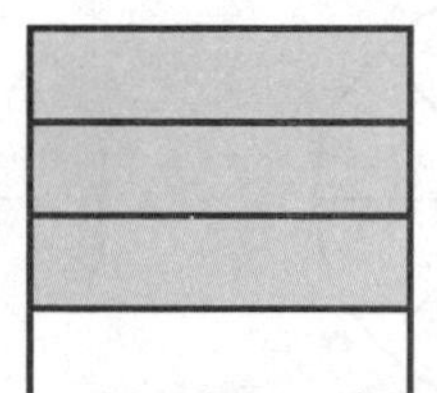

$\frac{3}{4}$ □ $\frac{4}{5}$

Name ______________________

Dare to Compare

Compare the fractions below. **Write** =, < or > in each box.

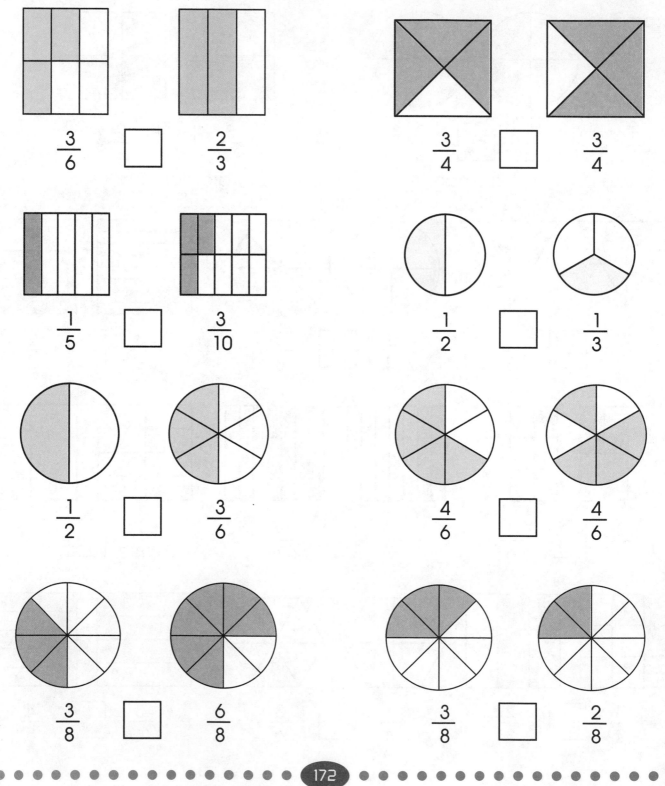

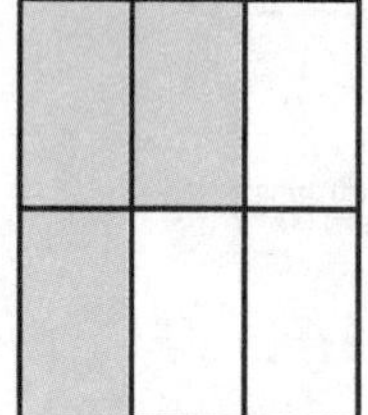 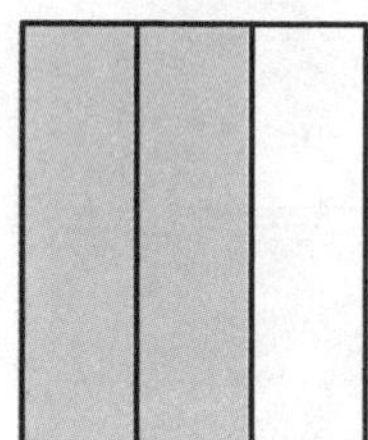

$\frac{3}{6}$ ☐ $\frac{2}{3}$

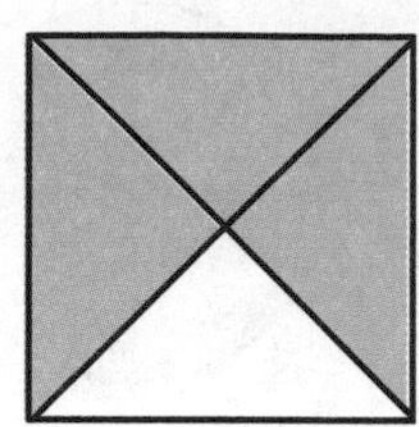 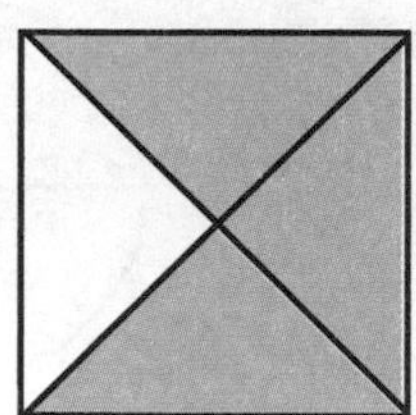

$\frac{3}{4}$ ☐ $\frac{3}{4}$

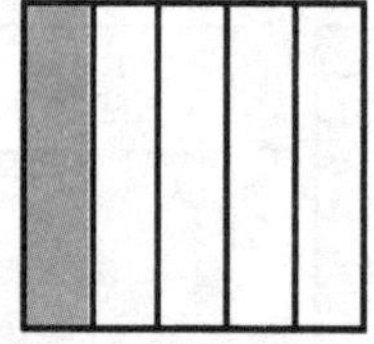 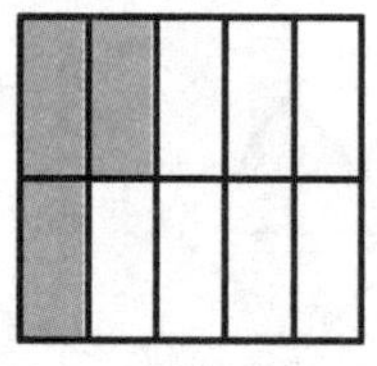

$\frac{1}{5}$ ☐ $\frac{3}{10}$

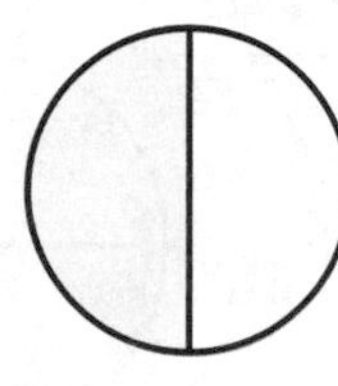 

$\frac{1}{2}$ ☐ $\frac{1}{3}$

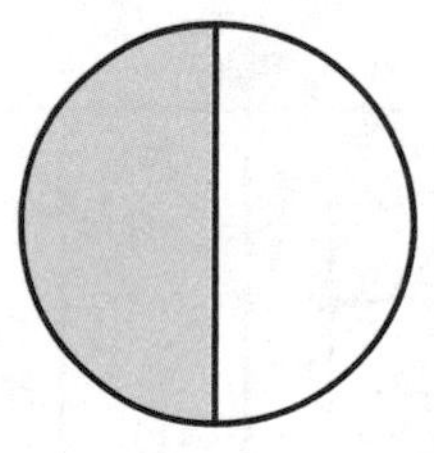 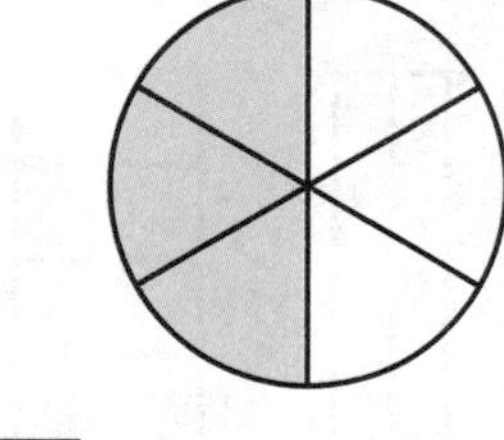

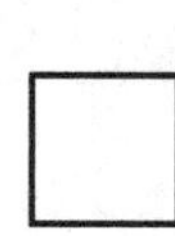

$\frac{1}{2}$ ☐ $\frac{3}{6}$

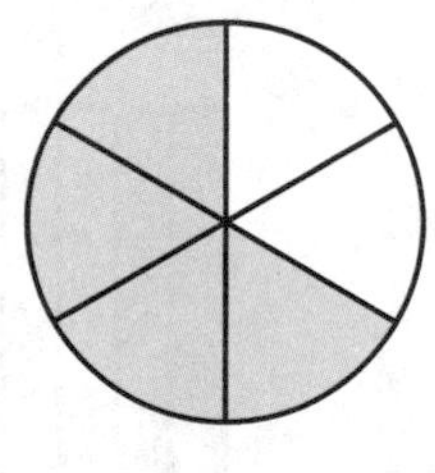 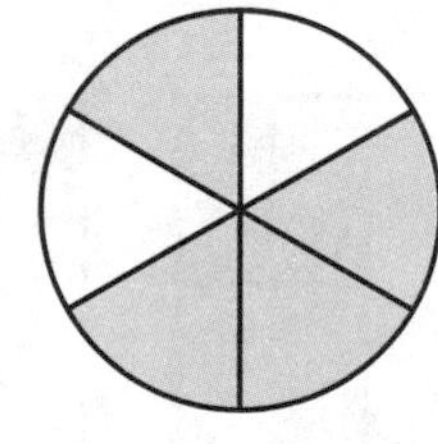

$\frac{4}{6}$ ☐ $\frac{4}{6}$

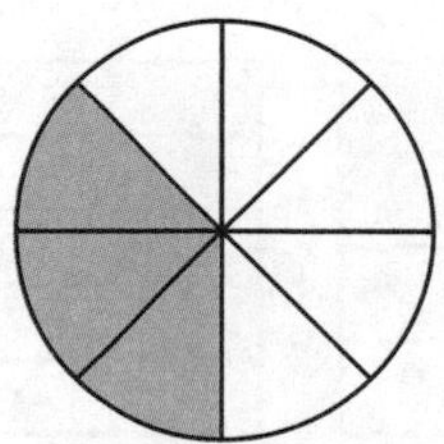 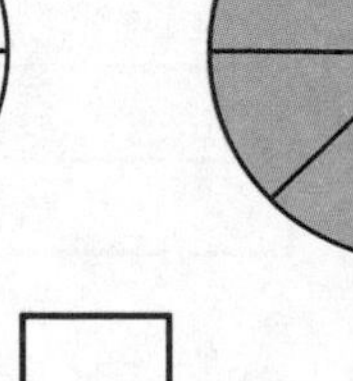

$\frac{3}{8}$ ☐ $\frac{6}{8}$

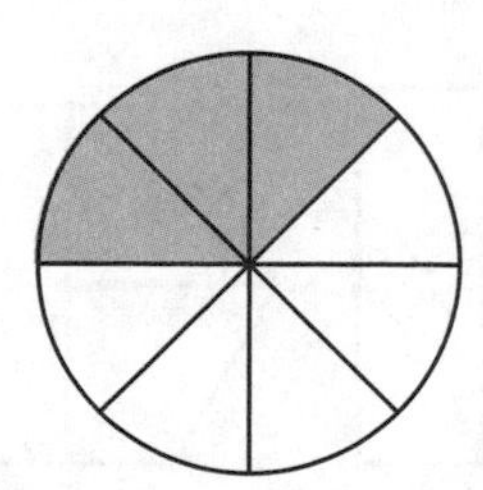 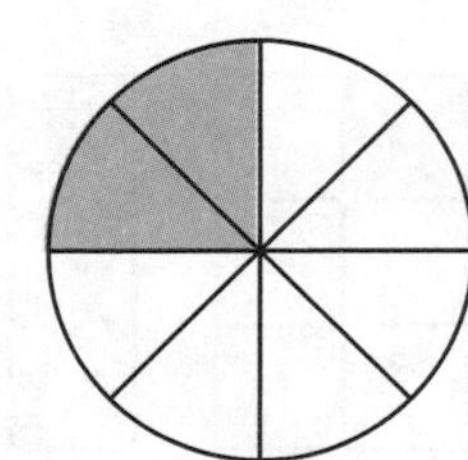

$\frac{3}{8}$ ☐ $\frac{2}{8}$

Name ______________________________

Exploring Equivalent Fractions

Equivalent fractions are two different fractions which represent the same number. For example, on page 172, the picture shows that 1/2 and 3/6 are the same or equivalent fractions.

Complete these equivalent fractions. **Use** your fraction bars.

1. $\frac{1}{3} = \frac{\quad}{6}$ 2. $\frac{1}{2} = \frac{\quad}{4}$ 3. $\frac{3}{4} = \frac{\quad}{8}$ 4. $\frac{1}{3} = \frac{\quad}{9}$

Circle the figure that shows a fraction equivalent to the first figure. **Write** the fractions for the shaded area under each figure.

5. 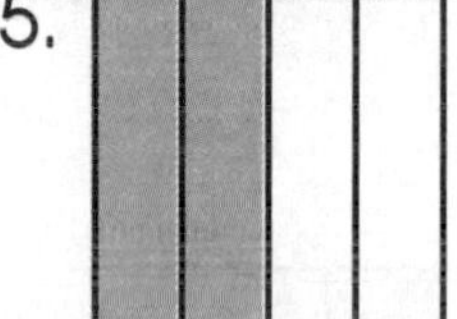 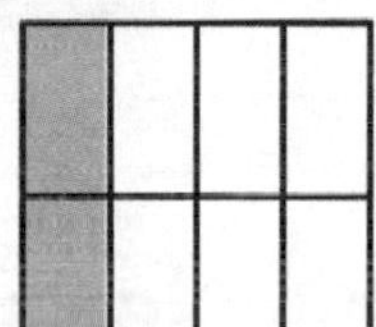 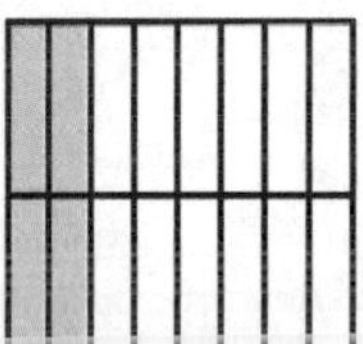 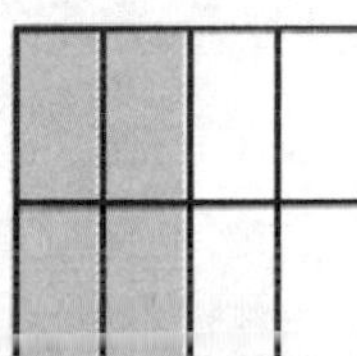

______ ______ ______ ______

6. 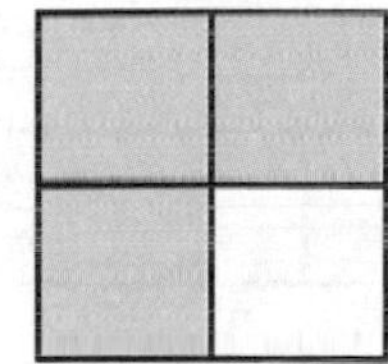 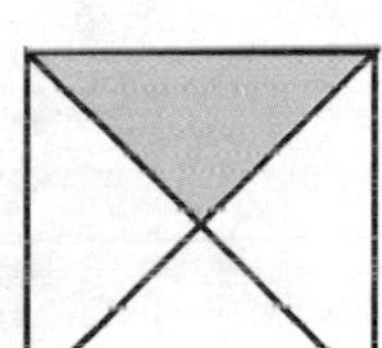 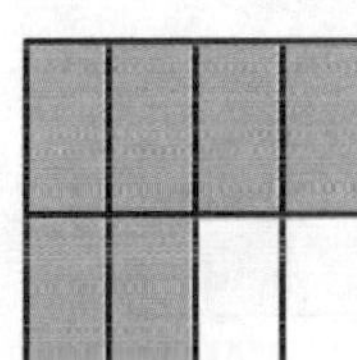 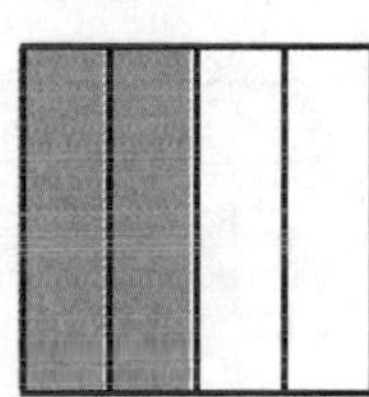

______ ______ ______ ______

Write two equivalent fractions for each fraction.

7. $\frac{1}{4}$, —, —   8. $\frac{1}{5}$, —, —   9. $\frac{2}{3}$, —, —   10. $\frac{3}{8}$, —, —

To find an equivalent fraction, **multiply** both parts of the fraction by the same number.

Example: $\frac{2}{3} \times \frac{3}{3} = \frac{6}{9}$

11. $\frac{1}{4} = \frac{\quad}{8}$ 12. $\frac{3}{4} = \frac{\quad}{8}$ 13. $\frac{4}{5} = \frac{8}{\quad}$ 14. $\frac{3}{8} = \frac{\quad}{24}$

Name ______________________

Match the Fractions

Above each bar, **write** a fraction for the shaded part. Then, **match** each fraction on the left with its equivalent fraction on the right.

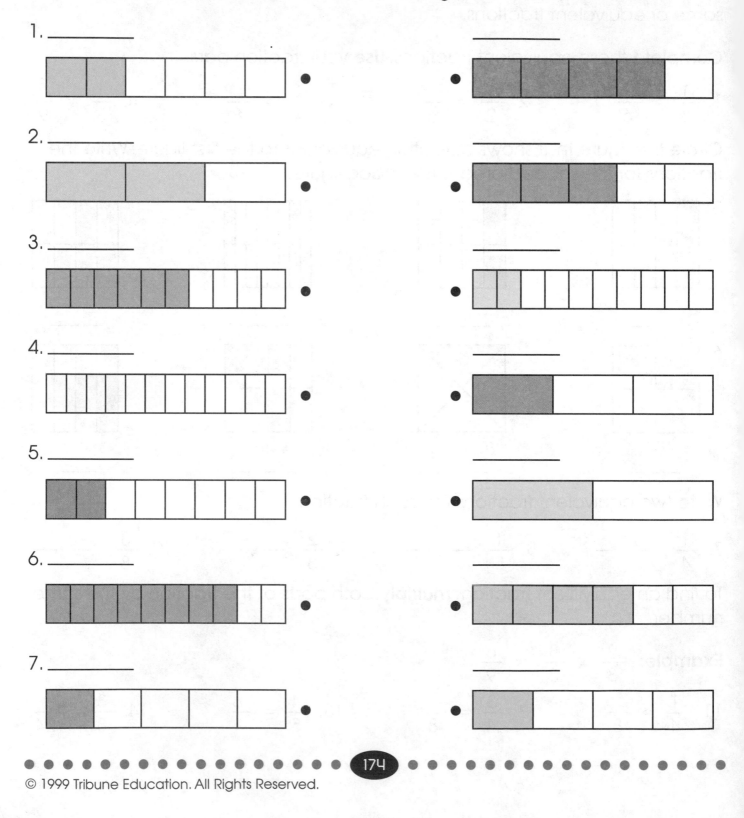

1. ________

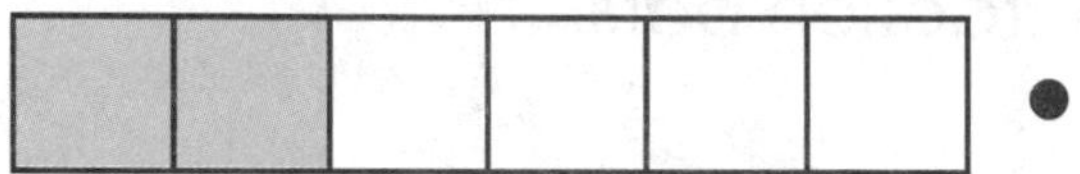

2. ________

3. ________

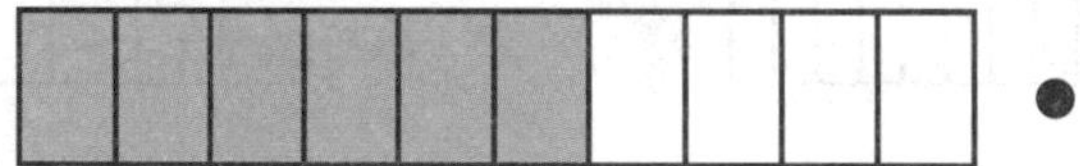

4. ________

5. ________

6. ________

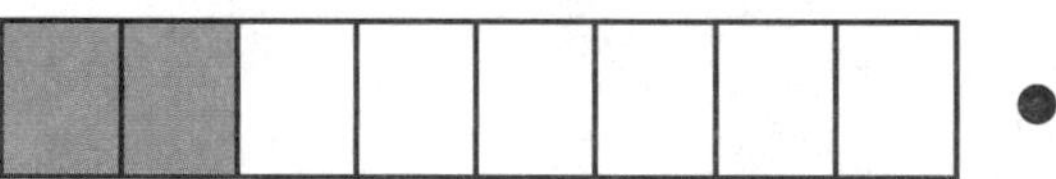

7. ________

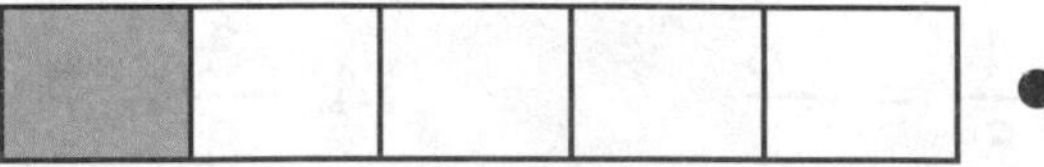

Name ______________________________

Fraction Patterns

Each row contains equivalent fractions except for one. **Find** which three fractions are equivalent for each row.
Draw an **X** on the fraction that is not equivalent. On the line, **write** a fraction that could be in the set. If necessary, **draw** a picture to help.

Example:

$\frac{1}{2}$	$\frac{2}{4}$	~~$\frac{3}{5}$~~ (X)	$\frac{4}{8}$

$$\frac{\text{Numerator (N)} \times 2}{\text{Denominator (D)} \times 2}$$

New Fraction: $\frac{8}{16}$

New Fraction

1.

$\frac{1}{8}$	$\frac{2}{16}$	$\frac{2}{24}$	$\frac{4}{32}$

____

2.

$\frac{3}{4}$	$\frac{6}{8}$	$\frac{12}{16}$	$\frac{20}{30}$

____

3.

$\frac{3}{10}$	$\frac{9}{30}$	$\frac{27}{90}$	$\frac{36}{180}$

____

4.

$\frac{1}{5}$	$\frac{3}{10}$	$\frac{3}{15}$	$\frac{4}{20}$

____

5.

$\frac{3}{7}$	$\frac{6}{14}$	$\frac{8}{21}$	$\frac{12}{28}$

____

6.

$\frac{1}{2}$	$\frac{4}{8}$	$\frac{16}{32}$	$\frac{62}{128}$

____

7.

$\frac{5}{8}$	$\frac{9}{16}$	$\frac{15}{24}$	$\frac{20}{32}$

____

Write a rule to find equivalent fractions.

____

Name ____________________

Alligator Problems

Complete each equivalent fraction below.

Example: $\frac{4 \times 3}{6 \times 3} = \frac{12}{18}$

$\frac{2}{3} = \frac{\quad}{15}$	$\frac{1}{6} = \frac{\quad}{36}$	$\frac{5}{7} = \frac{\quad}{49}$	$\frac{4}{5} = \frac{\quad}{20}$
$\frac{1}{2} = \frac{6}{\quad}$	$\frac{1}{3} = \frac{\quad}{12}$	$\frac{4}{9} = \frac{\quad}{27}$	$\frac{7}{9} = \frac{14}{\quad}$
$\frac{2}{3} = \frac{\quad}{12}$	$\frac{4}{9} = \frac{\quad}{27}$	$\frac{3}{8} = \frac{\quad}{24}$	$\frac{1}{6} = \frac{\quad}{24}$
$\frac{1}{2} = \frac{4}{\quad}$	$\frac{1}{2} = \frac{\quad}{16}$	$\frac{1}{4} = \frac{4}{\quad}$	$\frac{4}{7} = \frac{\quad}{28}$
$\frac{1}{8} = \frac{\quad}{16}$	$\frac{1}{3} = \frac{\quad}{24}$	$\frac{3}{6} = \frac{\quad}{12}$	$\frac{5}{10} = \frac{\quad}{20}$
$\frac{2}{5} = \frac{4}{\quad}$	$\frac{2}{3} = \frac{4}{\quad}$	$\frac{3}{7} = \frac{\quad}{21}$	
$\frac{2}{3} = \frac{\quad}{9}$			
$\frac{2}{5} = \frac{\quad}{25}$			
$\frac{2}{7} = \frac{\quad}{14}$			

Name ______________________________

More Than Peanuts

Write <, >, or = to compare the fractions below. **Draw** pictures or **write** equivalent fractions, if needed.

$\frac{3}{8}$ □ $\frac{2}{8}$ $\frac{2}{3}$ □ $\frac{3}{6}$ $\frac{3}{6}$ □ $\frac{1}{2}$

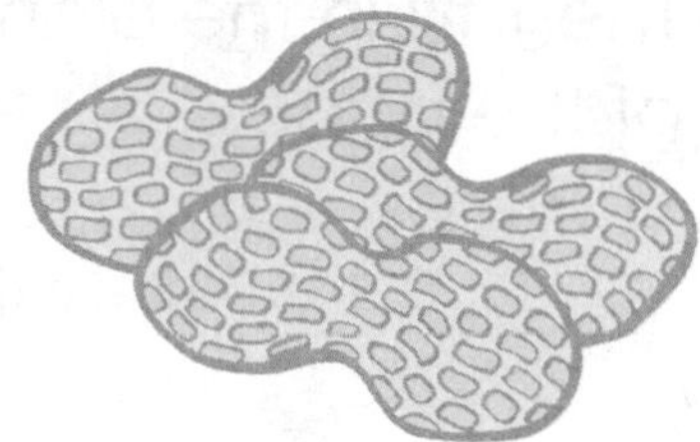

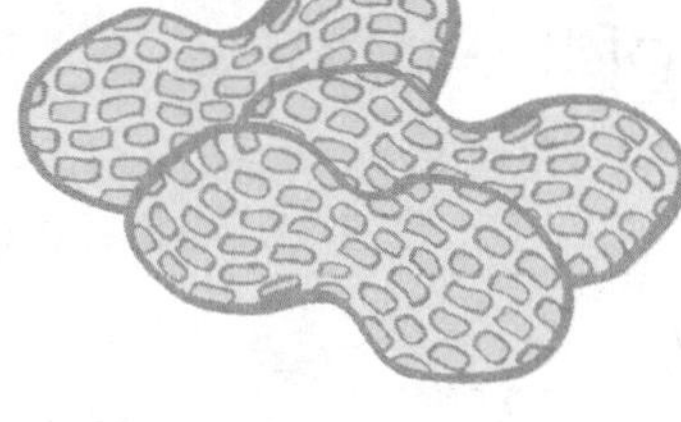

$\frac{4}{7}$ □ $\frac{4}{14}$ $\frac{1}{3}$ □ $\frac{6}{9}$ $\frac{7}{10}$ □ $\frac{2}{5}$

$\frac{8}{12}$ □ $\frac{3}{6}$ $\frac{7}{14}$ □ $\frac{1}{2}$ $\frac{4}{7}$ □ $\frac{3}{7}$ $\frac{4}{8}$ □ $\frac{8}{16}$

$\frac{1}{3}$ □ $\frac{2}{6}$ $\frac{2}{8}$ □ $\frac{1}{2}$ $\frac{1}{5}$ □ $\frac{3}{10}$ $\frac{6}{11}$ □ $\frac{5}{11}$

$\frac{6}{12}$ □ $\frac{1}{2}$ $\frac{2}{3}$ □ $\frac{2}{6}$ $\frac{7}{12}$ □ $\frac{2}{4}$ $\frac{5}{6}$ □ $\frac{1}{3}$

$\frac{7}{10}$ □ $\frac{3}{10}$ $\frac{1}{2}$ □ $\frac{8}{12}$ $\frac{1}{5}$ □ $\frac{8}{10}$ $\frac{7}{8}$ □ $\frac{2}{4}$

$\frac{3}{8}$ □ $\frac{1}{4}$ $\frac{2}{5}$ □ $\frac{5}{10}$

$\frac{5}{6}$ □ $\frac{2}{3}$ $\frac{6}{10}$ □ $\frac{2}{5}$

$\frac{6}{10}$ □ $\frac{3}{10}$ $\frac{3}{6}$ □ $\frac{6}{12}$

$\frac{1}{8}$ □ $\frac{1}{4}$ $\frac{1}{2}$ □ $\frac{1}{4}$

Name ____________________

Catch It If You Can

For each fraction below, determine if the fraction equals more or less than 1/2. For each fraction, **cross out** the ball that does not describe the fraction. Then, **fill in** the blanks with the letters left to solve the riddle at the bottom of the page.

	Less than	More than
1. $\frac{3}{8}$	 Y	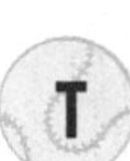 T
2. $\frac{4}{5}$	 H	 O
3. $\frac{1}{3}$	 U	 E
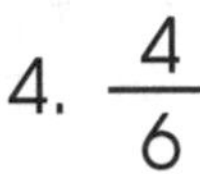 4. $\frac{4}{6}$	 S	 R
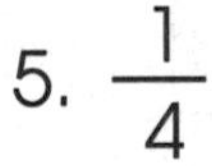 5. $\frac{1}{4}$	 B	 T

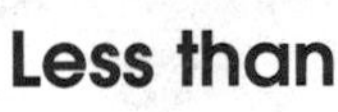

	Less than	More than
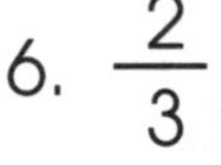 6. $\frac{2}{3}$	 L	 R
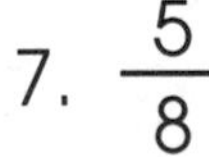 7. $\frac{5}{8}$	 R	 E
8. $\frac{7}{8}$	O	A
9. $\frac{1}{8}$	T	L
10. $\frac{1}{6}$	H	P

What is harder to catch the faster you run?

____ ____ ____ ____   ____ ____ ____ ____ ____ ____

Name ____________________________

Reduce, Reduce

To reduce a fraction, **divide** each number in the fraction by a common factor. A fraction is reduced when the numerator and the denominator have only a common factor of 1. This is called a fraction's **lowest terms**.

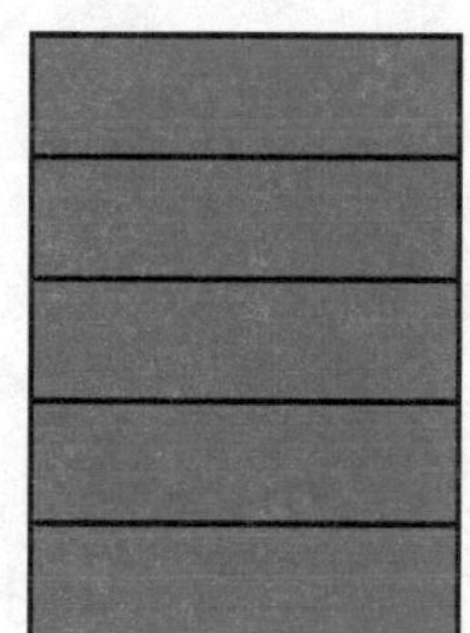

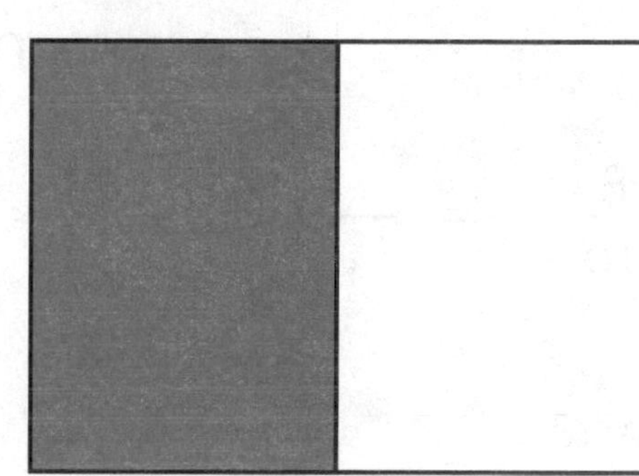

$\frac{5}{10} \div \frac{5}{5} = \frac{1}{2}$

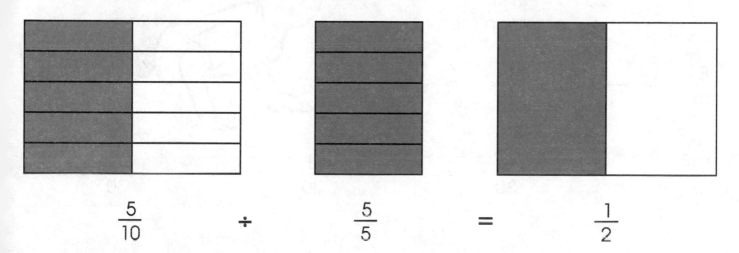

5 is a common factor of 5 and 10. (It can be divided into groups of five.)
Is there another number these both can be divided by? (Only the number 1.)

Example: $\frac{16}{20} \div \frac{2}{2} = \frac{8}{10}$ **Ask:** Is this the lowest? Is there another number these both can be divided by? (Yes, 2.)

$\frac{8}{10} \div \frac{2}{2} = \frac{4}{5}$ Can this still divided by a common number? (No.)

Reduce these fractions.

$\frac{9}{12} =$ $\frac{3}{15} =$ $\frac{12}{16} =$ $\frac{4}{5} =$ $\frac{2}{8} =$

$\frac{1}{8} =$ $\frac{4}{6} =$ $\frac{3}{9} =$ $\frac{7}{14} =$ $\frac{18}{24} =$

Name ____________________

Reduce the Fat

Reduce each fraction to its lowest terms.

Example: $\frac{5 \div 5}{25 \div 5} = \frac{1}{5}$ (common factors)

$\frac{8}{16} = \_\_$ $\frac{12}{18} = \_\_$

$\frac{10}{25} = \_\_$ $\frac{12}{30} = \_\_$ $\frac{3}{30} = \_\_$ $\frac{6}{30} = \_\_$

$\frac{12}{20} = \_\_$ $\frac{3}{18} = \_\_$ $\frac{3}{9} = \_\_$ $\frac{4}{26} = \_\_$

$\frac{4}{28} = \_\_$ $\frac{7}{21} = \_\_$ $\frac{16}{20} = \_\_$ $\frac{2}{10} = \_\_$

$\frac{3}{27} = \_\_$ $\frac{5}{60} = \_\_$ $\frac{21}{35} = \_\_$ $\frac{3}{12} = \_\_$

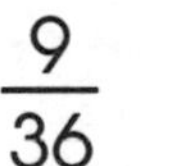

$\frac{9}{36} = \_\_$ $\frac{24}{40} = \_\_$ $\frac{8}{24} = \_\_$

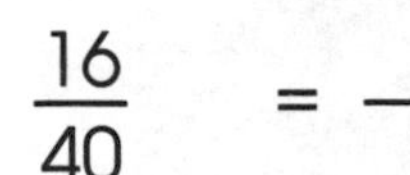

$\frac{16}{40} = \_\_$

Name ______________________________

Mix 'Em Up

A **mixed number** is a whole number with a fraction.

Example: $1\frac{2}{3}$ 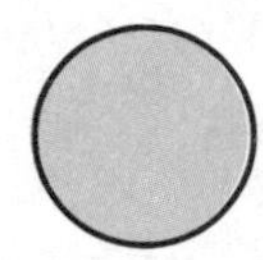 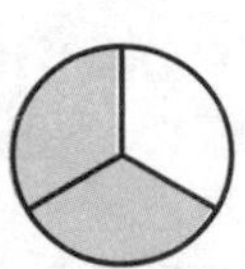

An **improper fraction** is a fraction representing a whole and a fraction. The numerator is larger than the denominator.

Example: $\frac{16}{3}$  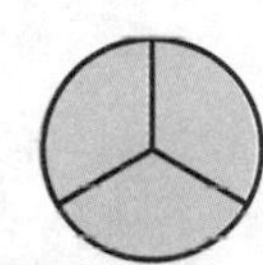    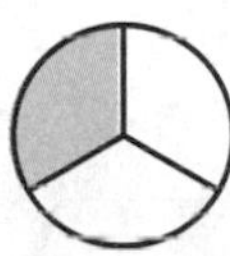

To change a mixed number to an improper fraction, **multiply** the whole number by the denominator.

Example: $2\frac{3}{4}$ 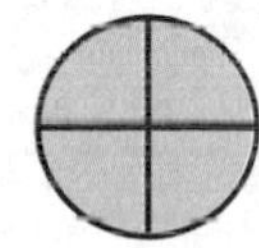 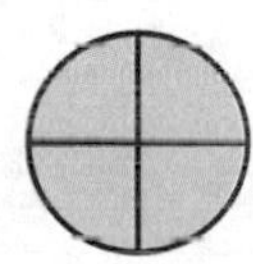 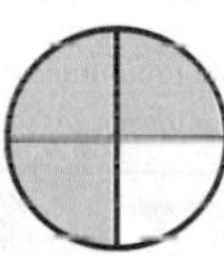 2 x 4 = 8 (How many fourths?)

Add the numerator to that number. 8 + 3 = 11

Write the fraction with the resulting number as numerator over the original denominator. $\frac{11}{4}$

$1\frac{1}{3}$ = $3\frac{2}{5}$ = $4\frac{3}{4}$ = $2\frac{2}{7}$ =

To change an improper fraction to a mixed number, **divide** the numerator by the denominator. $\frac{10}{3}$

(How many wholes can be made?) $3\overline{)10}$ = 3 R1

Write the quotient as the whole number and **write** any remainder as a fraction (with the denominator from the original problem).

$3\frac{1}{3}$ = 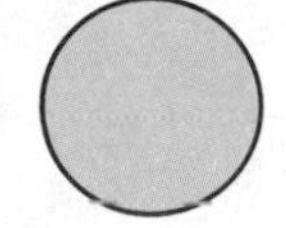 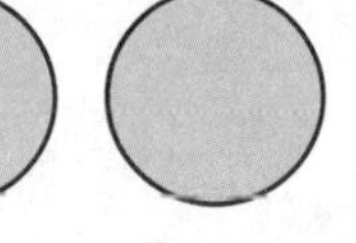

$\frac{5}{2}$ = $\frac{7}{6}$ = $\frac{4}{3}$ = $\frac{10}{4}$ =

Name ______________________________

Oh, My!

When the numerator is greater than the denominator (an improper fraction), write a mixed number or divide to write a whole number. A mixed number is made up of a whole number and a fraction. **Example:** $2\frac{1}{2}$

Draw the correct mouths on the animals by finding the whole or mixed number for each.

Example:

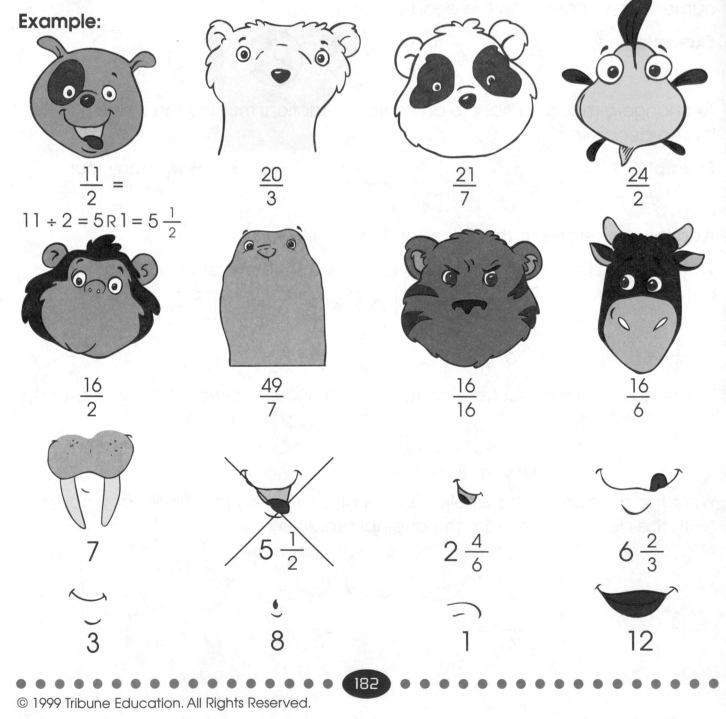

$\frac{11}{2} =$

$11 \div 2 = 5\text{R}1 = 5\frac{1}{2}$

$\frac{20}{3}$

$\frac{21}{7}$

$\frac{24}{2}$

$\frac{16}{2}$

$\frac{49}{7}$

$\frac{16}{16}$

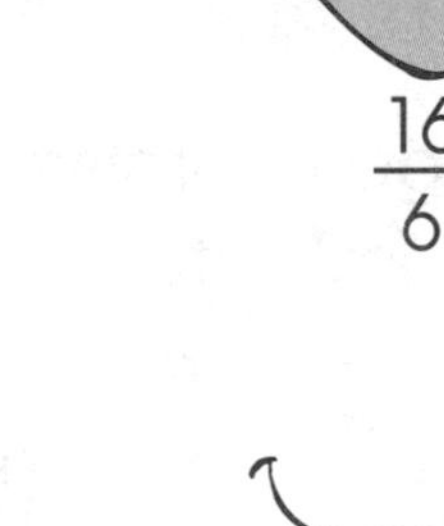

$\frac{16}{6}$

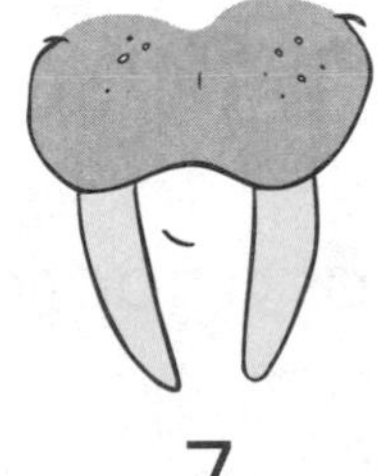

7

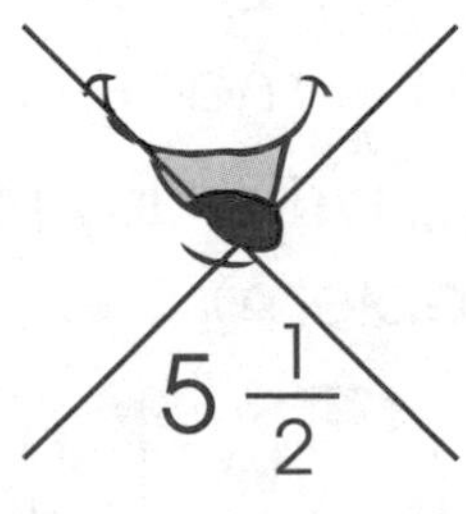

$5\frac{1}{2}$

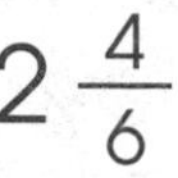

$2\frac{4}{6}$

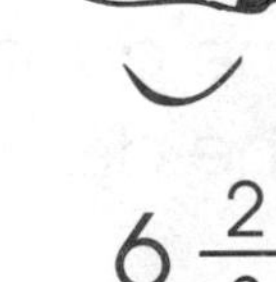

$6\frac{2}{3}$

3

8

1

12

Name ____________________

Figure It Out

Solve the problems. Then, **connect** the dots in the same order as the answers appear.

1. $3\frac{3}{4} = \frac{\quad}{4}$
2. $\frac{30}{11} = 2\frac{\quad}{11}$
3. $\frac{10}{6} = 1\frac{\quad}{6}$
4. $4\frac{1}{5} = \frac{\quad}{5}$
5. $\frac{13}{7} = 1\frac{\quad}{7}$
6. $1\frac{5}{6} = \frac{\quad}{6}$
7. $4\frac{1}{3} = \frac{\quad}{3}$
8. $2\frac{2}{5} = \frac{\quad}{5}$
9. $1\frac{1}{9} = \frac{\quad}{9}$
10. $1\frac{2}{5} = \frac{\quad}{5}$
11. $\frac{9}{2} = 4\frac{\quad}{2}$
12. $8\frac{1}{2} = \frac{\quad}{2}$
13. $4\frac{3}{8} = \frac{\quad}{8}$
14. $\frac{11}{3} = 3\frac{\quad}{3}$
15. $3\frac{5}{6} = \frac{\quad}{6}$
16. $\frac{13}{5} = 2\frac{\quad}{5}$
17. $\frac{12}{7} = 1\frac{\quad}{7}$
18. $6\frac{2}{5} = \frac{\quad}{5}$
19. $\frac{13}{8} = 1\frac{\quad}{8}$
20. $1\frac{1}{8} = \frac{\quad}{8}$

1 7 17 35 10 2 13 12 21 4 8 11 23 9 3 15 5 5 32 6

Name ____________________________________

The Ultimate Adding Machine

Find the sum for each problem. **Reduce** it to the lowest terms.

$\frac{7}{9} + \frac{1}{9} =$

$\frac{4}{12} + \frac{3}{12} =$

$\frac{3}{6} + \frac{2}{6} =$

$\frac{1}{9} + \frac{3}{9} =$

$\frac{4}{10} + \frac{4}{10} =$

$\frac{3}{6} + \frac{1}{6} =$

$\frac{5}{9} + \frac{3}{9} =$

$\frac{2}{5} + \frac{1}{5} =$

$\frac{5}{11} + \frac{5}{11} =$

$\frac{3}{7} + \frac{2}{7} =$

$\frac{4}{8} + \frac{1}{8} =$

$\frac{4}{12} + \frac{1}{12} =$

$\frac{5}{8} + \frac{2}{8} =$

$\frac{6}{12} + \frac{4}{12} =$

$\frac{4}{6} + \frac{1}{6} =$

$\frac{4}{11} + \frac{4}{11} =$

$\frac{2}{5} + \frac{2}{5} =$

$\frac{5}{8} + \frac{5}{8} =$

$\frac{1}{9} + \frac{2}{9} =$

$\frac{7}{10} + \frac{2}{10} =$

7+9+6+

Name ____________________________

Sea Math

Reduce each sum to a whole number or a mixed number in the lowest terms.

$\frac{6}{9} + \frac{6}{9}$ $\frac{4}{5} + \frac{6}{5}$ $\frac{3}{4} + \frac{2}{4}$ $\frac{8}{11} + \frac{8}{11}$ $\frac{2}{5} + \frac{3}{5}$

$\frac{8}{9} + \frac{3}{9}$ $\frac{4}{8} + \frac{6}{8}$ $\frac{5}{4} + \frac{2}{4}$ $\frac{4}{3} + \frac{2}{3}$ $\frac{5}{7} + \frac{6}{7}$

$\frac{8}{11} + \frac{3}{11}$ $\frac{3}{12} + \frac{10}{12}$ $\frac{3}{6} + \frac{3}{6}$ $\frac{6}{12} + \frac{8}{12}$ $\frac{4}{8} + \frac{4}{8}$ $\frac{5}{12} + \frac{8}{12}$

$\frac{5}{12} + \frac{10}{12}$

$\frac{7}{13} + \frac{6}{13}$ $\frac{8}{15} + \frac{14}{15}$ $\frac{5}{7} + \frac{6}{7}$

Name ____________________

Soaring Subtraction

Solve each subtraction problem. **Reduce** each difference to the lowest terms.

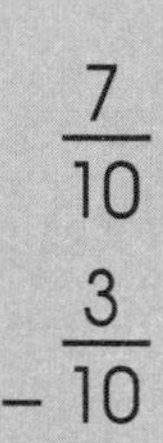

$\frac{7}{10} - \frac{3}{10}$ $\frac{14}{16} - \frac{7}{16}$ $\frac{7}{7} - \frac{3}{7}$

$\frac{6}{8} - \frac{2}{8}$ $\frac{9}{11} - \frac{7}{11}$ $\frac{16}{21} - \frac{9}{21}$ $\frac{9}{10} - \frac{6}{10}$ $\frac{17}{18} - \frac{6}{18}$ $\frac{9}{12} - \frac{7}{12}$

$\frac{15}{18} - \frac{7}{18}$ $\frac{11}{14} - \frac{8}{14}$ $\frac{17}{17} - \frac{8}{17}$ $\frac{14}{15} - \frac{8}{15}$ $\frac{11}{12} - \frac{2}{12}$ $\frac{9}{10} - \frac{5}{10}$

$\frac{8}{9} - \frac{7}{9}$ $\frac{4}{5} - \frac{3}{5}$ $\frac{8}{10} - \frac{5}{10}$ $\frac{2}{3} - \frac{1}{3}$ $\frac{4}{6} - \frac{3}{6}$ $\frac{8}{9} - \frac{5}{9}$

Take a Closer Look

What is a stamp collector called?

To find out, **solve** the following subtraction problems and **reduce** to the lowest terms. Then, **write** the letter above its matching answer at the bottom of the page.

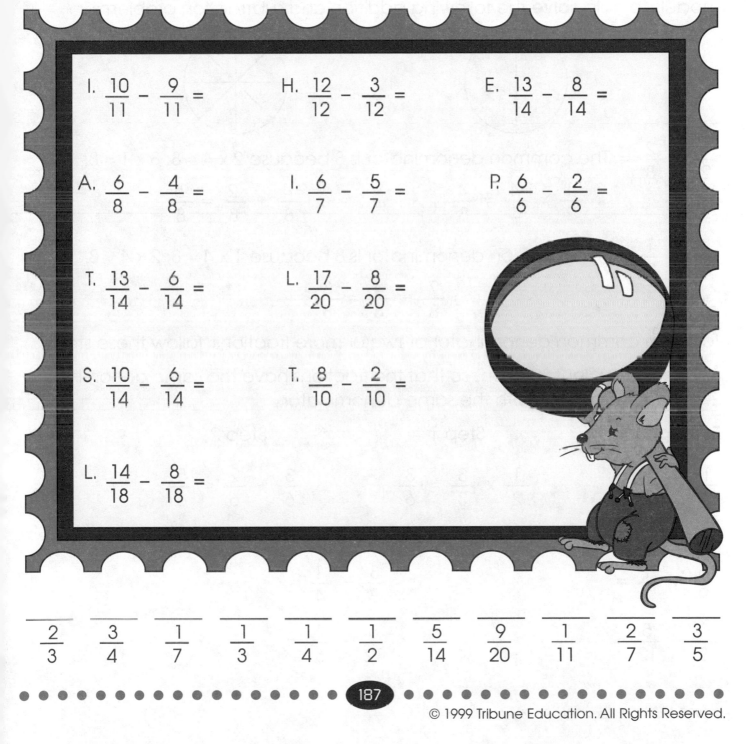

I. $\frac{10}{11} - \frac{9}{11} =$

H. $\frac{12}{12} - \frac{3}{12} =$

E. $\frac{13}{14} - \frac{8}{14} =$

A. $\frac{6}{8} - \frac{4}{8} =$

I. $\frac{6}{7} - \frac{5}{7} =$

P. $\frac{6}{6} - \frac{2}{6} =$

T. $\frac{13}{14} - \frac{6}{14} =$

L. $\frac{17}{20} - \frac{8}{20} =$

S. $\frac{10}{14} - \frac{6}{14} =$

T. $\frac{8}{10} - \frac{2}{10} =$

L. $\frac{14}{18} - \frac{8}{18} =$

___	___	___	___	___	___	___	___	___	___	___
$\frac{2}{3}$	$\frac{3}{4}$	$\frac{1}{7}$	$\frac{1}{3}$	$\frac{1}{4}$	$\frac{1}{2}$	$\frac{5}{14}$	$\frac{9}{20}$	$\frac{1}{11}$	$\frac{2}{7}$	$\frac{3}{5}$

Name ____________________

Finding a Common Denominator

When adding or subtracting fractions with different denominators, find a common denominator first. A **common denominator** is a common multiple of two or more denominators.

Cut a paper plate in half. **Cut** another paper plate into eighths. Use these models to help **solve** the following addition and subtraction problems.

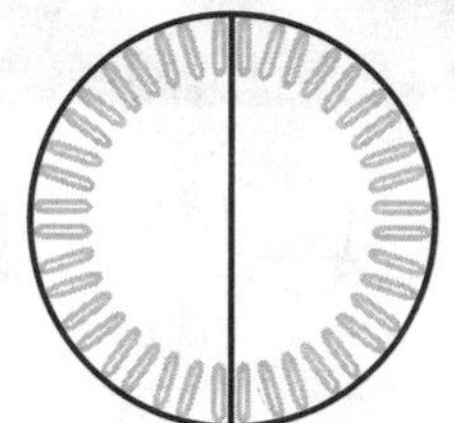

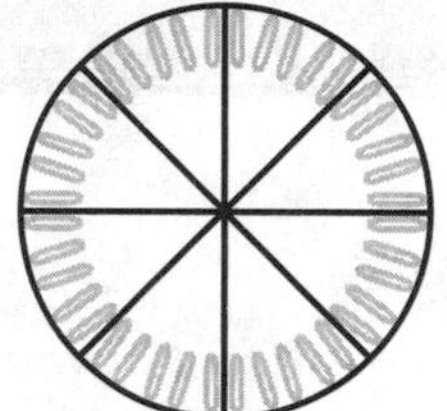

$\frac{1}{2} + \frac{2}{8} =$ The common denominator is 8 because 2 x 4 = 8; 8 x 1 = 8.

$\frac{1}{2} \times \frac{4}{4} = \frac{4}{8}$ $\frac{4}{8} + \frac{2}{8} = \frac{6}{8}$

$\frac{7}{8} - \frac{1}{2} =$ The common denominator is 8 because 1 x 4 = 8; 2 x 4 = 8.

$\frac{7}{8} - \frac{4}{8} = \frac{3}{8}$

To find a common denominator of two or more fractions, follow these steps:

1. Write equivalent fractions so that the fractions have the same denominator.
2. Write the fractions with the same denominator.

Example: Step 1 Step 2

$\frac{1}{2} + \frac{2}{6} =$ $\frac{1}{2} \times \frac{3}{3} = \frac{3}{6}$ $\frac{3}{6} + \frac{2}{6} = \frac{5}{6}$

Follow the steps above. Then, **add**. **Reduce** the answer to its lowest terms.

$\frac{5}{9} + \frac{1}{3} =$ $\frac{3}{8} - \frac{1}{4} =$

$\frac{1}{3} + \frac{5}{12} =$ $\frac{5}{12} - \frac{1}{6} =$

Name ____________________

Bug Me!

Solve the puzzle.

Down

1. $\frac{1}{15} + \frac{2}{5} =$ ________ fifteenths
4. $\frac{2}{12} + \frac{2}{6} =$ one ________
5. $\frac{3}{10} + \frac{7}{20} =$ thirteen ________
7. $\frac{1}{8} + \frac{1}{4} =$ three ________
8. $\frac{2}{6} + \frac{1}{12} =$ five ________
9. $\frac{3}{9} + \frac{1}{3} =$ two ________
11. $\frac{1}{8} + \frac{2}{16} =$ ________ fourth

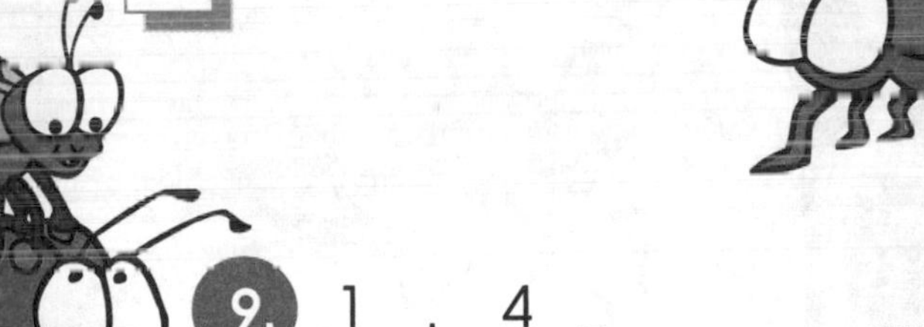

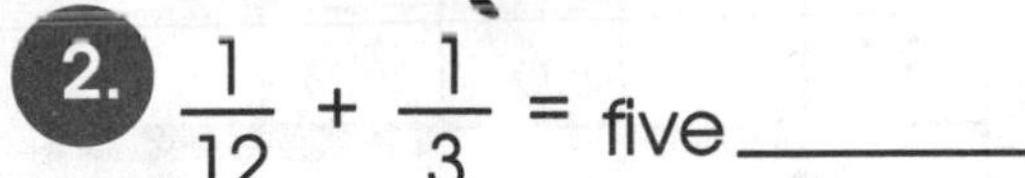

Across

2. $\frac{1}{12} + \frac{1}{3} =$ five ________
3. $\frac{5}{10} + \frac{2}{5} =$ nine ________
5. $\frac{7}{15} + \frac{1}{5} =$ ________ thirds
6. $\frac{1}{2} + \frac{2}{6} =$ ________ sixths
8. $\frac{1}{6} + \frac{1}{2} =$ ________ thirds
9. $\frac{1}{5} + \frac{4}{10} =$ ________ fifths
10. $\frac{1}{3} + \frac{3}{6} =$ ________ sixths
12. $\frac{2}{7} + \frac{1}{14} =$ five ________
13. $\frac{8}{14} + \frac{2}{7} =$ ________ sevenths

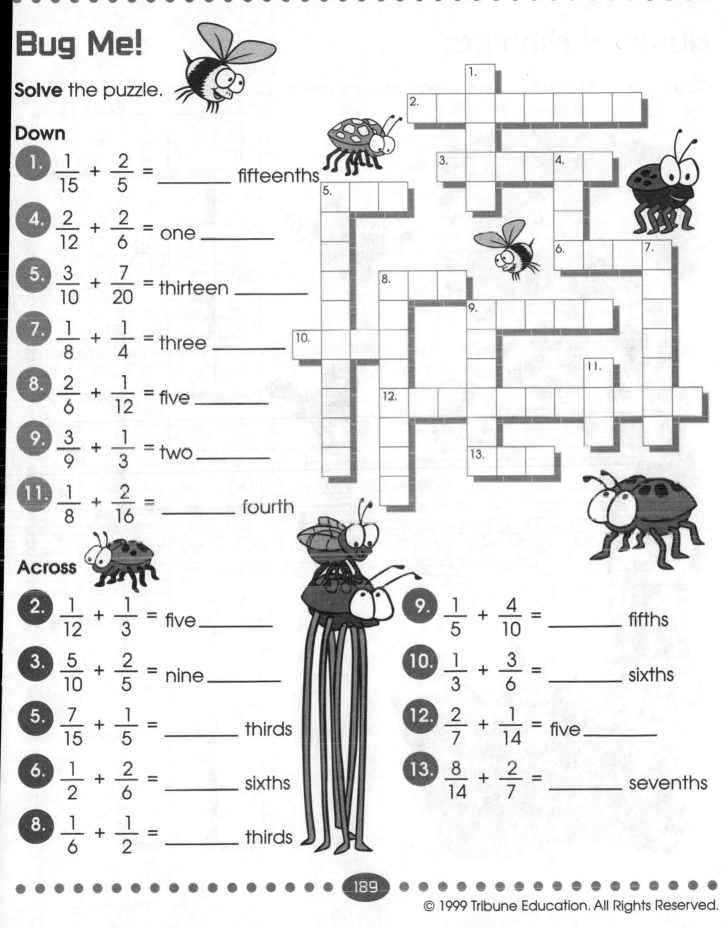

Name ____________________

Numeral Nibblers

Complete these equations. Use another sheet of paper to solve the problems, if needed.

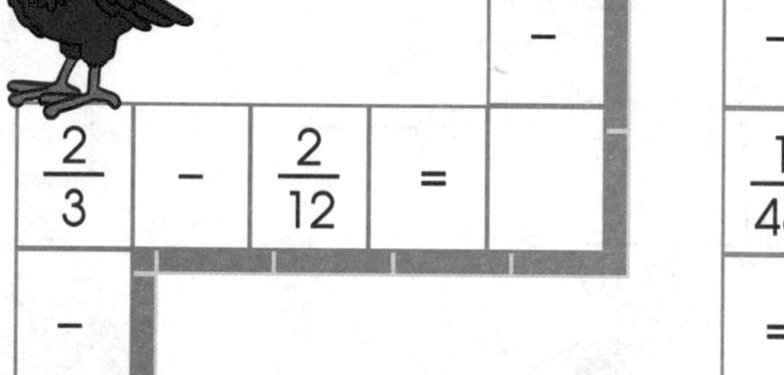

		$\frac{15}{16}$	−	$\frac{1}{2}$	=	
		−				
		$\frac{3}{4}$	−	$\frac{10}{16}$	=	
		=		−		
			−	$\frac{1}{8}$	=	
				−		−
$\frac{2}{3}$	−	$\frac{2}{12}$	=			$\frac{1}{48}$
−						=
$\frac{2}{9}$		$\frac{21}{24}$	−	$\frac{5}{6}$	=	
=		−		−		
		$\frac{3}{4}$	−	$\frac{7}{12}$	=	
		=		=		

Make a Wish

Solve these problems.

Example: $\frac{2}{9}$ of 27 = 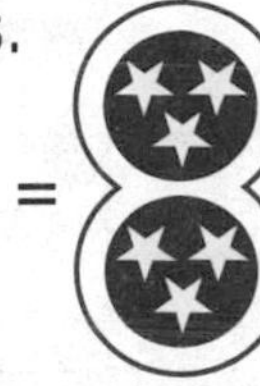    (27 ÷ 9) x 2 = 6

$\frac{7}{8}$ of 16 = $\frac{3}{7}$ of 49 = $\frac{4}{6}$ of 60 = $\frac{3}{6}$ of 54 =

$\frac{6}{8}$ of 24 = $\frac{9}{12}$ of 36 = $\frac{9}{12}$ of 24 = $\frac{2}{5}$ of 25 =

$\frac{3}{8}$ of 32 = $\frac{5}{7}$ of 42 = $\frac{3}{4}$ of 48 =

$\frac{3}{7}$ of 35 = $\frac{7}{9}$ of 36 =

$\frac{6}{8}$ of 64 = $\frac{8}{9}$ of 81 =

$\frac{3}{6}$ of 24 = $\frac{5}{6}$ of 30 =

$\frac{9}{10}$ of 40 = $\frac{6}{8}$ of 72 =

$\frac{9}{11}$ of 33 = $\frac{3}{8}$ of 48 =

Name ____________________

Make the Move

Complete the puzzle by writing the answers in words.

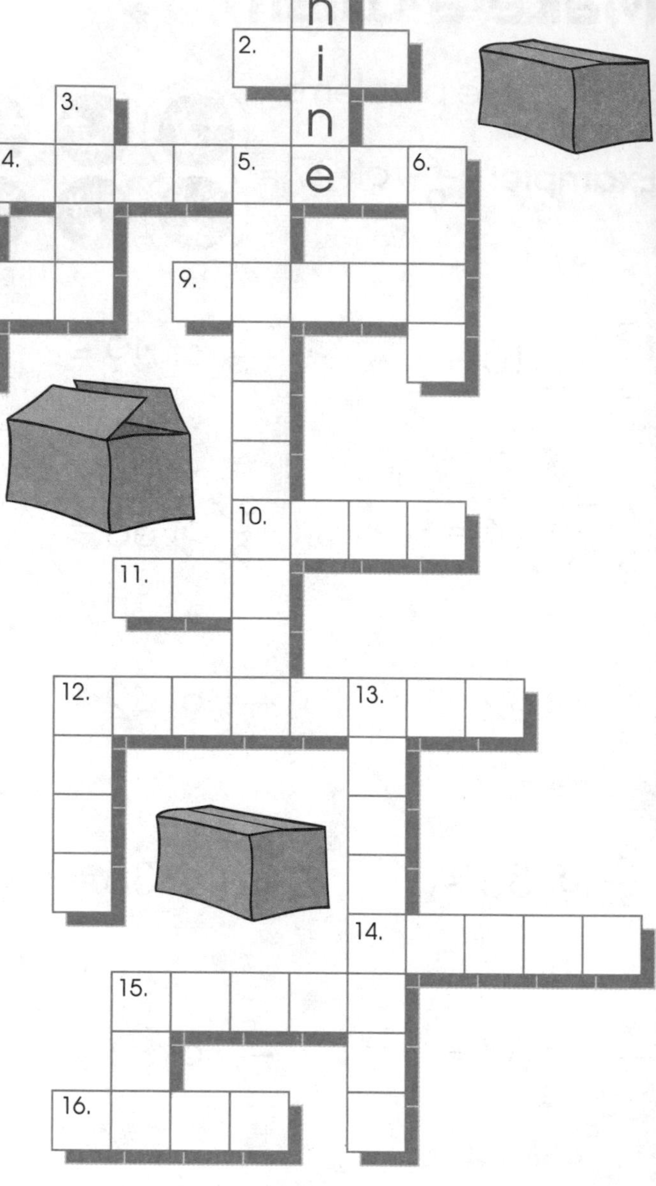

Down

Example: 1. $\frac{3}{4}$ of 12 =

(12 ÷ 4) x 3 = 9 nine

3. $\frac{1}{5}$ of 25 =

5. $\frac{8}{9}$ of 27 =

6. $\frac{3}{6}$ of 18 =

7. $\frac{3}{8}$ of 16 =

12. $\frac{2}{11}$ of 22 =

13. $\frac{3}{4}$ of 24 =

15. $\frac{1}{8}$ of 16 =

Across

2. $\frac{3}{10}$ of 20 =

4. $\frac{9}{10}$ of 20 =

8. $\frac{1}{3}$ of 15 =

9. $\frac{7}{9}$ of 9 =

10. $\frac{1}{3}$ of 12 =

11. $\frac{1}{8}$ of 16 =

12. $\frac{7}{8}$ of 16 =

14. $\frac{1}{5}$ of 15 =

15. $\frac{1}{6}$ of 18 =

16. $\frac{2}{5}$ of 10 =

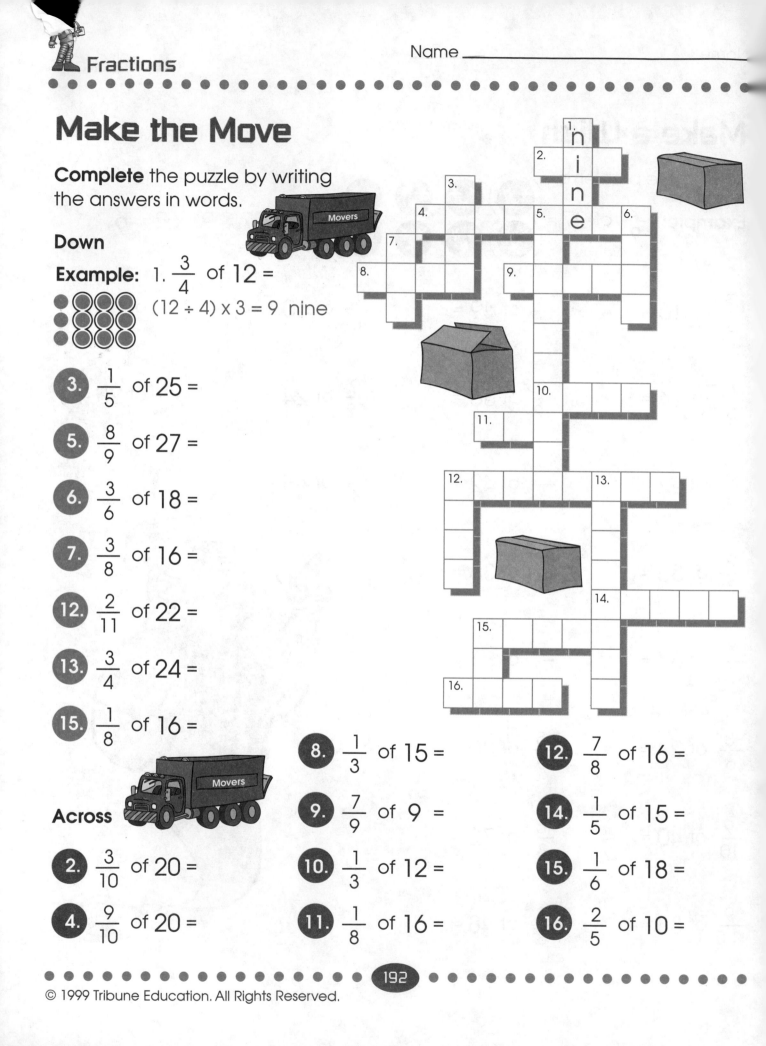

Name ____________________

Animals Bit by Bit

Color each animal a different color. Be sure it's a color that doesn't cover the numbers. Then, **cut** the puzzle pieces apart and mix them up. Assemble the pieces by solving the problems.

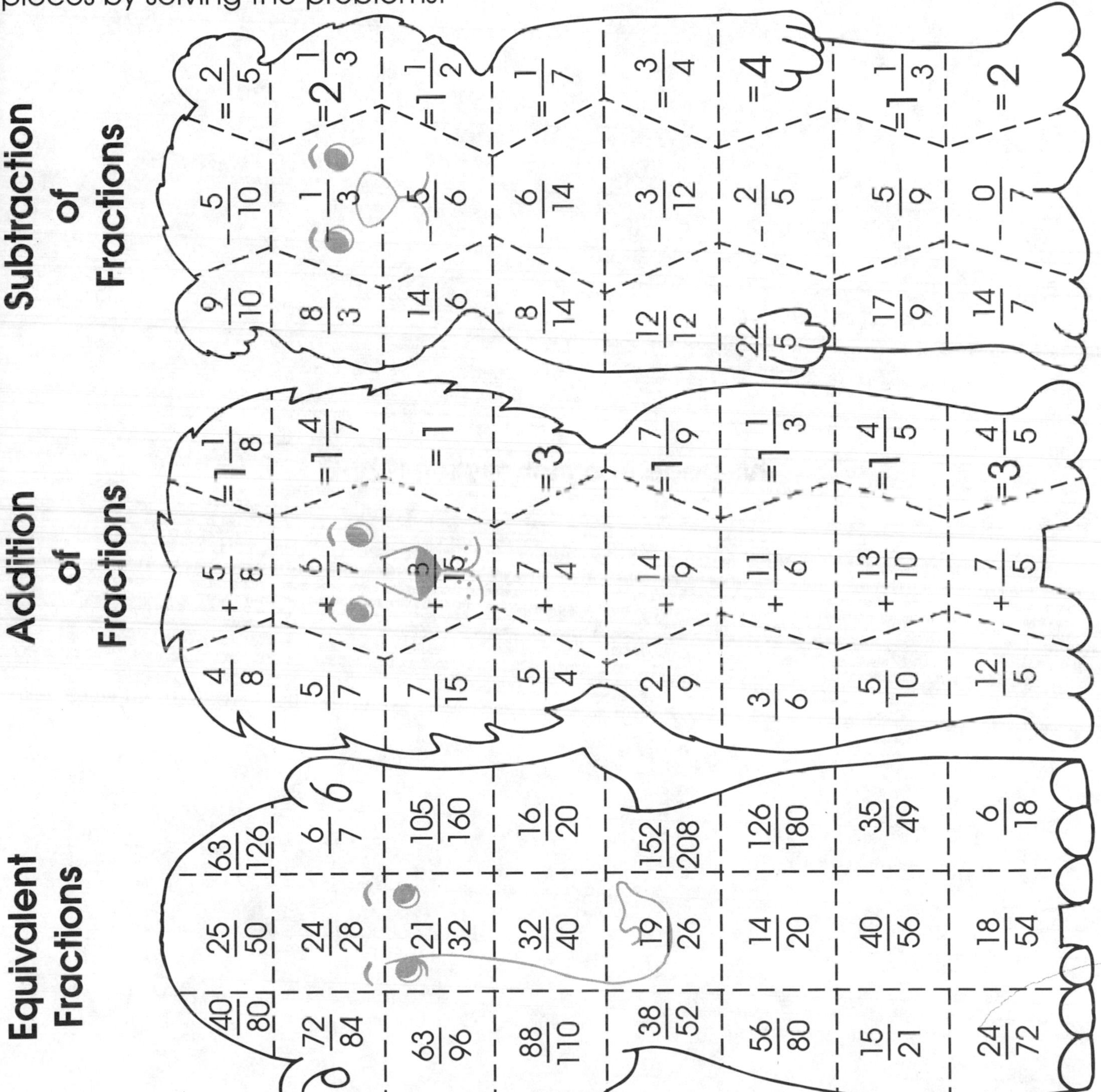

Subtraction of Fractions

$\frac{9}{10}$	$-\frac{5}{10}$	$=\frac{2}{5}$
$\frac{8}{3}$	$-\frac{1}{3}$	$=2\frac{1}{3}$
$\frac{14}{6}$	$-\frac{5}{6}$	$=1\frac{1}{2}$
$\frac{8}{14}$	$-\frac{6}{14}$	$=\frac{1}{7}$
$\frac{12}{12}$	$-\frac{3}{12}$	$=\frac{3}{4}$
$\frac{22}{5}$	$-\frac{2}{5}$	$=4$
$\frac{17}{9}$	$-\frac{5}{9}$	$=1\frac{1}{3}$
$\frac{14}{7}$	$-\frac{0}{7}$	$=2$

Addition of Fractions

$\frac{4}{8}$	$+\frac{5}{8}$	$=1\frac{1}{8}$
$\frac{5}{7}$	$+\frac{6}{7}$	$=1\frac{4}{7}$
$\frac{7}{15}$	$+\frac{3}{15}$	$=1$
$\frac{5}{4}$	$+\frac{7}{4}$	$=3$
$\frac{2}{9}$	$+\frac{14}{9}$	$=1\frac{7}{9}$
$\frac{3}{6}$	$+\frac{11}{6}$	$=1\frac{1}{3}$
$\frac{5}{10}$	$+\frac{13}{10}$	$=1\frac{4}{5}$
$\frac{12}{5}$	$+\frac{7}{5}$	$=3\frac{4}{5}$

Equivalent Fractions

$\frac{40}{80}$	$\frac{25}{50}$	$\frac{63}{126}$
$\frac{72}{84}$	$\frac{24}{28}$	$\frac{6}{7}$
$\frac{63}{96}$	$\frac{21}{32}$	$\frac{105}{160}$
$\frac{88}{110}$	$\frac{32}{40}$	$\frac{16}{20}$
$\frac{38}{52}$	$\frac{19}{26}$	$\frac{152}{208}$
$\frac{56}{80}$	$\frac{14}{20}$	$\frac{126}{180}$
$\frac{15}{21}$	$\frac{40}{56}$	$\frac{35}{49}$
$\frac{24}{72}$	$\frac{18}{54}$	$\frac{6}{18}$

This page intentionally left blank.

Name ______________________________

Picture the Problem

Use the picture to **solve** each problem.

1. Andy had two ropes of the same length. He cut one rope into 2 equal parts and gave the 2 halves to Bill. The other rope he cut into fourths and gave 2 of the fourths to Sue. Circle who got the most rope.

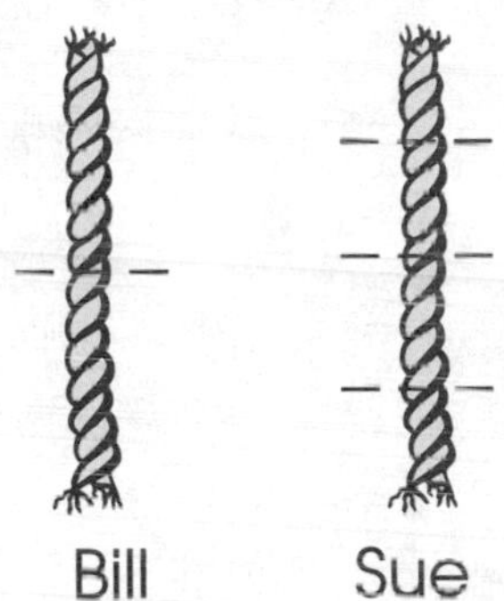

Bill Sue

3. Hannah cut an 8-foot log into 4 equal pieces and burned 2 of them in the fireplace. Joseph cut an 8-foot log into 8 equal pieces and put 3 of them in the fireplace. Circle who put the most wood in the fireplace.

Hannah Joseph

2. Mr. Johns built an office building with an aisle down the middle. He divided one side into 6 equal spaces. He divided the other side into 9 equal spaces. The Ace Company rented 5 of the ninths. The Best Company rented 4 of the sixths. Circle which company rented the larger space.

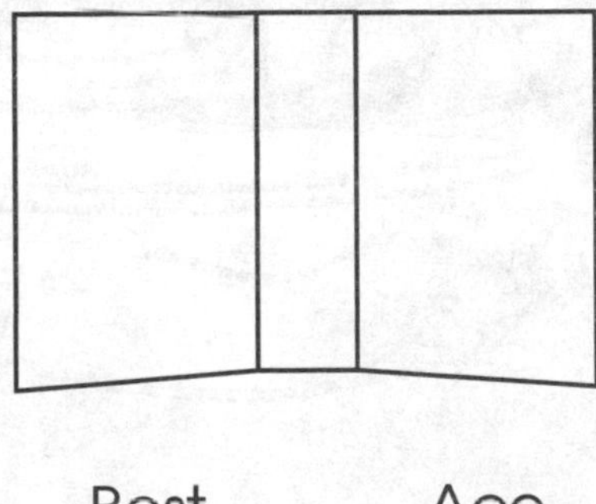

Best Ace

4. The 4-H Club display area at the state fair was divided into 2 equal areas. One of these sections had 12 booths, the other had 9 booths. The flower display covered 2 of the ninths, and the melon display covered 4 of the twelfths. Circle which display had the most room.

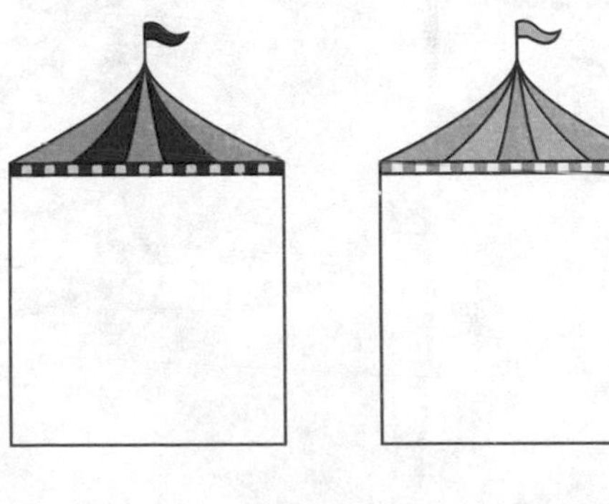

Flowers Melons

Section 8

Decimals

Name ________________________________

Doing Decimals

Just as a fraction stands for part of a whole number, a decimal also shows part of a whole number. And with decimals, the number is always broken into ten or a power of ten (hundred, thousand, etc.) parts. These place values are named tenths, hundredths, thousandths, etc.

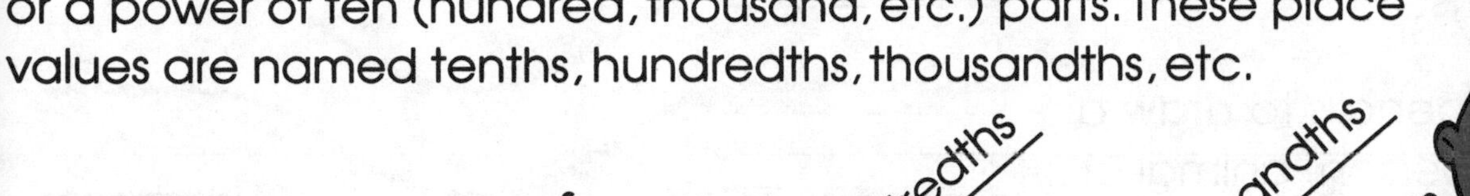

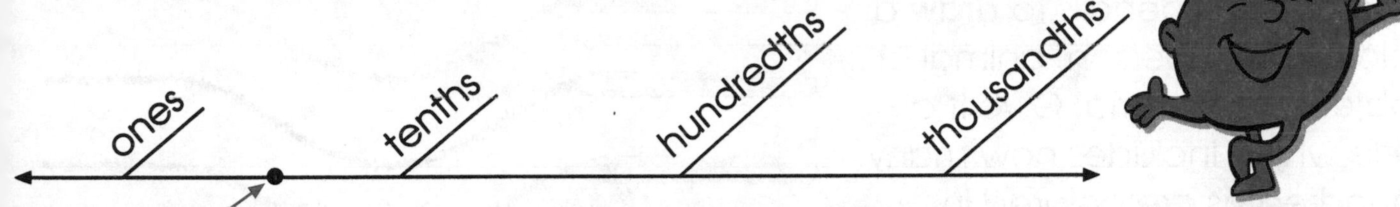

A **decimal point** is a dot placed between the ones place and the tenths place.

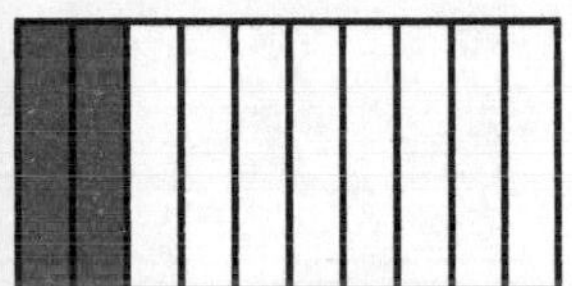

0.2 is read as "two tenths."

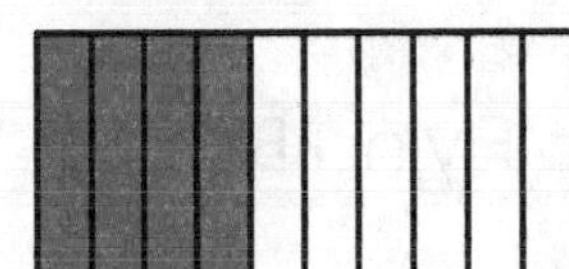

0.4 is four tenths

Write the answer as a decimal for the shaded parts.

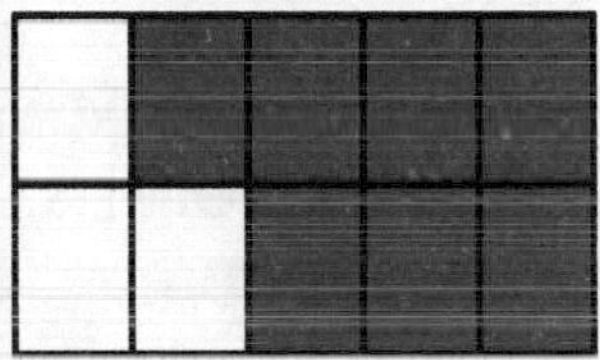

____

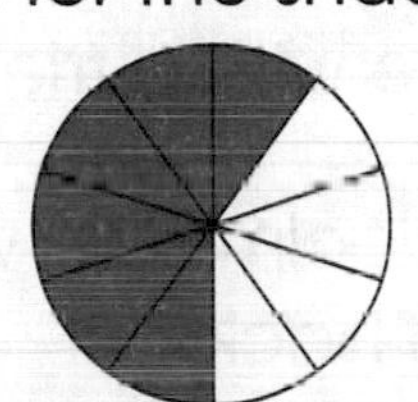

____

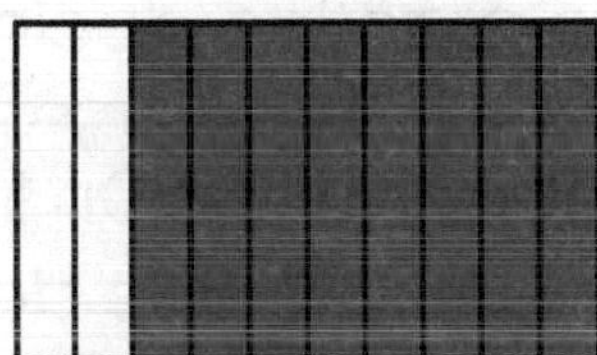

____

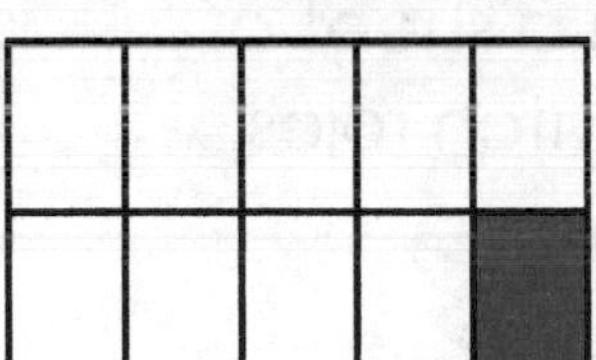

____

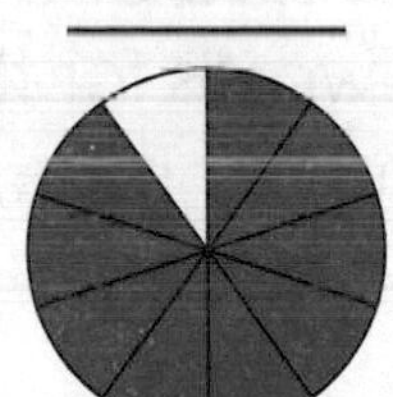

____

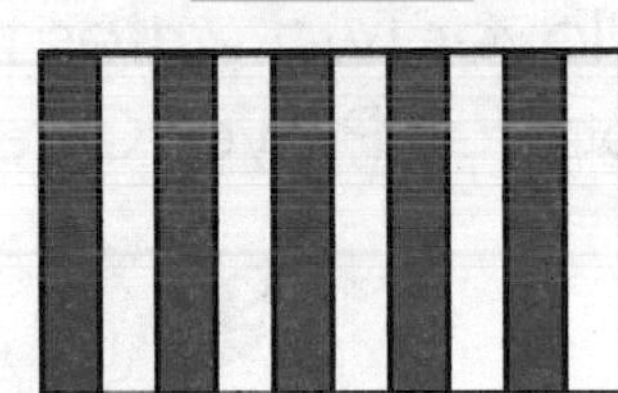

____

Color the parts that match the decimal numbers.

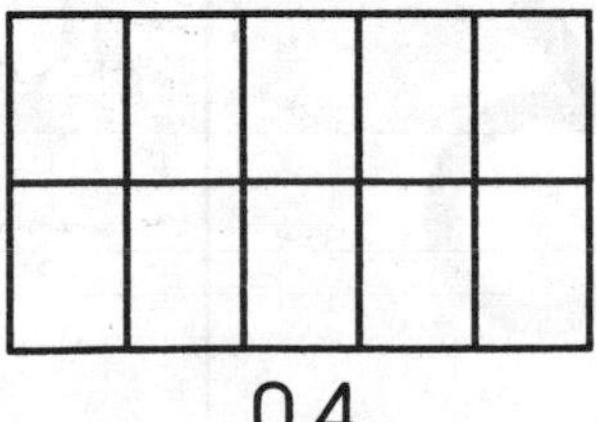

0.4

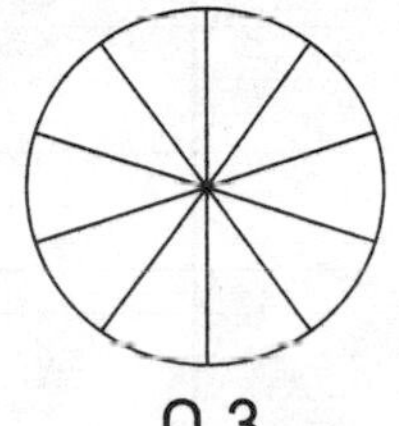

0.3

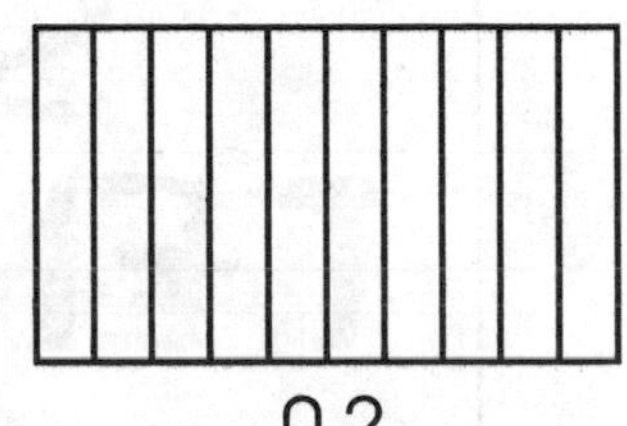

0.2

Name ____________________

Decimal Fun

The **Hundredth Picture Grid** on page 199 is divided into one hundred parts.

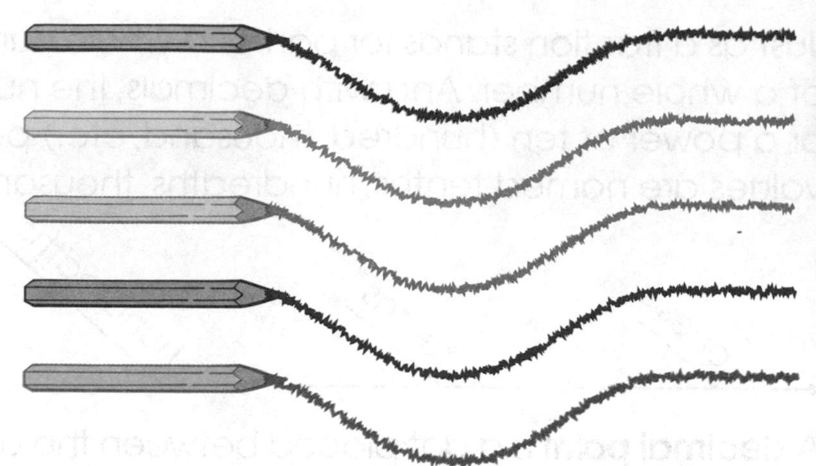

Use colored pencils to **draw** a picture of a person, animal or object on the grid. Give it a title which includes how many hundredths are colored in the drawing.

Example: "The 0.46 Flying Bird" or "A 0.82 Scuba Diver," etc.

To practice decimals, play this game with a friend.

Preparation: On index cards, write decimals in written form, such as six tenths. Then, write the decimal numbers on back.

Directions: Player One holds up either side of a card or says a decimal. Player Two writes the decimal or the words for the decimal on a sheet of paper. Player One checks his/her answer. Then, the players switch roles.

Name ________________________________

Hundredth Picture Grid

Name ____________________

Decimal Divisions

Decimals are often used with whole numbers.

Examples: 2.8

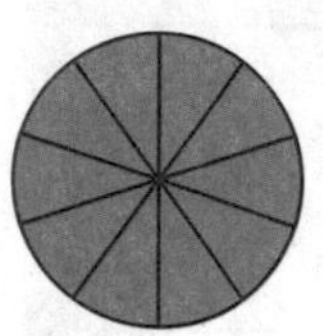 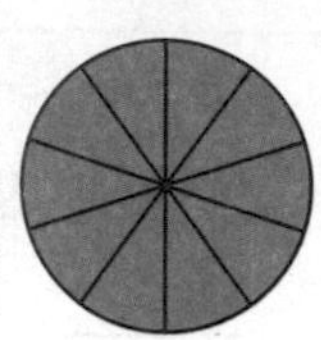 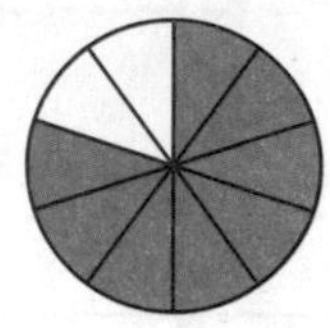

3.5

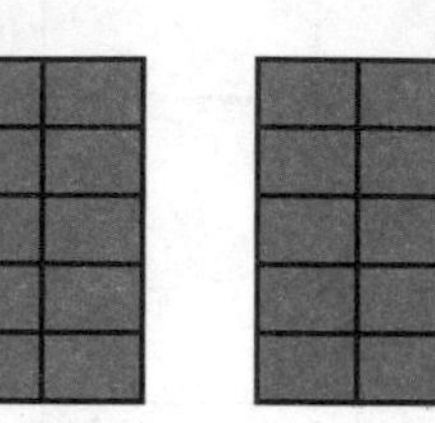 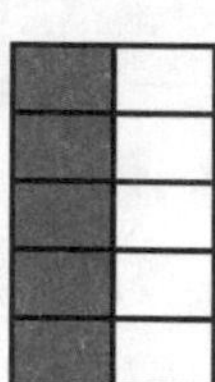

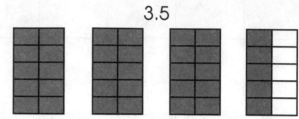

Write the decimal for each picture.

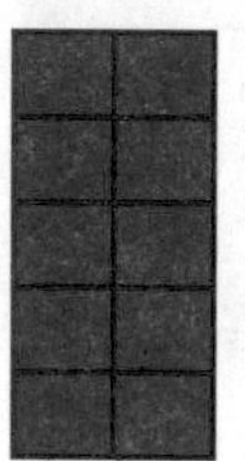 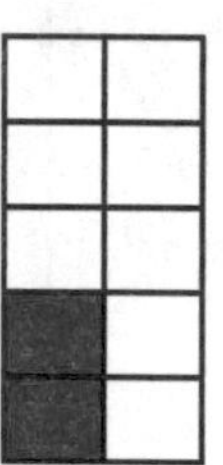

____

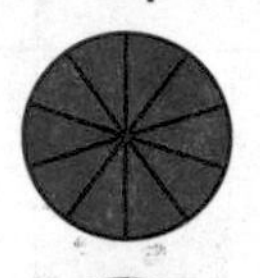  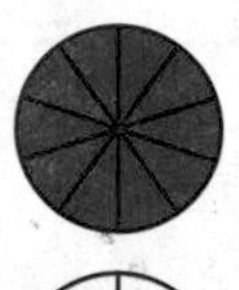

____

 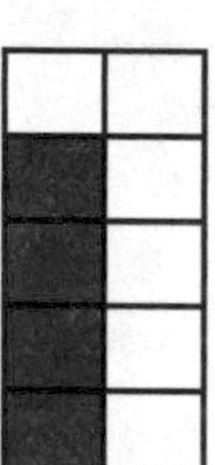 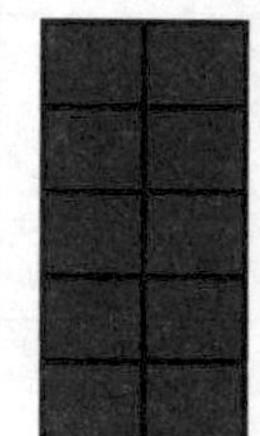

____

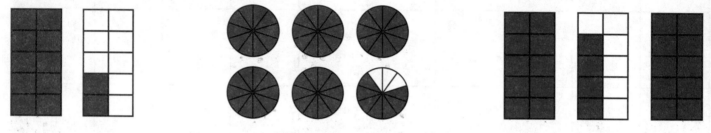

Shade in the picture to show the decimal number.

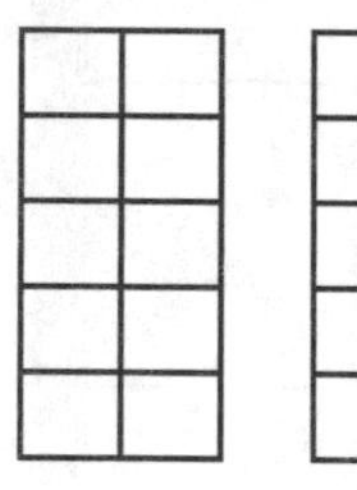

1.9

3.5

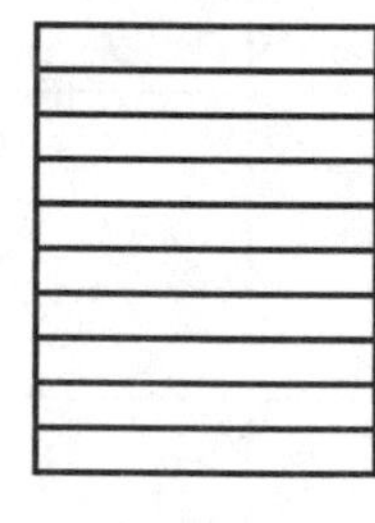

0.4

4.1

When reading decimals with whole numbers, say "point" or "and" for the decimal point.

Write the word names for each decimal from above.

1.9 ______________________________ 0.4 ______________________________

3.5 ______________________________ 4.1 ______________________________

Name ________________________________

How Hot Are You?

Write the number for each word name. **Cross off** the number in the cloud. The number that is left is your body temperature. **Hint:** Remember to add a zero to hold any place value not given.

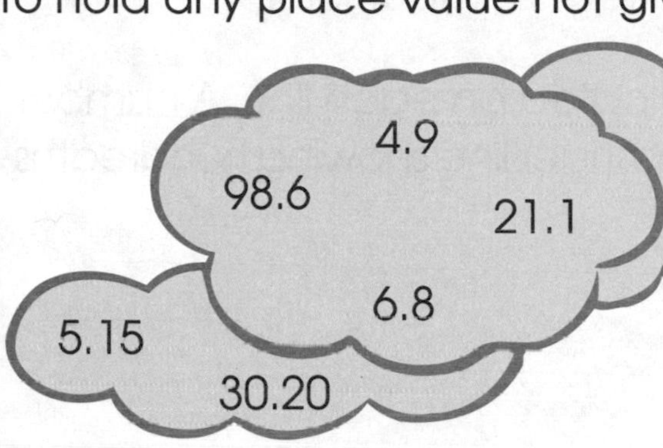

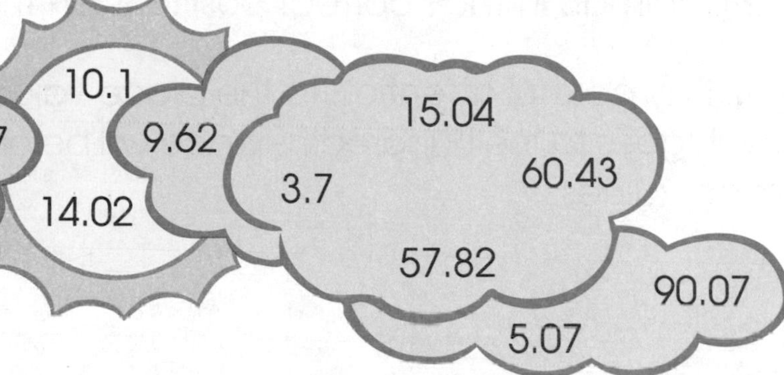

1. six and eight tenths ____________
2. four and nine tenths ____________
3. thirteen and seven tenths ____________
4. twenty-one and one tenth ____________
5. five and fifteen hundredths ____________
6. nine and sixty-two hundredths ____________
7. fifteen and four hundredths ____________
8. fifty-seven and eighty-two hundredths ____________
9. three and seven tenths ____________
10. sixty and forty-three hundredths ____________
11. ninety and seven hundredths ____________
12. fourteen and two hundredths ____________
13. five and seven hundredths ____________
14. ten and one tenth ____________
15. thirty and twenty hundredths ____________

Your body temperature is: ____________

Name ____________________

Order in the Line

Look at the number lines below. **Cut out** the decimal number squares on the next page. First, **find** the number line on which each number is located. **Glue** the decimals in their correct positions on the correct number line.

Hint: Pay careful attention to the place value indicated on each line. A number which goes to the hundredths place will be on a number line showing hundredths place values.

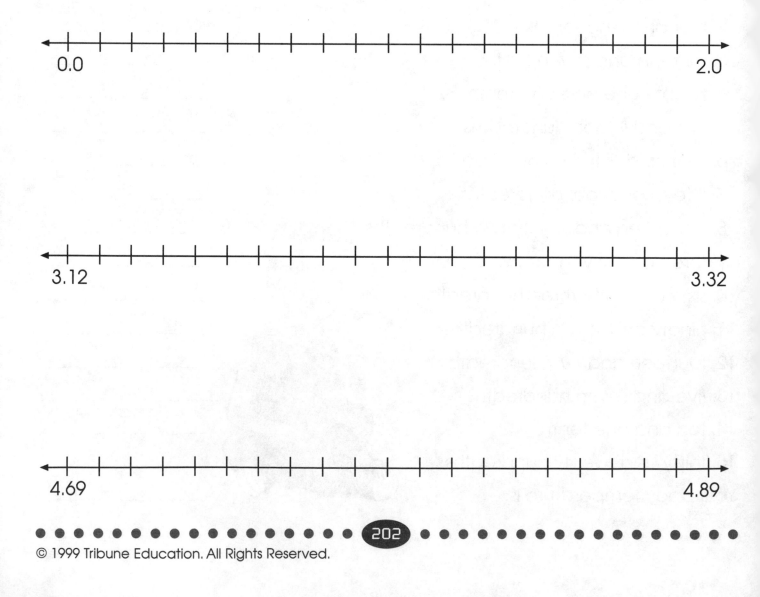

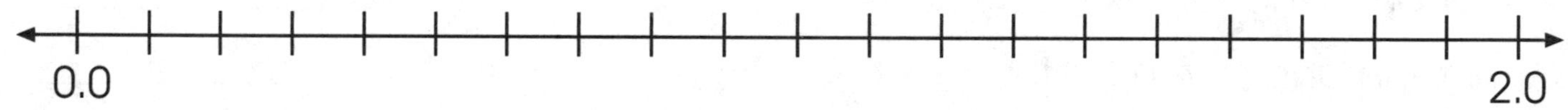

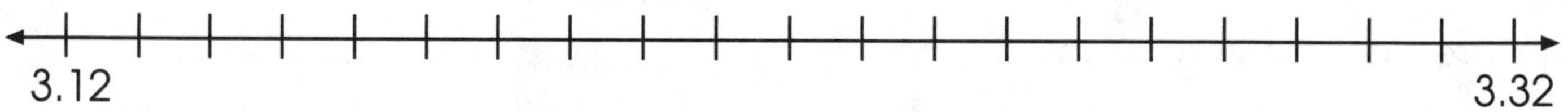

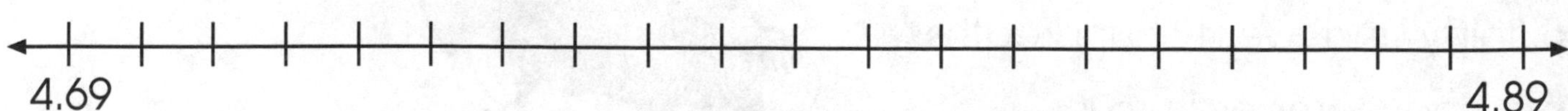

Name ______________________________

Order in the Line

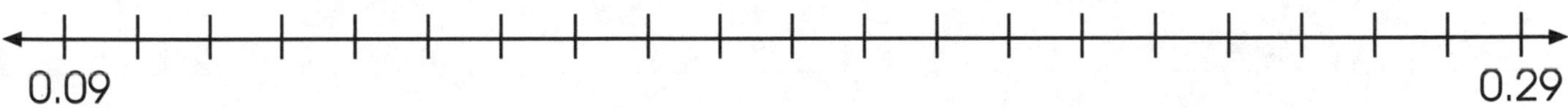

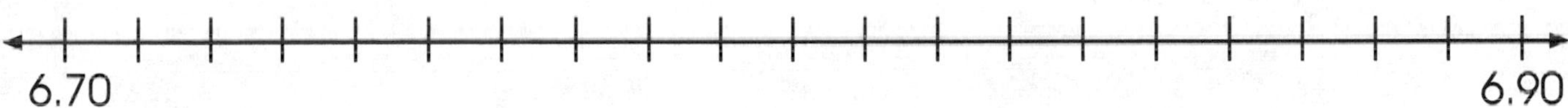

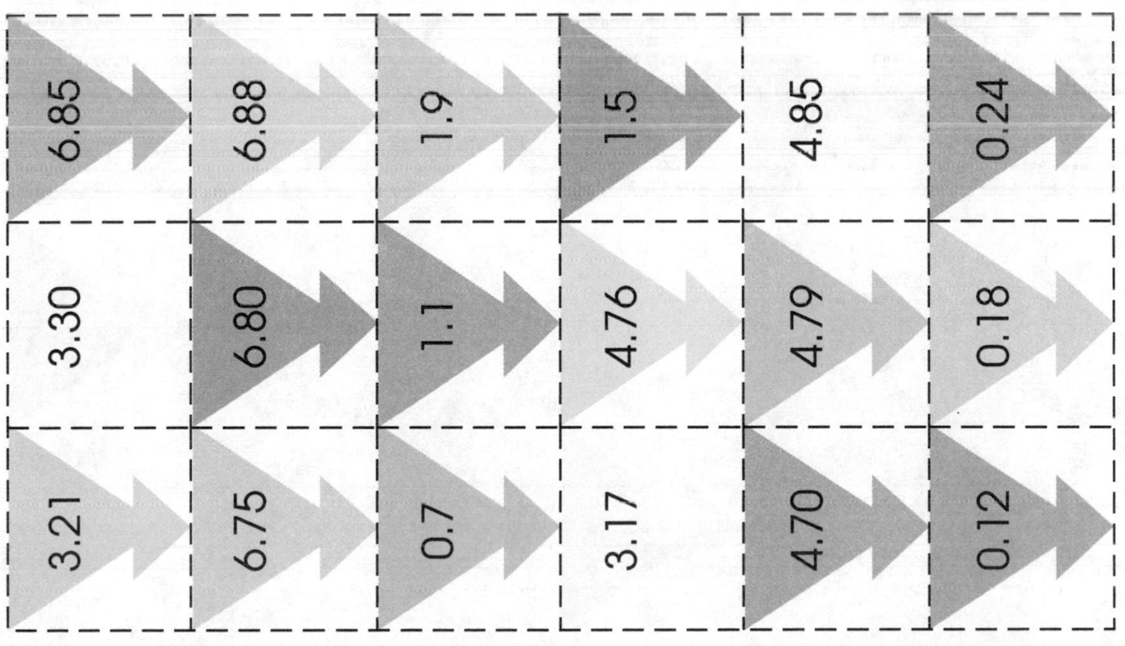

This page intentionally left blank.

Name ________________________________

Get the Point

When you add or subtract decimals, remember to include the decimal point.

Add. 3.6 + 3.3 = 6.9

Subtract. 6.8 − 2.6 = 4.2

Solve these problems.

4.2 +5.2	6.4 +1.4	3.1 +7.8	4.7 +3.2	4.9 +2.0	4.27 +5.52
5.9 −3.2	6.7 −5.6	7.8 −2.5	5.8 −3.3	3.9 −1.5	4.86 −1.76
0.23 +0.25	0.43 +0.16	0.26 +0.42	0.64 +0.15	0.68 +0.31	6.73 +1.15
0.87 −0.42	0.98 −0.35	0.79 −0.15	0.87 −0.67	0.83 −0.12	5.86 −3.83
3.13 +2.26	4.72 +1.15	6.87 +2.11	4.98 −2.32	5.97 −2.54	6.98 −1.45

Name ________________________

Animal Trivia

1. An earthworm is 14.9 cm long. A grasshopper is 8.7 cm long. What is the difference?

2. A pocket gopher has a hind foot 3.5 cm long. A ground squirrel's hind foot is 6.4 cm long. How much longer is the ground squirrel's hind foot?

3. A porcupine has a tail 30.0 cm long. An opossum has a tail 53.5 cm long. How much longer is the opossum's tail?

4. A wood rat has a tail which is 23.6 cm long. A deer mouse has a tail 12.2 cm long. What is the difference between the two?

5. A cottontail rabbit has ears which are 6.8 cm long. A jackrabbit has ears 12.9 cm long. How much shorter is the cottontail's ear?

6. The hind foot of a river otter is 14.6 cm long. The hind foot of a hog-nosed skunk is 9.0 cm long. What is the difference?

7. A rock mouse is 26.1 cm long. His tail adds another 14.4 cm. What is his total length from his nose to the tip of his tail?

Name ________________________________

Dueling Decimals

Preparation: To play "Dueling Decimals," you need 2 players. Each player needs a spinner and a place value card (see the example shown).

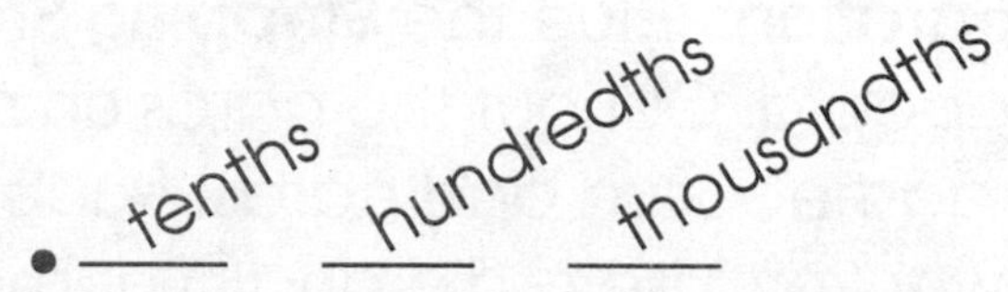

Directions: Player One should spin the spinner. The number that comes up should be recorded under the thousandths place column on the player's place value card. Player Two repeats the process. Player One then spins again, this time placing the number under the hundredths place column on his/her place value card.

Repeat until both players have a complete decimal number. Players should then compare the two numbers. The player with the larger number earns a point. Players have now completed the first round and should continue for four more rounds. The player with the most points after the fifth round wins "Dueling Decimals"!

Extension: Add your five decimal numbers. Compare the sums. Is the winner of the game also the player with a higher sum? ______________________________

Why? ____

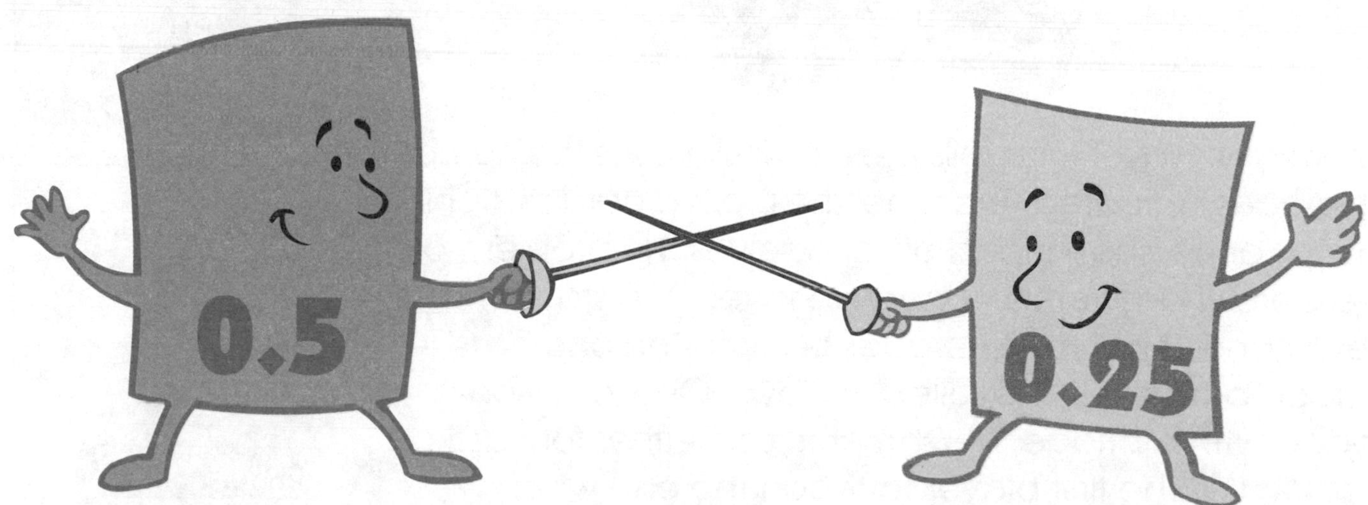

Name ____________________

Stepping Stones

Preparation: Glue the **Stepping Stones** gameboard on page 209 onto cardboard. Cut out the cards on pages 211–220. You may choose to laminate the gameboard and cards. Rubber band the cards together and make an answer key. Use a die and a game piece for each player. (You may also use a button or coin for each player to mark his/her place.)

Rules: This game involves 2–4 players. The player who rolls the lowest number is first. Play goes counterclockwise. Separate the stack of cards. Place them in five piles upside down by the board. Cards should always be returned to the bottom of the stack.

Each group of cards is different.
The pink set gives a game obstacle.
The gray set gives an addition problem with decimals.
The blue set gives a subtraction problem with decimals.
The yellow set gives two decimals to compare.
The purple set gives a decimal number to round.

Oops! Lost your balance. Move back 1 stone.

$$\begin{array}{r} 0.307 \\ +0.900 \\ \hline \end{array}$$

$$\begin{array}{r} 1.040 \\ -0.216 \\ \hline \end{array}$$

7.2 ◯ 7.5
< or >

3.5$\underline{3}$5
Round to the underlined number.

Directions: Player One rolls the die and moves the number of spaces indicated. Then, he/she picks a card matching the color he/she landed on and solves the problem on the card. If answered correctly, Player One stays on the new stone. If not, he/she goes back to the one he/she was on before he/she rolled. If Player One lands on a space with a bridge, he/she crosses it either forward or backward. The first player to reach the end wins.

Name ________________________________

Stepping Stones Gameboard

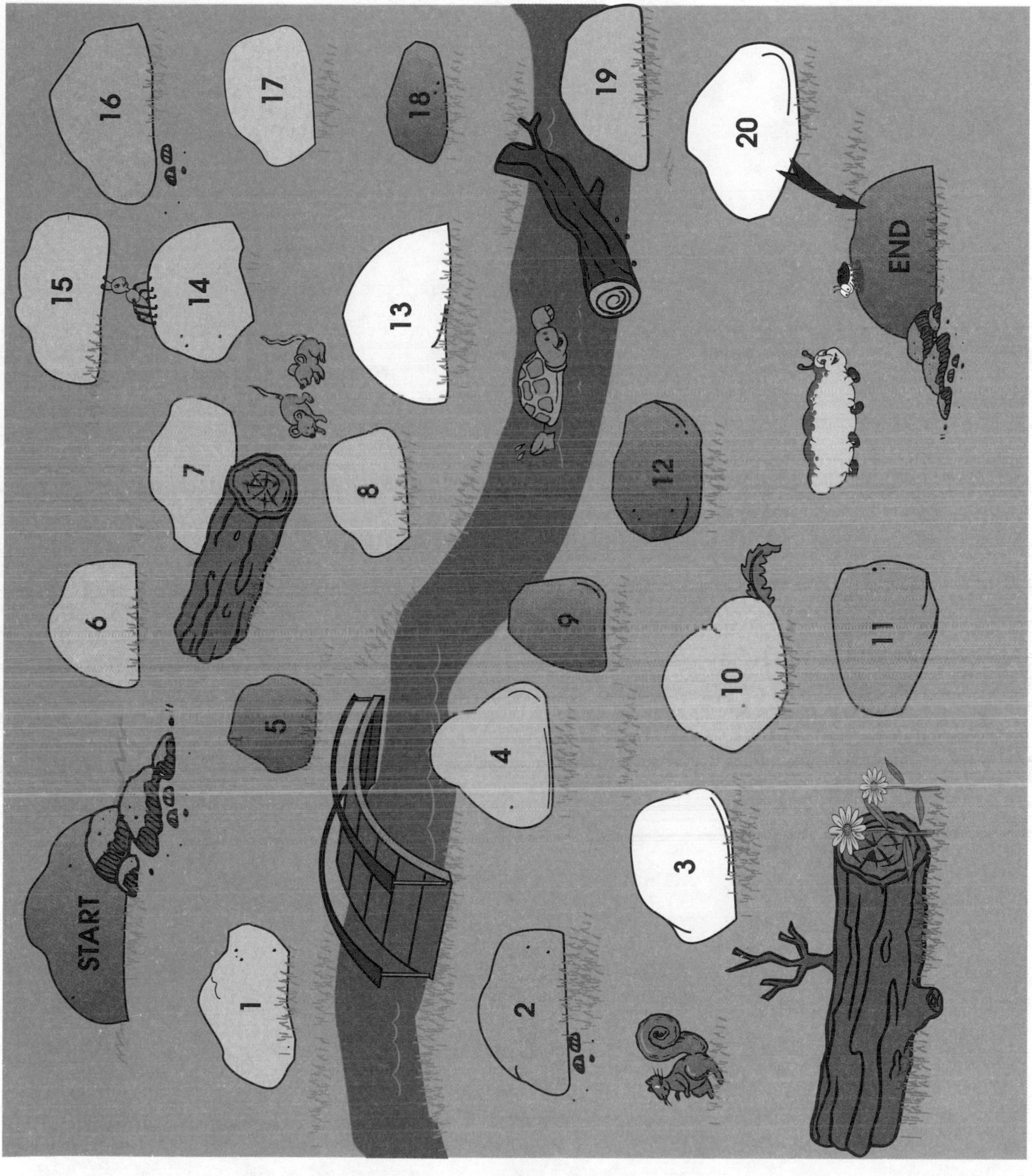

START

1 2 3 4 5 6 7 8 9 10 11 12 13 14 15 16 17 18 19 20

END

This page intentionally left blank.

Name ______________________

Subtraction Cards

1.040 − 0.216	5.5 − 3.2
0.350 − 0.128	8.6 − 4.8
0.609 − 0.317	1.30 − 0.17
0.87 − 0.49	0.94 − 0.53
0.704 − 0.326	2.3 − 1.4

Name ______________________________

Name ______________________________

Rounding Cards

$3.5\underline{3}5$ Round to the underlined number.	$\underline{9}.7$ Round to the underlined number.
$0.\underline{3}34$ Round to the underlined number.	$\underline{2}.09$ Round to the underlined number.
$\underline{5}.48$ Round to the underlined number.	$6.\underline{8}3$ Round to the underlined number.
$0.6\underline{1}2$ Round to the underlined number.	$0.\underline{0}51$ Round to the underlined number.
$7.7\underline{1}7$ Round to the underlined number.	$\underline{1}.842$ Round to the underlined number.

Name ______________________

Comparison Cards

7.2 ◯ 7.5 < or >	0.3 ◯ 3.0 < or >
4.9 ◯ 4.8 < or >	1.5 ◯ 1.7 < or >
3.23 ◯ 3.32 < or >	6.19 ◯ 6.2 < or >
2.08 ◯ 2.40 < or >	0.86 ◯ 0.88 < or >
5.61 ◯ 5.62 < or >	8.3 ◯ 8.06 < or >

Name ____________________

Name ______________________

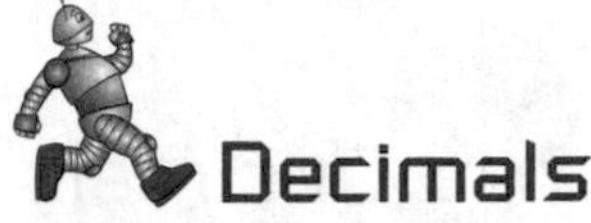

Addition Cards

0.307 + 0.900	0.64 + 0.33
0.78 + 0.21	0.65 + 0.65
1.29 + 4.50	0.442 + 0.784
0.704 + 0.127	0.946 + 0.035
4.76 + 2.25	2.12 + 3.79

Name ____________________

Game Obstacle Cards

Cross the closest bridge.	Cross the closest bridge.
There's a butterfly on the next rock. Step back one stone.	Step ahead to the next blue stone. If there isn't one, go to 14.
Oops! Lost your balance. Move back 1 stone.	You're a great leaper— jump ahead 1 stone.
No need to rest— take another turn.	Stop to tie your shoe. Lose a turn.
Rest for a minute— lose your turn.	Catch up with the sunbeam— take another turn.

Name ___________________________

Decimal Riddles

Read the clues to **write** the numbers.

1. Numbers: 4, 8, 2, 2
   Clues:
   - The numbers in the tens place and the tenths place are the same.
   - The greatest number is in the hundredths place.

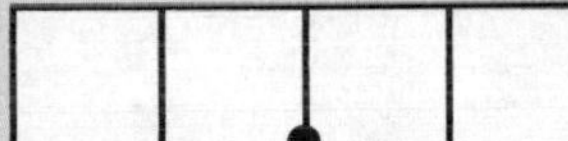

4. Numbers: 2, 3, 4, 6
   Clues:
   - The 3 is in the tenths place.
   - The number in the hundreds place is half the number in the tens place.
   - The number in the ones place is the sum of the numbers in the hundreds place and the tens place.

2. Numbers: 1, 2, 3, 8
   Clues:
   - The number in the tens place is 5 less than the number in the hundredths place.
   - The number in the tenths place is twice the number in the ones place.

5. Numbers: 0, 5, 6, 7, 8
   Clues:
   - The number in the hundredths place is 8 more than the number in the tenths place.
   - The 6 is in the tens place.
   - The number in the hundreds place is greater than the number in the ones place.

3. Numbers: 3, 5, 8, 9
   Clues:
   - The greatest number is in the hundredths place.
   - The number in the tenths place is 2 less than the number in the tens place.

6. Numbers: 2, 4, 6, 7, 8
   Clues:
   - The number in the hundredths place is twice the number in the tenths place.
   - The 7 is in the ones place.
   - The number in the hundreds place is three times the number in the tens place.

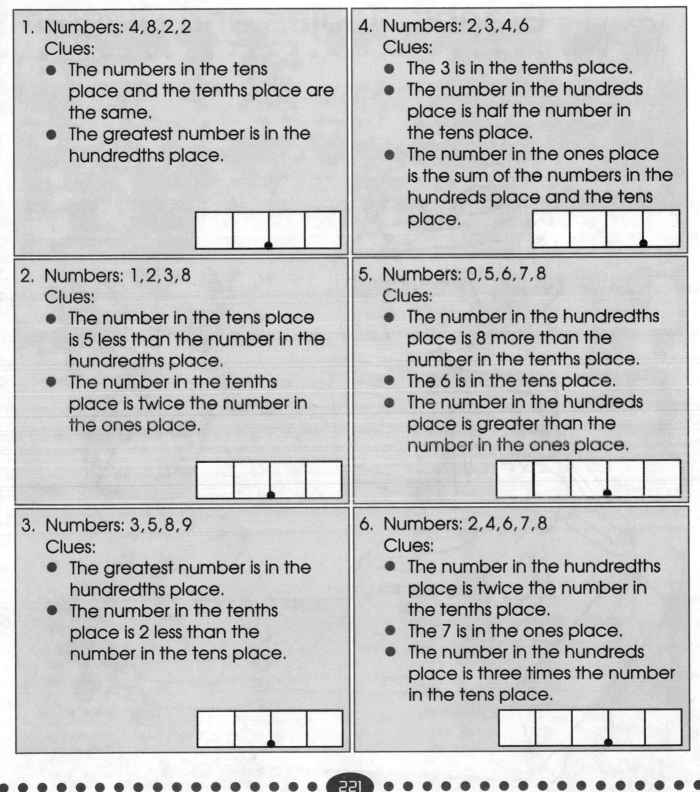

Graphs, Tables and Diagrams

BEHAVIOR
CHORES
TRASH
FEED DOG
CLEAN ROOM
DISHES
DUST

Name ______________________________

Flower Graph

A **pictograph** is a graph using pictures to give information.
Cut out the flowers and **glue** them onto the pictograph.

Daisies					
Sunflowers					
Tulips					
Roses					

How many tulips? ______

sunflowers? ______

roses? ______

daisies? ______

How many more tulips than roses? ______

How many more daisies than sunflowers? ______

How many sunflowers and tulips? ______

How many roses and daisies? ______

Each picture stands for 2 flowers.

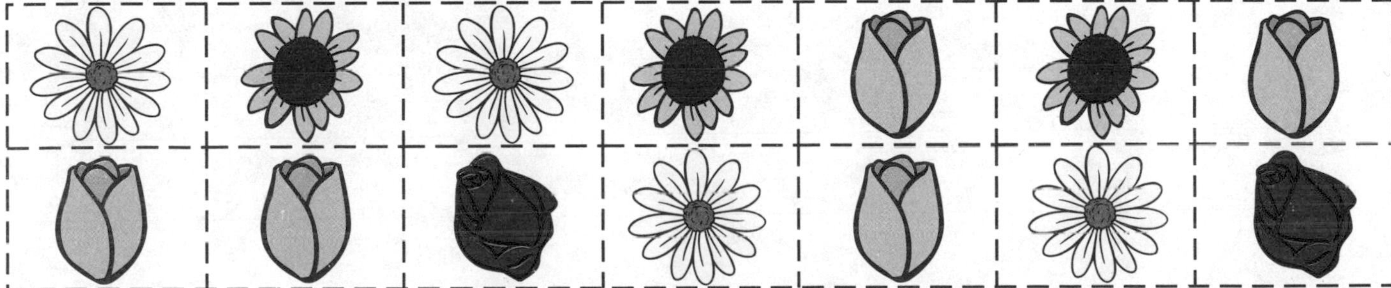

This page intentionally left blank.

Name ___________________________

Frog Bubbles

Complete the line graph to show how many bubbles each frog blew.

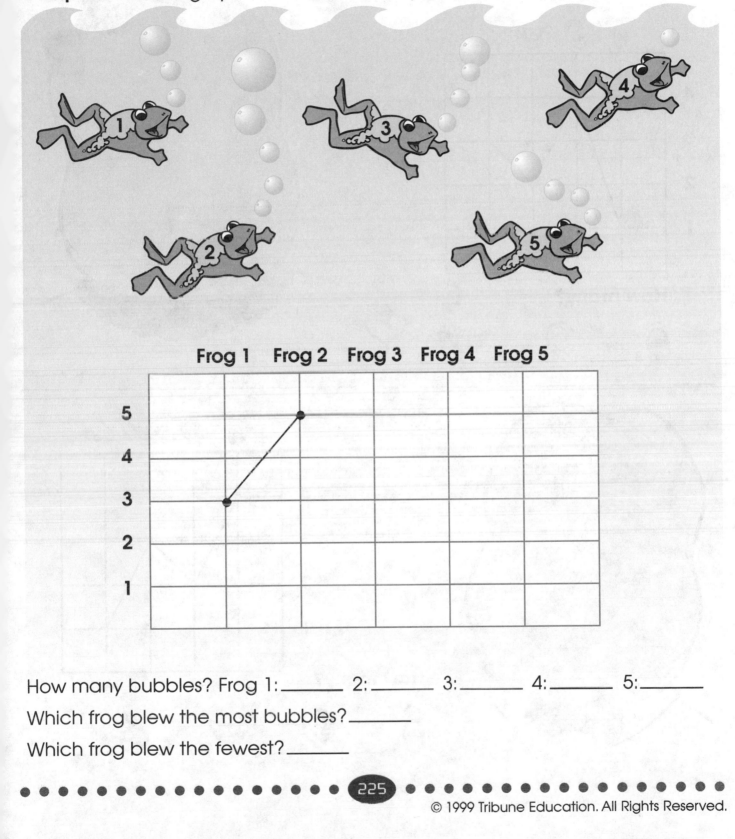

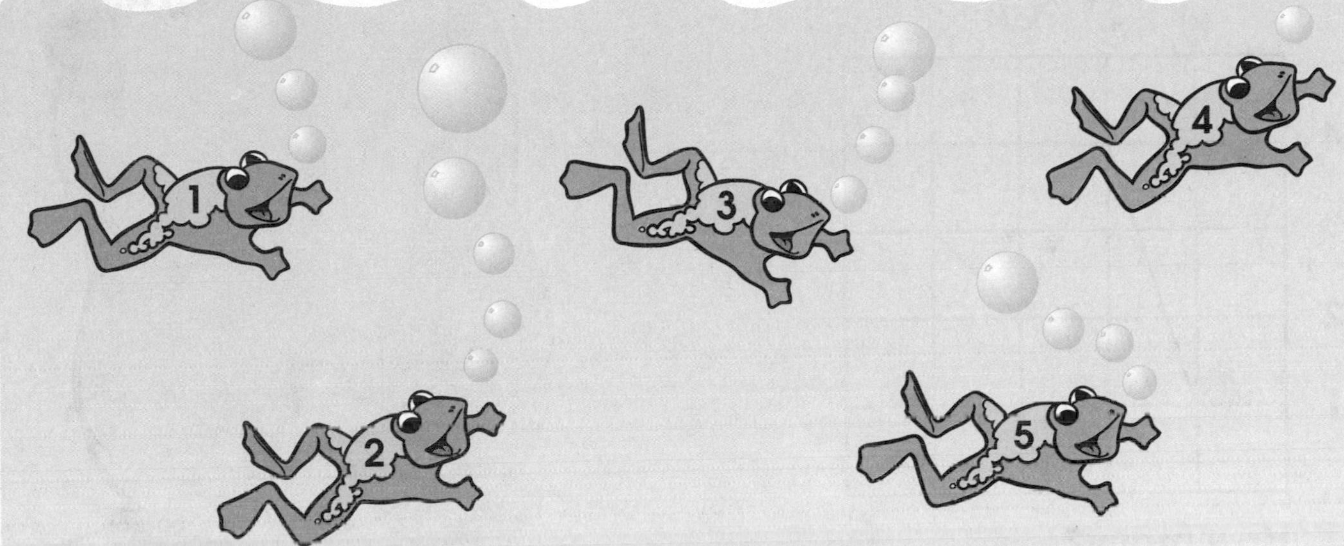

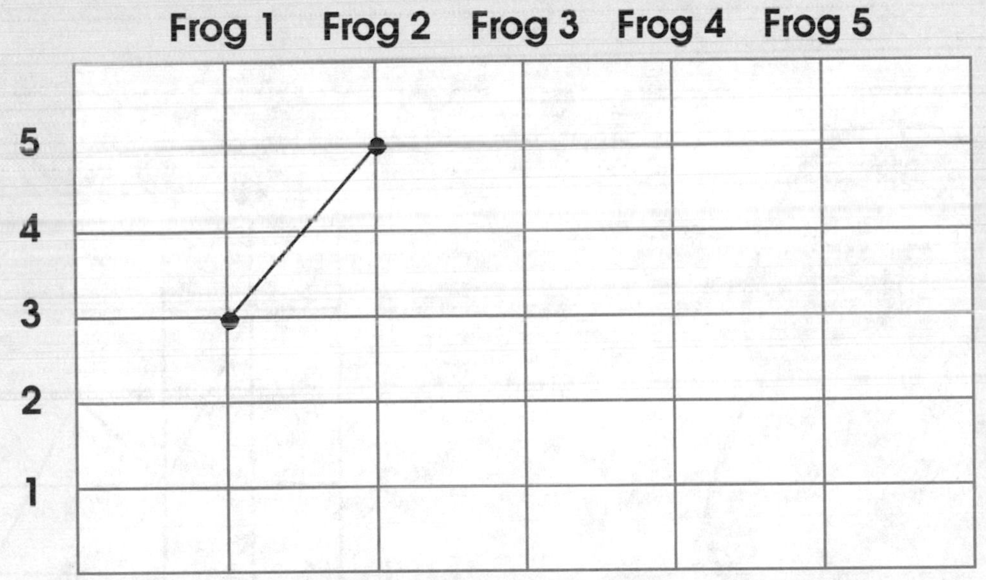

How many bubbles? Frog 1:______ 2:______ 3:______ 4:______ 5:______

Which frog blew the most bubbles?______

Which frog blew the fewest?______

Name ______________________

Potato Face

Read the line graphs to **draw** the potato faces.

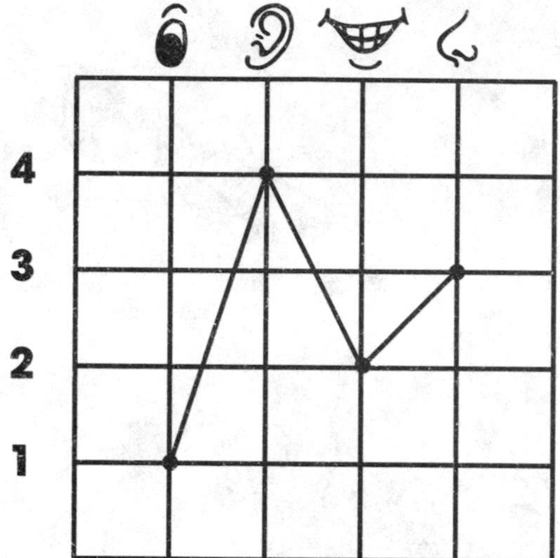

How many?

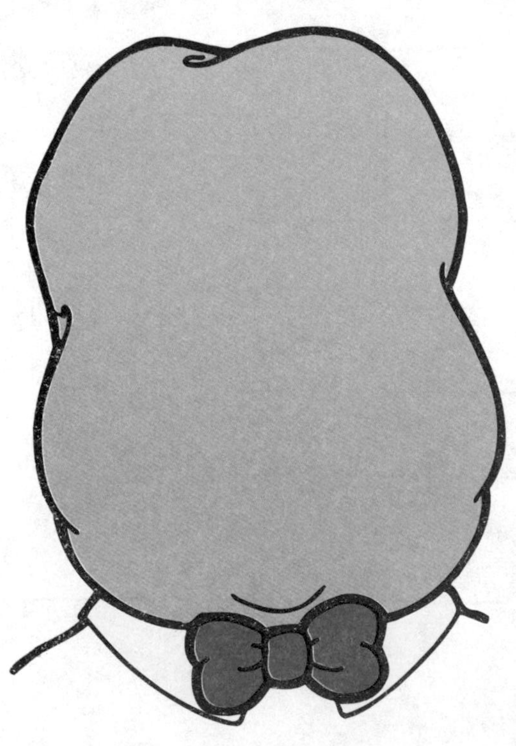

4
3
2
1

How many?

s ___ s ___ s ___ s ___

Vote for Me!

Middletown school had an election to choose the new members of the Student Council. Grace, Bernie, Laurie, Sherry and Sam all ran for the office of president. On the chart below are the five students' names with the number of the votes each received.

Grace	21	36	39
Bernie	47	32	26
Laurie	25	44	38
Sherry	34	37	40
Sam	48	33	29

Use the information and the clues below to see who became president and how many votes he or she received.

- The winning number of votes was an even number.
- The winning number of votes was between 30 and 40.
- The two digits added together are greater than 10.

______________ became the president of the Student Council with ______________ votes.

Who would have become president if the winning number was **odd** and the other clues remained the same?

____

Name ______________________________

School Statistics

Read each graph and follow the directions.

List the names of the students from the shortest to the tallest.

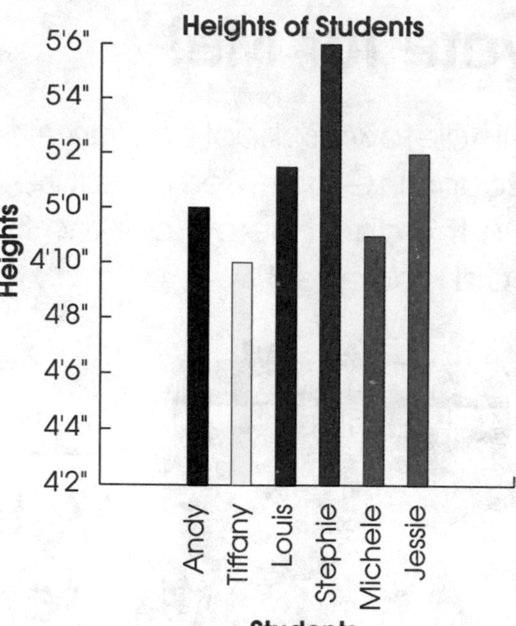

1. ____________________ 4. ____________________

2. ____________________ 5. ____________________

3. ____________________ 6. ____________________

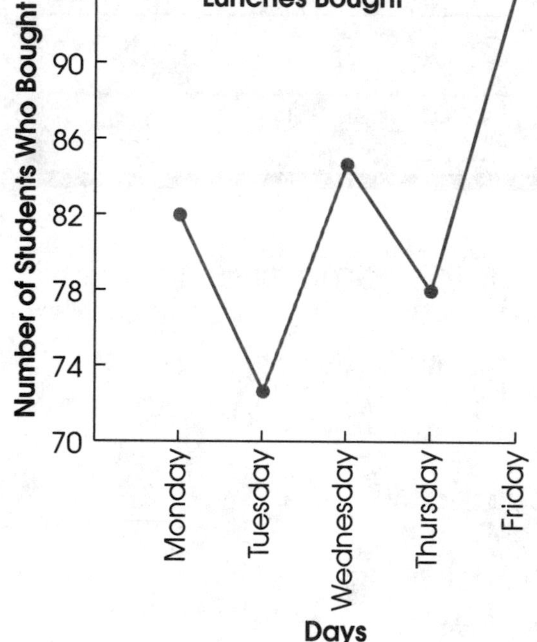

List how many lunches the students bought each day, from the day the most were bought to the least.

1. ____________________ 4. ____________________

2. ____________________ 5. ____________________

3. ____________________

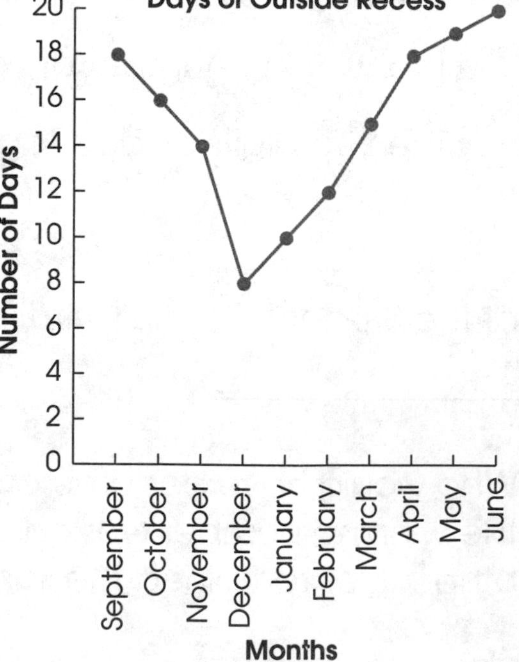

List the months in the order of the most number of outside recesses to the least number.

1. ____________________ 6. ____________________

2. ____________________ 7. ____________________

3. ____________________ 8. ____________________

4. ____________________ 9. ____________________

5. ____________________

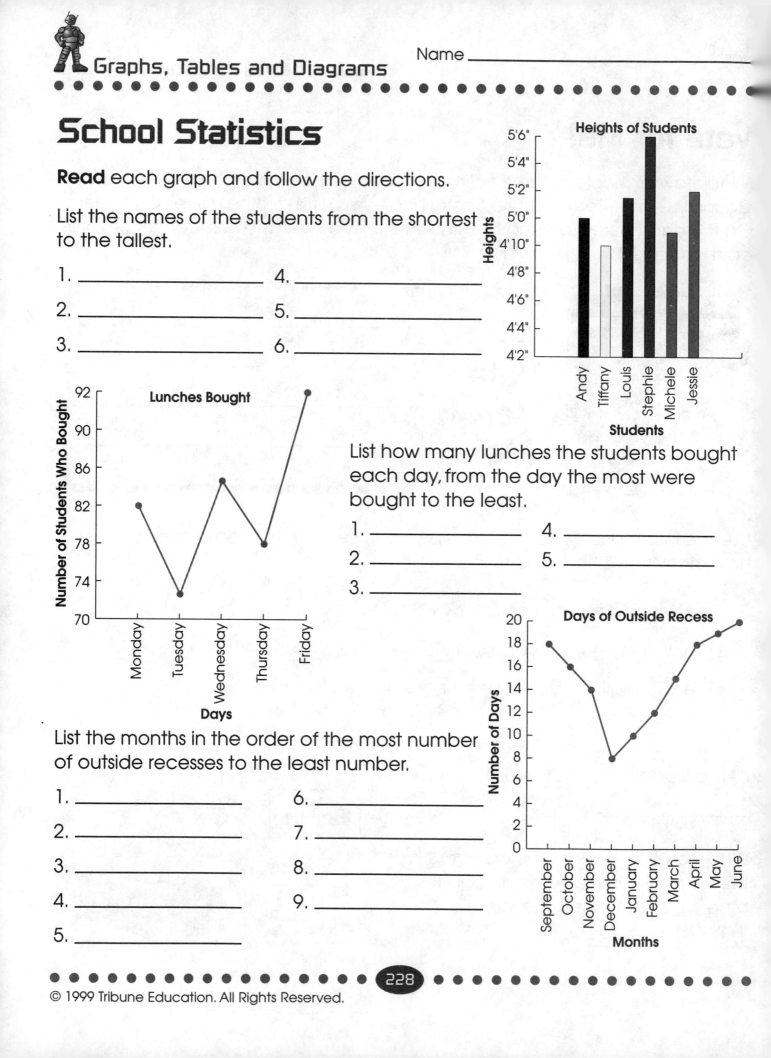

Name ______________________

Candy Sales 

Every year the students at Lincoln Elementary sell candy as a fund-raising project. These are the results of the sales for this year.

Grade Level	Number of Sales
Kindergarten	40
First	70
Second	50
Third	80
Fourth	85
Fifth	75

Color the bar graph to show the number of sales made at each grade level.

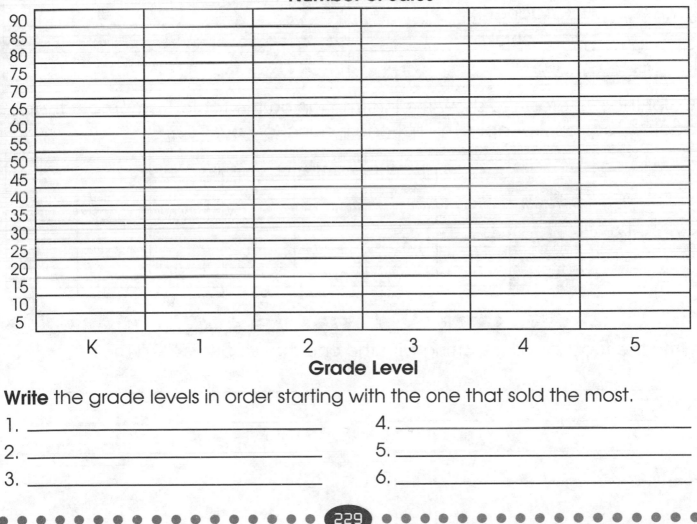

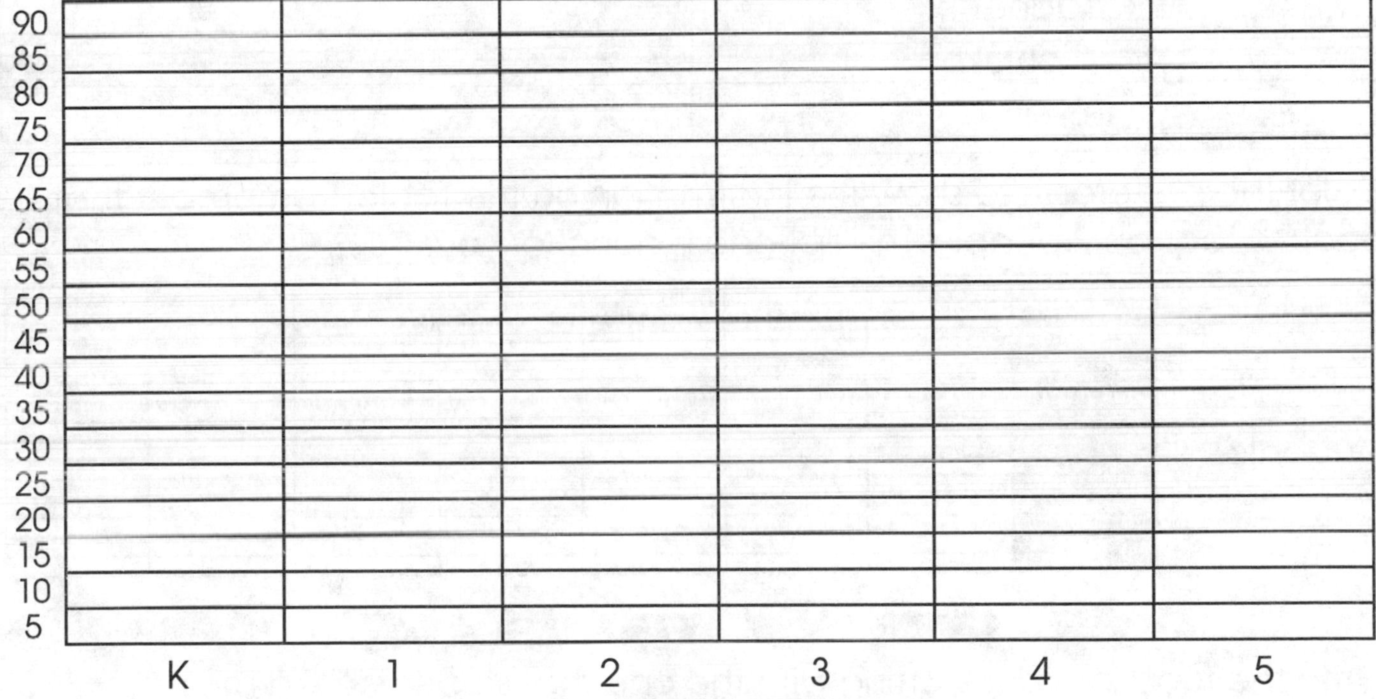

Write the grade levels in order starting with the one that sold the most.

1. ______________________ 4. ______________________

2. ______________________ 5. ______________________

3. ______________________ 6. ______________________

Name ___________________________

Hot Lunch Favorites

The cooks in the cafeteria asked each third- and fourth-grade class to rate the hot lunches. They wanted to know which food the children liked the best.

The table shows how the students rated the lunches.
Key: Each 🧍 equals 2 students.

Food	Number of students who liked it best
hamburgers	🧍🧍🧍🧍🧍🧍
hot dogs	🧍🧍🧍🧍🧍🧍🧍
tacos	🧍🧍🧍🧍🧍
chili	
soup and sandwiches	🧍
spaghetti	🧍🧍
fried chicken	🧍🧍🧍🧍
fish sticks	🧍🧍🧍

Color the bar graph to show the information on the table. Remember that each 🧍 equals 2 people. The first one is done for you.

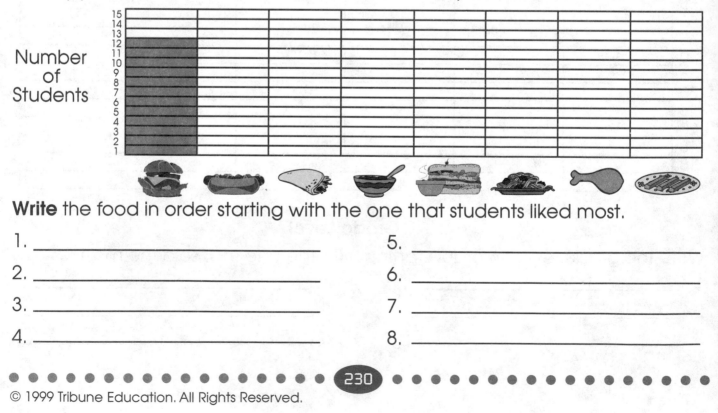

Write the food in order starting with the one that students liked most.

1. ___________________________
2. ___________________________
3. ___________________________
4. ___________________________
5. ___________________________
6. ___________________________
7. ___________________________
8. ___________________________

Gliding Graphics

Draw the lines as directed from point to point for each graph.

Draw a line from:

- F,7 to D,1
- D,1 to I,6
- I,6 to N,8
- N,8 to M,3
- M,3 to F,1
- F,1 to G,4
- G,4 to E,4
- E,4 to B,1
- B,1 to A,8
- A,8 to D,11
- D,11 to F,9
- F,9 to F,7
- F,7 to I,9
- I,9 to I,6
- I,6 to F,7

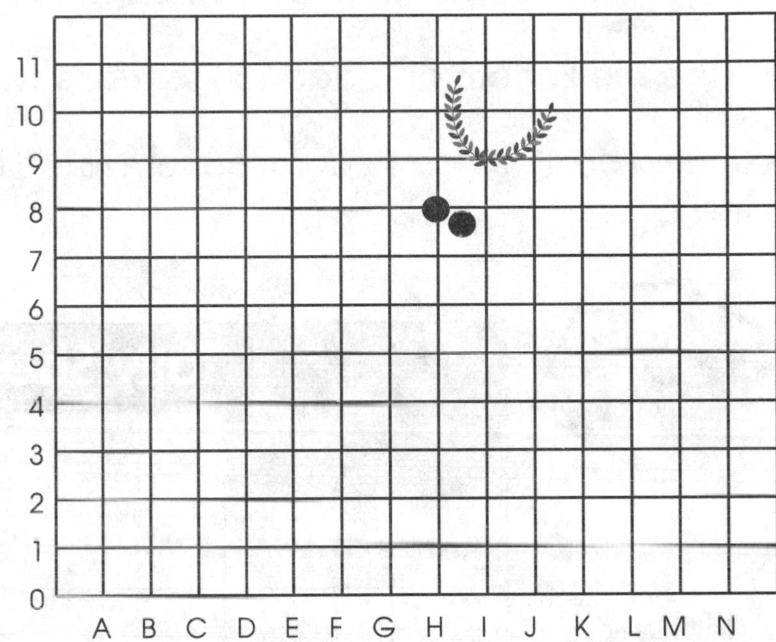

Draw a line from:

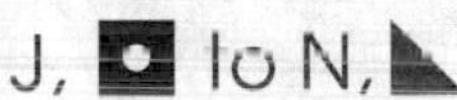
J, to N,
N, to U,
U, to Z,
Z, to X,
X, to U,
U, to S,
S, to N,
N, to N,
N, to J,
J, to L,
L, to Y,
Y, to Z,
Z, to L,
L, to J,
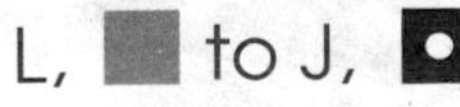

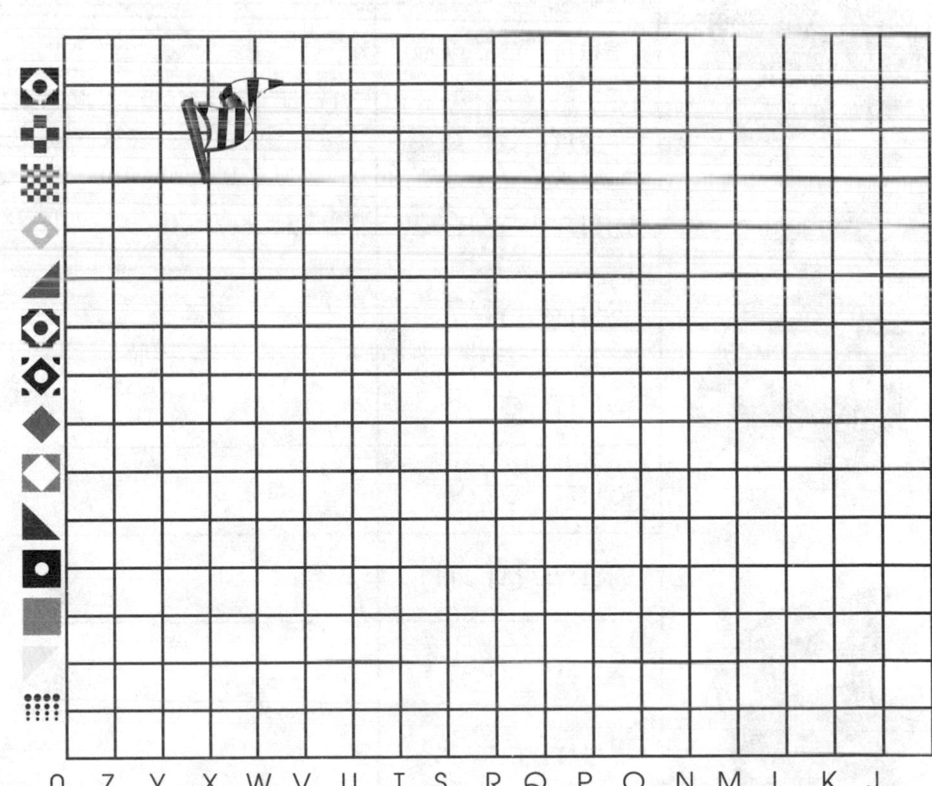

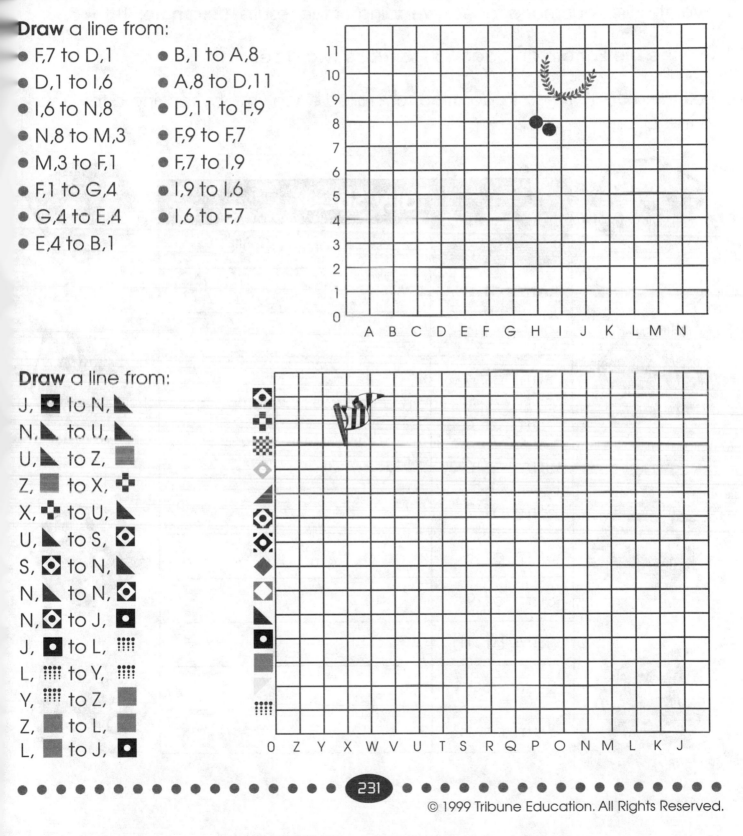

Name ____________________

Tally Ho!

A **tally mark** is a line to represent one. The fifth tally mark is written diagonally over the first four marks for easy reading of the results. (**Example:** ~~||||~~ = 5.)

Use the **Die Pattern** on page 233 to **make** two dice.

Roll the dice 10 times. **Record** the sum rolled each time by making a tally mark in the chart.

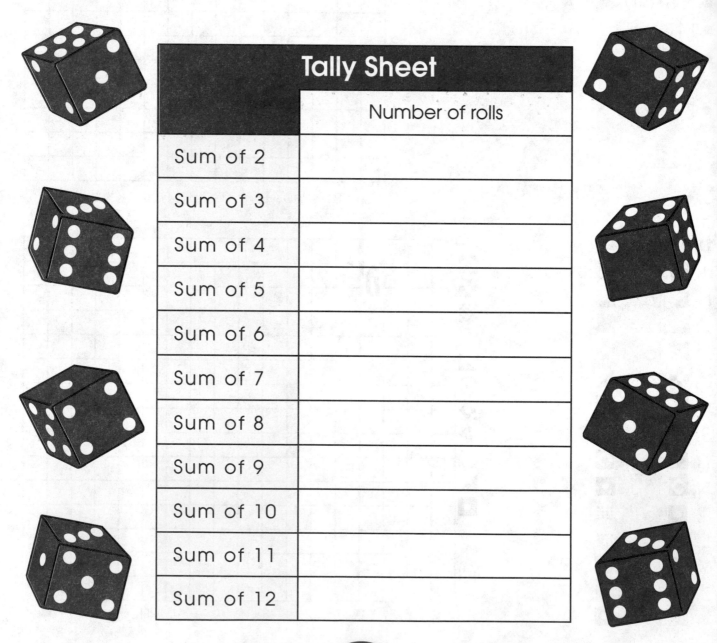

Tally Sheet	Number of rolls
Sum of 2	
Sum of 3	
Sum of 4	
Sum of 5	
Sum of 6	
Sum of 7	
Sum of 8	
Sum of 9	
Sum of 10	
Sum of 11	
Sum of 12	

Name ________________________________

Die Pattern

You will need: tape, glue, construction paper, two copies of this pattern

Directions: Glue the patterns to construction paper and cut them out. Fold on the dotted lines so that all the edges meet to form a cube. Glue the tabs in place and tape the edges of the cube together carefully.

This page intentionally left blank.

Name ______________________________

Roll 'Em!

Roll the die 20 times in a row. **Use** the following tally sheet to keep track of the number you roll each time.

Tally Sheet

Number rolled	Number of rolls
Number 1	
Number 2	
Number 3	
Number 4	
Number 5	
Number 6	

Answer the following questions about the tally sheet.

1. Which number was rolled most frequently? ____________________
2. Which number was rolled least frequently? ____________________
3. Were any numbers rolled the same number of times? ____________________

   Which ones? ____________________

   Why do you think this happened? ______________________________

Extension:

Do this exercise again and compare the first results with the second results.

Why did the results turn out the way they did? ____________________

Was there anything that could have been done to change the results?

____

Predict what would happen if the die were rolled 40 times? ________________

____

Name ______________________________

Pie Graph Survey

Step 1: Conducting a Survey

A **survey** is a mini-interview of many people to find out what they like or do not like. Possible topics might be a favorite television show, a food or a career choice. Choose a survey topic to create the survey table.

Directions: Create a title for the survey. Write it across the top of the chart below. Next, provide several choices for the survey. For example, if the title of the survey is "Favorite Subject," you would choose some popular subjects and write them vertically along the left margin of the chart. Next, you will survey sixteen people.

You may want to discuss the sample population and perhaps set limits. Will you survey a group of people that are all the same? Will you survey only friends your age? The first sixteen people you see on the street? Relatives?

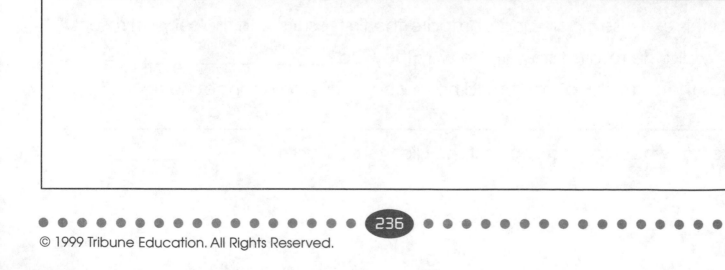

Favorite Desserts	
Ice cream	III
Pecan pie	I
Apple pie	II
Chocolate cake	III
Candy bar	II
Milkshake	~~IIII~~

Title:

Name ______________________________

Pie Graph Survey

Step 2: Creating Fractions

Directions: Convert the results of your survey into fractions. The denominator will be 16, because that is the number of people who make up the whole survey. Determine the numerator by counting the number of people who chose an item. (For example, if four people chose math as their favorite subject, the fraction would be 4/16.) When all tallied results have been converted into fractions, you are ready to create the pie graph.

Chocolate cake = 3/16 means three children out of sixteen picked the cake as their favorite dessert.

Step 3: Creating the Pie Graph

Directions: Shade in the number of sections that each numerator indicates, using a different color for each numerator, or choice from the survey. Write the choice, fraction and the color in the key. Now, copy your pie graph and key, cut them out, mount them and share them with the people you surveyed.

Key:
Pecan pie 1/16
Apple pie 2/16
Chocolate cake 3/16
Candy bar 2/16
Milkshake 5/16
Ice cream 3/16

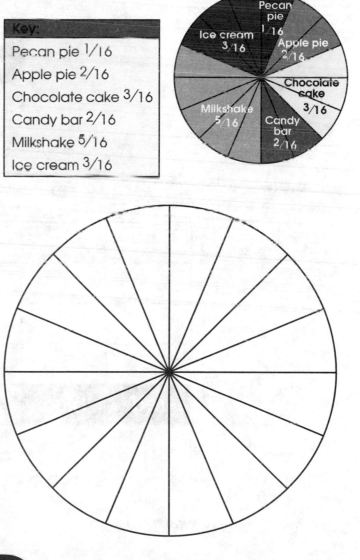

Key:

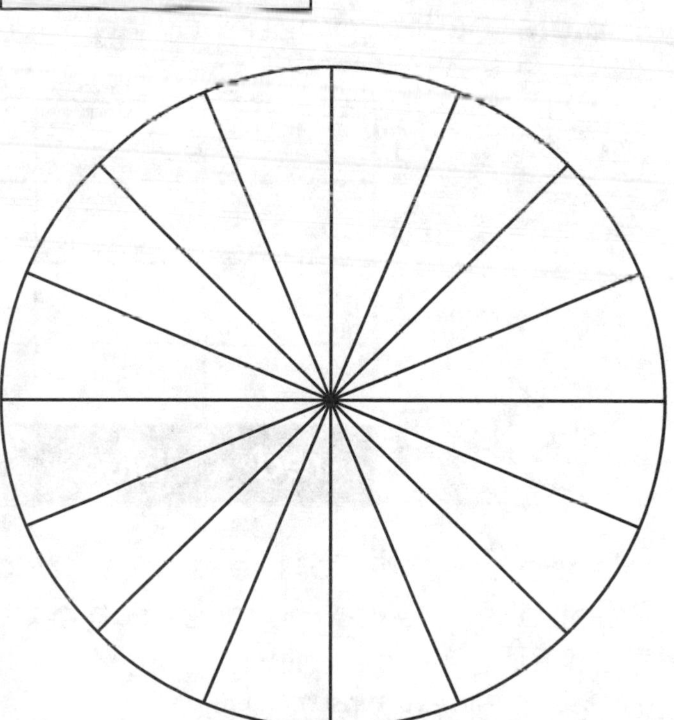

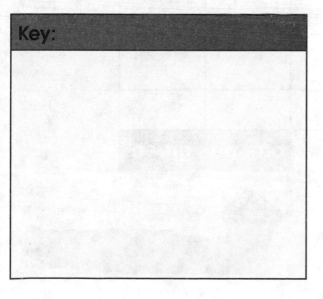

Name ______________________

Guess the Color

Probability shows the chance that a given event will happen. To show probability, write a fraction. The number of different possibilities is the denominator. The number of times the event could happen is the numerator. (Remember to reduce fractions to the lowest terms.)

Look at the spinner. What is the probability that the arrow will land on . . .

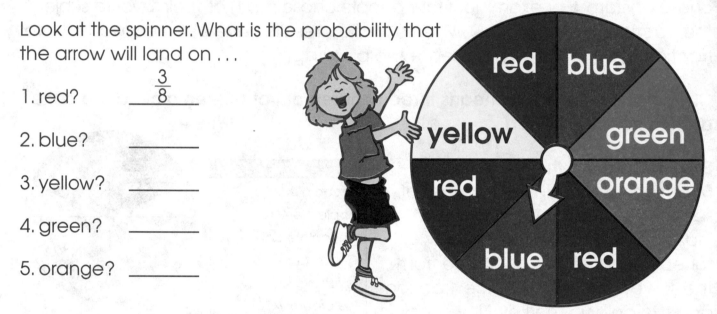

1. red? $\frac{3}{8}$
2. blue? ______
3. yellow? ______
4. green? ______
5. orange? ______

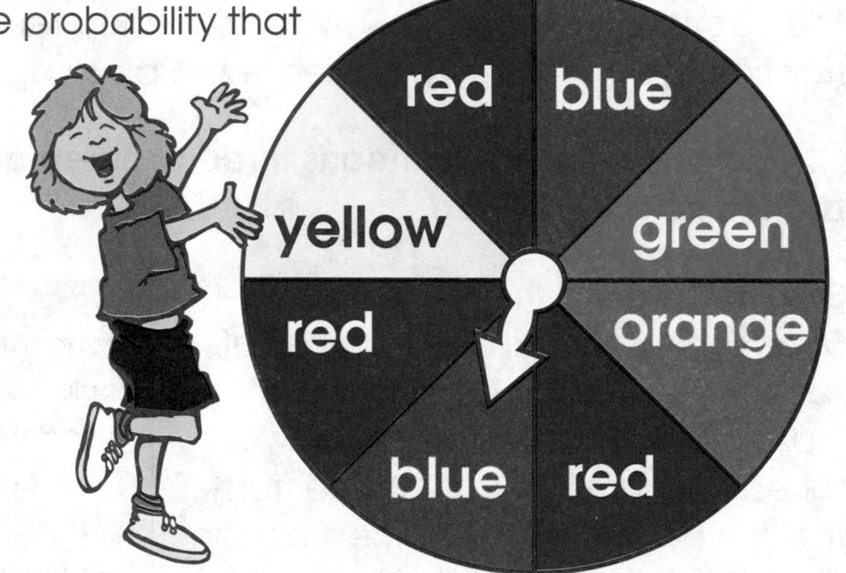

Complete the bar graph showing your answers (the data) from above.

Number of Probability					
8					
6					
4					
2					
	red	blue	yellow	orange	green

Circle the best title for the above bar graph.

a. Probability of Arrow Landing on a Color
b. Eight Turns of the Spinner
c. Which Color Is the Winner?

Name ______________________________

Spinner Fun

You will need: 2 brass fasteners, a piece of cardboard

Directions: Glue the patterns below to a piece of cardboard and cut them out. Pierce a hole in the arrows and in the center of each spinner. Using the brass fasteners, connect an arrow to each spinner.

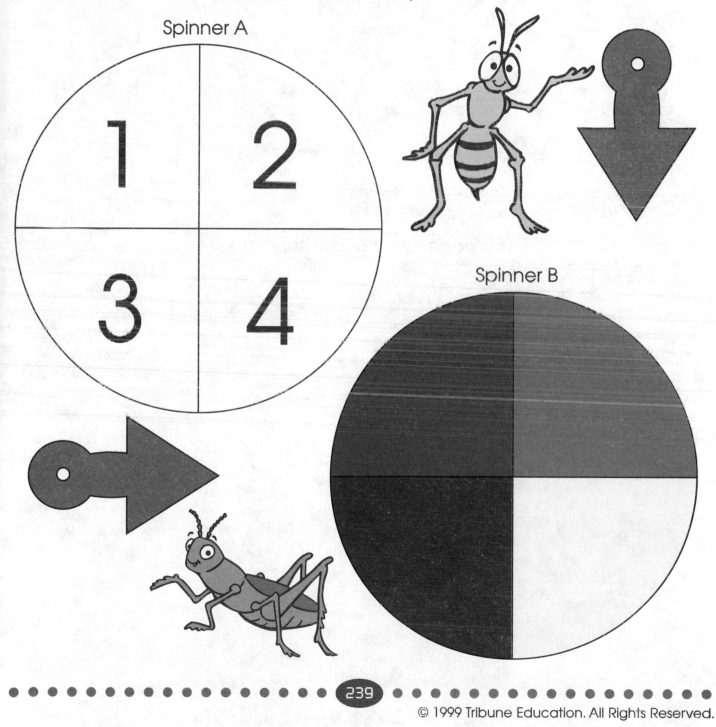

Spinner A

1 2

3 4

Spinner B

This page intentionally left blank.

Name ______________________________

Trees

Possible combinations of two events can be organized on trees. **Use** the spinners from page 239.

Part A: Complete the tree diagram by doing the following: Assume that you first spin Spinner A. Write the possibilities on the diagram. Then, spin Spinner B. Write the possibilities on the diagram. On the right, write the probability for each combination if you spun both spinners 16 times. Then, below the tree diagram, list all the possible combinations of the two spinners.

Probability

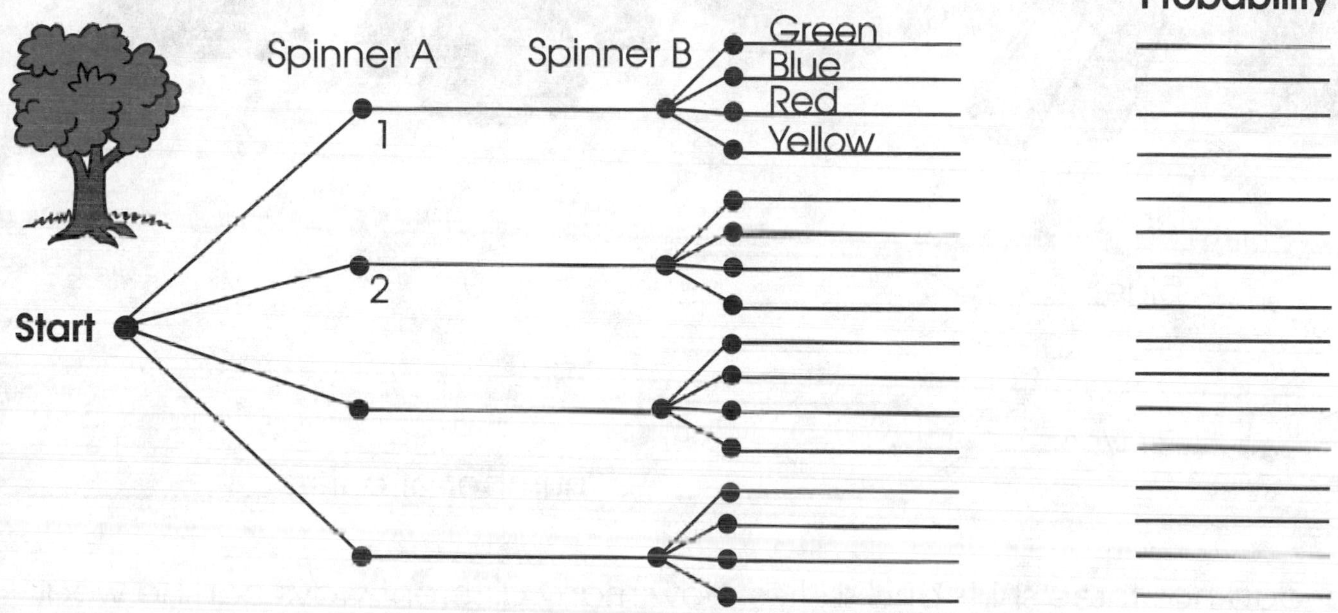

Part B: Spin Spinner A, then spin Spinner B. Do this 16 times. Record the outcomes below and compare them with the probabilities and possible combinations you listed above.

1. ________	5. ________	9. ________	13. ________
2. ________	6. ________	10. ________	14. ________
3. ________	7. ________	11. ________	15. ________
4. ________	8. ________	12. ________	16. ________

What do you notice? Why do you think that is? ______________________________

____

Name ______________________________

How Many Outfits?

Suppose you had two pairs of jeans (one blue and the other gray) and three shirts (orange, red and green). How many different outfits could you wear? **Use** a tree to help you with the answer.

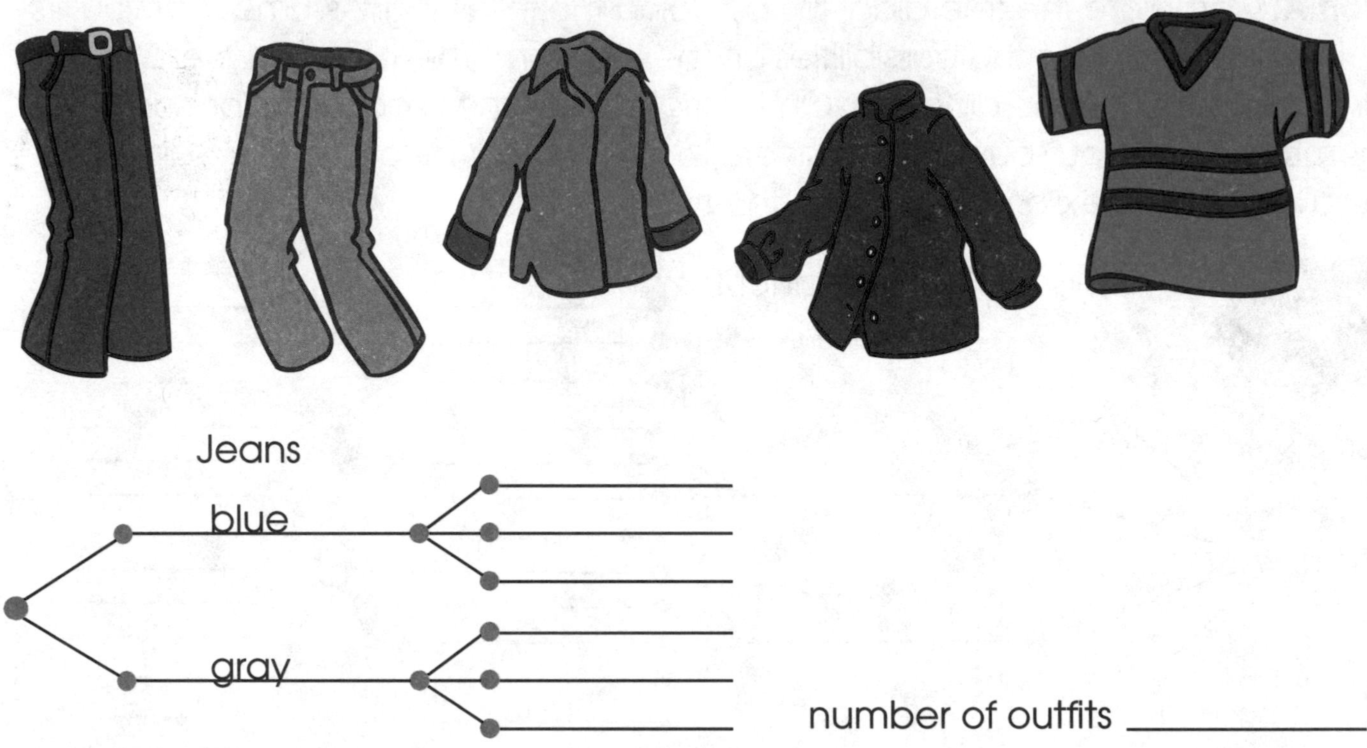

number of outfits __________

Your dad has three shirts and six ties. How many different ways can he wear his shirts and ties? **Draw** a tree to help you figure out the answer.

number of outfits __________

Name ______________________________

Keep Your Heads Up!

Collect 21 pennies. **Predict** the numbers of heads and tails that will turn up before you toss the pennies. Then, **toss** the coins ten times.

Does anything change about your predictions the more you guess?

____

Toss	Guess Heads	Guess Tails	Actual Heads	Actual Tails
1				
2				
3				
4				
5				
6				
7				
8				
9				
10				

Measurement

Name ____________________

Make a Tape Measure

Directions:

1. Cut out the rectangle pattern below on the solid lines.
2. Cut the rectangle into six strips by cutting on the dotted lines.
3. Put a little glue on the shaded end of one strip and glue it to the end of another strip. Press the strips together. Repeat this step until all the strips are joined to make one long strip.
4. Cut off the one leftover shaded end. You now have a tape measure.
5. Lay your tape measure out flat. Starting from the left side, mark off inches, 1/2 inches and 1/4 inches. Number the inches.
6. Reinforce your tape measure by putting clear tape on the back of it.

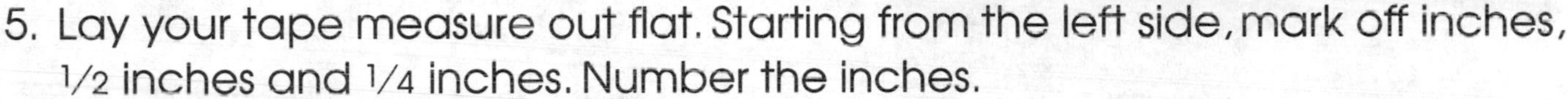

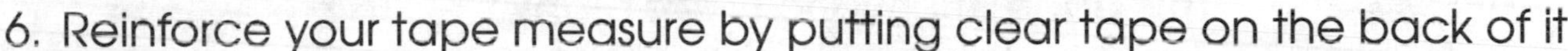

This page intentionally left blank.

Name ______________________________

How Does Your Home Measure Up?

Directions: Take a "measuring journey" through your house. To begin, brainstorm a list of various destinations around your house. Then, **list** five objects found in each room and **write** them on the left-hand side of a sheet of paper.

Example:

Kitchen	**Bathroom**	**Bedroom**
stove	toothbrush	books
teaspoon	hairbrush	desk/table
cookbook	soap	pillow
can opener	mirror	clock
box of cereal	bandage	hanger

Read through the objects on the list and **write** estimations of their measurements. Decide on a unit of measurement to use and whether to measure length, width or both. Then, **measure** the objects. (A tape measure or string may be used to measure the size or circumference of any oddly shaped objects.) Finally, compare your estimations with the actual measurements.

Object	Estimate	Actual

Name ______________________________

Growing String Beans

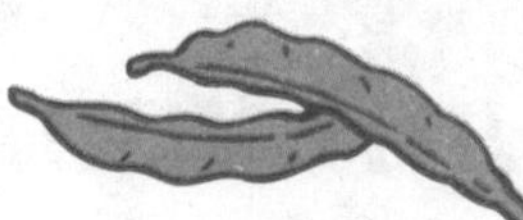

All plants with green leaves make food from the sun. They take water and nutrients from the soil, but they make their food from light.

You will measure in inches how fast a string bean plant grows. Record this information on the **Growing String Beans Bar Graph** on page 249.

You will need:
string bean seeds
potting soil
16 oz. plastic cup
12-inch ruler

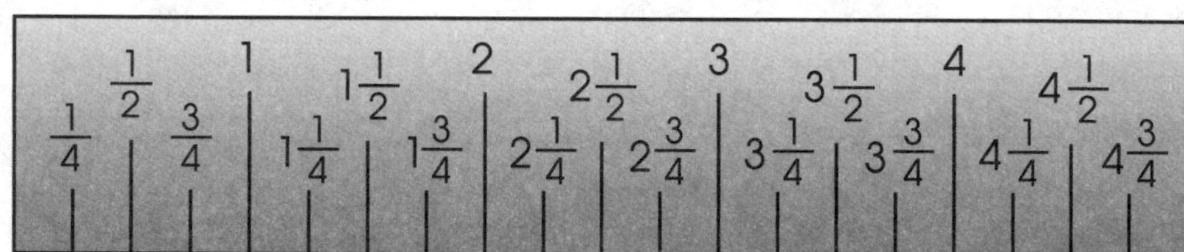

Directions:
1. Fill the cup 3/4 full with potting soil.
2. Use a pencil to make a hole 1-inch deep and drop in a bean seed. Gently cover the seed and lightly water it.
3. Water the plant regularly so that the soil does not become dried out.
4. Wait for the new plant to germinate and peek out of the soil.
5. Measure and record the plant's growth using the ruler. Record it on the bar graph at each specified interval.
6. When it has grown, enjoy the delicious string beans as a treat!

How To Measure: Place the ruler next to the plant, resting it on the soil. Measure from the top of the plant down to the soil.

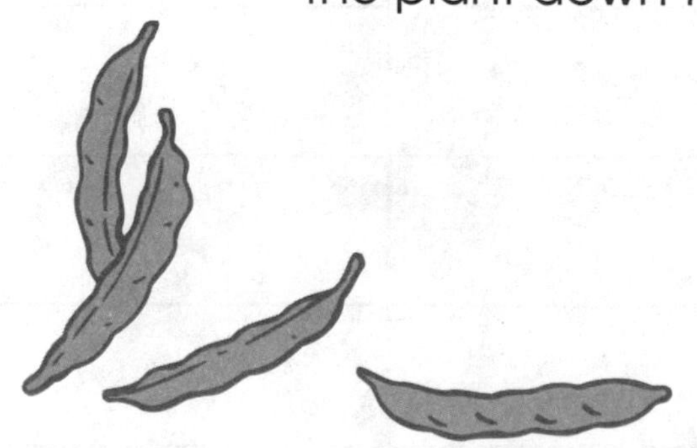

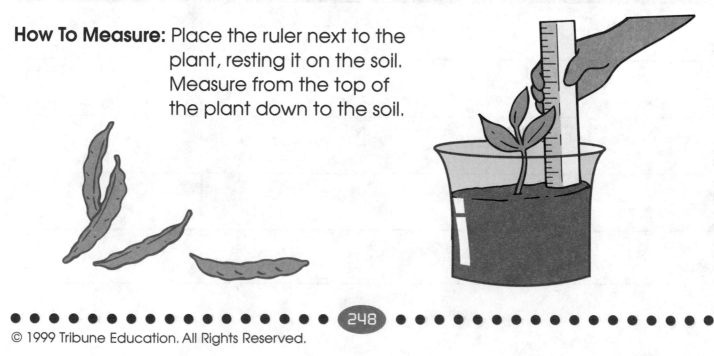

Name ______________________________

Growing String Beans

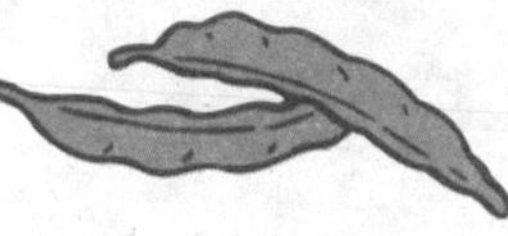

Bar Graph

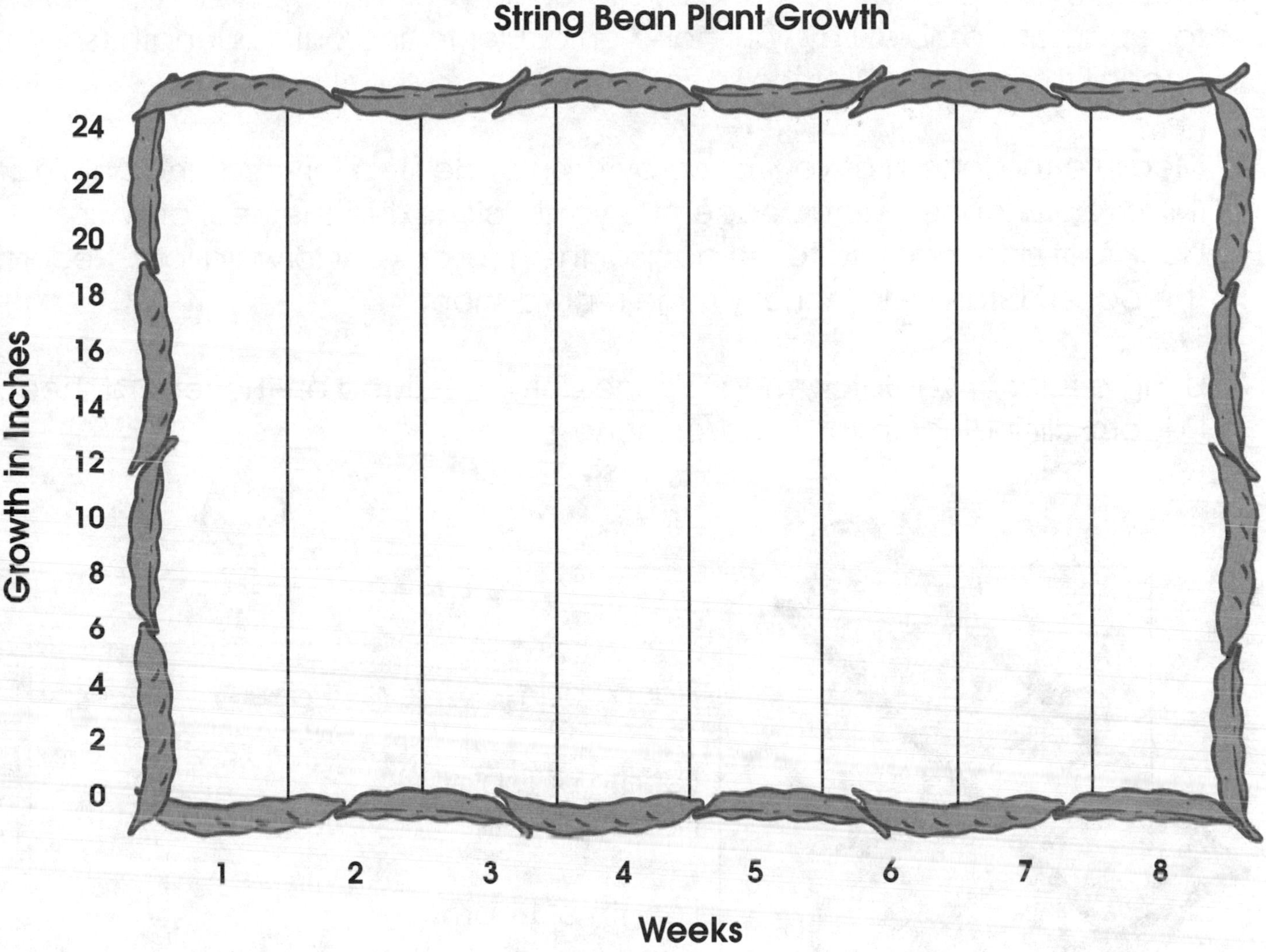

String Bean Plant Growth

Growth in Inches: 0, 2, 4, 6, 8, 10, 12, 14, 16, 18, 20, 22, 24

Weeks: 1, 2, 3, 4, 5, 6, 7, 8

Other Ideas:

Try growing a few other interesting plants like:

1. Carrot tops cut off and placed in a pie tin filled with water.
2. Plain popcorn seeds from the store (no oiled or treated). Plant them in the ground.
3. Go to your local plant nursery or hardware store and look at the selection of plant seeds available.
4. Plant a young tree in your yard and measure its growth each year.

Name ______________________

Hand—Foot—Ruler

Directions:

1. Measure the span of your hand by stretching your thumb and little finger as far apart as possible. Lay your hand on a ruler to find out this length (span). Record the inches (") of the span on the record sheet below.

2. Measure the length of your pace by taking one step forward and holding it. Have someone put the edge of a yardstick next to the heel of your back foot and measure to the back of the heel on your forward foot. Record the pace distance in inches on the record sheet.

3. Using a ruler or yardstick, measure the distances listed on the record sheet. Record all findings in feet and/or inches.

Hand Span ________" Pace ________"

Length of Table:
Hand Span ________ Ruler ________"

Length of Room:
Pace ________ Yardstick ________"

Height of Bookcase:
Hand Span ________ Ruler ________"

Width of Kitchen:
Pace ________ Yardstick ________"

Name ______________________

A Measurement of Our Own

Create your own new system of measurement. Brainstorm ideas on what and how you should base the new unit. For example, you may use the length of your finger, the length of a juice box, the length of your backpack, etc. as a base.

Next, **create** a ruler using your new unit of measurement. A foot is made of inches and a meter is made of centimeters. Break your standard unit into smaller units and **add** these to the ruler. When the ruler is complete, fill out the form below.

Answer the questions below.

1. What is the name of your unit of measurement? ______________________

2. What would your unit of measurement be best suited for measuring—long distances or microscopic organisms? ______________________

   Why? ______________________

3. Would you rather use your new unit of measurement versus the standard unit? __________ Why or why not? ______________________

4. Measure an object using your new ruler. What did it measure? __________
   If you were to tell someone that the object you measured was that long, do you think that person would be able to picture its length? __________

   Why or why not? ______________________

5. Why do you think everyone in the entire country uses the exact same unit of measurement? ______________________

Name ______________________________

Krab E. Krabby

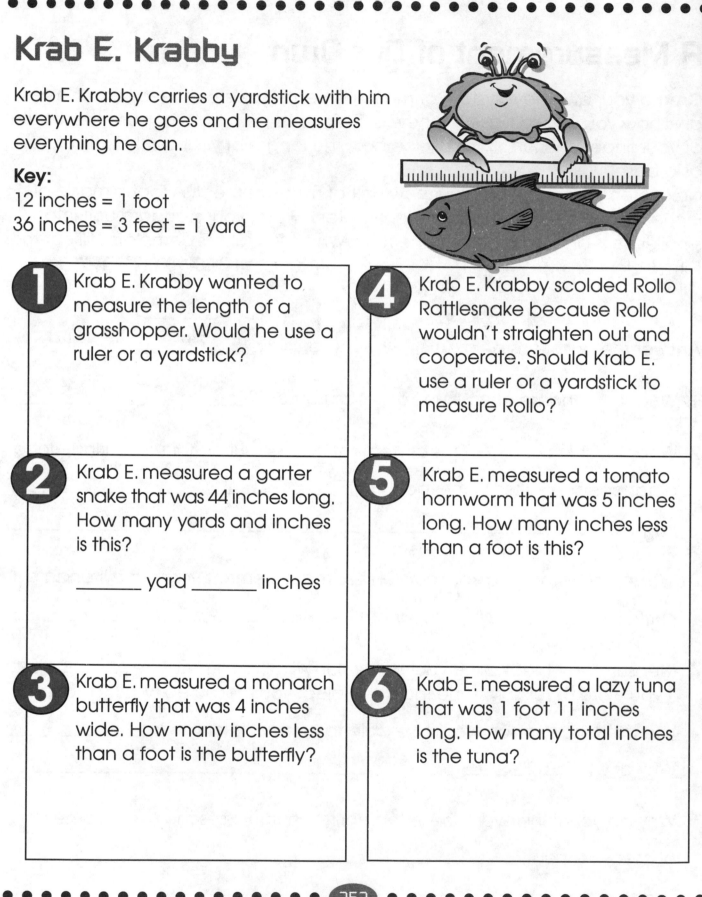

Krab E. Krabby carries a yardstick with him everywhere he goes and he measures everything he can.

Key:
12 inches = 1 foot
36 inches = 3 feet = 1 yard

1. Krab E. Krabby wanted to measure the length of a grasshopper. Would he use a ruler or a yardstick?

2. Krab E. measured a garter snake that was 44 inches long. How many yards and inches is this?

   _______ yard _______ inches

3. Krab E. measured a monarch butterfly that was 4 inches wide. How many inches less than a foot is the butterfly?

4. Krab E. Krabby scolded Rollo Rattlesnake because Rollo wouldn't straighten out and cooperate. Should Krab E. use a ruler or a yardstick to measure Rollo?

5. Krab E. measured a tomato hornworm that was 5 inches long. How many inches less than a foot is this?

6. Krab E. measured a lazy tuna that was 1 foot 11 inches long. How many total inches is the tuna?

Calculating Lengths

Use your yardstick to **calculate** and **write** the following lengths. Remember to write feet or yards. Some lengths may not be exactly in feet or yards, so be sure to write the inches too. Have a friend or parent help you **measure** these lengths.

1. How long is the biggest step you can take? ____________________
2. How far can a paper airplane fly? ____________________
3. From start to finish, how much distance do you cover when you do a somersault? ____________________
4. How far can you throw a feather? ____________________
5. How wide is your driveway? ____________________
6. How far can you walk balancing a book on your head? ____________________
7. How high can you stack wooden blocks before they fall? ____________________
8. How high can you jump? (Measure from where your finger touches to the floor.) ____________________
9. How far can you jump? (Begin with your feet together.) ____________________
10. How much distance is covered if you skip 10 times? ____________________
11. What is the distance you can hit a softball with your bat before it hits the ground? ____________________
12. What is the distance you can throw a baseball? ____________________
13. How far away were you when you caught your friend's throw? ____________________
14. How far can you spit a seed? ____________________
15. How much distance do you cover when you sprint for 3 seconds? ____________________

Name ______________________________

Animal Math

The chart below lists some of the body statistics of 15 endangered animals. Use these measurements to **solve** the problems below the chart.

Animal	Height	Weight	Length
Mountain gorilla	6 feet	450 pounds	
Black rhinoceros	5.5 feet	4,000 pounds	12 feet
Cheetah	2.5 feet	100 pounds	5 feet
Leopard	2 feet	150 pounds	4.5 feet
Spectacled bear	2.5 feet	300 pounds	5 feet
Giant armadillo		100 pounds	4 feet
Vicuna	2.5 feet	100 pounds	
Siberian tiger	38 inches	600 pounds	6 feet
Orangutan	4.5 feet	200 pounds	
Giant panda		300 pounds	6 feet
Polar bear		1,600 pounds	8 feet
Yak	5.5 feet	1,200 pounds	

1. What is the total height of a mountain gorilla, a vicuna and a yak? __________
2. What is the total weight of a leopard, a cheetah and a polar bear? __________
3. What is the total weight of a giant panda and a giant armadillo? __________
4. Add the lengths of a black rhinoceros, a spectacled bear and a Siberian tiger. __________
5. Add the heights of two leopards, three yaks and four orangutans. __________
6. Subtract the height of a vicuna from the height of a cheetah. __________
7. Add the weights of all the animals. __________
8. Write the lengths of the animals from longest to shortest.

____

____

____

Name ______________________________

Finding Weight Equivalents

In the United States, we use a standard weight system that includes ounces (oz.), pounds (lb.) and tons (tn.). Develop your own standard weight system below.

You will need: marbles, paper clips, ice-cream sticks, crayons, pencils, spoons, etc. (anything that has weight and can be counted), a scale or balance

Directions: Your standard weight is ______________________.

Now, use your scale to find out how much different objects weigh.

1. Place the object to be weighed on one side of the scale.
2. Find out, for example, how many of your standard weight it takes to equal the object being weighed.
3. When the scale is level, you have found your equivalent weight.
4. Weigh different objects and record the results below.

Example: bottle of glue weight: 16 crayons

object: ______________________ weight: ______________________

object: ______________________ weight: ______________________

object: ______________________ weight: ______________________

object: ______________________ weight: ______________________

object: ______________________ weight: ______________________

object: ______________________ weight: ______________________

object: ______________________ weight: ______________________

object: ______________________ weight: ______________________

object: ______________________ weight: ______________________

object: ______________________ weight: ______________________

object: ______________________ weight: ______________________

Name ______________________

Discovering Capacity

Capacity measures how much can fit inside an object.

You will need:

measuring cup (2 cup capacity)
pie tin
1 cup of salt
bathroom sink
1 gallon plastic jug
2 liter plastic jug
tablespoon
cake pan
1 cup of ice
baking pan
1 gallon freezer bag

Complete the tasks below to discover the capacity of objects around your house.

1. How many cups of water are there in a 1-gallon plastic jug? __________

2. How many tablespoons of salt does it take to fill up 1 cup? __________

   How many tablespoons of water does it take to fill up 1/2 cup? __________

3. Plug your bathroom sink. How many cups of water will it hold? __________

   How many gallons is that? __________

5. How many cups of water does it take to fill a pie tin? __________

6. Does a gallon-size plastic freezer bag really hold a gallon of something?

   __________ Count how many cups of water you can fit inside one. ______

   __________ Is that a gallon?

7. Fill a cake pan with water. Count how many cups it takes. __________

   If 2 cups = 1 pint, how many pints does it hold? __________

   If 2 pints = 1 quart, what is the quart capacity of your cake pan? ________

Name ________________________________

Discovering Capacity Equivalents

Gallons, quarts, cups and pints are used for measuring capacity in the U.S.A. You use them every day, but you probably don't measure them every time. When you pour milk on your cereal in the morning, you are estimating how much milk you need to cover your breakfast. We are always making estimates.

You will need:
1 cup capacity measuring cup, pint, quart and half gallon containers, two 1-gallon capacity plastic jugs, water

Directions:
Set the two 1-gallon jugs beside each other. Fill one with water. Then, fill the measuring cups with water from the jug to determine the number of cups, pints, quarts and gallons of water it will take to fill the other jug.

1 cup — How many cups do you think it will take to fill 1 gallon? ____________

The actual amount ____________

1 pint (2 cups) — How many pints do you think it will take to fill 1 gallon? ____________

The actual amount ____________

1 quart (2 pints) — How many quarts do you think it will take to fill 1 gallon? ____________

The actual amount ____________

1 half gallon (2 quarts) — How many half gallons do you think it will take to fill 1 gallon? ____________

The actual amount ____________

Name ____________________

Comparing Temperatures

Temperatures tell how warm or cold something is.
You will need: Fahrenheit thermometer
measuring cup (1 or 2 cup capacity)

Measure and **record** the temperatures of:

________ 1. Water from the tap

________ 2. The dairy section at the grocery store (Call or visit store to ask.)

________ 3. A pet's body temperature (Call or visit veterinarian.)

________ 4. Your freezer (Have your parents help you.)

________ 5. Bathtub water (Fill a cup from the bathtub and place the thermometer in it.)

________ 6. A cup of water outside in the sun

- Place a cup of water in a safe place with the thermometer resting inside.
- Let it set until the temperature stops rising.
- Record the temperature.

Is it the same as the temperature outside? ________

________ 7. A cup of ice water

________ 8. Your body temperature

Now, **compare**.

1. How many degrees warmer is the bathtub water than the tap water?

   ____

2. How many degrees difference is a pet's body temperature than yours?

   ________ Who is warmer? ____________________

3. What is the difference between your freezer's temperature and the temperature in the dairy section of your grocery store? ____________

4. What is the difference in temperature between a cup of water that has set out in the sun and a cup of ice water? ____________

Name ______________________________

Weather Page

Examine the weather page from the newspaper for two or more consecutive days (preferably the two days prior to this activity).

Look for the following information:
time of sunrise and sunset for each day,
low temperature for each day,
high temperature for each day,
high and low tides (if applicable.)

How accurate was the forecast for:
time of sunrise and sunset for each day?
low temperature for each day?
high temperature for each day?
high and low tides?

time of sunrise	
time of sunset	
low temperature	
high temperature	
times of high tides	
times of low tides	

Name ____________________

Today's Temperature

Record the indoor and outdoor temperatures in degrees Celsius and Fahrenheit. Post the daily temperature on poster paper on your refrigerator. If desired, use an almanac or newspaper to share record high and low temperatures for each day.

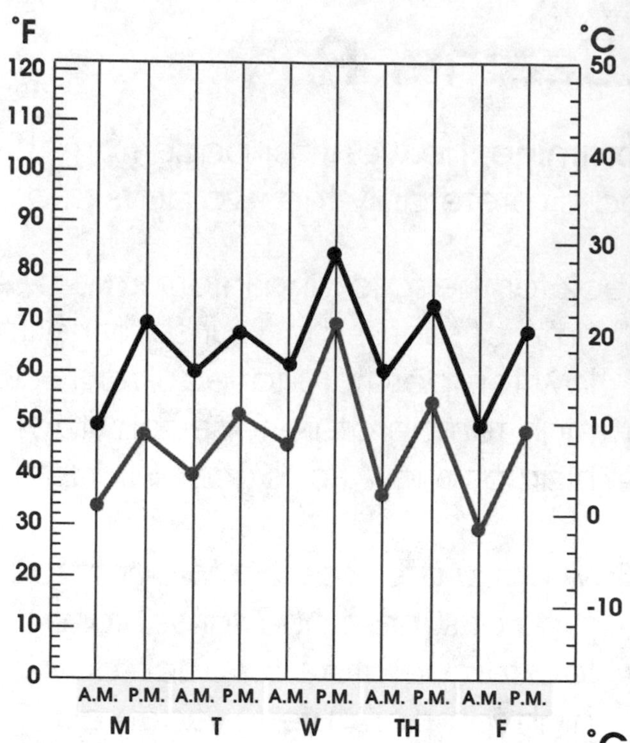

Indoor temperature
(8 A.M. and 3 P.M.)

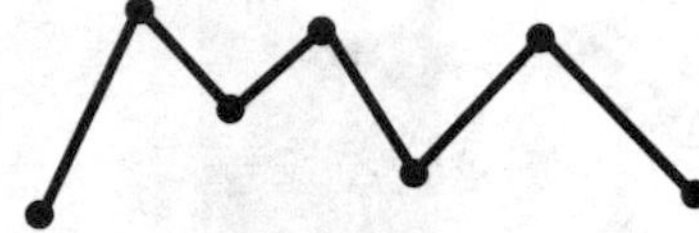

Outdoor temperature
(8 A.M. and 3 P.M.)

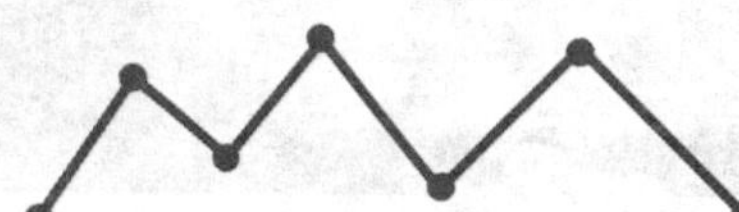

Extension: Create ongoing line graphs to show temperature differences. Each day, plot the temperatures. Display them near the daily temperature recordings.

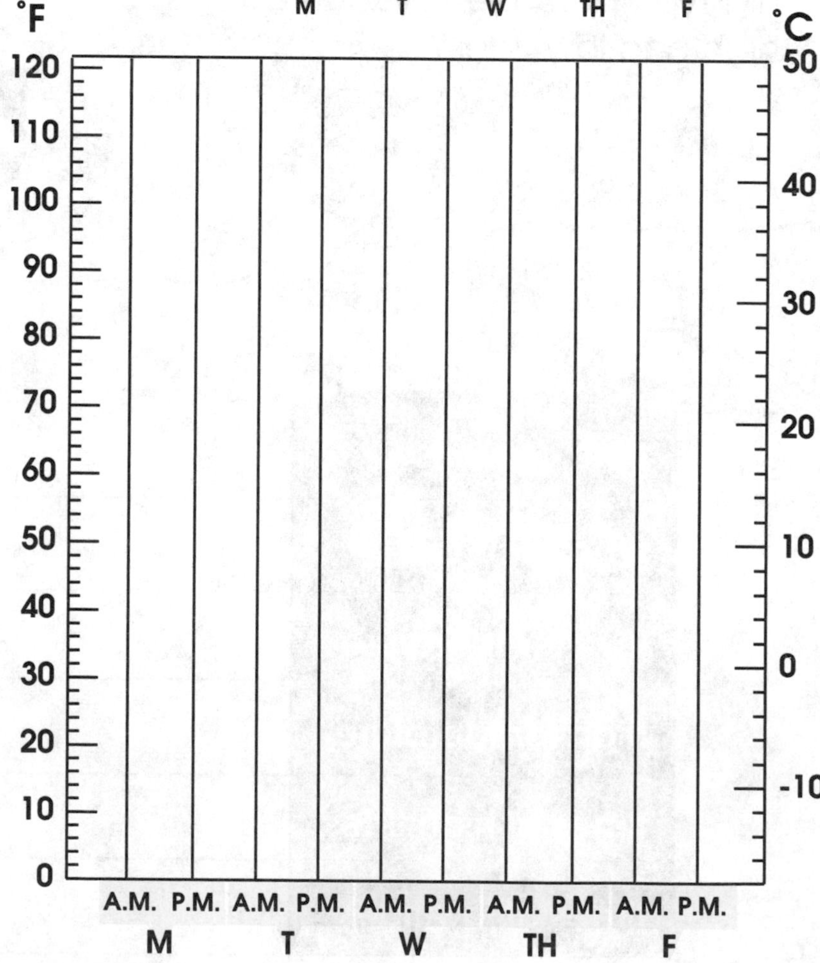

Super Shadows

Go outside to **measure** your shadow every hour on a sunny day. Have someone help you by **drawing** around your shadow with colored chalk. **Record** the time and length on your chart. Stand in the same place each time. Predict what will be different.

Were your predictions accurate? __________

8 A.M. Shadows

Everyone's shadow is taller than really,
The shadows of giants are taller than trees.
The shadows of children are big as their parents,
And shadows of trotting dogs bend at the knees.
Everyone's shadow is taller than really,
Everyone's shadow is thinner than thin,
8 A.M. shadows are long at the dawning,
Pulling the night away,
Coaxing the light to say:
"Welcome, all shadows,
Day, please begin!"

Patricia Hubbel

Time	Length of shadow

Time

My Schedule

Keep track of what you do all day for a week on several copies of this page. **Write** the day and date at the start of the day. Then, **write** what you do and the time you do it. Each time you change activities, you should **write** a new time entry. At the end of the day, **add** how much time was spent in each type of activity. Some activities can be grouped together (i.e., breakfast, lunch, dinner = eating; social studies, language, math = school subjects; etc.). Tally up your activities on Friday.

Extension: Use the information collected to plot a pie graph, bar graph, line graph or pictograph.

Day and date

Time	Activity

Totals

Name ______________________

Timely Fun

Predict how many times you can do each activity in 1 minute. Then, **time** yourself and see how accurate your predictions were.

Say the alphabet.

Estimate: ________ Actual: ________

Clap your hands.

Estimate: ________ Actual: ________

Do 20 jumping jacks.

Estimate: ________ Actual: ________

Count to 20.

Estimate: ________ Actual: ________

Hop on one foot.

Estimate: ________ Actual: ________

Count backward from 20 to 1.

Estimate: ________ Actual: ________

Name ___________________________

Time on My Hands

Draw the hour and minute hands to show each time below.

Example:

3:35

10:05

4:55

8:10

12:50

9:20

7:25

1:15

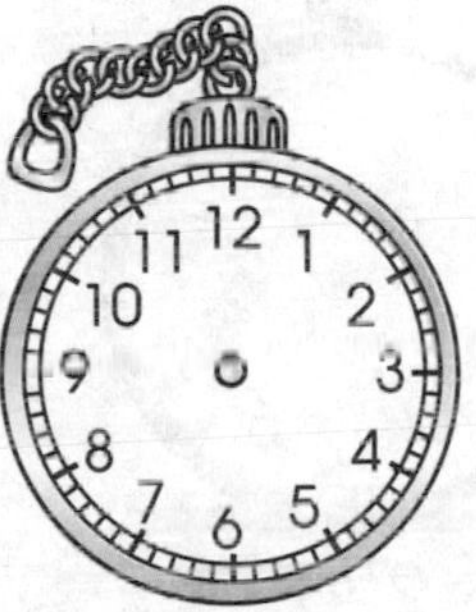

11:45

3:30

6:40

12:55

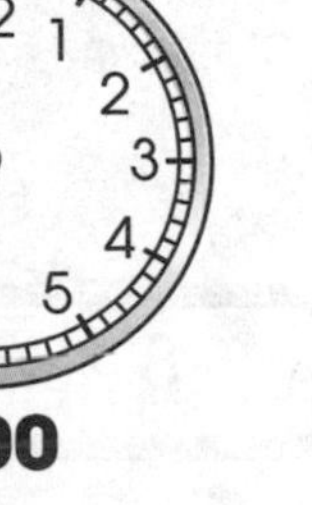

2:00

5:35

3:15

10:50

Minute Men

Draw the hour and minute hands on these clocks.

Example:

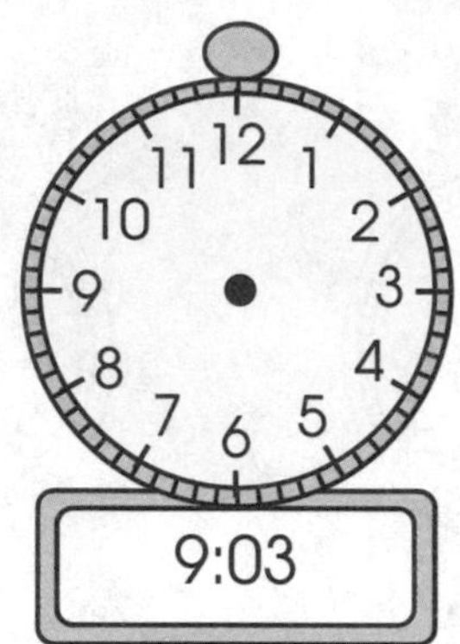

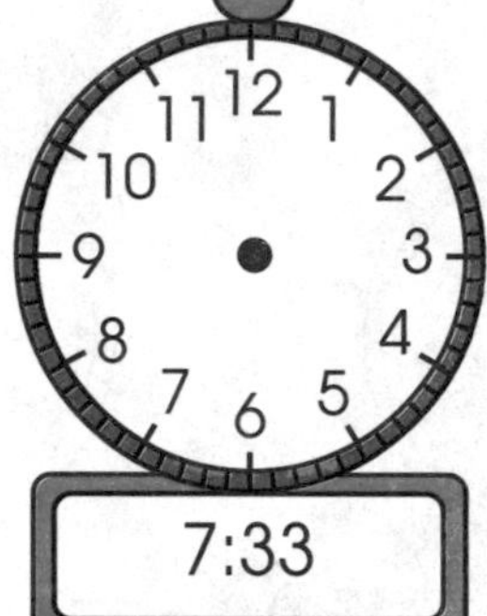

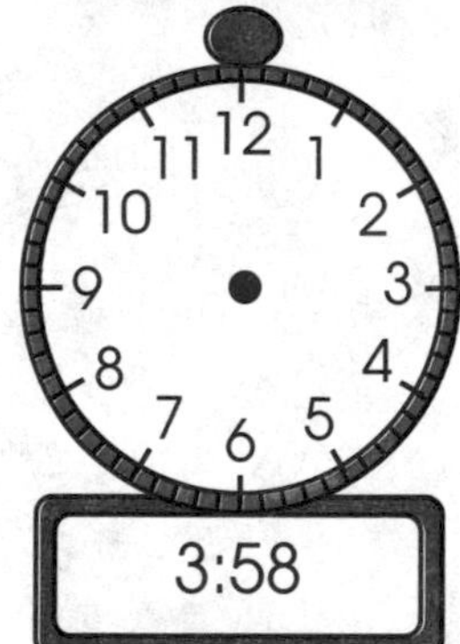

Name ______________________________

Take Time for These

Write the time shown on these clocks.

Example:

6:47 ______ ______ ______

______ ______ ______ ______

______ ______ ______ ______

Name ____________________

Father Time Teasers

Write the times below.

Example:

25 minutes ago

5:35

10 minutes later

______

40 minutes ago

______

35 minutes ago

______

50 minutes later

______

15 minutes ago

______

20 minutes later

______

45 minutes ago

______

5 minutes ago

______

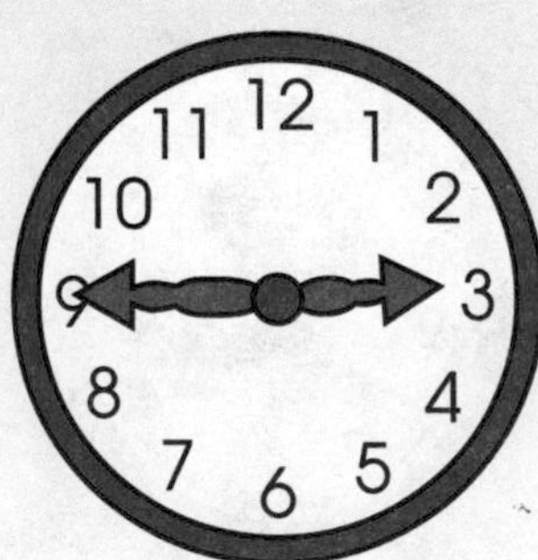

30 minutes later

______

55 minutes later

______

25 minutes ago

______

Time "Tables"

Draw the hands on these clocks.

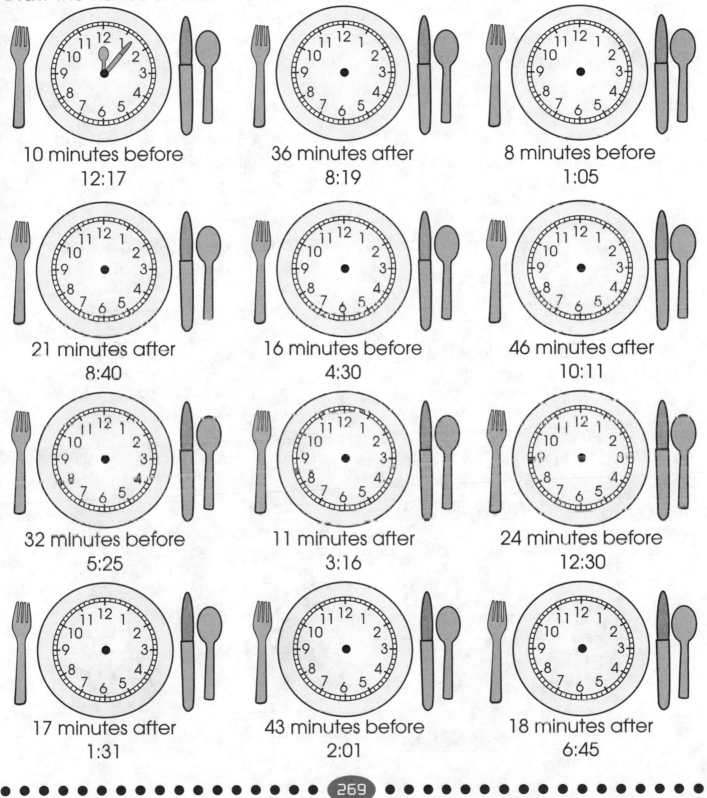

10 minutes before
12:17

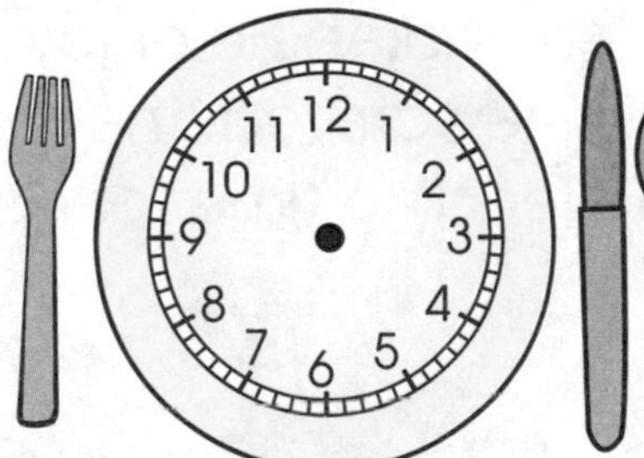

36 minutes after
8:19

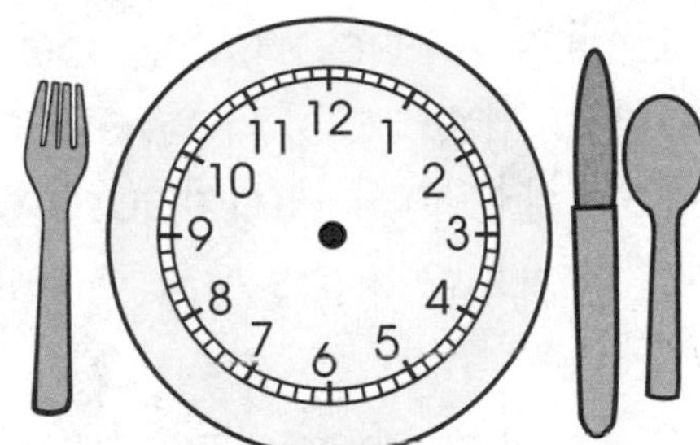

8 minutes before
1:05

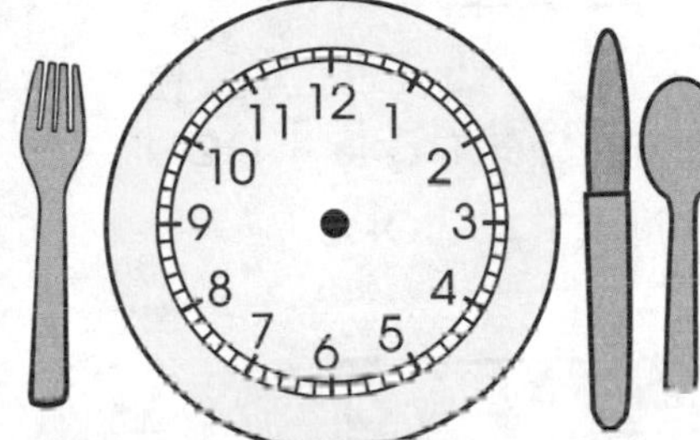

21 minutes after
8:40

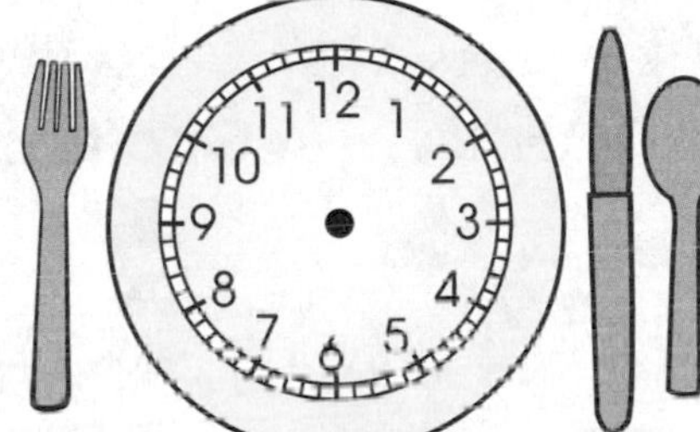

16 minutes before
4:30

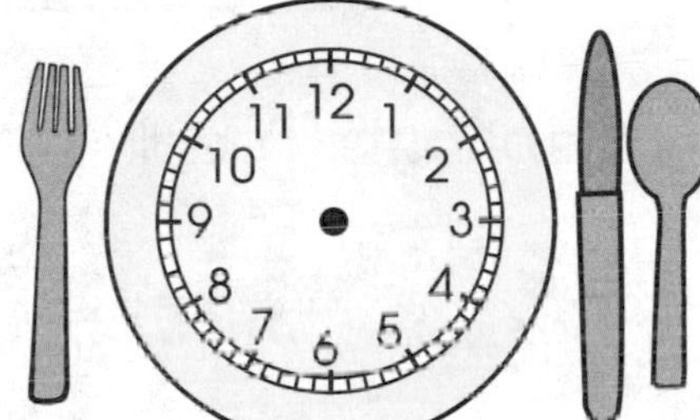

46 minutes after
10:11

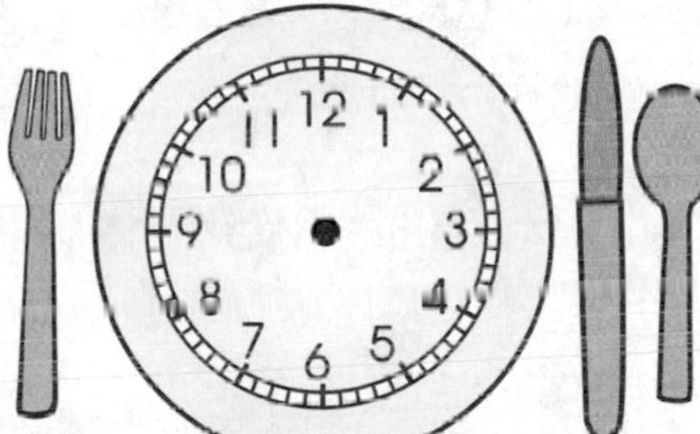

32 minutes before
5:25

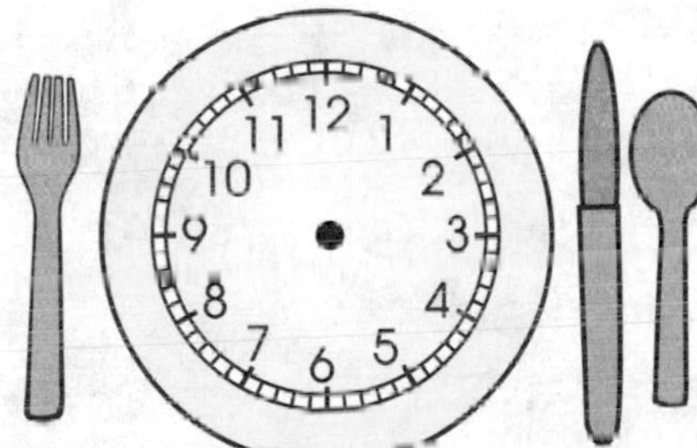

11 minutes after
3:16

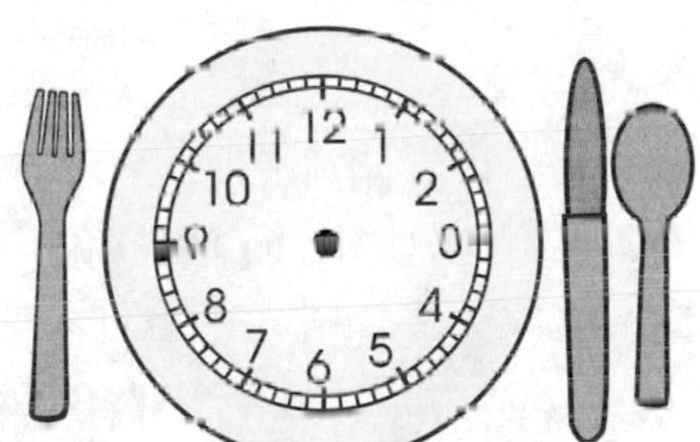

24 minutes before
12:30

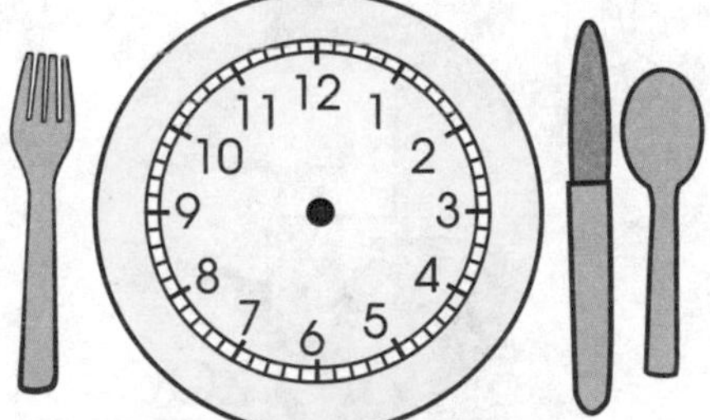

17 minutes after
1:31

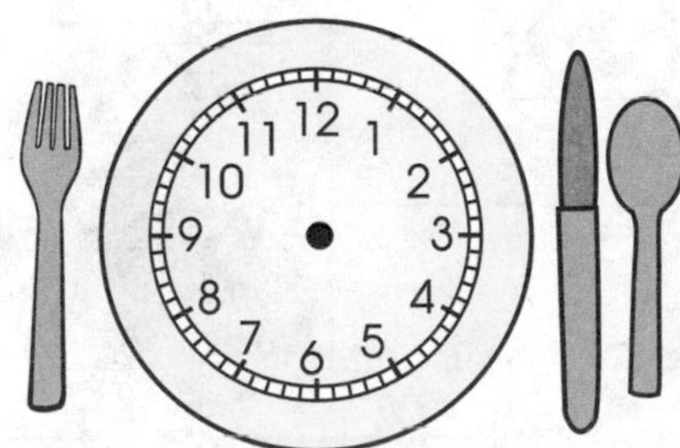

43 minutes before
2:01

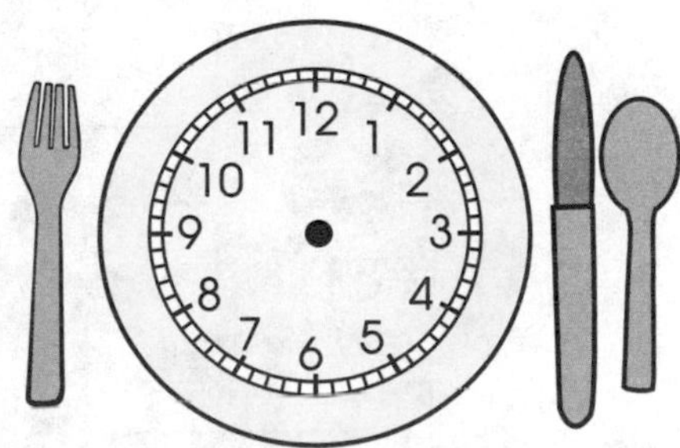

18 minutes after
6:45

Name 

Feeding Time

The abbreviations **A.M.** and **P.M.** help tell the time of day. At midnight, A.M. begins. At noon, P.M. begins. Ken and Angie enjoy watching the animals being fed at the zoo. However, when they arrived, they were a little confused by the signs. Help them figure out the feeding time for each kind of animal. Be sure to include if it's A.M. or P.M.

Zebras: Feeding time is 2 hours after the monkeys.

____

Tigers: Feeding time is 2 hours after 9:00 A.M.

____

Elephants: Feeding time is 1:00 P.M.

Giraffes: Feeding time is 1 hour before the lions.

____

Monkeys: Feeding time is 3 hours before the giraffes.

____

Lions: Feeding time is 3 hours after the elephants.

____

Now, **trace** the path in the zoo that Ken and Angie would take so that they could see all the animals being fed.

Name ______________________________

Monkeying Around

Nat can't tell time. He needs your help to **solve** these problems.

1. Nat is supposed to be at school in 10 minutes. What time should he get there?

____

2. Nat started breakfast at 7:10 A.M. It took him 15 minutes to eat. Mark the time he finished.

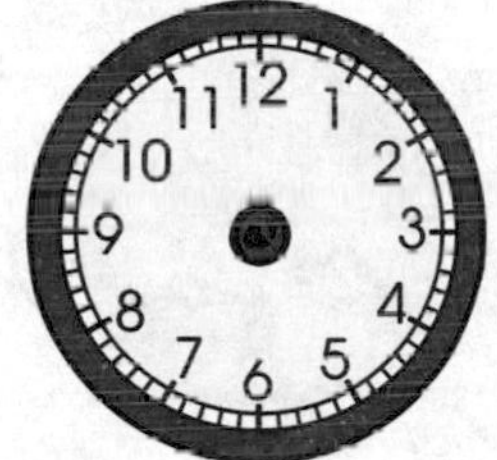

3. Nat will leave school in 5 minutes. What time will it be then?

____

4. Nat's family will eat dinner in 15 minutes. When will that be?

____

5. It is now 6:45 P.M. Nat must start his homework in 5 minutes. Mark the starting time on the clock.

6. Nat will go to the park in 15 minutes. It is now 1:25 P.M. Mark the time he will go to the park.

Name 

Minutes Make Up the Hours

Preparation: Cut out the game cards on pages 273 and 275. There are 12 pairs of card's. One card of each pair has minutes written on it. The other card has hours and minutes written on it (see the examples shown). M is on the back of the Minute cards. HM is on the back of the Hour/Minute cards. Put a rubber band around the Minute cards and one around the Hour/Minute cards. Make an answer key telling which Hour/Minute card matches each Minute card.

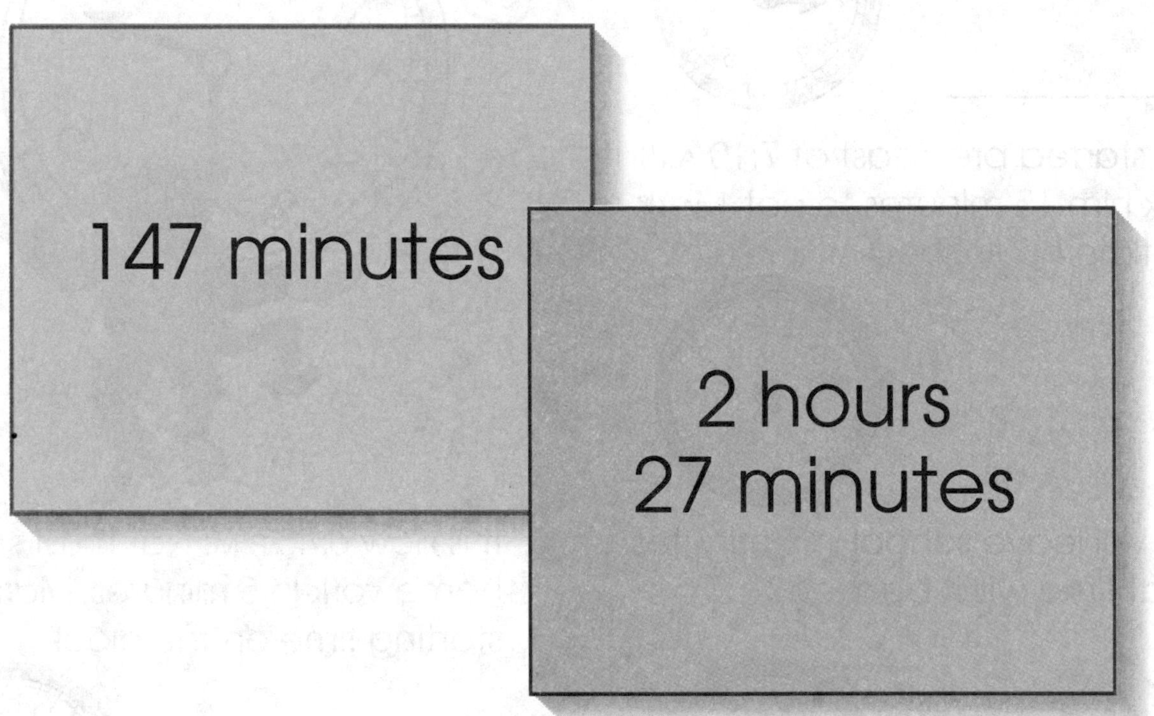

Rules: This game involves 2–4 players. The youngest player goes first and play goes clockwise. Lay the Minute cards facedown on one side of the playing area. Lay the Hour/Minute cards facedown on the other side. For another challenge, mix them together and lay them all in rows.

Directions: The game is played like "Memory." Player One turns a card up from each set of cards. If the cards are a pair, the player may take them. Otherwise, the cards should be put back facedown. Play continues until all pairs are matched. The player with the most pairs is the winner and goes first if playing another game. Use the key only if the players do not agree on a match.

Name ______________________

Minute Cards

233 minutes	200 minutes	120 minutes
65 minutes	280 minutes	147 minutes
74 minutes	35 minutes	360 minutes
122 minutes	97 minutes	109 minutes

Name 

Minute Cards

M	M	M
M	M	M
M	M	M
M	M	M

Name ______________________

Hour/Minute Cards

3 hours 53 minutes	3 hours 20 minutes	2 hours
1 hour 5 minutes	4 hours 40 minutes	2 hours 27 minutes
1 hour 14 minutes	(0 hours) 35 minutes	6 hours (0 minutes)
2 hours 2 minutes	1 hour 37 minutes	1 hour 49 minutes

Hour/Minute Cards

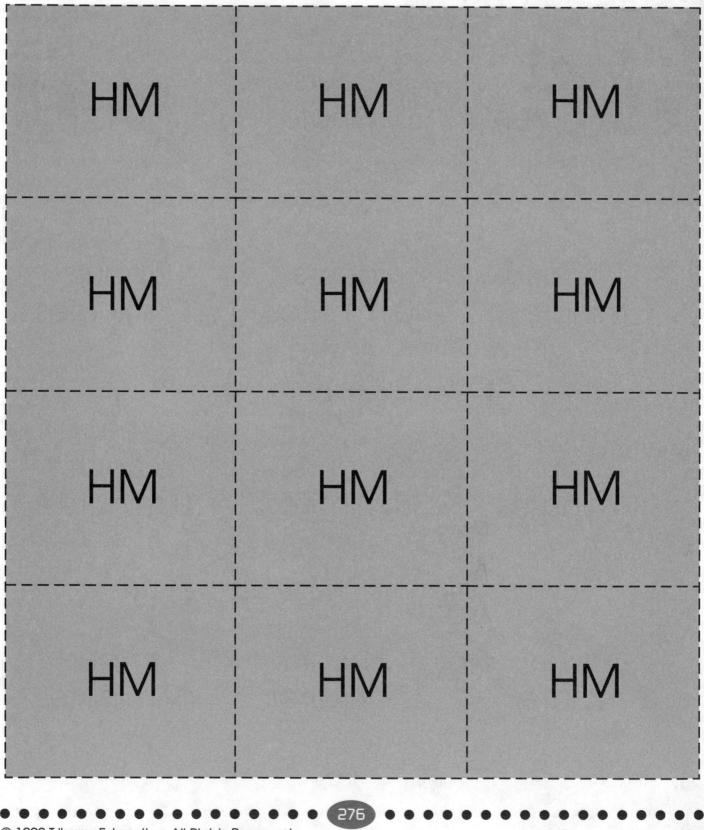

HM	HM	HM
HM	HM	HM
HM	HM	HM
HM	HM	HM

Name ______________________________

How Far Is It?

Drawing pictures can be a good problem-solving strategy. **Draw** pictures to help you **solve** the problems below. Each problem requires three answers.

1. Jimmy has to walk 12 blocks to get to the park where he likes to play ball. It takes him 3 minutes to walk one block. How many minutes will it take him to walk to the park?

   Distance ____________ Speed ____________ Time ____________

2. An airplane leaves the airport at 9:00 A.M. It flies at 200 miles per hour. When it lands at 11:00 A.M., how far will it have gone?

   Distance ____________ Speed ____________ Time ____________

3. It is 50 miles between Dakota City and Blue Falls. It takes Mr. Oliver 1 hour to make the drive. How fast does he drive?

   Distance ____________ Speed ____________ Time ____________

4. Tad rides his bike to his grandmother's house. It takes him 45 minutes to ride there. She lives 5 miles from his house. How many minutes does it take him to ride 1 mile?

   Distance ____________ Speed ____________ Time ____________

5. Rachel loves to visit her grandparents who live 150 miles from her house. When they make the trip, her dad drives. He averages 50 miles an hour. How many hours will the trip take?

   Distance ____________ Speed ____________ Time ____________

Name ____________________

Time Problems

Draw the hands on the clocks to show the starting time and the ending time. Then, **write** the answer to the question.

1. The bike race started at 2:55 P.M. and lasted 2 hours and 10 minutes. What time did the race end?

____

4. Sherry walked in the 12-mile Hunger Walk. She started at 12:30 P.M. and finished at 4:50 P.M. How long did she walk?

____

2. The 500-mile auto race started at 11:00 A.M. and lasted 2 hours and 25 minutes. What time did the race end?

____

5. The chili cook-off started at 10:00 A.M., and all the chili was cooked by 4:30 P.M. How long did it take to cook the chili?

____

3. The train left Indianapolis at 7:25 A.M. and arrived in Chicago at 10:50 A.M. How long did the trip take?

____

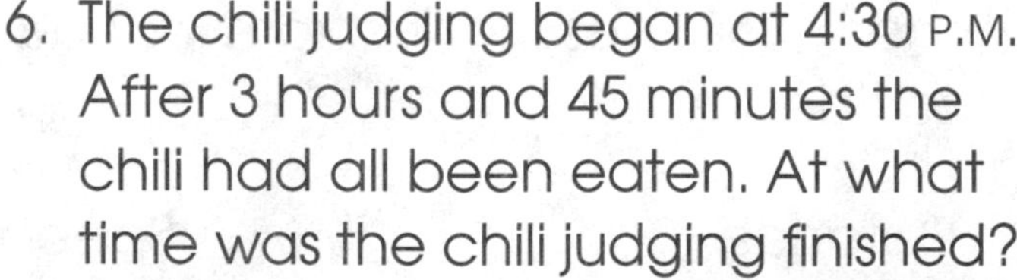

6. The chili judging began at 4:30 P.M. After 3 hours and 45 minutes the chili had all been eaten. At what time was the chili judging finished?

____

Name ________________________________

Time Zones

Clocks in various parts of the world do not show the same time. Suppose they did show the same time—3 P.M., for example. At that time, people in some countries would see the sun rise and people in other lands would see it high in the sky. In other countries, the sun could not be seen because 3 P.M. would occur at night. Instead, clocks in all locations show 12 o'clock at midday.

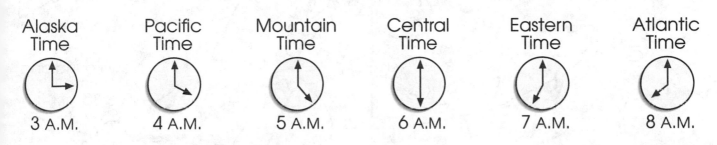

Alaska Time

3 A.M.

Pacific Time

4 A.M.

Mountain Time

5 A.M.

Central Time

6 A.M.

Eastern Time

7 A.M.

Atlantic Time

8 A.M.

The United States and Canada each have six standard time zones. Each zone uses a time 1 hour different from its neighboring zones. The hours are earlier to the west of each zone and later to the east. The Newfoundland Time Zone is not a true standard time zone because it differs from its neighboring zones by only a half hour. The boundaries between the zones are irregular so that neighboring communities can have the same time.

3:00 A.M.

St. Louis, MO

Directions:

Color each time zone a different color on **Map of North America** on page 280. Cut out **Hour Cards** from page 281 and **City Cards** from page 283.

Lay the **City Cards** facedown in a stack and spread out the **Hour Cards** faceup. Select one **Hour Card** and one **City Card**. This **City Card** will be referred to as the original city. Take another **City Card** from the stack. Find the **Hour Card** that tells what the time would be in this city. Do this several times, choosing other **City Cards** before changing the original city and time.

Name 

Map of North America

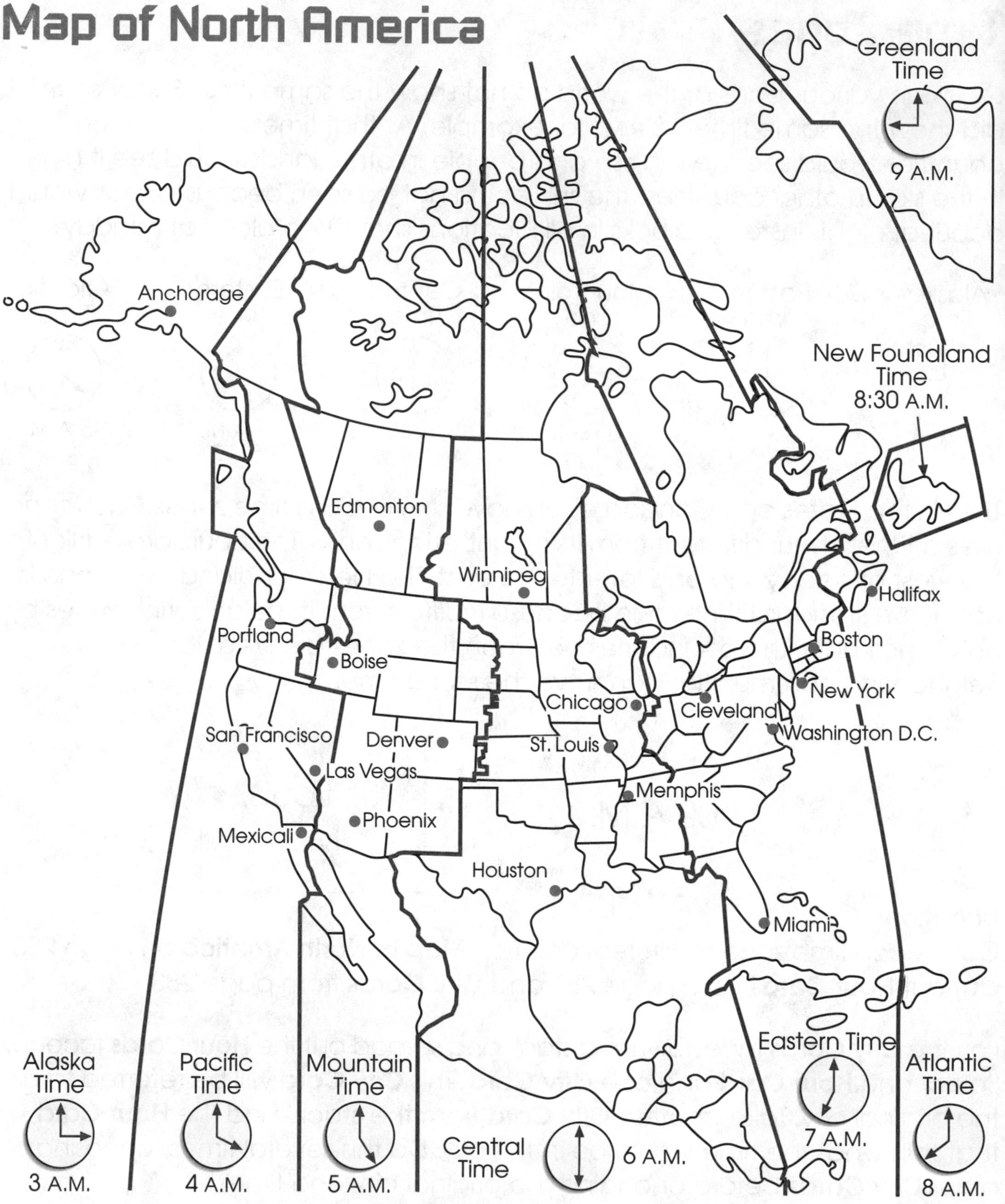

Greenland Time
9 A.M.

Anchorage

New Foundland Time
8:30 A.M.

Edmonton

Winnipeg

Halifax

Portland

Boise

Boston

Chicago

New York

Cleveland

San Francisco

Denver

St. Louis

Washington D.C.

Las Vegas

Memphis

Phoenix

Mexicali

Houston

Miami

Eastern Time
7 A.M.

Alaska Time
3 A.M.

Pacific Time
4 A.M.

Mountain Time
5 A.M.

Central Time
6 A.M.

Atlantic Time
8 A.M.

Name ______________________________

Hour Cards

12:00 A.M.	1:00 A.M.	2:00 A.M.	3:00 A.M.
4:00 A.M.	5:00 A.M.	6:00 A.M.	7:00 A.M.
8:00 A.M.	9:00 A.M.	10:00 A.M.	11:00 A.M.
12:00 P.M.	1:00 P.M.	2:00 P.M.	3:00 P.M.
4:00 P.M.	5:00 P.M.	6:00 P.M.	7:00 P.M.
8:00 P.M.	9:00 P.M.	10:00 P.M.	11:00 P.M.

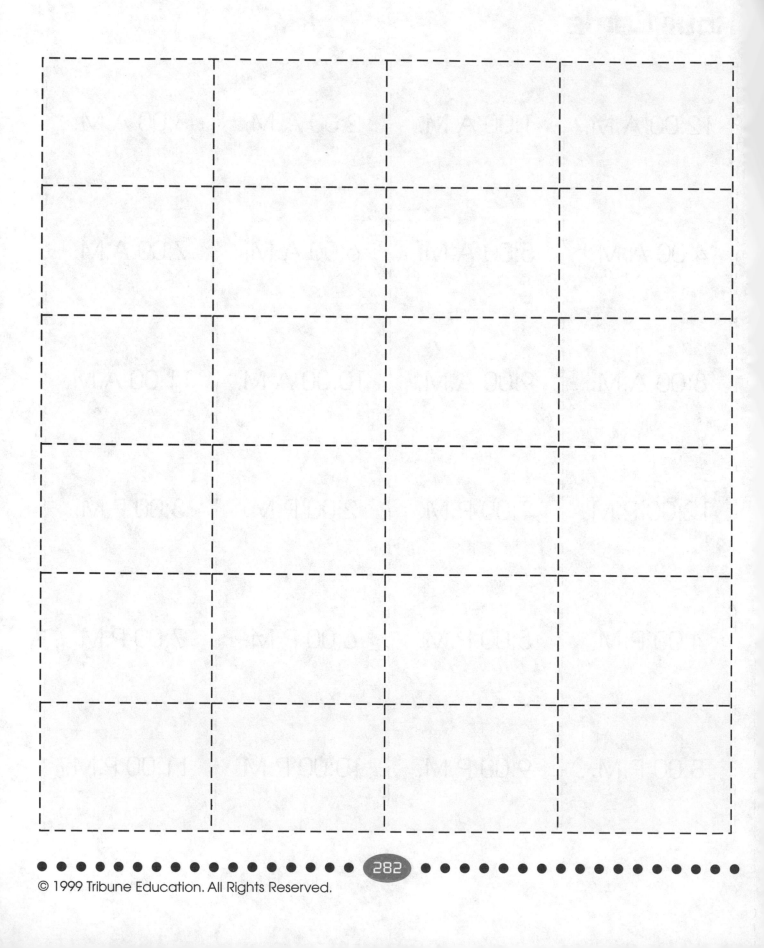

Name ____________________

Name ______________________

City Cards

Halifax, N.S.	Boston, MA	New York, NY	Miami, FL
Washington, D.C.	St. Louis, MO	Chicago, IL	Cleveland, OH
Winnipeg, MB	Houston, TX	Memphis, TN	Edmonton, AB
Denver, CO	Phoenix, AZ	Boise, ID	Las Vegas, NV
Portland, OR	Anchorage, AK	San Francisco, CA	Mexicali, Mexico

Name ______________________________

Name ________________________________

Racing Chimps

One chimpanzee in the forest always likes to brag that it can get more fruit than any other animal in the forest. So an older and wiser chimpanzee decided to challenge him to a race.

"Let us see who can bring back more bananas in 1 hour," said the older chimp. The race began.

Quickly, the younger chimp picked a bunch of five bananas and carried it back. He continued doing this every 5 minutes.

The older chimp was not quite as fast. Every 10 minutes he carried back eight bananas.

After 45 minutes, the young chimp decided to stop and eat one of his bananas before continuing. By the time he finished, the hour was over and the older chimp called out, "The race is over. Whose pile of bananas is bigger?"

Using the information above, figure out how many bananas were in each pile and which chimp won the race.

The younger chimp had ____________________ bananas in his pile.

The older chimp had ____________________ bananas in his pile.

The winner was the ____________________ chimp!

Money

Name ______________________________

Garage Sale

Use the fewest number of coins possible to equal the amount shown in each box. **Write** or **draw** the coins you would use in each box.

 17¢	 98¢	 24¢
 63¢	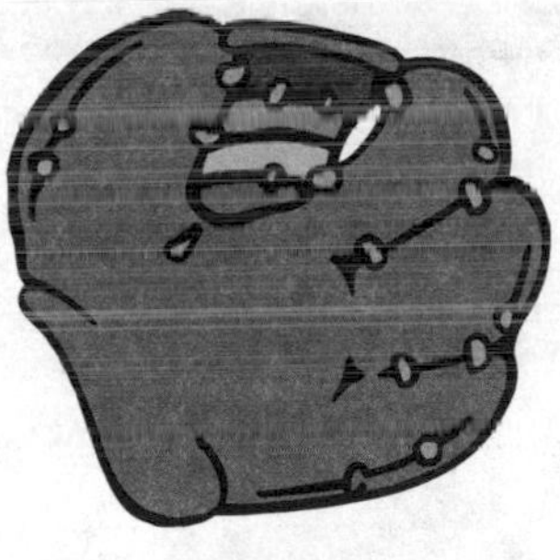 58¢	 35¢

Name ____________________

Your Answer's Safe With Me

Find the right "combination" to open each safe. **Draw** the bills and coins needed to make each amount.

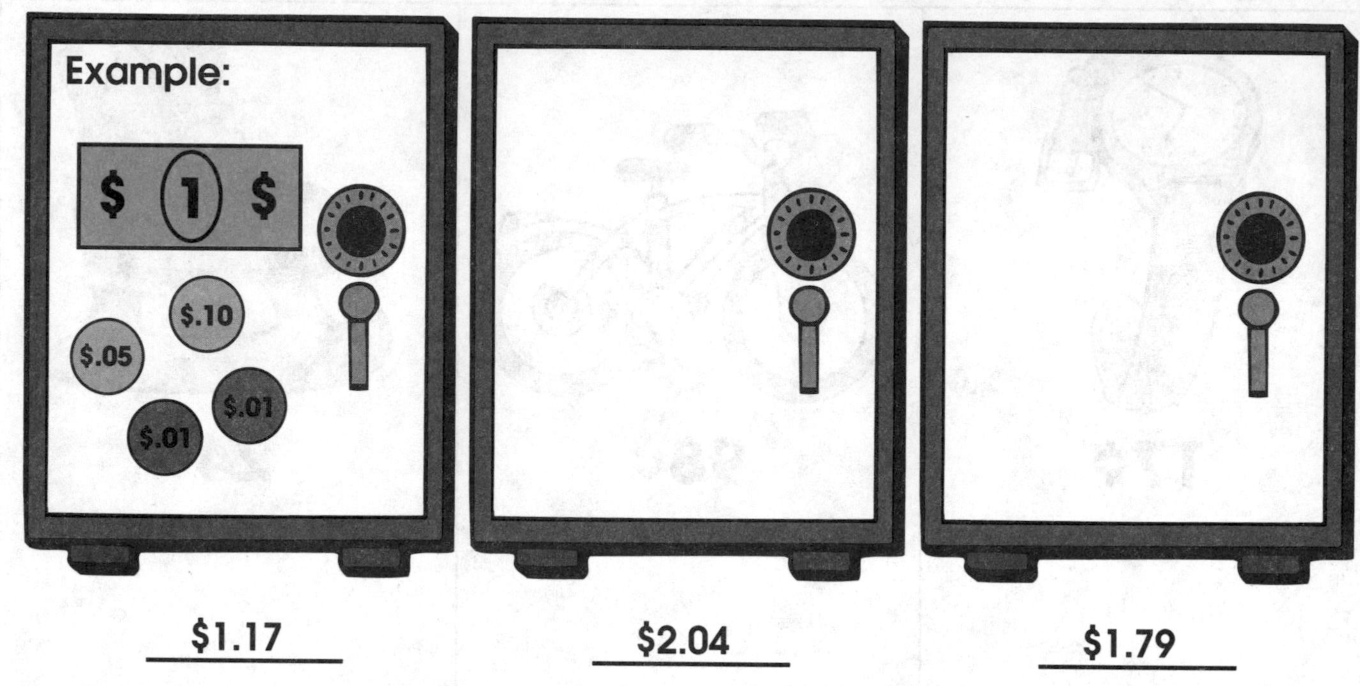

$1.17 $2.04 $1.79

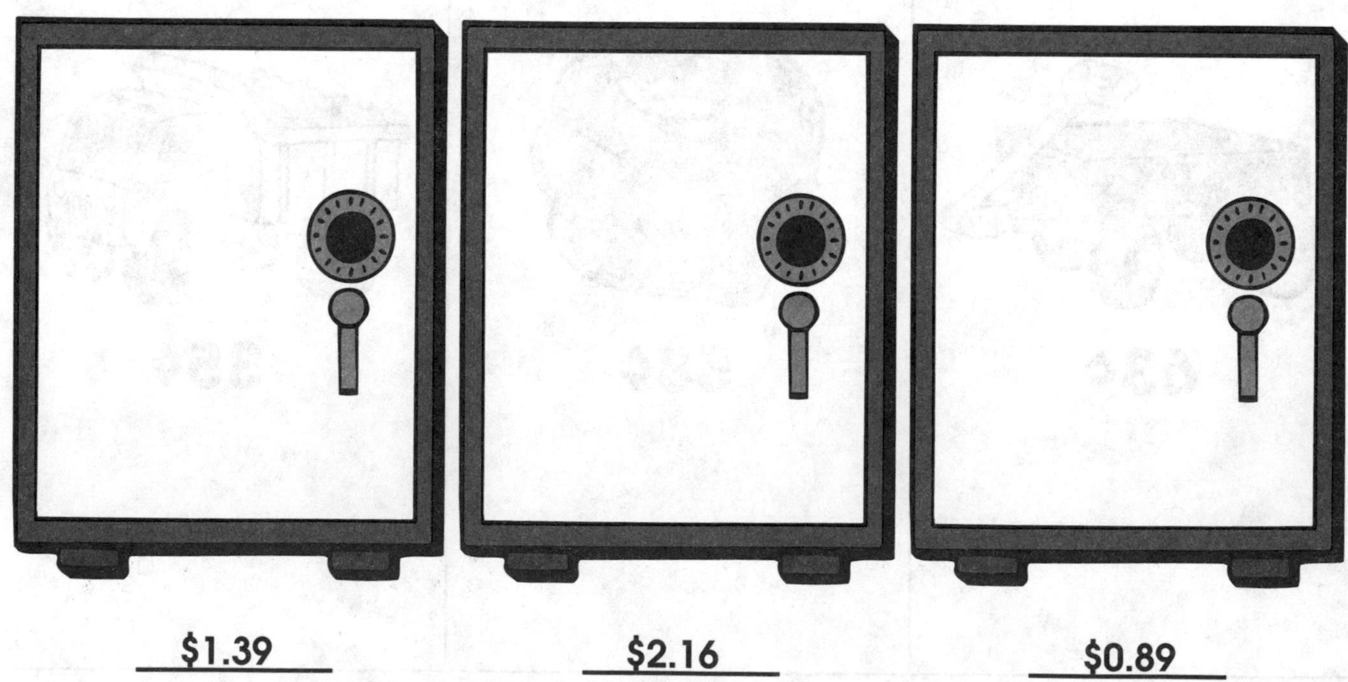

$1.39 $2.16 $0.89

ame ___________________________

Easy Street

What is each house worth? **Count** the money in each house on Easy Street. **Write** the amount on the line below it.

Example:

$2.40 ________ ________ ________ ________

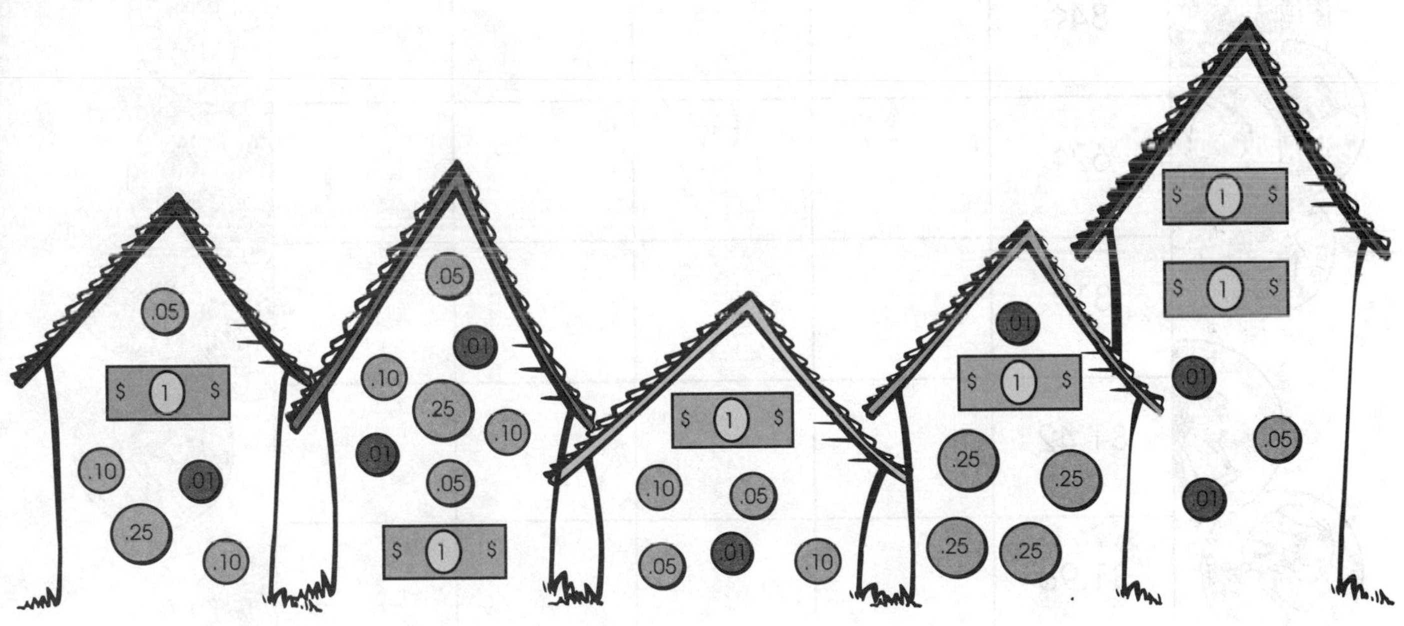

________ ________ ________ ________ ________

Name ____________________

A Collection of Coins

Write the number of coins needed to make the amount shown.

Money	Quarters	Dimes	Nickels	Pennies
76¢				
45¢				
98¢				
40¢				
84¢				
62¢				
31¢				
$1.42				
$1.98				

Name ______________________

Monetary Message

What's the smartest thing to do with your money? To find out, **solve** the following problems and **write** the matching letter above the answer.

___ ___ ___ ___ ___ ___,
$42.71 $33.94 $50.42 $100.73 $45.70 $2.39

___ ___ ___ ___ ___ ___ ___ ___ ___
$33.94 $26.13 $88.02 $45.70 $2.39 $51.12 $45.70 $11.01 $11.01

___ ___ ___ ___ ___!
$33.94 $88.02 $88.02 $55.76 $42.79

V = $42.13 + 8.29

A = $ 4.56 + 29.38

N = $ 4.65 + 21.48

S = $23.46 + 19.25

P = $ 9.31 + 33.48

L = $ 6.73 + 4.28

E = $81.49 + 19.24

T = $ .42 + 1.94 + .03

U = $50.84 + 4.92

I = $ 7.49 + 38.21

D = $ 3.04 + 84.98

W = $ 1.89 + 49.23

Name ____________________

Add 'Em Up!

Write the prices, then **add**. **Regroup**, when needed.

1. skateboard
   + ________ hat

2. dictionary
   + ________ radio

3. wallet
   + ________ goldfish

4. hot dog
   + ________ watch

5. dictionary
   + ________ kite

6. in-line skates
   + ________ trumpet

7. hot dog
   + ________ rocket

8. skateboard
   + ________ goldfish

9. hat
   + ________ kite

10. radio
    + ________ trumpet

11. rocket
    + ________ goldfish

12. skateboard
    + ________ in-line skates

Making Change

When you do not have the exact change to buy something at a store, the clerk must give you change. The first amount of money is what you give the clerk. The second amount is what the item costs. In the box, **list** the fewest number of coins and bills you will receive in change.

	Amount I Have	Cost of Item	Change
1	$3.75	$3.54	
2	$10.00	$5.63	
3	$7.00	$6.05	
4	$7.25	$6.50	
5	$7.50	$6.13	
6	$0.75	$0.37	
7	$7.00	$6.99	
8	$15.00	$12.75	

Name ______________________________

The Money Shuffle 

Cut out the game board on pages 295 and 297 and laminate it, if possible. To play the game, you will need two players. Place the gameboard on the floor or table top.

Player One takes his/her turn by placing a penny at the bottom of the paper and flicking it with his/her thumb and forefinger. The penny should land on a coin. (If it does not, Player One counts it as zero. Or, if desired, the player may "shoot" again.)

Player One must then remember that coin value while Player Two takes his/her turn and repeats the process. (If the players are still learning coin values, they may use paper and pencil.) Player One then receives a second turn. This time, however, Player One must add the new coin value to the coin value from his/her first turn. This procedure is repeated until one player makes a mental addition error and is "caught" by another player. His/her score returns to zero and the player must start all over. Players may use a calculator to help check the other players' sums.

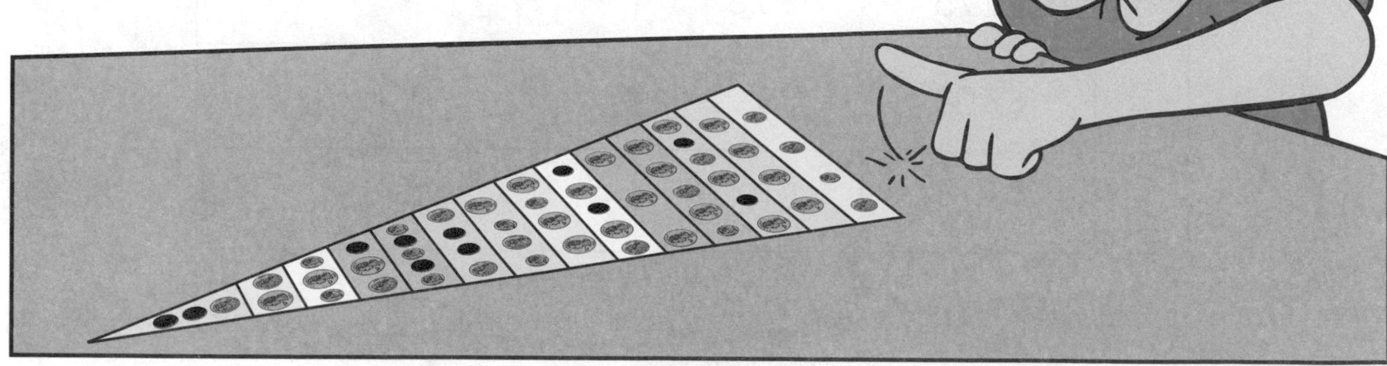

Name ______________________________

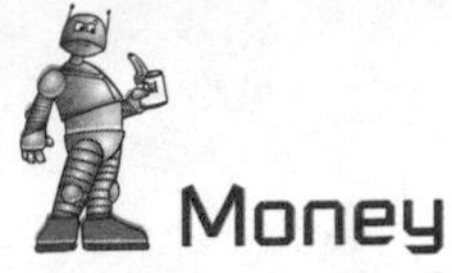

The Money Shuffle Gameboard

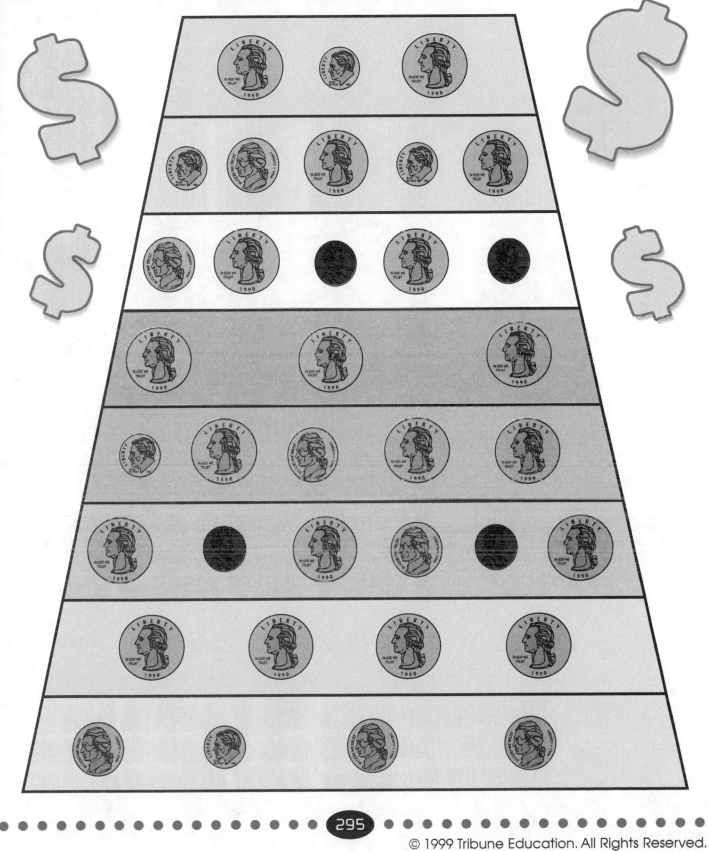

This page intentionally left blank.

Name ___________________________

The Money Shuffle Gameboard

This page intentionally left blank.

Name ____________________

Super Savers!

Add to find the amounts of money each person saved.

Sam's Account	Debbie's Account	Sarah's Account	Roberto's Account
\$8.03	\$45.32	\$85.42	
0.84	2.41	12.58	\$41.46
+ 5.47	+ 34.28	+ 2.21	+ 8.89

Alex's Account	Eva's Account	Bill's Account	Monica's Account
\$ 4.06	\$89.42	\$62.41	\$20.04
81.23	3.06	3.84	3.42
+ 2.84	+ 0.94	+ 64.21	+ 25.81

Tom's Account	Andy's Account	Earl's Account	Mark's Account
\$ 8.05	\$ 0.47	\$50.42	\$21.46
21.21	31.24	3.84	20.00
+ 0.98	+ 2.38	+ 0.98	+ 5.58

Katelyn's Account	Kimberly's Account
\$ 0.42	\$ 5.42
0.59	40.64
+ 3.42	+ 3.89

Whose account is the largest? ____________

Whose is the smallest? ____________

Whose is closest to \$50? ____________

Name ______________________________

Fast Food

Mealwormy is the latest restaurant of that famous fast food creator, Buggs I. Lyke. His Mealwormy Burger costs $1.69. An order of Roasted Roaches cost $0.59 for the regular size and $0.79 for the larger size. A Cricket Cola is $0.89.

1. You buy a Mealwormy Burger and a regular order of Roasted Roaches. What is the total?

2. Your teacher buys a Cricket Cola and a regular order of Roasted Roaches. What does it cost her?

3. Your mom goes to Mealwormy to buy your dinner. She spends $3.37. How much change does she get from a $5.00 bill?

4. Your best friend orders a Mealwormy Burger, a large order of Roasted Roaches and Cricket Cola. How much will it cost?

5. The principal is very hungry, so his bill comes to $14.37. How much change will he get from $20.00?

6. You have $1.17 in your bank. How much more do you need to pay for a Mealwormy Burger?

Name ____________________________

Spending Spree

Use the clues to figure out what each person bought. Then, **subtract** to find out how much change each had left.

$12.49 $9.31 $21.52 $13.45 $15.29 $2.43 $3.95 $52.28 $32.51 $47.29

		Clue:
1. David began with:	$40.25 – ______	He loves to see things zoom into the sky!
2. Mark started with:	$50.37 – ______	He likes to travel places with his hands free and a breeze in his face!
3. Eva started with:	$14.84 – ______	She loves to practice her jumping and exercise at the same time!
4. Bill brought:	$61.49 – ______	He wants to see the heavens for himself!
5. Michelle brought:	$40.29 ______	Fuzzy companions make such great friends!
6. Cheryl started with:	$16.80 – ______	She loves to hear music that is soft and beautiful!
7. Heather arrived with:	$20.48 – ______	She loves to put it down on paper for everyone to see!

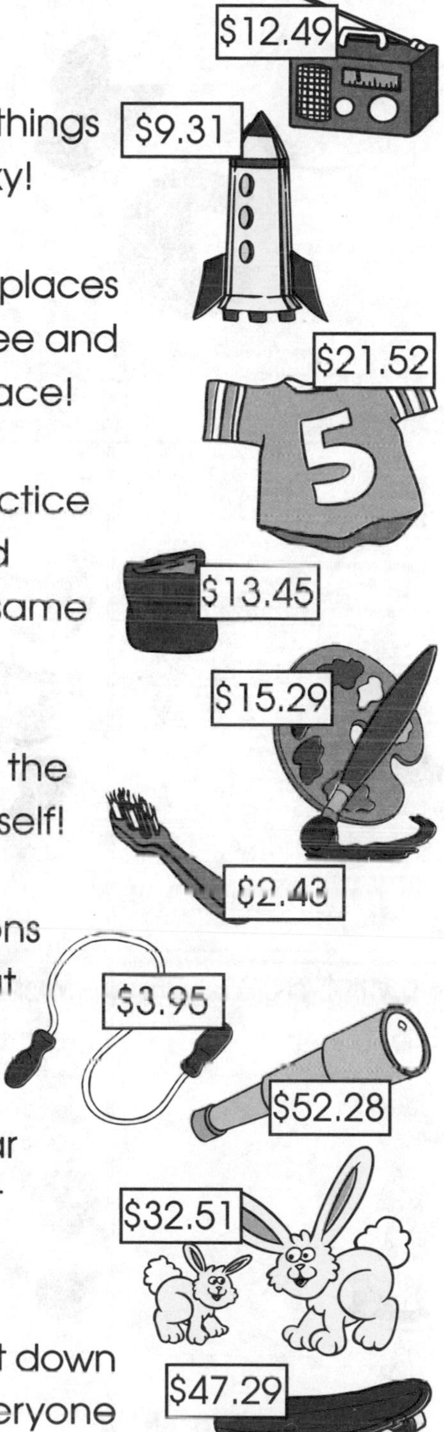

Name ____________________

One-Stop Shopping

Stash McCash is shopping. **Add** to find the total cost of the items. Then, **subtract** to find how much change Stash should receive.

Example:

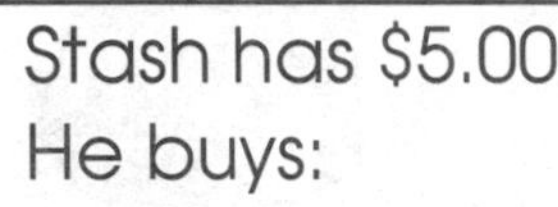

Stash has $5.00.
He buys:

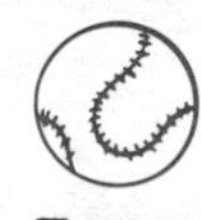

$ 0.88
0.77
\+ 1.54
$ 3.19

$ 5.00
− 3.19
$ 1.81 Change

Stash has $8.50.
He buys:

Change

Stash has $7.04.
He buys:

Change

Stash has $9.00.
He buys:

Change

Stash has $10.95.
He buys:

Change

Stash has $10.00.
He buys:

Change

Stash has $9.24.
He buys:

Change

Stash has $8.09.
He buys:

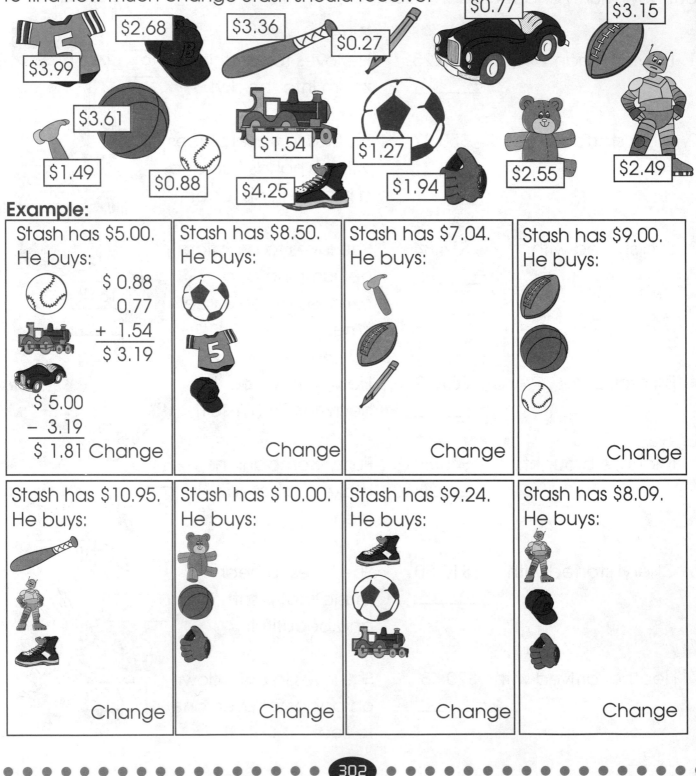

Change

Name ______________________________

Match the Sale

Which item did each child purchase? **Calculate** the amount. **Write** each purchase price below.

Jessica:	Tammy:	Heather:	Mark:	Eva:
\$17.43	\$43.21	\$10.06	\$52.46	\$65.04
– ______	– ______	– ______	– ______	– ______
\$9.14	\$34.86	\$1.64	\$14.17	\$36.94

Monica:	Katelyn:	David:	Curt:	Michele:
\$6.99	\$9.06	\$15.25	\$63.45	\$32.45
– ______	– ______	– ______	– ______	– ______
\$3.56	\$5.24	\$6.82	\$46.16	\$13.50

Gwen:	Thomas:
\$19.24	\$9.43
– ______	– ______
\$6.38	\$5.59

\$8.29 \$28.10 \$38.29 \$17.29 \$8.43 \$8.42 \$3.82 \$8.35 \$3.84 \$3.43 \$18.95 \$12.86

Frosted NEW OATS Cereal

ONE OF A KIND

What a Great Catch!

Solve these problems.

You buy fish A, C and H. Total cost: $2.47 2.18 + 2.54 $7.19	You have $4.00. You buy fish D. How much money is left?	You have $10.00. You buy fish E and J. How much money is left?
You buy 4 of fish I. Total cost:	You have $5.75. You buy fish G and C. How much money is left?	You buy fish D, F, J and B. Total cost:
You buy 6 of fish E. Total cost:	You buy 3 of fish J and 6 of fish D. Total cost:	You have $10.76. You buy 3 of fish A. How much money is left?

Name ______________________________

Dessert Included

Brenda and Doug really like chocolate—chocolate-covered raisins, chocolate candy, chocolate cake and hot chocolate! Most of all, they love chocolate sundaes with chocolate chip ice cream. When they find out that the Eats and Sweets Restaurant is offering a free chocolate dessert with any meal costing exactly $5.00, they decide to go there for dinner.

Menu

Meat		Potatoes/Vegetables	
Chicken	$1.95	Mashed Potatoes	$1.00
Roast Beef	$3.05	French Fries	$0.85
Shrimp	$3.50	Sweet Corn	$0.65
Roast Pork	$2.75	Green Beans	$0.50

Salad		Drinks	
Cole Slaw	$0.60	Milk	$0.40
Potato Salad	$0.95	Chocolate Milk	$0.45
Dinner Salad	$0.75	Orange Juice	$0.95
Macaroni Salad	$1.10	Soda Pop	$0.55

Choosing one item from each of the four categories, **list** four different meals Brenda and Doug could eat for exactly $5.00.

Meal # 1 ____________, ____________, ____________, ____________

Meal # 2 ____________, ____________, ____________, ____________

Meal # 3 ____________, ____________, ____________, ____________

Meal # 4 ____________, ____________, ____________, ____________

Name ________________________________

What's for Lunch?

Lunch Menu

Salad	$2.25	**Beverages**	
Hot Dog	$1.10	Milk	$0.50
Grilled cheese	$1.00	Orange Juice	$0.60
Pizza	$0.90	Soda	$0.75
Dessert			
Pudding	$0.90		
Ice Cream	$0.85		

Solve these problems.

1. Craig, Thomas and Laura stopped for lunch on their long trip. Craig had a late breakfast and only wanted some milk to drink. Thomas was feeling a little carsick, so he simply wanted a soda. Laura was very hungry. They spent a total of $4.25. What could Laura have had for lunch?

   ____

2. Beth and Michelle stopped for lunch during their busy day of shopping. They had worked up quite an appetite after all their bargain hunting! Beth exclaimed, "I'll buy you lunch today, Michelle. After all, you've helped me carry these packages all day!" "Thank you," Michelle replied. Beth reached into her pocket to be sure of the amount of money she had left. "Oh, no!" Beth cried, "I must have lost some money! I only have $3.50 left!" What could they have eaten for lunch?

   ____

3. Diane spent $1.60 on lunch. She was too full to get dessert. What could she have had for lunch?

   ____

4. The twins had too much pizza for dinner last night and certainly did not want it today. They each had the same meal, including pudding for dessert. They spent $5.50. What could they have eaten for lunch?

   ____

5. Sue is a vegetarian and she's allergic to milk. Bob ate two slices of pizza and a soda. Together, their lunch cost them $5.40. What did Sue have for lunch?

   ____

Name ______________________________

Multiplying Money

Money is multiplied in the same way other numbers are. The only difference is a dollar sign and a decimal point are added to the final product.

Steps:

1. Multiply by ones.
1. 4 x 8 = 32 (Carry the 3.)
2. 4 x 2 = 8 + 3 = 11 (Carry the 1.)
3. 4 x 4 = 16 + 1 = 17

```
   1 3
  $4.2 8
x    3 4
--------
 1 7 1 2
```

2. 1. Cross out the carried digits.
2. Add the zero.

```
  XX
 $4.2 8
x   3 4
-------
1 7 1 2
      0
```

3. Multiply by tens.
1. 3 x 8 = 24 (Carry the 2.)
2. 3 x 2 = 6 + 2 = 8
3. 3 x 4 = 12

```
       2
   $4. 2 8
x      3 4
----------
   1 7 1 2
 1 2 8 4 0
```

4. Add.
1,712 + 12,840 = 14,552

```
    $4. 2 8
 x      3 4
-----------
    1 7 1 2
+ 1 2 8 4 0
-----------
  1 4,5 5 2
```

5. Add the dollar sign and the decimal point.

```
    $4. 2 8
 x      3 4
-----------
    1 7 1 2
+ 1 2 8 4 0
-----------
  $1 4 5.5 2
```

Multiply.

```
 $3.4 2        $5.4 2
x   2 5       x   6 1
-------       -------

 $3.8 1        $8.2 0
x   4 6       x   5 5
-------       -------

 $9.4 2        $4.2 3
x   3 1       x   9 6
-------       -------
```

Name ____________________

Foxy Felix's Shop

Solve these problems.

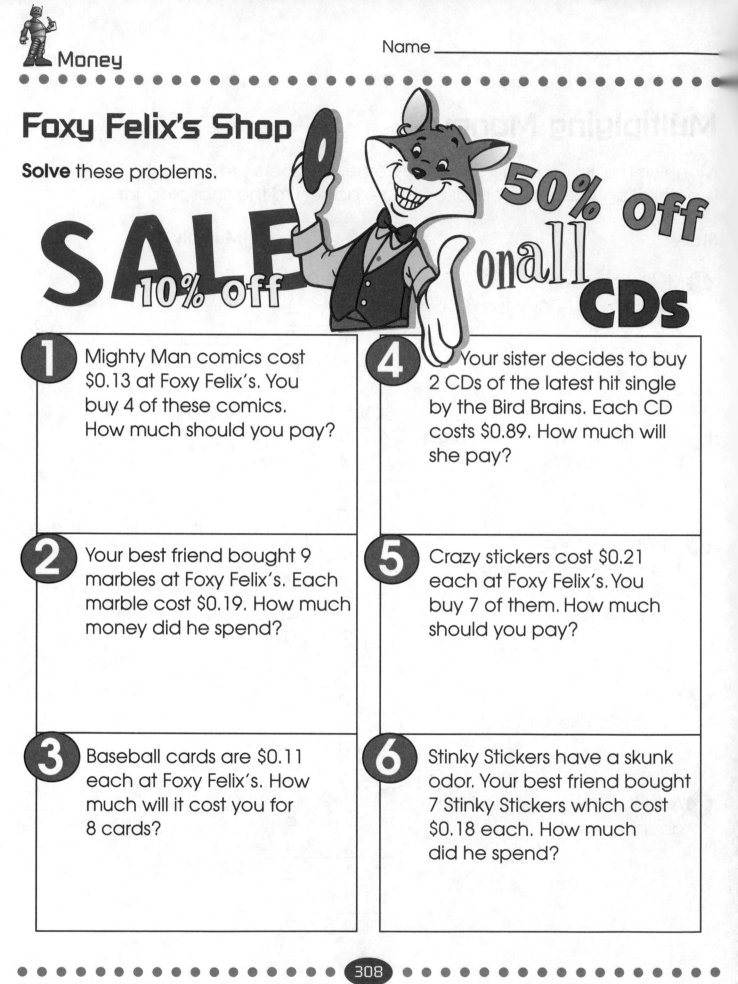

SALE
10% off
50% off
on all
CDs

1 Mighty Man comics cost $0.13 at Foxy Felix's. You buy 4 of these comics. How much should you pay?

2 Your best friend bought 9 marbles at Foxy Felix's. Each marble cost $0.19. How much money did he spend?

3 Baseball cards are $0.11 each at Foxy Felix's. How much will it cost you for 8 cards?

4 Your sister decides to buy 2 CDs of the latest hit single by the Bird Brains. Each CD costs $0.89. How much will she pay?

5 Crazy stickers cost $0.21 each at Foxy Felix's. You buy 7 of them. How much should you pay?

6 Stinky Stickers have a skunk odor. Your best friend bought 7 Stinky Stickers which cost $0.18 each. How much did he spend?

Money Math

Solve these problems. Remember the decimal point and dollar sign in your answers.

\$3.42 x 27	\$2.45 x 34	\$6.42 x 56	\$8.43 x 30
\$0.49 x 56	\$2.53 x 41	\$8.21 x 37	\$4.21 x 36
\$5.41 x 42	\$0.21 x 84	\$0.89 x 32	\$4.25 x 31

Name ____________________

Science Trip

The science class is planning a field trip to Chicago to visit the Museum of Science and Industry. There are 18 students in the class and each student needs $40.00 to cover the expenses. The class decided to sell candy to raise money.

Answer the questions using the chart below.

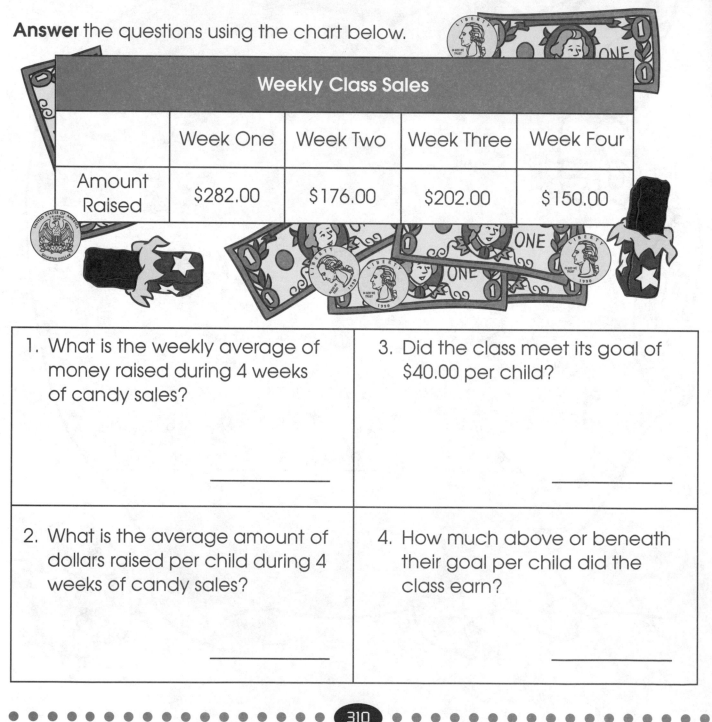

Weekly Class Sales				
	Week One	Week Two	Week Three	Week Four
Amount Raised	$282.00	$176.00	$202.00	$150.00

1. What is the weekly average of money raised during 4 weeks of candy sales?

   ____

2. What is the average amount of dollars raised per child during 4 weeks of candy sales?

   ____

3. Did the class meet its goal of $40.00 per child?

   ____

4. How much above or beneath their goal per child did the class earn?

   ____

Name ____________________

Too Much Information

Cross out the information not needed and **solve** the problems.

1. All 20 of the students from Sandy's class went to the movies. Tickets cost $3.50 each. Drinks cost $0.95 each. How much altogether did the students spend on tickets?

2. Five students had ice cream, 12 others had candy. Ice cream cost $0.75 per cup. How much did the students spend on ice cream?

3. Seven of the 20 students did not like the movie. Three of the 20 students had seen the movie before. How many students had not seen the movie before?

4. Six of the students spent a total of $16.50 for refreshments and $21.00 for their tickets. How much did each spend for refreshments?

5. Of the students, 11 were girls and 9 were boys. At $1.50 per ticket, how much did the boys' tickets cost altogether?

6. Mary paid $0.95 for an orange drink and $0.65 for a candy bar. Sarah paid $2.50 for popcorn. How much did Mary's refreshments cost her?

7. Ten of the students went back to see the movie again the next day. Each student paid $3.50 for a ticket, $2.50 for popcorn and $0.95 for a soft drink. How much did each student pay?

Name ______________________

Sam Sillicook's Donut Shop

Solve these problems.

1. Your mom bought 32 Jam-filled Cream Puffs. They cost $0.89 each. How much did your mom spend?

2. Harry D. Hulk bought 14 Banana Cream Donuts for his breakfast at $0.65 each. How much did they cost Harry?

3. Your best friend bought 12 Cinnamon Twists at $0.29 each. How much did he spend?

4. You love Jam-filled Cream Puffs. Your mother buys 17 for your birthday party at $0.89 each. How much do they cost?

5. Your dad decided to take the whole family out. He bought 24 Super Duper Jelly Donuts at $0.49 each. What was the total cost?

6. You took 40 Banana Cream Donuts to school. They cost $0.65 each. What was the total?

Name ____________________

Perplexing Problems

Solve these problems.

Mark, David, Curt and Jordan rented a motorized skateboard for 1 hour. What was the cost for each of them—split equally 4 ways? **Total:** $17.36 $ ________	Five students pitched in to buy Mr. Foley a birthday gift. How much did each of them contribute? **Total:** $9.60 $ ________	
Mary, Cheryl and Betty went to the skating rink. What was their individual cost? **Total:** $7.44 $ ________	Carol, Katelyn and Kimberly bought lunch at their favorite salad shop. What did each of them pay for lunch? **Total:** $12.63 $ ________	Debbie, Sarah, Michele and Kelly earned $6.56 altogether collecting cans. How much did each of them earn individually? **Total:** $6.56 $ ________
Five friends went to the Hot Spot Café for lunch. They all ordered the special. What did it cost? **Total:** $27.45 $ ________	Lee and Ricardo purchased an awesome model rocket together. What was the cost for each of them? **Total:** $9.52 $ ________	The total fee for Erik, Bill and Steve to enter the science museum was $8.76. What amount did each of them pay? **Total:** $8.76 $ ________

Name 

Let's Take a Trip!

You will plan a car trip to calculate approximately how much the trip will cost. You will calculate distances between locations and the amount of gasoline needed based upon miles per gallon of the car. Then, you will estimate the cost of the gasoline, hotel, food and entertainment.

Directions: Using graph paper, plot out your trip starting and ending at "point A." The trip should have five points of travel, including point A. Each square on the graph paper represents 10 miles. Calculate the mileage between points.

Use a copy of the **Expense Chart** on page 315 to keep track of your calculations. Use newspapers, travel brochures and menus to help you estimate the cost of food, gas, hotels, entertainment, etc. You will also want to use a calculator. When you have completed the **Expense Chart**, answer the questions below.

1. If two people go on this trip, how will the cost change? ________________
2. If a family of four goes on the trip, how will the cost change? ____________
3. Would the cost of gas change? ______________________________

   Why or why not? ______________________________
4. What else could change the cost of the trip? ________________
5. Why is this just an estimate?______________________________

____

Name ______________________________

Expense Chart

Distance to travel

Miles from Point A to Point B: ____________

Miles from Point B to Point C: ____________

Miles from Point C to Point D: ____________

Miles from Point D to Point E: ____________

Miles from Point E to Point A: ____________

Total miles to travel: ____________

Your car gets 22 miles per gallon of gas.

Total gas needed: ____________

Gas costs $1.19 per gallon.

Total amount needed for gas: ____________

You will stay at a hotel/motel for four nights at $79.00 per night.

Total cost for four nights: ____________

Estimated food cost per day (5 days)

breakfast—$2.50

lunch —$4.75

dinner—$9.25

Total per day: ____________

Total for 5 days: ____________

Estimated entertainment expenses

Admission to movies: ____________

Admission to museums: ____________

Admission to theme parks: ____________

Admission to sports events: ____________

Add all the entries to get a total estimate for the cost of the trip.

Total estimated cost of the trip: ______________________________

Name ______________________________

Mind-Bogglers

Solve these problems. Then, explain your strategies.

1. Marta receives an allowance of $2.25 a week. This week, her mom pays her in nickels, dimes and quarters. She received more dimes than quarters.

   What coins did her mom use to pay her? ______________________

   Strategy I used: ______________________________

2. Mr. Whitman takes his family on a trip to the amusement park. He brings $75 with him to buy the entrance tickets, food and souvenirs for the family. The tickets to get into the amusement park are $12.75 for adults and $8.45 for children. How much money will Mr. Whitman have for food and souvenirs after he buys entrance tickets for himself, Mrs. Whitman and their two children?

   Amount of money? ______________

   Strategy I used: ______________________________

3. There are four children who worked at the car wash. Kelly worked 4 hours. Jack worked for 3 hours. Matt and Tammy worked for 2 hours. They made $110.

   How much of that did Kelly earn?__________

   Jack?__________ Matt and Tammy?__________

   Strategy I used: ______________________________

4. Mrs. Downs gives her three children a weekly allowance. She pays them in dollar bills. Lauren is the first to get paid. She receives half the number of dollar bills her mom has. Don gets his allowance second. He receives half of the remaining dollar bills plus one. Mrs. Downs now has $2 left, which is Edith's allowance. How much allowance do Lauren and Don receive?

   Lauren __________ Don __________

   Strategy I used: ______________________________

Glossary

Acute angle: Any angle that is less than a right angle or 90°.
Angle: The part of a shape where two lines come together.
Area: The number of square units needed to cover a flat surface.
Average: A number that tells about how something is normally. Find an average by adding all the numbers together and dividing by the number of addends.
Capacity: The measure of how much can fit inside an object.
Circle: A round, closed figure.
Common denominator: One number that is a common multiple of two or more denominators.
Congruent figures: Figures that have the same shape and size.
Decimal: A dot placed between the ones place and the tenths place in a number.
Denominator: The bottom number of a fraction that numbers the total amount of equal pieces.
Diameter: A line segment with both points on the circle, which always passes through the center of the circles.
Difference: The answer in a subtraction problem.
Dividend: The number to be divided in a division problem.
Divisor: The number to divide by in a division problem.
Equivalent fractions: Two different fractions that represent the same number.
Factors: The two numbers multiplied together in a multiplication problem.
Fraction: One or more equal parts of a whole or part of a group.
Improper fractions: A fraction representing a whole and a fraction. The numerator is larger than the denominator.

Like Fractions: Fractions with the same denominator.
Mixed number: A number made up of a whole number and a fraction.
Multiplication: A quick way to add.
Numerator: The top number of a fraction that numbers the parts.
Obtuse angle: Any angle that is more than a right angle or 90°.
Ordered pair: A set of numbers used to find a point on a grid.
Perimeter: The distance around the outside of a shape.
Pictograph: A graph using pictures to give information.
Place value: The value of a numeral determined by its place in a number.
Polygon: A closed shape with straight sides.
Probability: The chance that a given event will happen.
Product: The answer in a multiplication problem.
Quotient: The answer in a division problem.
Radius: A line segment from the center of a circle to any point on the circle.
Regrouping: Borrowing or carrying numbers between places.
Remainder: The amount left over after dividing a number.
Right angle: Any angle that measures 90°. It forms a square corner.
Rounding: Changing an exact amount to an estimate of the number.
Sum: The answer in an addition problem.
Survey: A mini-interview of many people to find out what they like or do not like.
Symmetry: A figure with two parts that match exactly.
Tally mark: A line to represent one. The fifth tally of any grouping is written diagonally over the first four marks. **Example:** ~~||||~~
Temperature: The measure of how warm or cold something is.
Unlike fractions: Fractions with different denominators.
Volume: The measure of the inside of a shape.

Answer Key

The Complete Book of Math Grades 3–4

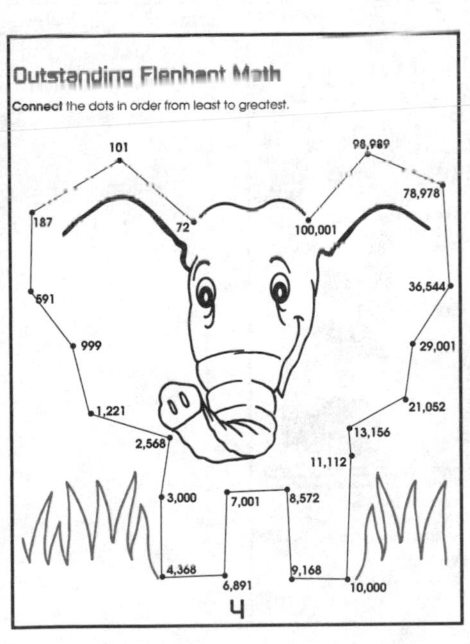

Outstanding Elephant Math

Connect the dots in order from least to greatest.

4

Place Value Riddles

Using the clues below, choose the number each riddle describes. As you read, draw an **X** on all the numbers that do not fit the clue. After you have read all the clues for each riddle, there should be only one number left.

(3005)

1. I am greater than 300.
2. I have a 5 in the ones place.
3. I have a zero in the hundreds place.
4. Circle the number.

(3,691)

1. I have a number greater than 6 in the tens place.
2. I am between 3,000 and 4,000.
3. I have a 6 in the hundreds place.
4. Circle the number.

(324)

1. I have a 2 in the tens place.
2. I am less than 1,000.
3. I have a 4 in the ones place.
4. Circle the number.

(5048)

1. I have a 4 in the tens place.
2. I am greater than 5,000.
3. I have a 0 in the hundreds place.
4. Circle the number.

Now, fold a blank sheet of paper in half three times to create eight boxes. Create eight of these place value riddles. You may want to use words like these when writing your clues:
ones, tens, hundreds ...
greater ...
less than ...
have a ___ somewhere

Answers will vary.

5

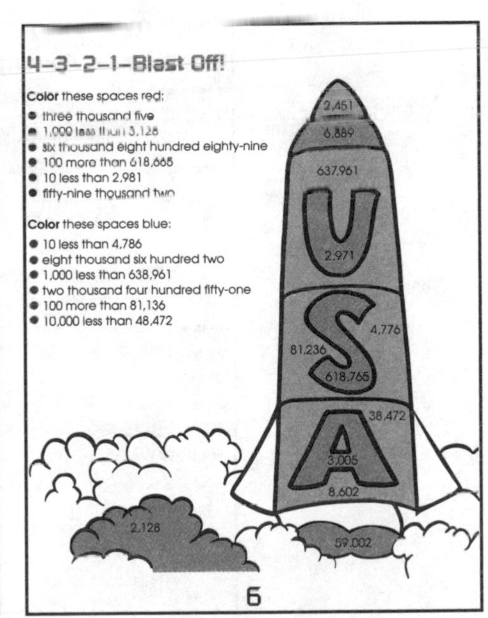

4–3–2–1–Blast Off!

Color these spaces red:

- three thousand five
- 1,000 less than 3,128
- six thousand eight hundred eighty-nine
- 100 more than 618,665
- 10 less than 2,981
- fifty-nine thousand two

Color these spaces blue:

- 10 less than 4,786
- eight thousand six hundred two
- 1,000 less than 638,961
- two thousand four hundred fifty-one
- 100 more than 81,136
- 10,000 less than 48,472

6

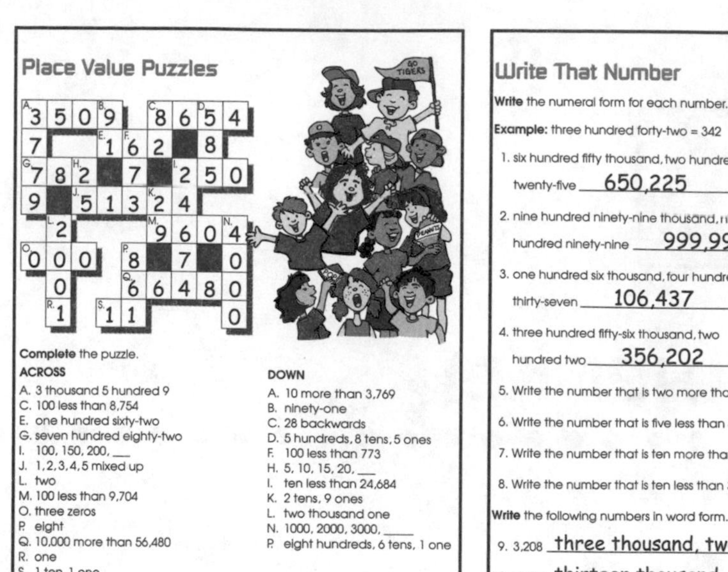

Place Value Puzzles

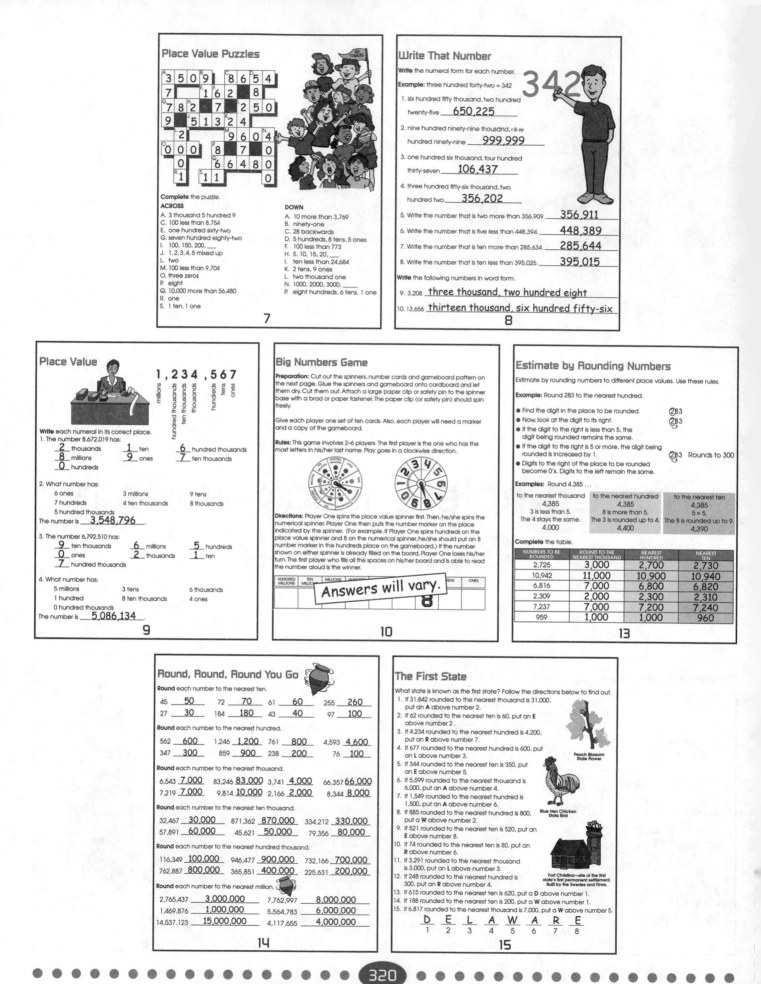

Complete the puzzle.

ACROSS
A. 3 thousand 5 hundred 9
C. 100 less than 8,754
E. one hundred sixty-two
G. seven hundred eighty-two
I. 100, 150, 200, ___
J. 1, 2, 3, 4, 5 mixed up
L. two
M. 100 less than 9,704
O. three zeros
P. eight
Q. 10,000 more than 56,480
R. one
S. 1 ten, 1 one

DOWN
A. 10 more than 3,769
B. ninety-one
C. 28 backwards
D. 5 hundreds, 8 tens, 5 ones
F. 100 less than 773
H. 5, 10, 15, 20, ___
I. ten less than 24,684
K. 2 tens, 9 ones
L. two thousand one
N. 1000, 2000, 3000, ____
P. eight hundreds, 6 tens, 1 one

7

Write That Number

Write the numeral form for each number.

Example: three hundred forty-two = 342

1. six hundred fifty thousand, two hundred twenty-five 650,225
2. nine hundred ninety-nine thousand, nine hundred ninety-nine 999,999
3. one hundred six thousand, four hundred thirty-seven 106,437
4. three hundred fifty-six thousand, two hundred two 356,202
5. Write the number that is two more than 356,909. 356,911
6. Write the number that is five less than 448,394. 448,389
7. Write the number that is ten more than 285,634. 285,644
8. Write the number that is ten less than 395,025. 395,015

Write the following numbers in word form.

9. 3,208 three thousand, two hundred eight
10. 13,656 thirteen thousand, six hundred fifty-six

8

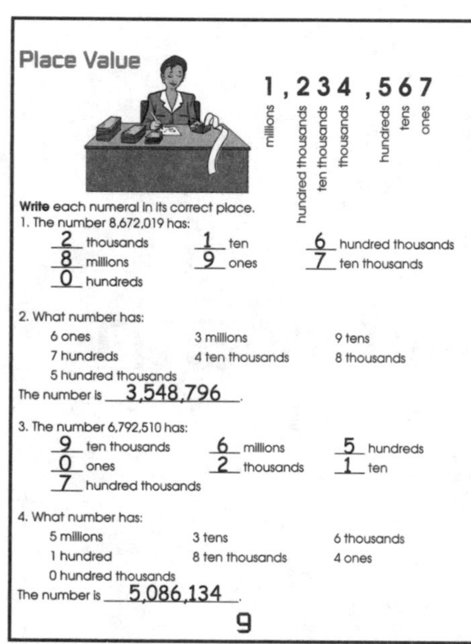

Place Value

1,234,567 — millions, hundred thousands, ten thousands, thousands, hundreds, tens, ones

Write each numeral in its correct place.

1. The number 8,672,019 has:
2 thousands, 8 millions, 0 hundreds, 1 ten, 9 ones, 6 hundred thousands, 7 ten thousands

2. What number has:
6 ones, 7 hundreds, 5 hundred thousands, 3 millions, 4 ten thousands, 9 tens, 8 thousands
The number is 3,548,796.

3. The number 6,792,510 has:
9 ten thousands, 0 ones, 7 hundred thousands, 6 millions, 2 thousands, 5 hundreds, 1 ten

4. What number has:
5 millions, 1 hundred, 0 hundred thousands, 3 tens, 8 ten thousands, 6 thousands, 4 ones
The number is 5,086,134.

9

Big Numbers Game

Preparation: Cut out the spinners, number cards and gameboard pattern on the next page. Glue the spinners and gameboard onto cardboard and let them dry. Cut them out. Attach a large paper clip or safety pin to the spinner base with a brad or paper fastener. The paper clip (or safety pin) should spin freely.

Give each player one set of ten cards. Also, each player will need a marker and a copy of the gameboard.

Rules: This game involves 2–6 players. The first player is the one who has the most letters in his/her last name. Play goes in a clockwise direction.

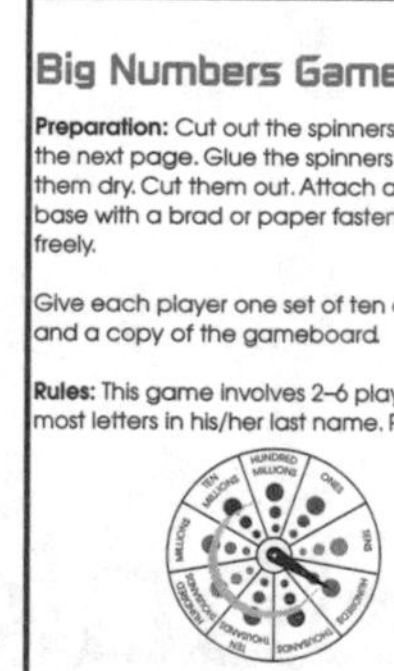

Directions: Player One spins the place value spinner first. Then, he/she spins the numerical spinner. Player One then puts the number marker on the place indicated by the spinner. (For example, if Player One spins hundreds on the place value spinner and 8 on the numerical spinner, he/she should put an 8 number marker in the hundreds place on the gameboard.) If the number shown on either spinner is already filled on the board, Player One loses his/her turn. The first player who fills all the spaces on his/her board and is able to read the number aloud is the winner.

HUNDRED MILLIONS
TEN MILLIONS
MILLIONS
TENS
ONES
Answers will vary.

10

Estimate by Rounding Numbers

Estimate by rounding numbers to different place values. Use these rules.

Example: Round 283 to the nearest hundred.

- Find the digit in the place to be rounded. 283
- Now, look at the digit to its right. 283
- If the digit to the right is less than 5, the digit being rounded remains the same.
- If the digit to the right is 5 or more, the digit being rounded is increased by 1. 283 Rounds to 300
- Digits to the right of the place to be rounded become 0's. Digits to the left remain the same.

Examples: Round 4,385 . . .

to the nearest thousand	to the nearest hundred	to the nearest ten
4,385 3 is less than 5. The 4 stays the same. 4,000	4,385 8 is more than 5. The 3 is rounded up to 4. 4,400	4,385 5 = 5. The 8 is rounded up to 9. 4,390

Complete the table.

NUMBERS TO BE ROUNDED	ROUND TO THE NEAREST THOUSAND	NEAREST HUNDRED	NEAREST TEN
2,725	3,000	2,700	2,730
10,942	11,000	10,900	10,940
6,816	7,000	6,800	6,820
2,309	2,000	2,300	2,310
7,237	7,000	7,200	7,240
959	1,000	1,000	960

13

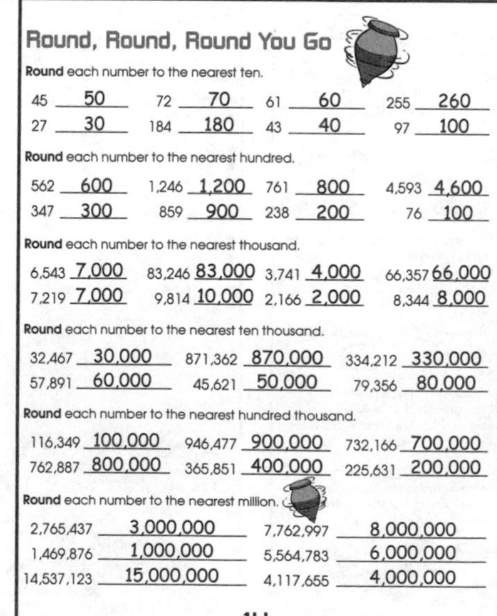

Round, Round, Round You Go

Round each number to the nearest ten.

45 50 · 72 70 · 61 60 · 255 260
27 30 · 184 180 · 43 40 · 97 100

Round each number to the nearest hundred.

562 600 · 1,246 1,200 · 761 800 · 4,593 4,600
347 300 · 859 900 · 238 200 · 76 100

Round each number to the nearest thousand.

6,543 7,000 · 83,246 83,000 · 3,741 4,000 · 66,357 66,000
7,219 7,000 · 9,814 10,000 · 2,166 2,000 · 8,344 8,000

Round each number to the nearest ten thousand.

32,467 30,000 · 871,362 870,000 · 334,212 330,000
57,891 60,000 · 45,621 50,000 · 79,356 80,000

Round each number to the nearest hundred thousand.

116,349 100,000 · 946,477 900,000 · 732,166 700,000
762,887 800,000 · 365,851 400,000 · 225,631 200,000

Round each number to the nearest million.

2,765,437 3,000,000 · 7,762,997 8,000,000
1,469,876 1,000,000 · 5,564,783 6,000,000
14,537,123 15,000,000 · 4,117,655 4,000,000

14

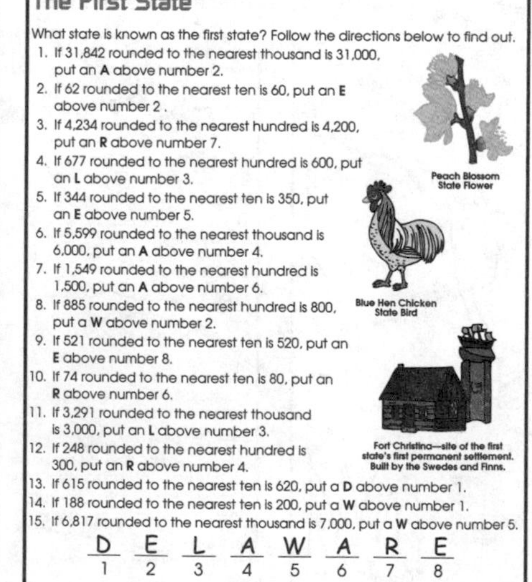

The First State

What state is known as the first state? Follow the directions below to find out.

1. If 31,842 rounded to the nearest thousand is 31,000, put an **A** above number 2.
2. If 62 rounded to the nearest ten is 60, put an **E** above number 2.
3. If 4,234 rounded to the nearest hundred is 4,200, put an **R** above number 7.
4. If 677 rounded to the nearest hundred is 600, put an **L** above number 3.
5. If 344 rounded to the nearest ten is 350, put an **E** above number 5.
6. If 5,599 rounded to the nearest thousand is 6,000, put an **A** above number 4.
7. If 1,549 rounded to the nearest hundred is 1,500, put an **A** above number 6.
8. If 885 rounded to the nearest hundred is 800, put a **W** above number 2.
9. If 521 rounded to the nearest ten is 520, put an **E** above number 8.
10. If 74 rounded to the nearest ten is 80, put an **R** above number 6.
11. If 3,291 rounded to the nearest thousand is 3,000, put an **L** above number 3.
12. If 248 rounded to the nearest hundred is 300, put an **R** above number 4.
13. If 615 rounded to the nearest ten is 620, put a **D** above number 1.
14. If 188 rounded to the nearest ten is 200, put a **W** above number 1.
15. If 6,817 rounded to the nearest thousand is 7,000, put a **W** above number 5.

Peach Blossom State Flower

Blue Hen Chicken State Bird

Fort Christina—site of the first state's first permanent settlement. Built by the Swedes and Finns.

D	E	L	A	W	A	R	E
1	2	3	4	5	6	7	8

15

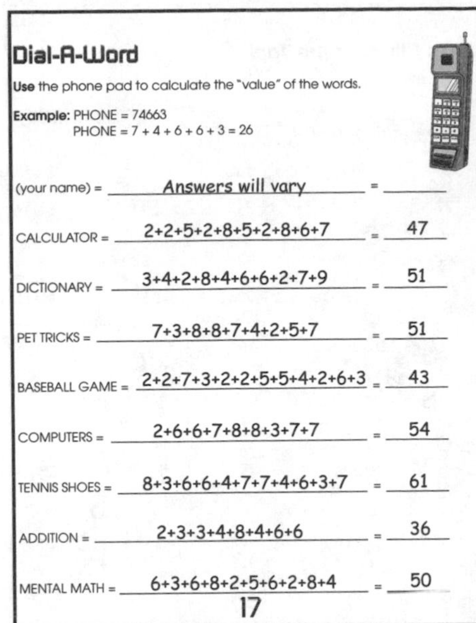

Dial-A-Word

Use the phone pad to calculate the "value" of the words.

Example: PHONE = 74663
PHONE = 7 + 4 + 6 + 6 + 3 = 26

(your name) =	Answers will vary	=
CALCULATOR =	2+2+5+2+8+5+2+8+6+7	= 47
DICTIONARY =	3+4+2+8+4+6+6+2+7+9	= 51
PET TRICKS =	7+3+8+8+7+4+2+5+7	= 51
BASEBALL GAME =	2+2+7+3+2+2+5+5+4+2+6+3	= 43
COMPUTERS =	2+6+6+7+8+8+3+7+7	= 54
TENNIS SHOES =	8+3+6+6+4+7+7+4+6+3+7	= 61
ADDITION =	2+3+3+4+8+4+6+6	= 36
MENTAL MATH =	6+3+6+8+2+5+6+2+8+4	= 50

17

Using Number Concepts

Cut out the set of cards on the next page. Use them to form number sentences that answer the questions below.

Sample answers below.

1. Use only two cards to list all the ways you can make the sum of 10.
   There are 11 different combinations.
   6 + 4 = 10 3 + 7 = 10 4 + 6 = 10 7 + 3 = 10
2. Use only two cards to list all the ways you can make the sum of 13.
   14 combinations
   8 + 5 = 13 10 + 3 = 13
3. Use only two cards to list all the ways you can make the sum of 16.
   17 combinations
4. Use only two cards to list all the ways you can make the sum of 12.
   13 combinations
5. Use only two cards to list all the ways you can make the sum of 15.
   16 combinations
6. Use only two cards to list all the ways you can make the sum of 17.
   18 combinations
7. How did you know you found all the ways?
   Answers will vary.

Extension: Repeat this exercise using three cards to make each sum.

18

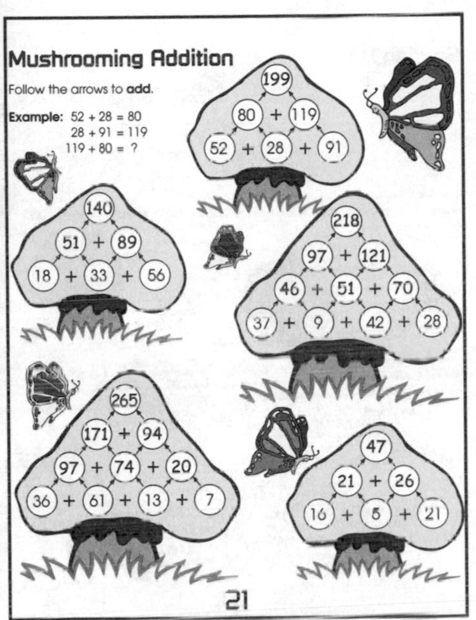

Mushrooming Addition

Follow the arrows to **add**.

Example: 52 + 28 = 80
28 + 91 = 119
119 + 80 = ?

21

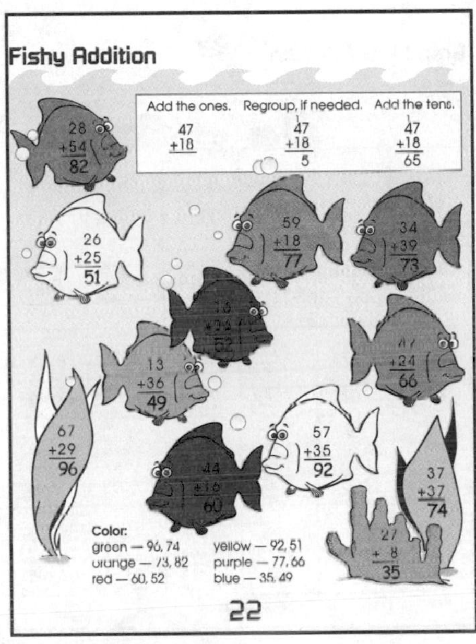

Fishy Addition

Add the ones.	Regroup, if needed.	Add the tens.
47 + 18	47 + 18 = 5	47 + 18 = 65

Color:
green — 96, 74 yellow — 92, 51
orange — 73, 82 purple — 77, 66
red — 60, 52 blue — 35, 49

22

Make the Windows Shine!

Add.

476 + 319 = 795
248 + 629 = 877
327 + 544 = 871
572 + 318 = 890
815 + 177 = 992
527 + 144 = 671
429 + 343 = 772
462 + 319 = 781
462 + 529 = 991
648 + 238 = 886
756 + 127 = 883
563 + 208 = 771
646 + 248 = 894
924 + 66 = 990
628 + 259 = 887
526 + 347 = 873
927 + 46 = 973
765 + 218 = 983

23

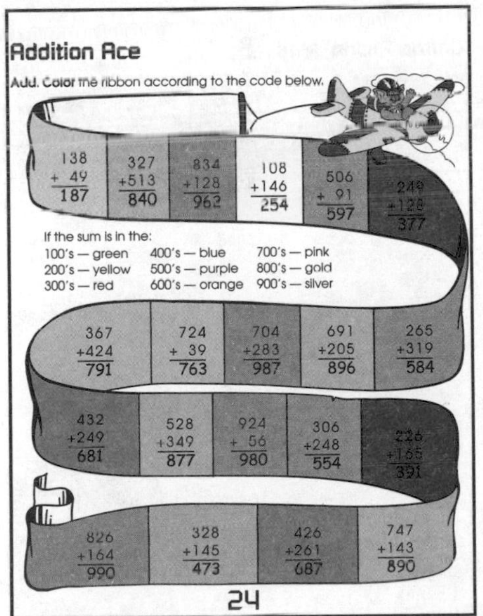

Addition Ace

Add. Color the ribbon according to the code below.

138 + 49 = 187
327 + 513 = 840
834 + 128 = 962
108 + 146 = 254
506 + 91 = 597
249 + 128 = 377
367 + 424 = 791
724 + 39 = 763
704 + 283 = 987
691 + 205 = 896
265 + 319 = 584
432 + 249 = 681
528 + 349 = 877
924 + 56 = 980
306 + 248 = 554
226 + 165 = 391
826 + 164 = 990
328 + 145 = 473
426 + 261 = 687
747 + 143 = 890

If the sum is in the:
100's — green 400's — blue 700's — pink
200's — yellow 500's — purple 800's — gold
300's — red 600's — orange 900's — silver

24

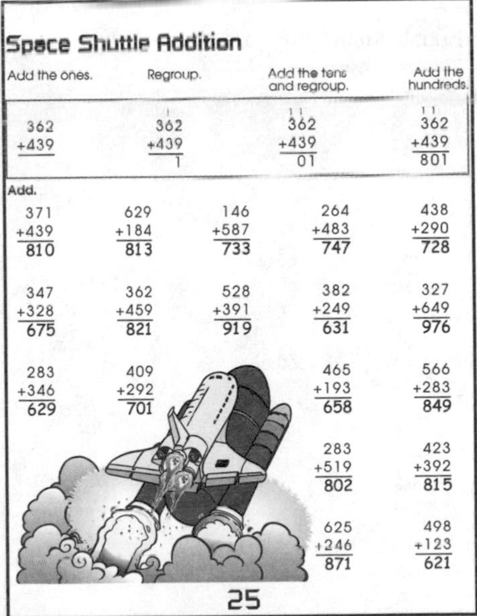

Space Shuttle Addition

Add the ones.	Regroup.	Add the tens and regroup.	Add the hundreds.
362 + 439	362 + 439 = 1	362 + 439 = 01	362 + 439 = 801

Add.

371 + 439 = 810	629 + 184 = 813	146 + 587 = 733	264 + 483 = 747	438 + 290 = 728
347 + 328 = 675	362 + 459 = 821	528 + 391 = 919	382 + 249 = 631	327 + 649 = 976
283 + 346 = 629	409 + 292 = 701		465 + 193 = 658	566 + 283 = 849
			283 + 519 = 802	423 + 392 = 815
			625 + 246 = 871	498 + 123 = 621

25

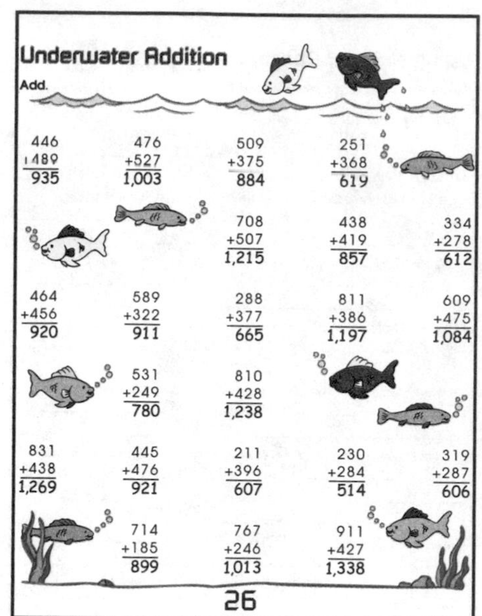

Underwater Addition

Add.

446 + 489 = 935; 476 + 527 = 1,003; 509 + 375 = 884; 251 + 368 = 619

708 + 507 = 1,215; 438 + 419 = 857; 334 + 278 = 612

464 + 456 = 920; 589 + 322 = 911; 288 + 377 = 665; 811 + 386 = 1,197; 609 + 475 = 1,084

531 + 249 = 780; 810 + 428 = 1,238

831 + 438 = 1,269; 445 + 476 = 921; 211 + 396 = 607; 230 + 284 = 514; 319 + 287 = 606

714 + 185 = 899; 767 + 246 = 1,013; 911 + 427 = 1,338

26

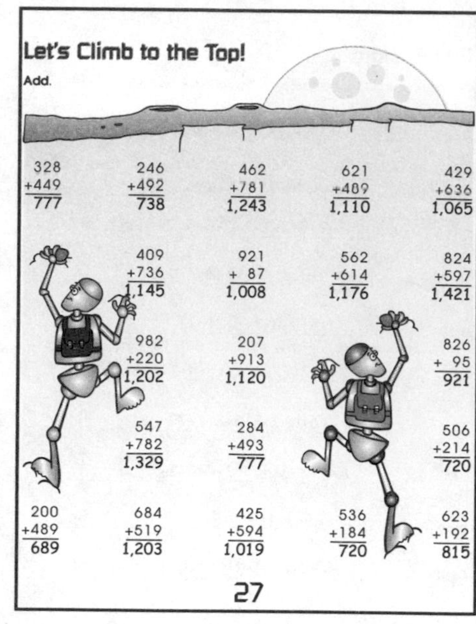

Let's Climb to the Top!

Add.

328 + 449 = 777; 246 + 492 = 738; 462 + 781 = 1,243; 621 + 489 = 1,110; 429 + 636 = 1,065

409 + 736 = 1,145; 921 + 87 = 1,008; 562 + 614 = 1,176; 824 + 597 = 1,421

982 + 220 = 1,202; 207 + 913 = 1,120; 826 + 95 = 921

547 + 782 = 1,329; 284 + 493 = 777; 506 + 214 = 720

200 + 489 = 689; 684 + 519 = 1,203; 425 + 594 = 1,019; 536 + 184 = 720; 623 + 192 = 815

27

Picnic Problems

Help the ant find a path to the picnic. **Solve** the problems. **Shade** the box if an answer has a 9 in it.

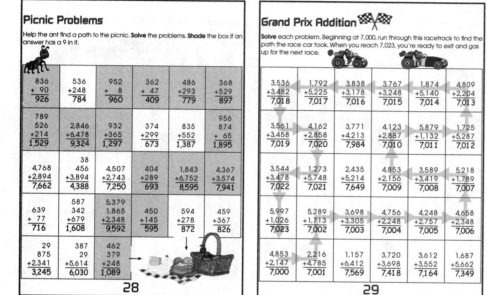

836 + 90 = 926	536 + 248 = 784	952 + 8 = 960	362 + 47 = 409	486 + 293 = 779	368 + 529 = 897
789 + 526 + 214 = 1,529	2,846 + 6,478 = 9,324	932 + 365 = 1,297	374 + 299 = 673	835 + 552 = 1,387	956 + 874 + 65 = 1,895
4,768 + 2,894 = 7,662	38 + 456 + 3,894 = 4,388	4,507 + 2,743 = 7,250	404 + 289 = 693	1,843 + 6,752 = 8,595	4,367 + 3,574 = 7,941
639 + 77 = 716	587 + 342 + 679 = 1,608	5,379 + 1,865 + 2,348 = 9,592	450 + 145 = 595	594 + 278 = 872	459 + 367 = 826
29 + 875 + 2,341 = 3,245	387 + 29 + 5,614 = 6,030	462 + 379 + 248 = 1,089			

28

Grand Prix Addition

Solve each problem. Beginning at 7,000, run through this racetrack to find the path the race car took. When you reach 7,023, you're ready to exit and gas up for the next race.

3,536 + 3,482 = 7,018	1,792 + 5,225 = 7,017	3,838 + 3,178 = 7,016	3,767 + 3,248 = 7,015	1,874 + 5,140 = 7,014	4,809 + 2,204 = 7,013
3,561 + 3,458 = 7,019	4,162 + 2,858 = 7,020	3,771 + 4,213 = 7,984	4,123 + 2,887 = 7,010	5,879 + 1,132 = 7,011	1,725 + 5,287 = 7,012
3,544 + 3,478 = 7,022	1,273 + 5,748 = 7,021	2,435 + 5,214 = 7,649	4,853 + 2,156 = 7,009	3,589 + 3,419 = 7,008	5,218 + 1,789 = 7,007
5,997 + 1,026 = 7,023	5,289 + 1,713 = 7,002	3,698 + 3,305 = 7,003	4,756 + 2,248 = 7,004	4,248 + 2,757 = 7,005	4,658 + 2,348 = 7,006
4,853 + 2,147 = 7,000	2,216 + 4,785 = 7,001	1,157 + 6,412 = 7,569	3,720 + 3,698 = 7,418	3,612 + 3,552 = 7,164	1,687 + 5,662 = 7,349

29

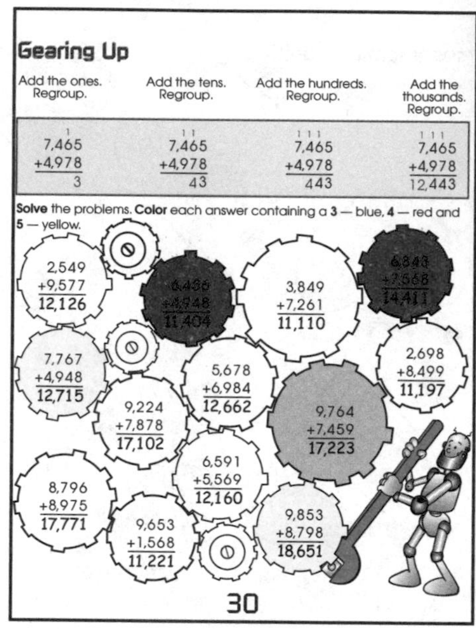

Gearing Up

Add the ones. Regroup.	Add the tens. Regroup.	Add the hundreds. Regroup.	Add the thousands. Regroup.
7,465 + 4,978 = 3	7,465 + 4,978 = 43	7,465 + 4,978 = 443	7,465 + 4,978 = 12,443

Solve the problems. **Color** each answer containing a **3** — blue, **4** — red and **5** — yellow.

2,549 + 9,577 = 12,126; 6,436 + 4,968 = 11,404; 3,849 + 7,261 = 11,110; 6,843 + 7,568 = 14,411; 7,767 + 4,948 = 12,715; 5,678 + 6,984 = 12,662; 2,698 + 8,499 = 11,197; 9,224 + 7,878 = 17,102; 9,764 + 7,459 = 17,223; 6,591 + 5,569 = 12,160; 8,796 + 8,975 = 17,771; 9,653 + 1,568 = 11,221; 9,853 + 8,798 = 18,651

30

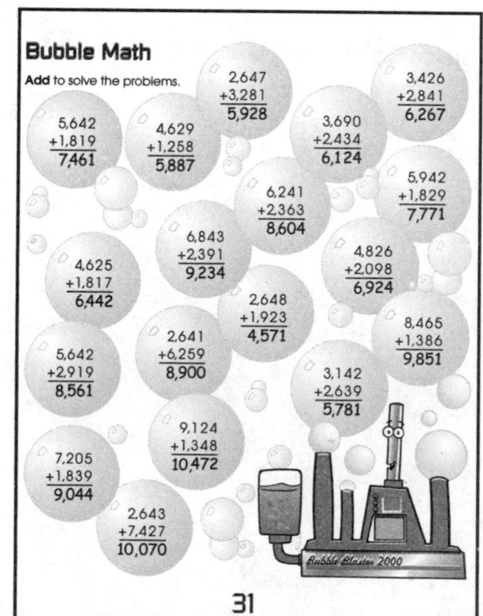

Bubble Math

Add to solve the problems.

2,647 + 3,281 = 5,928; 3,426 + 2,841 = 6,267; 5,642 + 1,819 = 7,461; 4,629 + 1,258 = 5,887; 3,690 + 2,434 = 6,124; 5,942 + 1,829 = 7,771; 6,241 + 2,363 = 8,604; 6,843 + 2,391 = 9,234; 4,826 + 2,098 = 6,924; 4,625 + 1,817 = 6,442; 2,648 + 1,923 = 4,571; 8,465 + 1,386 = 9,851; 5,642 + 2,919 = 8,561; 2,641 + 6,259 = 8,900; 3,142 + 2,639 = 5,781; 9,124 + 1,348 = 10,472; 7,205 + 1,839 = 9,044; 2,643 + 7,427 = 10,070

31

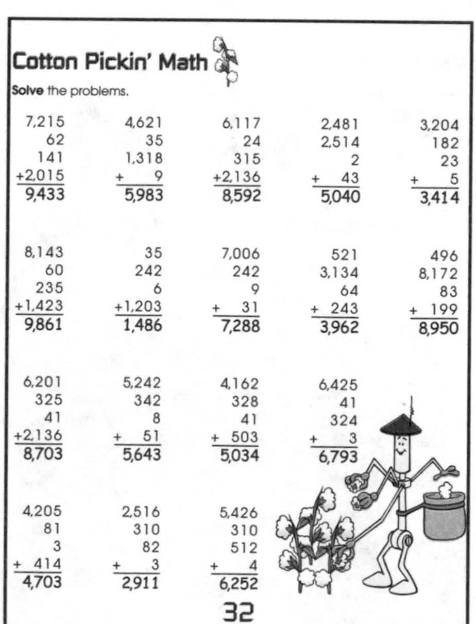

Cotton Pickin' Math

Solve the problems.

7,215 + 62 + 141 + 2,015 = 9,433; 4,621 + 35 + 1,318 + 9 = 5,983; 6,117 + 24 + 315 + 2,136 = 8,592; 2,481 + 2,514 + 2 + 43 = 5,040; 3,204 + 182 + 23 + 5 = 3,414

8,143 + 60 + 235 + 1,423 = 9,861; 35 + 242 + 6 + 1,203 = 1,486; 7,006 + 242 + 9 + 31 = 7,288; 521 + 3,134 + 64 + 243 = 3,962; 496 + 8,172 + 83 + 199 = 8,950

6,201 + 325 + 41 + 2,136 = 8,703; 5,242 + 342 + 8 + 51 = 5,643; 4,162 + 328 + 41 + 503 = 5,034; 6,425 + 41 + 324 + 3 = 6,793

4,205 + 81 + 3 + 414 = 4,703; 2,516 + 310 + 82 + 3 = 2,911; 5,426 + 310 + 512 + 4 = 6,252

32

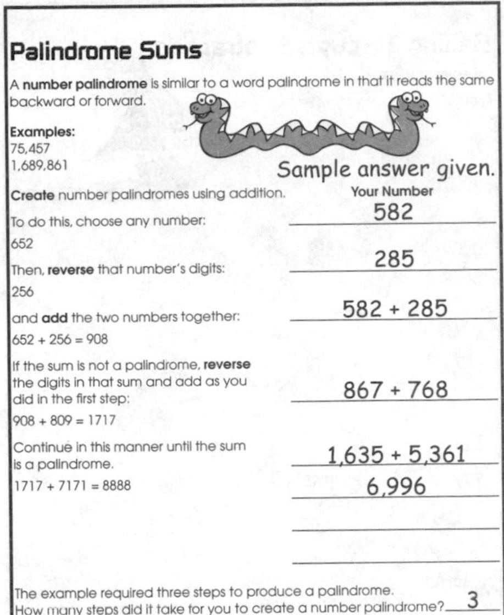

Palindrome Sums

A **number palindrome** is similar to a word palindrome in that it reads the same backward or forward.

Examples:
75,457
1,689,861

Sample answer given.

Create number palindromes using addition.

	Your Number
To do this, choose any number: 652	582
Then, **reverse** that number's digits: 256	285
and **add** the two numbers together: 652 + 256 = 908	582 + 285
If the sum is not a palindrome, **reverse** the digits in that sum and add as you did in the first step: 908 + 809 = 1717	867 + 768
Continue in this manner until the sum is a palindrome. 1717 + 7171 = 8888	1,635 + 5,361
	6,996

The example required three steps to produce a palindrome.
How many steps did it take for you to create a number palindrome? 3

33

Mountaintop Getaway

Solve the problems. **Find** a path to the cabin by shading in all answers that have a 3 in them.

			98 − 52 = 46	46 − 12 = 34	68 − 17 = 51
		79 − 53 = 26	65 − 23 = 42	63 − 31 = 32	86 − 32 = 54
	59 − 45 = 14	75 − 64 = 11	67 − 24 = 43	87 − 54 = 33	55 − 43 = 12
87 − 65 = 22	44 − 32 = 12	57 − 24 = 33	88 − 25 = 63	75 − 61 = 14	48 − 26 = 22
69 − 25 = 44	95 − 24 = 71	48 − 13 = 35	58 − 16 = 42	35 − 13 = 22	39 − 17 = 22

35

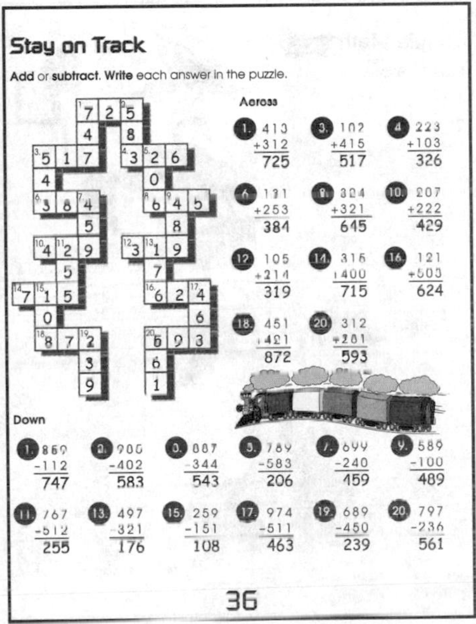

Stay on Track

Add or **subtract**. **Write** each answer in the puzzle.

Across

1. 413 + 312 = 725
3. 102 + 415 = 517
4. 223 + 103 = 326
6. 131 + 253 = 384
8. 324 + 321 = 645
10. 207 + 222 = 429
12. 105 + 214 = 319
14. 316 + 400 = 715
16. 121 + 503 = 624
18. 451 + 421 = 872
20. 312 + 281 = 593

Down

1. 859 − 112 = 747
2. 985 − 402 = 583
3. 887 − 344 = 543
5. 789 − 583 = 206
7. 699 − 240 = 459
9. 589 − 100 = 489
11. 767 − 512 = 255
13. 497 − 321 = 176
15. 259 − 151 = 108
17. 974 − 511 = 463
19. 689 − 450 = 239
20. 797 − 236 = 561

36

Subtracting Two-Digit Numbers
With Regrouping

Step 1: Decide whether to regroup. In the ones column, 3 is less than 9 so, regroup 4 tens 3 ones to 3 tens 13 ones.

Step 2: Subtract the ones.

Step 3: Subtract the tens.

43 − 19 = 24

Subtract to find the difference. **Regroup**, if needed.

67 − 34 = 33	85 − 12 = 73	86 − 47 = 39	91 − 48 = 43	44 − 27 = 17	61 − 34 = 27
32 − 14 = 18	97 − 36 = 61	60 − 45 = 15	52 − 22 = 30	71 − 19 = 52	83 − 15 = 68

37

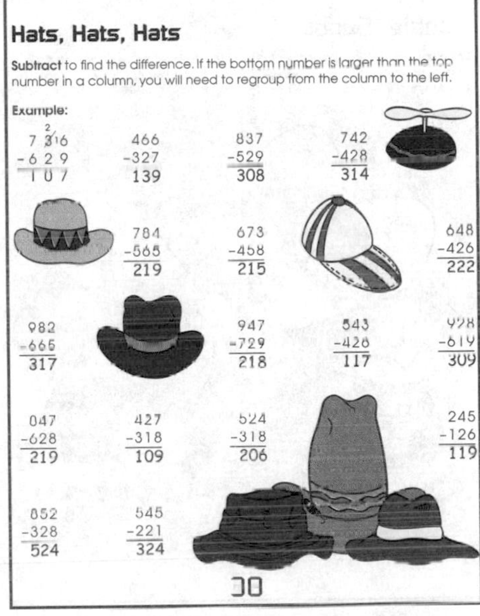

Hats, Hats, Hats

Subtract to find the difference. If the bottom number is larger than the top number in a column, you will need to regroup from the column to the left.

Example: 736 − 629 = 107

466 − 327 = 139
837 − 529 = 308
742 − 428 = 314
784 − 565 = 219
673 − 458 = 215
648 − 426 = 222
982 − 665 = 317
947 − 729 = 218
543 − 426 = 117
928 − 619 = 309
847 − 628 = 219
427 − 318 = 109
524 − 318 = 206
245 − 126 = 119
852 − 328 = 524
545 − 221 = 324

38

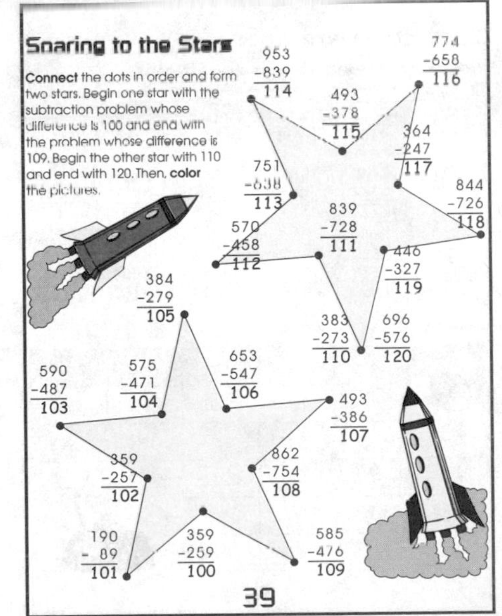

Soaring to the Stars

Connect the dots in order and form two stars. Begin one star with the subtraction problem whose difference is 100 and end with the problem whose difference is 109. Begin the other star with 110 and end with 120. Then, **color** the pictures.

953 − 839 = 114
774 − 658 = 116
493 − 378 = 115
364 − 247 = 117
751 − 638 = 113
844 − 726 = 118
839 − 728 = 111
570 − 458 = 112
446 − 327 = 119
384 − 279 = 105
383 − 273 = 110
696 − 576 = 120
590 − 487 = 103
575 − 471 = 104
653 − 547 = 106
493 − 386 = 107
359 − 257 = 102
862 − 754 = 108
190 − 89 = 101
359 − 259 = 100
585 − 476 = 109

39

Dino-Code

How is a T-Rex like an explosion?
To find out, **solve** the following problems and **write** the matching letter above each answer on the blanks.

He's . . . F(195) U(185) L(92) L(92) O(171) F(195) D(265) I(74) N(183) O(171) – M(93) I(74) G(45) H(181) T(191)!

Remember to regroup when the bottom number is larger than the top number in a column.

F = 348 − 153 = 195
L = 765 − 673 = 92
G = 427 − 382 = 45
T = 637 − 446 = 191
H = 878 − 697 = 181
U = 548 − 363 = 185
O = 824 − 653 = 171
N = 439 − 256 = 183
I = 447 − 373 = 74
M = 568 − 475 = 93
D = 748 − 483 = 265

40

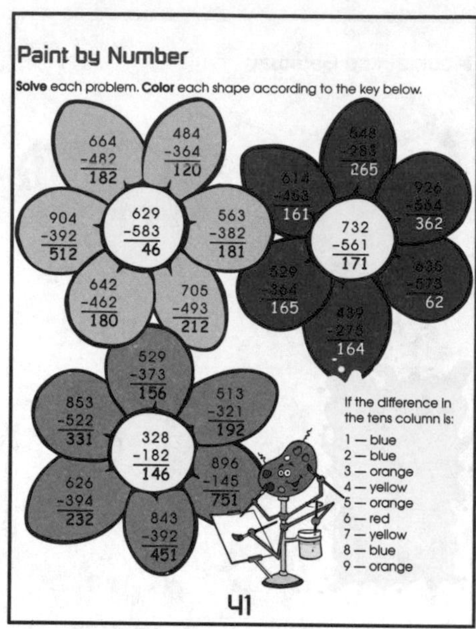

Paint by Number

Solve each problem. **Color** each shape according to the key below.

664 − 482 = 182 · 484 − 364 = 120 · 904 − 392 = 512 · 629 − 583 = 46 · 563 − 382 = 181 · 642 − 462 = 180 · 705 − 493 = 212

648 − 283 = 265 · 614 − 453 = 161 · 926 − 564 = 362 · 732 − 561 = 171 · 529 − 364 = 165 · 636 − 573 = 62 · 439 − 275 = 164

529 − 373 = 156 · 853 − 522 = 331 · 513 − 321 = 192 · 328 − 182 = 146 · 896 − 145 = 751 · 626 − 394 = 232 · 843 − 392 = 451

If the difference in the tens column is:
1 — blue
2 — blue
3 — orange
4 — yellow
5 — orange
6 — red
7 — yellow
8 — blue
9 — orange

41

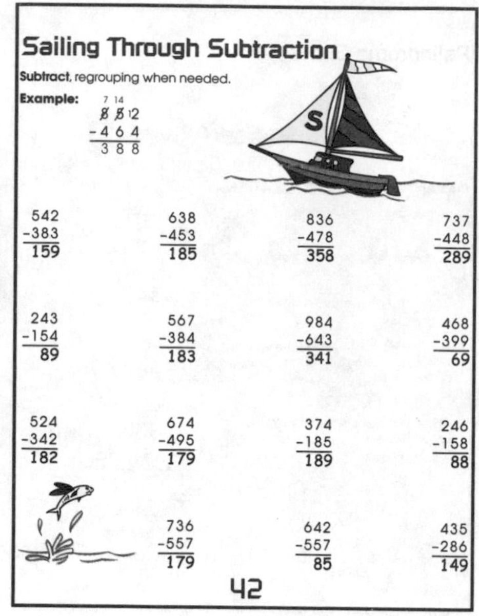

Sailing Through Subtraction

Subtract, regrouping when needed.

Example: 852 − 464 = 388

542 − 383 = 159 · 638 − 453 = 185 · 836 − 478 = 358 · 737 − 448 = 289

243 − 154 = 89 · 567 − 384 = 183 · 984 − 643 = 341 · 468 − 399 = 69

524 − 342 = 182 · 674 − 495 = 179 · 374 − 185 = 189 · 246 − 158 = 88

736 − 557 = 179 · 642 − 557 = 85 · 435 − 286 = 149

42

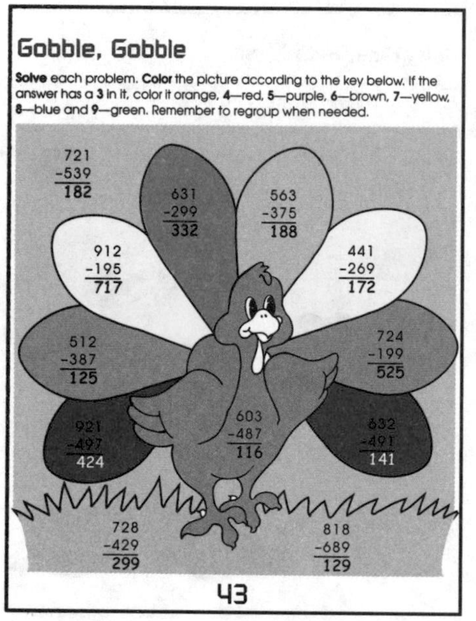

Gobble, Gobble

Solve each problem. **Color** the picture according to the key below. If the answer has a **3** in it, color it orange, **4**—red, **5**—purple, **6**—brown, **7**—yellow, **8**—blue and **9**—green. Remember to regroup when needed.

721 − 539 = 182 · 631 − 299 = 332 · 563 − 375 = 188 · 912 − 195 = 717 · 441 − 269 = 172 · 512 − 387 = 125 · 724 − 199 = 525 · 921 − 497 = 424 · 603 − 487 = 116 · 632 − 491 = 141 · 728 − 429 = 299 · 818 − 689 = 129

43

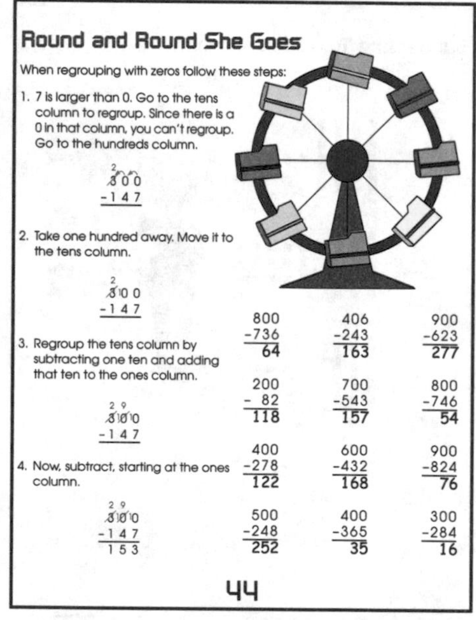

Round and Round She Goes

When regrouping with zeros follow these steps:

1. 7 is larger than 0. Go to the tens column to regroup. Since there is a 0 in that column, you can't regroup. Go to the hundreds column.
2. Take one hundred away. Move it to the tens column.
3. Regroup the tens column by subtracting one ten and adding that ten to the ones column.
4. Now, subtract, starting at the ones column. 300 − 147 = 153

800 − 736 = 64 · 406 − 243 = 163 · 900 − 623 = 277

200 − 82 = 118 · 700 − 543 = 157 · 800 − 746 = 54

400 − 278 = 122 · 600 − 432 = 168 · 900 − 824 = 76

500 − 248 = 252 · 400 − 365 = 35 · 300 − 284 = 16

44

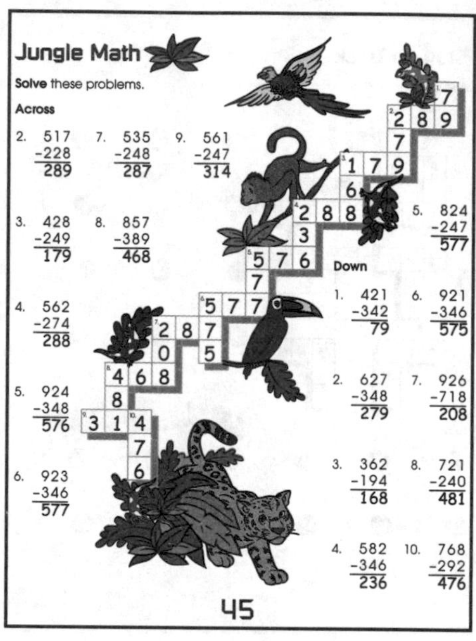

Jungle Math

Solve these problems.

Across

2. 517 − 228 = 289
7. 535 − 248 = 287
9. 561 − 247 = 314
3. 428 − 249 = 179
8. 857 − 389 = 468
4. 562 − 274 = 288
5. 924 − 348 = 576
6. 923 − 346 = 577
5. 824 − 247 = 577

Down

1. 421 − 342 = 79
6. 921 − 346 = 575
2. 627 − 348 = 279
7. 926 − 718 = 208
3. 362 − 194 = 168
8. 721 − 240 = 481
4. 582 − 346 = 236
10. 768 − 292 = 476

45

Timely Zeros

Subtract.

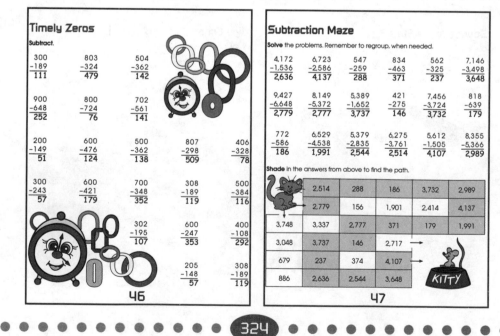

300 − 189 = 111 · 803 − 324 = 479 · 504 − 362 = 142

900 − 648 = 252 · 800 − 724 = 76 · 702 − 561 = 141

200 − 149 = 51 · 600 − 476 = 124 · 500 − 362 = 138 · 807 − 298 = 509 · 406 − 328 = 78

300 − 243 = 57 · 600 − 421 = 179 · 700 − 348 = 352 · 308 − 189 = 119 · 500 − 384 = 116

302 − 195 = 107 · 600 − 247 = 353 · 400 − 108 = 292

205 − 148 = 57 · 308 − 189 = 119

46

Subtraction Maze

Solve the problems. Remember to regroup, when needed.

4,172 − 1,536 = 2,636 · 6,723 − 2,586 = 4,137 · 547 − 259 = 288 · 834 − 463 = 371 · 562 − 325 = 237 · 7,146 − 3,498 = 3,648

9,427 − 6,648 = 2,779 · 8,149 − 5,372 = 2,777 · 5,389 − 1,652 = 3,737 · 421 − 275 = 146 · 7,456 − 3,724 = 3,732 · 818 − 639 = 179

772 − 586 = 186 · 6,529 − 4,538 = 1,991 · 5,379 − 2,835 = 2,544 · 6,275 − 3,761 = 2,514 · 5,612 − 1,505 = 4,107 · 8,355 − 5,366 = 2,989

Shade in the answers from above to find the path.

	2,514	288	186	3,732	2,989
	2,779	156	1,901	2,414	4,137
3,748	3,337	2,777	371	179	1,991
3,048	3,737	146	2,717 →		
679	237	374	4,107 →		
886	2,636	2,544	3,648		

KITTY

47

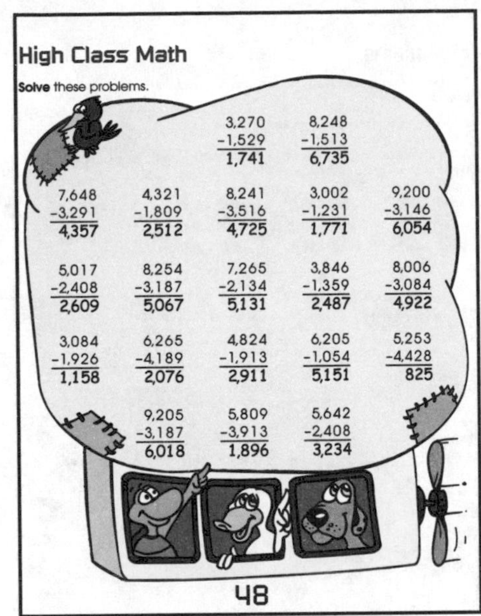

High Class Math

Solve these problems.

3,270 − 1,529 = 1,741
8,248 − 1,513 = 6,735

7,648 − 3,291 = 4,357
4,321 − 1,809 = 2,512
8,241 − 3,516 = 4,725
3,002 − 1,231 = 1,771
9,200 − 3,146 = 6,054

5,017 − 2,408 = 2,609
8,254 − 3,187 = 5,067
7,265 − 2,134 = 5,131
3,846 − 1,359 = 2,487
8,006 − 3,084 = 4,922

3,084 − 1,926 = 1,158
6,265 − 4,189 = 2,076
4,824 − 1,913 = 2,911
6,205 − 1,054 = 5,151
5,253 − 4,428 = 825

9,205 − 3,187 = 6,018
5,809 − 3,913 = 1,896
5,642 − 2,408 = 3,234

48

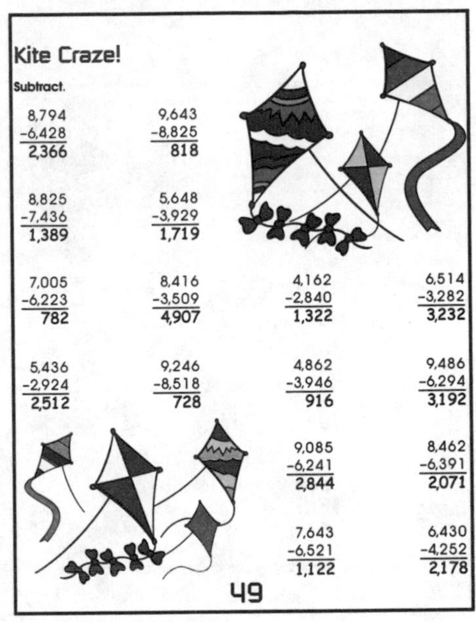

Kite Craze!

Subtract.

8,794 − 6,428 = 2,366
9,643 − 8,825 = 818

8,825 − 7,436 = 1,389
5,648 − 3,929 = 1,719

7,005 − 6,223 = 782
8,416 − 3,509 = 4,907
4,162 − 2,840 = 1,322
6,514 − 3,282 = 3,232

5,436 − 2,924 = 2,512
9,246 − 8,518 = 728
4,862 − 3,946 = 916
9,486 − 6,294 = 3,192

9,085 − 6,241 = 2,844
8,462 − 6,391 = 2,071

7,643 − 6,521 = 1,122
6,430 − 4,252 = 2,178

49

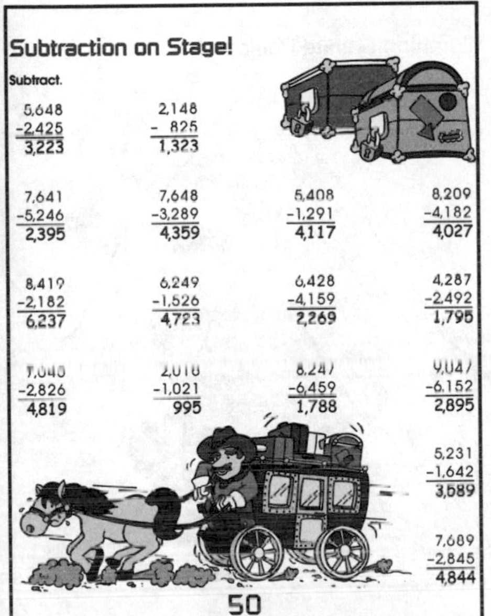

Subtraction on Stage!

Subtract.

5,648 − 2,425 = 3,223
2,148 − 825 = 1,323

7,641 − 5,246 = 2,395
7,648 − 3,289 = 4,359
5,408 − 1,291 = 4,117
8,209 − 4,182 = 4,027

8,419 − 2,182 = 6,237
6,249 − 1,526 = 4,723
6,428 − 4,159 = 2,269
4,287 − 2,492 = 1,795

[illegible] − 2,826 = 4,819
2,016 − 1,021 = 995
8,247 − 6,459 = 1,788
9,047 − 6,152 = 2,895

5,231 − 1,642 = 3,589

7,689 − 2,845 = 4,844

50

Subtraction Search

Solve each problem. **Find** the answer in the chart and **circle** it. The answers may go in any direction.

6,003 − 2,737 = 3,266
5,040 − 3,338 = 1,702
9,000 − 5,725 = 3,275

7,200 − 4,356 = 2,844
3,406 − 1,298 = 2,108
5,602 − 3,138 = 2,464

7,006 − 5,429 = 1,577
3,006 − 2,798 = 208
3,605 − 2,718 = 887

5,904 − 3,917 = 1,987
5,039 − 1,954 = 3,085
8,704 − 2,496 = 6,208

4,081 − 3,594 = 487
6,508 − 399 = 6,109
5,039 − 2,467 = 2,572
9,006 − 575 = 8,431
5,001 − 2,351 = 2,650

8,002 − 5,686 = 2,316
6,058 − 2,175 = 3,883
9,504 − 7,368 = 2,136
7,290 − 1,801 = 5,489

2	1	6	3	2	7	5
6	3	3	2	1	0	8
2	2	1	6	3	3	4
0	2	2	6	5	0	6
8	5	4	2	0	8	7
8	9	0	6	1	5	6
3	2	8	4	4	2	1
8	3	4	8	8	5	0
8	1	2	8	7	2	9
3	4	[illegible]	[illegible]	[illegible]	[illegible]	[illegible]
8	1	3	7	0	4	2
9	3	2	1	7	0	2

51

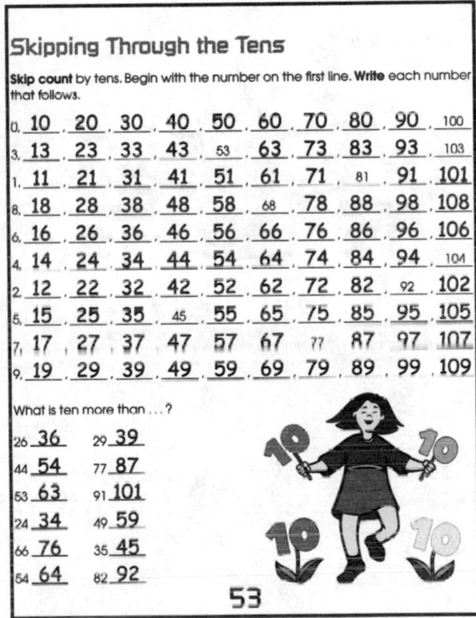

Skipping Through the Tens

Skip count by tens. Begin with the number on the first line. **Write** each number that follows.

0. 10, 20, 30, 40, 50, 60, 70, 80, 90, 100
3. 13, 23, 33, 43, 53, 63, 73, 83, 93, 103
1. 11, 21, 31, 41, 51, 61, 71, 81, 91, 101
8. 18, 28, 38, 48, 58, 68, 78, 88, 98, 108
6. 16, 26, 36, 46, 56, 66, 76, 86, 96, 106
4. 14, 24, 34, 44, 54, 64, 74, 84, 94, 104
2. 12, 22, 32, 42, 52, 62, 72, 82, 92, 102
5. 15, 25, 35, 45, 55, 65, 75, 85, 95, 105
7. 17, 27, 37, 47, 57, 67, 77, 87, 97, 107
9. 19, 29, 39, 49, 59, 69, 79, 89, 99, 109

What is ten more than . . . ?

26 36   29 39
44 54   77 87
53 63   91 101
24 34   49 59
66 76   35 45
54 64   82 92

53

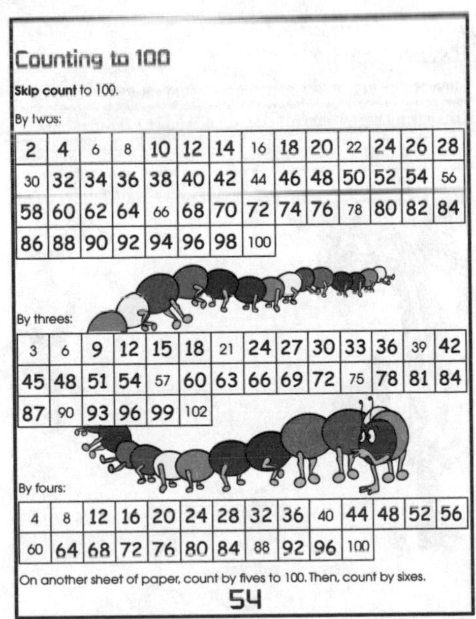

Counting to 100

Skip count to 100.

By twos:

2	4	6	8	10	12	14	16	18	20	22	24	26	28
30	32	34	36	38	40	42	44	46	48	50	52	54	56
58	60	62	64	66	68	70	72	74	76	78	80	82	84
86	88	90	92	94	96	98	100						

By threes:

3	6	9	12	15	18	21	24	27	30	33	36	39	42
45	48	51	54	57	60	63	66	69	72	75	78	81	84
87	90	93	96	99	102								

By fours:

4	8	12	16	20	24	28	32	36	40	44	48	52	56
60	64	68	72	76	80	84	88	92	96	100			

On another sheet of paper, count by fives to 100. Then, count by sixes.

54

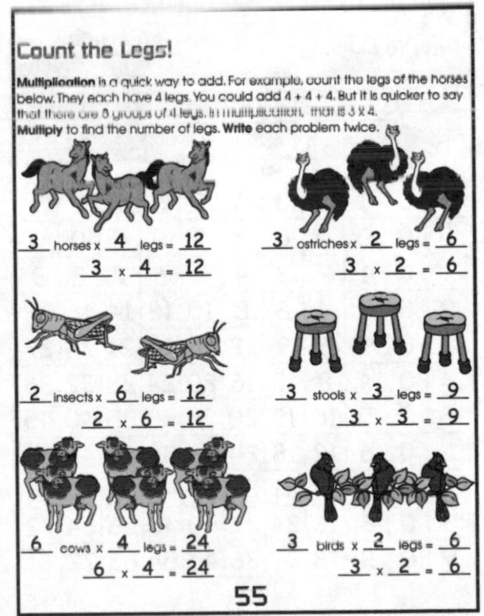

Count the Legs!

Multiplication is a quick way to add. For example, count the legs of the horses below. They each have 4 legs. You could add 4 + 4 + 4. But it is quicker to say that there are 3 groups of 4 legs. In multiplication, that is 3 x 4. **Multiply** to find the number of legs. **Write** each problem twice.

3 horses x 4 legs = 12
3 x 4 = 12

3 ostriches x 2 legs = 6
3 x 2 = 6

2 insects x 6 legs = 12
2 x 6 = 12

3 stools x 3 legs = 9
3 x 3 = 9

6 cows x 4 legs = 24
6 x 4 = 24

3 birds x 2 legs = 6
3 x 2 = 6

55

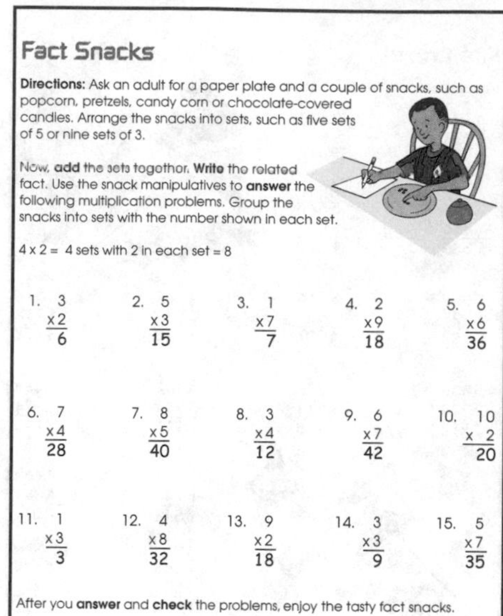

Fact Snacks

Directions: Ask an adult for a paper plate and a couple of snacks, such as popcorn, pretzels, candy corn or chocolate-covered candies. Arrange the snacks into sets, such as five sets of 5 or nine sets of 3.

Now, **add** the sets together. **Write** the related fact. Use the snack manipulatives to **answer** the following multiplication problems. Group the snacks into sets with the number shown in each set.

4 x 2 = 4 sets with 2 in each set = 8

1. 3 x 2 = 6
2. 5 x 3 = 15
3. 1 x 7 = 7
4. 2 x 9 = 18
5. 6 x 6 = 36
6. 7 x 4 = 28
7. 8 x 5 = 40
8. 3 x 4 = 12
9. 6 x 7 = 42
10. 10 x 2 = 20
11. 1 x 3 = 3
12. 4 x 8 = 32
13. 9 x 2 = 18
14. 3 x 3 = 9
15. 5 x 7 = 35

After you **answer** and **check** the problems, enjoy the tasty fact snacks.

56

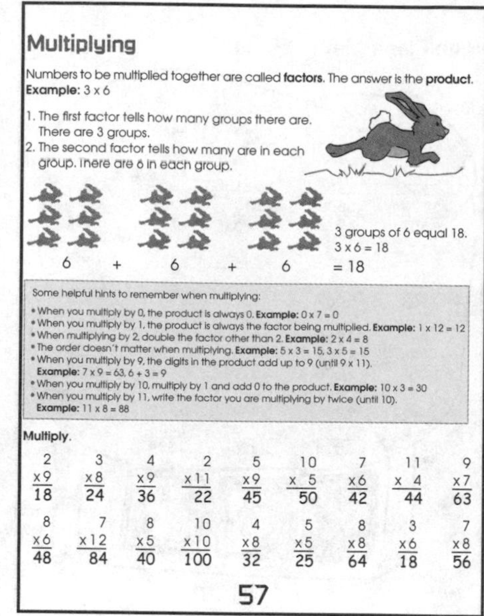

Multiplying

Numbers to be multiplied together are called **factors**. The answer is the **product**.
Example: 3 x 6

1. The first factor tells how many groups there are. There are 3 groups.
2. The second factor tells how many are in each group. There are 6 in each group.

6 + 6 + 6 = 18

3 groups of 6 equal 18.
3 x 6 = 18

Some helpful hints to remember when multiplying:

- When you multiply by 0, the product is always 0. **Example:** 0 x 7 = 0
- When you multiply by 1, the product is always the factor being multiplied. **Example:** 1 x 12 = 12
- When multiplying by 2, double the factor other than 2. **Example:** 2 x 4 = 8
- The order doesn't matter when multiplying. **Example:** 5 x 3 = 15, 3 x 5 = 15
- When you multiply by 9, the digits in the product add up to 9 (until 9 x 11). **Example:** 7 x 9 = 63, 6 + 3 = 9
- When you multiply by 10, multiply by 1 and add 0 to the product. **Example:** 10 x 3 = 30
- When you multiply by 11, write the factor you are multiplying by twice (until 10). **Example:** 11 x 8 = 88

Multiply.

2 x 9 = 18; 3 x 8 = 24; 4 x 9 = 36; 2 x 11 = 22; 5 x 9 = 45; 10 x 5 = 50; 7 x 6 = 42; 11 x 4 = 44; 9 x 7 = 63

8 x 6 = 48; 7 x 12 = 84; 8 x 5 = 40; 10 x 10 = 100; 4 x 8 = 32; 5 x 5 = 25; 8 x 8 = 64; 3 x 6 = 18; 7 x 8 = 56

57

Factor Fun

When you change the order of the factors, you have the same product.

4 x 3 = 12; 3 x 4 = 12

Multiply.

7 x 3 = 21; 3 x 7 = 21; 6 x 5 = 30; 5 x 6 = 30; 2 x 3 = 6; 3 x 2 = 6

4 x 6 = 24; 6 x 4 = 24; 2 x 9 = 18; 9 x 2 = 18; 8 x 4 = 32; 4 x 8 = 32

7 x 2 = 14; 2 x 7 = 14; 3 x 6 = 18; 6 x 3 = 18; 9 x 4 = 36; 4 x 9 = 36

8 x 3 = 24; 3 x 8 = 24; 5 x 2 = 10; 2 x 5 = 10; 9 x 3 = 27; 3 x 9 = 27

58

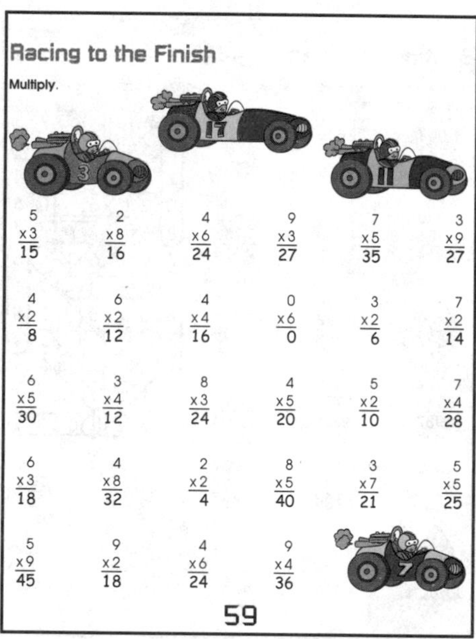

Racing to the Finish

Multiply.

5 x 3 = 15; 2 x 8 = 16; 4 x 6 = 24; 9 x 3 = 27; 7 x 5 = 35; 3 x 9 = 27

4 x 2 = 8; 6 x 2 = 12; 4 x 4 = 16; 0 x 6 = 0; 3 x 2 = 6; 7 x 2 = 14

6 x 5 = 30; 3 x 4 = 12; 8 x 3 = 24; 4 x 5 = 20; 5 x 2 = 10; 7 x 4 = 28

6 x 3 = 18; 4 x 8 = 32; 2 x 2 = 4; 8 x 5 = 40; 3 x 7 = 21; 5 x 5 = 25

5 x 9 = 45; 9 x 2 = 18; 4 x 6 = 24; 9 x 4 = 36

59

Climbing Granite Boulders!

Multiply.

9 x 1 = 9; 6 x 1 = 6; 3 x 9 = 27; 6 x 7 = 42; 2 x 6 = 12; 8 x 8 = 64

2 x 9 = 18; 8 x 9 = 72; 7 x 8 = 56; 8 x 7 = 56; 7 x 7 = 49; 5 x 9 = 45; 5 x 7 = 35

3 x 3 = 9
4 x 4 = 16
9 x 9 = 81
6 x 6 = 36
9 x 0 = 0
8 x 6 = 48
4 x 8 = 32
7 x 2 = 14
3 x 5 = 15
2 x 8 = 16
3 x 7 = 21
3 x 6 = 18
6 x 6 = 36
5 x 6 = 30
2 x 2 = 4
2 x 3 = 6
6 x 9 = 54
4 x 7 = 28
4 x 6 = 24
0 x 4 = 0
7 x 9 = 63
5 x 5 = 25

60

Time To Multiply

Complete the table. Try to do it in less than 3 minutes.

X	0	1	2	3	4	5	6	7	8	9
0	0	0	0	0	0	0	0	0	0	0
1	0	1	2	3	4	5	6	7	8	9
2	0	2	4	6	8	10	12	14	16	18
3	0	3	6	9	12	15	18	21	24	27
4	0	4	8	12	16	20	24	28	32	36
5	0	5	10	15	20	25	30	35	40	45
6	0	6	12	18	24	30	36	42	48	54
7	0	7	14	21	28	35	42	49	56	63
8	0	8	16	24	32	40	48	56	64	72
9	0	9	18	27	36	45	54	63	72	81

65

Double Trouble

Solve each multiplication problem. Below each answer, **write** the letter from the code that matches the answer. **Read** the coded question and **write** the answer in the space provided.

1	4	9	16	25	36	49	64	81	100	121	144
E	G	H	I	N	O	S	T	U	W	X	Y

10 x 10	3 x 3	6 x 6
100	9	36
W	H	O

4 x 4	7 x 7
16	49
I	S

7 x 7	4 x 4	8 x 8	8 x 8	4 x 4	5 x 5	2 x 2
49	16	64	64	16	25	4
S	I	T	T	I	N	G

5 x 5	1 x 1	11 x 11	8 x 8
25	1	121	64
N	E	X	T

8 x 8	6 x 6
64	36
T	O

12 x 12	6 x 6	9 x 9
144	36	81
Y	O	U

?

Answer: *Answers will vary.*

66

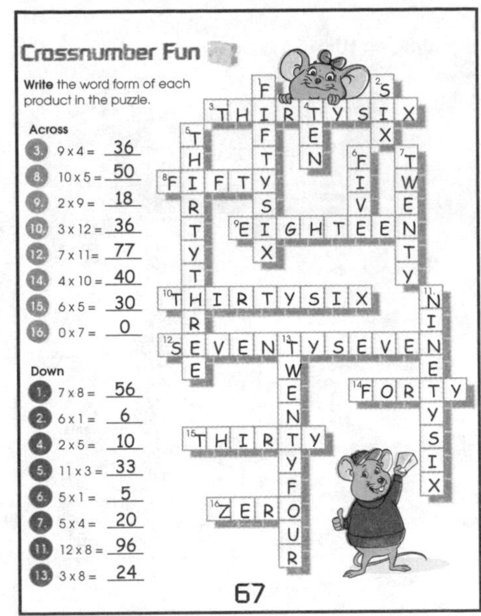

Crossnumber Fun

Write the word form of each product in the puzzle.

Across

3. 9 x 4 = 36
8. 10 x 5 = 50
9. 2 x 9 = 18
10. 3 x 12 = 36
12. 7 x 11 = 77
14. 4 x 10 = 40
15. 6 x 5 = 30
16. 0 x 7 = 0

Down

1. 7 x 8 = 56
2. 6 x 1 = 6
4. 2 x 5 = 10
5. 11 x 3 = 33
6. 5 x 1 = 5
7. 5 x 4 = 20
11. 12 x 8 = 96
13. 3 x 8 = 24

67

Hmm, What Should I Do?

Example: 52 (+) 9 = 61

8 (X) 4 = 32

Write the correct symbols in the circles.

7 (x) 8 = 56	81 (−) 6 = 75	55 (−) 3 = 52
54 (÷) 9 = 6	2 (x) 1 = 2	40 (−) 2 = 38
36 (−) 5 = 31	0 (+) 2 = 2	8 (x) 8 = 64
12 (+) 6 = 18	9 (x) 8 = 72	18 (+) 5 = 23
72 (−) 7 = 65		32 (+) 5 = 37
0 (x) 1 = 0		48 (÷) 6 = 8
9 (x) 1 = 9		32 (÷) 4 = 8
45 (÷) 9 = 5		6 (x) 7 = 42

68

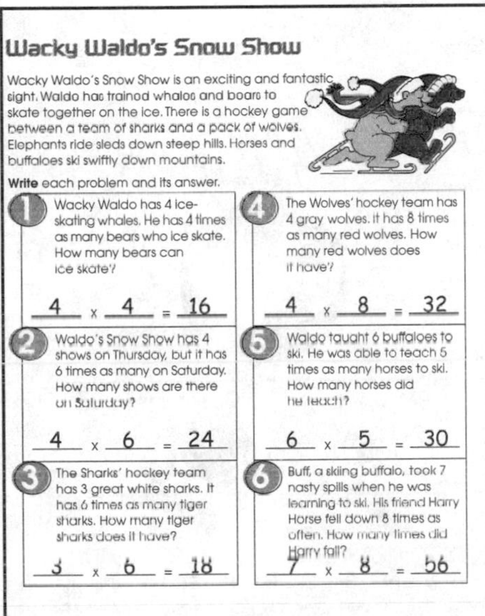

Wacky Waldo's Snow Show

Wacky Waldo's Snow Show is an exciting and fantastic sight. Waldo has trained whales and bears to skate together on the ice. There is a hockey game between a team of sharks and a pack of wolves. Elephants ride sleds down steep hills. Horses and buffaloes ski swiftly down mountains.

Write each problem and its answer.

1. Wacky Waldo has 4 ice-skating whales. He has 4 times as many bears who ice skate. How many bears can ice skate? 4 x 4 = 16
2. Waldo's Snow Show has 4 shows on Thursday, but it has 6 times as many on Saturday. How many shows are there on Saturday? 4 x 6 = 24
3. The Sharks' hockey team has 3 great white sharks. It has 6 times as many tiger sharks. How many tiger sharks does it have? 3 x 6 = 18
4. The Wolves' hockey team has 4 gray wolves. It has 8 times as many red wolves. How many red wolves does it have? 4 x 8 = 32
5. Waldo taught 6 buffaloes to ski. He was able to teach 5 times as many horses to ski. How many horses did he teach? 6 x 5 = 30
6. Buff, a skiing buffalo, took 7 nasty spills when he was learning to ski. His friend Harry Horse fell down 8 times as often. How many times did Harry fall? 7 x 8 = 56

69

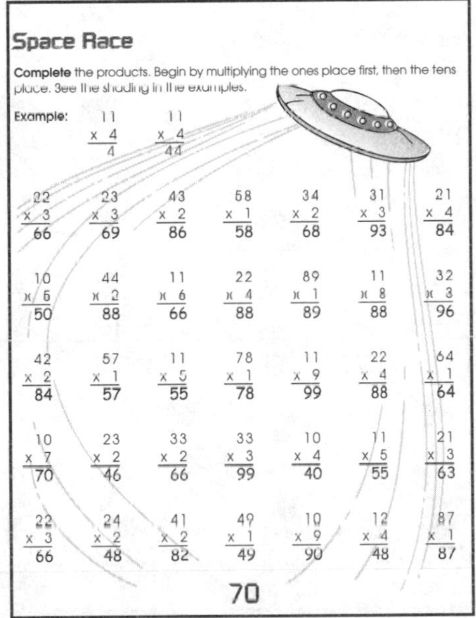

Space Race

Complete the products. Begin by multiplying the ones place first, then the tens place. See the shading in the examples.

Example: 11 x 4 = 4; 11 x 4 = 44

22 x 3 = 66	23 x 3 = 69	43 x 2 = 86	58 x 1 = 58	34 x 2 = 68	31 x 3 = 93	21 x 4 = 84
10 x 5 = 50	44 x 2 = 88	11 x 6 = 66	22 x 4 = 88	89 x 1 = 89	11 x 8 = 88	32 x 3 = 96
42 x 2 = 84	57 x 1 = 57	11 x 5 = 55	78 x 1 = 78	11 x 9 = 99	22 x 4 = 88	64 x 1 = 64
10 x 7 = 70	23 x 2 = 46	33 x 2 = 66	33 x 3 = 99	10 x 4 = 40	11 x 5 = 55	21 x 3 = 63
22 x 3 = 66	24 x 2 = 48	41 x 2 = 82	49 x 1 = 49	10 x 9 = 90	12 x 4 = 48	87 x 1 = 87

70

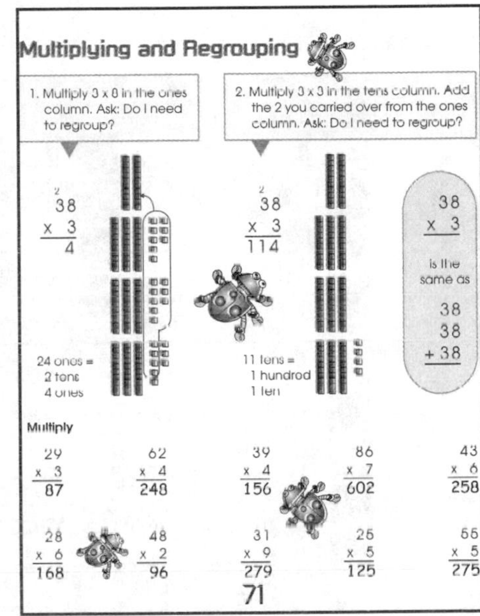

Multiplying and Regrouping

1. Multiply 3 x 8 in the ones column. Ask: Do I need to regroup?
2. Multiply 3 x 3 in the tens column. Add the 2 you carried over from the ones column. Ask: Do I need to regroup?

38 x 3 = 4 (2 carried) — 24 ones = 2 tens 4 ones

38 x 3 = 114 — 11 tens = 1 hundred 1 ten

38 x 3 is the same as 38 + 38 + 38

Multiply

29 x 3 = 87	62 x 4 = 248	39 x 4 = 156	86 x 7 = 602	43 x 6 = 258
28 x 6 = 168	48 x 2 = 96	31 x 9 = 279	25 x 5 = 125	55 x 5 = 275

71

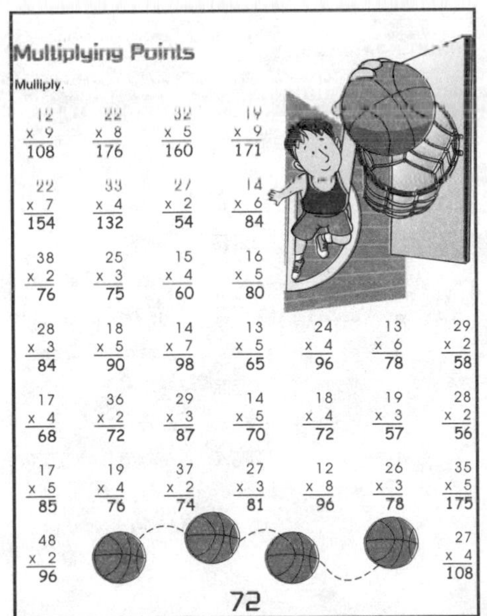

Multiplying Points

Multiply.

12 x 9 = 108	22 x 8 = 176	32 x 5 = 160	19 x 9 = 171			
22 x 7 = 154	33 x 4 = 132	27 x 2 = 54	14 x 6 = 84			
38 x 2 = 76	25 x 3 = 75	15 x 4 = 60	16 x 5 = 80			
28 x 3 = 84	18 x 5 = 90	14 x 7 = 98	13 x 5 = 65	24 x 4 = 96	13 x 6 = 78	29 x 2 = 58
17 x 4 = 68	36 x 2 = 72	29 x 3 = 87	14 x 5 = 70	18 x 4 = 72	19 x 3 = 57	28 x 2 = 56
17 x 5 = 85	19 x 4 = 76	37 x 2 = 74	27 x 3 = 81	12 x 8 = 96	26 x 3 = 78	35 x 5 = 175
48 x 2 = 96						27 x 4 = 108

72

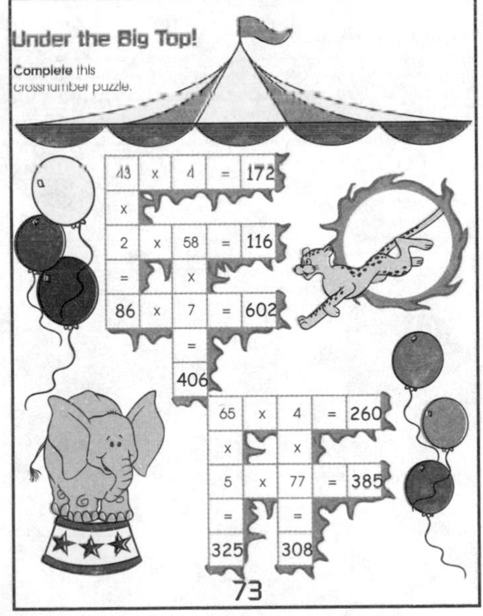

Under the Big Top!

Complete this crossnumber puzzle.

43 x 4 = 172

2 x 58 = 116

86 x 7 = 602

4 x 7 = ... 58 x 7 = 406

65 x 4 = 260

5 x 77 = 385

65 x 5 = 325; 4 x 77 = 308

73

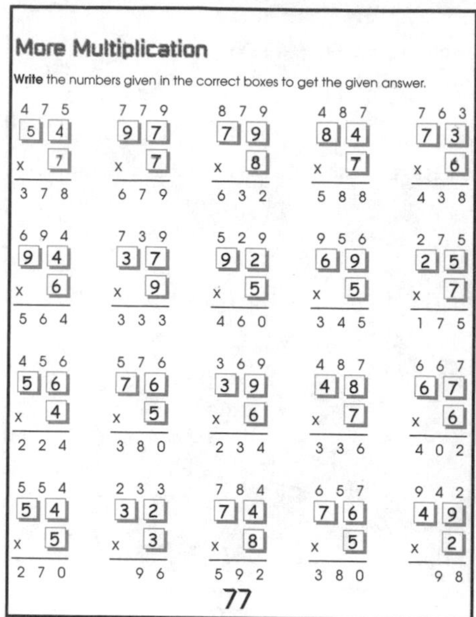

More Multiplication

Write the numbers given in the correct boxes to get the given answer.

Numbers given	Problem	Answer
4 7 5	54 x 7	378
7 7 9	97 x 7	679
8 7 9	79 x 8	632
4 8 7	84 x 7	588
7 6 3	73 x 6	438
6 9 4	94 x 6	564
7 3 9	37 x 9	333
5 2 9	92 x 5	460
9 5 6	69 x 5	345
2 7 5	25 x 7	175
4 5 6	56 x 4	224
5 7 6	76 x 5	380
3 6 9	39 x 6	234
4 8 7	48 x 7	336
6 6 7	67 x 6	402
5 5 4	54 x 5	270
2 3 3	32 x 3	96
7 8 4	74 x 8	592
6 5 7	76 x 5	380
9 4 2	49 x 2	98

77

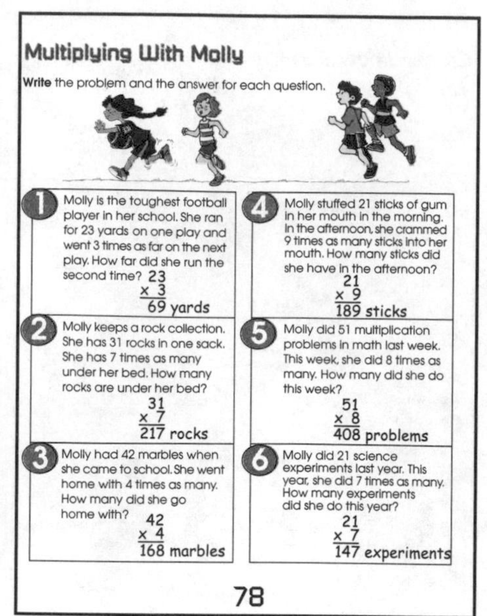

Multiplying With Molly

Write the problem and the answer for each question.

1. Molly is the toughest football player in her school. She ran for 23 yards on one play and went 3 times as far on the next play. How far did she run the second time? 23 x 3 = 69 yards
2. Molly keeps a rock collection. She has 31 rocks in one sack. She has 7 times as many under her bed. How many rocks are under her bed? 31 x 7 = 217 rocks
3. Molly had 42 marbles when she came to school. She went home with 4 times as many. How many did she go home with? 42 x 4 = 168 marbles
4. Molly stuffed 21 sticks of gum in her mouth in the morning. In the afternoon, she crammed 9 times as many sticks into her mouth. How many sticks did she have in the afternoon? 21 x 9 = 189 sticks
5. Molly did 51 multiplication problems in math last week. This week, she did 8 times as many. How many did she do this week? 51 x 8 = 408 problems
6. Molly did 21 science experiments last year. This year, she did 7 times as many. How many experiments did she do this year? 21 x 7 = 147 experiments

78

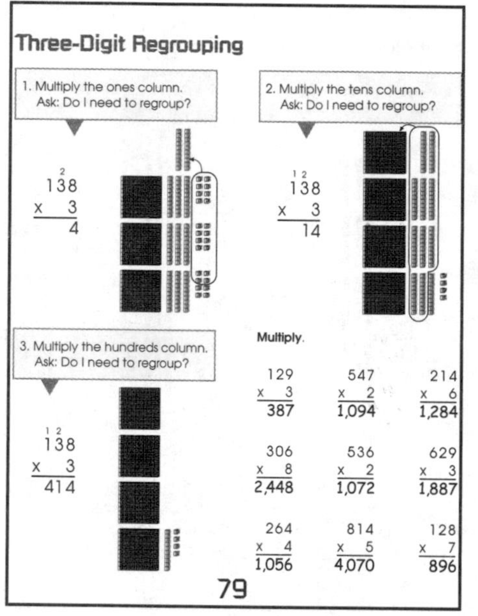

Three-Digit Regrouping

1. Multiply the ones column. Ask: Do I need to regroup? 138 x 3 = 4 (carry 2)
2. Multiply the tens column. Ask: Do I need to regroup? 138 x 3 = 14 (carry 1 2)
3. Multiply the hundreds column. Ask: Do I need to regroup? 138 x 3 = 414

Multiply.

129 x 3 = 387	547 x 2 = 1,094	214 x 6 = 1,284
306 x 8 = 2,448	536 x 2 = 1,072	629 x 3 = 1,887
264 x 4 = 1,056	814 x 5 = 4,070	128 x 7 = 896

79

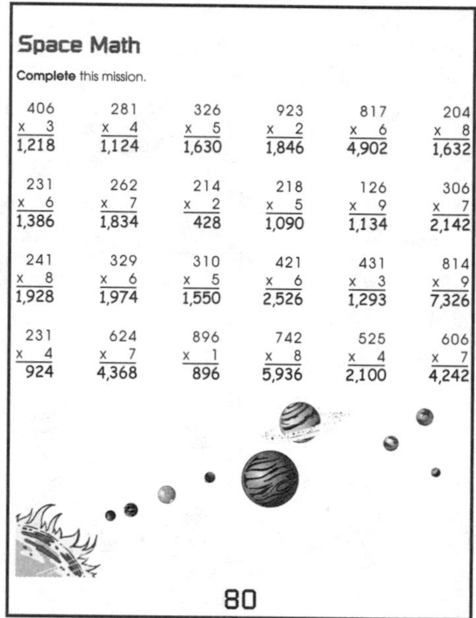

Space Math

Complete this mission.

406 x 3 = 1,218	281 x 4 = 1,124	326 x 5 = 1,630	923 x 2 = 1,846	817 x 6 = 4,902	204 x 8 = 1,632
231 x 6 = 1,386	262 x 7 = 1,834	214 x 2 = 428	218 x 5 = 1,090	126 x 9 = 1,134	306 x 7 = 2,142
241 x 8 = 1,928	329 x 6 = 1,974	310 x 5 = 1,550	421 x 6 = 2,526	431 x 3 = 1,293	814 x 9 = 7,326
231 x 4 = 924	624 x 7 = 4,368	896 x 1 = 896	742 x 8 = 5,936	525 x 4 = 2,100	606 x 7 = 4,242

80

Solve It!

What set of ridges and loops are different on every person? To find out, **solve** the following problems and **write** the matching letter above each answer at the bottom of the page.

I. 303 x 3 = 9	303 x 3 = 09	303 x 3 = 909	R. 214 x 2 = 428	N. 413 x 2 = 826
N. 142 x 2 = 284			R. 211 x 4 = 844	F. 104 x 2 = 208
T. 131 x 2 = 262	P. 232 x 3 = 696		E. 301 x 2 = 602	I. 134 x 1 = 134
G. 244 x 2 = 488	S. 334 x 2 = 668			

F	I	N	G	E	R	P	R	I	N	T	S
208	909	826	488	602	844	696	428	134	284	262	668

81

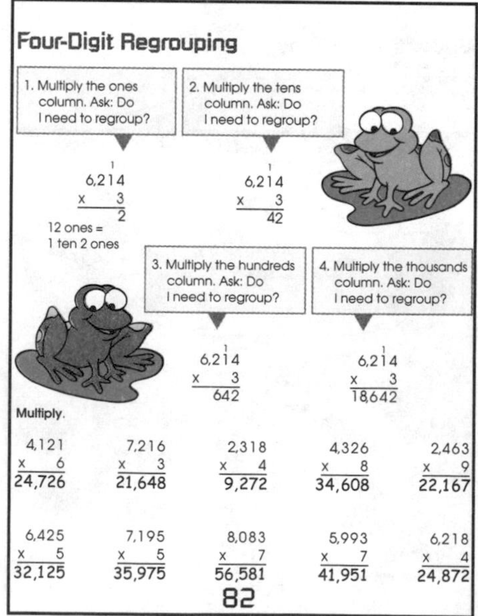

Four-Digit Regrouping

1. Multiply the ones column. Ask: Do I need to regroup? 6,214 x 3 = 2 (12 ones = 1 ten 2 ones)
2. Multiply the tens column. Ask: Do I need to regroup? 6,214 x 3 = 42
3. Multiply the hundreds column. Ask: Do I need to regroup? 6,214 x 3 = 642
4. Multiply the thousands column. Ask: Do I need to regroup? 6,214 x 3 = 18,642

Multiply.

4,121 x 6 = 24,726	7,216 x 3 = 21,648	2,318 x 4 = 9,272	4,326 x 8 = 34,608	2,463 x 9 = 22,167
6,425 x 5 = 32,125	7,195 x 5 = 35,975	8,083 x 7 = 56,581	5,993 x 7 = 41,951	6,218 x 4 = 24,872

82

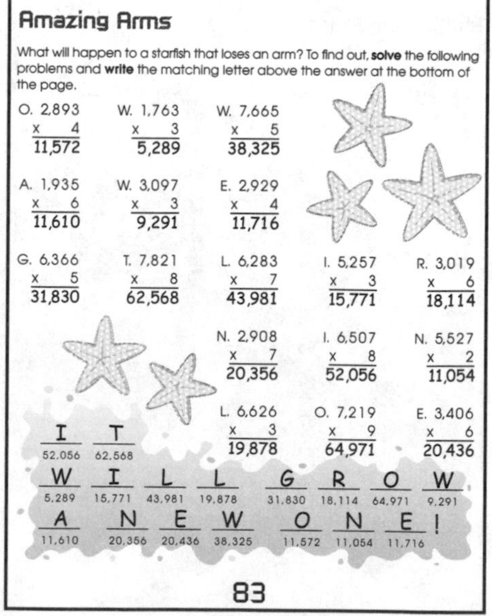

Amazing Arms

What will happen to a starfish that loses an arm? To find out, **solve** the following problems and **write** the matching letter above the answer at the bottom of the page.

O. 2,893 x 4 = 11,572	W. 1,763 x 3 = 5,289	W. 7,665 x 5 = 38,325		
A. 1,935 x 6 = 11,610	W. 3,097 x 3 = 9,291	E. 2,929 x 4 = 11,716		
G. 6,366 x 5 = 31,830	T. 7,821 x 8 = 62,568	L. 6,283 x 7 = 43,981	I. 5,257 x 3 = 15,771	R. 3,019 x 6 = 18,114
		N. 2,908 x 7 = 20,356	I. 6,507 x 8 = 52,056	N. 5,527 x 2 = 11,054
		L. 6,626 x 3 = 19,878	O. 7,219 x 9 = 64,971	E. 3,406 x 6 = 20,436

I	T
52,056	62,568

W	I	L	L	G	R	O	W
5,289	15,771	43,981	19,878	31,830	18,114	64,971	9,291

A	N	E	W	O	N	E	!
11,610	20,356	20,436	38,325	11,572	11,054	11,716	

83

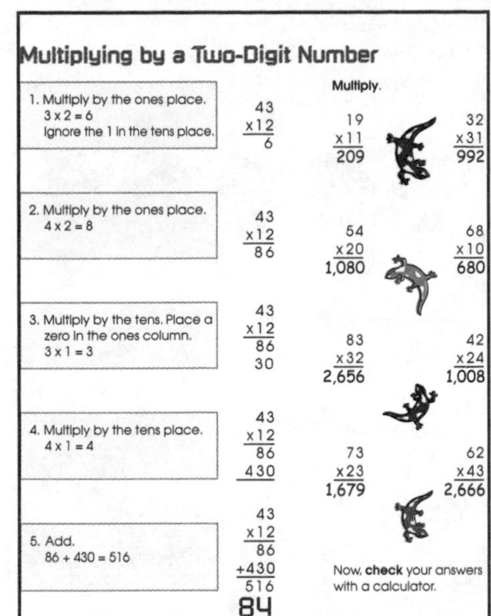

Multiplying by a Two-Digit Number

1. Multiply by the ones place. 3 x 2 = 6 Ignore the 1 in the tens place. — 43 x12 = 6
2. Multiply by the ones place. 4 x 2 = 8 — 43 x12 = 86
3. Multiply by the tens. Place a zero in the ones column. 3 x 1 = 3 — 43 x12: 86, 30
4. Multiply by the tens place. 4 x 1 = 4 — 43 x12: 86, 430
5. Add. 86 + 430 = 516 — 43 x12: 86 +430 = 516

Multiply.

19 x 11 = 209	32 x 31 = 992
54 x 20 = 1,080	68 x 10 = 680
83 x 32 = 2,656	42 x 24 = 1,008
73 x 23 = 1,679	62 x 43 = 2,666

Now, **check** your answers with a calculator.

84

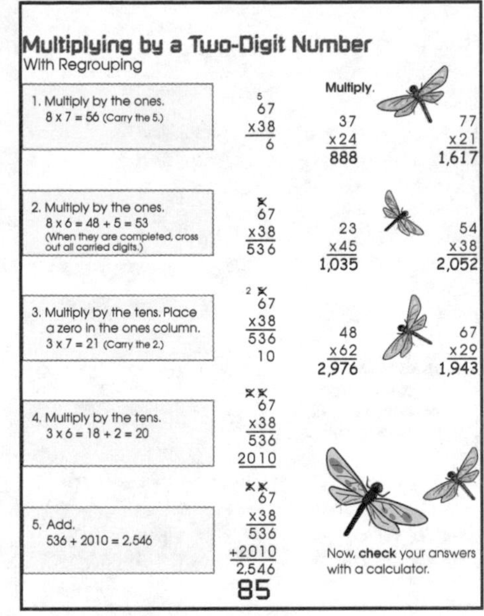

Multiplying by a Two-Digit Number

With Regrouping

1. Multiply by the ones. 8 x 7 = 56 (Carry the 5.) — 67 x38 = 6
2. Multiply by the ones. 8 x 6 = 48 + 5 = 53 (When they are completed, cross out all carried digits.) — 67 x38 = 536
3. Multiply by the tens. Place a zero in the ones column. 3 x 7 = 21 (Carry the 2.) — 67 x38: 536, 10
4. Multiply by the tens. 3 x 6 = 18 + 2 = 20 — 67 x38: 536, 2010
5. Add. 536 + 2010 = 2,546 — 67 x38: 536 +2010 = 2,546

Multiply.

37 x 24 = 888	77 x 21 = 1,617
23 x 45 = 1,035	54 x 38 = 2,052
48 x 62 = 2,976	67 x 29 = 1,943

Now, **check** your answers with a calculator.

85

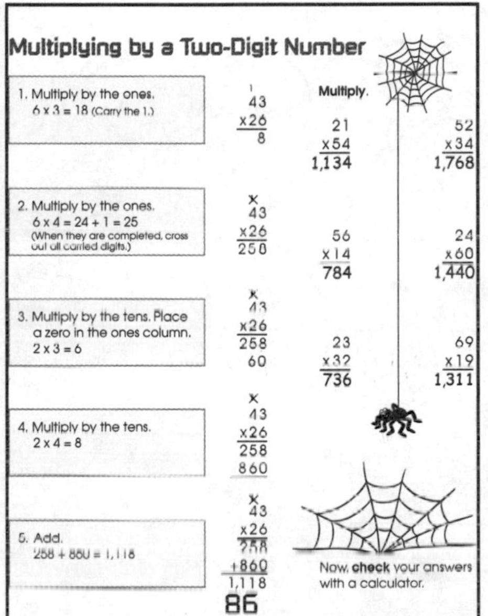

Multiplying by a Two-Digit Number

1. Multiply by the ones. 6 x 3 = 18 (Carry the 1.) — 43 x26 = 8
2. Multiply by the ones. 6 x 4 = 24 + 1 = 25 (When they are completed, cross out all carried digits.) — 43 x26 = 258
3. Multiply by the tens. Place a zero in the ones column. 2 x 3 = 6 — 43 x26: 258, 60
4. Multiply by the tens. 2 x 4 = 8 — 43 x26: 258, 860
5. Add. 258 + 860 = 1,118 — 43 x26: 258 +860 = 1,118

Multiply.

21 x 54 = 1,134	52 x 34 = 1,768
56 x 14 = 784	24 x 60 = 1,440
23 x 32 = 736	69 x 19 = 1,311

Now, **check** your answers with a calculator.

86

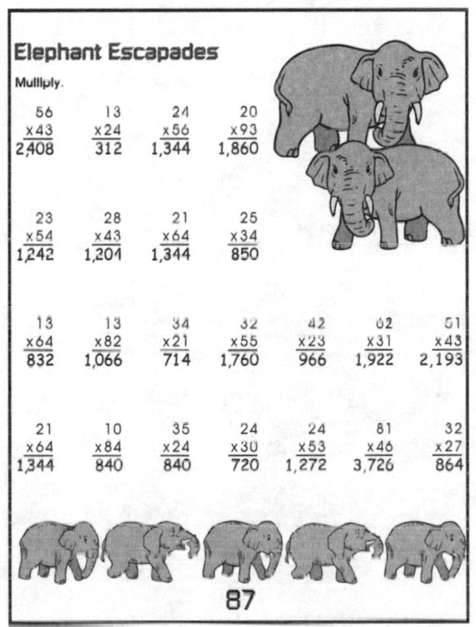

Elephant Escapades

Multiply.

56 x 43 = 2,408	13 x 24 = 312	24 x 56 = 1,344	20 x 93 = 1,860			
23 x 54 = 1,242	28 x 43 = 1,204	21 x 64 = 1,344	25 x 34 = 850			
13 x 64 = 832	13 x 82 = 1,066	34 x 21 = 714	32 x 55 = 1,760	42 x 23 = 966	62 x 31 = 1,922	51 x 43 = 2,193
21 x 64 = 1,344	10 x 84 = 840	35 x 24 = 840	24 x 30 = 720	24 x 53 = 1,272	81 x 46 = 3,726	32 x 27 = 864

87

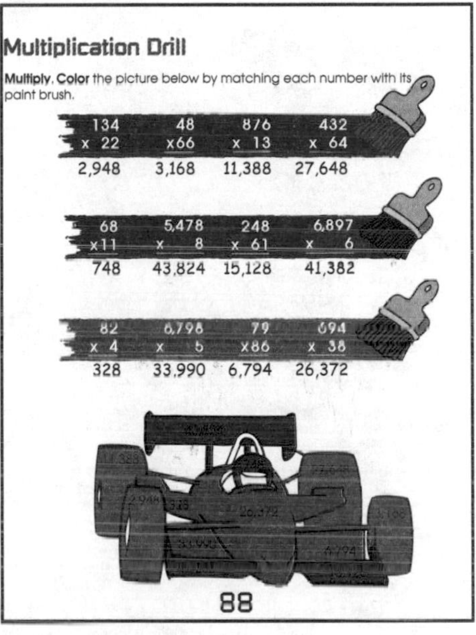

Multiplication Drill

Multiply. Color the picture below by matching each number with its paint brush.

134 x 22 = 2,948	48 x 66 = 3,168	876 x 13 = 11,388	432 x 64 = 27,648
68 x 11 = 748	5,478 x 8 = 43,824	248 x 61 = 15,128	6,897 x 6 = 41,382
82 x 4 = 328	6,798 x 5 = 33,990	79 x 86 = 6,794	694 x 38 = 26,372

88

Step by Step

Read the problems below. **Write** each answer in the space provided.

Work space

1. One battalion of ants marches with 25 ants in a row. There are 35 rows of ants in each battalion. How many ants are in one battalion?
   875 ants
2. The Ant Army finds a picnic! Now, they need to figure out how many ants should carry each piece of food. A team of 137 ants moves a celery stick. They need 150 ants to carry a carrot stick. A troop of 121 ants carries a very large radish. How many ants in all are needed to move the vegetables?
   408 ants
3. Now, the real work begins—the big pieces of food that would feed their whole colony. It takes 1,259 ants to haul a peanut butter and jelly sandwich. It takes a whole battalion of 2,067 ants to lug the lemonade back, and it takes 1,099 ants to steal the pickle jar. How many soldiers carry these big items?
   4,425 ants
4. Look-outs are posted all around the picnic blanket. It takes 53 soldiers to watch in front of the picnic basket. Another group of 69 ants watch out by the grill. Three groups of 77 watch the different trails in the park. How many ant soldiers are on the look-out?
   353 ants

89

Equally Alike

Label six shoe boxes with one of these numbers: 12, 18, 20, 24, 36 and 48. **Fill** each box with the **number of objects** on its label. For example, 12 game pieces may be in one box and 18 marbles in another.

Directions:
1. **Count** the number of objects in each box.
2. **Divide** the number of objects into different sets of equal numbers. **Write** all possible multiplication sentences for each one. Try to **write** the related division sentences as well.
3. **Complete** the activity chart below.

Sample answers below.

Box #	Number in set	Multiplication problem	Related division problem
12	4	3 x 4 4 x 3	12 ÷ 4 12 ÷ 3
18	9	2 x 9 9 x 2	18 ÷ 9 18 ÷ 2
20	5	4 x 5 5 x 4	20 ÷ 5 20 ÷ 4
24	3	3 x 8 8 x 3	24 ÷ 3 24 ÷ 8
36	4	4 x 9 9 x 4	36 ÷ 4 36 ÷ 9
48	6	6 x 8 8 x 6	48 ÷ 6 48 ÷ 8

90

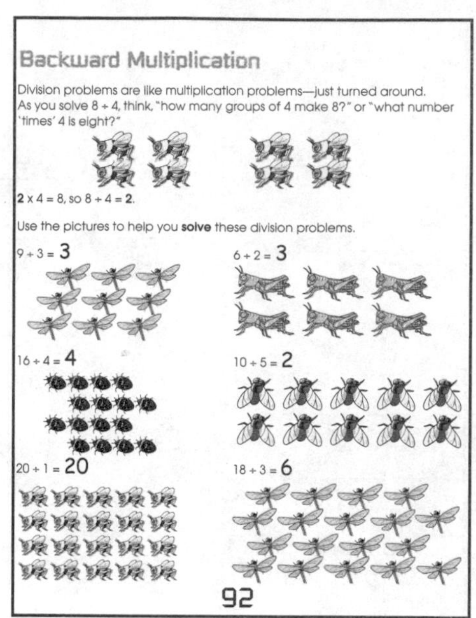

Backward Multiplication

Division problems are like multiplication problems—just turned around. As you solve $8 \div 4$, think, "how many groups of 4 make 8?" or "what number 'times' 4 is eight?"

2 $\times 4 = 8$, so $8 \div 4 =$ **2**.

Use the pictures to help you **solve** these division problems.

$9 \div 3 =$ 3 $\quad 6 \div 2 =$ 3

$16 \div 4 =$ 4 $\quad 10 \div 5 =$ 2

$20 \div 1 =$ 20 $\quad 18 \div 3 =$ 6

92

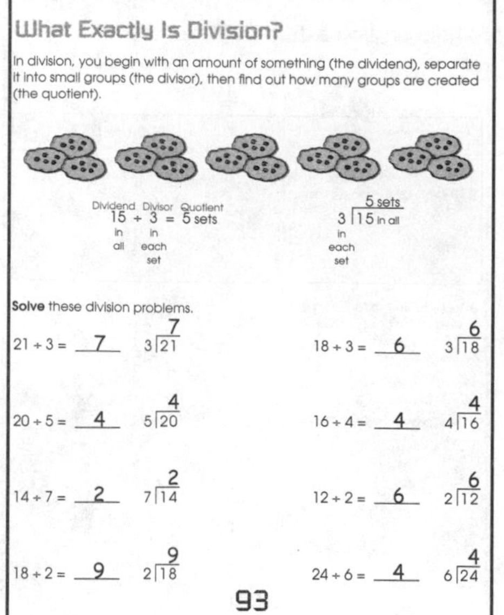

What Exactly Is Division?

In division, you begin with an amount of something (the dividend), separate it into small groups (the divisor), then find out how many groups are created (the quotient).

Dividend Divisor Quotient
15 ÷ 3 = 5 sets
in all / in each set

$\overset{5 \text{ sets}}{3\overline{)15 \text{ in all}}}$
in each set

Solve these division problems.

$21 \div 3 =$ 7 $\quad \overset{7}{3\overline{)21}}$ $\qquad 18 \div 3 =$ 6 $\quad \overset{6}{3\overline{)18}}$

$20 \div 5 =$ 4 $\quad \overset{4}{5\overline{)20}}$ $\qquad 16 \div 4 =$ 4 $\quad \overset{4}{4\overline{)16}}$

$14 \div 7 =$ 2 $\quad \overset{2}{7\overline{)14}}$ $\qquad 12 \div 2 =$ 6 $\quad \overset{6}{2\overline{)12}}$

$18 \div 2 =$ 9 $\quad \overset{9}{2\overline{)18}}$ $\qquad 24 \div 6 =$ 4 $\quad \overset{4}{6\overline{)24}}$

93

Sandwich Cookie

Oops! This recipe below makes 24 dozen or 288 cookies. Reduce the ingredients to make four dozen or 48 cookies. Then, follow the directions to bake the cookies. (We divided 24 dozen by 6 to get 4 dozen. Divide the rest of the ingredients by 6 also.)

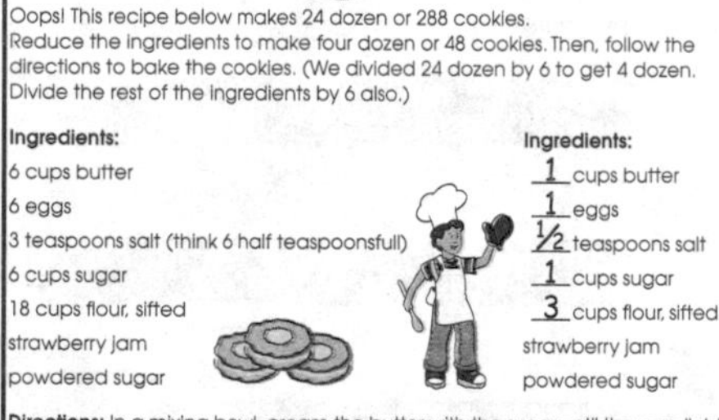

Ingredients:	**Ingredients:**
6 cups butter	1 cups butter
6 eggs	1 eggs
3 teaspoons salt (think 6 half teaspoonsfull)	½ teaspoons salt
6 cups sugar	1 cups sugar
18 cups flour, sifted	3 cups flour, sifted
strawberry jam	strawberry jam
powdered sugar	powdered sugar

Directions: In a mixing bowl, cream the butter with the sugar until they are light and fluffy. Beat in the eggs. Sift the flour and salt into the butter/egg mixture. Mix until well blended. Refrigerate for 1 hour. Divide the dough in half and keep one-half in the refrigerator until needed. Preheat oven to 375°.

Bottom Cookie: Roll out the first half of the dough to 1/8" thickness on a lightly floured surface. Cut out the dough using a 2"-3" round cookie cutter. Place the dough shapes on a cookie sheet. Bake for 10 to 12 minutes.

Top Cookie: Roll out the other half of the dough. Cut the dough using the same cookie cutter, but after it is cut, use a very small cookie cutter or a small bottle cap, floured, to cut a hole in the center of each dough shape. Place the shapes on a cookie sheet and bake them for 10 to 12 minutes. While they are cooling, sprinkle them lightly with powdered sugar.

When both sets of cookies are cool, spread jam on the bottom cookie. Cover it with the top cookie.

94

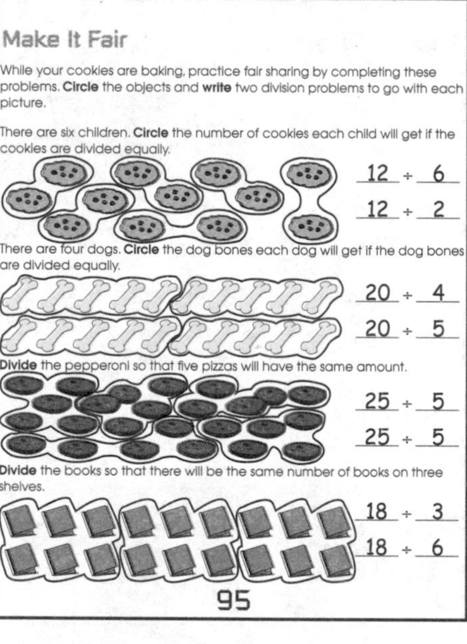

Make It Fair

While your cookies are baking, practice fair sharing by completing these problems. **Circle** the objects and **write** two division problems to go with each picture.

There are six children. **Circle** the number of cookies each child will get if the cookies are divided equally.

$12 \div 6$
$12 \div 2$

There are four dogs. **Circle** the dog bones each dog will get if the dog bones are divided equally.

$20 \div 4$
$20 \div 5$

Divide the pepperoni so that five pizzas will have the same amount.

$25 \div 5$
$25 \div 5$

Divide the books so that there will be the same number of books on three shelves.

$18 \div 3$
$18 \div 6$

95

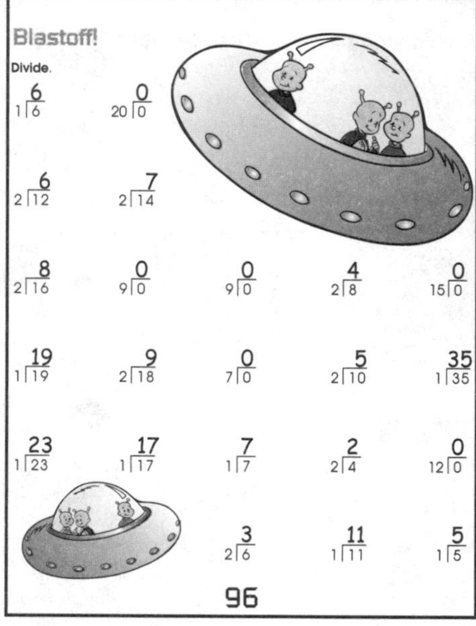

Blastoff!

Divide.

$\overset{6}{1\overline{)6}}$ $\quad \overset{0}{20\overline{)0}}$

$\overset{6}{2\overline{)12}}$ $\quad \overset{7}{2\overline{)14}}$

$\overset{8}{2\overline{)16}}$ $\quad \overset{0}{9\overline{)0}}$ $\quad \overset{0}{9\overline{)0}}$ $\quad \overset{4}{2\overline{)8}}$ $\quad \overset{0}{15\overline{)0}}$

$\overset{19}{1\overline{)19}}$ $\quad \overset{9}{2\overline{)18}}$ $\quad \overset{0}{7\overline{)0}}$ $\quad \overset{5}{2\overline{)10}}$ $\quad \overset{35}{1\overline{)35}}$

$\overset{23}{1\overline{)23}}$ $\quad \overset{17}{1\overline{)17}}$ $\quad \overset{7}{1\overline{)7}}$ $\quad \overset{2}{2\overline{)4}}$ $\quad \overset{0}{12\overline{)0}}$

$\overset{3}{2\overline{)6}}$ $\quad \overset{11}{1\overline{)11}}$ $\quad \overset{5}{1\overline{)5}}$

96

Carrier Math Messengers

Divide.

$\overset{4}{3\overline{)12}}$ $\quad \overset{6}{8\overline{)48}}$ $\quad \overset{9}{2\overline{)18}}$

$\overset{5}{5\overline{)25}}$ $\quad \overset{8}{9\overline{)72}}$ $\quad \overset{6}{4\overline{)24}}$

$\overset{7}{6\overline{)42}}$ $\quad \overset{5}{8\overline{)40}}$ $\quad \overset{2}{2\overline{)4}}$ $\quad \overset{8}{7\overline{)56}}$ $\quad \overset{7}{9\overline{)63}}$

$\overset{5}{9\overline{)45}}$ $\quad \overset{1}{7\overline{)7}}$ $\quad \overset{5}{3\overline{)15}}$ $\quad \overset{4}{2\overline{)8}}$ $\quad \overset{9}{7\overline{)63}}$

$\overset{8}{3\overline{)24}}$ $\quad \overset{5}{6\overline{)30}}$ $\quad \overset{6}{9\overline{)54}}$

$\overset{9}{9\overline{)81}}$ $\quad \overset{4}{7\overline{)28}}$ $\quad \overset{8}{4\overline{)32}}$

97

Bath Math!

Divide.

$\overset{4}{8\overline{)32}}$ $\quad \overset{6}{6\overline{)36}}$ $\quad \overset{1}{7\overline{)7}}$

$\overset{5}{8\overline{)40}}$ $\quad \overset{8}{7\overline{)56}}$ $\quad \overset{8}{9\overline{)72}}$

$\overset{2}{6\overline{)12}}$ $\quad \overset{4}{9\overline{)36}}$

$\overset{7}{6\overline{)42}}$ $\quad \overset{8}{6\overline{)48}}$ $\quad \overset{3}{7\overline{)21}}$

$\overset{4}{7\overline{)28}}$ $\quad \overset{3}{8\overline{)24}}$

$\overset{2}{8\overline{)16}}$ $\quad \overset{9}{9\overline{)81}}$ $\quad \overset{9}{6\overline{)54}}$ $\quad \overset{3}{6\overline{)18}}$

$\overset{1}{8\overline{)8}}$ $\quad \overset{4}{6\overline{)24}}$ $\quad \overset{2}{9\overline{)18}}$ $\quad \overset{5}{7\overline{)35}}$ $\quad \overset{6}{8\overline{)48}}$

$\overset{5}{9\overline{)45}}$

$\overset{7}{9\overline{)63}}$ $\quad \overset{3}{9\overline{)27}}$

98

Division Tic-Tac-Toe

Solve the problems. **Draw** an **X** on the odd (9, 7, 5, 3) answers. **Draw** an **O** on the even (8, 6, 4, 2) answers.

X 9	O 6	O 2
O 8	O 8	X 5
X 7	X 5	X 3

O 8	X 3	O 6
X 7	X 5	X 5
O 4	O 2	X 3

O 6	X 9	X 7
X 9	O 4	O 2
O 4	X 3	O 6

X 5	O 2	O 4
O 8	O 4	X 7
O 8	X 3	X 3

O 2	O 2	O 6
X 9	X 7	O 8
X 9	O 6	X 3

O 2	X 9	O 4
X 5	X 9	O 6
O 2	X 5	X 9

X 3	O 2	X 9
O 6	X 5	X 7
O 8	O 2	O 4

X 9	X 7	O 4
O 6	X 7	O 8
X 5	O 2	X 9

X 7	O 6	X 9
O 4	O 8	X 3
X 5	X 3	O 2

99

Jersey Division

Write the numbers in the correct footballs to get the given answer.

712	423	972
21 ÷ 7 = 3	24 ÷ 3 = 8	27 ÷ 9 = 3
848	819	554
48 ÷ 8 = 6	18 ÷ 9 = 2	45 ÷ 5 = 9
274	658	794
42 ÷ 7 = 6	56 ÷ 8 = 7	49 ÷ 7 = 7
376	663	804
63 ÷ 7 = 9	36 ÷ 6 = 6	40 ÷ 8 = 5

100

Lizzy the Lizard Bags Her Bugs

Lizzy the Lizard separates her bugs into separate bags so that her lunch is ready for the week. Help her decide how to divide the bugs.

1. Lizzy caught 45 cockroaches. She put 5 into each bag. How many bags did she use?
   45 ÷ 5 = 9 bags
2. Lizzy found 32 termites. She put 4 into each bag. How many bags did she need?
   32 ÷ 4 = 8 bags
3. Lizzy captured 49 stinkbugs. She put them into 7 bags. How many stinkbugs were in each bag?
   49 ÷ 7 = 7 stinkbugs
4. Lizzy bagged 27 horn beetles. She used 3 bags. How many beetles went into each bag?
   27 ÷ 3 = 9 beetles
5. Lizzy lassoed 36 butterflies. She put 9 into each bag. How many bags did she need?
   36 ÷ 9 = 4 bags
6. Lizzy went fishing and caught 48 water beetles. She used 6 bags for her catch. How many beetles went into each bag?
   48 ÷ 6 = 8 beetles

101

Two-Digit Quotients

Steps:

1. Ask: Is the tens digit large enough to divide into? (Yes.) Divide. Multiply the partial quotient (2) by the divisor (4) and subtract from the partial dividend (8).
   4)84 → 2; 4 × 2; −8; 0

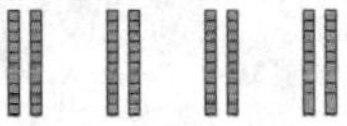

8 tens divided into 4 groups. How many are in each group? (2)

2. Carry down the 4 in the ones column. Ask: How many groups of 4 are there in 4? (1) Divide. Multiply the partial quotient (1) by the divisor (4) and subtract from the partial dividend (4).
   4)84 → 21; −8; 04; −4 (4 × 1); 0

3. When 84 things are divided into 4 groups, there will be 21 in each group.

84 ÷ 4 = 21 + 21 + 21 + 21

4)84 → 21; −8; 04; −4; 0

Divide.

3)63 = 21 (−6, 03, −3, 0)
2)72 = 36
4)48 = 12
2)56 = 28
3)96 = 32
2)82 = 41

102

Snowball Bash

Divide this mound of giant snowballs!

7)84 = 12 (−7, 14, −14, 0)
5)75 = 15
3)45 = 15
9)99 = 11
4)88 = 22
5)80 = 16
4)64 = 16
3)57 = 19
3)78 = 26
3)72 = 24
8)96 = 12
2)86 = 43
2)38 = 19
6)66 = 11
5)65 = 13
4)52 = 13
4)68 = 17
6)78 = 13
7)91 = 13
2)42 = 21
6)72 = 12

103

Three-Digit Quotients

Steps:

1. Ask: Is the hundreds digit large enough to divide into? (Yes.) Divide. Multiply the partial quotient by the divisor and subtract from the partial dividend.
   7)938 → 1; −7; 2
2. Ask: Can I divide the remaining 2 by 7? (No.) Bring down the 3 tens.
   7)938 → 1; −7; 23 — 2 hundreds + 3 tens = 23 tens
3. Divide the 23 tens by 7. Multiply the partial quotient by the divisor and subtract.
   7)938 → 13; −7; 23; −21; 2
4. Ask: Can I divide the remaining 2 by 7? (No.) Bring down 8 ones.
   7)938 → 13; −7; 23; −21; 28 — 2 tens + 8 ones = 28 ones
5. Divide the 28 ones by 7. Multiply the partial quotient by the divisor and subtract.
   7)938 → 134; −7; 23; −21; 28; −28; 0

Divide.

6)888 = 148 (−6, 28, −24, 48, −48, 0)
2)542 = 271
3)693 = 231
4)544 = 136
7)896 = 128
5)635 = 127

104

On-Stage Division

Divide.

6)888 = 148 (−6, 28, −24, 48, −48, 0)
2)956 = 478
2)712 = 356
4)860 = 215
5)845 = 169

6)750 = 125
9)999 = 111
8)968 = 121
3)774 = 258
5)735 = 147
8)920 = 115

8)984 = 123
4)500 = 125
2)846 = 423
4)712 = 178

105

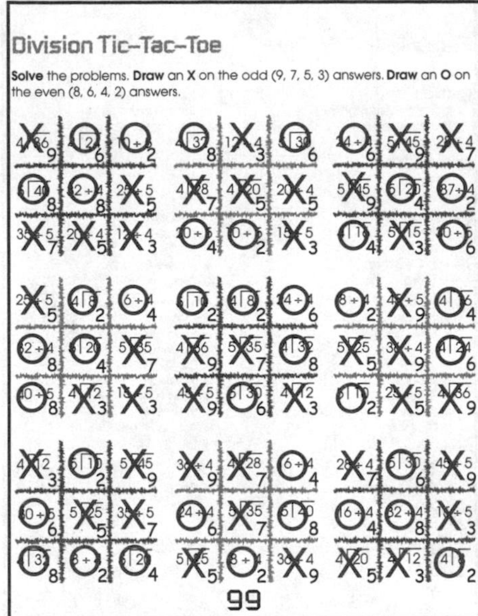

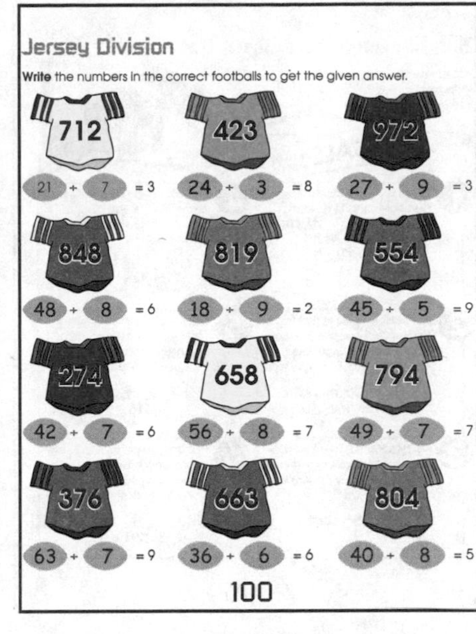

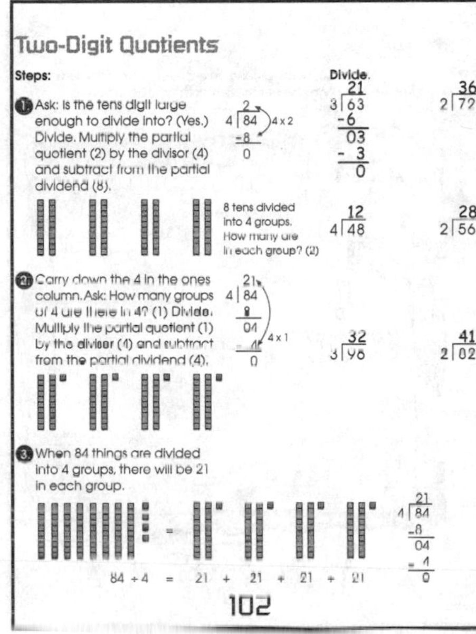

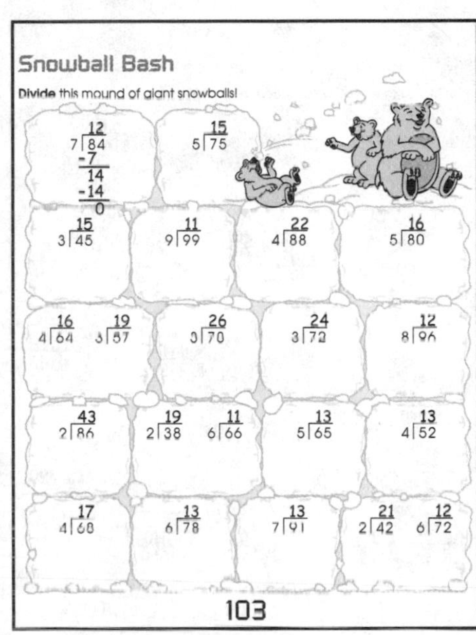

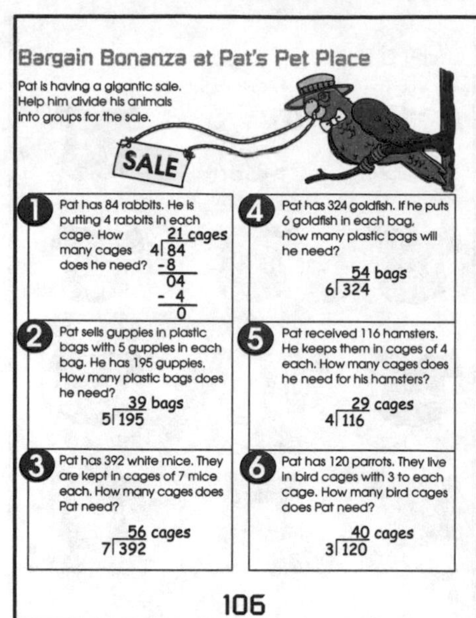

Bargain Bonanza at Pat's Pet Place

Pat is having a gigantic sale. Help him divide his animals into groups for the sale.

SALE

1. Pat has 84 rabbits. He is putting 4 rabbits in each cage. How many cages does he need? **21 cages** (4⟌84; −8; 04; −4; 0)
2. Pat sells guppies in plastic bags with 5 guppies in each bag. He has 195 guppies. How many plastic bags does he need? **39 bags** (5⟌195)
3. Pat has 392 white mice. They are kept in cages of 7 mice each. How many cages does Pat need? **56 cages** (7⟌392)
4. Pat has 324 goldfish. If he puts 6 goldfish in each bag, how many plastic bags will he need? **54 bags** (6⟌324)
5. Pat received 116 hamsters. He keeps them in cages of 4 each. How many cages does he need for his hamsters? **29 cages** (4⟌116)
6. Pat has 120 parrots. They live in bird cages with 3 to each cage. How many bird cages does Pat need? **40 cages** (3⟌120)

106

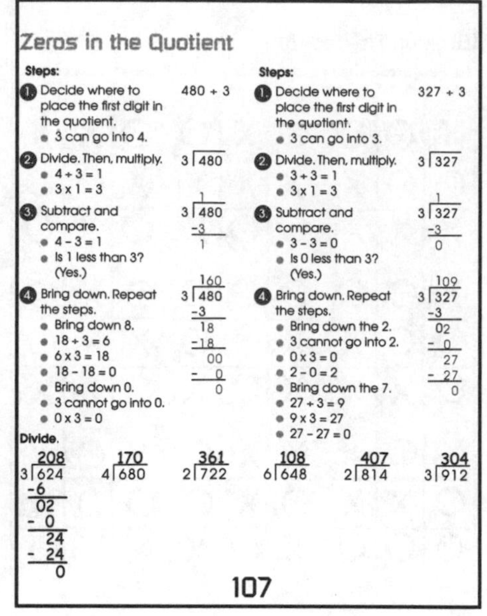

Zeros in the Quotient

Steps: 480 ÷ 3

1. Decide where to place the first digit in the quotient.
   - 3 can go into 4.
2. Divide. Then, multiply. (3⟌480)
   - 4 ÷ 3 = 1
   - 3 x 1 = 3
3. Subtract and compare. (3⟌480; −3; 1)
   - 4 − 3 = 1
   - Is 1 less than 3? (Yes.)
4. Bring down. Repeat the steps. (160: 3⟌480; −3; 18; −18; 00; −0; 0)
   - Bring down 8.
   - 18 ÷ 3 = 6
   - 6 x 3 = 18
   - 18 − 18 = 0
   - Bring down 0.
   - 3 cannot go into 0.
   - 0 x 3 = 0

Steps: 327 ÷ 3

1. Decide where to place the first digit in the quotient.
   - 3 can go into 3.
2. Divide. Then, multiply. (3⟌327)
   - 3 ÷ 3 = 1
   - 3 x 1 = 3
3. Subtract and compare. (3⟌327; −3; 0)
   - 3 − 3 = 0
   - Is 0 less than 3? (Yes.)
4. Bring down. Repeat the steps. (109: 3⟌327; −3; 02; −0; 27; −27; 0)
   - Bring down the 2.
   - 3 cannot go into 2.
   - 0 x 3 = 0
   - 2 − 0 = 2
   - Bring down the 7.
   - 27 ÷ 3 = 9
   - 9 x 3 = 27
   - 27 − 27 = 0

Divide.

3⟌624 = 208 (−6; 02; −0; 24; −24; 0)   4⟌680 = 170   2⟌722 = 361   6⟌648 = 108   2⟌814 = 407   3⟌912 = 304

107

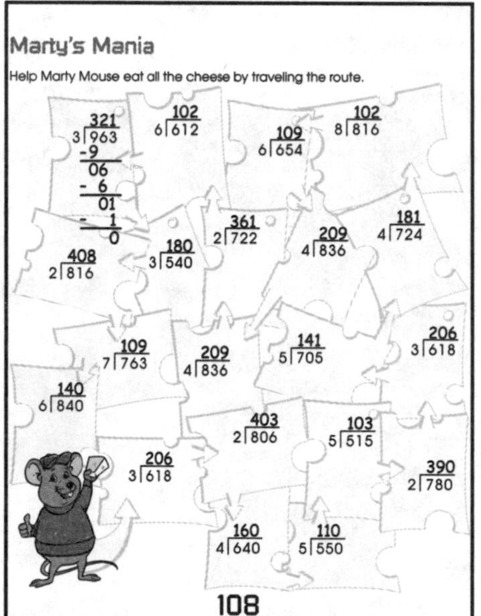

Marty's Mania

Help Marty Mouse eat all the cheese by traveling the route.

3⟌963 = 321 (−9; 06; −6; 01; −1; 0)
6⟌612 = 102
6⟌654 = 109
8⟌816 = 102
2⟌816 = 408
3⟌540 = 180
2⟌722 = 361
4⟌836 = 209
4⟌724 = 181
7⟌763 = 109
4⟌836 = 209
5⟌705 = 141
3⟌618 = 206
6⟌840 = 140
2⟌806 = 403
5⟌515 = 103
3⟌618 = 206
2⟌780 = 390
4⟌640 = 160
5⟌550 = 110

108

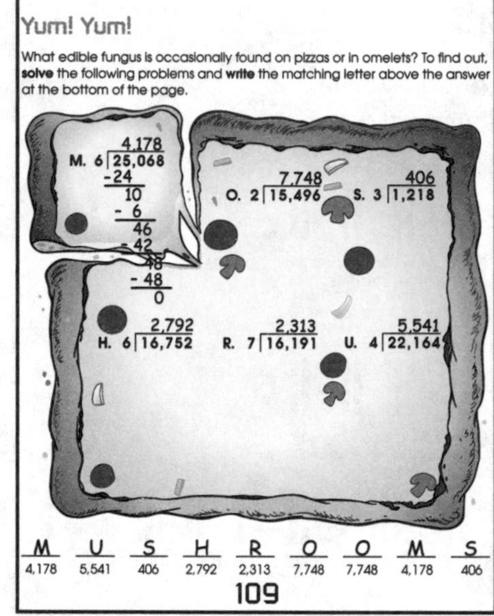

Yum! Yum!

What edible fungus is occasionally found on pizzas or in omelets? To find out, **solve** the following problems and **write** the matching letter above the answer at the bottom of the page.

M. 6⟌25,068 = 4,178 (−24; 10; −6; 46; −42; 48; −48; 0)
O. 2⟌15,496 = 7,748
S. 3⟌1,218 = 406
H. 6⟌16,752 = 2,792
R. 7⟌16,191 = 2,313
U. 4⟌22,164 = 5,541

M	U	S	H	R	O	O	M	S
4,178	5,541	406	2,792	2,313	7,748	7,748	4,178	406

109

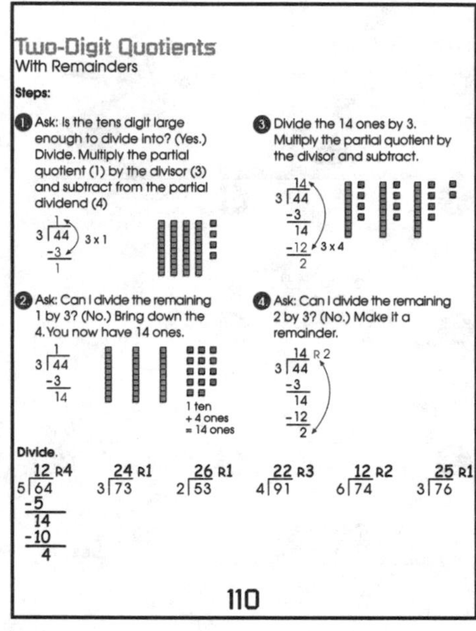

Two-Digit Quotients

With Remainders

Steps:

1. Ask: Is the tens digit large enough to divide into? (Yes.) Divide. Multiply the partial quotient (1) by the divisor (3) and subtract from the partial dividend (4). (3⟌44; 3 x 1; −3; 1)
2. Ask: Can I divide the remaining 1 by 3? (No.) Bring down the 4. You now have 14 ones. (3⟌44; −3; 14) 1 ten + 4 ones = 14 ones
3. Divide the 14 ones by 3. Multiply the partial quotient by the divisor and subtract. (14: 3⟌44; −3; 14; −12; 2; 3 x 4)
4. Ask: Can I divide the remaining 2 by 3? (No.) Make it a remainder. (14 R2: 3⟌44; −3; 14; −12; 2)

Divide.

5⟌64 = 12 R4 (−5; 14; −10; 4)   3⟌73 = 24 R1   2⟌53 = 26 R1   4⟌91 = 22 R3   6⟌74 = 12 R2   3⟌76 = 25 R1

110

Mr. R Means Business

Solve the division problems below. **Write** the quotient and the remainder.

Use me when a problem doesn't come out even.

No Remainder	Remainder
4⟌22 = 6; −24	4⟌22 = 5 R2; −20; 2

5⟌28 = 5 R3 (−25; 3)   4⟌19 = 4 R3 (−16; 3)   8⟌26 = 3 R2   7⟌45 = 6 R3

3⟌26 = 8 R2   2⟌19 = 9 R1   6⟌51 = 8 R3   9⟌65 = 7 R2

8⟌43 = 5 R3   9⟌59 = 6 R5   7⟌33 = 4 R5   4⟌27 = 6 R3

111

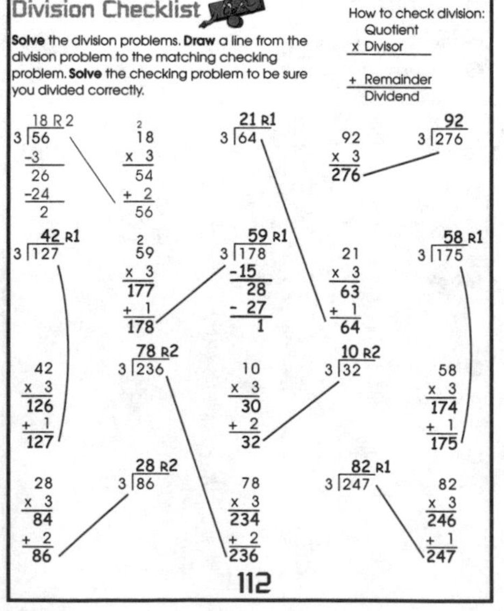

Division Checklist

Solve the division problems. **Draw** a line from the division problem to the matching checking problem. **Solve** the checking problem to be sure you divided correctly.

How to check division:
Quotient
x Divisor
+ Remainder
Dividend

3⟌56 = 18 R2 (−3; 26; −24; 2) — 18 x 3 = 54; + 2 = 56
3⟌64 = 21 R1 — 21 x 3 = 63; + 1 = 64
3⟌276 = 92 — 92 x 3 = 276
3⟌127 = 42 R1 — 42 x 3 = 126; + 1 = 127
3⟌178 = 59 R1 (−15; 28; −27; 1) — 59 x 3 = 177; + 1 = 178
3⟌175 = 58 R1 — 58 x 3 = 174; + 1 = 175
3⟌236 = 78 R2 — 78 x 3 = 234; + 2 = 236
3⟌32 = 10 R2 — 10 x 3 = 30; + 2 = 32
3⟌86 = 28 R2 — 28 x 3 = 84; + 2 = 86
3⟌247 = 82 R1 — 82 x 3 = 246; + 1 = 247

112

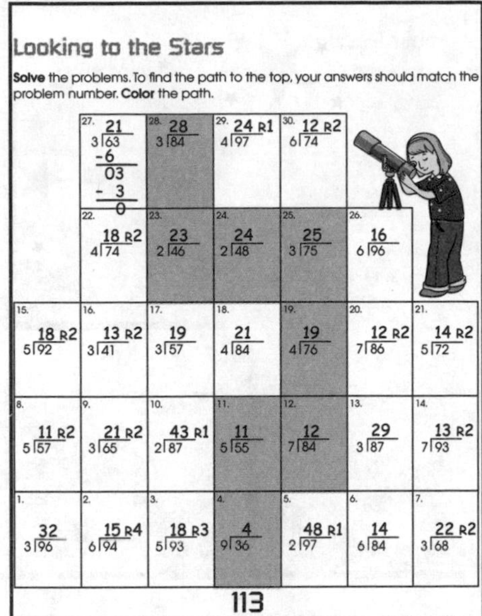

Looking to the Stars

Solve the problems. To find the path to the top, your answers should match the problem number. **Color** the path.

	27. 3⟌63 = 21	28. 3⟌84 = 28	29. 4⟌97 = 24 R1	30. 6⟌74 = 12 R2		
	22. 4⟌74 = 18 R2	23. 2⟌46 = 23	24. 2⟌48 = 24	25. 3⟌75 = 25	26. 6⟌96 = 16	
15. 5⟌92 = 18 R2	16. 3⟌41 = 13 R2	17. 3⟌57 = 19	18. 4⟌84 = 21	19. 4⟌76 = 19	20. 7⟌86 = 12 R2	21. 5⟌72 = 14 R2
8. 5⟌57 = 11 R2	9. 3⟌65 = 21 R2	10. 2⟌87 = 43 R1	11. 5⟌55 = 11	12. 7⟌84 = 12	13. 3⟌87 = 29	14. 7⟌93 = 13 R2
1. 3⟌96 = 32	2. 6⟌94 = 15 R4	3. 5⟌93 = 18 R3	4. 9⟌36 = 4	5. 2⟌97 = 48 R1	6. 6⟌84 = 14	7. 3⟌68 = 22 R2

113

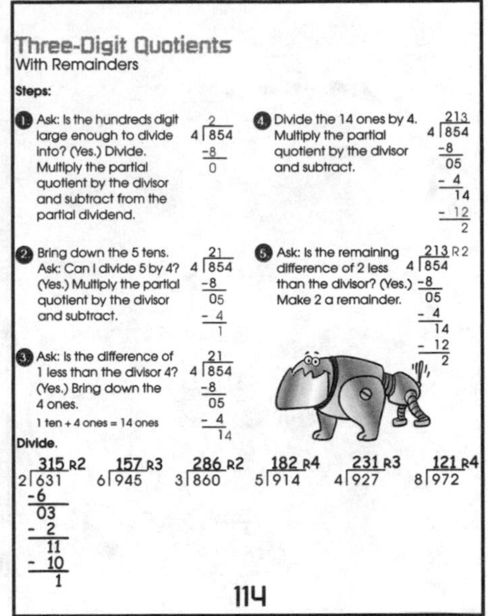

Three-Digit Quotients
With Remainders

Steps:

1. Ask: Is the hundreds digit large enough to divide into? (Yes.) Divide. Multiply the partial quotient by the divisor and subtract from the partial dividend.
2. Bring down the 5 tens. Ask: Can I divide 5 by 4? (Yes.) Multiply the partial quotient by the divisor and subtract.
3. Ask: Is the difference of 1 less than the divisor 4? (Yes.) Bring down the 4 ones. 1 ten + 4 ones = 14 ones
4. Divide the 14 ones by 4. Multiply the partial quotient by the divisor and subtract.
5. Ask: Is the remaining difference of 2 less than the divisor? (Yes.) Make 2 a remainder.

4⟌854 = 213 R2

Divide.

2⟌631 = 315 R2 6⟌945 = 157 R3 3⟌860 = 286 R2 5⟌914 = 182 R4 4⟌927 = 231 R3 8⟌972 = 121 R4

114

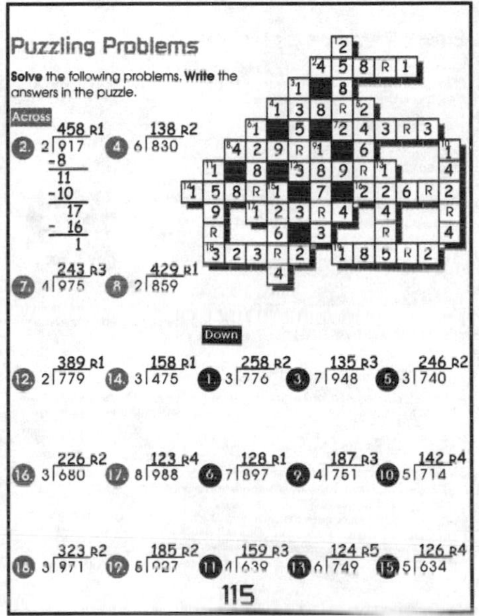

Puzzling Problems

Solve the following problems. **Write** the answers in the puzzle.

Across

2. 2⟌917 = 458 R1
4. 6⟌830 = 138 R2
7. 4⟌975 = 243 R3
8. 2⟌859 = 429 R1

Down

12. 2⟌779 = 389 R1
14. 3⟌475 = 158 R1
1. 3⟌776 = 258 R2
3. 7⟌948 = 135 R3
5. 3⟌740 = 246 R2
16. 3⟌680 = 226 R2
17. 8⟌988 = 123 R4
6. 7⟌897 = 128 R1
9. 4⟌751 = 187 R3
10. 5⟌714 = 142 R4
18. 3⟌971 = 323 R2
19. 5⟌927 = 185 R2
11. 4⟌639 = 159 R3
13. 6⟌749 = 124 R5
15. 5⟌634 = 126 R4

115

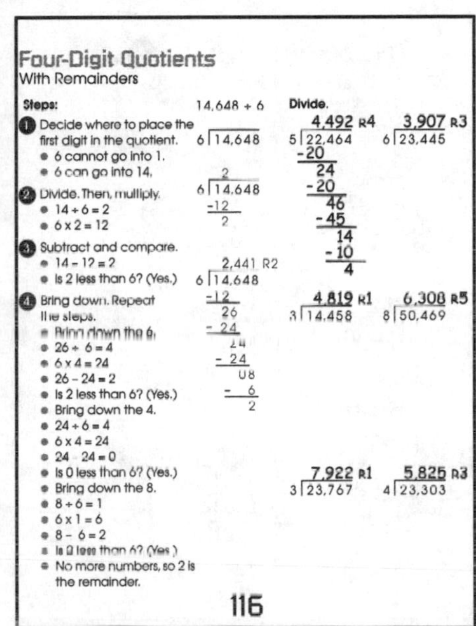

Four-Digit Quotients
With Remainders

Steps: 14,648 ÷ 6

1. Decide where to place the first digit in the quotient.
   - 6 cannot go into 1.
   - 6 can go into 14.
2. Divide. Then, multiply.
   - 14 ÷ 6 = 2
   - 6 x 2 = 12
3. Subtract and compare.
   - 14 − 12 = 2
   - Is 2 less than 6? (Yes.)
4. Bring down. Repeat the steps.
   - Bring down the 6.
   - 26 ÷ 6 = 4
   - 6 x 4 = 24
   - 26 − 24 = 2
   - Is 2 less than 6? (Yes.)
   - Bring down the 4.
   - 24 ÷ 6 = 4
   - 6 x 4 = 24
   - 24 − 24 = 0
   - Is 0 less than 6? (Yes.)
   - Bring down the 8.
   - 8 ÷ 6 = 1
   - 6 x 1 = 6
   - 8 − 6 = 2
   - Is 2 less than 6? (Yes.)
   - No more numbers, so 2 is the remainder.

6⟌14,648 = 2,441 R2

Divide.

5⟌22,464 = 4,492 R4 6⟌23,445 = 3,907 R3
3⟌14,458 = 4,819 R1 8⟌50,469 = 6,308 R5
3⟌23,767 = 7,922 R1 4⟌23,303 = 5,825 R3

116

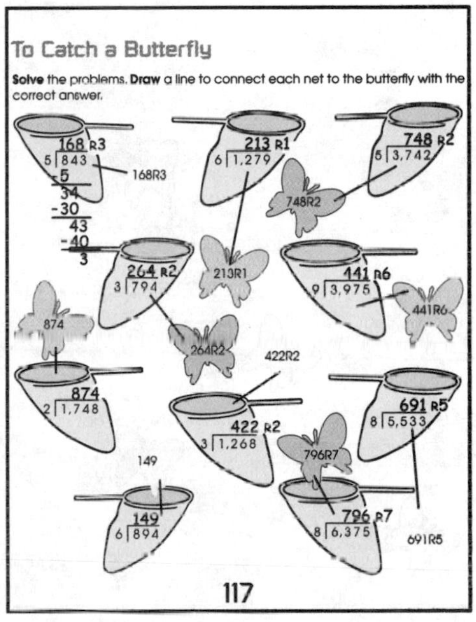

To Catch a Butterfly

Solve the problems. **Draw** a line to connect each net to the butterfly with the correct answer.

5⟌843 = 168 R3 6⟌1,279 = 213 R1 5⟌3,742 = 748 R2
3⟌794 = 264 R2 9⟌3,975 = 441 R6
2⟌1,748 = 874 3⟌1,268 = 422 R2 8⟌5,533 = 691 R5
6⟌894 = 149 8⟌6,375 = 796 R7

117

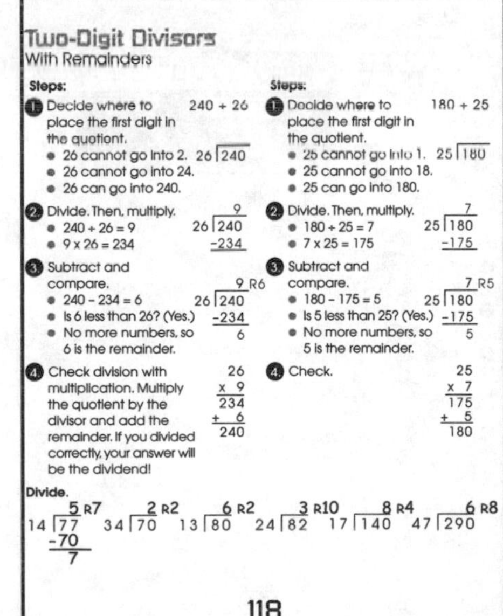

Two-Digit Divisors
With Remainders

Steps: 240 ÷ 26

1. Decide where to place the first digit in the quotient.
   - 26 cannot go into 2.
   - 26 cannot go into 24.
   - 26 can go into 240.
2. Divide. Then, multiply.
   - 240 ÷ 26 = 9
   - 9 x 26 = 234
3. Subtract and compare.
   - 240 − 234 = 6
   - Is 6 less than 26? (Yes.)
   - No more numbers, so 6 is the remainder.
4. Check division with multiplication. Multiply the quotient by the divisor and add the remainder. If you divided correctly, your answer will be the dividend!

26 x 9 = 234, 234 + 6 = 240

Steps: 180 ÷ 25

1. Decide where to place the first digit in the quotient.
   - 25 cannot go into 1.
   - 25 cannot go into 18.
   - 25 can go into 180.
2. Divide. Then, multiply.
   - 180 ÷ 25 = 7
   - 7 x 25 = 175
3. Subtract and compare.
   - 180 − 175 = 5
   - Is 5 less than 25? (Yes.)
   - No more numbers, so 5 is the remainder.
4. Check.

25 x 7 = 175, 175 + 5 = 180

Divide.

14⟌77 = 5 R7 34⟌70 = 2 R2 13⟌80 = 6 R2 24⟌82 = 3 R10 17⟌140 = 8 R4 47⟌290 = 6 R8

118

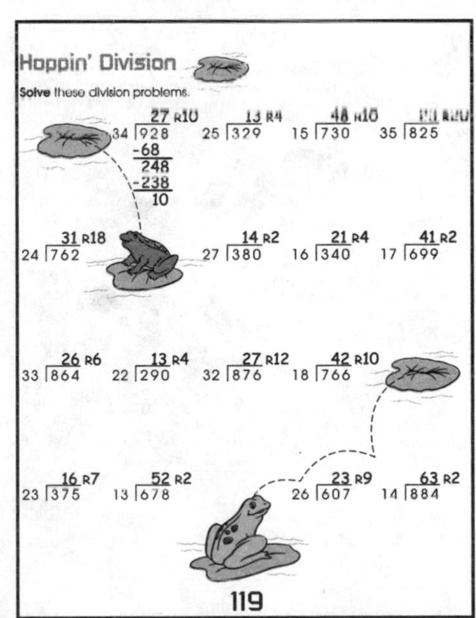

Hoppin' Division

Solve these division problems.

34⟌928 = 27 R10 25⟌329 = 13 R4 15⟌730 = 48 R10 35⟌825 = 23 R20
24⟌762 = 31 R18 27⟌380 = 14 R2 16⟌340 = 21 R4 17⟌699 = 41 R2
33⟌864 = 26 R6 22⟌290 = 13 R4 32⟌876 = 27 R12 18⟌766 = 42 R10
23⟌375 = 16 R7 13⟌678 = 52 R2 26⟌607 = 23 R9 14⟌884 = 63 R2

119

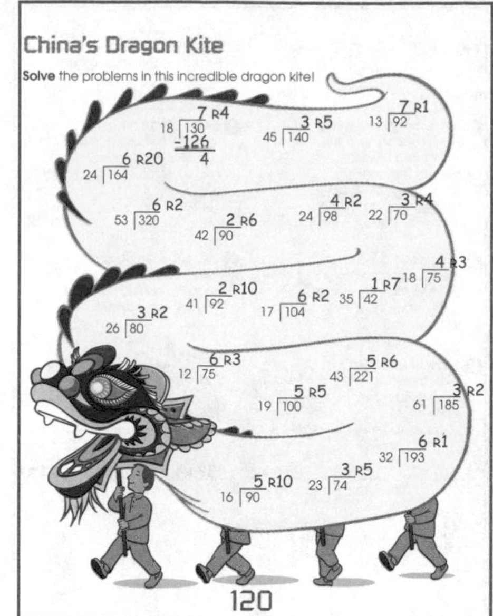

China's Dragon Kite

Solve the problems in this incredible dragon kite!

- 18 ⟌ 130 = 7 R4 (−126, 4)
- 45 ⟌ 140 = 3 R5
- 13 ⟌ 92 = 7 R1
- 24 ⟌ 164 = 6 R20
- 53 ⟌ 320 = 6 R2
- 42 ⟌ 90 = 2 R6
- 24 ⟌ 98 = 4 R2
- 22 ⟌ 70 = 3 R4
- 18 ⟌ 75 = 4 R3
- 41 ⟌ 92 = 2 R10
- 17 ⟌ 104 = 6 R2
- 35 ⟌ 42 = 1 R7
- 26 ⟌ 80 = 3 R2
- 12 ⟌ 75 = 6 R3
- 43 ⟌ 221 = 5 R6
- 19 ⟌ 100 = 5 R5
- 61 ⟌ 185 = 3 R2
- 32 ⟌ 193 = 6 R1
- 16 ⟌ 90 = 5 R10
- 23 ⟌ 74 = 3 R5

120

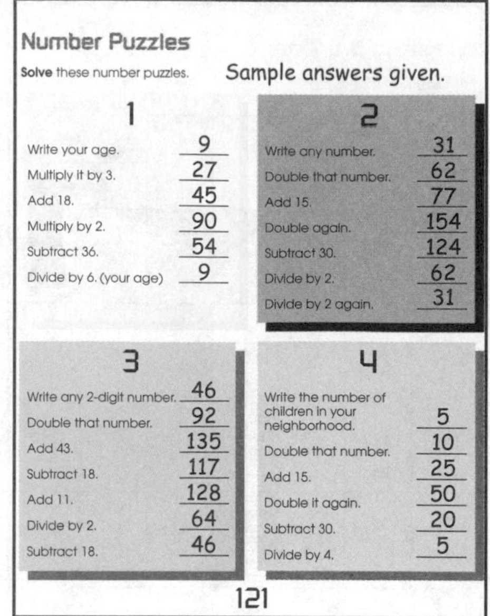

Number Puzzles

Solve these number puzzles. Sample answers given.

1

Write your age.	9
Multiply it by 3.	27
Add 18.	45
Multiply by 2.	90
Subtract 36.	54
Divide by 6. (your age)	9

2

Write any number.	31
Double that number.	62
Add 15.	77
Double again.	154
Subtract 30.	124
Divide by 2.	62
Divide by 2 again.	31

3

Write any 2-digit number.	46
Double that number.	92
Add 43.	135
Subtract 18.	117
Add 11.	128
Divide by 2.	64
Subtract 18.	46

4

Write the number of children in your neighborhood.	5
Double that number.	10
Add 15.	25
Double it again.	50
Subtract 30.	20
Divide by 4.	5

121

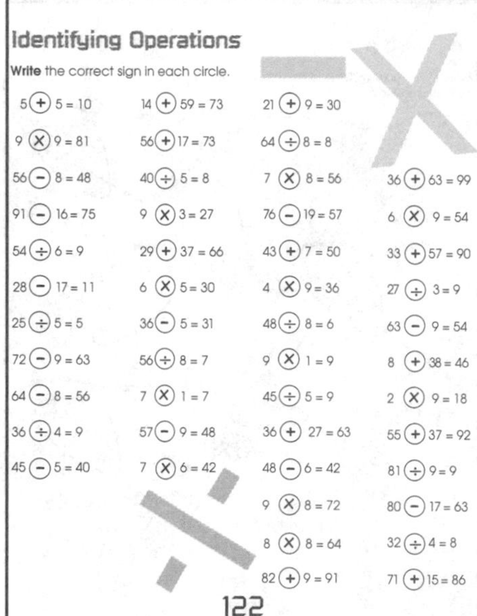

Identifying Operations

Write the correct sign in each circle.

5 (+) 5 = 10	14 (+) 59 = 73	21 (+) 9 = 30	
9 (×) 9 = 81	56 (+) 17 = 73	64 (÷) 8 = 8	
56 (−) 8 = 48	40 (÷) 5 = 8	7 (×) 8 = 56	36 (+) 63 = 99
91 (−) 16 = 75	9 (×) 3 = 27	76 (−) 19 = 57	6 (×) 9 = 54
54 (÷) 6 = 9	29 (+) 37 = 66	43 (+) 7 = 50	33 (+) 57 = 90
28 (−) 17 = 11	6 (×) 5 = 30	4 (×) 9 = 36	27 (÷) 3 = 9
25 (÷) 5 = 5	36 (−) 5 = 31	48 (÷) 8 = 6	63 (−) 9 = 54
72 (−) 9 = 63	56 (÷) 8 = 7	9 (×) 1 = 9	8 (+) 38 = 46
64 (−) 8 = 56	7 (×) 1 = 7	45 (÷) 5 = 9	2 (×) 9 = 18
36 (÷) 4 = 9	57 (−) 9 = 48	36 (+) 27 = 63	55 (+) 37 = 92
45 (−) 5 = 40	7 (×) 6 = 42	48 (−) 6 = 42	81 (÷) 9 = 9
		9 (×) 8 = 72	80 (−) 17 = 63
		8 (×) 8 = 64	32 (÷) 4 = 8
		82 (+) 9 = 91	71 (+) 15 = 86

122

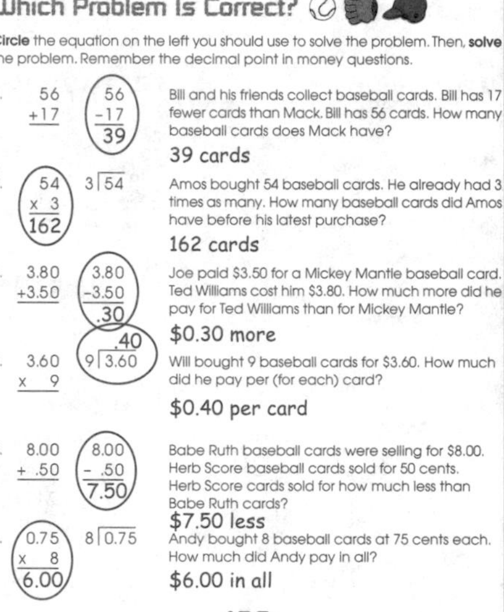

Which Problem Is Correct?

Circle the equation on the left you should use to solve the problem. Then, **solve** the problem. Remember the decimal point in money questions.

1. 56 + 17 | (56 − 17 = 39) — Bill and his friends collect baseball cards. Bill has 17 fewer cards than Mack. Bill has 56 cards. How many baseball cards does Mack have? **39 cards**
2. (54 × 3 = 162) | 3 ⟌ 54 — Amos bought 54 baseball cards. He already had 3 times as many. How many baseball cards did Amos have before his latest purchase? **162 cards**
3. 3.80 + 3.50 | (3.80 − 3.50 = .30) — Joe paid $3.50 for a Mickey Mantle baseball card. Ted Williams cost him $3.80. How much more did he pay for Ted Williams than for Mickey Mantle? **$0.30 more**
4. 3.60 × 9 | (9 ⟌ 3.60 = .40) — Will bought 9 baseball cards for $3.60. How much did he pay per (for each) card? **$0.40 per card**
5. 8.00 + .50 | (8.00 − .50 = 7.50) — Babe Ruth baseball cards were selling for $8.00. Herb Score baseball cards sold for 50 cents. Herb Score cards sold for how much less than Babe Ruth cards? **$7.50 less**
6. (0.75 × 8 = 6.00) | 8 ⟌ 0.75 — Andy bought 8 baseball cards at 75 cents each. How much did Andy pay in all? **$6.00 in all**

123

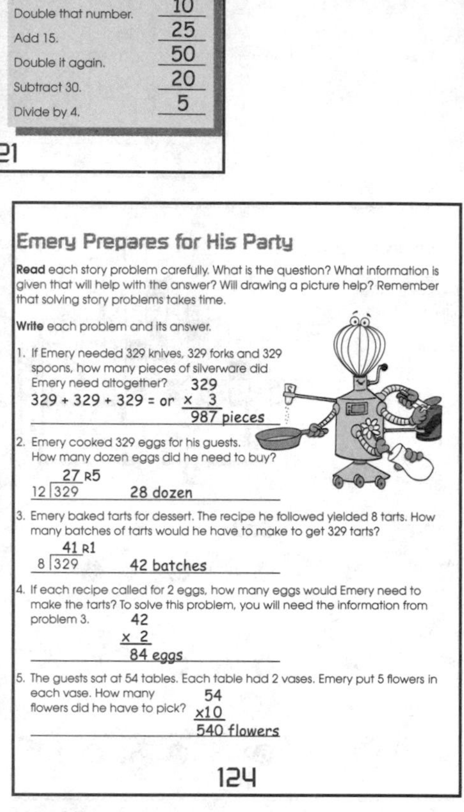

Emery Prepares for His Party

Read each story problem carefully. What is the question? What information is given that will help with the answer? Will drawing a picture help? Remember that solving story problems takes time.

Write each problem and its answer.

1. If Emery needed 329 knives, 329 forks and 329 spoons, how many pieces of silverware did Emery need altogether? 329 + 329 + 329 = or 329 × 3 = **987 pieces**
2. Emery cooked 329 eggs for his guests. How many dozen eggs did he need to buy? 12 ⟌ 329 = 27 R5 **28 dozen**
3. Emery baked tarts for dessert. The recipe he followed yielded 8 tarts. How many batches of tarts would he have to make to get 329 tarts? 8 ⟌ 329 = 41 R1 **42 batches**
4. If each recipe called for 2 eggs, how many eggs would Emery need to make the tarts? To solve this problem, you will need the information from problem 3. 42 × 2 = **84 eggs**
5. The guests sat at 54 tables. Each table had 2 vases. Emery put 5 flowers in each vase. How many flowers did he have to pick? 54 × 10 = **540 flowers**

124

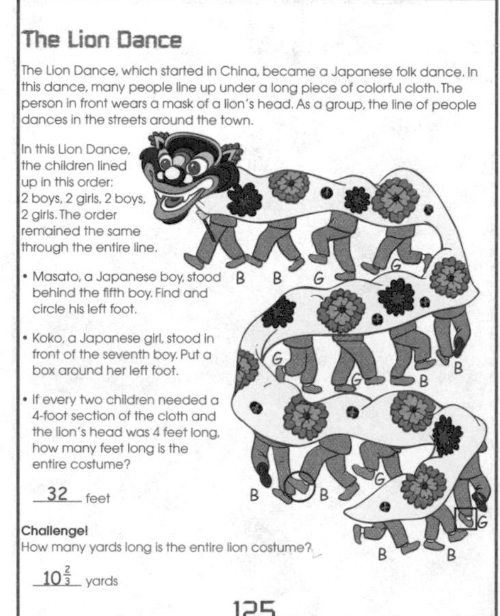

The Lion Dance

The Lion Dance, which started in China, became a Japanese folk dance. In this dance, many people line up under a long piece of colorful cloth. The person in front wears a mask of a lion's head. As a group, the line of people dances in the streets around the town.

In this Lion Dance, the children lined up in this order: 2 boys, 2 girls, 2 boys, 2 girls. The order remained the same through the entire line.

- Masato, a Japanese boy, stood behind the fifth boy. Find and circle his left foot.
- Koko, a Japanese girl, stood in front of the seventh boy. Put a box around her left foot.
- If every two children needed a 4-foot section of the cloth and the lion's head was 4 feet long, how many feet long is the entire costume?

32 feet

Challenge!
How many yards long is the entire lion costume?

$10\frac{2}{3}$ yards

125

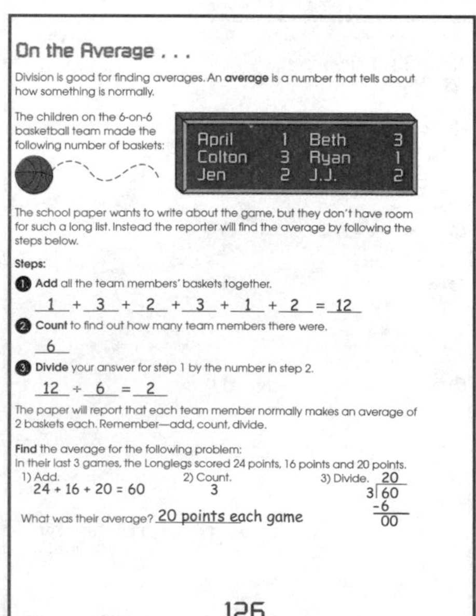

On the Average . . .

Division is good for finding averages. An **average** is a number that tells about how something is normally.

The children on the 6-on-6 basketball team made the following number of baskets:

April	1	Beth	3
Colton	3	Ryan	1
Jen	2	J.J.	2

The school paper wants to write about the game, but they don't have room for such a long list. Instead the reporter will find the average by following the steps below.

Steps:

1. **Add** all the team members' baskets together. 1 + 3 + 2 + 3 + 1 + 2 = 12
2. **Count** to find out how many team members there were. 6
3. **Divide** your answer for step 1 by the number in step 2. 12 ÷ 6 = 2

The paper will report that each team member normally makes an average of 2 baskets each. Remember—add, count, divide.

Find the average for the following problem:
In their last 3 games, the Longlegs scored 24 points, 16 points and 20 points.
1) Add. 24 + 16 + 20 = 60 2) Count. 3 3) Divide. 3 ⟌ 60 = 20 (−6, 00)

What was their average? 20 points each game

126

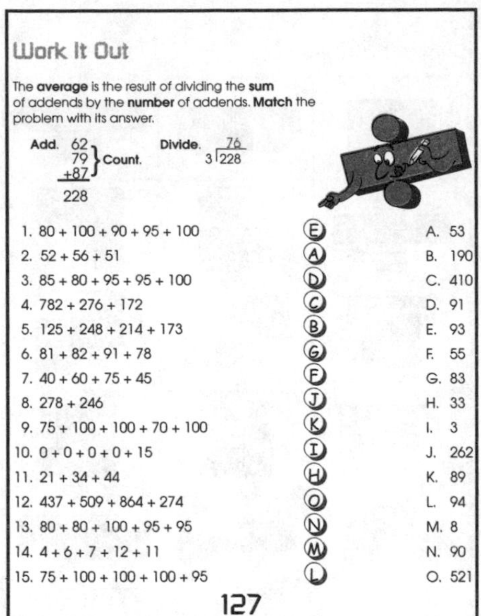

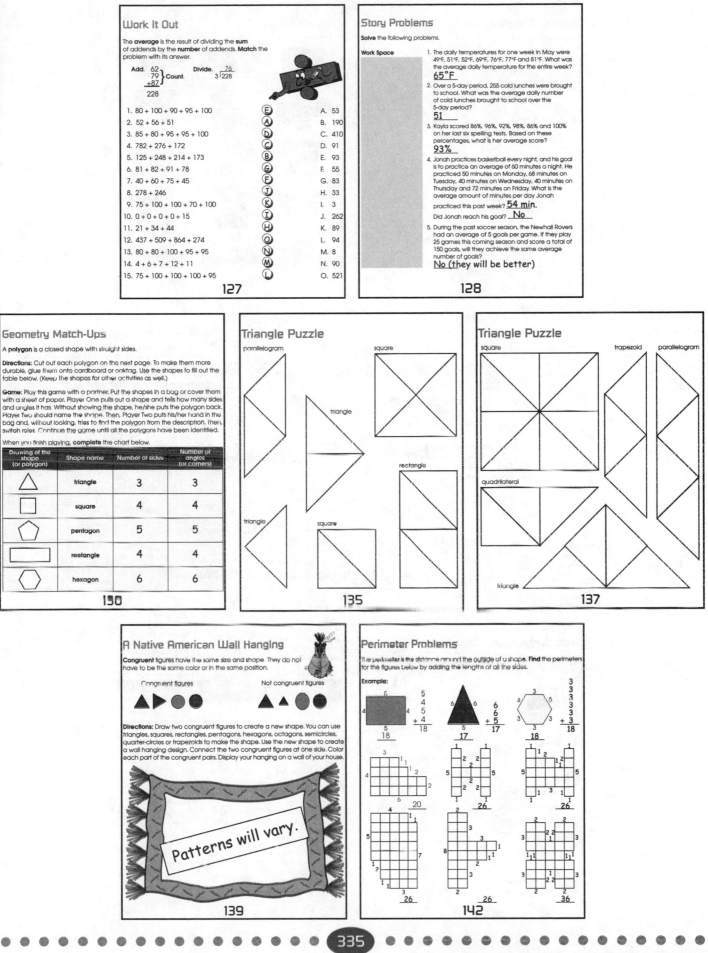

Work It Out

The **average** is the result of dividing the **sum** of addends by the **number** of addends. **Match** the problem with its answer.

Add. 62, 79, +87 } Count. 228

Divide. $3\overline{)228}$ = 76

1. 80 + 100 + 90 + 95 + 100 — (E)
2. 52 + 56 + 51 — (A)
3. 85 + 80 + 95 + 95 + 100 — (D)
4. 782 + 276 + 172 — (C)
5. 125 + 248 + 214 + 173 — (B)
6. 81 + 82 + 91 + 78 — (G)
7. 40 + 60 + 75 + 45 — (F)
8. 278 + 246 — (J)
9. 75 + 100 + 100 + 70 + 100 — (K)
10. 0 + 0 + 0 + 0 + 15 — (I)
11. 21 + 34 + 44 — (H)
12. 437 + 509 + 864 + 274 — (O)
13. 80 + 80 + 100 + 95 + 95 — (N)
14. 4 + 6 + 7 + 12 + 11 — (M)
15. 75 + 100 + 100 + 100 + 95 — (L)

A. 53
B. 190
C. 410
D. 91
E. 93
F. 55
G. 83
H. 33
I. 3
J. 262
K. 89
L. 94
M. 8
N. 90
O. 521

127

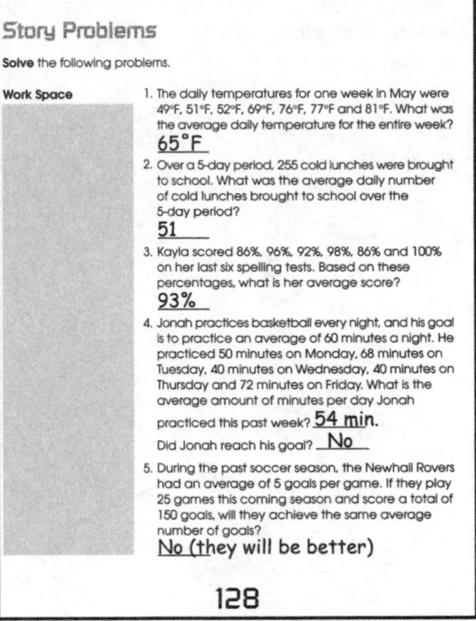

Story Problems

Solve the following problems.

Work Space

1. The daily temperatures for one week in May were 49°F, 51°F, 52°F, 69°F, 76°F, 77°F and 81°F. What was the average daily temperature for the entire week? 65°F
2. Over a 5-day period, 255 cold lunches were brought to school. What was the average daily number of cold lunches brought to school over the 5-day period? 51
3. Kayla scored 86%, 96%, 92%, 98%, 86% and 100% on her last six spelling tests. Based on these percentages, what is her average score? 93%
4. Jonah practices basketball every night, and his goal is to practice an average of 60 minutes a night. He practiced 50 minutes on Monday, 68 minutes on Tuesday, 40 minutes on Wednesday, 40 minutes on Thursday and 72 minutes on Friday. What is the average amount of minutes per day Jonah practiced this past week? 54 min.
   Did Jonah reach his goal? No
5. During the past soccer season, the Newhall Rovers had an average of 5 goals per game. If they play 25 games this coming season and score a total of 150 goals, will they achieve the same average number of goals? No (they will be better)

128

Geometry Match-Ups

A **polygon** is a closed shape with straight sides.

Directions: Cut out each polygon on the next page. To make them more durable, glue them onto cardboard or oaktag. Use the shapes to fill out the table below. (Keep the shapes for other activities as well.)

Game: Play this game with a partner. Put the shapes in a bag or cover them with a sheet of paper. Player One pulls out a shape and tells how many sides and angles it has. Without showing the shape, he/she puts the polygon back. Player Two should name the shape. Then, Player Two puts his/her hand in the bag and, without looking, tries to find the polygon from the description. Then, switch roles. Continue the game until all the polygons have been identified.

When you finish playing, **complete** the chart below.

Drawing of the shape (or polygon)	Shape name	Number of sides	Number of angles (or corners)
	triangle	3	3
	square	4	4
	pentagon	5	5
	rectangle	4	4
	hexagon	6	6

130

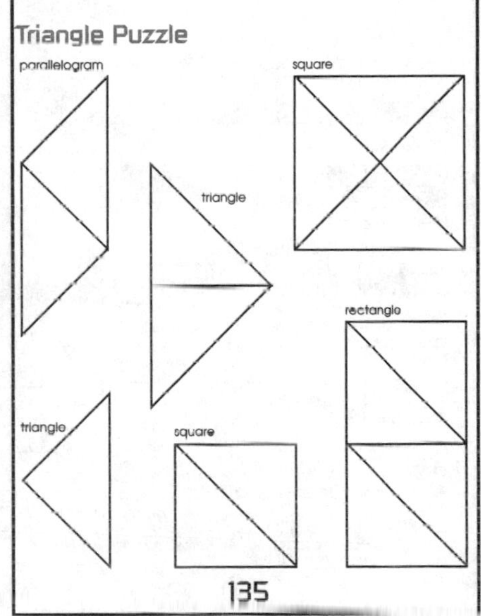

Triangle Puzzle

135

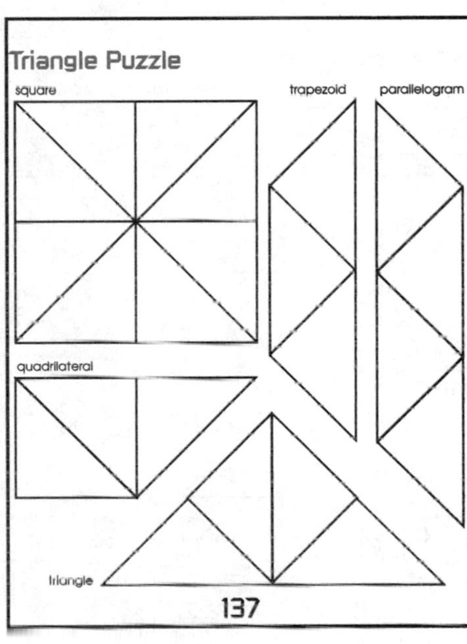

Triangle Puzzle

137

A Native American Wall Hanging

Congruent figures have the same size and shape. They do not have to be the same color or in the same position.

Congruent figures — Not congruent figures

Directions: Draw two congruent figures to create a new shape. You can use triangles, squares, rectangles, pentagons, hexagons, octagons, semicircles, quarter-circles or trapezoids to make the shape. Use the new shape to create a wall hanging design. Connect the two congruent figures at one side. Color each part of the congruent pairs. Display your hanging on a wall of your house.

139

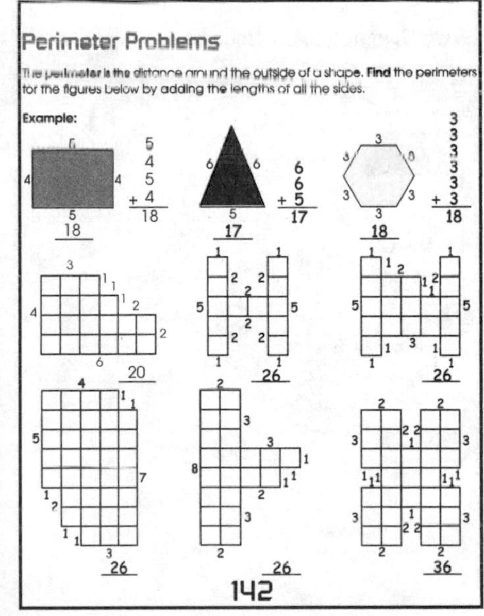

Perimeter Problems

The **perimeter** is the distance around the outside of a shape. **Find** the perimeters for the figures below by adding the lengths of all the sides.

Example:

Rectangle: 5 + 4 + 5 + 4 = 18
Triangle: 6 + 6 + 5 = 17
Hexagon: 3 + 3 + 3 + 3 + 3 + 3 = 18

Answers: 20, 26, 26, 26, 26, 36

142

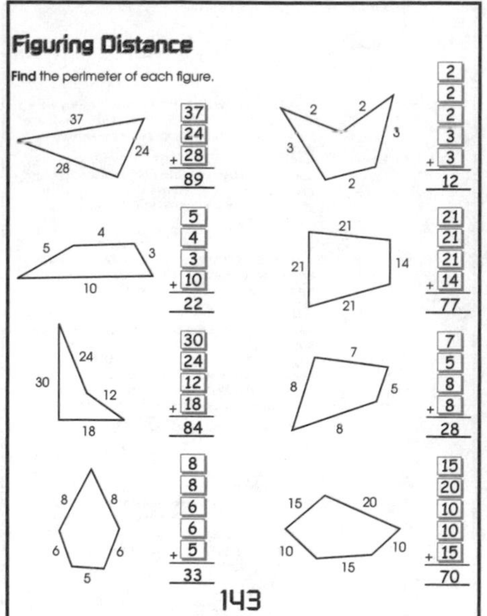

Figuring Distance

Find the perimeter of each figure.

37 + 24 + 28 = 89

2 + 2 + 2 + 3 + 3 = 12

5 + 4 + 3 + 10 = 22

21 + 21 + 21 + 14 = 77

30 + 24 + 12 + 18 = 84

7 + 5 + 8 + 8 = 28

8 + 8 + 6 + 6 + 5 = 33

15 + 20 + 10 + 10 + 15 = 70

143

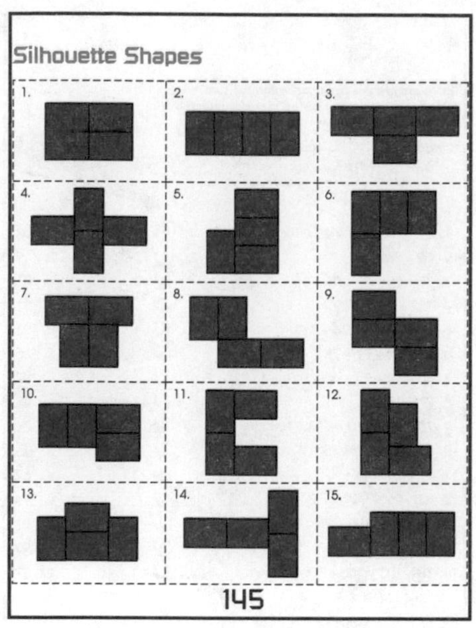

Silhouette Shapes

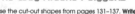

1. 2. 3. 4. 5. 6. 7. 8. 9. 10. 11. 12. 13. 14. 15.

145

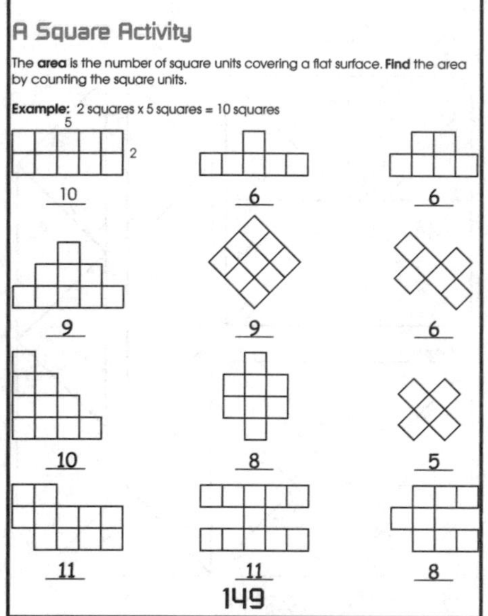

A Square Activity

The **area** is the number of square units covering a flat surface. **Find** the area by counting the square units.

Example: 2 squares x 5 squares = 10 squares

10 6 6

9 9 6

10 8 5

11 11 8

149

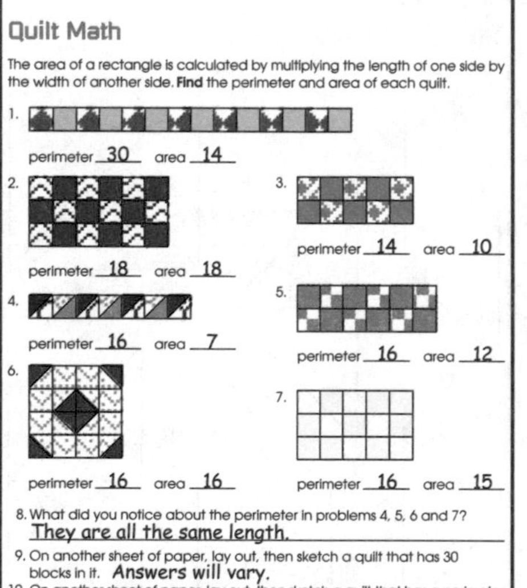

Quilt Math

The area of a rectangle is calculated by multiplying the length of one side by the width of another side. **Find** the perimeter and area of each quilt.

1. perimeter 30 area 14
2. perimeter 18 area 18
3. perimeter 14 area 10
4. perimeter 16 area 7
5. perimeter 16 area 12
6. perimeter 16 area 16
7. perimeter 16 area 15
8. What did you notice about the perimeter in problems 4, 5, 6 and 7? *They are all the same length.*
9. On another sheet of paper, lay out, then sketch a quilt that has 30 blocks in it. *Answers will vary.*
10. On another sheet of paper, lay out, then sketch a quilt that has a perimeter of 14 units. *Answers will vary.*

150

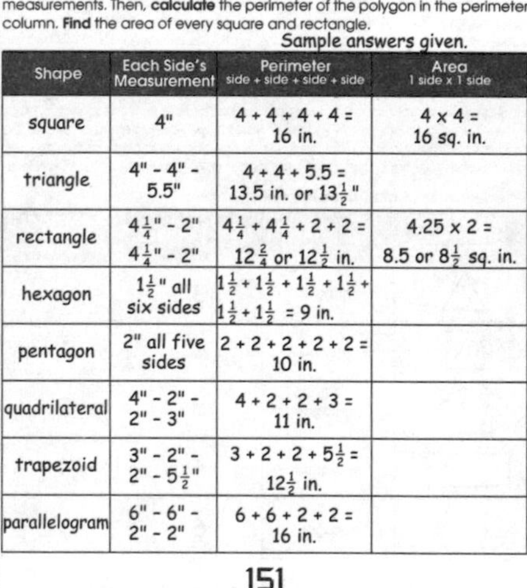

The Way Around Polygons

Use the cut-out shapes from pages 131–137. **Write** the name of each shape in the shape column. **Measure** the sides of each polygon and **record** its measurements. Then, **calculate** the perimeter of the polygon in the perimeter column. **Find** the area of every square and rectangle.

Sample answers given.

Shape	Each Side's Measurement	Perimeter side + side + side + side	Area 1 side x 1 side
square	4"	4 + 4 + 4 + 4 = 16 in.	4 x 4 = 16 sq. in.
triangle	4" - 4" - 5.5"	4 + 4 + 5.5 = 13.5 in. or $13\frac{1}{2}$"	
rectangle	$4\frac{1}{4}$" - 2" $4\frac{1}{4}$" - 2"	$4\frac{1}{4} + 4\frac{1}{4} + 2 + 2 = 12\frac{2}{4}$ or $12\frac{1}{2}$ in.	4.25 x 2 = 8.5 or $8\frac{1}{2}$ sq. in.
hexagon	$1\frac{1}{2}$" all six sides	$1\frac{1}{2} + 1\frac{1}{2} + 1\frac{1}{2} + 1\frac{1}{2} + 1\frac{1}{2} + 1\frac{1}{2}$ = 9 in.	
pentagon	2" all five sides	2 + 2 + 2 + 2 + 2 = 10 in.	
quadrilateral	4" - 2" - 2" - 3"	4 + 2 + 2 + 3 = 11 in.	
trapezoid	3" - 2" - 2" - $5\frac{1}{2}$"	$3 + 2 + 2 + 5\frac{1}{2} = 12\frac{1}{2}$ in.	
parallelogram	6" - 6" - 2" - 2"	6 + 6 + 2 + 2 = 16 in.	

151

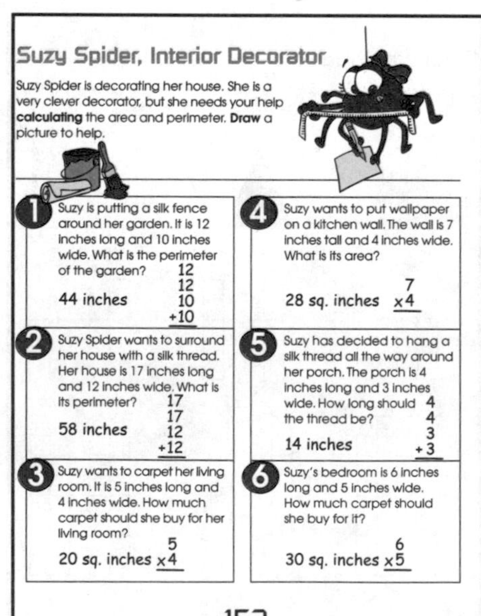

Suzy Spider, Interior Decorator

Suzy Spider is decorating her house. She is a very clever decorator, but she needs your help **calculating** the area and perimeter. **Draw** a picture to help.

1. Suzy is putting a silk fence around her garden. It is 12 inches long and 10 inches wide. What is the perimeter of the garden? 12 + 12 + 10 + 10 — **44 inches**
2. Suzy Spider wants to surround her house with a silk thread. Her house is 17 inches long and 12 inches wide. What is its perimeter? 17 + 17 + 12 + 12 — **58 inches**
3. Suzy wants to carpet her living room. It is 5 inches long and 4 inches wide. How much carpet should she buy for her living room? 5 x 4 — **20 sq. inches**
4. Suzy wants to put wallpaper on a kitchen wall. The wall is 7 inches tall and 4 inches wide. What is its area? 7 x 4 — **28 sq. inches**
5. Suzy has decided to hang a silk thread all the way around her porch. The porch is 4 inches long and 3 inches wide. How long should the thread be? 4 + 4 + 3 + 3 — **14 inches**
6. Suzy's bedroom is 6 inches long and 5 inches wide. How much carpet should she buy for it? 6 x 5 — **30 sq. inches**

152

"State"istics

Choose ten states. Then, **research** their "lengths" and "heights" and **multiply** them to find their areas.

Sample answers given. Numbers are approximate.

State Name	Approximate Miles E-W	Approximate Miles N-S	Area in Square Miles
Montana			147,000
Nebraska			77,000
Nevada			110,000
New Hampshire			9,000
New Jersey			8,000
New Mexico			122,000
New York			49,000
North Carolina			53,000
North Dakota			70,000
Ohio			41,000

153

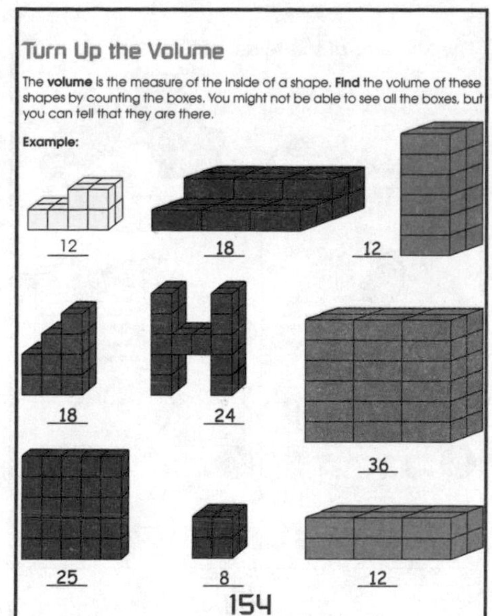

Turn Up the Volume

The **volume** is the measure of the inside of a shape. **Find** the volume of these shapes by counting the boxes. You might not be able to see all the boxes, but you can tell that they are there.

Example:

12 | 18 | 12

18 | 24 | 36

25 | 8 | 12

154

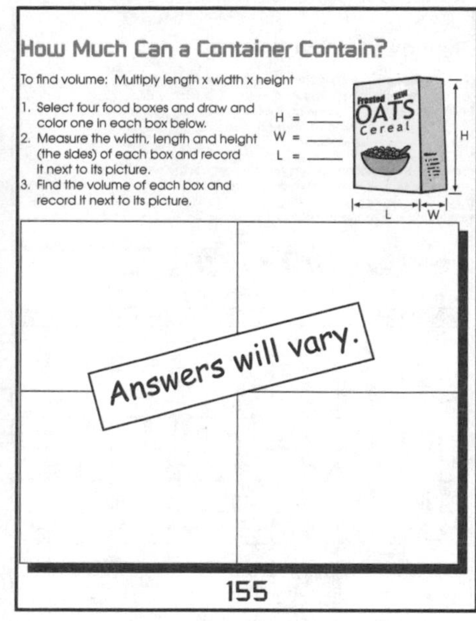

How Much Can a Container Contain?

To find volume: Multiply length x width x height

1. Select four food boxes and draw and color one in each box below.
2. Measure the width, length and height (the sides) of each box and record it next to its picture.
3. Find the volume of each box and record it next to its picture.

H = ____
W = ____
L = ____

Answers will vary.

155

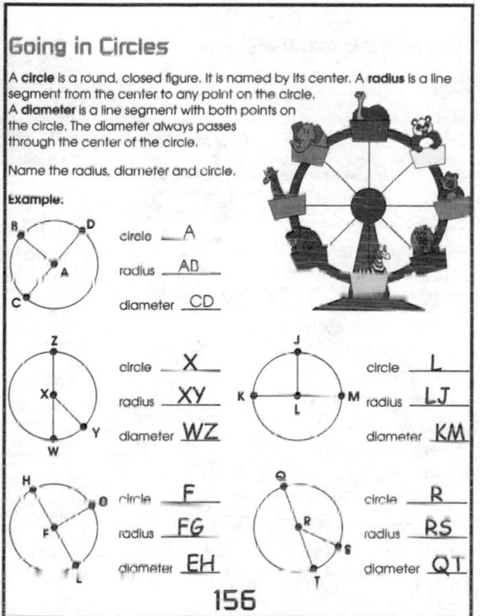

Going in Circles

A **circle** is a round, closed figure. It is named by its center. A **radius** is a line segment from the center to any point on the circle. A **diameter** is a line segment with both points on the circle. The diameter always passes through the center of the circle.

Name the radius, diameter and circle.

Example:

circle A
radius AD
diameter CD

circle X
radius XY
diameter WZ

circle L
radius LJ
diameter KM

circle F
radius FG
diameter EH

circle R
radius RS
diameter QT

156

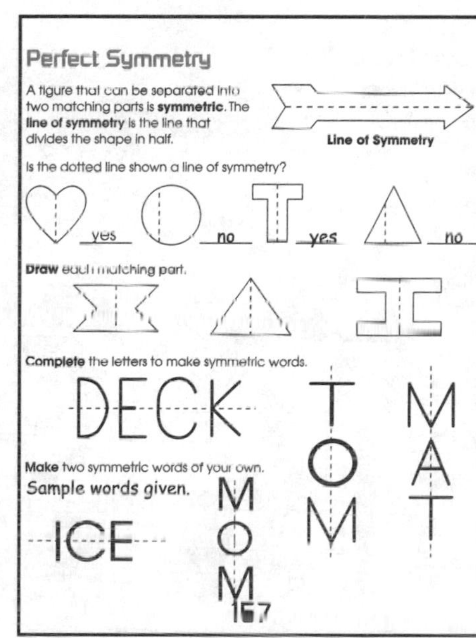

Perfect Symmetry

A figure that can be separated into two matching parts is **symmetric**. The **line of symmetry** is the line that divides the shape in half.

Line of Symmetry

Is the dotted line shown a line of symmetry?

yes | no | yes | no

Draw each matching part.

Complete the letters to make symmetric words.

DECK | TOM | MAT

Make two symmetric words of your own.

Sample words given.

ICE | MOM | MOM

157

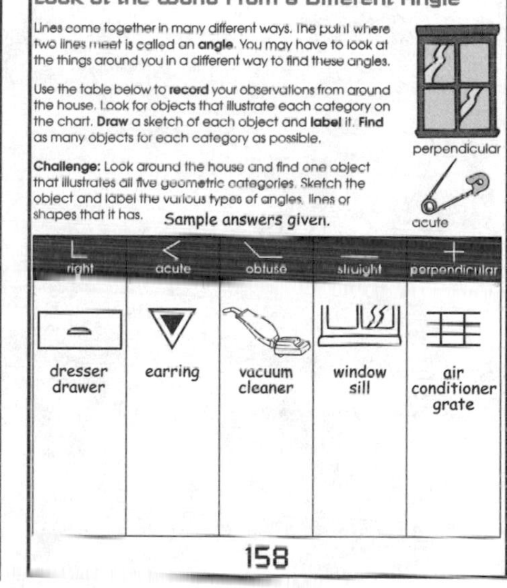

Look at the World From a Different Angle

Lines come together in many different ways. The point where two lines meet is called an **angle**. You may have to look at the things around you in a different way to find these angles.

Use the table below to **record** your observations from around the house. Look for objects that illustrate each category on the chart. **Draw** a sketch of each object and **label** it. **Find** as many objects for each category as possible.

Challenge: Look around the house and find one object that illustrates all five geometric categories. Sketch the object and label the various types of angles, lines or shapes that it has.

Sample answers given.

perpendicular

acute

right	acute	obtuse	straight	perpendicular
dresser drawer	earring	vacuum cleaner	window sill	air conditioner grate

158

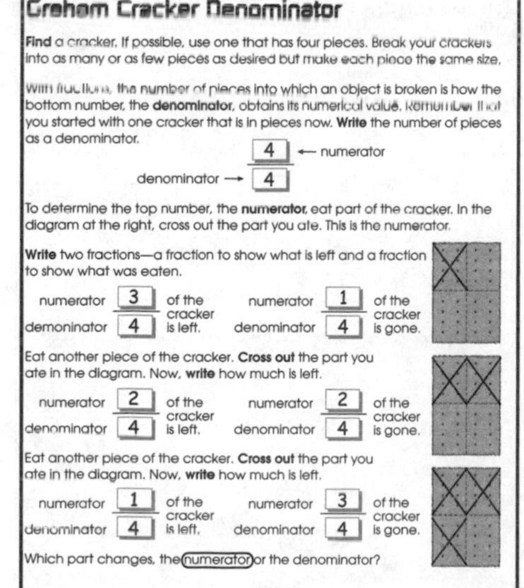

Graham Cracker Denominator

Find a cracker. If possible, use one that has four pieces. Break your crackers into as many or as few pieces as desired but make each piece the same size.

With fractions, the number of pieces into which an object is broken is how the bottom number, the **denominator**, obtains its numerical value. Remember that you started with one cracker that is in pieces now. **Write** the number of pieces as a denominator.

4 ← numerator
denominator → 4

To determine the top number, the **numerator**, eat part of the cracker. In the diagram at the right, cross out the part you ate. This is the numerator.

Write two fractions—a fraction to show what is left and a fraction to show what was eaten.

numerator 3 / denominator 4 of the cracker is left. numerator 1 / denominator 4 of the cracker is gone.

Eat another piece of the cracker. **Cross out** the part you ate in the diagram. Now, **write** how much is left.

numerator 2 / denominator 4 of the cracker is left. numerator 2 / denominator 4 of the cracker is gone.

Eat another piece of the cracker. **Cross out** the part you ate in the diagram. Now, **write** how much is left.

numerator 1 / denominator 4 of the cracker is left. numerator 3 / denominator 4 of the cracker is gone.

Which part changes, the (numerator) or the denominator?

160

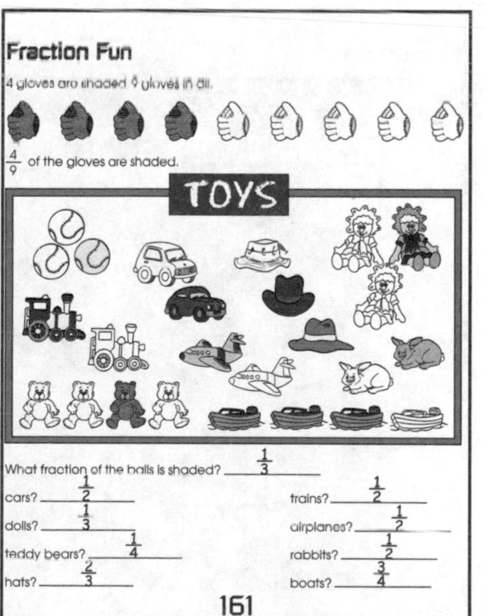

Fraction Fun

4 gloves are shaded. 9 gloves in all.

$\frac{4}{9}$ of the gloves are shaded.

TOYS

What fraction of the balls is shaded? $\frac{1}{3}$

cars? $\frac{1}{2}$ | trains? $\frac{1}{2}$

dolls? $\frac{1}{3}$ | airplanes? $\frac{1}{2}$

teddy bears? $\frac{1}{4}$ | rabbits? $\frac{1}{2}$

hats? $\frac{2}{3}$ | boats? $\frac{3}{4}$

161

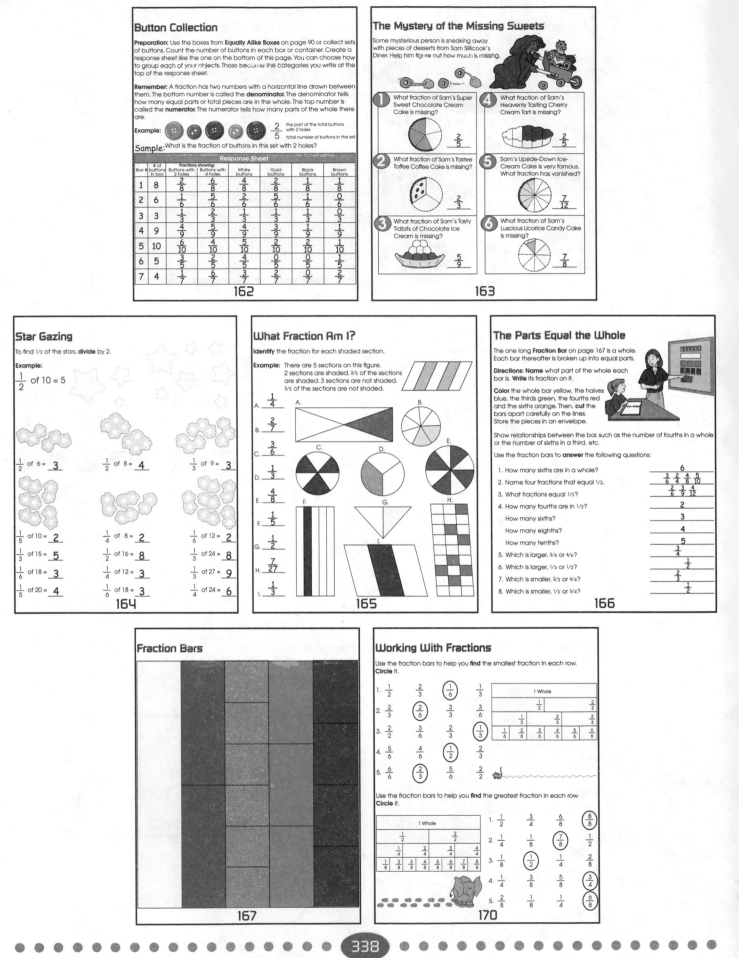

Button Collection

Preparation: Use the boxes from **Equally Alike Boxes** on page 90 or collect sets of buttons. Count the number of buttons in each box or container. Create a response sheet like the one on the bottom of this page. You can choose how to group each of your objects. These become the categories you write at the top of the response sheet.

Remember: A fraction has two numbers with a horizontal line drawn between them. The bottom number is called the **denominator.** The denominator tells how many equal parts or total pieces are in the whole. The top number is called the **numerator.** The numerator tells how many parts of the whole there are.

Example: $\frac{2}{5}$ the part of the total buttons with 2 holes / total number of buttons in the set

Sample: What is the fraction of buttons in this set with 2 holes?

Response Sheet							
Box #	# of buttons in box	Fractions showing: Buttons with 2 holes	Buttons with 4 holes	White buttons	Gold buttons	Black buttons	Brown buttons
1	8	$\frac{2}{8}$	$\frac{6}{8}$	$\frac{4}{8}$	$\frac{2}{8}$	$\frac{1}{8}$	$\frac{1}{8}$
2	6	$\frac{1}{6}$	$\frac{5}{6}$	$\frac{2}{6}$	$\frac{5}{6}$	$\frac{1}{6}$	$\frac{0}{6}$
3	3	$\frac{1}{3}$	$\frac{2}{3}$	$\frac{1}{3}$	$\frac{1}{3}$	$\frac{1}{3}$	$\frac{0}{3}$
4	9	$\frac{4}{9}$	$\frac{5}{9}$	$\frac{4}{9}$	$\frac{3}{9}$	$\frac{1}{9}$	$\frac{1}{9}$
5	10	$\frac{6}{10}$	$\frac{4}{10}$	$\frac{5}{10}$	$\frac{2}{10}$	$\frac{2}{10}$	$\frac{1}{10}$
6	5	$\frac{3}{5}$	$\frac{2}{5}$	$\frac{4}{5}$	$\frac{0}{5}$	$\frac{0}{5}$	$\frac{1}{5}$
7	4	$\frac{1}{7}$	$\frac{6}{7}$	$\frac{3}{7}$	$\frac{2}{7}$	$\frac{0}{7}$	$\frac{2}{7}$

162

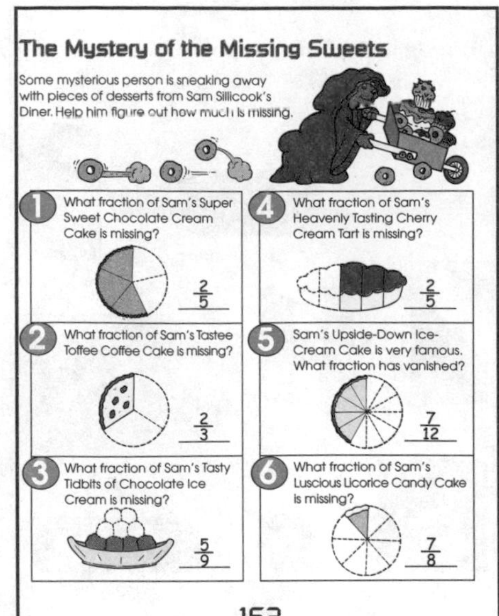

The Mystery of the Missing Sweets

Some mysterious person is sneaking away with pieces of desserts from Sam Sillicook's Diner. Help him figure out how much is missing.

1. What fraction of Sam's Super Sweet Chocolate Cream Cake is missing? $\frac{2}{5}$
2. What fraction of Sam's Tastee Toffee Coffee Cake is missing? $\frac{2}{3}$
3. What fraction of Sam's Tasty Tidbits of Chocolate Ice Cream is missing? $\frac{5}{9}$
4. What fraction of Sam's Heavenly Tasting Cherry Cream Tart is missing? $\frac{2}{5}$
5. Sam's Upside-Down Ice-Cream Cake is very famous. What fraction has vanished? $\frac{7}{12}$
6. What fraction of Sam's Luscious Licorice Candy Cake is missing? $\frac{7}{8}$

163

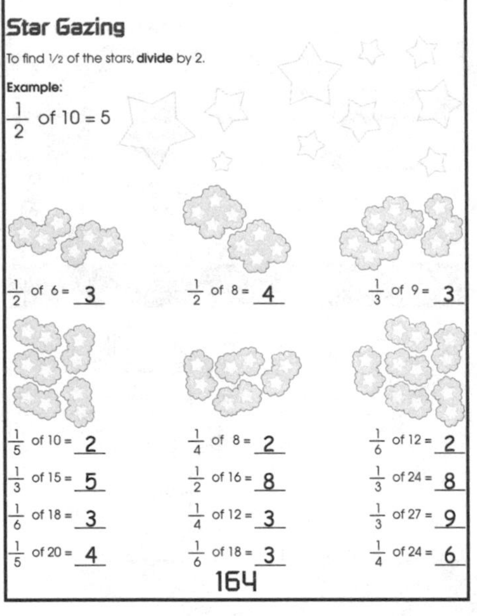

Star Gazing

To find 1/2 of the stars, **divide** by 2.

Example:

$\frac{1}{2}$ of 10 = 5

$\frac{1}{2}$ of 6 = 3 | $\frac{1}{2}$ of 8 = 4 | $\frac{1}{3}$ of 9 = 3

$\frac{1}{5}$ of 10 = 2 | $\frac{1}{4}$ of 8 = 2 | $\frac{1}{6}$ of 12 = 2

$\frac{1}{3}$ of 15 = 5 | $\frac{1}{2}$ of 16 = 8 | $\frac{1}{3}$ of 24 = 8

$\frac{1}{6}$ of 18 = 3 | $\frac{1}{4}$ of 12 = 3 | $\frac{1}{3}$ of 27 = 9

$\frac{1}{5}$ of 20 = 4 | $\frac{1}{6}$ of 18 = 3 | $\frac{1}{4}$ of 24 = 6

164

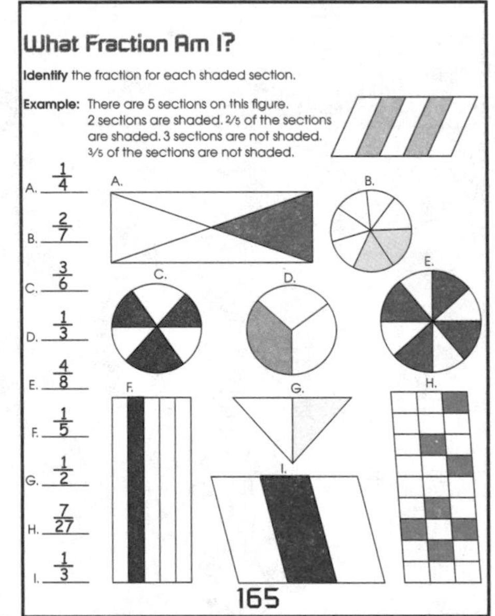

What Fraction Am I?

Identify the fraction for each shaded section.

Example: There are 5 sections on this figure. 2 sections are shaded. 2/5 of the sections are shaded. 3 sections are not shaded. 3/5 of the sections are not shaded.

A. $\frac{1}{4}$
B. $\frac{2}{7}$
C. $\frac{3}{6}$
D. $\frac{1}{3}$
E. $\frac{4}{8}$
F. $\frac{1}{5}$
G. $\frac{1}{2}$
H. $\frac{7}{27}$
I. $\frac{1}{3}$

165

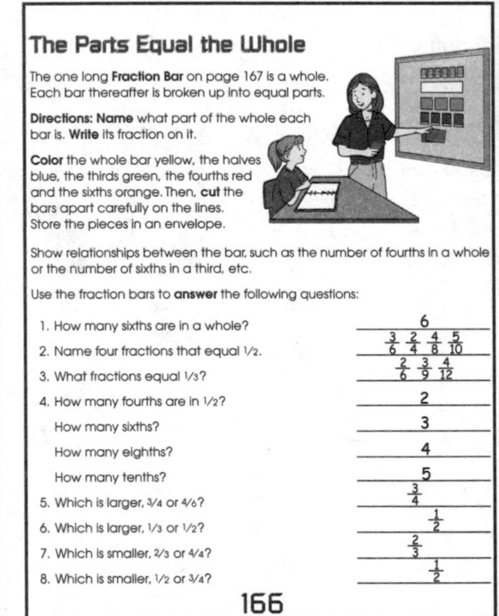

The Parts Equal the Whole

The one long **Fraction Bar** on page 167 is a whole. Each bar thereafter is broken up into equal parts.

Directions: Name what part of the whole each bar is. **Write** its fraction on it.

Color the whole bar yellow, the halves blue, the thirds green, the fourths red and the sixths orange. Then, **cut** the bars apart carefully on the lines. Store the pieces in an envelope.

Show relationships between the bar, such as the number of fourths in a whole or the number of sixths in a third, etc.

Use the fraction bars to **answer** the following questions:

1. How many sixths are in a whole? 6
2. Name four fractions that equal 1/2. $\frac{3}{6}$ $\frac{2}{4}$ $\frac{4}{8}$ $\frac{5}{10}$
3. What fractions equal 1/3? $\frac{2}{6}$ $\frac{3}{9}$ $\frac{4}{12}$
4. How many fourths are in 1/2? 2
   How many sixths? 3
   How many eighths? 4
   How many tenths? 5
5. Which is larger, 3/4 or 4/6? $\frac{3}{4}$
6. Which is larger, 1/3 or 1/2? $\frac{1}{2}$
7. Which is smaller, 2/3 or 4/4? $\frac{2}{3}$
8. Which is smaller, 1/2 or 3/4? $\frac{1}{2}$

166

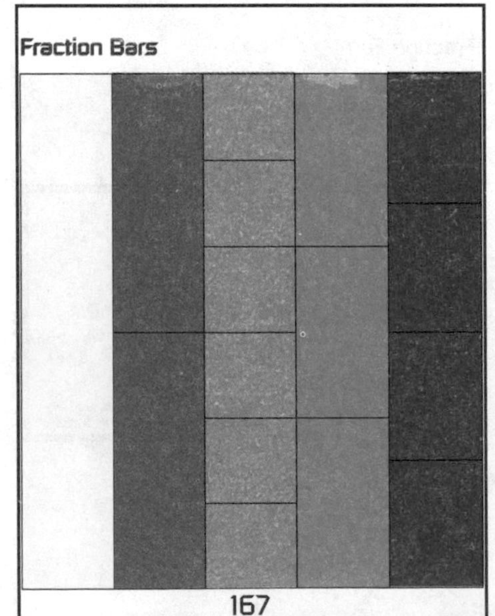

Fraction Bars

167

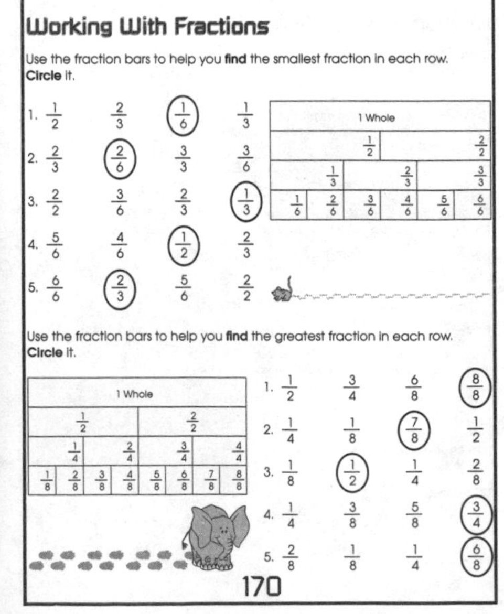

Working With Fractions

Use the fraction bars to help you **find** the smallest fraction in each row. **Circle** it.

1. $\frac{1}{2}$ $\frac{2}{3}$ ($\frac{1}{6}$) $\frac{1}{3}$
2. $\frac{2}{3}$ ($\frac{2}{6}$) $\frac{3}{3}$ $\frac{3}{6}$
3. $\frac{2}{2}$ $\frac{3}{6}$ $\frac{2}{3}$ ($\frac{1}{3}$)
4. $\frac{5}{6}$ $\frac{4}{6}$ ($\frac{1}{2}$) $\frac{2}{3}$
5. $\frac{6}{6}$ ($\frac{2}{3}$) $\frac{5}{6}$ $\frac{2}{2}$

Use the fraction bars to help you **find** the greatest fraction in each row. **Circle** it.

1. $\frac{1}{2}$ $\frac{3}{4}$ $\frac{6}{8}$ ($\frac{8}{8}$)
2. $\frac{1}{4}$ $\frac{1}{8}$ ($\frac{7}{8}$) $\frac{1}{2}$
3. $\frac{1}{8}$ ($\frac{1}{2}$) $\frac{1}{4}$ $\frac{2}{8}$
4. $\frac{1}{4}$ $\frac{3}{8}$ $\frac{5}{8}$ ($\frac{3}{4}$)
5. $\frac{2}{8}$ $\frac{1}{8}$ $\frac{1}{4}$ ($\frac{6}{8}$)

170

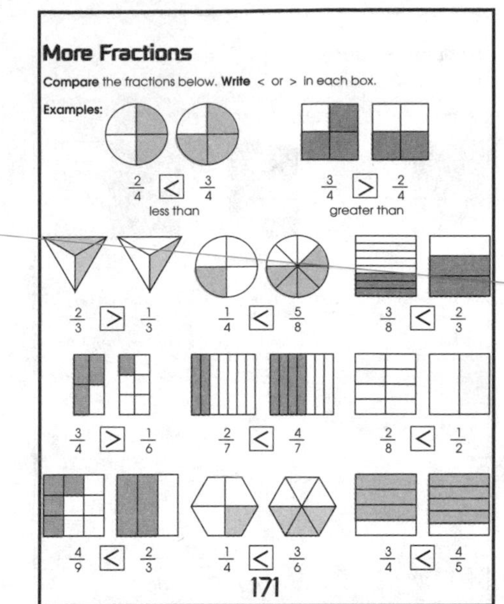

More Fractions

Compare the fractions below. **Write** < or > in each box.

Examples: $\frac{2}{4} < \frac{3}{4}$ less than; $\frac{3}{4} > \frac{2}{4}$ greater than

$\frac{2}{3} > \frac{1}{3}$ $\frac{1}{4} < \frac{5}{8}$ $\frac{3}{8} < \frac{2}{3}$

$\frac{3}{4} > \frac{1}{6}$ $\frac{2}{7} < \frac{4}{7}$ $\frac{2}{8} < \frac{1}{2}$

$\frac{4}{9} < \frac{2}{3}$ $\frac{1}{4} < \frac{3}{6}$ $\frac{3}{4} < \frac{4}{5}$

171

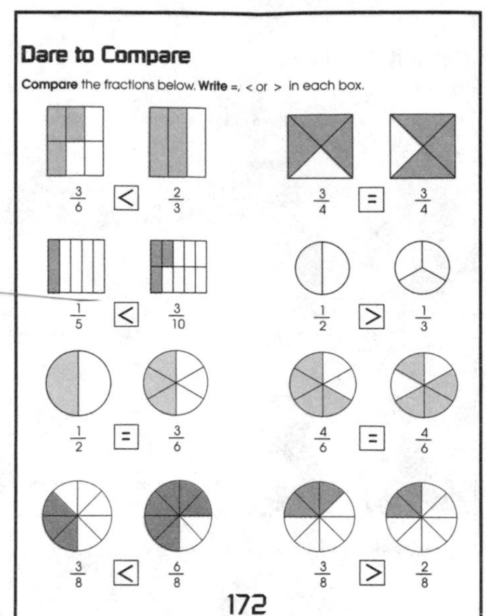

Dare to Compare

Compare the fractions below. **Write** =, < or > in each box.

$\frac{3}{6} < \frac{2}{3}$ $\frac{3}{4} = \frac{3}{4}$

$\frac{1}{5} < \frac{3}{10}$ $\frac{1}{2} > \frac{1}{3}$

$\frac{1}{2} = \frac{3}{6}$ $\frac{4}{6} = \frac{4}{6}$

$\frac{3}{8} < \frac{6}{8}$ $\frac{3}{8} > \frac{2}{8}$

172

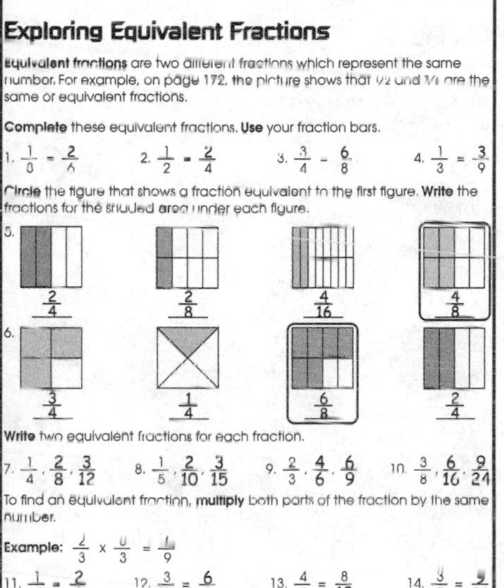

Exploring Equivalent Fractions

Equivalent fractions are two different fractions which represent the same number. For example, on page 172, the picture shows that 1/2 and 3/6 are the same or equivalent fractions.

Complete these equivalent fractions. **Use** your fraction bars.

1. $\frac{1}{3} = \frac{2}{6}$ 2. $\frac{1}{2} = \frac{2}{4}$ 3. $\frac{3}{4} = \frac{6}{8}$ 4. $\frac{1}{3} = \frac{3}{9}$

Circle the figure that shows a fraction equivalent to the first figure. **Write** the fractions for the shaded area under each figure.

5. $\frac{2}{4}$ $\frac{2}{8}$ $\frac{4}{16}$ $\frac{4}{8}$

6. $\frac{3}{4}$ $\frac{1}{4}$ $\frac{6}{8}$ $\frac{2}{4}$

Write two equivalent fractions for each fraction.

7. $\frac{1}{4}$, $\frac{2}{8}$, $\frac{3}{12}$ 8. $\frac{1}{5}$, $\frac{2}{10}$, $\frac{3}{15}$ 9. $\frac{2}{3}$, $\frac{4}{6}$, $\frac{6}{9}$ 10. $\frac{3}{8}$, $\frac{6}{16}$, $\frac{9}{24}$

To find an equivalent fraction, **multiply** both parts of the fraction by the same number.

Example: $\frac{2}{3} \times \frac{3}{3} = \frac{6}{9}$

11. $\frac{1}{4} = \frac{2}{8}$ 12. $\frac{3}{4} = \frac{6}{8}$ 13. $\frac{4}{5} = \frac{8}{10}$ 14. $\frac{3}{8} = \frac{9}{24}$

173

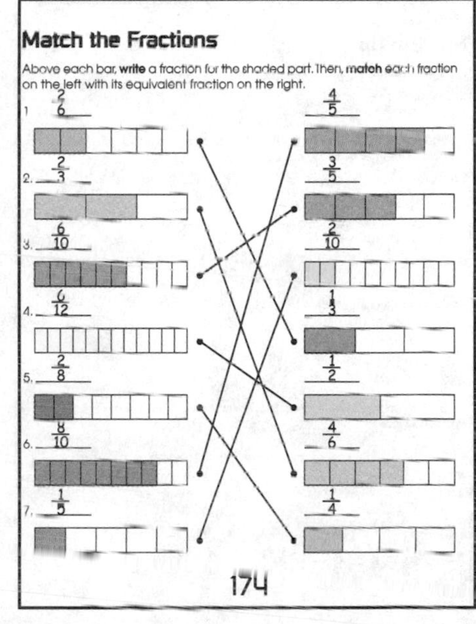

Match the Fractions

Above each bar, **write** a fraction for the shaded part. Then, **match** each fraction on the left with its equivalent fraction on the right.

1. $\frac{2}{6}$ 2. $\frac{2}{3}$ 3. $\frac{6}{10}$ 4. $\frac{6}{12}$ 5. $\frac{2}{8}$ 6. $\frac{8}{10}$ 7. $\frac{1}{5}$

$\frac{4}{5}$ $\frac{3}{5}$ $\frac{2}{10}$ $\frac{1}{3}$ $\frac{1}{2}$ $\frac{4}{6}$ $\frac{1}{4}$

174

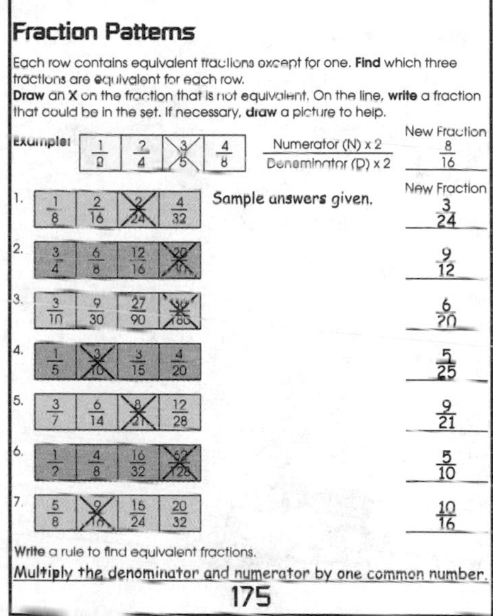

Fraction Patterns

Each row contains equivalent fractions except for one. **Find** which three fractions are equivalent for each row.

Draw an X on the fraction that is not equivalent. On the line, **write** a fraction that could be in the set. If necessary, **draw** a picture to help.

Example: $\frac{1}{2}$ $\frac{2}{4}$ $\frac{3}{5}$ (X) $\frac{4}{8}$ — $\frac{\text{Numerator (N)} \times 2}{\text{Denominator (D)} \times 2}$ — New Fraction $\frac{8}{16}$

Sample answers given.

					New Fraction
1.	1/8	2/16	2/24 (X)	4/32	3/24
2.	3/4	6/8	12/16	20/? (X)	9/12
3.	3/10	9/30	27/90	?/160 (X)	6/20
4.	1/5	?/10 (X)	3/15	4/20	5/25
5.	3/7	6/14	8/21 (X)	12/28	9/21
6.	1/2	4/8	16/32	?/128 (X)	5/10
7.	5/8	?/16 (X)	15/24	20/32	10/16

Write a rule to find equivalent fractions.

Multiply the denominator and numerator by one common number.

175

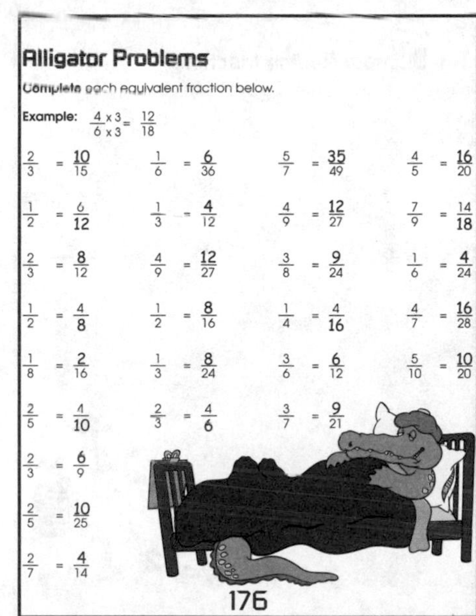

Alligator Problems

Complete each equivalent fraction below.

Example: $\frac{4 \times 3}{6 \times 3} = \frac{12}{18}$

$\frac{2}{3} = \frac{10}{15}$ $\frac{1}{6} = \frac{6}{36}$ $\frac{5}{7} = \frac{35}{49}$ $\frac{4}{5} = \frac{16}{20}$

$\frac{1}{2} = \frac{6}{12}$ $\frac{1}{3} = \frac{4}{12}$ $\frac{4}{9} = \frac{12}{27}$ $\frac{7}{9} = \frac{14}{18}$

$\frac{2}{3} = \frac{8}{12}$ $\frac{4}{9} = \frac{12}{27}$ $\frac{3}{8} = \frac{9}{24}$ $\frac{1}{6} = \frac{4}{24}$

$\frac{1}{2} = \frac{4}{8}$ $\frac{1}{2} = \frac{8}{16}$ $\frac{1}{4} = \frac{4}{16}$ $\frac{4}{7} = \frac{16}{28}$

$\frac{1}{8} = \frac{2}{16}$ $\frac{1}{3} = \frac{8}{24}$ $\frac{3}{6} = \frac{6}{12}$ $\frac{5}{10} = \frac{10}{20}$

$\frac{2}{5} = \frac{4}{10}$ $\frac{2}{3} = \frac{4}{6}$ $\frac{3}{7} = \frac{9}{21}$

$\frac{2}{3} = \frac{6}{9}$

$\frac{2}{5} = \frac{10}{25}$

$\frac{2}{7} = \frac{4}{14}$

176

More Than Peanuts

Write <, >, or = to compare the fractions below. **Draw** pictures or **write** equivalent fractions, if needed.

$\frac{3}{8} > \frac{2}{8}$ $\frac{2}{3} > \frac{3}{6}$ $\frac{3}{6} = \frac{1}{2}$

$\frac{4}{7} > \frac{4}{14}$ $\frac{1}{3} < \frac{6}{9}$ $\frac{7}{10} > \frac{2}{5}$

$\frac{8}{12} > \frac{3}{6}$ $\frac{7}{14} = \frac{1}{2}$ $\frac{4}{7} > \frac{3}{7}$ $\frac{4}{8} = \frac{8}{16}$

$\frac{1}{3} = \frac{2}{6}$ $\frac{2}{8} < \frac{1}{2}$ $\frac{1}{5} < \frac{3}{10}$ $\frac{6}{11} > \frac{5}{11}$

$\frac{6}{12} = \frac{1}{2}$ $\frac{2}{3} > \frac{2}{6}$ $\frac{7}{12} > \frac{2}{4}$ $\frac{5}{6} > \frac{1}{3}$

$\frac{7}{10} > \frac{3}{10}$ $\frac{1}{2} < \frac{8}{12}$ $\frac{1}{5} < \frac{8}{10}$ $\frac{7}{8} > \frac{2}{4}$

$\frac{3}{8} > \frac{1}{4}$ $\frac{2}{5} < \frac{5}{10}$

$\frac{5}{6} > \frac{2}{3}$ $\frac{6}{10} > \frac{2}{5}$

$\frac{6}{10} > \frac{3}{10}$ $\frac{3}{6} = \frac{6}{12}$

$\frac{1}{8} < \frac{1}{4}$ $\frac{1}{2} > \frac{1}{4}$

177

Catch It If You Can

For each fraction below, determine if the fraction equals more or less than 1/2. For each fraction, **cross out** the ball that does not describe the fraction. Then, **fill in** the blanks with the letters left to solve the riddle at the bottom of the page.

	Less than	More than
1. $\frac{3}{8}$	Y	X
2. $\frac{4}{5}$	X	O
3. $\frac{1}{3}$	U	X
4. $\frac{4}{6}$	X	R
5. $\frac{1}{4}$	B	X
6. $\frac{2}{3}$	X	R
7. $\frac{5}{8}$	X	E
8. $\frac{7}{8}$	X	A
9. $\frac{1}{8}$	T	X
10. $\frac{1}{6}$	H	X

What is harder to catch the faster you run?

Y O U R B R E A T H

178

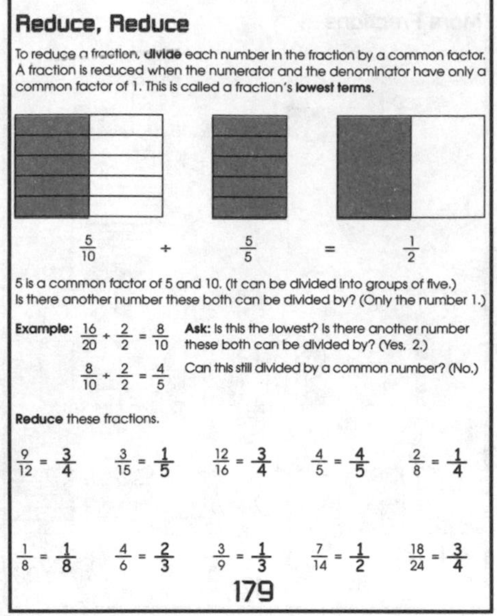

Reduce, Reduce

To reduce a fraction, **divide** each number in the fraction by a common factor. A fraction is reduced when the numerator and the denominator have only a common factor of 1. This is called a fraction's **lowest terms.**

$\frac{5}{10} \div \frac{5}{5} = \frac{1}{2}$

5 is a common factor of 5 and 10. (It can be divided into groups of five.) Is there another number these both can be divided by? (Only the number 1.)

Example: $\frac{16}{20} \div \frac{2}{2} = \frac{8}{10}$ **Ask:** Is this the lowest? Is there another number these both can be divided by? (Yes, 2.)

$\frac{8}{10} \div \frac{2}{2} = \frac{4}{5}$ Can this still divided by a common number? (No.)

Reduce these fractions.

$\frac{9}{12} = \frac{3}{4}$ $\frac{3}{15} = \frac{1}{5}$ $\frac{12}{16} = \frac{3}{4}$ $\frac{4}{5} = \frac{4}{5}$ $\frac{2}{8} = \frac{1}{4}$

$\frac{1}{8} = \frac{1}{8}$ $\frac{4}{6} = \frac{2}{3}$ $\frac{3}{9} = \frac{1}{3}$ $\frac{7}{14} = \frac{1}{2}$ $\frac{18}{24} = \frac{3}{4}$

179

Reduce the Fat

Reduce each fraction to its lowest terms.

Example: $\frac{5 \div 5}{25 \div 5} = \frac{1}{5}$ common factors

$\frac{8}{16} = \frac{1}{2}$ $\frac{12}{18} = \frac{2}{3}$

$\frac{10}{25} = \frac{2}{5}$ $\frac{12}{30} = \frac{2}{5}$ $\frac{3}{30} = \frac{1}{10}$ $\frac{6}{30} = \frac{1}{5}$

$\frac{12}{20} = \frac{3}{5}$ $\frac{3}{18} = \frac{1}{6}$ $\frac{3}{9} = \frac{1}{3}$ $\frac{4}{26} = \frac{2}{13}$

$\frac{4}{28} = \frac{1}{7}$ $\frac{7}{21} = \frac{1}{3}$ $\frac{16}{20} = \frac{4}{5}$ $\frac{2}{10} = \frac{1}{5}$

$\frac{3}{27} = \frac{1}{9}$ $\frac{5}{60} = \frac{1}{12}$ $\frac{21}{35} = \frac{3}{5}$ $\frac{3}{12} = \frac{1}{4}$

$\frac{9}{36} = \frac{1}{4}$ $\frac{24}{40} = \frac{3}{5}$ $\frac{8}{24} = \frac{1}{3}$

$\frac{16}{40} = \frac{2}{5}$

180

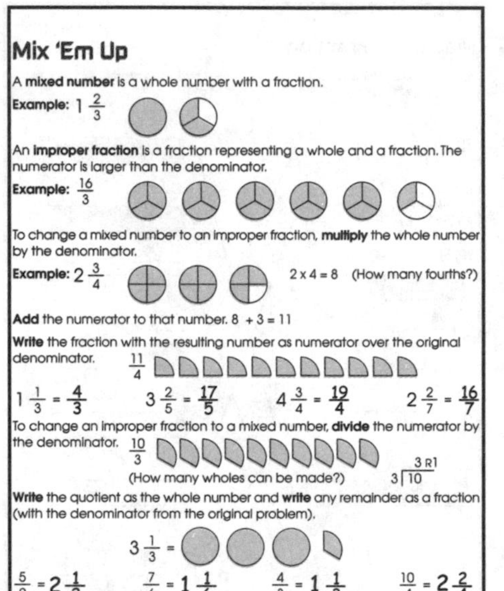

Mix 'Em Up

A **mixed number** is a whole number with a fraction.

Example: $1\frac{2}{3}$

An **improper fraction** is a fraction representing a whole and a fraction. The numerator is larger than the denominator.

Example: $\frac{16}{3}$

To change a mixed number to an improper fraction, **multiply** the whole number by the denominator.

Example: $2\frac{3}{4}$ 2 x 4 = 8 (How many fourths?)

Add the numerator to that number. 8 + 3 = 11

Write the fraction with the resulting number as numerator over the original denominator. $\frac{11}{4}$

$1\frac{1}{3} = \frac{4}{3}$ $3\frac{2}{5} = \frac{17}{5}$ $4\frac{3}{4} = \frac{19}{4}$ $2\frac{2}{7} = \frac{16}{7}$

To change an improper fraction to a mixed number, **divide** the numerator by the denominator. $\frac{10}{3}$

(How many wholes can be made?) 3 R1 over $3\overline{)10}$

Write the quotient as the whole number and **write** any remainder as a fraction (with the denominator from the original problem).

$3\frac{1}{3} =$

$\frac{5}{2} = 2\frac{1}{2}$ $\frac{7}{6} = 1\frac{1}{6}$ $\frac{4}{3} = 1\frac{1}{3}$ $\frac{10}{4} = 2\frac{2}{4}$

181

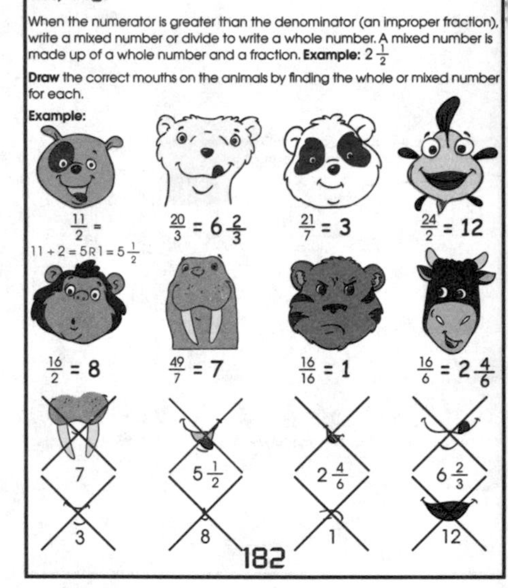

Oh, My!

When the numerator is greater than the denominator (an improper fraction), write a mixed number or divide to write a whole number. A mixed number is made up of a whole number and a fraction. **Example:** $2\frac{1}{2}$

Draw the correct mouths on the animals by finding the whole or mixed number for each.

Example:

$\frac{11}{2} =$ 11 ÷ 2 = 5R1 = $5\frac{1}{2}$ $\frac{20}{3} = 6\frac{2}{3}$ $\frac{21}{7} = 3$ $\frac{24}{2} = 12$

$\frac{16}{2} = 8$ $\frac{49}{7} = 7$ $\frac{16}{16} = 1$ $\frac{16}{6} = 2\frac{4}{6}$

7 $5\frac{1}{2}$ $2\frac{4}{6}$ $6\frac{2}{3}$

3 8 1 12

182

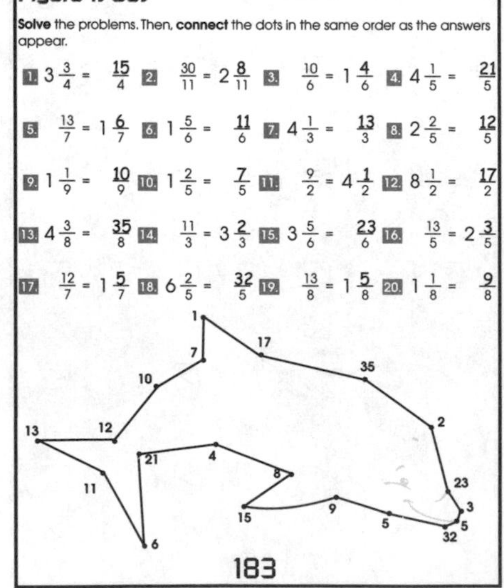

Figure It Out

Solve the problems. Then, **connect** the dots in the same order as the answers appear.

1. $3\frac{3}{4} = \frac{15}{4}$ 2. $\frac{30}{11} = 2\frac{8}{11}$ 3. $\frac{10}{6} = 1\frac{4}{6}$ 4. $4\frac{1}{5} = \frac{21}{5}$

5. $\frac{13}{7} = 1\frac{6}{7}$ 6. $1\frac{5}{6} = \frac{11}{6}$ 7. $4\frac{1}{3} = \frac{13}{3}$ 8. $2\frac{2}{5} = \frac{12}{5}$

9. $1\frac{1}{9} = \frac{10}{9}$ 10. $1\frac{2}{5} = \frac{7}{5}$ 11. $\frac{9}{2} = 4\frac{1}{2}$ 12. $8\frac{1}{2} = \frac{17}{2}$

13. $4\frac{3}{8} = \frac{35}{8}$ 14. $\frac{11}{3} = 3\frac{2}{3}$ 15. $3\frac{5}{6} = \frac{23}{6}$ 16. $\frac{13}{5} = 2\frac{3}{5}$

17. $\frac{12}{7} = 1\frac{5}{7}$ 18. $6\frac{2}{5} = \frac{32}{5}$ 19. $\frac{13}{8} = 1\frac{5}{8}$ 20. $1\frac{1}{8} = \frac{9}{8}$

183

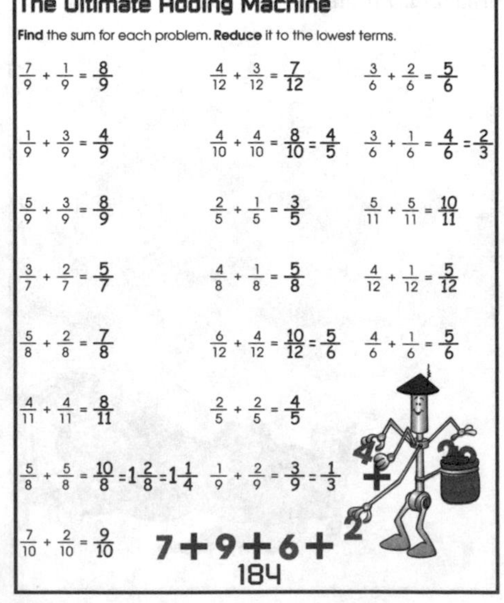

The Ultimate Adding Machine

Find the sum for each problem. **Reduce** it to the lowest terms.

$\frac{7}{9} + \frac{1}{9} = \frac{8}{9}$ $\frac{4}{12} + \frac{3}{12} = \frac{7}{12}$ $\frac{3}{6} + \frac{2}{6} = \frac{5}{6}$

$\frac{1}{9} + \frac{3}{9} = \frac{4}{9}$ $\frac{4}{10} + \frac{4}{10} = \frac{8}{10} = \frac{4}{5}$ $\frac{3}{6} + \frac{1}{6} = \frac{4}{6} = \frac{2}{3}$

$\frac{5}{9} + \frac{3}{9} = \frac{8}{9}$ $\frac{2}{5} + \frac{1}{5} = \frac{3}{5}$ $\frac{5}{11} + \frac{5}{11} = \frac{10}{11}$

$\frac{3}{7} + \frac{2}{7} = \frac{5}{7}$ $\frac{4}{8} + \frac{1}{8} = \frac{5}{8}$ $\frac{4}{12} + \frac{1}{12} = \frac{5}{12}$

$\frac{5}{8} + \frac{2}{8} = \frac{7}{8}$ $\frac{6}{12} + \frac{4}{12} = \frac{10}{12} = \frac{5}{6}$ $\frac{4}{6} + \frac{1}{6} = \frac{5}{6}$

$\frac{4}{11} + \frac{4}{11} = \frac{8}{11}$ $\frac{2}{5} + \frac{2}{5} = \frac{4}{5}$

$\frac{5}{8} + \frac{5}{8} = \frac{10}{8} = 1\frac{2}{8} = 1\frac{1}{4}$ $\frac{1}{9} + \frac{2}{9} = \frac{3}{9} = \frac{1}{3}$

$\frac{7}{10} + \frac{2}{10} = \frac{9}{10}$

184

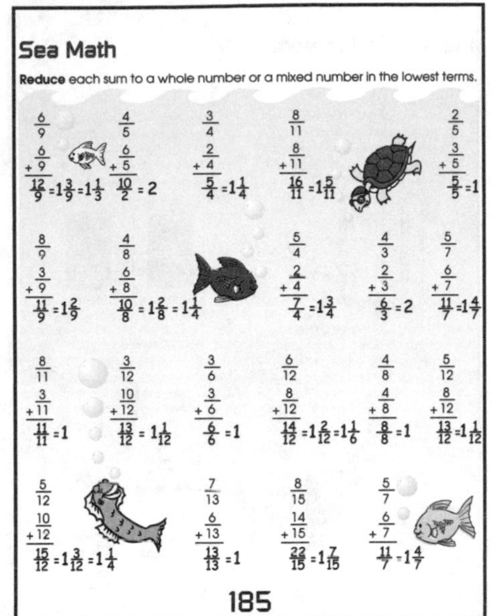

Sea Math

Reduce each sum to a whole number or a mixed number in the lowest terms.

$\frac{6}{9} + \frac{6}{9} = \frac{12}{9} = 1\frac{3}{9} = 1\frac{1}{3}$ $\frac{4}{5} + \frac{6}{5} = \frac{10}{2} = 2$ $\frac{3}{4} + \frac{2}{4} = \frac{5}{4} = 1\frac{1}{4}$ $\frac{8}{11} + \frac{8}{11} = \frac{16}{11} = 1\frac{5}{11}$ $\frac{2}{5} + \frac{3}{5} = \frac{5}{5} = 1$

$\frac{8}{9} + \frac{3}{9} = \frac{11}{9} = 1\frac{2}{9}$ $\frac{4}{8} + \frac{6}{8} = \frac{10}{8} = 1\frac{2}{8} = 1\frac{1}{4}$ $\frac{5}{4} + \frac{2}{4} = \frac{7}{4} = 1\frac{3}{4}$ $\frac{4}{3} + \frac{2}{3} = \frac{6}{3} = 2$ $\frac{5}{7} + \frac{6}{7} = \frac{11}{7} = 1\frac{4}{7}$

$\frac{8}{11} + \frac{3}{11} = \frac{11}{11} = 1$ $\frac{3}{12} + \frac{10}{12} = \frac{13}{12} = 1\frac{1}{12}$ $\frac{3}{6} + \frac{3}{6} = \frac{6}{6} = 1$ $\frac{6}{12} + \frac{8}{12} = \frac{14}{12} = 1\frac{2}{12} = 1\frac{1}{6}$ $\frac{4}{8} + \frac{4}{8} = \frac{8}{8} = 1$ $\frac{5}{12} + \frac{8}{12} = \frac{13}{12} = 1\frac{1}{12}$

$\frac{5}{12} + \frac{10}{12} = \frac{15}{12} = 1\frac{3}{12} = 1\frac{1}{4}$ $\frac{7}{13} + \frac{6}{13} = \frac{13}{13} = 1$ $\frac{8}{15} + \frac{14}{15} = \frac{22}{15} = 1\frac{7}{15}$ $\frac{5}{7} + \frac{6}{7} = \frac{11}{7} = 1\frac{4}{7}$

185

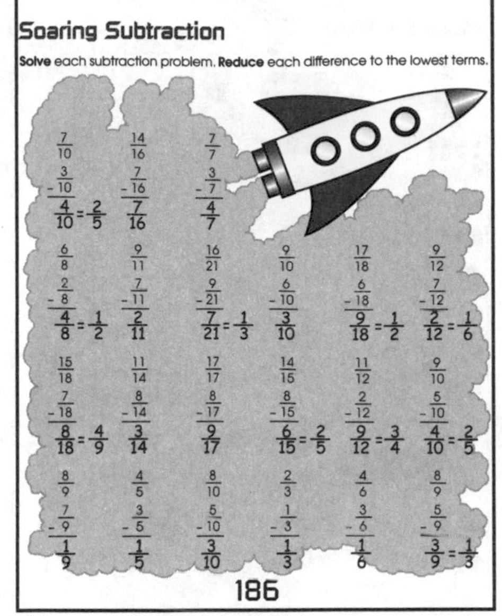

Soaring Subtraction

Solve each subtraction problem. **Reduce** each difference to the lowest terms.

$\frac{7}{10} - \frac{3}{10} = \frac{4}{10} = \frac{2}{5}$ $\frac{14}{16} - \frac{7}{16} = \frac{7}{16}$ $\frac{7}{7} - \frac{3}{7} = \frac{4}{7}$

$\frac{6}{8} - \frac{2}{8} = \frac{4}{8} = \frac{1}{2}$ $\frac{9}{11} - \frac{7}{11} = \frac{2}{11}$ $\frac{16}{21} - \frac{9}{21} = \frac{7}{21} = \frac{1}{3}$ $\frac{9}{10} - \frac{6}{10} = \frac{3}{10}$ $\frac{17}{18} - \frac{6}{18} = \frac{9}{18} = \frac{1}{2}$ $\frac{9}{12} - \frac{7}{12} = \frac{2}{12} = \frac{1}{6}$

$\frac{15}{18} - \frac{7}{18} = \frac{8}{18} = \frac{4}{9}$ $\frac{11}{14} - \frac{8}{14} = \frac{3}{14}$ $\frac{17}{17} - \frac{8}{17} = \frac{9}{17}$ $\frac{14}{15} - \frac{8}{15} = \frac{6}{15} = \frac{2}{5}$ $\frac{11}{12} - \frac{2}{12} = \frac{9}{12} = \frac{3}{4}$ $\frac{9}{10} - \frac{5}{10} = \frac{4}{10} = \frac{2}{5}$

$\frac{8}{9} - \frac{7}{9} = \frac{1}{9}$ $\frac{4}{5} - \frac{3}{5} = \frac{1}{5}$ $\frac{8}{10} - \frac{5}{10} = \frac{3}{10}$ $\frac{2}{3} - \frac{1}{3} = \frac{1}{3}$ $\frac{4}{6} - \frac{3}{6} = \frac{1}{6}$ $\frac{8}{9} - \frac{5}{9} = \frac{3}{9} = \frac{1}{3}$

186

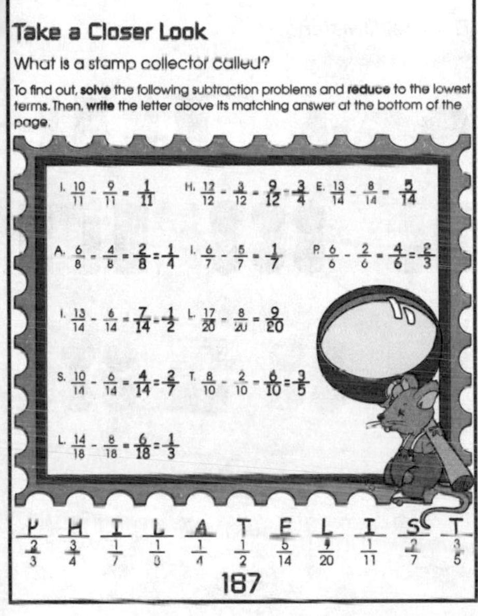

Take a Closer Look

What is a stamp collector called?

To find out, **solve** the following subtraction problems and **reduce** to the lowest terms. Then, **write** the letter above its matching answer at the bottom of the page.

I. $\frac{10}{11} - \frac{9}{11} = \frac{1}{11}$ H. $\frac{12}{12} - \frac{3}{12} = \frac{9}{12} = \frac{3}{4}$ E. $\frac{13}{14} - \frac{8}{14} = \frac{5}{14}$

A. $\frac{6}{8} - \frac{4}{8} = \frac{2}{8} = \frac{1}{4}$ I. $\frac{6}{7} - \frac{5}{7} = \frac{1}{7}$ P. $\frac{6}{6} - \frac{2}{6} = \frac{4}{6} = \frac{2}{3}$

I. $\frac{13}{14} - \frac{6}{14} = \frac{7}{14} = \frac{1}{2}$ L. $\frac{17}{20} - \frac{8}{20} = \frac{9}{20}$

S. $\frac{10}{14} - \frac{6}{14} = \frac{4}{14} = \frac{2}{7}$ T. $\frac{8}{10} - \frac{2}{10} = \frac{6}{10} = \frac{3}{5}$

L. $\frac{14}{18} - \frac{8}{18} = \frac{6}{18} = \frac{1}{3}$

P	H	I	L	A	T	E	L	I	S	T
$\frac{2}{3}$	$\frac{3}{4}$	$\frac{1}{7}$	$\frac{1}{3}$	$\frac{1}{4}$	$\frac{1}{2}$	$\frac{5}{14}$	$\frac{9}{20}$	$\frac{1}{11}$	$\frac{2}{7}$	$\frac{3}{5}$

187

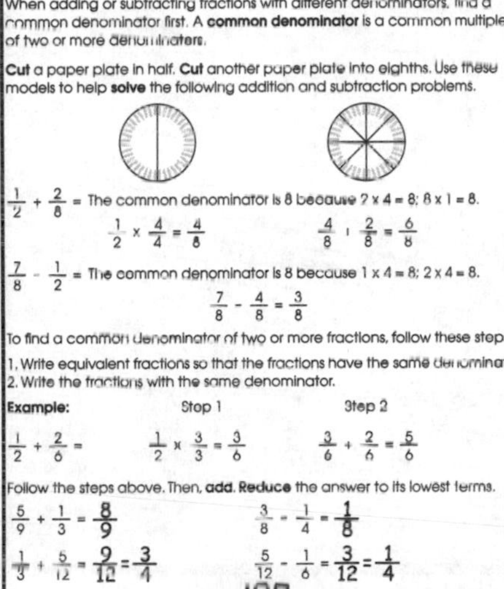

Finding a Common Denominator

When adding or subtracting fractions with different denominators, find a common denominator first. A **common denominator** is a common multiple of two or more denominators.

Cut a paper plate in half. **Cut** another paper plate into eighths. Use these models to help **solve** the following addition and subtraction problems.

$\frac{1}{2} + \frac{2}{8} =$ The common denominator is 8 because $2 \times 4 = 8$; $8 \times 1 = 8$.

$\frac{1}{2} \times \frac{4}{4} = \frac{4}{8}$ $\frac{4}{8} + \frac{2}{8} = \frac{6}{8}$

$\frac{7}{8} - \frac{1}{2} =$ The common denominator is 8 because $1 \times 4 = 8$; $2 \times 4 = 8$.

$\frac{7}{8} - \frac{4}{8} = \frac{3}{8}$

To find a common denominator of two or more fractions, follow these steps:

1. Write equivalent fractions so that the fractions have the same denominator.
2. Write the fractions with the same denominator.

Example: Step 1 Step 2

$\frac{1}{2} + \frac{2}{6} =$ $\frac{1}{2} \times \frac{3}{3} = \frac{3}{6}$ $\frac{3}{6} + \frac{2}{6} = \frac{5}{6}$

Follow the steps above. Then, **add**. **Reduce** the answer to its lowest terms.

$\frac{5}{9} + \frac{1}{3} = \frac{8}{9}$ $\frac{3}{8} - \frac{1}{4} = \frac{1}{8}$

$\frac{1}{3} + \frac{5}{12} = \frac{9}{12} = \frac{3}{4}$ $\frac{5}{12} - \frac{1}{6} = \frac{3}{12} = \frac{1}{4}$

188

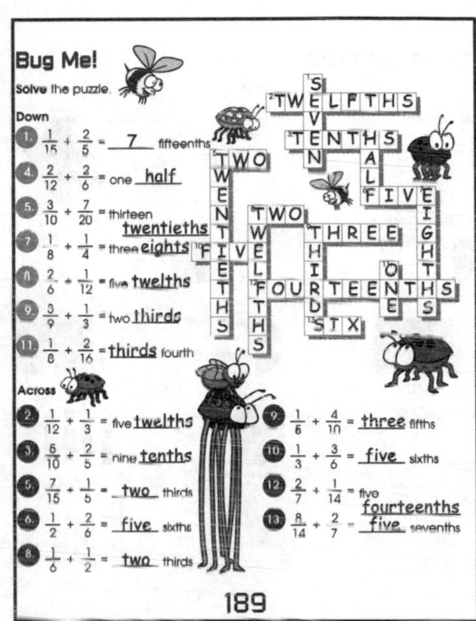

Bug Me!

Solve the puzzle.

Down

1. $\frac{1}{15} + \frac{2}{5} =$ 7 fifteenths
4. $\frac{2}{12} + \frac{2}{6} =$ one half
5. $\frac{3}{10} + \frac{7}{20} =$ thirteen twentieths
7. $\frac{1}{8} + \frac{1}{4} =$ three eights
8. $\frac{2}{6} + \frac{1}{12} =$ five twelths
9. $\frac{3}{9} + \frac{1}{3} =$ two thirds
11. $\frac{1}{8} + \frac{2}{16} =$ thirds fourth

Across

2. $\frac{1}{12} + \frac{1}{3} =$ five twelths
3. $\frac{5}{10} + \frac{2}{5} =$ nine tenths
5. $\frac{7}{15} + \frac{1}{5} =$ two thirds
6. $\frac{1}{2} + \frac{2}{6} =$ five sixths
8. $\frac{1}{6} + \frac{1}{2} =$ two thirds
9. $\frac{1}{5} + \frac{4}{10} =$ three fifths
10. $\frac{1}{3} + \frac{3}{6} =$ five sixths
12. $\frac{2}{7} + \frac{1}{14} =$ five fourteenths
13. $\frac{8}{14} + \frac{2}{7} =$ five sevenths

189

Numeral Nibblers

Complete these equations. Use another sheet of paper to solve the problems, if needed.

$\frac{15}{16} - \frac{1}{2} = \frac{7}{16}$

$\frac{3}{4} - \frac{10}{16} = \frac{1}{8}$

$\frac{3}{16} - \frac{1}{8} = \frac{1}{16}$

$\frac{2}{3} - \frac{2}{12} = \frac{1}{2}$

$\frac{21}{24} - \frac{5}{6} = \frac{1}{24}$

$\frac{3}{4} - \frac{7}{12} = \frac{1}{6}$

$\frac{15}{16} - \frac{3}{4} = \frac{3}{16}$

$\frac{10}{16} - \frac{1}{8} = \frac{1}{2}$

$\frac{1}{16} - \frac{1}{48} = \frac{1}{24}$

$\frac{2}{3} - \frac{2}{9} = \frac{4}{9}$

$\frac{21}{24} - \frac{3}{4} = \frac{1}{8}$

$\frac{5}{6} - \frac{7}{12} = \frac{1}{4}$

190

Make a Wish

Solve these problems.

Example: $\frac{2}{9}$ of 27 = $(27 \div 9) \times 2 = 6$

$\frac{7}{8}$ of 16 = 14 $\frac{3}{7}$ of 49 = 21 $\frac{4}{6}$ of 60 = 40 $\frac{3}{6}$ of 54 = 27

$\frac{6}{8}$ of 24 = 18 $\frac{9}{12}$ of 36 = 27 $\frac{9}{12}$ of 24 = 18 $\frac{2}{5}$ of 25 = 10

$\frac{3}{8}$ of 32 = 12 $\frac{5}{7}$ of 42 = 30 $\frac{3}{4}$ of 48 = 36

$\frac{3}{7}$ of 35 = 15 $\frac{7}{9}$ of 36 = 28

$\frac{6}{8}$ of 64 = 48 $\frac{8}{9}$ of 81 = 72

$\frac{3}{6}$ of 24 = 12 $\frac{5}{6}$ of 30 = 25

$\frac{9}{10}$ of 40 = 36 $\frac{6}{8}$ of 72 = 54

$\frac{9}{11}$ of 33 = 27 $\frac{3}{8}$ of 48 = 18

191

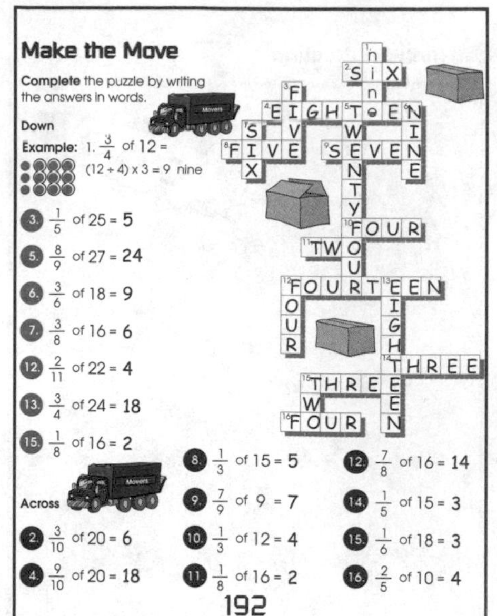

Make the Move

Complete the puzzle by writing the answers in words.

Down

Example: 1. $\frac{3}{4}$ of 12 = (12 ÷ 4) x 3 = 9 nine

3. $\frac{1}{5}$ of 25 = 5
5. $\frac{8}{9}$ of 27 = 24
6. $\frac{3}{6}$ of 18 = 9
7. $\frac{3}{8}$ of 16 = 6
12. $\frac{2}{11}$ of 22 = 4
13. $\frac{3}{4}$ of 24 = 18
15. $\frac{1}{8}$ of 16 = 2

Across

2. $\frac{3}{10}$ of 20 = 6
4. $\frac{9}{10}$ of 20 = 18
8. $\frac{1}{3}$ of 15 = 5
9. $\frac{7}{9}$ of 9 = 7
10. $\frac{1}{3}$ of 12 = 4
11. $\frac{1}{8}$ of 16 = 2
12. $\frac{7}{8}$ of 16 = 14
14. $\frac{1}{5}$ of 15 = 3
15. $\frac{1}{6}$ of 18 = 3
16. $\frac{2}{5}$ of 10 = 4

192

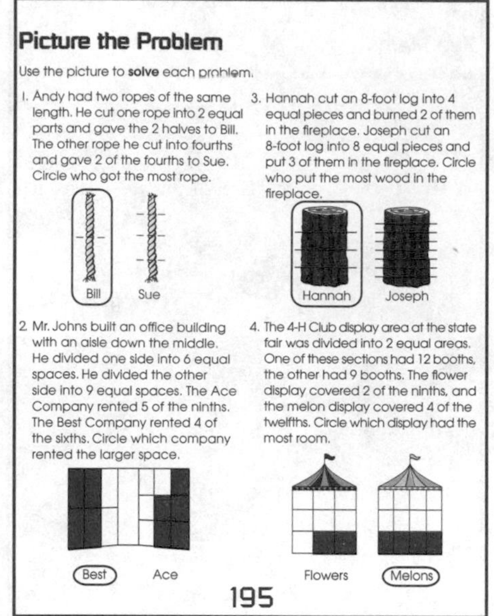

Picture the Problem

Use the picture to **solve** each problem.

1. Andy had two ropes of the same length. He cut one rope into 2 equal parts and gave the 2 halves to Bill. The other rope he cut into fourths and gave 2 of the fourths to Sue. Circle who got the most rope.

2. Mr. Johns built an office building with an aisle down the middle. He divided one side into 6 equal spaces. He divided the other side into 9 equal spaces. The Ace Company rented 5 of the ninths. The Best Company rented 4 of the sixths. Circle which company rented the larger space.

3. Hannah cut an 8-foot log into 4 equal pieces and burned 2 of them in the fireplace. Joseph cut an 8-foot log into 8 equal pieces and put 3 of them in the fireplace. Circle who put the most wood in the fireplace.

4. The 4-H Club display area at the state fair was divided into 2 equal areas. One of these sections had 12 booths, the other had 9 booths. The flower display covered 2 of the ninths, and the melon display covered 4 of the twelfths. Circle which display had the most room.

195

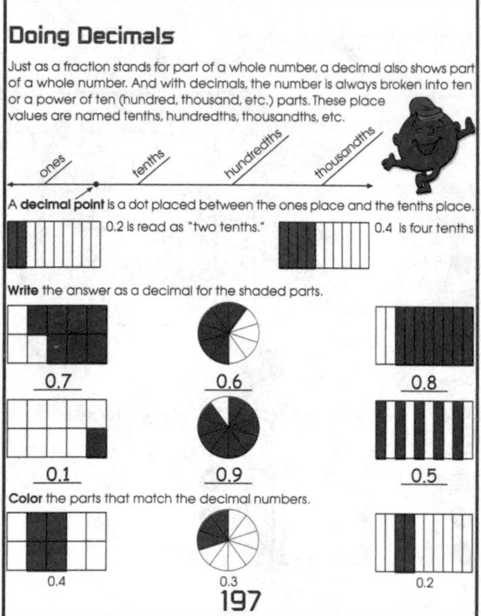

Doing Decimals

Just as a fraction stands for part of a whole number, a decimal also shows part of a whole number. And with decimals, the number is always broken into ten or a power of ten (hundred, thousand, etc.) parts. These place values are named tenths, hundredths, thousandths, etc.

A **decimal point** is a dot placed between the ones place and the tenths place.

0.2 is read as "two tenths." 0.4 is four tenths

Write the answer as a decimal for the shaded parts.

0.7 0.6 0.8

0.1 0.9 0.5

Color the parts that match the decimal numbers.

0.4 0.3 0.2

197

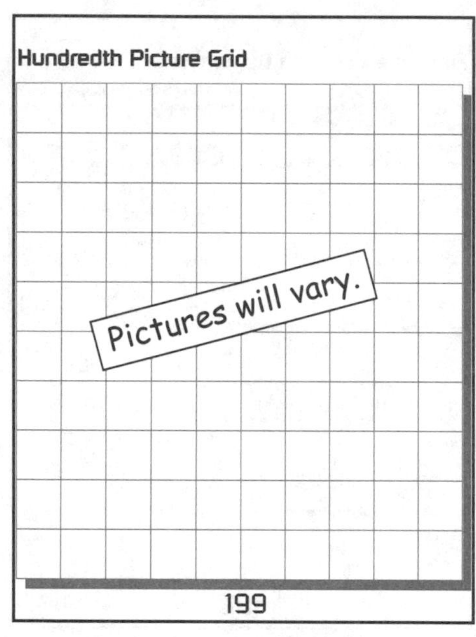

Hundredth Picture Grid

199

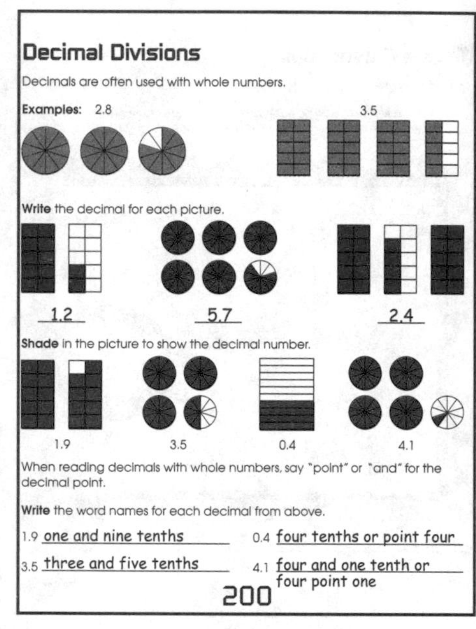

Decimal Divisions

Decimals are often used with whole numbers.

Examples: 2.8 3.5

Write the decimal for each picture.

1.2 5.7 2.4

Shade in the picture to show the decimal number.

1.9 3.5 0.4 4.1

When reading decimals with whole numbers, say "point" or "and" for the decimal point.

Write the word names for each decimal from above.

1.9 one and nine tenths

0.4 four tenths or point four

3.5 three and five tenths

4.1 four and one tenth or four point one

200

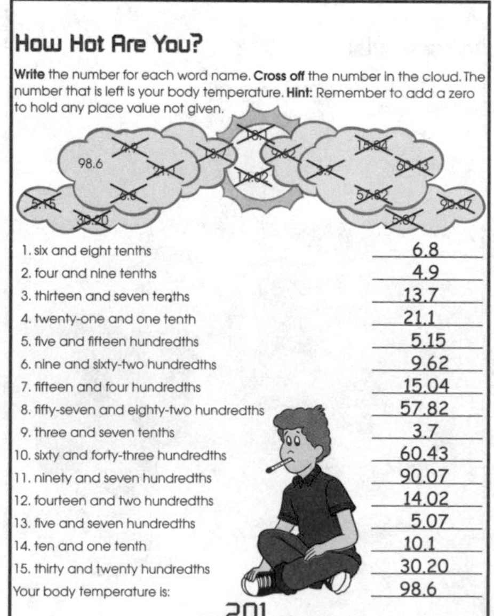

How Hot Are You?

Write the number for each word name. **Cross off** the number in the cloud. The number that is left is your body temperature. **Hint:** Remember to add a zero to hold any place value not given.

1. six and eight tenths 6.8
2. four and nine tenths 4.9
3. thirteen and seven tenths 13.7
4. twenty-one and one tenth 21.1
5. five and fifteen hundredths 5.15
6. nine and sixty-two hundredths 9.62
7. fifteen and four hundredths 15.04
8. fifty-seven and eighty-two hundredths 57.82
9. three and seven tenths 3.7
10. sixty and forty-three hundredths 60.43
11. ninety and seven hundredths 90.07
12. fourteen and two hundredths 14.02
13. five and seven hundredths 5.07
14. ten and one tenth 10.1
15. thirty and twenty hundredths 30.20

Your body temperature is: 98.6

201

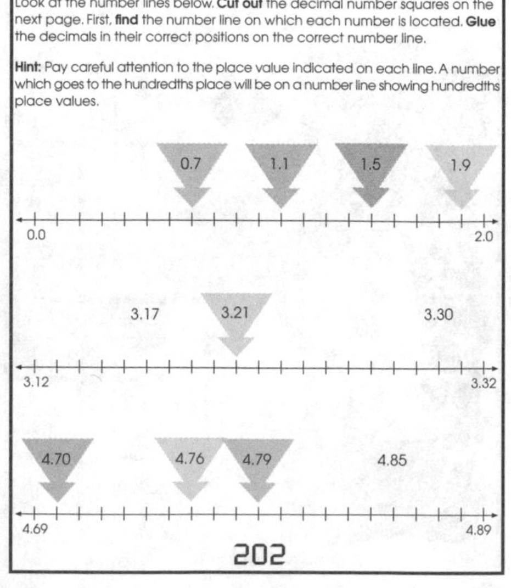

Order in the Line

Look at the number lines below. **Cut out** the decimal number squares on the next page. First, **find** the number line on which each number is located. **Glue** the decimals in their correct positions on the correct number line.

Hint: Pay careful attention to the place value indicated on each line. A number which goes to the hundredths place will be on a number line showing hundredths place values.

202

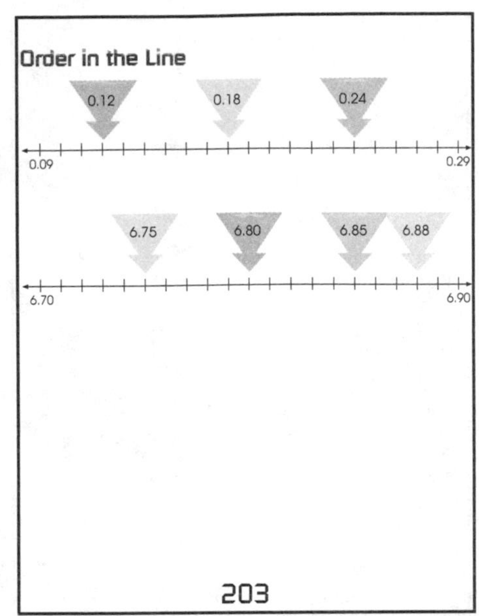

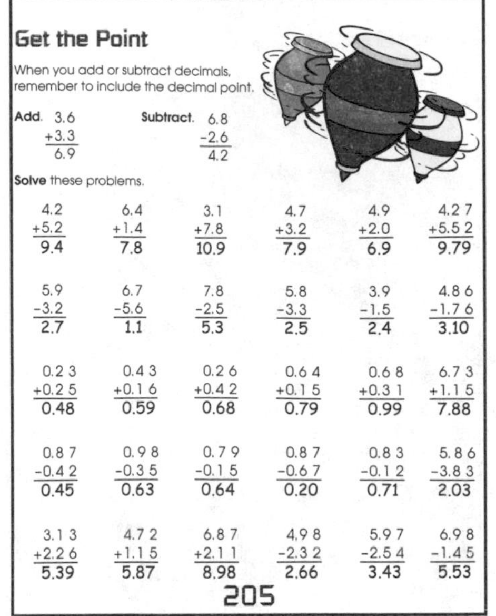

Get the Point

When you add or subtract decimals, remember to include the decimal point.

Add. 3.6 + 3.3 = 6.9 **Subtract.** 6.8 − 2.6 = 4.2

Solve these problems.

4.2 + 5.2 = 9.4	6.4 + 1.4 = 7.8	3.1 + 7.8 = 10.9	4.7 + 3.2 = 7.9	4.9 + 2.0 = 6.9	4.27 + 5.52 = 9.79
5.9 − 3.2 = 2.7	6.7 − 5.6 = 1.1	7.8 − 2.5 = 5.3	5.8 − 3.3 = 2.5	3.9 − 1.5 = 2.4	4.86 − 1.76 = 3.10
0.23 + 0.25 = 0.48	0.43 + 0.16 = 0.59	0.26 + 0.42 = 0.68	0.64 + 0.15 = 0.79	0.68 + 0.31 = 0.99	6.73 + 1.15 = 7.88
0.87 − 0.42 = 0.45	0.98 − 0.35 = 0.63	0.79 − 0.15 = 0.64	0.87 − 0.67 = 0.20	0.83 − 0.12 = 0.71	5.86 − 3.83 = 2.03
3.13 + 2.26 = 5.39	4.72 + 1.15 = 5.87	6.87 + 2.11 = 8.98	4.98 − 2.32 = 2.66	5.97 − 2.54 = 3.43	6.98 − 1.45 = 5.53

205

Animal Trivia

1. An earthworm is 14.9 cm long. A grasshopper is 8.7 cm long. What is the difference?
   6.2 cm
2. A pocket gopher has a hind foot 3.5 cm long. A ground squirrel's hind foot is 6.4 cm long. How much longer is the ground squirrel's hind foot?
   2.9 cm
3. A porcupine has a tail 30.0 cm long. An opossum has a tail 53.5 cm long. How much longer is the opossum's tail?
   23.5 cm
4. A wood rat has a tail which is 23.6 cm long. A deer mouse has a tail 12.2 cm long. What is the difference between the two?
   11.4 cm
5. A cottontail rabbit has ears which are 6.8 cm long. A jackrabbit has ears 12.9 cm long. How much shorter is the cottontail's ear?
   6.1 cm
6. The hind foot of a river otter is 14.6 cm long. The hind foot of a hog-nosed skunk is 9.0 cm long. What is the difference?
   5.6 cm
7. A rock mouse is [illegible] cm long. His tail adds another 14.4 cm. What is his total length from his nose to the tip of his tail?
   40.5 cm

206

Subtraction Cards

1.040 − 0.216 = 0.824	5.5 − 3.2 = 2.3
0.350 − 0.128 = 0.222	8.6 − 4.8 = 3.8
0.609 − 0.317 = 0.292	1.30 − 0.17 = 1.13
0.87 − 0.49 = 0.38	0.94 − 0.53 = 0.41
0.704 − 0.326 = 0.378	2.3 − 1.4 = 0.9

211

Rounding Cards

$3.5\underline{3}5$ 3.54 Round to the underlined number.	$\underline{9}.7$ 10.0 Round to the underlined number.
$0.\underline{3}34$ 0.3 Round to the underlined number.	$\underline{2}.09$ 2.0 Round to the underlined number.
$\underline{5}.48$ 5.0 Round to the underlined number.	$6.\underline{8}3$ 6.8 Round to the underlined number.
$0.6\underline{1}2$ 0.61 Round to the underlined number.	$0.\underline{0}51$ 0.1 Round to the underlined number.
7.717 7.72 Round to the underlined number.	$\underline{1}.842$ 2.0 Round to the underlined number.

213

Comparison Cards

7.2 (<) 7.5 < or >	0.3 (<) 3.0 < or >
4.9 (>) 4.8 < or >	1.5 (<) 1.7 < or >
3.23 (<) 3.32 < or >	6.19 (<) 6.2 < or >
2.08 (<) 2.40 < or >	0.86 (<) 0.88 < or >
5.61 (<) 5.62 < or >	8.3 (>) 8.06 < or >

215

Addition Cards

0.307 + 0.900 = 1.207	0.64 + 0.33 = 0.97
0.78 + 0.21 = 0.99	0.65 + 0.65 = 1.30
1.29 + 4.50 = 5.79	0.442 + 0.784 = 1.226
0.704 + 0.127 = 0.831	0.946 + 0.035 = 0.981
4.76 + 2.25 = 7.01	2.12 + 3.79 = 5.91

217

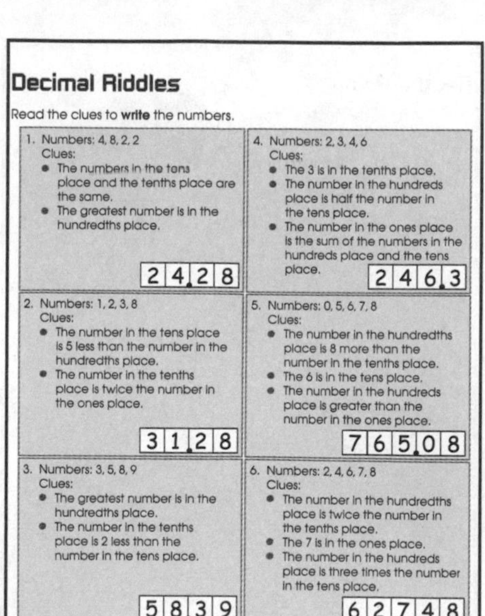

Decimal Riddles

Read the clues to **write** the numbers.

1. Numbers: 4, 8, 2, 2
   Clues:
   - The numbers in the tens place and the tenths place are the same.
   - The greatest number is in the hundredths place.

   24.28

2. Numbers: 1, 2, 3, 8
   Clues:
   - The number in the tens place is 5 less than the number in the hundredths place.
   - The number in the tenths place is twice the number in the ones place.

   31.28

3. Numbers: 3, 5, 8, 9
   Clues:
   - The greatest number is in the hundredths place.
   - The number in the tenths place is 2 less than the number in the tens place.

   58.39

4. Numbers: 2, 3, 4, 6
   Clues:
   - The 3 is in the tenths place.
   - The number in the hundreds place is half the number in the tens place.
   - The number in the ones place is the sum of the numbers in the hundreds place and the tens place.

   246.3

5. Numbers: 0, 5, 6, 7, 8
   Clues:
   - The number in the hundredths place is 8 more than the number in the tenths place.
   - The 6 is in the tens place.
   - The number in the hundreds place is greater than the number in the ones place.

   765.08

6. Numbers: 2, 4, 6, 7, 8
   Clues:
   - The number in the hundredths place is twice the number in the tenths place.
   - The 7 is in the ones place.
   - The number in the hundreds place is three times the number in the tens place.

   627.48

221

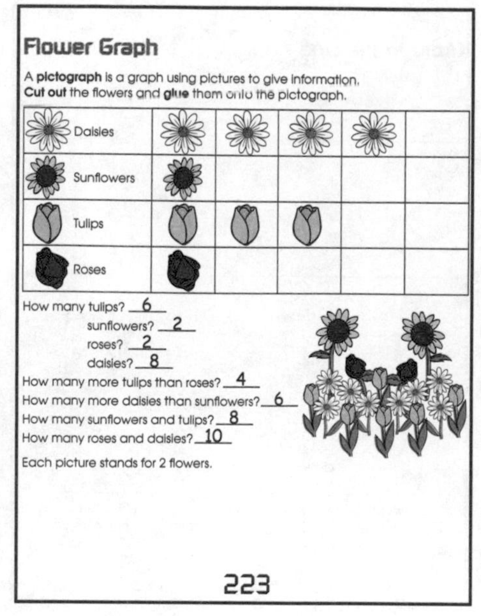

Flower Graph

A **pictograph** is a graph using pictures to give information.
Cut out the flowers and **glue** them onto the pictograph.

Daisies
Sunflowers
Tulips
Roses

How many tulips? 6
sunflowers? 2
roses? 2
daisies? 8
How many more tulips than roses? 4
How many more daisies than sunflowers? 6
How many sunflowers and tulips? 8
How many roses and daisies? 10

Each picture stands for 2 flowers.

223

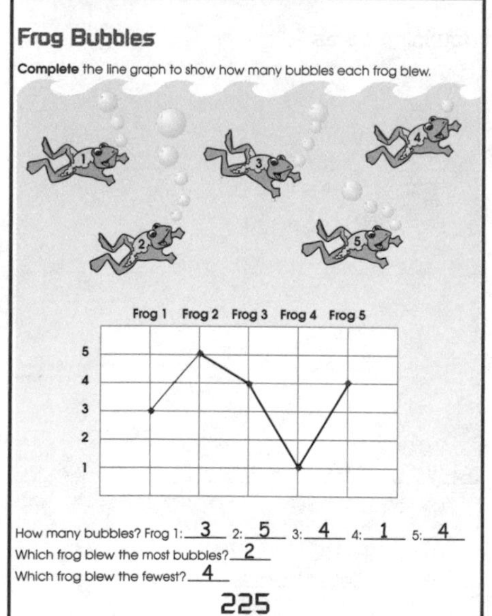

Frog Bubbles

Complete the line graph to show how many bubbles each frog blew.

How many bubbles? Frog 1: 3 2: 5 3: 4 4: 1 5: 4
Which frog blew the most bubbles? 2
Which frog blew the fewest? 4

225

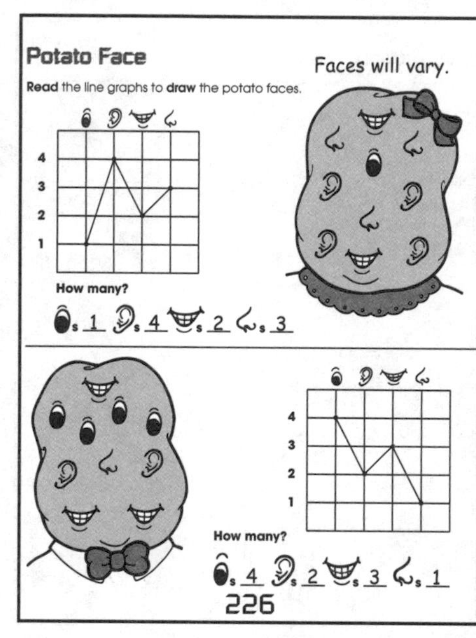

Potato Face

Read the line graphs to **draw** the potato faces.

Faces will vary.

How many?
1, 4, 2, 3

How many?
4, 2, 3, 1

226

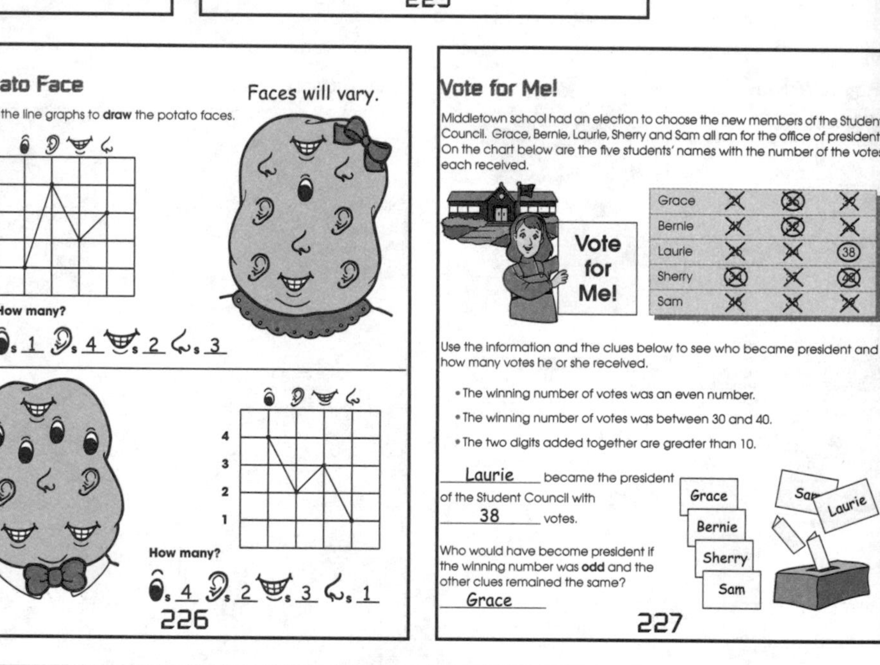

Vote for Me!

Middletown school had an election to choose the new members of the Student Council. Grace, Bernie, Laurie, Sherry and Sam all ran for the office of president. On the chart below are the five students' names with the number of the votes each received.

Use the information and the clues below to see who became president and how many votes he or she received.

- The winning number of votes was an even number.
- The winning number of votes was between 30 and 40.
- The two digits added together are greater than 10.

Laurie became the president of the Student Council with 38 votes.

Who would have become president if the winning number was **odd** and the other clues remained the same?
Grace

227

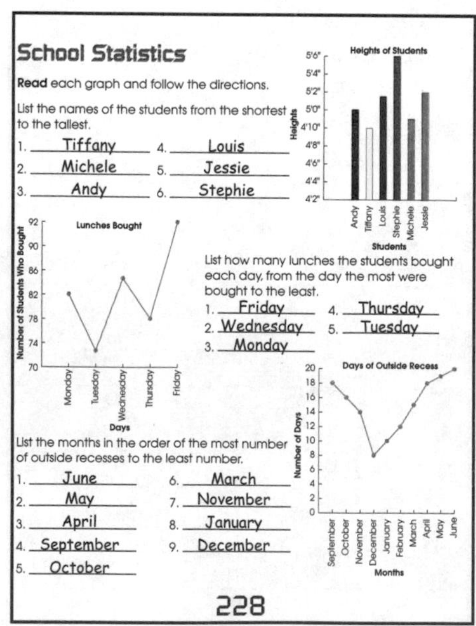

School Statistics

Read each graph and follow the directions.

List the names of the students from the shortest to the tallest.

1. Tiffany
2. Michele
3. Andy
4. Louis
5. Jessie
6. Stephie

List how many lunches the students bought each day, from the day the most were bought to the least.

1. Friday
2. Wednesday
3. Monday
4. Thursday
5. Tuesday

List the months in the order of the most number of outside recesses to the least number.

1. June
2. May
3. April
4. September
5. October
6. March
7. November
8. January
9. December

228

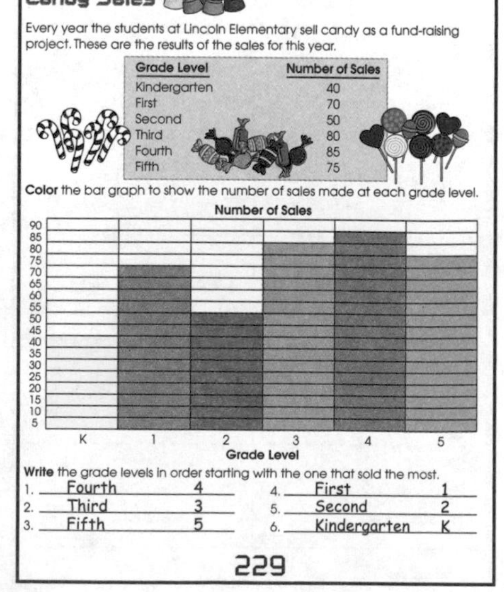

Candy Sales

Every year the students at Lincoln Elementary sell candy as a fund-raising project. These are the results of the sales for this year.

Grade Level	Number of Sales
Kindergarten	40
First	70
Second	50
Third	80
Fourth	85
Fifth	75

Color the bar graph to show the number of sales made at each grade level.

Write the grade levels in order starting with the one that sold the most.

1. Fourth 4
2. Third 3
3. Fifth 5
4. First 1
5. Second 2
6. Kindergarten K

229

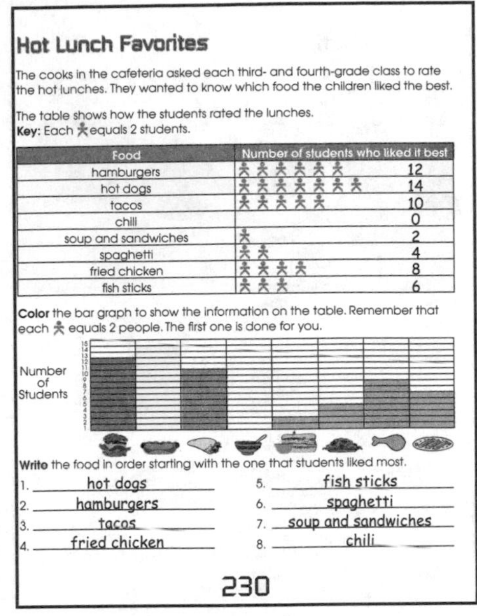

Hot Lunch Favorites

The cooks in the cafeteria asked each third- and fourth-grade class to rate the hot lunches. They wanted to know which food the children liked the best.

The table shows how the students rated the lunches.
Key: Each 🯅 equals 2 students.

Food	Number of students who liked it best
hamburgers	12
hot dogs	14
tacos	10
chili	0
soup and sandwiches	2
spaghetti	4
fried chicken	8
fish sticks	6

Color the bar graph to show the information on the table. Remember that each 🯅 equals 2 people. The first one is done for you.

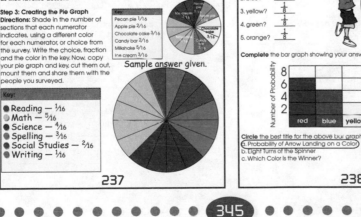

Write the food in order starting with the one that students liked most.

1. hot dogs
2. hamburgers
3. tacos
4. fried chicken
5. fish sticks
6. spaghetti
7. soup and sandwiches
8. chili

230

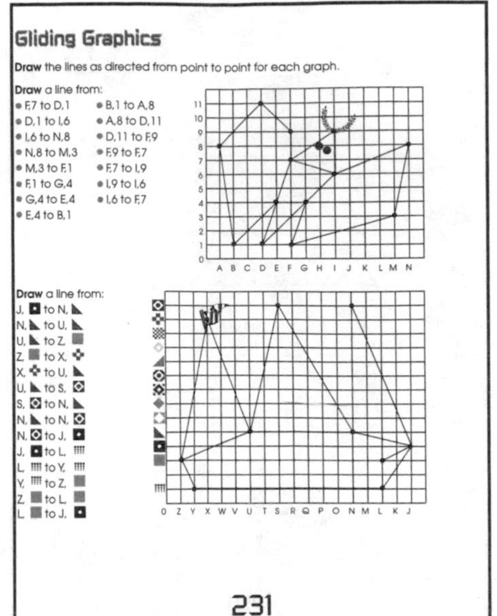

Gliding Graphics

Draw the lines as directed from point to point for each graph.

Draw a line from:

- F,7 to D,1
- D,1 to I,6
- I,6 to N,8
- N,8 to M,3
- M,3 to F,1
- F,1 to G,4
- G,4 to E,4
- E,4 to B,1
- B,1 to A,8
- A,8 to D,11
- D,11 to F,9
- F,9 to F,7
- F,7 to I,9
- I,9 to I,6
- I,6 to F,7

Draw a line from:

J, ■ to N, ◣
N, ◣ to U, ◣
U, ◣ to Z, ■
Z, ■ to X, ✣
X, ✣ to U, ◣
U, ◣ to S, ⊠
S, ⊠ to N, ◣
N, ◣ to N, ⊠
N, ⊠ to J, ■
J, ■ to L, ▥
L, ▥ to Y, ▥
Y, ▥ to Z, ■
Z, ■ to L, ■
L, ■ to J, ■

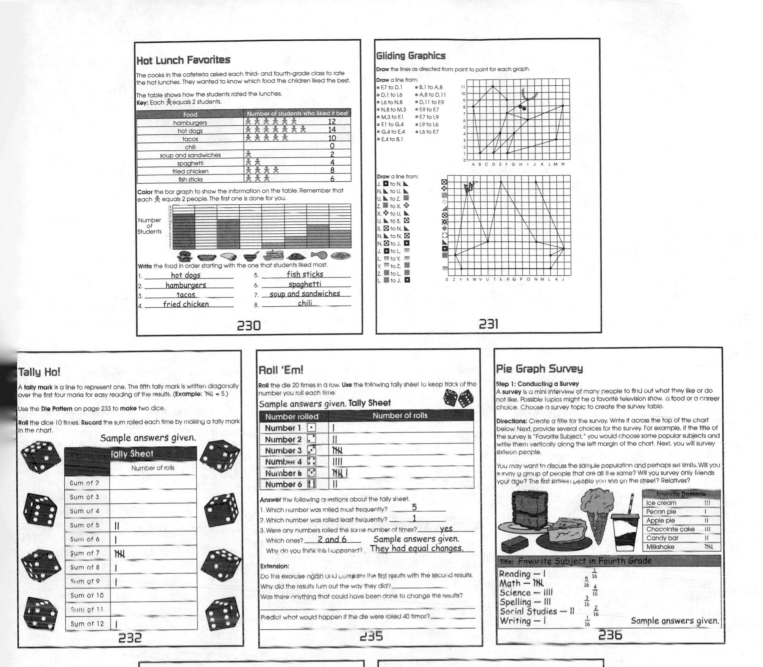

231

Tally Ho!

A **tally mark** is a line to represent one. The fifth tally mark is written diagonally over the first four marks for easy reading of the results. (**Example:** 卌 = 5.)

Use the **Die Pattern** on page 233 to **make** two dice.

Roll the dice 10 times. **Record** the sum rolled each time by making a tally mark in the chart.

Sample answers given.

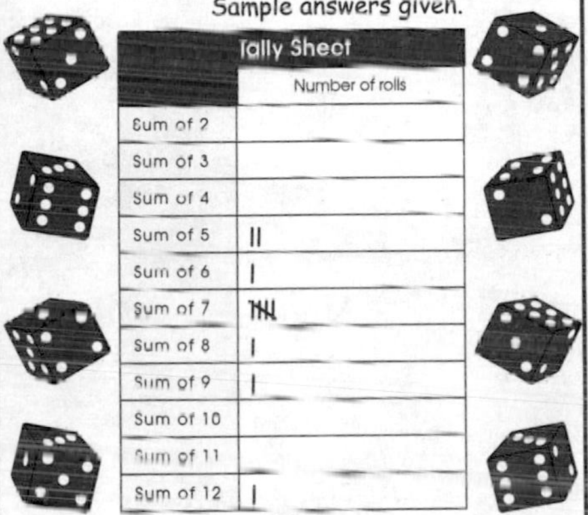

Tally Sheet

	Number of rolls
Sum of 2	
Sum of 3	
Sum of 4	
Sum of 5	||
Sum of 6	|
Sum of 7	卌
Sum of 8	|
Sum of 9	|
Sum of 10	
Sum of 11	
Sum of 12	|

232

Roll 'Em!

Roll the die 20 times in a row. **Use** the following tally sheet to keep track of the number you roll each time.

Sample answers given. **Tally Sheet**

Number rolled	Number of rolls
Number 1 ⚀	|
Number 2 ⚁	||
Number 3 ⚂	卌
Number 4 ⚃	||||
Number 5 ⚄	卌 |
Number 6 ⚅	||

Answer the following questions about the tally sheet.

1. Which number was rolled most frequently? 5
2. Which number was rolled least frequently? 1
3. Were any numbers rolled the same number of times? yes
   Which ones? 2 and 6 Sample answers given.
   Why do you think this happened? They had equal changes.

Extension:

Do this exercise again and compare the first results with the second results.
Why did the results turn out the way they did? ______
Was there anything that could have been done to change the results? ______

Predict what would happen if the die were rolled 40 times? ______

235

Pie Graph Survey

Step 1: Conducting a Survey
A **survey** is a mini interview of many people to find out what they like or do not like. Possible topics might be a favorite television show, a food or a career choice. Choose a survey topic to create the survey table.

Directions: Create a title for the survey. Write it across the top of the chart below. Next, provide several choices for the survey. For example, if the title of the survey is "Favorite Subject," you would choose some popular subjects and write them vertically along the left margin of the chart. Next, you will survey sixteen people.

You may want to discuss the sample population and perhaps set limits. Will you survey a group of people that are all the same? Will you survey only friends your age? The first sixteen people you see on the street? Relatives?

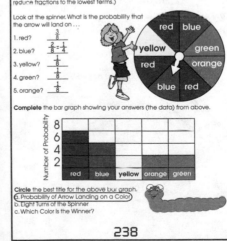

Favorite Desserts	
Ice cream	|||
Pecan pie	|
Apple pie	||
Chocolate cake	|||
Candy bar	||
Milkshake	卌

Title: Favorite Subject in Fourth Grade

Reading — |	$\frac{1}{16}$
Math — 卌	$\frac{5}{16}$
Science — ||||	$\frac{4}{16}$
Spelling — |||	$\frac{3}{16}$
Social Studies — ||	$\frac{2}{16}$
Writing — |	$\frac{1}{16}$

Sample answers given.

236

Pie Graph Survey

Step 2: Creating Fractions
Directions: Convert the results of your survey into fractions. The denominator will be 16, because that is the number of people who make up the whole survey. Determine the numerator by counting the number of people who chose an item. (For example, if four people chose math as their favorite subject, the fraction would be 4/16.) When all tallied results have been converted into fractions, you are ready to create the pie graph.

Chocolate cake = 3/16 means three children out of sixteen picked the cake as their favorite dessert.

Step 3: Creating the Pie Graph
Directions: Shade in the number of sections that each numerator indicates, using a different color for each numerator, or choice from the survey. Write the choice, fraction and the color in the key. Now, copy your pie graph and key, cut them out, mount them and share them with the people you surveyed.

Key:
Pecan pie 1/16
Apple pie 2/16
Chocolate cake 3/16
Candy bar 2/16
Milkshake 5/16
Ice cream 3/16

Sample answer given.

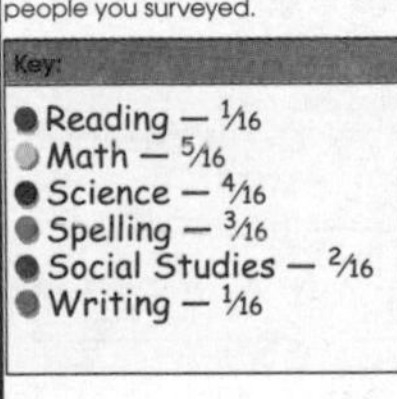

Key:
- Reading — 1/16
- Math — 5/16
- Science — 4/16
- Spelling — 3/16
- Social Studies — 2/16
- Writing — 1/16

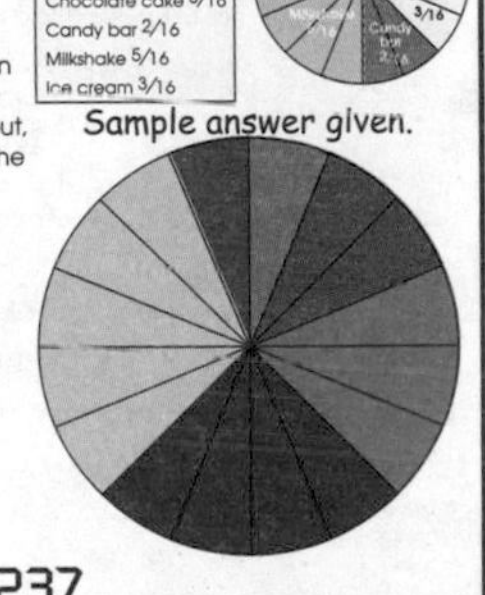

237

Guess the Color

Probability shows the chance that a given event will happen. To show probability, write a fraction. The number of different possibilities is the denominator. The number of times the event could happen is the numerator. (Remember to reduce fractions to the lowest terms.)

Look at the spinner. What is the probability that the arrow will land on . . .

1. red? $\frac{3}{8}$
2. blue? $\frac{2}{8} = \frac{1}{4}$
3. yellow? $\frac{1}{8}$
4. green? $\frac{1}{8}$
5. orange? $\frac{1}{8}$

Complete the bar graph showing your answers (the data) from above.

Number of Probability: 8, 6, 4, 2 — red, blue, yellow, orange, green

Circle the best title for the above bar graph.
a. Probability of Arrow Landing on a Color (circled)
b. Eight Turns of the Spinner
c. Which Color Is the Winner?

238

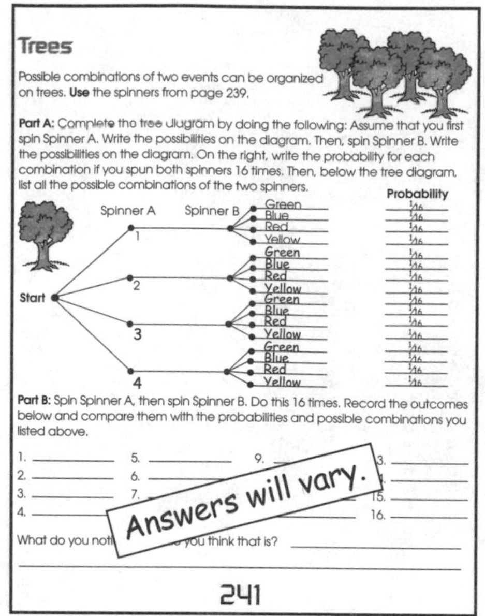

Trees

Possible combinations of two events can be organized on trees. **Use** the spinners from page 239.

Part A: Complete the tree diagram by doing the following: Assume that you first spin Spinner A. Write the possibilities on the diagram. Then, spin Spinner B. Write the possibilities on the diagram. On the right, write the probability for each combination if you spun both spinners 16 times. Then, below the tree diagram, list all the possible combinations of the two spinners.

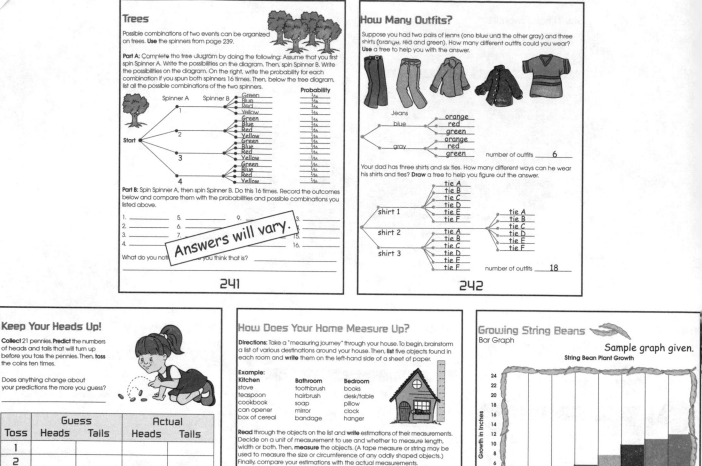

Part B: Spin Spinner A, then spin Spinner B. Do this 16 times. Record the outcomes below and compare them with the probabilities and possible combinations you listed above.

1. ______ 5. ______ 9. ______ 13. ______
2. ______ 6. ______ 10. ______ 14. ______
3. ______ 7. ______ 11. ______ 15. ______
4. ______ 8. ______ 12. ______ 16. ______

What do you notice? Why do you think that is? ______

Answers will vary.

241

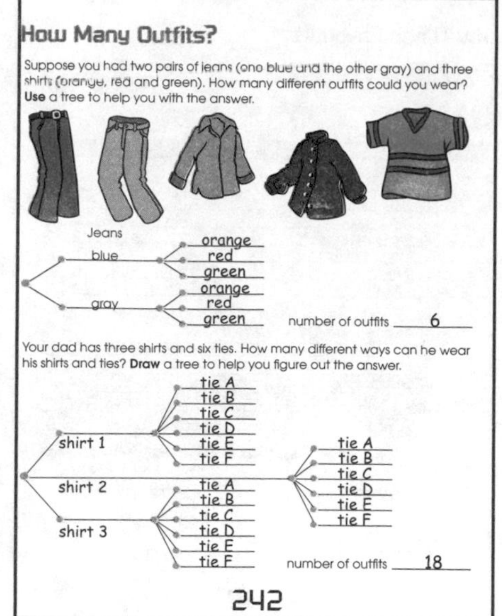

How Many Outfits?

Suppose you had two pairs of jeans (one blue and the other gray) and three shirts (orange, red and green). How many different outfits could you wear? **Use** a tree to help you with the answer.

number of outfits 6

Your dad has three shirts and six ties. How many different ways can he wear his shirts and ties? **Draw** a tree to help you figure out the answer.

number of outfits 18

242

Keep Your Heads Up!

Collect 21 pennies. **Predict** the numbers of heads and tails that will turn up before you toss the pennies. Then, **toss** the coins ten times.

Does anything change about your predictions the more you guess? ______

Toss	Guess		Actual	
	Heads	Tails	Heads	Tails
1				
2				
3				
4				
5				
6				
7				
8				
9				
10				

Answers will vary.

243

How Does Your Home Measure Up?

Directions: Take a "measuring journey" through your house. To begin, brainstorm a list of various destinations around your house. Then, **list** five objects found in each room and **write** them on the left-hand side of a sheet of paper.

Example:

Kitchen	Bathroom	Bedroom
stove	toothbrush	books
teaspoon	hairbrush	desk/table
cookbook	soap	pillow
can opener	mirror	clock
box of cereal	bandage	hanger

Read through the objects on the list and **write** estimations of their measurements. Decide on a unit of measurement to use and whether to measure length, width or both. Then, **measure** the objects. (A tape measure or string may be used to measure the size or circumference of any oddly shaped objects.) Finally, compare your estimations with the actual measurements.

Sample answers given.

Object	Estimate	Actual
box of cereal	12 in. by 6 in.	11 in. by 8 in.
soap	2 in. by 3 in.	3 in. by 4 in.
pillow	24 in. by 18 in.	26 in. by 20 in.
foot stool	24 in. by 18 in.	27 in. by 24 in.
table top	40 in. by 28 in.	42 in. by 30 in.

247

Growing String Beans

Bar Graph

Sample graph given.

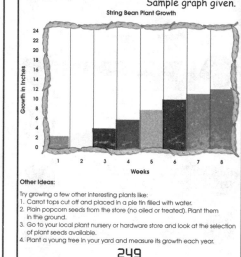

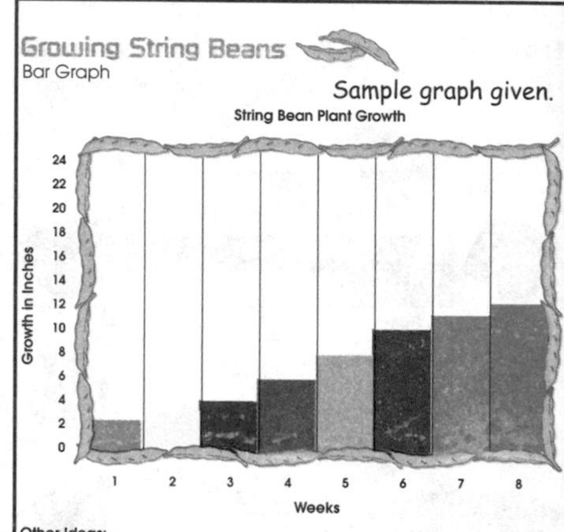

Other Ideas:

Try growing a few other interesting plants like:

1. Carrot tops cut off and placed in a pie tin filled with water.
2. Plain popcorn seeds from the store (no oiled or treated). Plant them in the ground.
3. Go to your local plant nursery or hardware store and look at the selection of plant seeds available.
4. Plant a young tree in your yard and measure its growth each year.

249

Hand—Foot—Ruler

Directions:

1. Measure the span of your hand by stretching your thumb and little finger as far apart as possible. Lay your hand on a ruler to find out this length (span). Record the inches (") of the span on the record sheet below.
2. Measure the length of your pace by taking one step forward and holding it. Have someone put the edge of a yardstick next to the heel of your back foot and measure to the back of the heel on your forward foot. Record the pace distance in inches on the record sheet.
3. Using a ruler or yardstick, measure the distances listed on the record sheet. Record all findings in feet and/or inches.

Sample answers given.

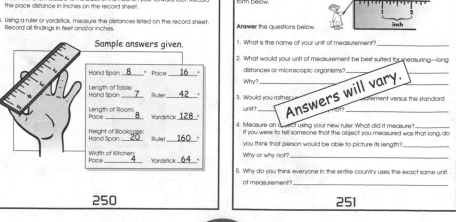

Hand Span 8 " Pace 16 "

Length of Table: Hand Span 7 Ruler 42 "

Length of Room: Pace 8 Yardstick 128 "

Height of Bookcase: Hand Span 20 Ruler 160 "

Width of Kitchen: Pace 4 Yardstick 64 "

250

A Measurement of Our Own

Create your own new system of measurement. Brainstorm ideas on what and how you should base the new unit. For example, you may use the length of your finger, the length of a juice box, the length of your backpack, etc. as a base.

Next, **create** a ruler using your new unit of measurement. A foot is made of inches and a meter is made of centimeters. Break your standard unit into smaller units and **add** these to the ruler. When the ruler is complete, fill out the form below.

Answer the questions below.

1. What is the name of your unit of measurement? ______
2. What would your unit of measurement be best suited for measuring—long distances or microscopic organisms? ______ Why? ______
3. Would you rather use your unit of measurement versus the standard unit? ______ Why or why not? ______
4. Measure an object using your new ruler. What did it measure? ______ If you were to tell someone that the object you measured was that long, do you think that person would be able to picture its length? ______ Why or why not? ______
5. Why do you think everyone in the entire country uses the exact same unit of measurement? ______

Answers will vary.

251

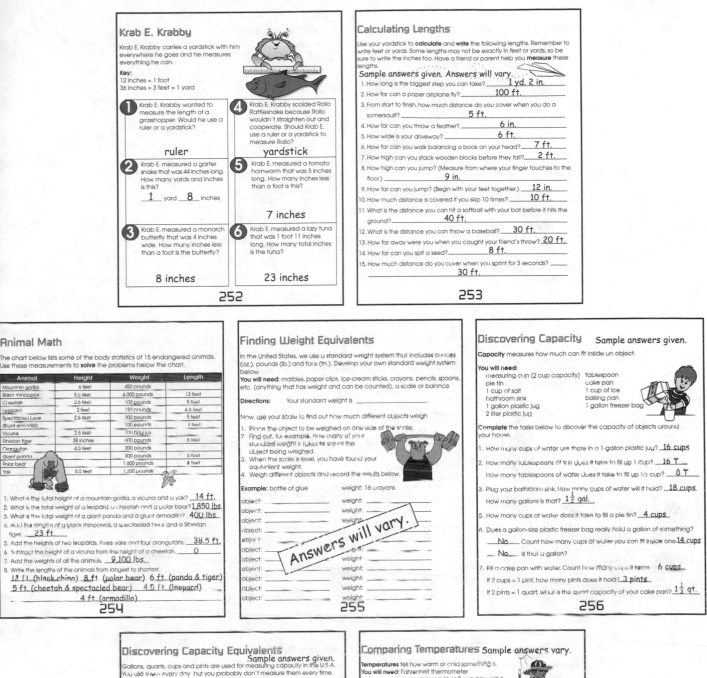

Krab E. Krabby

Krab E. Krabby carries a yardstick with him everywhere he goes and he measures everything he can.

Key:
12 inches = 1 foot
36 inches = 3 feet = 1 yard

1. Krab E. Krabby wanted to measure the length of a grasshopper. Would he use a ruler or a yardstick?
   ruler
2. Krab E. measured a garter snake that was 44 inches long. How many yards and inches is this?
   1 yard 8 inches
3. Krab E. measured a monarch butterfly that was 4 inches wide. How many inches less than a foot is the butterfly?
   8 inches
4. Krab E. Krabby scolded Rollo Rattlesnake because Rollo wouldn't straighten out and cooperate. Should Krab E. use a ruler or a yardstick to measure Rollo?
   yardstick
5. Krab E. measured a tomato hornworm that was 5 inches long. How many inches less than a foot is this?
   7 inches
6. Krab E. measured a lazy tuna that was 1 foot 11 inches long. How many total inches is the tuna?
   23 inches

252

Calculating Lengths

Use your yardstick to **calculate** and **write** the following lengths. Remember to write feet or yards. Some lengths may not be exactly in feet or yards, so be sure to write the inches too. Have a friend or parent help you **measure** these lengths.

Sample answers given. Answers will vary.

1. How long is the biggest step you can take? 1 yd. 2 in.
2. How far can a paper airplane fly? 100 ft.
3. From start to finish, how much distance do you cover when you do a somersault? 5 ft.
4. How far can you throw a feather? 6 in.
5. How wide is your driveway? 6 ft.
6. How far can you walk balancing a book on your head? 7 ft.
7. How high can you stack wooden blocks before they fall? 2 ft.
8. How high can you jump? (Measure from where your finger touches to the floor.) 9 in.
9. How far can you jump? (Begin with your feet together.) 12 in.
10. How much distance is covered if you skip 10 times? 10 ft.
11. What is the distance you can hit a softball with your bat before it hits the ground? 40 ft.
12. What is the distance you can throw a baseball? 30 ft.
13. How far away were you when you caught your friend's throw? 20 ft.
14. How far can you spit a seed? 8 ft.
15. How much distance do you cover when you sprint for 3 seconds? 30 ft.

253

Animal Math

The chart below lists some of the body statistics of 15 endangered animals. Use these measurements to **solve** the problems below the chart.

Animal	Height	Weight	Length
Mountain gorilla	6 feet	450 pounds	
Black rhinoceros	5.5 feet	4,000 pounds	12 feet
Cheetah	2.5 feet	100 pounds	5 feet
Leopard	2 feet	150 pounds	4.5 feet
Spectacled bear	2.5 feet	300 pounds	5 feet
Giant armadillo		100 pounds	4 feet
Vicuna	2.5 feet	100 pounds	
Siberian tiger	38 inches	600 pounds	6 feet
Orangutan	4.5 feet	200 pounds	
Giant panda		300 pounds	6 feet
Polar bear		1,600 pounds	8 feet
Yak	5.5 feet	1,200 pounds	

1. What is the total height of a mountain gorilla, a vicuna and a yak? 14 ft.
2. What is the total weight of a leopard, a cheetah and a polar bear? 1,850 lbs.
3. What is the total weight of a giant panda and a giant armadillo? 400 lbs.
4. Add the lengths of a black rhinoceros, a spectacled bear and a Siberian tiger. 23 ft.
5. Add the heights of two leopards, three yaks and four orangutans. 38.5 ft.
6. Subtract the height of a vicuna from the height of a cheetah. 0
7. Add the weights of all the animals. 9,100 lbs.
8. Write the lengths of the animals from longest to shortest.
   12 ft. (black rhino) 8 ft. (polar bear) 6 ft. (panda & tiger) 5 ft. (cheetah & spectacled bear) 4.5 ft. (leopard) 4 ft. (armadillo)

254

Finding Weight Equivalents

In the United States, we use a standard weight system that includes ounces (oz.), pounds (lb.) and tons (tn.). Develop your own standard weight system below.

You will need: marbles, paper clips, ice-cream sticks, crayons, pencils, spoons, etc. (anything that has weight and can be counted), a scale or balance

Directions: Your standard weight is ____________.

Now, use your scale to find out how much different objects weigh.

1. Place the object to be weighed on one side of the scale.
2. Find out, for example, how many of your standard weight it takes to equal the object being weighed.
3. When the scale is level, you have found your equivalent weight.
4. Weigh different objects and record the results below.

Example: bottle of glue — weight: 16 crayons

object: ________ weight: ________
object: ________ weight: ________
object: ________ weight: ________
object: ________ weight: ________
object: ________ weight: ________
object: ________ weight: ________
object: ________ weight: ________
object: ________ weight: ________
object: ________ weight: ________
object: ________ weight: ________
object: ________ weight: ________

Answers will vary.

255

Discovering Capacity

Sample answers given.

Capacity measures how much can fit inside an object.

You will need:
measuring cup (2 cup capacity), tablespoon, pie tin, cake pan, 1 cup of salt, 1 cup of ice, bathroom sink, baking pan, 1 gallon plastic jug, 1 gallon freezer bag, 2 liter plastic jug

Complete the tasks below to discover the capacity of objects around your house.

1. How many cups of water are there in a 1-gallon plastic jug? 16 cups
2. How many tablespoons of salt does it take to fill up 1 cup? 16 T
   How many tablespoons of water does it take to fill up 1/2 cup? 8 T
3. Plug your bathroom sink. How many cups of water will it hold? 18 cups
   How many gallons is that? $1\frac{1}{2}$ gal.
5. How many cups of water does it take to fill a pie tin? 4 cups
6. Does a gallon-size plastic freezer bag really hold a gallon of something?
   No Count how many cups of water you can fit inside one. 14 cups
   No Is that a gallon?
7. Fill a cake pan with water. Count how many cups it takes. 6 cups
   If 2 cups = 1 pint, how many pints does it hold? 3 pints
   If 2 pints = 1 quart, what is the quart capacity of your cake pan? $1\frac{1}{3}$ qt.

256

Discovering Capacity Equivalents

Sample answers given.

Gallons, quarts, cups and pints are used for measuring capacity in the U.S.A. You use them every day but you probably don't measure them every time. When you pour milk on your cereal in the morning, you are estimating how much milk you need to cover your breakfast. We are always making estimates.

You will need:
1 cup capacity measuring cup, pint, quart and half gallon containers, two 1-gallon capacity plastic jugs, water

Directions:
Set the two 1-gallon jugs beside each other. Fill one with water. Then, fill the measuring cups with water from the jug to determine the number of cups, pints, quarts and gallons of water it will take to fill the other jug.

1 cup — How many cups do you think it will take to fill 1 gallon? 16 cups
The actual amount 15 cups

1 pint (2 cups) — How many pints do you think it will take to fill 1 gallon? 8 pints
The actual amount $7\frac{1}{2}$ pints

1 quart (2 pints) — How many quarts do you think it will take to fill 1 gallon? 4 quarts
The actual amount 4 quarts

1 half gallon (2 quarts) — How many half gallons do you think it will take to fill 1 gallon? 2 half gallons
The actual amount 2 half gallons

257

Comparing Temperatures

Sample answers vary.

Temperatures tell how warm or cold something is.
You will need: Fahrenheit thermometer, measuring cup (1 or 2 cup capacity)

Measure and **record** the temperatures of:

70° 1. Water from the tap
40° 2. The dairy section at the grocery store (Call or visit store to ask.)
102° 3. A pet's body temperature (Call or visit veterinarian.)
0° 4. Your freezer (Have your parents help you.)
100° 5. Bathtub water (Fill a cup from the bathtub and place the thermometer in it.)
85° 6. A cup of water outside in the sun
- Place a cup of water in a safe place with the thermometer resting inside.
- Let it set until the temperature stops rising.
- Record the temperature.

Is it the same as the temperature outside? NO

63° 7. A cup of ice water
98.6° 8. Your body temperature

Now, **compare.**

1. How many degrees warmer is the bathtub water than the tap water? 30°
2. How many degrees difference is a pet's body temperature than yours? 2.2° Who is warmer? pet
3. What is the difference between your freezer's temperature and the temperature in the dairy section of your grocery store? 40°
4. What is the difference in temperature between a cup of water that has set out in the sun and a cup of ice water? 22°

258

Weather Page

Examine the weather page from the newspaper for two or more consecutive days (preferably the two days prior to this activity).

Look for the following information:
- time of sunrise and sunset for each day,
- low temperature for each day,
- high temperature for each day,
- high and low tides (if applicable.)

How accurate was the forecast for:
- time of sunrise and sunset for each day?
- low temperature for each day?
- high temperature for each day?
- high and low tides?

time of sunrise	
time of sunset	
low temperature	
high tem...	
times...	
times of low tides	

Answers will vary.

259

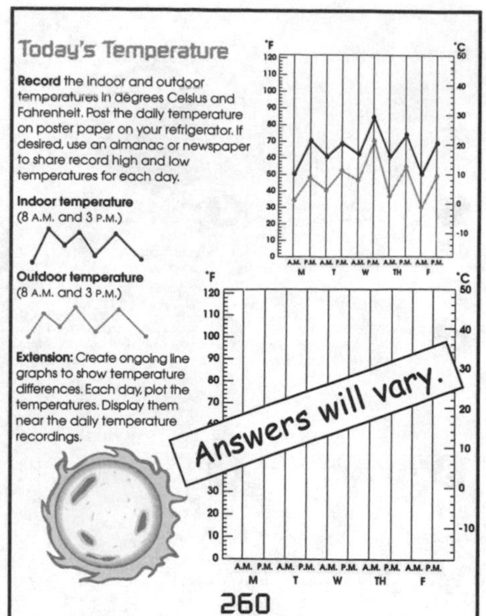

Today's Temperature

Record the indoor and outdoor temperatures in degrees Celsius and Fahrenheit. Post the daily temperature on poster paper on your refrigerator. If desired, use an almanac or newspaper to share record high and low temperatures for each day.

Indoor temperature
(8 A.M. and 3 P.M.)

Outdoor temperature
(8 A.M. and 3 P.M.)

Extension: Create ongoing line graphs to show temperature differences. Each day, plot the temperatures. Display them near the daily temperature recordings.

Answers will vary.

260

Super Shadows

Go outside to **measure** your shadow every hour on a sunny day. Have someone help you by **drawing** around your shadow with colored chalk. **Record** the time and length on your chart. Stand in the same place each time. Predict what will be different.

Were your predictions accurate? Answers will vary.

8 A.M. Shadows

Everyone's shadow is taller than really,
The shadows of giants are taller than trees.
The shadows of children are big as their parents,
And shadows of trotting dogs bend at the knees.
Everyone's shadow is taller than really,
Everyone's shadow is thinner than thin,
8 A.M. shadows are long at the dawning,
Pulling the night away,
Coaxing the light to say:
"Welcome, all shadows,
Day, please begin!"

Patricia Hubbel

Sample answers given.

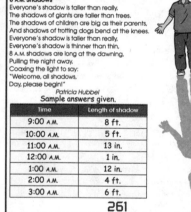

Time	Length of shadow
9:00 A.M.	8 ft.
10:00 A.M.	5 ft.
11:00 A.M.	13 in.
12:00 A.M.	1 in.
1:00 A.M.	12 in.
2:00 A.M.	4 ft.
3:00 A.M.	6 ft.

261

My Schedule

Keep track of what you do all day for a week on several copies of this page. **Write** the day and date at the start of the day. Then, **write** what you do and the time you do it. Each time you change activities, you should **write** a new time entry. At the end of the day, **add** how much time was spent in each type of activity. Some activities can be grouped together (i.e., breakfast, lunch, dinner = eating; social studies, language, math = school subjects; etc.). Tally up your activities on Friday.

Extension: Use the information collected to plot a pie graph, bar graph, line graph or pictograph.

Day and date

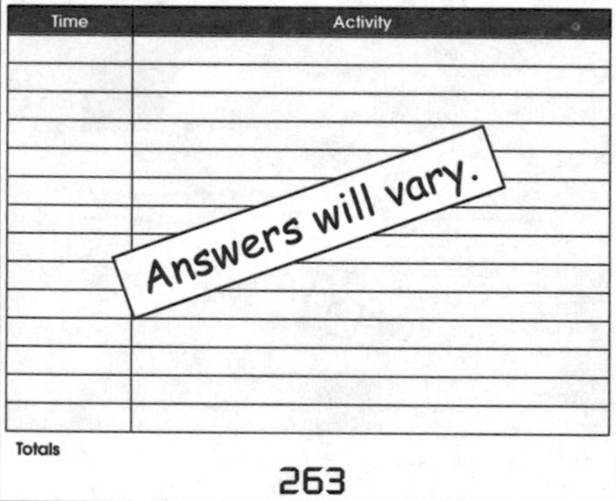

Time	Activity

Answers will vary.

Totals

263

Timely Fun

Sample answers given.

Predict how many times you can do each activity in 1 minute. Then, **time** yourself and see how accurate your predictions were.

Activity	Estimate	Actual
Say the alphabet.	20	14
Clap your hands.	60	42
Do 20 jumping jacks.	20	15
Count to 20.	10	8
Hop on one foot.	25	20
Count backward from 20 to 1.	10	8

264

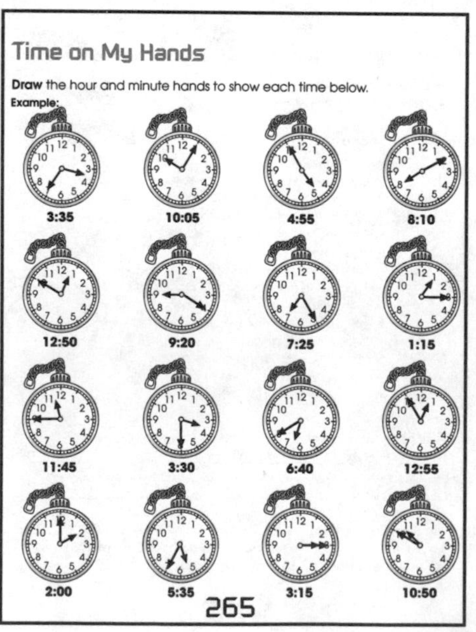

Time on My Hands

Draw the hour and minute hands to show each time below.

Example:

265

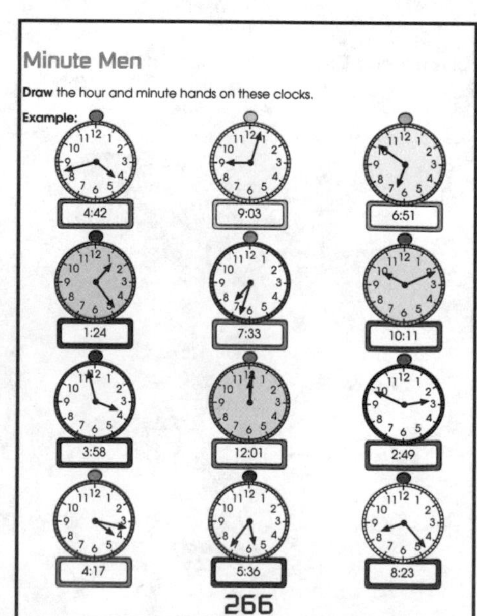

Minute Men

Draw the hour and minute hands on these clocks.

Example:

266

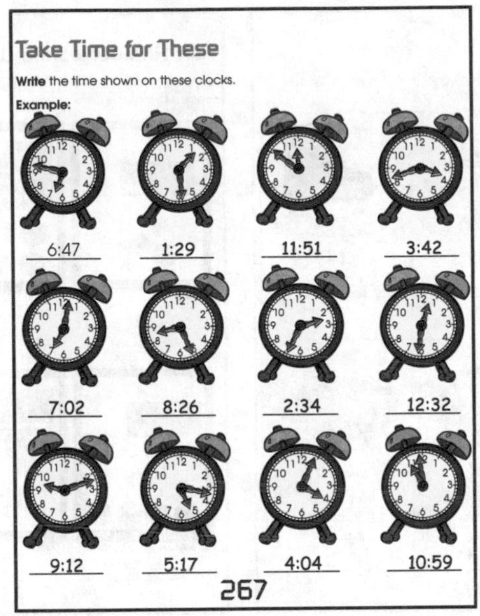

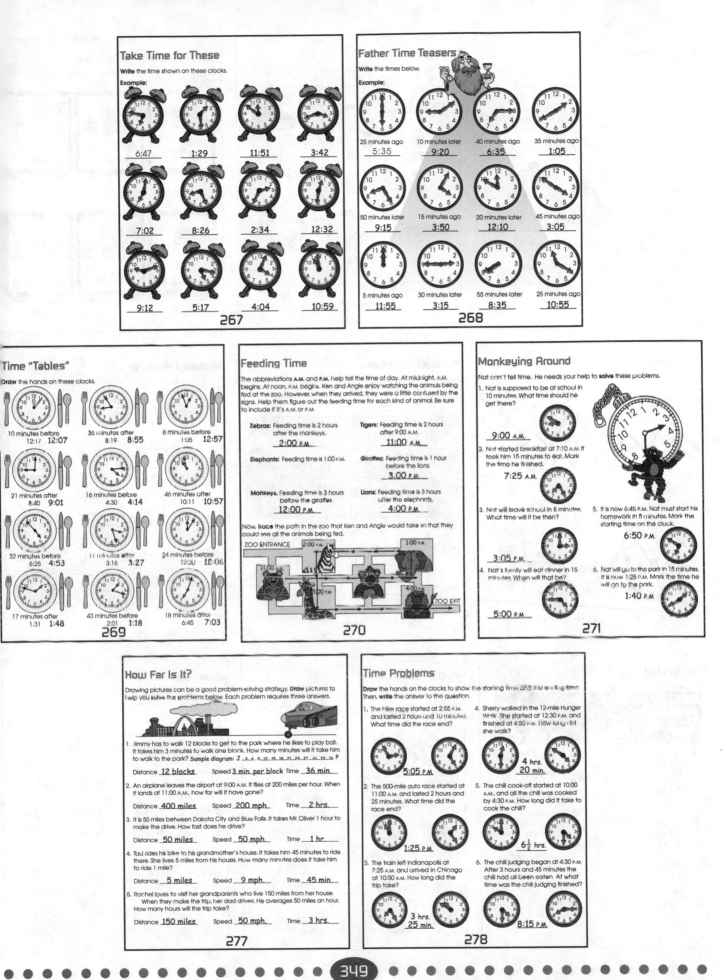

Take Time for These

Write the time shown on these clocks.

Example:

6:47	1:29	11:51	3:42
7:02	8:26	2:34	12:32
9:12	5:17	4:04	10:59

267

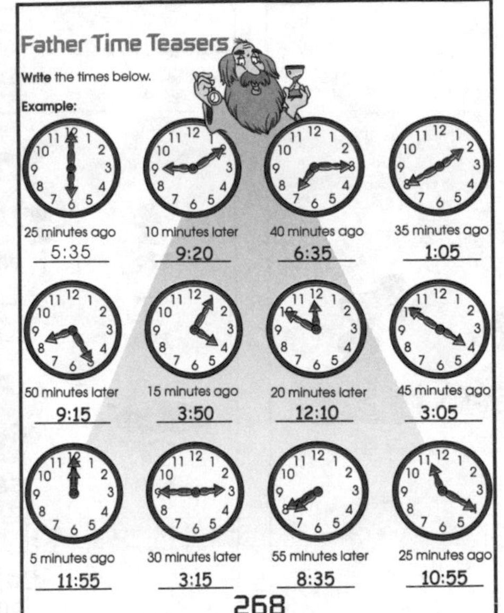

Father Time Teasers

Write the times below.

Example:

25 minutes ago 5:35	10 minutes later 9:20	40 minutes ago 6:35	35 minutes ago 1:05
50 minutes later 9:15	15 minutes ago 3:50	20 minutes later 12:10	45 minutes ago 3:05
5 minutes ago 11:55	30 minutes later 3:15	55 minutes later 8:35	25 minutes ago 10:55

268

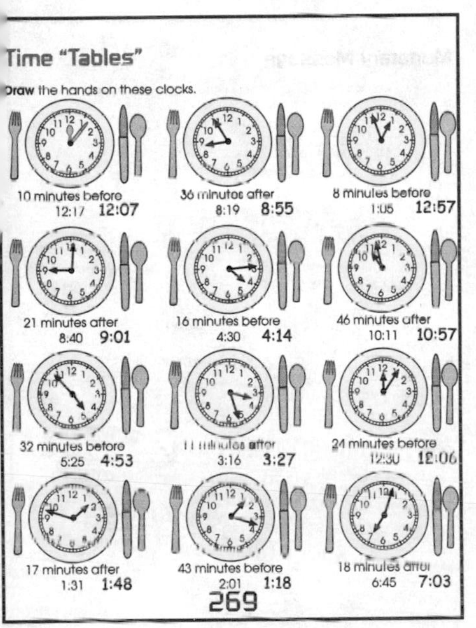

Time "Tables"

Draw the hands on these clocks.

10 minutes before 12:17 **12:07**	36 minutes after 8:19 **8:55**	8 minutes before 1:05 **12:57**
21 minutes after 8:40 **9:01**	16 minutes before 4:30 **4:14**	46 minutes after 10:11 **10:57**
32 minutes before 5:25 **4:53**	11 minutes after 3:16 **3:27**	24 minutes before 12:30 **12:06**
17 minutes after 1:31 **1:48**	43 minutes before 2:01 **1:18**	18 minutes after 6:45 **7:03**

269

Feeding Time

The abbreviations **A.M.** and **P.M.** help tell the time of day. At midnight, A.M. begins. At noon, P.M. begins. Ken and Angie enjoy watching the animals being fed at the zoo. However, when they arrived, they were a little confused by the signs. Help them figure out the feeding time for each kind of animal. Be sure to include if it's A.M. or P.M.

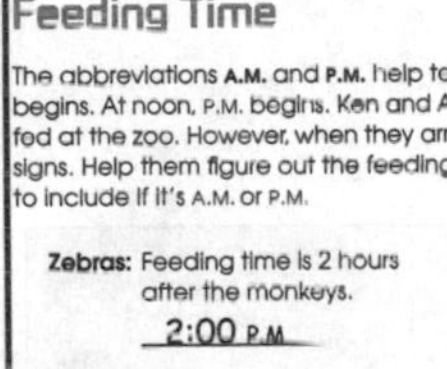

Zebras: Feeding time is 2 hours after the monkeys. 2:00 P.M.

Tigers: Feeding time is 2 hours after 9:00 A.M. 11:00 A.M.

Elephants: Feeding time is 1:00 P.M.

Giraffes: Feeding time is 1 hour before the lions. 3:00 P.M.

Monkeys: Feeding time is 3 hours before the giraffes. 12:00 P.M.

Lions: Feeding time is 3 hours after the elephants. 4:00 P.M.

Now, **trace** the path in the zoo that Ken and Angie would take so that they could see all the animals being fed.

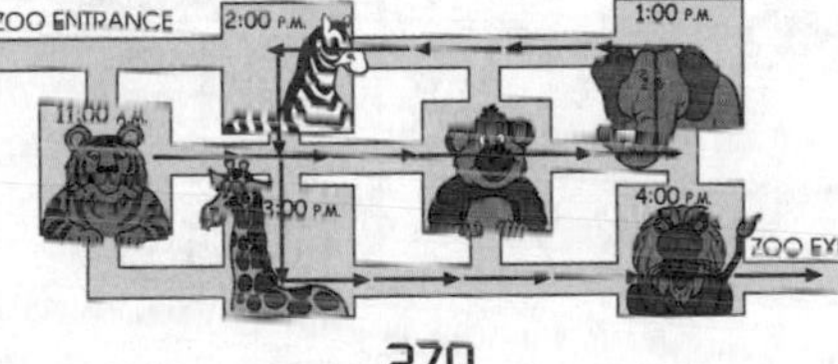

270

Monkeying Around

Nat can't tell time. He needs your help to **solve** these problems.

1. Nat is supposed to be at school in 10 minutes. What time should he get there?

9:00 A.M.

2. Nat started breakfast at 7:10 A.M. It took him 15 minutes to eat. Mark the time he finished.

7:25 A.M.

3. Nat will leave school in 5 minutes. What time will it be then?

3:05 P.M.

4. Nat's family will eat dinner in 15 minutes. When will that be?

5:00 P.M.

5. It is now 6:45 P.M. Nat must start his homework in 5 minutes. Mark the starting time on the clock.

6:50 P.M.

6. Nat will go to the park in 15 minutes. It is now 1:25 P.M. Mark the time he will go to the park.

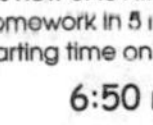

1:40 P.M.

271

How Far Is It?

Drawing pictures can be a good problem-solving strategy. **Draw** pictures to help you solve the problems below. Each problem requires three answers.

1. Jimmy has to walk 12 blocks to get to the park where he likes to play ball. It takes him 3 minutes to walk one block. How many minutes will it take him to walk to the park? **Sample diagram:** J 3 6 9 12 15 18 21 24 27 30 33 36 P

Distance 12 blocks Speed 3 min. per block Time 36 min.

2. An airplane leaves the airport at 9:00 A.M. It flies at 200 miles per hour. When it lands at 11:00 A.M., how far will it have gone?

Distance 400 miles Speed 200 mph. Time 2 hrs.

3. It is 50 miles between Dakota City and Blue Falls. It takes Mr. Oliver 1 hour to make the drive. How fast does he drive?

Distance 50 miles Speed 50 mph. Time 1 hr.

4. Tad rides his bike to his grandmother's house. It takes him 45 minutes to ride there. She lives 5 miles from his house. How many minutes does it take him to ride 1 mile?

Distance 5 miles Speed 9 mph. Time 45 min.

5. Rachel loves to visit her grandparents who live 150 miles from her house. When they make the trip, her dad drives. He averages 50 miles an hour. How many hours will the trip take?

Distance 150 miles Speed 50 mph. Time 3 hrs.

277

Time Problems

Draw the hands on the clocks to show the starting time and the ending time. Then, **write** the answer to the question.

1. The bike race started at 2:55 P.M. and lasted 2 hours and 10 minutes. What time did the race end?

5:05 P.M.

4. Sherry walked in the 12-mile Hunger Walk. She started at 12:30 P.M. and finished at 4:50 P.M. How long did she walk?

4 hrs. 20 min.

2. The 500-mile auto race started at 11:00 A.M. and lasted 2 hours and 25 minutes. What time did the race end?

1:25 P.M.

5. The chili cook-off started at 10:00 A.M., and all the chili was cooked by 4:30 P.M. How long did it take to cook the chili?

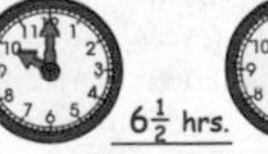

$6\frac{1}{2}$ hrs.

3. The train left Indianapolis at 7:25 A.M. and arrived in Chicago at 10:50 A.M. How long did the trip take?

3 hrs. 25 min.

6. The chili judging began at 4:30 P.M. After 3 hours and 45 minutes the chili had all been eaten. At what time was the chili judging finished?

8:15 P.M.

278

Racing Chimps

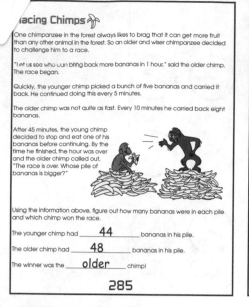

One chimpanzee in the forest always likes to brag that it can get more fruit than any other animal in the forest. So an older and wiser chimpanzee decided to challenge him to a race.

"Let us see who can bring back more bananas in 1 hour," said the older chimp. The race began.

Quickly, the younger chimp picked a bunch of five bananas and carried it back. He continued doing this every 5 minutes.

The older chimp was not quite as fast. Every 10 minutes he carried back eight bananas.

After 45 minutes, the young chimp decided to stop and eat one of his bananas before continuing. By the time he finished, the hour was over and the older chimp called out, "The race is over. Whose pile of bananas is bigger?"

Using the information above, figure out how many bananas were in each pile and which chimp won the race.

The younger chimp had 44 bananas in his pile.

The older chimp had 48 bananas in his pile.

The winner was the older chimp!

285

Garage Sale

Use the fewest number of coins possible to equal the amount shown in each box. **Write** or **draw** the coins you would use in each box.

17¢	98¢	24¢
1 dime, 1 nickel, 2 pennies	3 quarters, 2 dimes, 3 pennies	2 dimes, 4 pennies
63¢	**58¢**	**35¢**
2 quarters, 1 dime, 3 pennies	2 quarters, 1 nickel, 3 pennies	1 quarter, 1 dime

287

Your Answer's Safe With Me

Find the right "combination" to open each safe. **Draw** the bills and coins needed to make each amount.

Example:

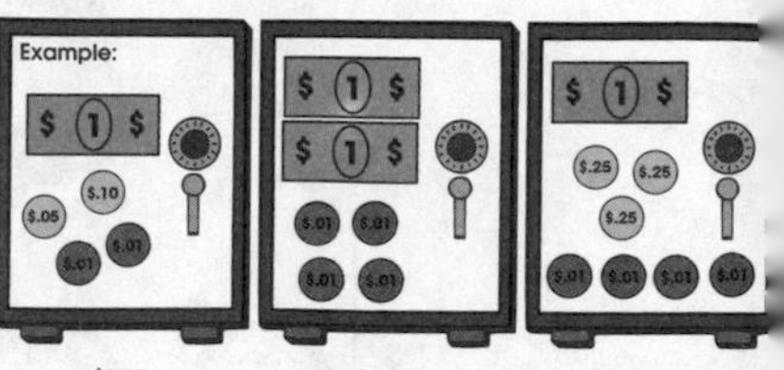

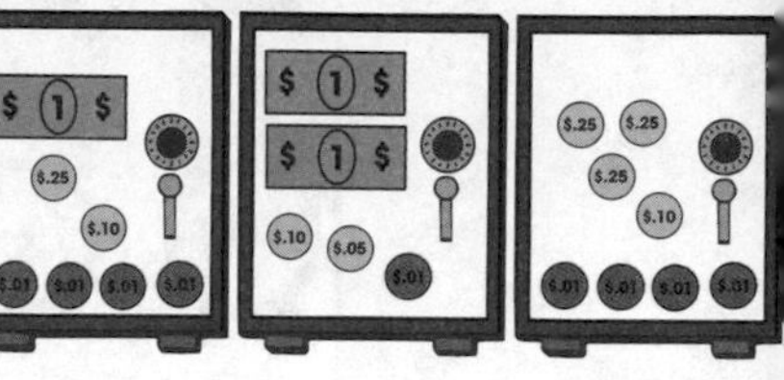

288

Easy Street

What is each house worth? **Count** the money in each house on Easy Street. **Write** the amount on the line below it.

Example:

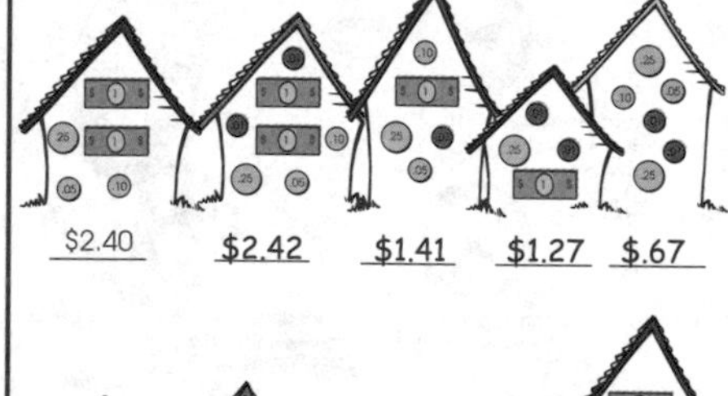

$2.40 $2.42 $1.41 $1.27 $.67

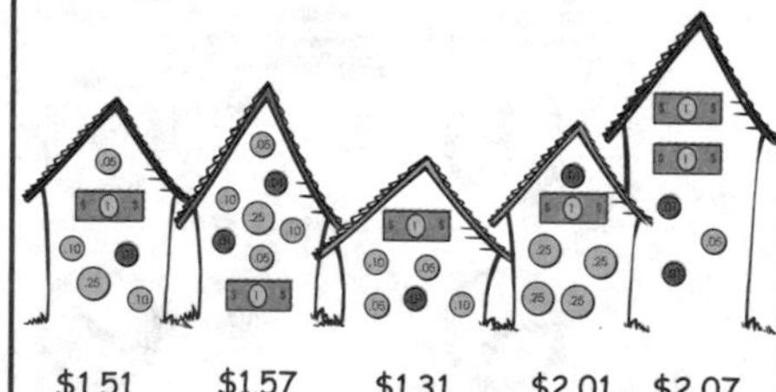

$1.51 $1.57 $1.31 $2.01 $2.07

289

A Collection of Coins

Write the number of coins needed to make the amount shown.

Money	Quarters	Dimes	Nickels	Pennies
76¢	3	0	0	1
45¢	1	2	0	0
98¢	3	2	0	3
40¢	1	1	1	0
84¢	3	0	1	4
62¢	2	1	0	2
31¢	1	0	1	1
$1.42	5	1	1	2
$1.98	7	2	0	3

290

Monetary Message

What's the smartest thing to do with your money? To find out, **solve** the following problems and **write** the matching letter above the answer.

S A V E I T, A N D I T W I L L A D D U P!

(S $42.71, A $33.94, V $50.42, E $100.73, I $45.70, T $2.39, A $33.94, N $26.13, D $88.02, I $45.70, T $2.39, W $51.12, I $45.70, L $11.01, L $11.01, A $33.94, D $88.02, D $88.02, U $55.76, P $42.79)

V = $42.13 + 8.29 = $50.42
A = $4.56 + 29.38 = $33.94
N = $4.65 + 21.48 = $26.13
S = $23.46 + 19.25 = $42.71

P = $9.31 + 33.48 = $42.79
L = $6.73 + 4.28 = $11.01
E = $81.49 + 19.24 = $100.73
T = $.42 + 1.94 + .03 = $2.39

U = $50.84 + 4.92 = $55.76
I = $7.49 + 38.21 = $45.70

D = $3.04 + 84.98 = $88.02
W = $1.89 + 49.23 = $51.12

291

Add 'Em Up!

Write the prices, then **add**. **Regroup**, when needed.

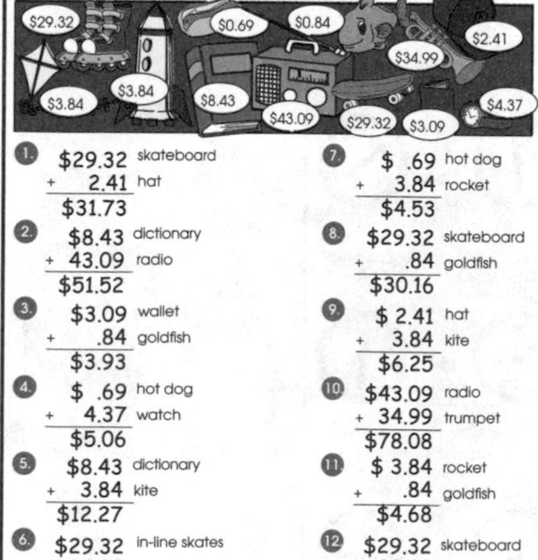

1. $29.32 skateboard + 2.41 hat = $31.73
2. $8.43 dictionary + 43.09 radio = $51.52
3. $3.09 wallet + .84 goldfish = $3.93
4. $ .69 hot dog + 4.37 watch = $5.06
5. $8.43 dictionary + 3.84 kite = $12.27
6. $29.32 in-line skates + 34.99 trumpet = $64.31
7. $ .69 hot dog + 3.84 rocket = $4.53
8. $29.32 skateboard + .84 goldfish = $30.16
9. $ 2.41 hat + 3.84 kite = $6.25
10. $43.09 radio + 34.99 trumpet = $78.08
11. $ 3.84 rocket + .84 goldfish = $4.68
12. $29.32 skateboard + 29.32 in-line skates = $58.64

292

Making Change

When you do not have the exact change to buy something at a store, the clerk must give you change. The first amount of money is what you give the clerk. The second amount is what the item costs. In the box, **list** the fewest number of coins and bills you will receive in change.

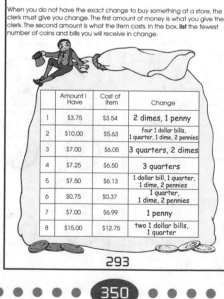

	Amount I Have	Cost of Item	Change
1	$3.75	$3.54	2 dimes, 1 penny
2	$10.00	$5.63	four 1 dollar bills, 1 quarter, 1 dime, 2 pennies
3	$7.00	$6.05	3 quarters, 2 dimes
4	$7.25	$6.50	3 quarters
5	$7.50	$6.13	1 dollar bill, 1 quarter, 1 dime, 2 pennies
6	$0.75	$0.37	1 quarter, 1 dime, 2 pennies
7	$7.00	$6.99	1 penny
8	$15.00	$12.75	two 1 dollar bills, 1 quarter

293

Super Savers!

Add to find the amounts of money each person saved.

Sam's Account: $8.03 + 0.84 + 5.47 = $14.34
Debbie's Account: $45.32 + 2.41 + 34.28 = $82.01
Sarah's Account: $85.42 + 12.58 + 2.21 = $100.21
Roberto's Account: $41.46 + 8.89 = $50.35

Alex's Account: $4.06 + 81.23 + 2.84 = $88.13
Eva's Account: $89.42 + 3.06 + 0.94 = $93.42
Bill's Account: $62.41 + 3.84 + 64.21 = $130.46
Monica's Account: $20.04 + 3.42 + 25.81 = $49.27

Tom's Account: $8.05 + 21.21 + 0.98 = $30.24
Andy's Account: $0.47 + 31.24 + 2.38 = $34.09
Earl's Account: $50.42 + 3.84 + 0.98 = $55.24
Mark's Account: $21.46 + 20.00 + 5.58 = $47.04

Katelyn's Account: $0.42 + 0.59 + 3.42 = $4.43
Kimberly's Account: $5.42 + 40.64 + 3.89 = $49.95

Whose account is the largest? Bill's

Whose is the smallest? Katelyn's

Whose is closest to $50? Kimberly's

299

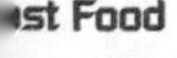

...st Food

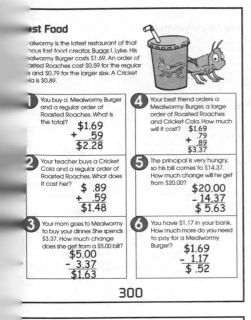

...alwormy is the latest restaurant of that ...ous fast food creator, Buggs I. Lyke. His ...ealwormy Burger costs $1.69. An order of ...asted Roaches cost $0.59 for the regular ...e and $0.79 for the larger size. A Cricket ...la is $0.89.

1. You buy a Mealwormy Burger and a regular order of Roasted Roaches. What is the total? $1.69 + .59 = $2.28
2. Your teacher buys a Cricket Cola and a regular order of Roasted Roaches. What does it cost her? $ .89 + .59 = $1.48
3. Your mom goes to Mealwormy to buy your dinner. She spends $3.37. How much change does she get from a $5.00 bill? $5.00 − 3.37 = $1.63
4. Your best friend orders a Mealwormy Burger, a large order of Roasted Roaches and Cricket Cola. How much will it cost? $1.69 + .79 + .89 = $3.37
5. The principal is very hungry, so his bill comes to $14.37. How much change will he get from $20.00? $20.00 − 14.37 = $ 5.63
6. You have $1.17 in your bank. How much more do you need to pay for a Mealwormy Burger? $1.69 − 1.17 = $ .52

300

Spending Spree

Use the clues to figure out what each person bought. Then, **subtract** to find out how much change each had left.

		Clue:
1. David began with:	$40.25 − 9.31 = $30.94	He loves to see things zoom into the sky!
2. Mark started with:	$50.37 − 47.29 = $3.08	He likes to travel places with his hands free and a breeze in his face!
3. Eva started with:	$14.84 − 3.95 = $10.89	She loves to practice her jumping and exercise at the same time!
4. Bill brought:	$61.49 − 52.28 = $9.21	He wants to see the heavens for himself!
5. Michelle brought:	$40.29 − 32.51 = $7.78	Fuzzy companions make such great friends!
6. Cheryl started with:	$16.80 − 12.49 = $4.31	She loves to hear music that is soft and beautiful!
7. Heather arrived with:	$20.48 − 15.29 = $5.19	She loves to put it down on paper for everyone to see!

$12.49 $9.31 $21.52 $13.45 $15.29 $2.43 $3.95 $52.28 $32.51 $47.29

301

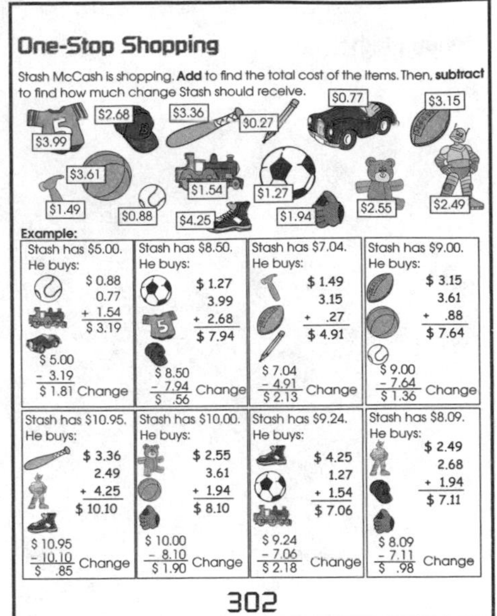

One-Stop Shopping

Stash McCash is shopping. **Add** to find the total cost of the items. Then, **subtract** to find out how much change Stash should receive.

$3.99 $2.68 $3.36 $0.27 $0.77 $3.15 $3.61 $1.54 $1.27 $1.49 $0.88 $4.25 $1.94 $2.55 $2.49

Example:

Stash has $5.00. He buys:	Stash has $8.50. He buys:	Stash has $7.04. He buys:	Stash has $9.00. He buys:
$ 0.88 + 0.77 + 1.54 = $ 3.19; $ 5.00 − 3.19 = $ 1.81 Change	$ 1.27 + 3.99 + 2.68 = $ 7.94; $ 8.50 − 7.94 = $ .56 Change	$ 1.49 + 3.15 + .27 = $ 4.91; $ 7.04 − 4.91 = $ 2.13 Change	$ 3.15 + 3.61 + .88 = $ 7.64; $ 9.00 − 7.64 = $ 1.36 Change
Stash has $10.95. He buys:	**Stash has $10.00. He buys:**	**Stash has $9.24. He buys:**	**Stash has $8.09. He buys:**
$ 3.36 + 2.49 + 4.25 = $ 10.10; $ 10.95 − 10.10 = $ .85 Change	$ 2.55 + 3.61 + 1.94 = $ 8.10; $ 10.00 − 8.10 = $ 1.90 Change	$ 4.25 + 1.27 + 1.54 = $ 7.06; $ 9.24 − 7.06 = $ 2.18 Change	$ 2.49 + 2.68 + 1.94 = $ 7.11; $ 8.09 − 7.11 = $ .98 Change

302

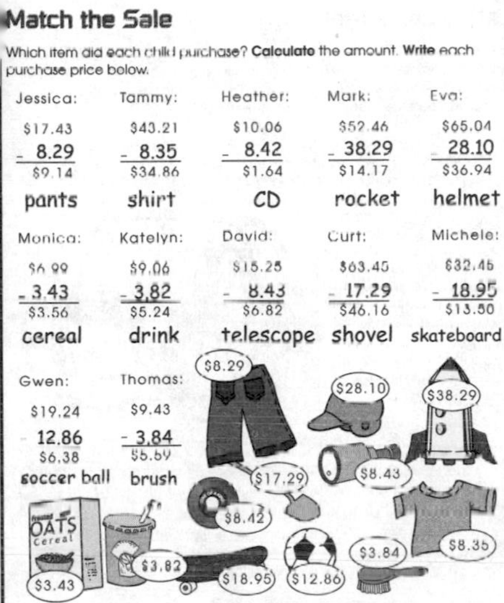

Match the Sale

Which item did each child purchase? **Calculate** the amount. **Write** each purchase price below.

Jessica:	Tammy:	Heather:	Mark:	Eva:
$17.43 − 8.29 = $9.14	$43.21 − 8.35 = $34.86	$10.06 − 8.42 = $1.64	$52.46 − 38.29 = $14.17	$65.04 − 28.10 = $36.94
pants	shirt	CD	rocket	helmet
Monica:	**Katelyn:**	**David:**	**Curt:**	**Michele:**
$6.99 − 3.43 = $3.56	$9.06 − 3.82 = $5.24	$15.25 − 8.43 = $6.82	$63.45 − 17.29 = $46.16	$32.45 − 18.95 = $13.50
cereal	drink	telescope	shovel	skateboard
Gwen:	**Thomas:**			
$19.24 − 12.86 = $6.38	$9.43 − 3.84 = $5.59			
soccer ball	brush			

$8.29 $28.10 $38.29 $17.29 $8.43 $8.42 $8.35 $3.82 $3.84 $18.95 $12.86 $3.43

303

What a Great Catch!

Solve these problems.

A $2.47; B $1.69; C $2.18; D $2.36; E $3.29; F $3.62; G $1.77; H $2.54; I $4.39; J $3.76

You buy fish A, C and H. Total cost: $2.47 + 2.10 + 2.64 = $7.19	You have $4.00. You buy fish D. How much money is left? $4.00 − 2.36 = $1.64	You have $10.00. You buy fish E and J. How much money is left? $3.29 + 3.76 = $7.05; $10.00 − 7.05 = $2.95
You buy 4 of fish I. $4.39 × 4 = $17.56 Total cost: $17.56	You have $5.75. You buy fish G and C. How much money is left? $1.77 + 2.18 = $3.95; $5.75 − 3.95 = $1.80	You buy fish D, F, J and B. $2.36 + 3.62 + 3.76 + 1.69 Total cost: $11.43
You buy 6 of fish E. $3.29 × 6 Total cost: $19.74	You buy 3 of fish J and 6 of fish D. $3.76 × 3 = $11.28; $2.36 × 6 = $14.16; $14.16 + 11.28 Total cost: $25.44	You have $10.76. You buy 3 of fish A. How much money is left? $2.47 × 3 = $7.41; $10.76 − 7.41 = $3.35

304

Dessert Included

Brenda and Doug really like chocolate—chocolate-covered raisins, chocolate candy, chocolate cake and hot chocolate! Most of all, they love chocolate sundaes with chocolate chip ice cream. When they find out that the Eats and Sweets Restaurant is offering a free chocolate dessert with any meal costing exactly $5.00, they decide to go there for dinner.

Menu

Meat		Potatoes/Vegetables	
Chicken	$1.95	Mashed Potatoes	$1.00
Roast Beef	$3.05	French Fries	$0.85
Shrimp	$3.50	Sweet Corn	$0.65
Roast Pork	$2.75	Green Beans	$0.50
Salad		**Drinks**	
Cole Slaw	$0.60	Milk	$0.40
Potato Salad	$0.95	Chocolate Milk	$0.45
Dinner Salad	$0.75	Orange Juice	$0.95
Macaroni Salad	$1.10	Soda Pop	$0.55

Choosing one item from each of the four categories, **list** four different meals Brenda and Doug could eat for exactly $5.00. Answers include:

Meal # 1 Chicken, Potatoes, Mac. Salad, O.J.
Meal # 2 Pork, Fr. Fries, Pot. Salad, Choc. Milk
Meal # 3 Beef, Corn, Dinner Salad, Pop
Meal # 4 Shrimp, Gr. Beans, Cole Slaw, Milk

305

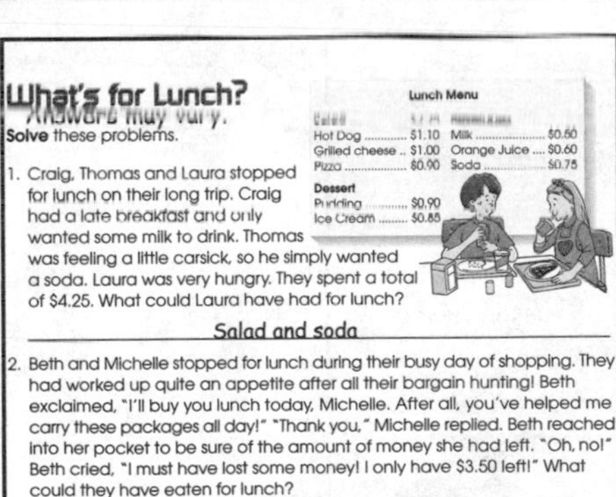

What's for Lunch?

Answers may vary.

Solve these problems.

Lunch Menu			
Hot Dog	$1.10	Milk	$0.60
Grilled cheese	$1.00	Orange Juice	$0.60
Pizza	$0.90	Soda	$0.75
Dessert			
Pudding	$0.90		
Ice Cream	$0.85		

1. Craig, Thomas and Laura stopped for lunch on their long trip. Craig had a late breakfast and only wanted some milk to drink. Thomas was feeling a little carsick, so he simply wanted a soda. Laura was very hungry. They spent a total of $4.25. What could Laura have had for lunch? Salad and soda
2. Beth and Michelle stopped for lunch during their busy day of shopping. They had worked up quite an appetite after all their bargain hunting! Beth exclaimed, "I'll buy you lunch today, Michelle. After all, you've helped me carry these packages all day!" "Thank you," Michelle replied. Beth reached into her pocket to be sure of the amount of money she had left. "Oh, no!" Beth cried. "I must have lost some money! I only have $3.50 left!" What could they have eaten for lunch? Grilled cheese and soda
3. Diane spent $1.60 on lunch. She was too full to get dessert. What could she have had for lunch? Hot dog and milk
4. The twins had too much pizza for dinner last night and certainly did not want it today. They each had the same meal, including pudding for dessert. They spent $5.50. What could they have eaten for lunch? Hot dogs, sodas and pudding
5. Sue is a vegetarian and she's allergic to milk. Bob ate two slices of pizza and a soda. Together, their lunch cost them $5.40. What did Sue have for lunch? Salad and O.J.

306

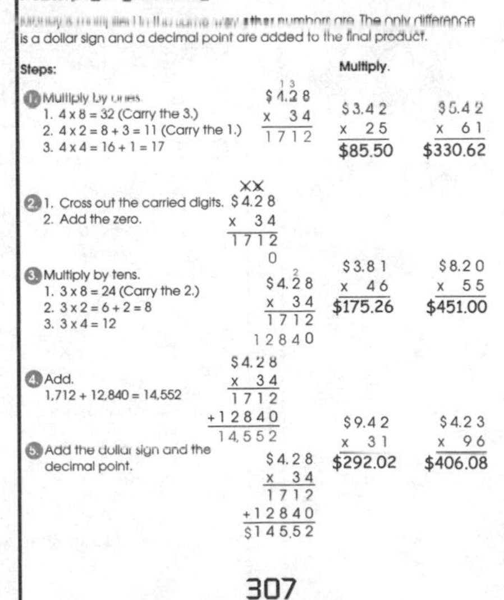

Multiplying Money

Money is multiplied in the same way other numbers are. The only difference is a dollar sign and a decimal point are added to the final product.

Steps:

1. Multiply by ones.
   1. 4 x 8 = 32 (Carry the 3.)
   2. 4 x 2 = 8 + 3 = 11 (Carry the 1.)
   3. 4 x 4 = 16 + 1 = 17

   $4.28 × 34 → 1712
2. 1. Cross out the carried digits.
   2. Add the zero.

   $4.28 × 34 → 1712, 0
3. Multiply by tens.
   1. 3 x 8 = 24 (Carry the 2.)
   2. 3 x 2 = 6 + 2 = 8
   3. 3 x 4 = 12

   $4.28 × 34 → 1712, 12840
4. Add. 1,712 + 12,840 = 14,552

   $4.28 × 34 → 1712 + 12840 = 14552
5. Add the dollar sign and the decimal point.

   $4.28 × 34 → 1712 + 12840 = $145.52

Multiply.

$3.42 × 25 = $85.50	$5.42 × 61 = $330.62
$3.81 × 46 = $175.26	$8.20 × 55 = $451.00
$9.42 × 31 = $292.02	$4.23 × 96 = $406.08

307

Foxy Felix's Shop

Solve these problems.

1. Mighty Man comics cost $0.13 at Foxy Felix's. You buy 4 of these comics. How much should you pay? $0.13 × 4 = $ .52
2. Your best friend bought 9 marbles at Foxy Felix's. Each marble cost $0.19. How much money did he spend? $0.19 × 9 = $1.71
3. Baseball cards are $0.11 each at Foxy Felix's. How much will it cost you for 8 cards? $0.11 × 8 = $ .88
4. Your sister decides to buy 2 CDs of the latest hit single by the Bird Brains. Each CD costs $0.89. How much will she pay? $ .89 × 2 = $1.78
5. Crazy stickers cost $0.21 each at Foxy Felix's. You buy 7 of them. How much should you pay? $0.21 × 7 = $1.47
6. Stinky Stickers have a skunk odor. Your best friend bought 7 Stinky Stickers which cost $0.18 each. How much did he spend? $0.18 × 7 = $1.26

308

Money Math

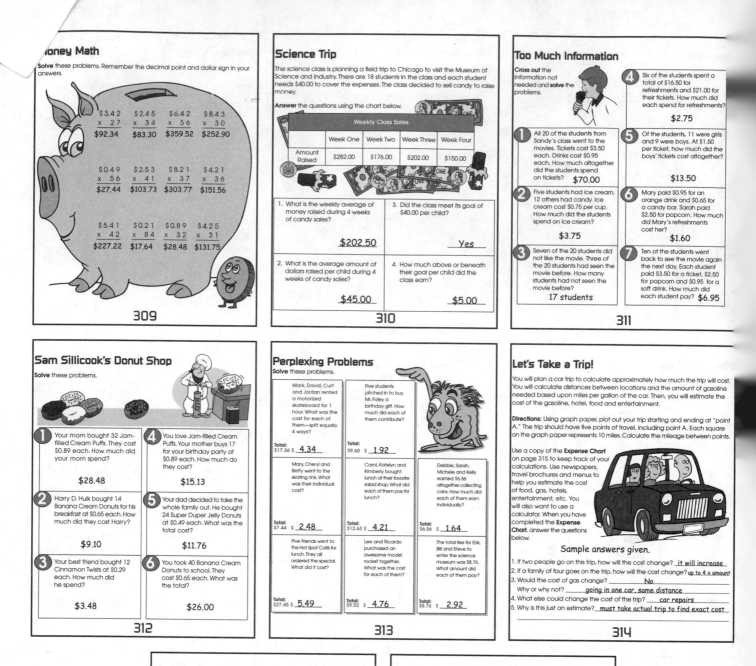

Solve these problems. Remember the decimal point and dollar sign in your answers.

$3.42 × 27 = $92.34	$2.45 × 34 = $83.30	$6.42 × 56 = $359.52	$8.43 × 30 = $252.90
$0.49 × 56 = $27.44	$2.53 × 41 = $103.73	$8.21 × 37 = $303.77	$4.21 × 36 = $151.56
$5.41 × 42 = $227.22	$0.21 × 84 = $17.64	$0.89 × 32 = $28.48	$4.25 × 31 = $131.75

309

Science Trip

The science class is planning a field trip to Chicago to visit the Museum of Science and Industry. There are 18 students in the class and each student needs $40.00 to cover the expenses. The class decided to sell candy to raise money.

Answer the questions using the chart below.

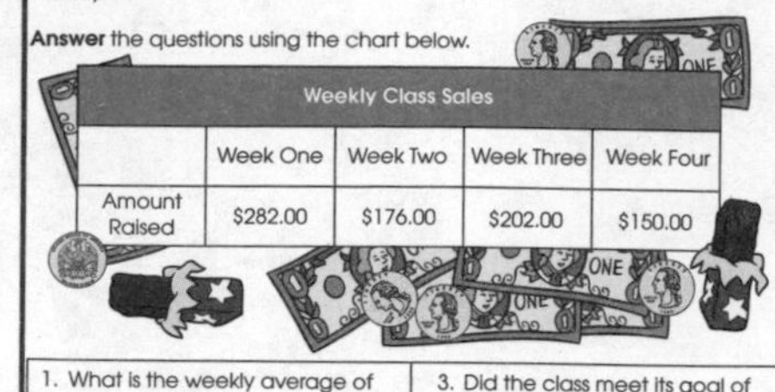

Weekly Class Sales

	Week One	Week Two	Week Three	Week Four
Amount Raised	$282.00	$176.00	$202.00	$150.00

1. What is the weekly average of money raised during 4 weeks of candy sales? $202.50
2. What is the average amount of dollars raised per child during 4 weeks of candy sales? $45.00
3. Did the class meet its goal of $40.00 per child? Yes
4. How much above or beneath their goal per child did the class earn? $5.00

310

Too Much Information

Cross out the information not needed and **solve** the problems.

1. All 20 of the students from Sandy's class went to the movies. Tickets cost $3.50 each. Drinks cost $0.95 each. How much altogether did the students spend on tickets? $70.00
2. Five students had ice cream, 12 others had candy. Ice cream cost $0.75 per cup. How much did the students spend on ice cream? $3.75
3. Seven of the 20 students did not like the movie. Three of the 20 students had seen the movie before. How many students had not seen the movie before? 17 students
4. Six of the students spent a total of $16.50 for refreshments and $21.00 for their tickets. How much did each spend for refreshments? $2.75
5. Of the students, 11 were girls and 9 were boys. At $1.50 per ticket, how much did the boys' tickets cost altogether? $13.50
6. Mary paid $0.95 for an orange drink and $0.65 for a candy bar. Sarah paid $2.50 for popcorn. How much did Mary's refreshments cost her? $1.60
7. Ten of the students went back to see the movie again the next day. Each student paid $3.50 for a ticket, $2.50 for popcorn and $0.95 for a soft drink. How much did each student pay? $6.95

311

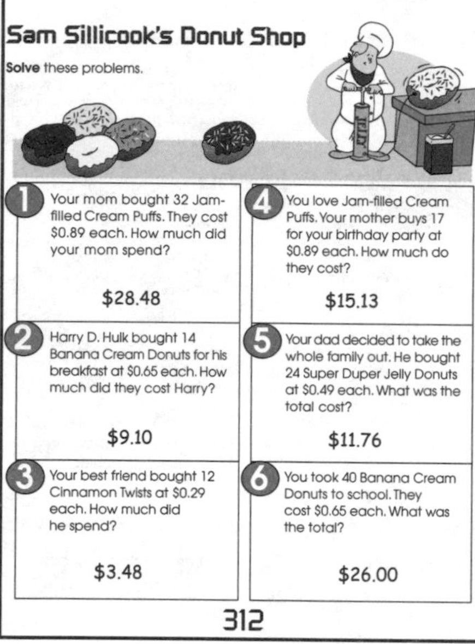

Sam Sillicook's Donut Shop

Solve these problems.

1. Your mom bought 32 Jam-filled Cream Puffs. They cost $0.89 each. How much did your mom spend? $28.48
2. Harry D. Hulk bought 14 Banana Cream Donuts for his breakfast at $0.65 each. How much did they cost Harry? $9.10
3. Your best friend bought 12 Cinnamon Twists at $0.29 each. How much did he spend? $3.48
4. You love Jam-filled Cream Puffs. Your mother buys 17 for your birthday party at $0.89 each. How much do they cost? $15.13
5. Your dad decided to take the whole family out. He bought 24 Super Duper Jelly Donuts at $0.49 each. What was the total cost? $11.76
6. You took 40 Banana Cream Donuts to school. They cost $0.65 each. What was the total? $26.00

312

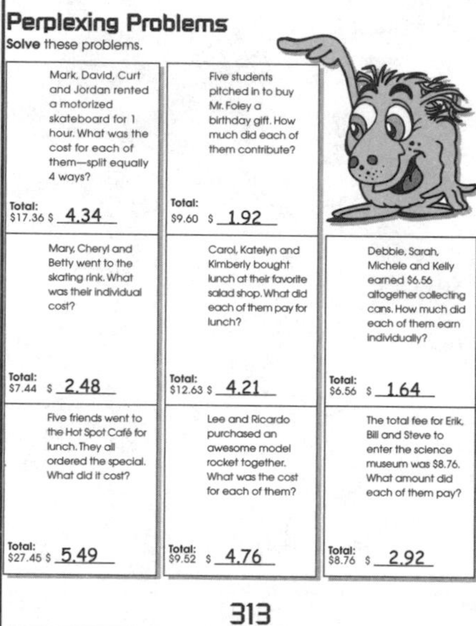

Perplexing Problems

Solve these problems.

- Mark, David, Curt and Jordan rented a motorized skateboard for 1 hour. What was the cost for each of them—split equally 4 ways? Total: $17.36 $ 4.34
- Five students pitched in to buy Mr. Foley a birthday gift. How much did each of them contribute? Total: $9.60 $ 1.92
- Mary, Cheryl and Betty went to the skating rink. What was their individual cost? Total: $7.44 $ 2.48
- Carol, Katelyn and Kimberly bought lunch at their favorite salad shop. What did each of them pay for lunch? Total: $12.63 $ 4.21
- Debbie, Sarah, Michele and Kelly earned $6.56 altogether collecting cans. How much did each of them earn individually? Total: $6.56 $ 1.64
- Five friends went to the Hot Spot Café for lunch. They all ordered the special. What did it cost? Total: $27.45 $ 5.49
- Lee and Ricardo purchased an awesome model rocket together. What was the cost for each of them? Total: $9.52 $ 4.76
- The total fee for Erik, Bill and Steve to enter the science museum was $8.76. What amount did each of them pay? Total: $8.76 $ 2.92

313

Let's Take a Trip!

You will plan a car trip to calculate approximately how much the trip will cost. You will calculate distances between locations and the amount of gasoline needed based upon miles per gallon of the car. Then, you will estimate the cost of the gasoline, hotel, food and entertainment.

Directions: Using graph paper, plot out your trip starting and ending at "point A." The trip should have five points of travel, including point A. Each square on the graph paper represents 10 miles. Calculate the mileage between points.

Use a copy of the **Expense Chart** on page 315 to keep track of your calculations. Use newspapers, travel brochures and menus to help you estimate the cost of food, gas, hotels, entertainment, etc. You will also want to use a calculator. When you have completed the **Expense Chart**, answer the questions below.

Sample answers given.

1. If two people go on this trip, how will the cost change? it will increase
2. If a family of four goes on the trip, how will the cost change? up to 4 x amount
3. Would the cost of gas change? No
   Why or why not? going in one car, same distance
4. What else could change the cost of the trip? car repairs
5. Why is this just an estimate? must take actual trip to find exact cost

314

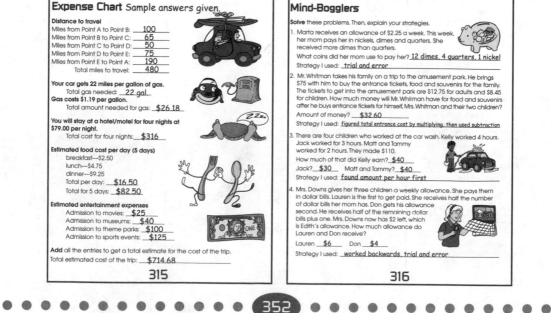

Expense Chart Sample answers given.

Distance to travel

Miles from Point A to Point B: 100
Miles from Point B to Point C: 65
Miles from Point C to Point D: 50
Miles from Point D to Point E: 75
Miles from Point E to Point A: 190
Total miles to travel: 480

Your car gets 22 miles per gallon of gas.
Total gas needed: 22 gal.
Gas costs $1.19 per gallon.
Total amount needed for gas: $26.18

You will stay at a hotel/motel for four nights at $79.00 per night.
Total cost for four nights: $316

Estimated food cost per day (5 days)
breakfast—$2.50
lunch—$4.75
dinner—$9.25
Total per day: $16.50
Total for 5 days: $82.50

Estimated entertainment expenses
Admission to movies: $25
Admission to museums: $40
Admission to theme parks: $100
Admission to sports events: $125

Add all the entries to get a total estimate for the cost of the trip.
Total estimated cost of the trip: $714.68

315

Mind-Bogglers

Solve these problems. Then, explain your strategies.

1. Marta receives an allowance of $2.25 a week. This week, her mom pays her in nickels, dimes and quarters. She received more dimes than quarters.
   What coins did her mom use to pay her? 12 dimes, 4 quarters, 1 nickel
   Strategy I used: trial and error
2. Mr. Whitman takes his family on a trip to the amusement park. He brings $75 with him to buy the entrance tickets, food and souvenirs for the family. The tickets to get into the amusement park are $12.75 for adults and $8.45 for children. How much money will Mr. Whitman have for food and souvenirs after he buys entrance tickets for himself, Mrs. Whitman and their two children?
   Amount of money? $32.60
   Strategy I used: figured total entrance cost by multiplying, then used subtraction
3. There are four children who worked at the car wash. Kelly worked 4 hours. Jack worked for 3 hours. Matt and Tammy worked for 2 hours. They made $110.
   How much of that did Kelly earn? $40
   Jack? $30 Matt and Tammy? $40
   Strategy I used: found amount per hour first
4. Mrs. Downs gives her three children a weekly allowance. She pays them in dollar bills. Lauren is the first to get paid. She receives half the number of dollar bills her mom has. Don gets his allowance second. He receives half of the remaining dollar bills plus one. Mrs. Downs now has $2 left, which is Edith's allowance. How much allowance do Lauren and Don receive?
   Lauren $6 Don $4
   Strategy I used: worked backwards, trial and error

316

OCR Revise Psychology

AS

OCR and Heinemann are working together to provide better support for you

Fiona Lintern
with Priya Bradshaw

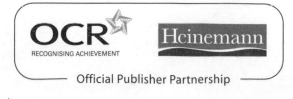

Official Publisher Partnership

Heinemann is an imprint of Pearson Education Limited, a company incorporated in England and Wales, having its registered office at Edinburgh Gate, Harlow, Essex, CM20 2JE. Registered company number: 872828

www.heinemann.co.uk
Heinemann is a registered trademark of Pearson Education Limited

First published 2009

13 12 11 10 09
10 9 8 7 6 5 4 3 2

British Library Cataloguing in Publication Data
A catalogue record for this book is available from the British Library

ISBN 978 0 435807 72 6

Edited by Caroline Compton-McPherson
Designed by Wooden Ark
Typeset by Phoenix Photosetting, Chatham, Kent
Original illustrations © Pearson Education 2009
Illustrated by Phoenix Photosetting and Saxon
Cover design by Pearson Education
Picture research by Zooid Pictures Ltd / Cristina Lombardo
Cover photo/illustration © I-Stock Photo
Printed in Malaysia, (CTP-KHL)

Photographs:
The authors and publisher would like to thank the following organisations and individuals for permission to reproduce photographs:

Page 78: 2003 Getty Images/Getty Images

Every effort has been made to contact copyright holders of material reproduced in this book. Any omissions will be rectified in subsequent printings if notice is given to the publishers.

Contents

Introduction

This book has been designed to support your revision for OCR AS Psychology. This is a revision guide rather than a textbook and should be used in conjunction with your class or lecture notes and your textbook.

References to pages in the textbook throughout this guide refer to the OCR AS Psychology text also published by Heinemann.

How to use this book

This book starts with the fifteen Core Studies. The key points of each study are given and you should read these carefully. If there is anything that you do not understand you should go back to your textbook and read the more detailed version. Once you are happy that you understand and can remember the key point summary you can test yourself with a set of multiple choice questions. These are simply testing your knowledge and understanding of the studies. Following this page, there is a page of questions designed to get you thinking about the studies. Answers are provided for both this page and the multiple choice questions.

Front

Study:	
Aim:	
Participants	Results
Method	Conclusions

For example, what were the strengths and weaknesses of the method that was used, what might happen if a different sample was used, and so on? Finally there is a mind map for you to complete with the key evaluation issues.

Once you have finished a whole study, you could copy and complete the revision card from the back of the book. This is designed to be photocopied and provide you with a 'pocket sized' revision guide. On the front of each card you can complete the key points about the study and on the back you can make notes about the important evaluation issues.

Back

Study	
Evaluation Issue 1	Evaluation Issue 2
Evaluation Issue 3	Evaluation Issue 4
Evaluation Issue 5	Evaluation Issue 6

Following all fifteen Core Studies there is a section on bringing it all together, which tests your knowledge and understanding of these studies. This section includes some activities such as crosswords and a wordsearch. These are useful activities just to check that you are remembering the key points.

The final section on the Core Studies is the Exam Café. You should be familiar with the format of this from your textbook, but just to remind you, this is a section which looks specifically at exam practice. In this section you will revise the approaches and perspectives and have a look at some exam style questions and answers.

The section on Psychological Investigations follows a similar format. The first section includes key point summaries on each of the research methods followed by multiple choice questions and other revision activities. The more of these activities you complete the more familiar you will become with the material. The Exam Café for the Psychological Investigations section also gives you the opportunity to compare two answers to a specimen question and identify the strengths and weaknesses of each.

Revision tips

- Ensure that you have a complete set of notes. You should have information on each of the fifteen Core Studies and on Research Methods. You may have separate notes on the approaches/ perspectives or you may have information within your Core Studies notes. Why not sit down with someone from your class and check your files?
- Make yourself a checklist of all your revision topics so you can tick them off when you are happy that you know them.
- Don't write out lengthy notes but try to summarise the material into key words and phrases. Our 'cut-out' revision card should help you with this.
- Use colour in your revision notes – why not use one colour for strengths and one colour for weaknesses when you are noting evaluation points?
- Why not put your revision material on the wall where you can see it? You could draw mind maps for each study or simply use Post-it® notes to remind you of key points.
- Revise with a friend! Working together can be very productive. Why not explain the method of a key study to someone else or ask them to test you?

Top exam tips

- Ask your tutor to show you some past papers or specimen papers so you are familiar with the layout of the paper. Do you know how many questions there are going to be and how long you have got to answer them?
- Read the questions carefully before you start writing. This will prevent you from answering the question that you thought was on the paper rather than the one that was really there. You can write on exam papers so why not underline the key words as you are reading.
- Do you know what the different 'command' words mean? What is the difference between 'describe' and 'evaluate'? What is the difference between 'explain' and 'outline'?
- Remember the 'mark a minute' rule. Your AS papers are both based on this formula. If a question is worth two marks then you have two minutes to answer it. If a question is worth 12 marks you have 12 minutes to answer it. It is important to remember this rule so that you do not waste too much time on very short questions.
- Planning is important where questions are asking for more than a simple piece of information. An answer to a ten mark question is likely to be improved by spending a minute or two thinking and planning. This is likely to be particularly true in the Psychological Investigations exam where you might be asked to design a piece of research.
- If you have time at the end of the exam, read your answers again, check for mistakes and see if there is anything you can add.

Cognitive Studies

This study is covered on pages 12–19 of your textbook

Loftus and Palmer (1974) Reconstruction of automobile destruction: an example of the interaction between language and memory

What do I need to know?

Aim

To investigate the effect of leading questions on the accuracy of eyewitness testimony. Will the use of more severe sounding verbs to describe an accident lead participants to:

- produce a higher estimate of speed?
- be more likely to (incorrectly) recall the presence of broken glass?

Study 1

Participants

- 45 students
- Five groups of nine

Method

- Laboratory experiment
- Seven clips of traffic accidents
- Asked to write a short account of what they had seen
- Asked to complete a questionnaire
- Critical question was, 'About how fast were the cars going when they ****** each other?'
- Five different verbs (one per condition) were smashed, collided, bumped, hit, contacted
- IV = Verb used in question
- DV = Estimate of speed

Results

- The more severe-sounding the verb used in the critical question, the higher the speed estimate. For example the word 'smashed' produced a mean estimate of 40.8 mph while 'contacted' produced a mean estimate of 31.8 mph.

Conclusions

- Interpretations:
  1 The verb distorts actual memory.
  2 Response bias (demand characteristics).
- A second study was conducted to explore these possible interpretations.

Study 2

Participants

- 150 students
- Three groups of 50

Methods

- Procedure similar to Study 1 but three conditions
- Group 1 – How fast were the cars going when they smashed into each other?
- Group 2 – How fast were the cars going when they hit each other?
- Group 3 – Control (not asked to estimate speed)

One week later

- All subjects questioned again.
- Critical question 'Did you see any broken glass?'
- (There was no broken glass in the film.)

Results

Group	Number reporting broken glass
'Smashed'	16/50
'Hit'	7/50
Control	6/50

- The wording of the question affected the participants' memory of the event. Those that heard the verb 'smashed' were more than twice as likely to recall seeing broken glass.

Conclusions

- Study 2 offers more support for the first interpretation – that the information we receive in the question can cause an actual distortion of the memory.
- Loftus and Palmer suggest that there are two types of information that go into making up a memory of a complex event and these are:
  1 The information that we get from perceiving an event.
  2 The information that we get after the event.

Test your knowledge

Answer the multiple choice questions below by ticking the correct answer(s) to test your knowledge of the study. You will find the answers at the bottom of the page.

1 *Which of the following was the Independent Variable in Study 1?*

a) the speed estimate
b) the verb used in the question
c) whether the question was leading or not
d) whether the participant was a student or not

2 *How many participants took part in Study 1?*

a) 45
b) 9
c) 150
d) 25

3 *How many verb conditions were there in Study 1?*

a) 6
b) 5
c) 4
d) 3

4 *Which of the following best describes the results of Study 1?*

a) people are not very good at estimating speed
b) the less severe the verb sounded, the higher the estimate of speed
c) the more severe the verb sounded, the higher the estimate of speed
d) people were not influenced by the verbs used

5 *How many participants took part in Study 2?*

a) 150
b) 50
c) 200
d) 45

6 *How many groups were there in Study 2?*

a) 3
b) 4
c) 5
d) 6

7 *Which group was more likely to say that they had seen broken glass?*

a) 'smashed'
b) 'hit'
c) control
d) none of them

8 *Loftus and Palmer conclude that there are two types of information that make our memory of an event. Which are they?*

a) information from directly perceiving the event
b) information received after the event
c) information from the other participants
d) information received before the event

What do you think?

It has been suggested that this study has low ecological validity as it was conducted in a laboratory environment and the car accident was on film. Think about all the differences between viewing a car accident in a controlled situation like this one and viewing a real accident. Discuss this with your teacher or with other students.

Answers: 1 b; 2 c; 3 b; 4 c; 5 a; 6 a; 7 a; 8 a and b

Test your understanding

Use the questions below to evaluate the study. Suggested answers can be found at the back of the book.

1 The sample used in this study were all students. Suggest one strength and one weakness with using this sample.

Strength

They are less likely to have memory problems or anomalies

Weakness

They are not representative of the general population. Results cannot be generalised.

2 Suggest another sample that could have been used for this experiment and suggest the effect that this might have on the results.

Alternative sample

Pensioners

Possible effect

having a poorer memor

3 This study was a laboratory experiment. Suggest one strength and one weakness with the use of this method to investigate eyewitness testimony.

Strength

Weakness

4 Suggest how eyewitness testimony could be investigated outside of the laboratory and identify the strengths and weaknesses of your suggested alternative.

Alternative

Strengths/Weaknesses

Mind mapping

Using the mind map below make brief notes on the issues that can be used to evaluate this study. Some of the bubbles have been started for you and you should use the list below to select two further evaluation issues for this study. These issues are covered in detail on pages 176–187 of your textbook.

Ecological validity	Application to everyday life	Representativeness/generalisability
Ethics	Nature–nurture	Individual–situational explanations
Reliability	Validity	Qualitative and quantitative data
Control	Reductionism	Determinism

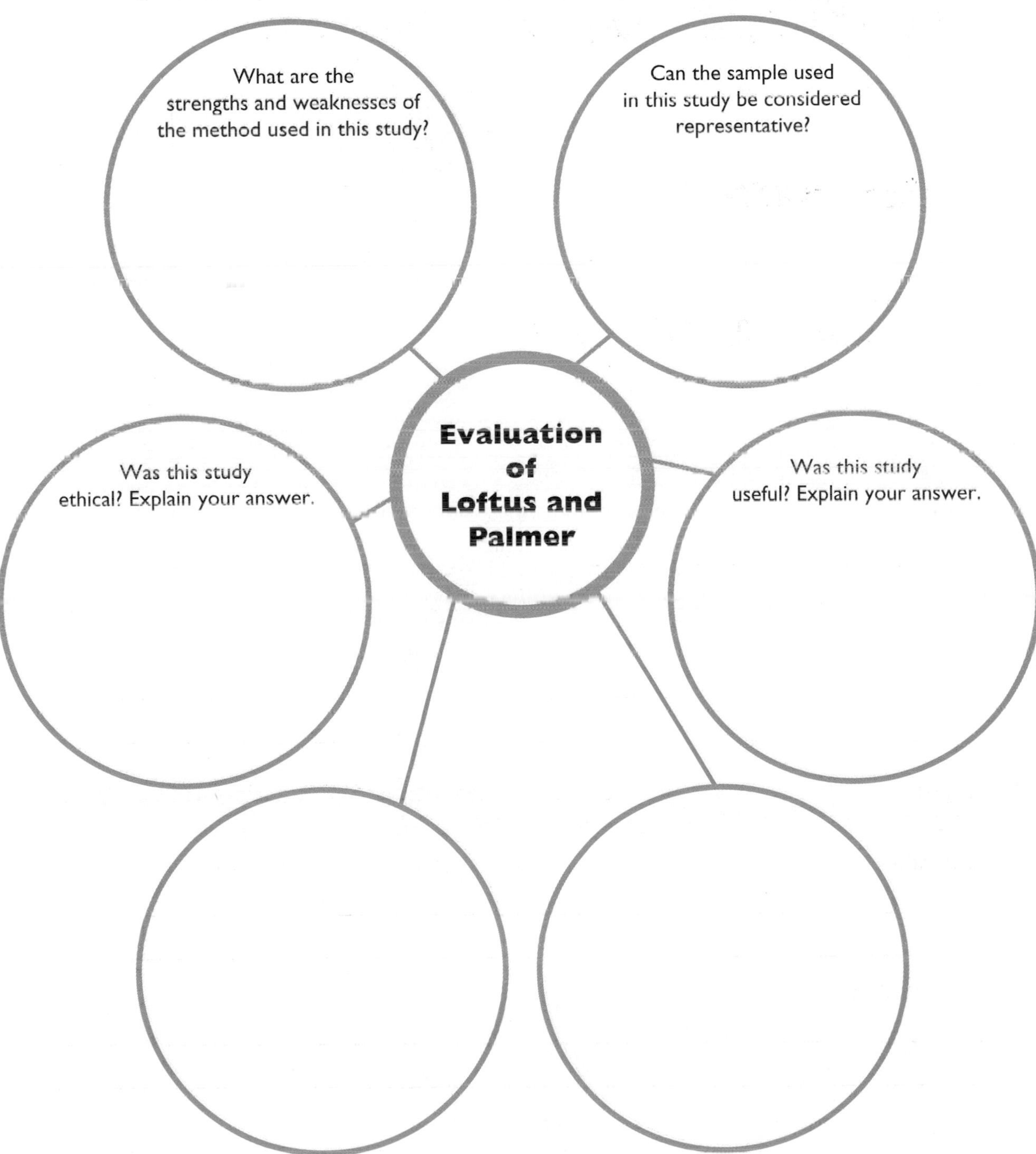

Evaluation of Loftus and Palmer
What are the strengths and weaknesses of the method used in this study?
Can the sample used in this study be considered representative?
Was this study ethical? Explain your answer.
Was this study useful? Explain your answer.

This study is covered on pages 20–27 in your textbook

Baron-Cohen et al (1997) Another advanced test of theory of mind: evidence from very high-functioning adults with autism or Asperger's Syndrome

What do I need to know?

Aim

The aim of this study was to provide more support for the cognitive explanation of autism; that autistic adults lack theory of mind skills. The theory of mind test used in this study is the Eyes Test, in which people have to choose the best word to describe the emotion displayed in a photograph of a person's eyes.

Participants

- Three groups

Group 1

- 16 participants
- 13 male, three female
- Four with high-functioning autism and 12 with Asperger's Syndrome
- Mean IQ of 105.3

Group 2

- 50 participants
- 25 male and 25 female
- Drawn from general population of Cambridge
- Assumed to have IQs in the normal range

Group 3

- Ten participants
- Eight male, two female
- Aged matched with Group 1
- All with Tourette's Syndrome
- Mean IQ of 103.5

Method

- Quasi-experiment
- Eyes Task – 25 standardised black and white photos of eyes
- Shown for three seconds
- Forced choice between two mental state terms
- Asked, 'Which word best describes what this person is feeling or thinking?'
- Strange Stories task – used to test concurrent validity of the Eyes Task
- Control tasks – Gender Recognition and Basic Emotion Recognition

Results

- Group 1 scores significantly lower on the Eyes Task than the other two groups.
- No difference between Group 2 and Group 3 on the Eyes Task.

Group	Mean score on the Eyes Task
1. Autism/Asperger's Syndrome	16.3
2. Control ('normal')	20.3
3. Tourette's Syndrome	20.4

- Group 1 were significantly more likely to make errors on the Strange Stories task than the other two groups.
- No difference between the groups on the Gender Recognition or Basic Emotion task.
- Females in the 'normal' group performed significantly better than males on the Eyes Task.

Conclusions

- The lack of a theory of mind is a core deficit in autistic spectrum disorders.
- They also explain that poor performance on the Eyes Task could not be due to low IQ (as the participants in Group 1 were in the normal or above normal range of intelligence) OR to developmental neuro-psychiatric disability since the participants with Tourette's Syndrome had no difficulties with the task.

Test your knowledge

Answer the multiple choice questions below by ticking the correct answer(s) to test your knowledge of the study. You will find the answers at the bottom of the page.

1 *Which of the following is not a group of participants in this study?*

a) ☐ people with autism/Asperger's Syndrome
b) ☐ 'normal' controls
c) ☐ people with Tourette's Syndrome
d) ☐ people with Down's Syndrome

2 *Why is this described as a quasi-experiment?*

a) ☐ because the experimenter had no direct control over the IV
b) ☐ because the experimenter had direct control over the IV
c) ☐ because the experimenter had no direct control over the DV
d) ☐ because the experimenter had direct control over the DV

3 *Which is the question used in the Eyes Task?*

a) ☐ 'What do you think this person is thinking?'
b) ☐ 'What emotion is shown in this picture?'
c) ☐ 'Which word best describes what this person is feeling or thinking?'
d) ☐ 'Which word would you use to describe this person?'

4 *Concurrent validity is based on the assumption that two measures of the same variable should produce the same results. Which other test was used to check the validity of the Eyes Task?*

a) ☐ Happe's strange stories
b) ☐ the Gender Recognition task
c) ☐ the basic Emotion Recognition task
d) ☐ the IQ test

5 *Why was the Gender Recognition task included?*

a) ☐ to check whether the results were due to IQ
b) ☐ to check whether the results were due to gender
c) ☐ to check whether the results were due to general deficits in face/social perception
d) ☐ to check whether the results were due to autism

6 *Which group performed worst on the Eyes Task?*

a) ☐ autistic/Asperger's Syndrome
b) ☐ control
c) ☐ Tourette's
d) ☐ there was no difference

7 *What was the difference between 'normal' males and 'normal' females' on the Eyes Task?*

a) ☐ they were both very poor at the task
b) ☐ there was no difference
c) ☐ males did better than females
d) ☐ females did better than males

8 *Which of the following is a conclusion from the study?*

a) ☐ low IQ is a core cognitive deficit in autism
b) ☐ neuro-psychiatric disability is a core cognitive deficit in autism
c) ☐ lack of theory of mind is a core cognitive deficit in autism
d) ☐ presence of theory of mind is a core cognitive deficit in autism

What do you think?

What everyday problems might be experienced by someone who lacks theory of mind? Discuss this with your teacher or with other students.

Answers: 1 d; 2 a; 3 c; 4 a; 5 c; 6 a; 7 d; 8 c

Test your understanding

Use the questions below to evaluate the study. Suggested answers can be found at the back of the book.

1 Suggest one improvement that could be made to this study and explain why you would make this improvement.

Suggested improvement

Reason for improvement

What effect do you think this improvement might have on the research?

2 The data collected in this study was quantitative data. Outline one strength and one weakness with collecting quantitative data in this study.

Strength

Weakness

Suggest how qualitative data might have been collected in this study.

What strengths and weaknesses would this have?

Strength

Weakness

Mind mapping

Using the mind map below make brief notes on the issues that can be used to evaluate this study. Some of the bubbles have been started for you and you should use the list below to select two further evaluation issues for this study. These issues are covered in detail on pages 176–187 of your textbook.

Ecological validity	Application to everyday life	Representativeness/generalisability
Ethics	Nature–nurture	Individual–situational explanations
Reliability	Validity	Qualitative and quantitative data
Control	Reductionism	Determinism

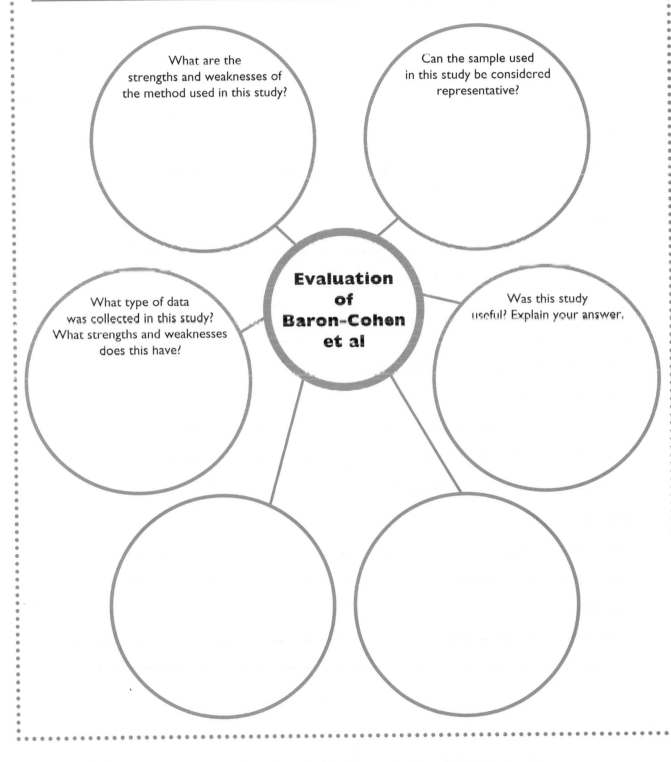

Evaluation of Baron-Cohen et al

What are the strengths and weaknesses of the method used in this study?

Can the sample used in this study be considered representative?

What type of data was collected in this study? What strengths and weaknesses does this have?

Was this study useful? Explain your answer.

This study is covered on pages 28–35 of your textbook

Savage-Rumbaugh et al (1986) Spontaneous symbol acquisition and communicative use by pygmy chimpanzees

What do I need to know?

Aim

To study language acquisition in two pygmy chimpanzees and to compare their language acquisition to two common chimpanzees.

Participants

- Two pygmy chimpanzees
- Kanzi (main subject of the research) aged four when report was written
- Mulika aged three (Kanzi's sister)
- Two common chimpanzees
- Sherman and Austin
- Aged nine and ten

Method

- Longitudinal study
- Ten year span
- This study reports on a 17 month period
- Quasi-experiment comparing species (IV) and measuring language acquisition (DV)
- Medium of communication:
  1. Lexigram – geometric symbols which brighten when touched and attached to speech synthesiser
  2. Pointing board for outside
  3. Spoken English and gestures accompanied experimenters' use of lexigram
  4. Modelling approach rather than formal training
- Differences in rearing environments

Kanzi and Mulika	Sherman and Austin
Observational setting	Training environment
Speech synthesiser	No speech synthesiser
Used pointing board outside laboratory	Used pointing board outside laboratory

Data recorded

- Kanzi – all lexigram utterances for 17 months (from age two and a half).
- Mulika – all lexigram utterances for ten months (from age 11 months).
- All utterances classified as:
  1. correct/incorrect
  2. spontaneous/imitated/structured
- Acquisition criteria – utterances must:
  1. be appropriate
  2. appear spontaneously nine out of ten times
  3. demonstrate concordance nine out of ten times.
- Observers ratings checked – 100% agreement.

Results

- Four main differences found.
- Kanzi and Mulika comprehended the lexigrams with far more ease and used them far more spontaneously without the need for training than Austin and Sherman did.
- Kanzi and Mulika were far more able to comprehend spoken English words.
- Kanzi and Mulika used lexigrams far more specifically (e.g. to differentiate between cake and juice) than Sherman and Austin who used broader categories (e.g. food).
- Kanzi was able to refer to requests involving others. Austin and Sherman never formed requests in which someone other than themselves was the beneficiary.

Conclusions

Pygmy chimpanzees exhibit symbolic and auditory perceptual skills that are significantly different from those of common chimpanzees. This is a somewhat surprising finding given how closely related the two species are.

Test your knowledge

Answer the multiple choice questions below by ticking the correct answer(s) to test your knowledge of the study. You will find the answers at the bottom of the page.

1 *Which two species were compared in this study?*

a) ☐ pygmy chimpanzees and humans
b) ☐ pygmy chimpanzees and common chimpanzees
c) ☐ common chimpanzees and humans
d) ☐ pygmy chimpanzees and bonobos

2 *What time period of the study does this cover?*

a) ☐ 10 years
b) ☐ 17 years
c) ☐ 10 months
d) ☐ 17 months

3 *Why is this best described as quasi-experimental?*

a) ☐ because species was experimentally manipulated
b) ☐ because it is not possible to experimentally manipulate species
c) ☐ because it was longitudinal
d) ☐ because there was more than one chimpanzee

4 *What is a lexigram?*

a) ☐ a system of flash cards
b) ☐ sign language
c) ☐ a system of geometric symbols
d) ☐ none of these

5 *Which two criteria had to be met before a word could be included in Kanzi and Mulika's vocabulary?*

a) ☐ symbol production should be appropriate
b) ☐ spontaneity/concordance
c) ☐ both a and b
d) ☐ none of these

6 *The coding for this criteria was checked. What level of agreement was found?*

a) ☐ 50%
b) ☐ 75%
c) ☐ 90%
d) ☐ 100%

7 *Which of the following correctly describes the differences between the species in using the lexigram?*

a) ☐ Kanzi and Mulika used the lexigrams more spontaneously than Sherman and Austin
b) ☐ Kanzi and Mulika used the lexigrams more specifically than Sherman and Austin
c) ☐ Sherman and Austin used the lexigrams more specifically than Kanzi and Mulika
d) ☐ Both a and b

8 *Which of the following is the best summary of the conclusion reached by Savage-Rumbaugh et al?*

a) ☐ pygmy chimps exhibit symbolic and auditory perceptual skills that are distinctly different from those of humans
b) ☐ pygmy chimps exhibit symbolic and auditory perceptual skills that are distinctly different from those of common chimpanzees
c) ☐ pygmy chimps exhibit symbolic and auditory perceptual skills that are distinctly different from those of bonobos
d) ☐ humans exhibit symbolic and auditory perceptual skills that are distinctly different from those of common chimpanzees

What do you think?

Is research with animals of any use to psychologists? Discuss this with your teacher or with other students.

Answers: 1 b; 2 d; 3 b; 4 c; 5 c; 6 d; 7 d; 8 b

Test your understanding

Use the questions below to evaluate the study. Suggested answers can be found at the back of the book.

1 This study was a longitudinal study. Outline two strengths of using a longitudinal study to study language acquisition in chimpanzees.

Strength 1

Strength 2

Outline one weakness with the way this study was conducted.

Suggest how this weakness could be overcome.

What effect might this have on the results of the study?

2 Research with animals raises a number of ethical issues. Identify two ethical issues that are raised by this study and consider whether this study should have been conducted.

Issue 1

Issue 2

Should the study have been conducted?

Mind mapping

Using the mind map below make brief notes on the issues that can be used to evaluate this study. Some of the bubbles have been started for you and you should use the list below to select two further evaluation issues for this study. These issues are covered in detail on pages 176–187 of your textbook.

Ecological validity	Application to everyday life	Representativeness/generalisability
Ethics	Nature–nurture	Individual–situational explanations
Reliability	Validity	Qualitative and quantitative data
Control	Reductionism	Determinism

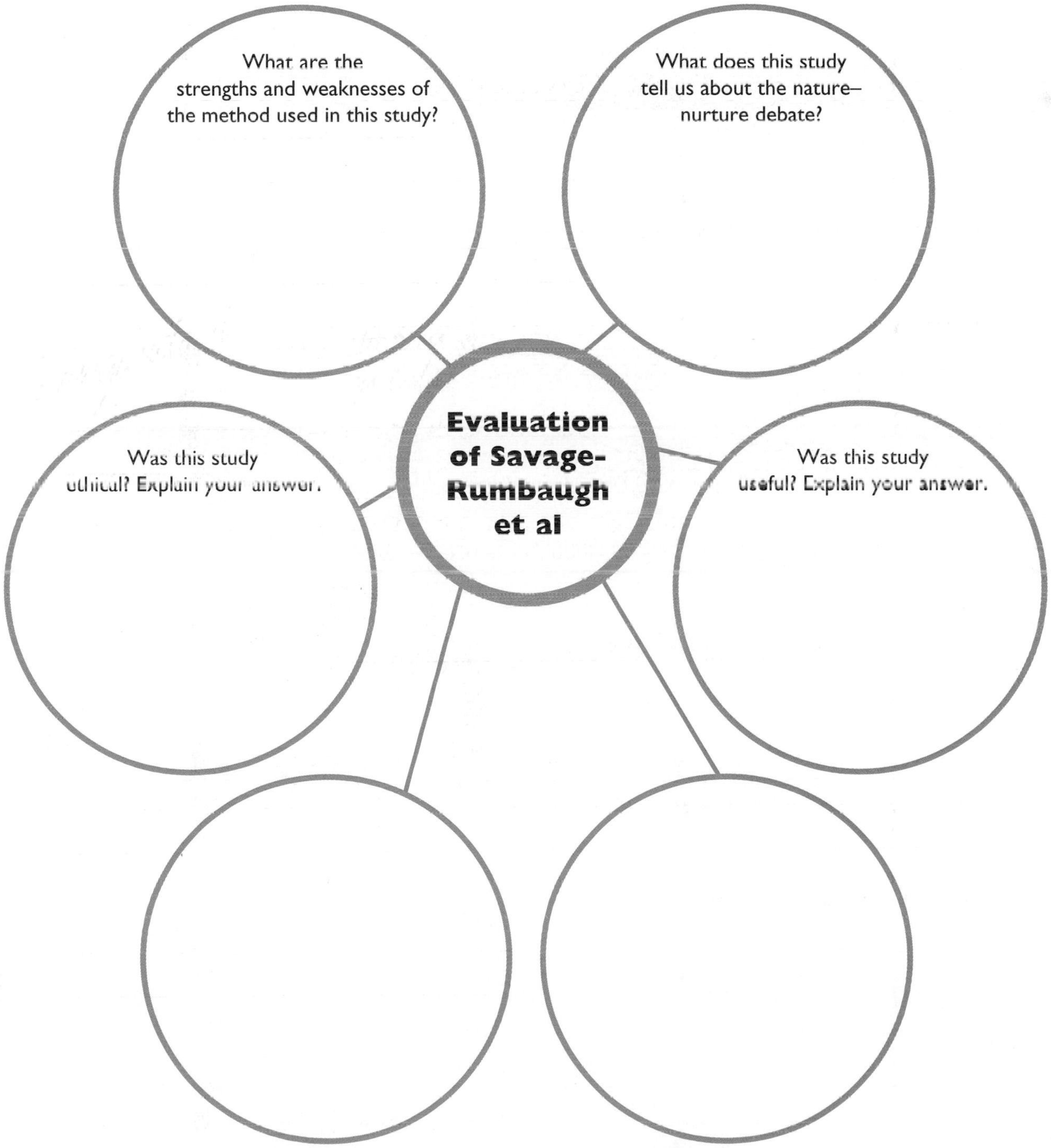

Evaluation of Savage-Rumbaugh et al

What are the strengths and weaknesses of the method used in this study?

What does this study tell us about the nature–nurture debate?

Was this study ethical? Explain your answer.

Was this study useful? Explain your answer.

Strengths and weaknesses of approach

The following tables suggest some strengths and weaknesses of the Cognitive Approach in psychology. Using the three studies from this section try to complete the 'examples' column with one or more example to illustrate the strength or weakness. The first one has been done for you.

Strengths of COGNITIVE approach		**Example from Core Study**
1	High levels of control in laboratory conditions	Loftus and Palmer controlled many variables
2	May be able to help those with cognitive problems and may lead to practical applications for teaching/ treatment	
3	Increases our understanding of cognitive abilities of other species	
4	Can you think of any more strengths?	

Weaknesses of COGNITIVE approach		**Example from Core Study**
1	Laboratory research may have low ecological validity	Eyes Task may not be the same as real life (Baron-Cohen et al)
2	Cognitive research tends to be reductionist	
3	Cognitive research tends to use quantitative rather than qualitative measures	
4	Can you think of any more weaknesses?	

Cognitive Studies crossword

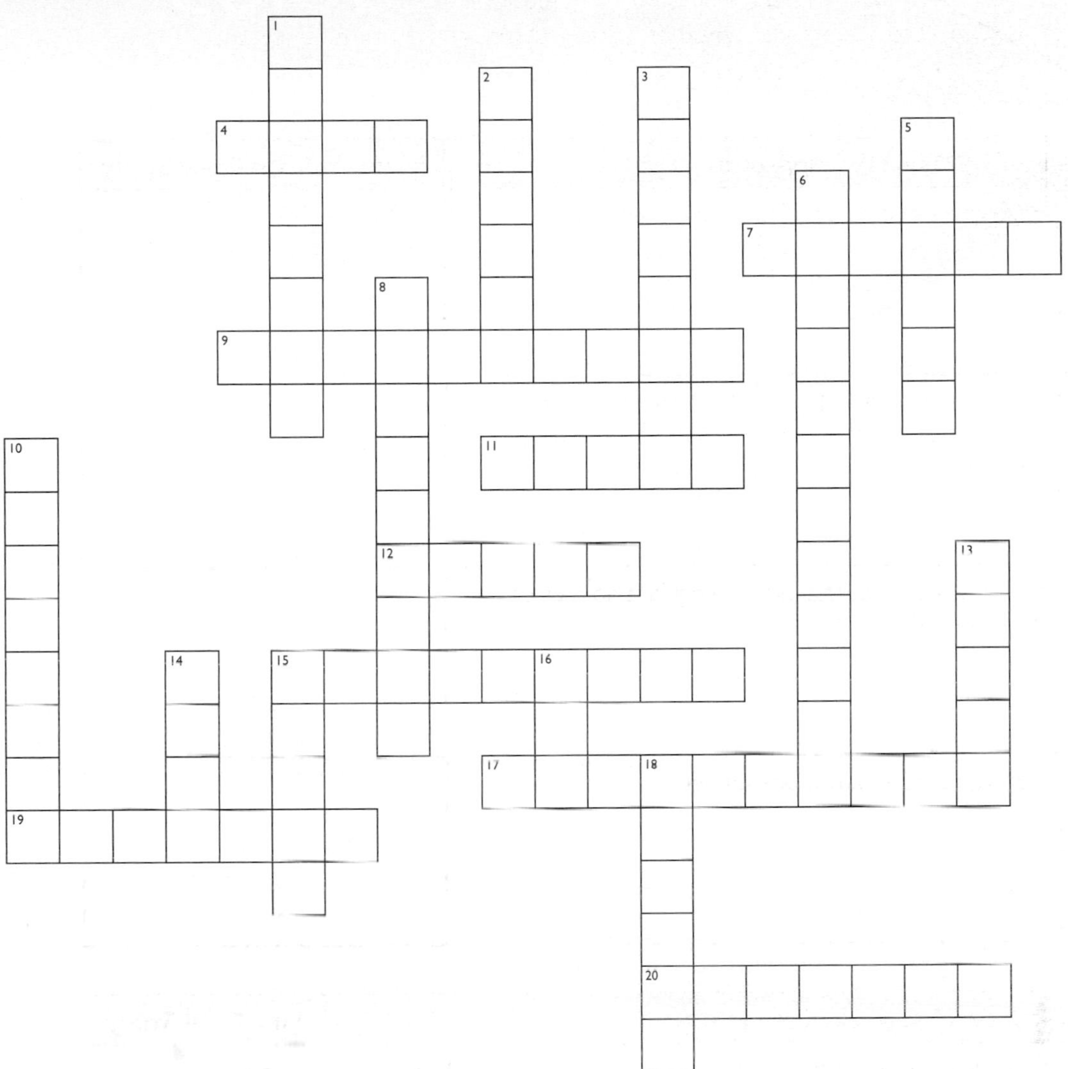

Clues

Across

4. the number of groups in Study 1 by Loftus and Palmer (4)
7. Sherman and Austin were this type of chimpanzee (6)
9. where Loftus and Palmer conducted their research (10)
11. Kanzi was this type of chimpanzee (5)
12. the number of groups in Study 2 by Loftus and Palmer (5)
15. the number of months that the report by Savage-Rumbaugh covers (9)
17. the term used for the words or symbols that a person or animals can use (10)
19. the word used in one of the questions in Study 2 by Loftus and Palmer (7)
20. the number of autistic/Asperger's participants in the study by Baron-Cohen (7)

Down

1. the important question in Loftus and Palmer is referred to as the ____ question (8)
2. Kanzi's sister (6)
3. Kanzi and Mulika communicated using this (8)
5. this group did better on the Eyes Task (6)
6. a study that covers a long time period (12)
8. lack of theory of mind is a ____ deficit (9)
10. Loftus and Palmer's participants (8)
13. the number of 'normal' participants in the study by Baron-Cohen (5)
14. the task used by Baron-Cohen (4)
15. the participants in Lotus and Palmer's study had to estimate this (5)
16. the number of criteria used to assess vocabulary acquisition in the study by Savage-Rumbaugh (3)
18. a disorder characterised by lack of theory of mind (6)

Answers:
Across: 4. five; 7. common; 9. laboratory; 11. pygmy; 12. three; 15. seventeen; 17. vocabulary; 19. smashed; 20. sixteen
Down: 1. critical; 2. Mulika; 3. lexigram; 5. female; 6. longitudinal; 8. cognitive; 10. students; 13. fifty; 14. Eyes; 15. speed; 16. two; 18. autism

Developmental Studies

This study is covered on pages 40–47 of the textbook

Samuel and Bryant (1984) Asking only one question in the conservation experiment

What do I need to know?

Aim

Samuel and Bryant were critical of the technique used by Piaget in his conservation studies. They believed that children were more likely to give the incorrect answer as they had been asked the question twice. This study was designed to test the hypothesis that asking only one question in the conservation task will lead to more correct answers.

Participants

- 252 boys and girls
- From a variety of schools and pre-schools in Devon
- Divided into four groups by age
- Each group had 63 children and the mean age for each group was 5 years and 3 months, 6 years and 3 months, 7 years and 3 months and 8 years and 3 months
- Each group was then subdivided into three groups of 21 and each group was tested under a different experimental condition

Mean age of group	Standard condition	One-judgement condition	Fixed-array condition	Total number of children
5 years, 3 months	N = 21	N = 21	N = 21	63
6 years, 3 months	N = 21	N = 21	N = 21	63
7 years, 3 months	N = 21	N = 21	N = 21	63
8 years, 3 months	N = 21	N = 21	N = 21	63
Total number of children	84	84	84	252

Method

- Three independent variables tested:
  1 type of questioning
  2 age
  3 type of task
- Laboratory experiment as the main independent variable (which type of questioning the child experienced) was manipulated by the experimenter. There were three experimental conditions:
  1 Standard. Asked before and after transformation as in Piagetian research
  2 One-judgement. Asked question only after transformation has taken place
  3 Fixed-array (control). Child only shown the post-transformational display and then asked the question
- 21 children from each group were tested in each condition making a total of 84 children in each condition. This allowed age differences to be compared as well.
- Children were only tested in one of the above conditions but each child was tested four times using each of the following tasks, as this is also an independent variable:
  1 counters for number
  2 plasticine for mass
  3 liquid in a glass for volume.

Results

Variable 1: Type of questioning
Results by mean number of errors (maximum 12)

Mean age of group	Standard condition	One-judgement condition	Fixed-array condition
5 years, 3 months	8.5	7.3	8.5
6 years, 3 months	5.7	4.3	6.4
7 years, 3 months	3.2	2.5	4.8
8 years, 3 months	1.6	1.3	3.3

From this table we can see that:

- All age groups make fewer errors on the one question condition than the other two conditions.
- The fixed array (control) condition produced the highest number of errors.

Variable 2: Age

- From the above table we can also see that older children make fewer errors than younger children.

Variable 3: Type of task
Results by mean number of errors on different types of task (maximum four).

	Standard	One-judgement	Fixed array
Mass	1.5	1.2	1.7
Number	1.4	1.0	1.5
Volume	1.8	1.6	2.5

From this table we can see that:

- Children make fewer errors on the conservation of mass task and most errors on the conservation of volume task.
- They make fewer errors in the one-judgement condition and most on the fixed array condition (particularly for volume).

Conclusions

- The hypothesis that children make more errors because they are asked the question twice is supported.
- However this evidence does not entirely negate Piaget's theory.
- This study confirms that children's conservation skills improve with age and also that conservation of number is easier than the other two tasks.

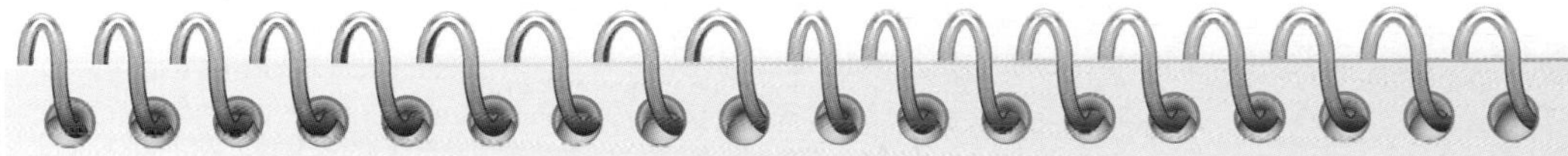

What do you think?

How could these results be applied to education? Would it be useful for primary school teachers to be taught about Piaget's work and the work of Samuel and Bryant? Discuss this with your teacher or with other students.

Test your knowledge

Answer the multiple choice questions below by ticking the correct answer(s) to test your knowledge of the study. You will find the answers at the bottom of the page.

1 *What does 'conservation' mean in Piagetian theory?*

a) ☐ the ability to attribute human characteristics to inanimate objects
b) ☐ the understanding that if the shape of something is changed it will still have the same mass, volume or number
c) ☐ the ability to reverse mental operations
d) ☐ saving the planet

2 *Why did Samuel and Bryant want to replicate Piaget's work?*

a) ☐ because they thought that he had confused the children by asking the same question twice
b) ☐ because they thought Piaget was wrong
c) ☐ because they thought the children should be asked more questions
d) ☐ because Piaget's research was very old

3 *How many children took part in Samuel and Bryant's study?*

a) ☐ 63 children
b) ☐ 100 children
c) ☐ 252 children
d) ☐ 6 children

4 *What was the total number of trials per child?*

a) ☐ 12
b) ☐ 6
c) ☐ 8
d) ☐ 24

5 *Which of the following is the best description of the one-judgement condition?*

a) ☐ the question was asked before and after the transformation
b) ☐ the question was only asked after the transformation
c) ☐ the children were not allowed to see the transformation
d) ☐ the children were not asked any questions

6 *How did age affect the childrens' ability to conserve?*

a) ☐ younger children made fewer errors than older children
b) ☐ older children made fewer errors than younger children
c) ☐ age had no affect on conservation skills
d) ☐ older children got bored more quickly

7 *Which experimental condition led to the fewest number of errors?*

a) ☐ the standard condition
b) ☐ the one-judgement condition
c) ☐ the fixed array (control) condition
d) ☐ none of them

8 *Which of the following statements is the best account of the conclusions drawn by Samuel and Bryant?*

a) ☐ Piaget was wrong
b) ☐ Piaget was right
c) ☐ Piaget's results were supported in that older children can conserve better than younger children although the standard condition where two questions were asked seemed to confuse the children
d) ☐ never work with children

Answers: 1 b; 2 a; 3 c; 4 a; 5 b; 6 b; 7 b; 8 c

Test your understanding

Use the questions below to evaluate the study. Suggested answers can be found at the back of the book.

1 The sample was 252 boys and girls from a variety of Devon schools and pre-schools.

a Suggest one problem with generalising from this sample.

b Suggest an alternative sample that could have been used for this study.

c Outline one effect of using this alternative sample.

2 The experiment collected quantitative data.

a Outline one strength and one weakness of the quantitative data collected in this study.

Strength

Weakness

b Suggest how qualitative data might have been collected in this study.

3 **a** Suggest one improvement that could have been made to this study.

b Outline the effect of this improvement on the results.

Mind mapping

Using the mind map below make brief notes on the issues that can be used to evaluate this study. Some of the bubbles have been started for you and you should use the list below to select two further evaluation issues for this study. These issues are covered in detail on pages 176–187 of your textbook.

Ecological validity	Application to everyday life	Representativeness/generalisability
Ethics	Nature–nurture	Individual–situational explanations
Reliability	Validity	Qualitative and quantitative data
Control	Reductionism	Determinism

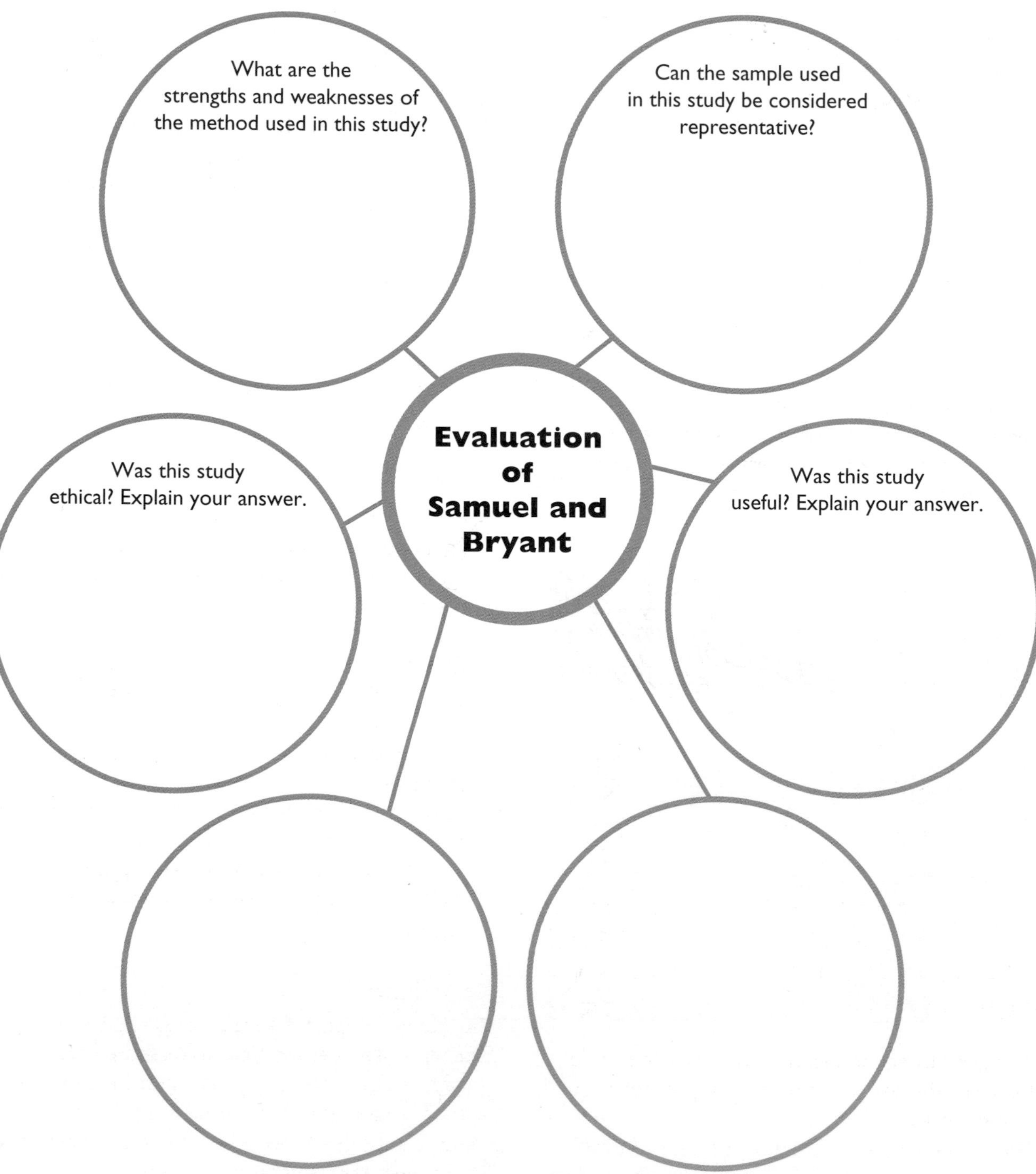
What are the strengths and weaknesses of the method used in this study?
Can the sample used in this study be considered representative?
Evaluation of Samuel and Bryant
Was this study ethical? Explain your answer.
Was this study useful? Explain your answer.

Bandura, Ross and Ross (1961) Transmission of aggression through imitation of aggressive models

This study is covered on pages 48–55 of your textbook

What do I need to know?

Aim

This study investigates the imitation of aggression and is based on the principles of Social Learning Theory. Four hypotheses were tested:

1 Children exposed to an adult behaving aggressively towards a toy will imitate this behaviour in the absence of the model.
2 Children exposed to a non-aggressive model will show less aggressive behaviour.
3 Children will imitate same-sex models more than opposite-sex models.
4 Boys may be more predisposed to imitate aggressive models than girls.

Participants

- 72 children between 37 and 69 months old
- All attended the nursery at Stanford University
- Equal numbers of boys and girls

Method

- Laboratory experiment
- Children were either exposed to a same-sex aggressive model, an opposite-sex aggressive model, a same-sex non-aggressive model, an opposite-sex non-aggressive model or not exposed to adult models

Group	No of children	Sex of children	Sex of model	Aggressive/ non-aggressive model
1	6	M	M	A
2	6	M	M	NA
3	6	M	F	A
4	6	M	F	NA
5	6	F	M	A
6	6	F	M	NA
7	6	F	F	A
8	6	F	F	NA
Control	24			

- This gives three independent variables: the sex of the child, the sex of the model and the behaviour of the model
- The children were matched on the basis of their pre-existing levels of aggression, which was rated on five-point scales by the experimenter and a nursery school teacher before the experiment began
- The dependent variable is the behaviour of the children and this was measured at stage 3 of the experiment (see below)
- The experiment took place in three stages:
  1 Children exposed to adult model (individually). In the aggressive condition the model acted out a series of pre-planned aggressive acts towards the Bobo doll. In the non-aggressive condition the model played quietly
  2 Mild aggression arousal where children were briefly shown some attractive toys and then told that they weren't allowed to play with them
  3 Observation of delayed imitation – lasted 20 minutes while child was in room containing aggressive and non aggressive toys and a Bobo doll. Observers watched through a one way mirror and three measures of imitation were obtained:
  - imitative physical aggression
  - imitative verbal aggression
  - imitative non-aggressive verbal responses (Non-imitative physical and verbal aggression was also noted.)

Results

- Children in the aggressive condition reproduced (imitated) a lot of the physical and verbal aggression used by the model, whereas children in the non-aggressive and control conditions showed virtually none of this behaviour.
- Children in the aggressive condition also copied the model's non-aggressive verbal responses and none of the children in the other conditions did.
- Boys produced more imitative physical aggression than girls.
- Children were more likely to imitate the same-sex model rather than the opposite-sex model.
- The children were shocked and surprised at the female model displaying physical and verbal aggression.

Conclusions

The results support the ideas of Social Learning Theory as they demonstrate that children will imitate the behaviours of others in the absence of reward/reinforcement. The results also suggest that there may be gender differences in the likelihood of aggressive behaviours being imitated.

Test your knowledge

Answer the multiple choice questions below by ticking the correct answer(s) to test your knowledge of the study. You will find the answers at the bottom of the page.

1 *Social Learning Theory predicts that people learn through:*

a) ☐ reinforcement
b) ☐ punishment
c) ☐ observation
d) ☐ playing

2 *Which of the following correctly describes the sample of the study?*

a) ☐ 72 children between 37 months and 69 months
b) ☐ 102 children between 37 months and 69 months
c) ☐ 12 children between 37 months and 69 months
d) ☐ 6 children aged 6 years

3 *The experiment was conducted in three stages. In the first stage, what did the children in the aggressive model condition observe?*

a) ☐ the model playing with tinker toys quietly
b) ☐ the model acting out a series of planned aggressive acts towards another person
c) ☐ the model acting out a series of planned aggressive acts towards a Bobo doll
d) ☐ other children acting aggressively

4 *Why was it necessary to include the second stage (aggression arousal)?*

a) ☐ to ensure that the children had some desire to act aggressively
b) ☐ to ensure that the children had no desire to act aggressively
c) ☐ to punish the children
d) ☐ as a control

5 *The observers recorded three types of aggression. Which of the following was not observed?*

a) ☐ imitative physical aggression
b) ☐ imitative verbal aggression
c) ☐ imitative non-aggressive verbal responses
d) ☐ imitative non-aggressive physical responses

6 *How long did the observation at stage 3 last?*

a) ☐ 5 minutes
b) ☐ 10 minutes
c) ☐ 20 minutes
d) ☐ 30 minutes

7 *What differences were found between boys and girls?*

a) ☐ boys produced more imitative physical aggression than girls
b) ☐ girls produced more imitative physical aggression than boys
c) ☐ girls produced more imitative verbal aggression than boys
d) ☐ boys produced more imitative verbal aggression than girls

8 *Which social issue could the findings of this study be applied to?*

a) ☐ the issue of television violence
b) ☐ the issue of computer game violence
c) ☐ the issue of domestic violence
d) ☐ all of the above

What do you think?

What other data could the researchers have collected? Discuss this with your teacher or with other students.

Answers: 1 c; 2 a; 3 c; 4 a; 5 d; 6 c; 7 a; 8 d

Test your understanding

Use the questions below to evaluate the study. Suggested answers can be found at the back of the book.

1 This study was conducted in a laboratory.

a Outline one strength and one weakness of conducting research in a laboratory.

Strength

Weakness

b Describe how this research might have been conducted outside of a laboratory environment.

c Identify one strength and one weakness with the suggested alternative.

Strength

Weakness

2 a Identify one ethical issue with this study.

b Describe one way of improving the ethics of the study.

c What effect do you think that this would have on the results?

Mind mapping

Using the mind map below make brief notes on the issues that can be used to evaluate this study. Some of the bubbles have been started for you and you should use the list below to select two further evaluation issues for this study. These issues are covered in detail on pages 176–187 of your textbook.

Ecological validity	Application to everyday life	Representativeness/generalisability
Ethics	Nature–nurture	Individual–situational explanations
Reliability	Validity	Qualitative and quantitative data
Control	Reductionism	Determinism

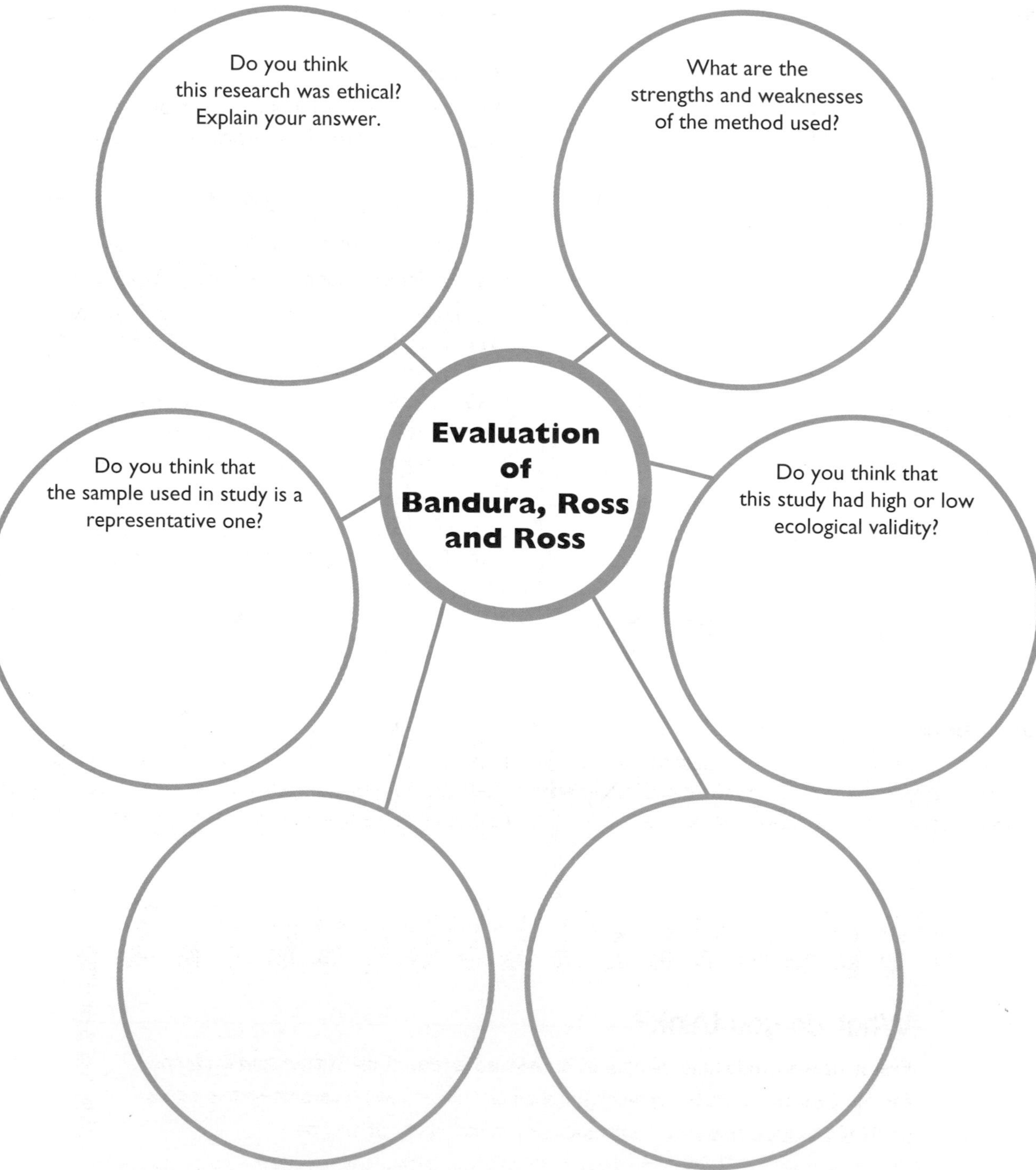
Evaluation of Bandura, Ross and Ross
Do you think this research was ethical? Explain your answer.
What are the strengths and weaknesses of the method used?
Do you think that the sample used in study is a representative one?
Do you think that this study had high or low ecological validity?

Freud (1909): Analysis of a phobia in a five-year-old boy

This study is covered on pages 56–61 of the textbook

What do I need to know?

Aim

In specific terms this study investigates the causes of a phobia of horses in a five-year-old boy. More generally it is a detailed account of the development of one child and allowed Freud to test his theory of infantile sexuality, the Oedipus complex and the use of psychoanalytic theory in general

Participant

- One child referred to as Little Hans
- Aged three at start of study (1906)
- Aged five when the reports of the phobia of horses were first made

Method

- Case study (Freud's only case study of a child)
- Hans' parents were great admirers of Freud's work and were attempting to bring Hans up in a relatively liberal way (for the time) in the hope that he would not develop any of the neuroses described by Freud in his earlier books
- Letters from Hans' father to Freud describing child's behaviour
- Freud would reply with his interpretations

Results

Some of the behaviours (in order of occurrence) together with Freud's interpretations are given below.

Behaviour	Interpretation
Interest in his 'widdler'	Evidence for Phallic stage of development
Desire to get into bed with mother	Evidence for Oedipus complex (desire for mother)
Fear of bath	Unconscious fear that mother loved Hans' baby sister more than him and thus would not hold on to him as tightly in the bath and he might slip and drown
Fear of white horses	Symbolic of fear of his father (evidence for castration anxiety seen during Phallic stage of development)
Fantasy about giraffes	Evidence for Oedipus complex (fantasy of taking mother away from father)
Fantasy about being his own father	Evidence for Oedipus complex (desire to replace father in mother's affection) and start of resolution of Oedipus complex
Fantasy about plumber giving him 'a bigger widdler and a bigger behind'	Wanting to be like his father (evidence for possible resolution of Oedipus complex)

Conclusions

The original case study is over 100 pages long and makes up only a tiny part of Freud's writings. At the end of the case study he concludes that Hans was experiencing the Oedipus complex and he used this case to support his notions of infantile sexuality, his theories of psychosexual development and his work on phobias.

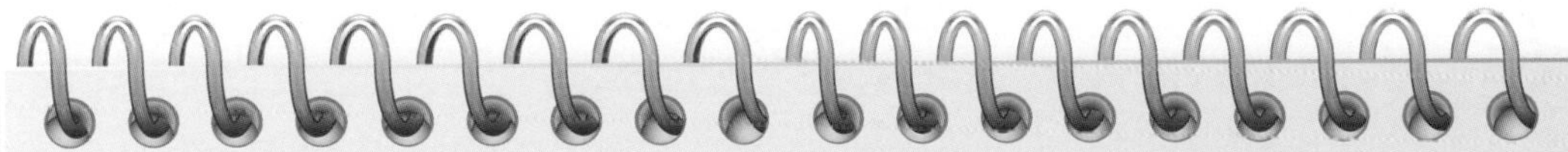

What do you think?

Freud interpreted Hans' phobia of horses as a fear of his father and evidence for the Oedipus complex. How might a behaviourist have interpreted the same phobia? Discuss this with your teacher or with other students.

Test your knowledge

Answer the multiple choice questions below by ticking the correct answer(s) to test your knowledge of the study. You will find the answers at the bottom of the page.

1 *This is a case study. Which of the following is the correct definition of a case study?*

a) ☐ a study that takes place over a long period of time
b) ☐ a study with a single participant
c) ☐ a study with lots of participants
d) ☐ a snapshot study

2 *What is the Oedipus complex?*

a) ☐ fear of castration
b) ☐ interest in own genitals
c) ☐ a phobia of horses
d) ☐ a desire to replace the father in the mother's affection

3 *How old was Hans at the start of the study?*

a) ☐ 5
b) ☐ 3
c) ☐ 4
d) ☐ 6

4 *Hans' father used to write to Freud describing Hans' behaviour. Which of the following are problems associated with this technique?*

a) ☐ Freud had not seen the behaviour for himself
b) ☐ Hans' father might have been biased in his reports
c) ☐ Hans' father was already a follower of Freud's work and used to offer his own interpretations
d) ☐ all of the above

5 *How was Hans' fear of the bath interpreted by Freud?*

a) ☐ as anxiety that his mother loved his sister more than him
b) ☐ as evidence for castration anxiety
c) ☐ as evidence that Hans wished to be more like his father
d) ☐ as a desire to take his mother away from his father

6 *How was the fantasy of the giraffes interpreted by Freud?*

a) ☐ as evidence for castration anxiety
b) ☐ as a desire to take his mother away from his father
c) ☐ as a desire to take his father away from his mother
d) ☐ as evidence of his anxiety over his baby sister

7 *Hans developed a phobia of horses. Who did Freud say the horse represented?*

a) ☐ his father
b) ☐ his mother
c) ☐ his sister
d) ☐ his whole family

8 *How was the fantasy of the plumber interpreted by Freud?*

a) ☐ as evidence for castration anxiety
b) ☐ as evidence of his anxiety over his baby sister
c) ☐ as evidence that Hans wished to be more like his father
d) ☐ as a desire to take his mother away from his father

Answers: 1 b; 2 d; 3 b; 4 d; 5 a; 6 b; 7 a; 8 c

Test your understanding

Use the questions below to evaluate the study. Suggested answers can be found at the back of the book.

1 This study was a case study. Outline one strength and one weakness of case studies.

Strength

They provide a large amount of qualitive data

Weakness

They focus on a very small population which makes it hard to generalise.

2 Outline one strength and one weakness of the way data was collected in this study.

Strength

Rich, qualitive data from father.

Weakness

Father may be biased in answers.

3 **a** Outline two improvements that could be made to this study.

Improvement one

Improvement two

b Suggest how each of these improvements might affect the results of the study.

Effect of improvement one

Effect of improvement two

Mind mapping

Using the mind map below make brief notes on the issues that can be used to evaluate this study. Some of the bubbles have been started for you and you should use the list below to select two further evaluation issues for this study. These issues are covered in detail on pages 176–187 of your textbook.

Ecological validity	Application to everyday life	Representativeness/generalisability
Ethics	Nature–nurture	Individual–situational explanations
Reliability	Validity	Qualitative and quantitative data
Control	Reductionism	Determinism

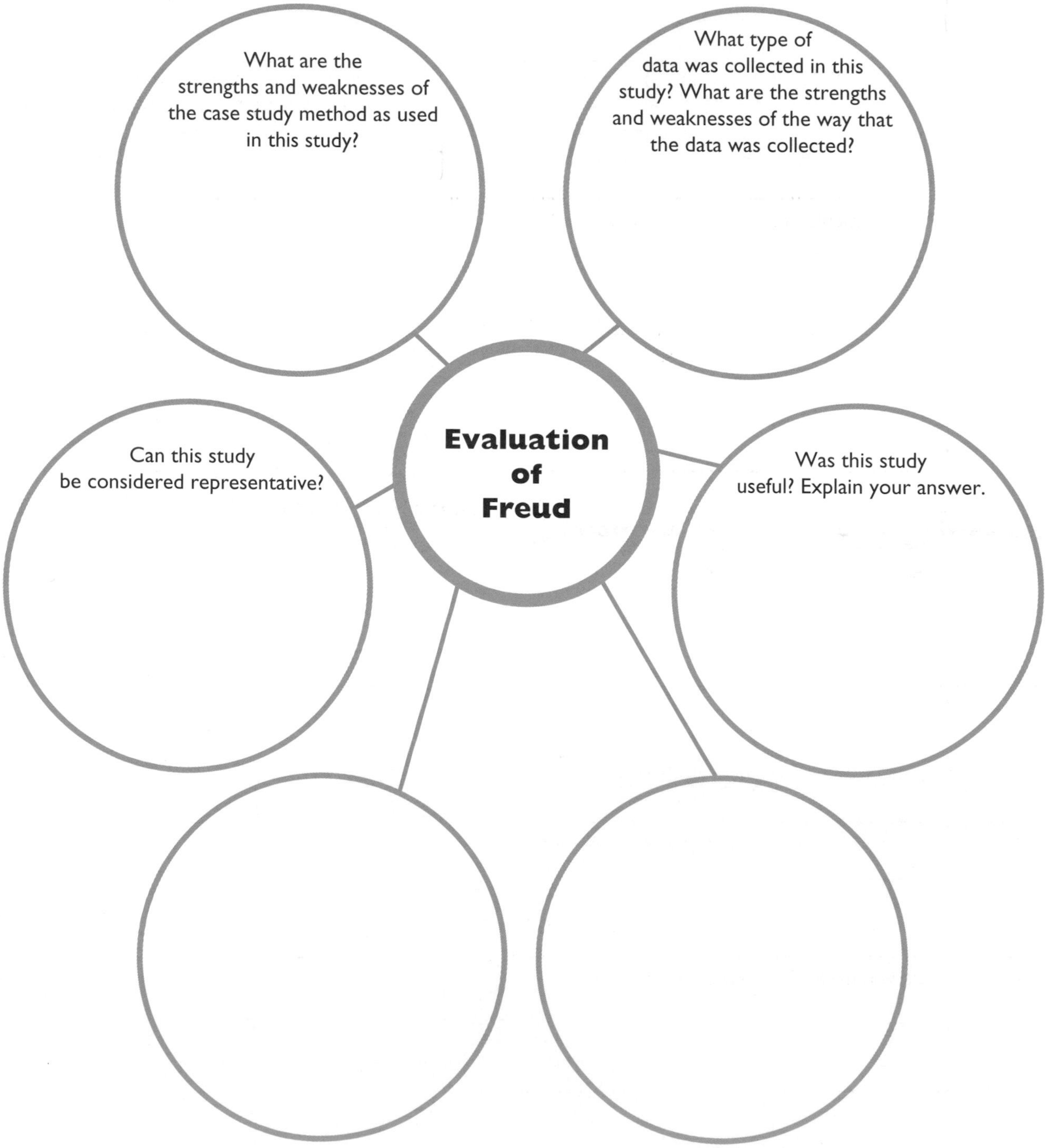

Evaluation of Freud

What are the strengths and weaknesses of the case study method as used in this study?

What type of data was collected in this study? What are the strengths and weaknesses of the way that the data was collected?

Can this study be considered representative?

Was this study useful? Explain your answer.

Strengths and weaknesses of approach

The following tables suggest some strengths and weaknesses of the Developmental Approach in psychology. Using the three studies from this section try to complete the 'examples' column with one or more example to illustrate the strength or weakness. The first one has been done for you.

Strengths of DEVELOPMENTAL approach		Example from Core Study
1	Allows us to see the effects of maturation (aging) on behaviour	Samuel and Bryant's study show us how conservation skills increase with age
2	Allows us to see the effect of different types of experience on behaviour	
3	Case studies can be extremely useful in studying unusual cases	
4	Developmental research can have many useful applications to child care, education etc	
5	Can you think of any more strengths?	

Weaknesses of DEVELOPMENTAL approach		Example from Core Study
1	Research with children may raise ethical issues	The children in Bandura's study may have been distressed or otherwise adversely affected by their experiences
2	Case studies are difficult to generalise from	
3	Laboratory research in this area may suffer from problems of low ecological validity	
4	Can you think of any more weaknesses?	

Developmental Approach crossword

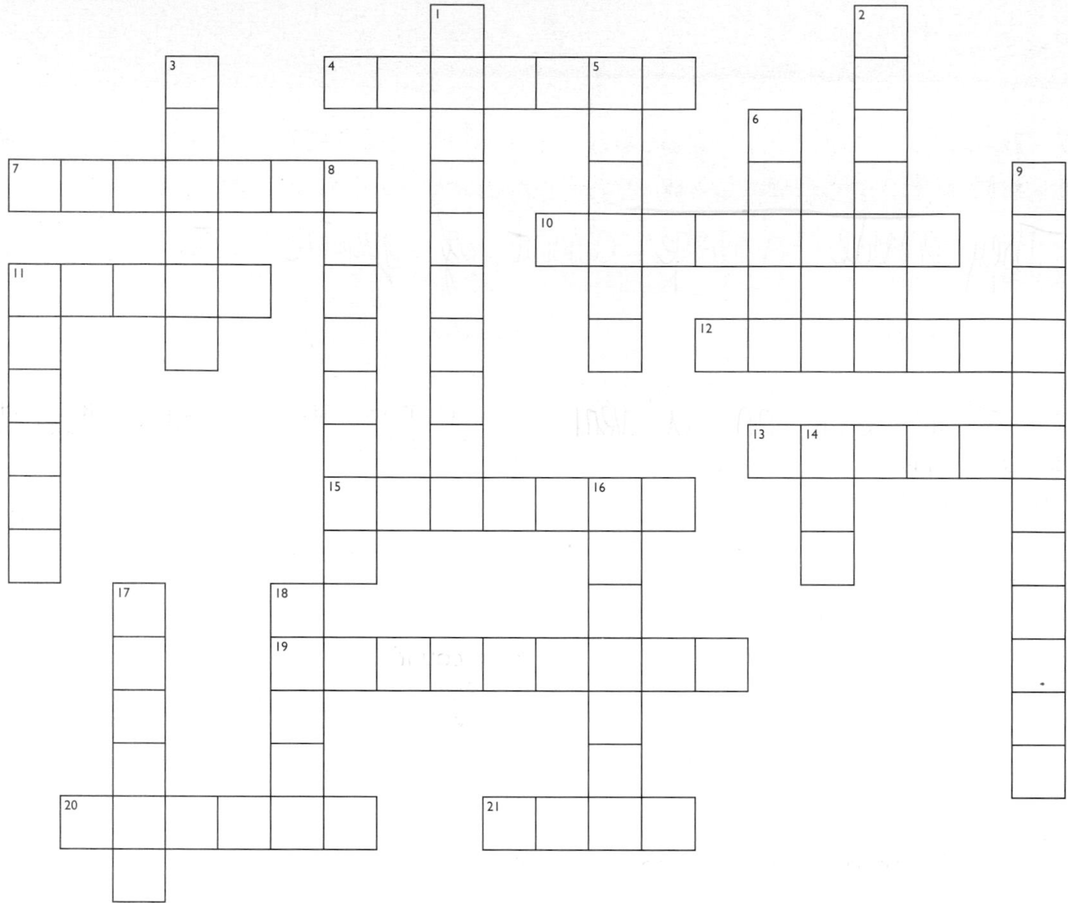

Clues

Across

4. Freud's first name (7)
7. the animal in Hans' fantasy (7)
10. someone who watches and records (8)
11. the person that is imitated (5)
12. Hans' father sent lots of these to Freud (7)
13. the object of Hans' jealousy (6)
15. this group is used for comparison purposes (7)
19. copying someone else's behaviour (9)
20. the number of minutes that the children in Bandura's study were observed for (6)
21. a type of study with a single participant (4)

Down

1. the behaviour studied by Bandura (10)
2. parents should give this before a child takes part in an experiment (7)
3. he proposed the original theory of cognitive development (6)
5. the type of conservation task that the children found the easiest (6)
6. the number of measures of aggression in the Bandura study (5)
8. material offered in support of a theory (8)
9. recognising that mass, volume or number remain the same despite changes in appearance (12)
11. the Bobo doll was hit with this (6)
14. conservation skills increase with this (3)
16. the complex where a boy desires his mother (7)
17. Hans had a phobia of these (6)
18. the total number of experimental conditions in the Bandura study (5)

Answers:
Across: 4. Sigmund; 7. giraffe; 10. observer; 11. model; 12. letters; 13. father; 15. control; 19. imitation; 20. twenty; 21. case
Down: 1. aggression; 2. consent; 3. Piaget; 5. number; 6. three; 8. evidence; 9. conservation; 11. mallet; 14. age; 16. Oedipus; 17. horses; 18. eight

Physiological Studies

Maguire et al (2000): Navigation – related structural changes in the hippocampi of taxi drivers

This study is covered on pages 68–75 of the textbook

What do I need to know?

Aim

The aim of the study was to investigate whether the hippocampus changes as a result of experience. In other words, do the hippocampi of licensed taxi drivers have a greater volume than the hippocampi of those without significant navigational experiences.

Participants

Experimental group

- 16 male licensed cab drivers who had passed 'The Knowledge'
- All right-handed
- Between 32 and 62 years of age with a mean age of 44
- All been licensed for at least 18 months (mean was 14.3 years)
- All described as having healthy medical, neurological and psychiatric profiles

Control group

- 50 healthy, right-handed males
- Aged between 32 and 62
- Mean ages and spread of ages similar to taxi drivers group
- None of this group were taxi drivers
- The researchers simply selected 50 scans from the MRI scan database at the same centre where the taxi drivers were screened

Method

- Quasi-experiment
- Independent Variable – whether someone was a taxi driver or not
- Data was collected from two different methods of analysing MRI scans:
  1 Voxel Based Morphology (VBM)
  2 pixel counting
- This data was then correlated with the length of time that taxi drivers had been licensed

Results

VBM results

- Taxi drivers had increased grey matter volume in the right and the left hippocampus. This difference was found in the posterior hippocampus.
- Control group had greater grey matter volume in the anterior hippocampus compared to the taxi drivers.

Pixel counting

- Showed no significant difference in overall volume of hippocampi between the two groups but confirmed the regional differences described above.

Correlations

- Significant positive correlation between the volume of the right posterior hippocampus and the length of time spent as a taxi driver.
- Negative correlation between size of anterior hippocampus and length of time spent as a taxi driver.

Conclusions

- The results suggest that the hippocampus shows 'plasticity', that is that its volume increases with navigational experience.
- Although it is possible that the taxi drivers might have had larger volumes of grey matter in their hippocampus before studying for 'The Knowledge' and this may have predisposed them to a navigational career, the correlational results suggest that change has taken place since qualifying. The longer they had been a taxi driver the greater the volume of their right posterior hippocampus.

What do you think?

Think about the nature–nurture debate. What does this study tell us about this debate? Discuss this with your teacher or with other students.

Test your knowledge

Answer the multiple choice questions below by ticking the correct answer(s) to test your knowledge of the study. You will find the answers at the bottom of the page.

1 *One of the major functions of the hippocampus is:*

a) ☐ language
b) ☐ navigation
c) ☐ singing
d) ☐ spelling

2 *Which of the following statements best describes the aim of this study?*

a) ☐ to determine whether the hippocampus is involved in navigation
b) ☐ to determine whether the hippocampus is involved in language
c) ☐ to determine whether changes in the volume of grey matter in the hippocampus can be related to navigational experience
d) ☐ to determine the effects of driving a taxi

3 *Which of the following best describes the sample of licensed taxi drivers?*

a) ☐ 16 males between 32 and 62, all right-handed and with healthy medical, neurological and psychiatric profiles
b) ☐ 16 females between 32 and 62, all right-handed and with healthy medical, neurological and psychiatric profiles
c) ☐ 50 males
d) ☐ 50 females

4 *What is 'The Knowledge'?*

a) ☐ an intelligence test
b) ☐ a driving test
c) ☐ a detailed knowledge of all major routes within the UK
d) ☐ a detailed knowledge of the 25,000 roads within a six mile radius of Charing Cross, as well as more general knowledge of the major routes throughout the rest of London

5 *What is a quasi-experiment?*

a) ☐ a badly controlled experiment
b) ☐ an experiment where the independent variable is not manipulated by the experimenter but occurs naturally
c) ☐ an experiment with more than two conditions
d) ☐ an experiment conducted outside the laboratory

6 *How does an MRI scan work?*

a) ☐ the person is given an injection of a radioactive marker which enables the scan to work out where glucose metabolism is greatest
b) ☐ it beams low-level light waves into the brain and measures the amount of reflection
c) ☐ it aligns atomic particles in the body tissues by magnetism and then bombards them with radio waves, causing the particles to give off radio signals that differ according to what type of tissue is present
d) ☐ it measures the electrical patterns created by the rhythmic oscillations of neurons

7 *One of the following statements is NOT a finding from this study. Identify which is the incorrect statement.*

a) ☐ taxi drivers had a greater grey matter volume in the posterior hippocampus compared to controls
b) ☐ controls had a greater grey matter volume in the anterior hippocampus compared to taxi drivers
c) ☐ there was a significant positive correlation between the volume of the right posterior hippocampus and the length of time spent as a taxi driver
d) ☐ there was a significant negative correlation between the volume of the right posterior hippocampus and the length of time spent as a taxi driver

8 *Which of the following statements best describes the conclusions that can be drawn from this study?*

a) ☐ the hippocampus cannot change its size
b) ☐ people with small hippocampi make poor taxi drivers
c) ☐ the hippocampus is able to increase its size with navigational experience
d) ☐ the hippocampus will get smaller over time

Answers: 1 b; 2 c; 3 a; 4 d; 5 b; 6 c; 7 d; 8 c

Test your understanding

Use the questions below to evaluate the study. Suggested answers can be found at the back of the book.

1 Outline one strength and one weakness of this study.

Strength

Weakness

2 This study collected quantitative data from MRI scans. Outline two strengths associated with the data collection in this study.

Strength 1

Strength 2

3 The sample of this study were all licensed taxi drivers.

a Suggest one advantage of using a highly discrete sample of this type for this study.

b Suggest an alternative sample that could have been used for this study.

4 a Suggest one improvement/change that could have been made to this study.

b Outline the possible effects of this change.

5 Suggest one practical application of the findings of this study.

Mind mapping

Using the mind map below make brief notes on the issues that can be used to evaluate this study. Some of the bubbles have been started for you and you should use the list below to select two further evaluation issues for this study. These issues are covered in detail on pages 176–187 of your textbook.

Ecological validity	Application to everyday life	Representativeness/generalisability
Ethics	Nature–nurture	Individual–situational explanations
Reliability	Validity	Qualitative and quantitative data
Control	Reductionism	Determinism

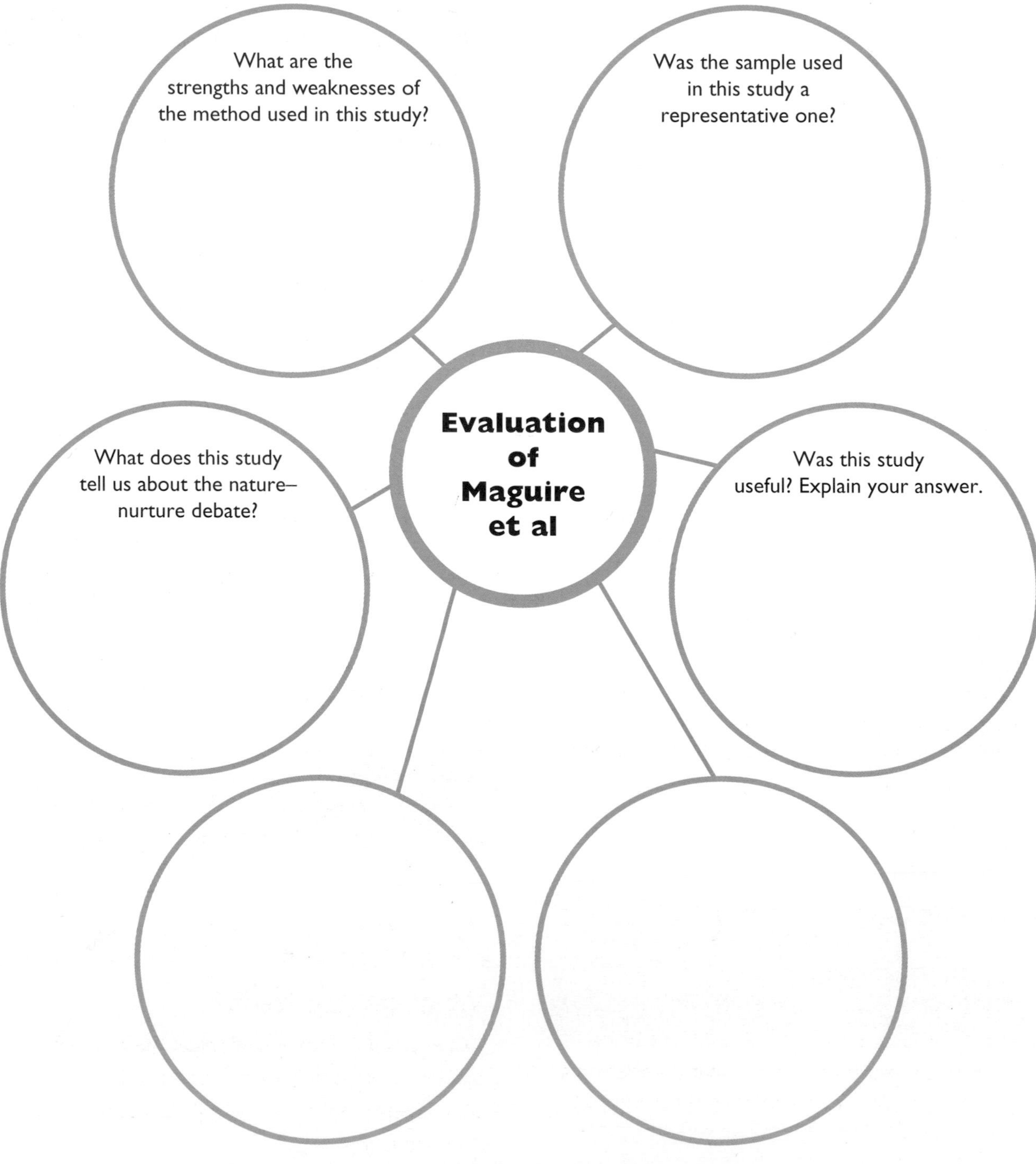
Evaluation of Maguire et al
What are the strengths and weaknesses of the method used in this study?
Was the sample used in this study a representative one?
What does this study tell us about the nature–nurture debate?
Was this study useful? Explain your answer.

Dement and Kleitman: The relation of eye movements during sleep to dream activity

This study is covered on pages 76–83 of the textbook

What do I need to know?

Aim

The aim of the study was to determine the relationship between eye movement and dreaming. There were three specific research questions:

1 Are dreams recalled more often during REM sleep than during non-REM sleep?
2 Would subjective estimates of dream length correlate with length of REM?
3 Is there a relationship between the content of the dream and the direction of eye movements?

Participants

- Seven adult males and two adult females
- Five of these participants were studied intensively
- Data collected from the other four to confirm the results from the original five

Method

- Laboratory experiment
- Participants reported to the laboratory just before their normal bedtime
- Asked to avoid alcohol and caffeine
- Electrodes attached near the eyes to measure eye movement
- Electrodes also attached to the scalp to measure electrical activity of the brain (to determine which stage of sleep they were in)
- Electrodes attached to EEG machine which ran continually throughout the night
- Participants woken at various times during the night
- Woken by a bell and spoke into a tape recorder
- They had to state whether they had been dreaming and if they had, to report the content of the dream

Results

Research Question 1

Woken during REM sleep		Woken during non-REM sleep	
Recalled dreams	**No recall**	**Recalled dreams**	**No recall**
152	39	11	149

- From these results we can see that the there is a far greater likelihood of reporting dreams when woken in REM sleep than when woken in non-REM sleep.

Research Question 2

- Asking people to estimate the length of their dreams turned out to be too complex so the procedure was simplified.
- Participants were woken randomly, either 5 or 15 minutes into REM sleep and asked to estimate whether they had been dreaming for 5 or 15 minutes.

51 tests		60 tests	
Woken after 5 minutes of REM		**Woken after 15 minutes of REM**	
Correct	**Incorrect**	**Correct**	**Incorrect**
45	6	47	13

- The results show that participants were mostly correct in their estimation of dream length.

Research Question 3

- Initially, the researchers asked the participants to try and describe the directions they had looked during their dreams.
- As with Research question 2, this proved too complex and the researchers simplified the procedure.
- When a particular pattern of eye movements was observed (mainly vertical, mainly horizontal, both vertical and horizontal or very little/no eye movement) participants were woken and asked to describe their dreams.
- Results include a participant who showed very little eye movement describing dreaming that he was driving a car and staring at the road ahead and a participant with mainly vertical eye movements reporting a dream of throwing basketballs in a net. There are more examples of this in your textbook on page 81.

Conclusions

- The research supports the notion that eye movements during sleep are related to dreaming.

What do you think?

Dement and Kleitman controlled the amount of caffeine and alcohol – what else could they have controlled? Discuss this with your teacher or with other students.

Test your knowledge

Answer the multiple choice questions below by ticking the correct answer(s) to test your knowledge of the study. You will find the answers at the bottom of the page.

1 *REM means:*

a) ☐ Rapid Electric Motion
b) ☐ Rapid Eye Motion
c) ☐ Rapid Eye Movement
d) ☐ Rapid Electric Movement

2 *Which of the following statements best describes the aim of the study?*

a) ☐ to investigate the meaning of dreams
b) ☐ to investigate why we sleep
c) ☐ to investigate the effect of caffeine and alcohol on dreams
d) ☐ to investigate the relationship between eye movements and dreaming

3 *How were the participants awoken in the study?*

a) ☐ by the experimenter knocking on the door
b) ☐ by an alarm clock
c) ☐ by the experimenter coming into the room
d) ☐ by a bell

4 *These are the results for the first research question.*

Woken during REM sleep		Woken during non-REM sleep	
Recalled dreams	**No recall**	**Recalled dreams**	**No recall**
152	39	11	149

Which of the following statements is the most appropriate conclusion that can be drawn from these results?

a) ☐ dreaming only takes place during REM sleep
b) ☐ participants always remember their dreams when woken during REM sleep
c) ☐ participants are more likely to recall dreaming when woken during REM sleep than when woken during non-REM sleep
d) ☐ some people don't dream

5 *Which of the following statements best describes the results for the second research question?*

a) ☐ participants were mostly accurate in their estimation of dream length
b) ☐ participants were mostly inaccurate in their estimation of dream length
c) ☐ dreams take either 5 or 15 minutes
d) ☐ some people's dreams last longer than others

6 *The final research question looked at the relationship between the direction of eye movements and the content of the dream. Participants were asked to describe their dreams. What type of data is this?*

a) ☐ quantitative
b) ☐ qualitative
c) ☐ anecdotes
d) ☐ not very useful

7 *One strength of this experiment is:*

a) ☐ the large number of participants
b) ☐ the level of control provided by the laboratory
c) ☐ the 'naturalness' of the surroundings
d) ☐ the number of research questions

8 *One weakness of this experiment is:*

a) ☐ the artificial environment in which the participants had to sleep
b) ☐ the use of highly scientific equipment
c) ☐ the number of research questions
d) ☐ the fact that participants didn't know they were in an experiment.

Answers: 1 c; 2 d; 3 d; 4 c; 5 a; 6 b; 7 b; 8 a

Test your understanding

Use the questions below to evaluate the study. Suggested answers can be found at the back of the book.

1 The sample for this study consisted of nine participants.

a Outline one advantage of using this sample.

They can be studied intensively as each patient was able to be studied in a highly controlled enviornment.

b Outline one disadvantage of using this sample.

2 a Identify one example of quantitative data collected in this study and one example of qualitative data collected in this study.

Quantitative data

Qualitative data

b Suggest one strength and one weakness of quantitative data.

Strength

Weakness

c Suggest one strength and one weakness of qualitative data.

Strength

Weakness

3 This study was conducted in a laboratory and may be considered to have low ecological validity.

a Explain why this study may be considered to have low ecological validity.

b Suggest how the ecological validity of this study may be improved and outline the possible effects that this alternative method may have on the results.

Mind mapping

Using the mind map below make brief notes on the issues that can be used to evaluate this study. Some of the bubbles have been started for you and you should use the list below to select two further evaluation issues for this study. These issues are covered in detail on pages 176–187 of your textbook.

Ecological validity	Application to everyday life	Representativeness/generalisability
Ethics	Nature–nurture	Individual–situational explanations
Reliability	Validity	Qualitative and quantitative data
Control	Reductionism	Determinism

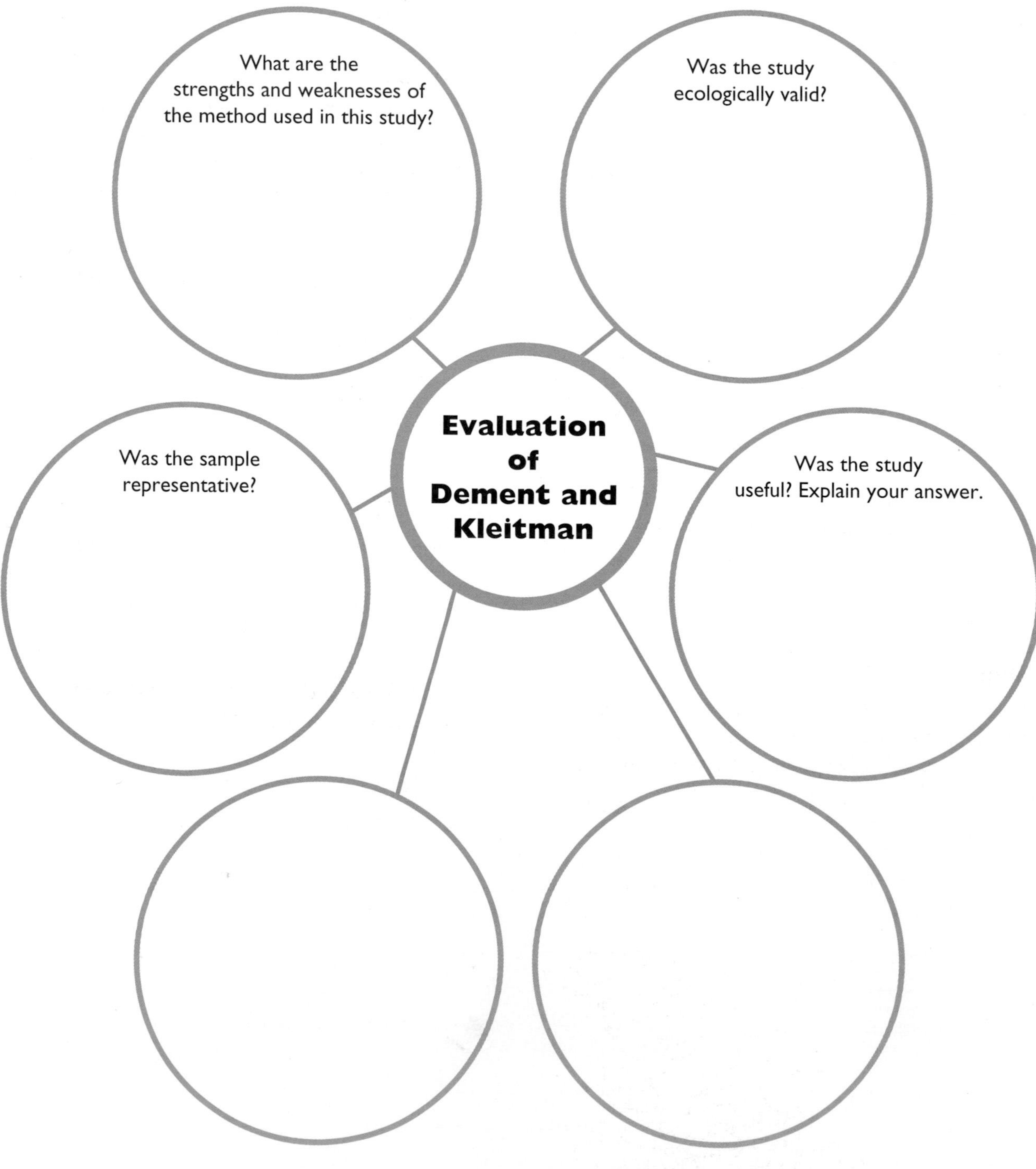

Evaluation of Dement and Kleitman
What are the strengths and weaknesses of the method used in this study?
Was the study ecologically valid?
Was the sample representative?
Was the study useful? Explain your answer.

Sperry (1968): Hemisphere deconnection and unity in conscious awareness

This study is covered on pages 84–91 of your textbook

What do I need to know?

Aim

To test the functioning of separated and independent hemispheres.

Participants

- Opportunity sample
- 11 participants
- All had undergone radical surgery to sever their corpus callosum (to control severe epilepsy and not for purposes of research)

Method

- Specialised laboratory equipment was designed that allowed information to be presented to just one hemisphere (see page 86 of your textbook for more detail).
- For example, vision is divided into left and right visual fields and their hands are screened from view. They have one eye covered and are asked to centre their gaze on a designated fixation point on a screen in front of them. Stimuli (words or images) can be flashed on this screen for $\frac{1}{10}$ second.
- For tactile tasks, objects can be placed in one of the subject's hands (which are screened from view) and thus the sensory information is received by one hemisphere only. The subjects then have to find the object again either with the same or the opposite hand.

Results

Taken overall, the results are described as suggesting that these patients act as if they have two minds in one body. Some of the key findings are given in the next column.

- Information seen by one hemisphere can only be recognised by the same hemisphere. The other hemisphere will respond as if it is seeing an object for the first time.
- Visual material seen by the left hemisphere can be described in speech and writing. If the same information is shown to the right hemisphere the person will insist that they did not see anything. However the person may be able to identify the object non-verbally (e.g. by pointing).
- If a different figure is flashed to each visual field and the participant is asked to draw with their left hand what they have just seen, they will draw the image that was seen in the left visual field. If you ask them what they have drawn they will name the object that appeared in the right visual field.
- An object placed in the right hand can be easily named and described. An object placed in the left hand leads participants to make wild guesses or to have no awareness even that anything is in their hand. However, they can still select it from an array of objects.
- If two objects are placed one in each hand, each hand searches independently for its own object and will reject the object originally placed in the other hand.

Conclusions

These findings confirm that patients who have had their corpus callosum severed effectively have 'two minds in one body'. These results have helped enormously in the development of knowledge about the functioning of the different hemispheres and Sperry was awarded the Noble Prize for his contribution to this area of research.

Test your knowledge

Answer the multiple choice questions below by ticking the correct answer(s) to test your knowledge of the study. You will find the answers at the bottom of the page.

1 *Which of the following statements is correct?*

a) ☐ the right hemisphere receives information from the right visual field
b) ☐ the right hemisphere receives information from the left visual field
c) ☐ the left hemisphere receives information from the left visual field
d) ☐ the left hemisphere does not receive any visual information

2 *How many participants took part in Sperry's research?*

a) ☐ 1
b) ☐ 100
c) ☐ 11
d) ☐ 12

3 *These participants had all had radical surgery to sever their corpus callosum. Why had they had this surgery?*

a) ☐ to control schizophrenic episodes
b) ☐ because Sperry asked them to
c) ☐ to control severe epilepsy
d) ☐ to control severe depression

4 *Which is the best description of the sample used by Sperry?*

a) ☐ random
b) ☐ opportunity
c) ☐ stratified
d) ☐ snowball

5 *Why did the participants have one eye covered?*

a) ☐ to stop them cheating
b) ☐ to prevent tiny eye movements which could have led to information being transferred to the other visual field
c) ☐ to make the task harder
d) ☐ to make the task more like real life

6 *If the visual fields are divided and one piece of information is sent to the left visual field (and hence to the right hemisphere) it can only be recognised again if:*

a) ☐ it is shown to the right visual field
b) ☐ it is shown to both visual fields at once
c) ☐ it is shown again within five minutes
d) ☐ it is shown to the same visual field again

7 *If visual information is shown to the right visual field (left hemisphere) it:*

a) ☐ can be described in speech and writing
b) ☐ cannot be described in speech and writing
c) ☐ can only be drawn
d) ☐ can only be pointed at

8 *If the person has their hands screened from sight and a different object is placed in each hand:*

a) ☐ the person gets confused
b) ☐ only the left hand will search
c) ☐ only the right hand will search
d) ☐ each hand will look for its own object

What do you think?

What other 'unusual' cases could be studied using the quasi-experimental method? Discuss this with your teacher or with other students.

Answers: 1 b; 2 c; 3 c; 4 b; 5 b; 6 d; 7 a; 8 d

Test your understanding

Use the questions below to evaluate the study. Suggested answers can be found at the back of the book.

1 Sperry conducted a natural or quasi-experiment as he did not have full control over the independent variable (whether someone had had the operation to sever their corpus callosum).

a Outline one advantage of conducting quasi-experimental research.

b Outline one disadvantage of conducting quasi-experimental research.

2 The sample of Sperry's study consisted of just 11 participants.

a Explain whether you think that this can be considered a representative sample for this research.

b Outline one problem in drawing conclusions about normal brain functioning from the results gained from these 11 participants.

3 Suggest one way that data could have been collected from these participants outside the laboratory. What strengths and weaknesses do you think that this method would have?

4 How useful do you think Sperry's work is? Explain your answer.

Mind mapping

Using the mind map below make brief notes on the issues that can be used to evaluate this study. Some of the bubbles have been started for you and you should use the list below to select two further evaluation issues for this study. These issues are covered in detail on pages 176–187 of your textbook.

Ecological validity	Application to everyday life	Representativeness/generalisability
Ethics	Nature–nurture	Individual–situational explanations
Reliability	Validity	Qualitative and quantitative data
Control	Reductionism	Determinism

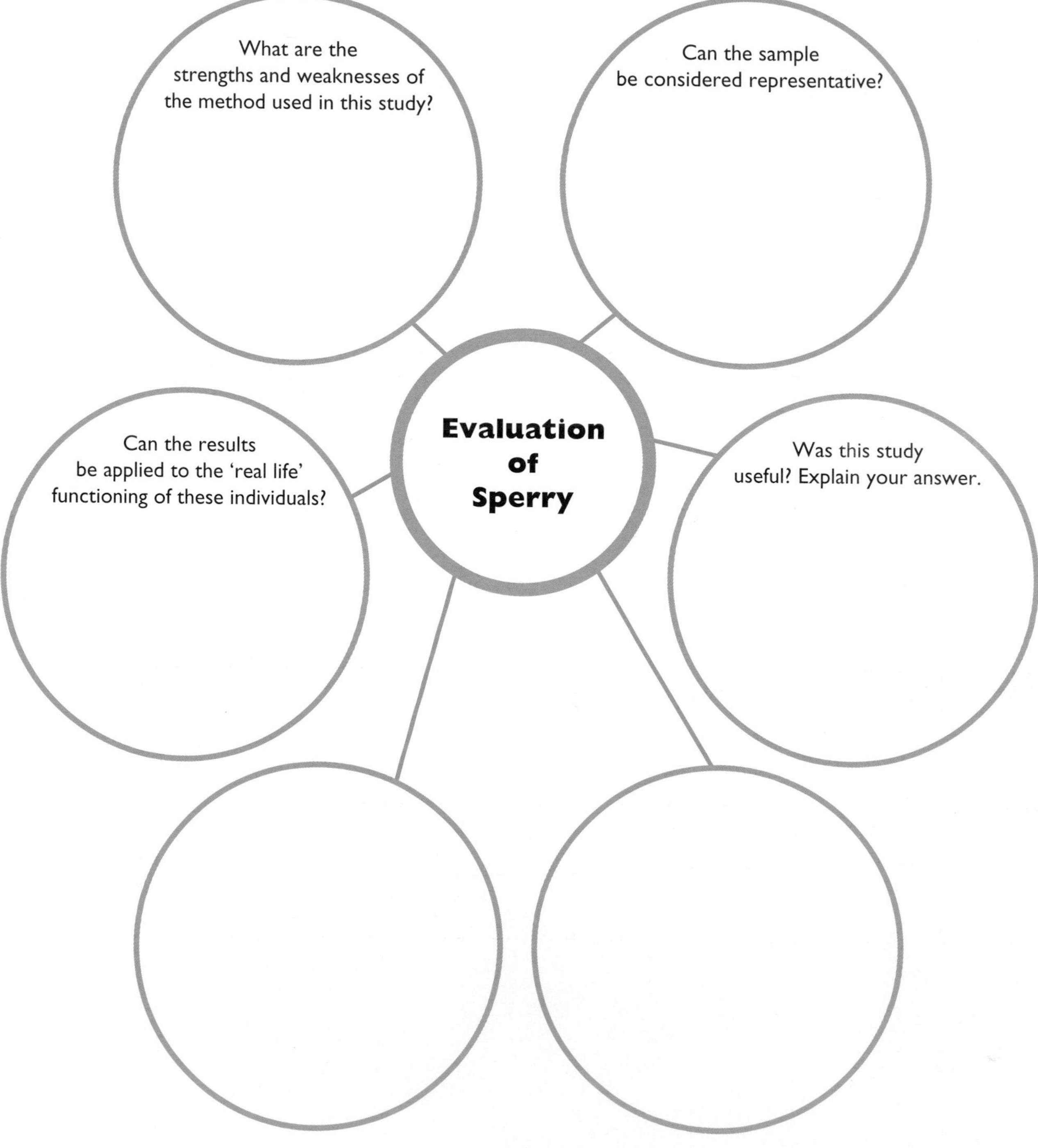

Evaluation of Sperry
What are the strengths and weaknesses of the method used in this study?
Can the sample be considered representative?
Can the results be applied to the 'real life' functioning of these individuals?
Was this study useful? Explain your answer.

Strengths and weaknesses of approach

The following tables suggest some strengths and weaknesses of the Physiological Approach in psychology. Using the three studies from this section try to complete the 'examples' column with one or more example to illustrate the strength or weakness. The first one has been done for you.

Strengths of PHYSIOLOGICAL approach		Example from Core Study
1	Uses highly controlled conditions and/or highly specialised techniques	MRI scans used in Maguire's research
2	Can demonstrate a link between brain activity and cognitive processes/behaviour	
3	Contributes to our understanding of the nature–nurture debate	
4	Can you think of any more strengths?	

Weaknesses of PHYSIOLOGICAL approach		Example from Core Study
1	Tasks may lack ecological validity	Sperry's use of highly specialised equipment
2	May be considered reductionist	
3	Some research may raise ethical concerns	
4	Can you think of any more weaknesses?	

Physiological Approach crossword

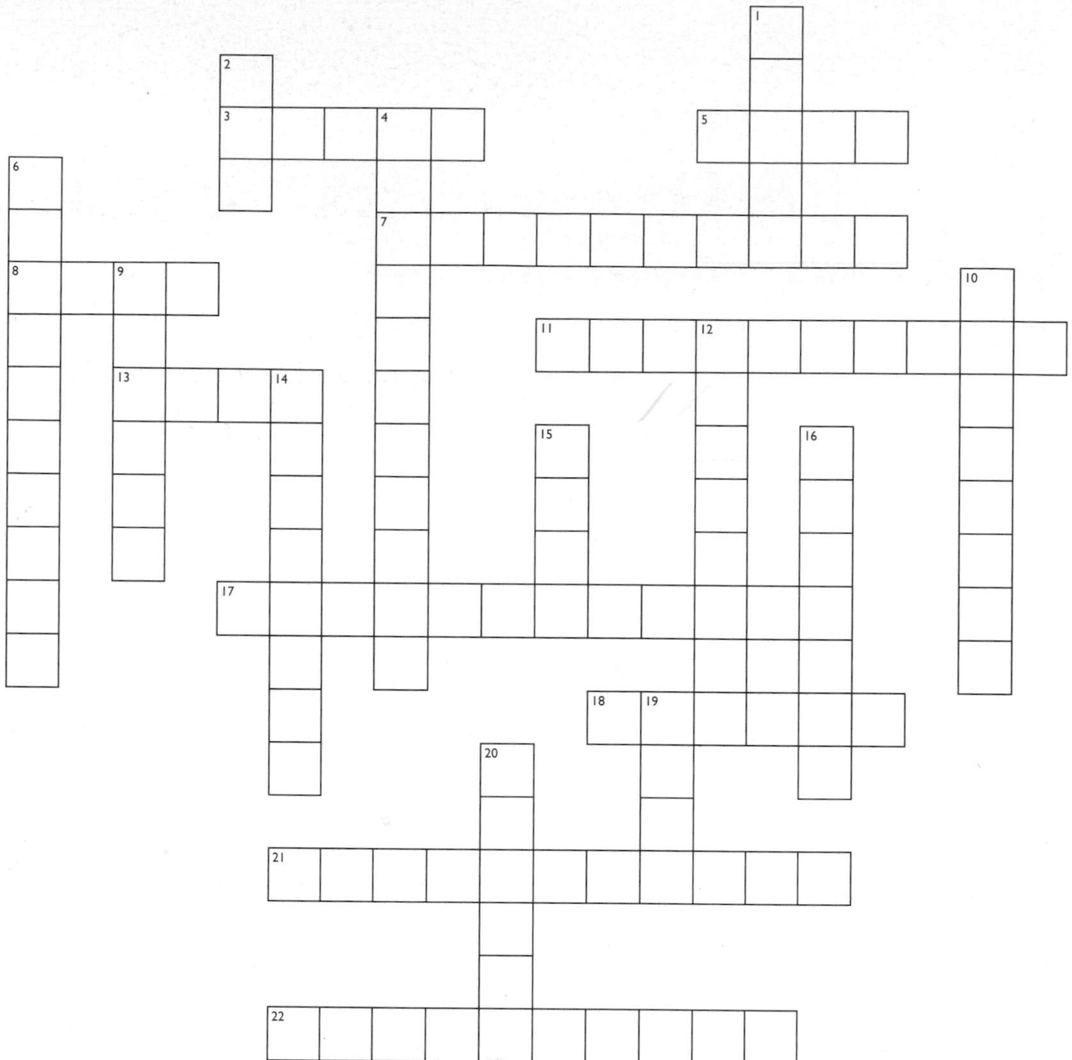

Clues

Across

3. the hemisphere which receives information from the left visual field (5)
5. the gender of the participants in the Maguire study (4)
7. Maguire's results suggest that the hippocampus has this characteristic (10)
8. used to wake the participants in the Dement and Kleitman study (4)
11. these were attached to the participants' heads (10)
13. the number of participants in the study by Dement and Kleitman (4)
17. physiological research is sometimes criticised for being this (12)
18. the number of participants in Sperry's study (6)
21. a relationship between variables (11)
22. your brain has two of them (10)

Down

1. the type of experiment used by Maguire (5)
2. the scan used in Maguire's study (11)
6. the type of experiment used by Dement and Kleitman (10)
9. Dement and Kleitman asked participants to estimate the ____ of their dreams (6)
10. someone dreaming of throwing basketballs into a net would be showing this type of eye movement (8)
12. Dement and Kleitman's participants were asked to avoid alcohol and ?
14. the participants in Sperry's study suffered from this disorder (8)
15. participants in Maguire's study drove one of these (4)
16. the number of licensed taxi drivers in the Maguire study (7)
19. the hemisphere that receives information from the right visual field (4)
20. they occur while we are asleep (6)

Answers:
Across: 3. right; 5. male; 7. plasticity; 8. bell; 11. electrodes; 13. nine; 17. reductionist; 18. eleven; 21. correlation; 22. hemisphere **Down:** 1. quasi; 2. MRI; 4. hippocampus; 6. laboratory; 9. length; 10. vertical; 12. caffeine; 14. epilepsy; 15. taxi; 16. sixteen; 19. left; 20. dreams

Milgram (1963) Behavioural study of obedience

This study is covered on pages 96–103 of your textbook

What do I need to know?

Aim

To study obedience in a laboratory situation.

Participants

- 40 males
- Aged between 20 and 50
- Range of occupations
- Recruited through direct mailing and advertisements
- Told the study was about the relationship between punishment and learning
- Paid $4.50 for participating

Method

- Laboratory observation (controlled observation)
- Rigged draw to ensure that participant was always the teacher
- Confederate to play role of learner
- Teacher given sample shock
- Learner strapped to chair and electrodes attached to wrist
- Learner (in presence of teacher) told that shocks would be painful but no permanent tissue damage would be caused
- Teacher sat in front of shock generator (15 volts to 450 volts)
- Teacher tested learner on word pairs
- Incorrect answers given on standard ratio of 3:1
- Shocks to be given for an incorrect answer starting at 15 volts and increasing in 15 volt increments to 450 shocks (shocks were not real)
- At 300 volt level learner pounded on wall
- Standard prods given by experimenter
- Full debrief and friendly reconciliation with learner

Results

- All subjects obeyed up to the 300 volt level
- Five refused after the 300 volt level
- Four refused after the 315 level
- Two refused at 330 volts
- One refused at 345, 360 and 375
- 26 continued till the 450 volt level
- Extreme tension was noted (nervous laughter etc.)
- Milgram defined obedience as continuing until the final shock level had been delivered, thus 65% (26) were defined as obedient and the remaining 35% (14) were defined as defying the experimenter's instructions.

Conclusions

Milgram suggests several explanations for this obedience. These include the location of the study at a prestigious university, the payment, the original commitment to participate, the belief that the shocks were not harmful and the fact that the learner continued to participate without complaining until the 20th shock. He concludes that obedience can be elicited from any individual given the right situational conditions. He also concludes that the extreme tension showed by the participants was due to the conflict between the desire not to hurt another person and the tendency to obey those in authority.

Test your knowledge

Answer the multiple choice questions below by ticking the correct answer(s) to test your knowledge of the study. You will find the answers at the bottom of the page.

1 *How were the participants recruited for this study?*

a) ☐ from the university
b) ☐ by adverts and direct mailing
c) ☐ they were friends of the experimenter
d) ☐ none of the above

2 *How many participants took part in the study?*

a) ☐ 40 males
b) ☐ 40 females
c) ☐ 65 males
d) ☐ 65 females

3 *Why was the draw to choose who would be the learner and who would be the teacher rigged?*

a) ☐ so that the participant would always be the learner
b) ☐ so that the participant would always be the teacher
c) ☐ so that no one would be deceived
d) ☐ so that no one would be distressed

4 *What was the predetermined ratio of wrong answers to right answers given by the learner?*

a) ☐ 2:1
b) ☐ 3:1
c) ☐ 4:1
d) ☐ 5:1

5 *At what shock level did the learner pound on the wall?*

a) ☐ 200 volts
b) ☐ 215 volts
c) ☐ 275 volts
d) ☐ 300 volts

6 *How many participants continued to 450 volts?*

a) ☐ 5
b) ☐ 26
c) ☐ 27
d) ☐ 28

7 *Which of the following are ethical concerns with the study?*

a) ☐ the deception
b) ☐ the distress
c) ☐ the results
d) ☐ both a and b

8 *Which of the following is a conclusion that can be drawn from the results of this study?*

a) ☐ our behaviour is determined by our personality
b) ☐ our behaviour is determined by the situation
c) ☐ people are inherently good
d) ☐ people are inherently evil

What do you think?

What factors would make it easier for someone to defy authority? Discuss this with your teacher or with other students.

Answers: 1 b; 2 a; 3 b; 4 b; 5 d; 6 b; 7 d; 8 b

Test your understanding

Use the questions below to evaluate the study. Suggested answers can be found at the back of the book.

1 One of the major concerns with this study involves the ethics. Outline two ethical issues that this study raises.

Issue 1

Issue 2

Suggest an alternative method that could be used for this study that would not break ethical guidelines.

What effect do you think that this alternative would have on:

The results?

The application of the results to real life?

The experience of the participants?

2 Suggest one other improvement that could be made to the original study and suggest what effect this improvement might have.

Improvement

Effect

Mind mapping

Using the mind map below make brief notes on the issues that can be used to evaluate this study. Some of the bubbles have been started for you and you should use the list below to select two further evaluation issues for this study. These issues are covered in detail on pages 176–187 of your textbook.

Ecological validity	Application to everyday life	Representativeness/generalisability
Ethics	Nature–nurture	Individual–situational explanations
Reliability	Validity	Qualitative and quantitative data
Control	Reductionism	Determinism

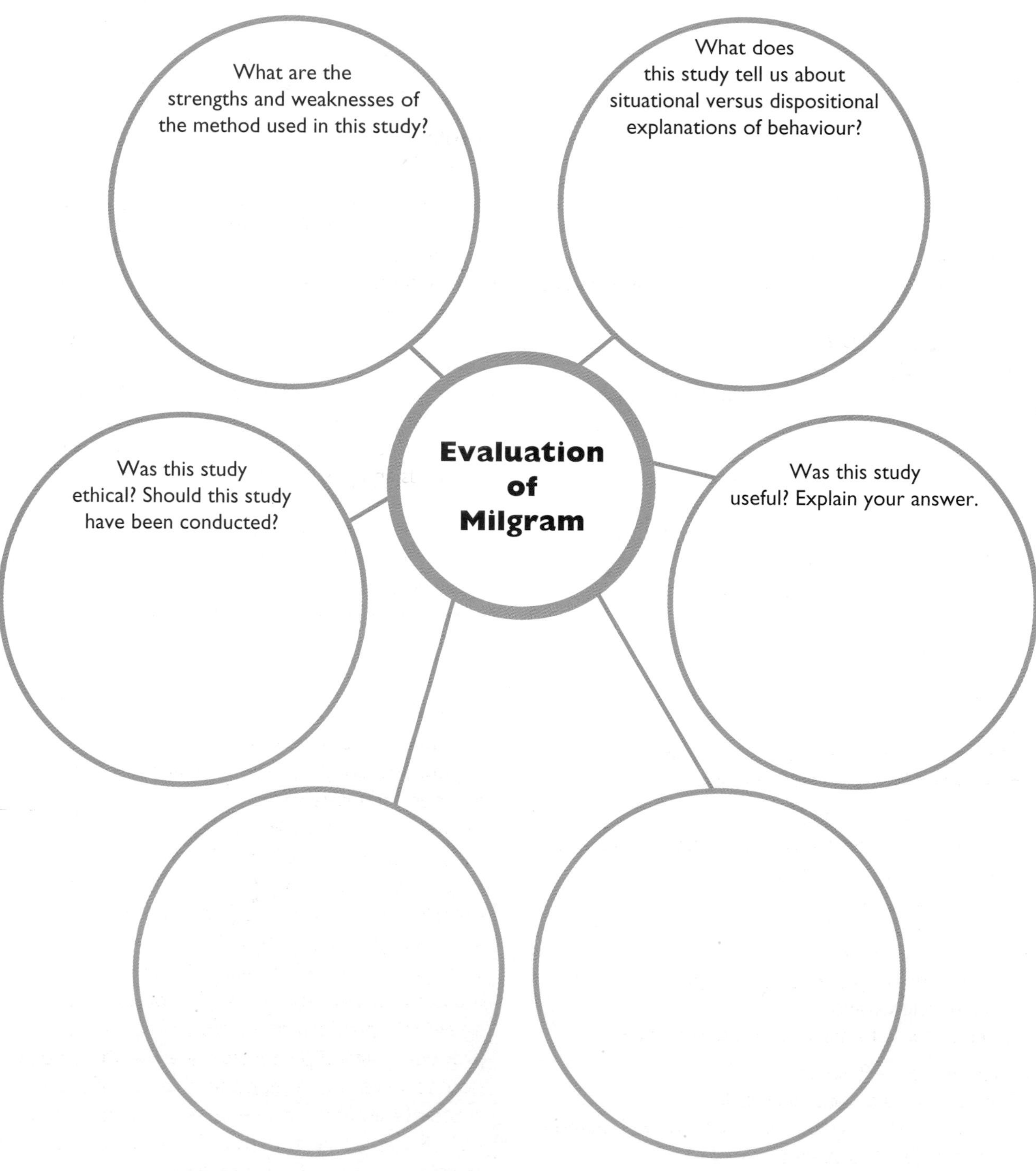

What are the strengths and weaknesses of the method used in this study?
What does this study tell us about situational versus dispositional explanations of behaviour?
Evaluation of Milgram
Was this study ethical? Should this study have been conducted?
Was this study useful? Explain your answer.

Reicher and Haslam (2006) Rethinking the psychology of tyranny: the BBC prison study

This study is covered on pages 104–111 of your textbook

What do I need to know?

Aim

The most important aim of the study was to analyse the conditions that lead individuals to identify with their groups and the conditions that lead individuals to accept or challenge intergroup inequalities. The study also aimed to provide data on interactions between groups of unequal status and to examine the role of social, organisational and clinical factors in group behaviour.

Participants

- 15 males
- Selected from an original pool of 332 who responded to adverts in national press and leaflets
- Screening process to ensure that only well adjusted and pro-social participants were included
- Conducted in three stages:
  1. psychometric tests to assess a range of social and clinical variables
  2. full weekend assessment by independent clinical psychologists
  3. medical and character references and police checks
- Final choice was made to ensure diversity of age, social class and ethnic background
- Final 15 allocated into five groups of three closely matched on personality variables
- One of each group randomly selected to be a guard and the other two to be prisoners.
- Nine prisoners and five guards at the start of the study
- The 10th prisoner was introduced later (see below)

Method

- Laboratory study
- Prison environment constructed in television studio
- Prisoners in lockable three-person cells

Induction process – Guards:

- Invited to hotel the evening before the study started
- Told they would be guards
- Given prison timetable
- Told their responsibility was to ensure that the institution ran smoothly
- Asked to draw up a series of punishments for prisoner rule violation
- Given uniform: formal trousers, shirt and tie

Induction process – Prisoners:

- Nine prisoners arrived individually
- Heads shaved and given uniform: t-shirt with number, loose trousers and sandals
- Given list of prison rules and prisoners' rights

Independent variables:

- Day 3: told movement between groups was no longer possible
- Day 6: told that allocation to prisoner/guard was in fact random (i.e. no differences existed between groups)
- Day 7: new prisoner introduced (trade union official)

Dependent variables:

- social, organisational and clinical variables measured via the following:
  1. video and audio recordings wherever participants were
  2. daily psychometric testing
  3. daily saliva swabs

Results

- Prisoners' behaviour was compliant to begin with
- Manipulation on Day 3 created stronger sense of group and lack of cooperation with guards and compliance with rules
- Manipulation on Day 5 also led to marked decrease in compliance
- New prisoner on Day 7 led to organised breakout and collapse of the prisoner–guard structure
- Prisoners and guards established a 'self-governing, self-disciplining commune'
- Some lost faith with this and a number of former guards and prisoners decided to become the new guards – asked for black berets and dark glasses to symbolise their desired authoritarian regime
- Remainder did nothing to defend commune – lack of individual and collective will
- For ethical reasons the study was terminated on Day 8

Conclusions

The study is compared to the Stanford Prison Experiment conducted by Zimbardo and others. Reicher and Haslam suggest that although the results of their study are similar, the path that the participants took to reach this outcome is very different. They claim that events were determined by the failure of the guards to develop a shared identity and the failure of the commune, which prevented any positive change, hence the authoritarian regime was accepted. They agree with previous researchers that tyranny is a product of group processes but argue that people do not mindlessly conform to roles and do not automatically abuse power when in a group. Group identification occurs when it makes sense to people to identify with a group and their values.

Test your knowledge

Answer the multiple choice questions below by ticking the correct answer(s) to test your knowledge of the study. You will find the answers at the bottom of the page.

1 *How long was the experiment intended to last for?*

a) ☐ 6 days
b) ☐ 8 days
c) ☐ 10 days
d) ☐ 12 days

2 *How many phases of screening were there?*

a) ☐ 1
b) ☐ 2
c) ☐ 3
d) ☐ 4

3 *What did the psychometric tests measure?*

a) ☐ social and clinical variables
b) ☐ intelligence
c) ☐ psychoticism
d) ☐ altruism

4 *What happened on Day 3?*

a) ☐ told movement between groups was no longer possible
b) ☐ told that allocation to prisoner/guard was in fact random
c) ☐ new prisoner introduced (trade union official)
d) ☐ the study was stopped

5 *What happened on Day 6?*

a) ☐ told movement between groups was no longer possible
b) ☐ told that allocation to prisoner/guard was in fact random
c) ☐ new prisoner introduced (trade union official)
d) ☐ the study was stopped

6 *What happened on Day 7?*

a) ☐ told movement between groups was no longer possible
b) ☐ told that allocation to prisoner/guard was in fact random
c) ☐ new prisoner introduced (trade union official)
d) ☐ the study was stopped

7 *Why did the prisoners' compliance with rules drop after Day 3?*

a) ☐ because they were told that there was no chance of them being promoted to guards
b) ☐ because they were bored
c) ☐ because a new prisoner had been introduced
d) ☐ because the experimenters told them to stop obeying the guards

8 *Why did the new guards ask for black berets and dark glasses?*

a) ☐ because they thought they would look cool
b) ☐ because it was symbolic of the new liberal regime
c) ☐ because it was symbolic of the new democratic regime
d) ☐ because it was symbolic of the new authoritarian regime

What do you think?

This study was broadcast on television. What effects could the knowledge that they were going to be on television have had on the participants' behaviour? Discuss this with your teacher or with other students.

Answers: 1 c; 2 c; 3 a; 4 a; 5 b; 6 c; 7 a; 8 d

Test your understanding

Use the questions below to evaluate the study. Suggested answers can be found at the back of the book.

1 This study collected a huge amount of different sorts of data. Give one example of quantitative data that was collected in this study and one example of qualitative data that was collected in this study.

Quantitative data

Qualitative data

Suggest one strength and one weakness with each example that you have given above.

Strength of quantitative data

Weakness

Strength of qualitative data

Weakness

2 Outline one weakness with the way that the study was conducted and suggest how you would overcome this.

What effect do you think this would have on the results?

Mind mapping

Using the mind map below make brief notes on the issues that can be used to evaluate this study. Some of the bubbles have been started for you and you should use the list below to select two further evaluation issues for this study. These issues are covered in detail on pages 176–187 of your textbook.

Ecological validity	Application to everyday life	Representativeness/generalisability
Ethics	Nature–nurture	Individual–situational explanations
Reliability	Validity	Qualitative and quantitative data
Control	Reductionism	Determinism

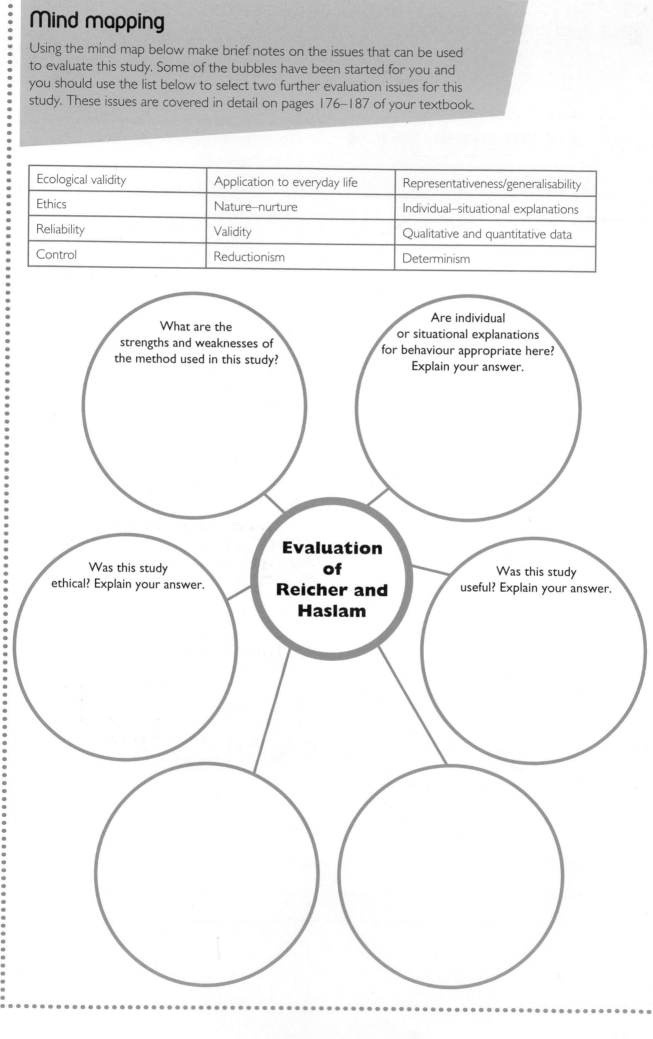

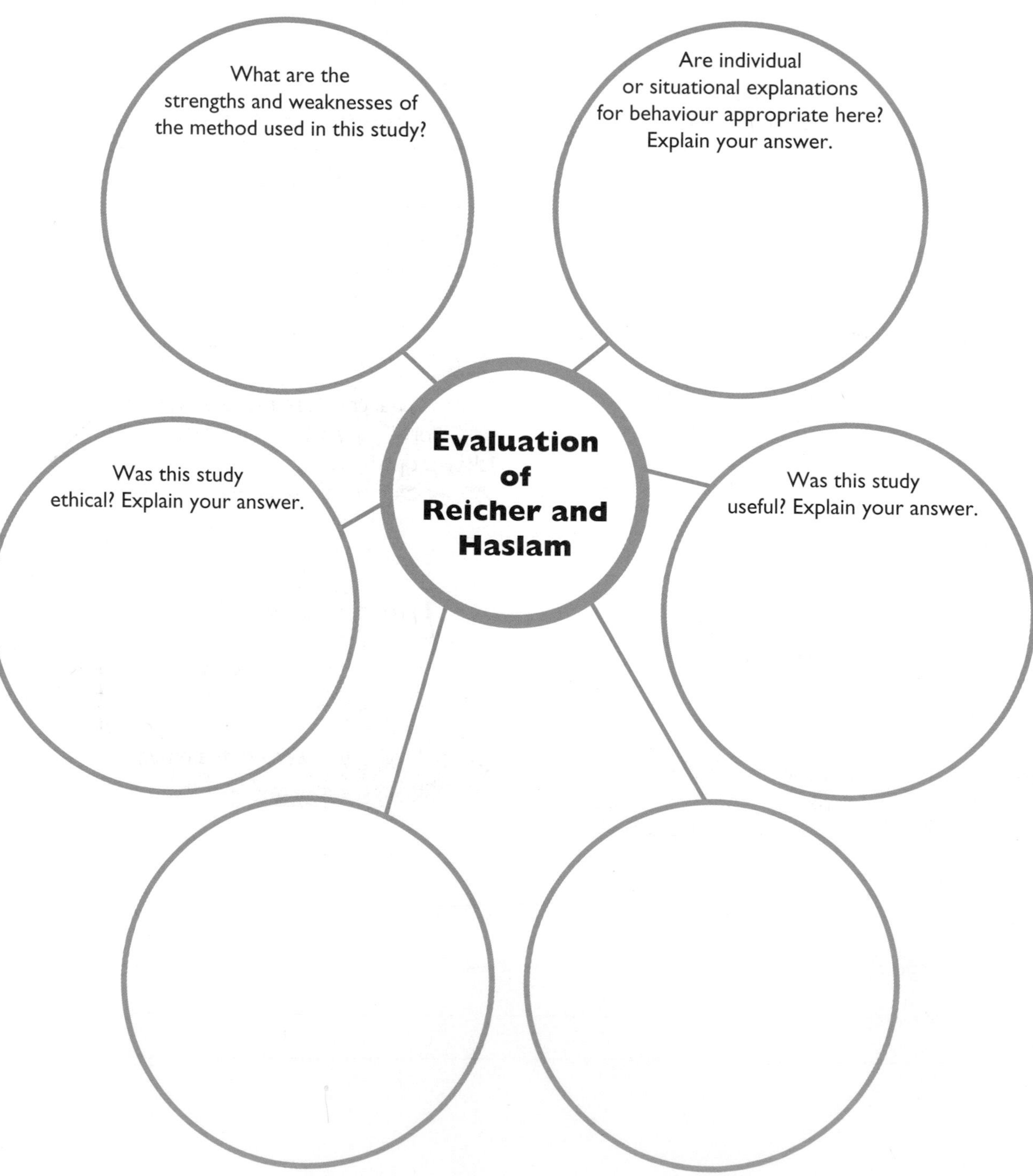

Evaluation of Reicher and Haslam
What are the strengths and weaknesses of the method used in this study?
Are individual or situational explanations for behaviour appropriate here? Explain your answer.
Was this study ethical? Explain your answer.
Was this study useful? Explain your answer.

Piliavin, Rodin and Piliavin (1969) Good Samaritanism: An underground phenomenon

This study is covered on pages 112–119 of your textbook

What do I need to know?

Aim

To investigate a situational explanation of bystander behaviour; how features of an emergency situation (race of victim, state of victim, no. of bystanders and presence of model) influence helping behaviour.

Participants

- 4450
- Men and women
- Average 45% black 55% white
- Using train between 11am and 3pm
- Over period of two months in 1968

Method

- Field experiment
- On New York subway
- Seven and a half minute journey
- 103 trials carried out
- Four teams of four people (two observers, victim, model)
- Emergency staged 70 seconds into journey
- Victim staggered forward and collapsed

Conditions (independent variables):

- Black victim
- White victim
- Drunk victim
- Ill victim
- Early model (critical/adjacent area)
- Late model (critical/adjacent area)
- Number of bystanders present varied naturally on each journey

Observers recorded (dependent variables):

- The time taken for the first passenger to help
- The total number of passengers who helped
- The gender, race and location of every helper
- The time taken for the first passenger to offer help after the model had assisted

Controls:

- Standardised procedure e.g. victim always collapsed in same way
- The victim in each team wore same clothes
- Observers recorded unobtrusively
- After each trial confederates got on the train going in the opposite direction to avoid the same passengers

Results

- More help given to the ill victim
- Men were most often first to help (90%)
- Some tendency for same race helping (drunk condition)
- No evidence of diffusion of responsibility
- Effect of model difficult to assess

Conclusions

Piliavin et al conclude that their research supports a situational explanation of bystander behaviour and they propose the Arousal: Cost–Reward Model; an heuristic device that can be used to predict helping behaviour in emergency situations. This proposes that emergency situations create arousal and this is increased with identification/empathy with the victim, proximity to the victim and the length of time the emergency continues without help being offered. Arousal is reduced by helping (directly or indirectly), leaving the scene of the emergency or rejecting the victim as undeserving of help. In this study, leaving the scene of the emergency was not possible.

Test your knowledge

Answer the multiple choice questions below by ticking the correct answer(s) to test your knowledge of the study. You will find the answers at the bottom of the page.

1 *What does a 'situational explanation' suggest about bystander behaviour?*

a) ☐ personality determines whether someone will help
b) ☐ characteristics of the emergency situation determines whether help is given
c) ☐ a person chooses whether or not to help (free will)
d) ☐ none of the above

2 *The purpose of the 'model' in the subway study was:*

a) ☐ to see if someone helping would increase helping
b) ☐ to provide assistance if no one else helped.
c) ☐ to encourage others to help
d) ☐ both a and b

3 *The method used in the subway study was a:*

a) ☐ laboratory experiment
b) ☐ case study
c) ☐ field experiment
d) ☐ self report

4 *Which of the following was an independent variable in the study?*

a) ☐ race of the victim
b) ☐ gender of the victim
c) ☐ both a and b
d) ☐ amount of helping

5 *'Diffusion of responsibility' refers to:*

a) ☐ more help being given the greater the number of other bystanders present
b) ☐ the amount of help given
c) ☐ less help being given the greater the number of other bystanders present
d) ☐ the amount of responsibility experienced by bystanders

6 *Piliavin, Rodin and Piliavin proposed which explanation of bystander behaviour?*

a) ☐ the Arousal: Cost–Reward Model
b) ☐ Social Learning Theory
c) ☐ imitation
d) ☐ modelling

7 *How many participants took part in the subway study?*

a) ☐ 450
b) ☐ 4000
c) ☐ 4450
d) ☐ 2450

8 *How was data collected in the subway study?*

a) ☐ self report
b) ☐ observation
c) ☐ psychometric testing
d) ☐ none of the above

What do you think?

What other methods could be used to investigate helping behaviour? Discuss this with your teacher or with other students.

Answers: 1 b; 2 d; 3 c; 4 c; 5 c; 6 a; 7 c; 8 b

Test your understanding

Use the questions below to evaluate the study. Suggested answers can be found at the back of the book.

1 The sample was approximately 4450 men and women who used the trains on weekdays between the hours of 11am and 3pm.

a Suggest an alternative sample for this study.

b Describe one strength and one weakness of this alternative sample.

Strength

Weakness

2 This study was a field experiment. Describe an alternative method that could be used to investigate the same characteristics of bystander behaviour.

Outline one strength and one weakness of this alternative method.

Strength

Weakness

What effect might this alternative method have on the results?

3 Suggest one way of improving the ethics of this study.

Explain one methodological implication of this change.

Mind mapping.

Using the mind map below make brief notes on the issues that can be used to evaluate this study. Some of the bubbles have been started for you and you should use the list below to select two further evaluation issues for this study. These issues are covered in detail on pages 176–187 of your textbook.

Ecological validity	Application to everyday life	Representativeness/generalisability
Ethics	Nature–nurture	Individual–situational explanations
Reliability	Validity	Qualitative and quantitative data
Control	Reductionism	Determinism

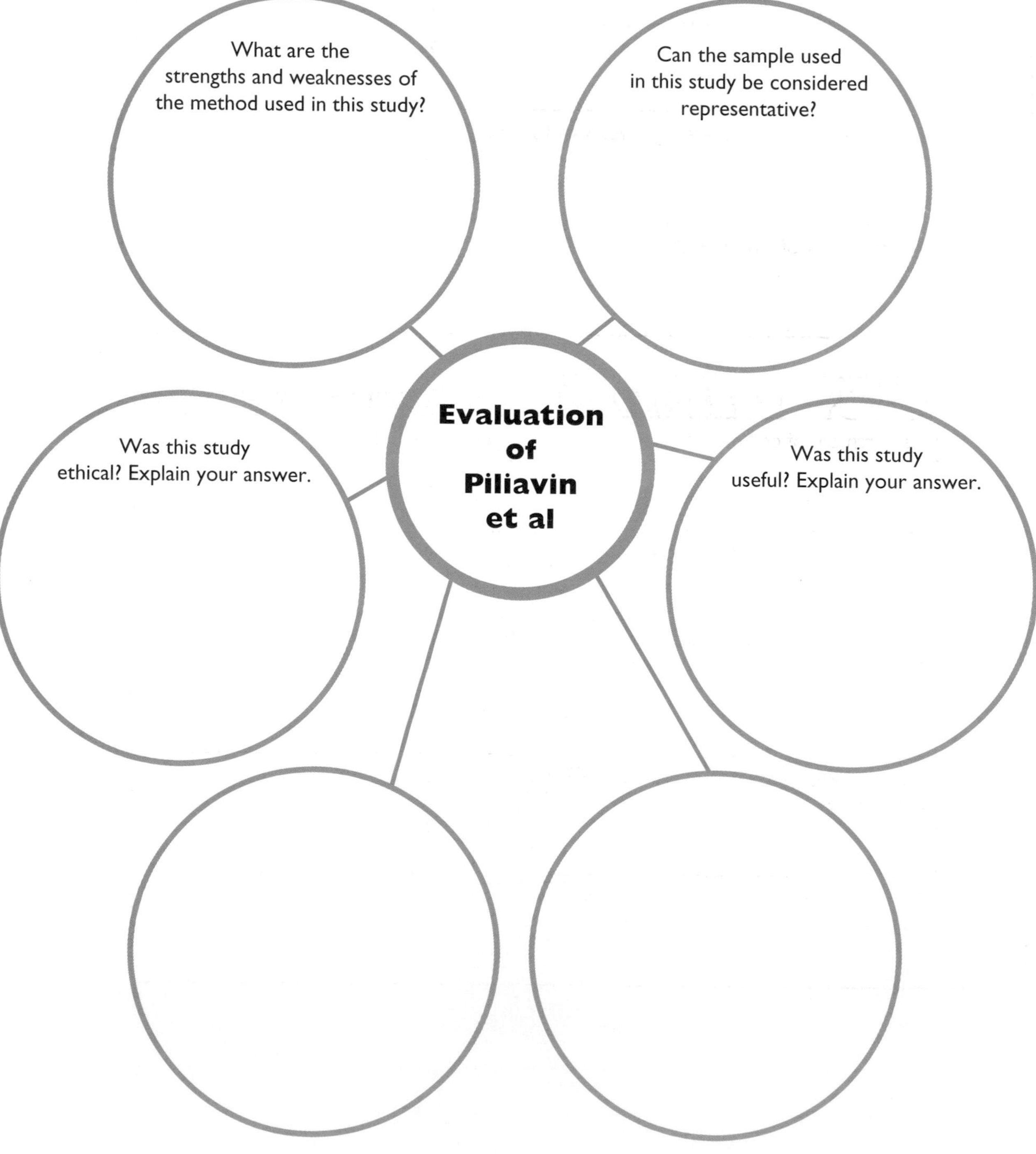

Evaluation of Piliavin et al
What are the strengths and weaknesses of the method used in this study?
Can the sample used in this study be considered representative?
Was this study ethical? Explain your answer.
Was this study useful? Explain your answer.

Strengths and weaknesses of approach

The following tables suggest some strengths and weaknesses of the Social Approach in psychology. Using the three studies from this section try to complete the 'examples' column with one or more examples to illustrate the strength or weakness. The first one has been done for you.

Strengths of SOCIAL approach		Example from Core Study
1	Demonstrates the extent to which situational factors affect behaviour	Milgram showed the power of authority
2	Demonstrates the power of interpersonal factors and group membership	
3	Field studies have high ecological validity	
4	Investigates issues which are highly relevant to society	
5	Can you think of any more strengths?	

Weaknesses of SOCIAL approach		Example from Core Study
1	Research can often be unethical	Deception in Piliavin
2	Laboratory studies can have low ecological validity	
3	Demand characteristics can be high	
4	May be dependent on culture, society, historical context etc.	
5	Can you think of any more weaknesses?	

Social Studies crossword

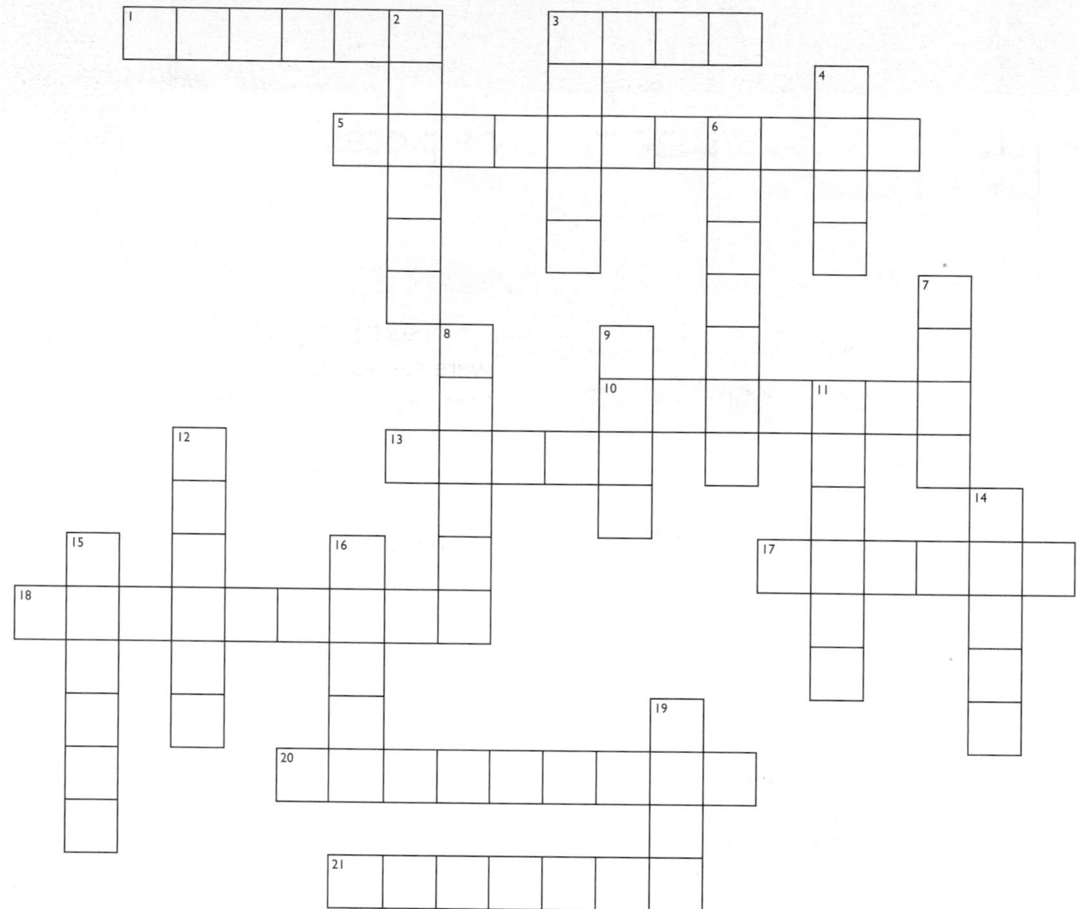

Clues

Across

1. there were five of these in the Reicher and Haslam study (6)
3. the number of recipients who refused to carry on shocking the learner after 300 volts (4)
5. Milgram conducted a controlled version of this (11)
10. Piliavin claimed that an emergency situation creates this in a bystander (7)
17. he would help if nobody else did in the Piliavin et al study (6)
18. there were ten of these in the Reicher and Haslam study (9)
20. Milgram's study could be described as this (9)
21. this was created by the participants in the Reicher and Haslam study (7)

Down

2. where Piliavin et al conducted their research (6)
3. the number of participants in the Milgram study (5)
4. the number of prods used in the Milgram study (4)
6. Milgram suggested that the experiment created this in participants (7)
7. the learner pounded on this in the Milgram study (4)
8. Reicher and Haslam studied the way these work (6)
9. the gender of the participants in the Reicher and Haslam study (4)
11. daily swabs of this were taken in the Reicher and Haslam study (6)
12. Reicher and Haslam created a mock one (6)
14. the type of experiment conducted by Piliavin et al (5)
15. 103 of these in the Piliavin study (6)
16. the day that the new prisoner was introduced in the Reicher and Haslam study (5)
19. the university where Milgram conducted his research (4)

Answers:
Across: 1. guards; 3. five; 5. observation; 10. arousal; 13. model; 17. victim; 18. prisoners; 20. unethical; 21. commune
Down: 2. subway; 3. forty; 4. four; 6. tension; 7. wall; 8. groups; 9. male; 11. saliva; 12. prison; 14. field; 15. trials; 16. seven; 19. Yale

Individual Differences Studies

Rosenhan (1973) On being sane in insane places

This study is covered on pages 124–131 of your textbook

What do I need to know?

Aim

This study aimed to test the hypothesis that psychiatric diagnosis was neither reliable nor valid. Is it possible to distinguish the sane from the insane within a psychiatric institution?

Study one

Participants

- Staff at 12 different psychiatric hospitals in America
- Range of old and new hospitals
- The staff did not know that the research was taking place

Method

- Participant observation
- Eight pseudo-patients including Rosenhan himself
- Three women and five men
- Range of occupations
- Each contacted the hospital for an appointment
- Claimed that they were hearing voices (of the same sex as them) saying words like 'empty', 'hollow' and 'thud'
- Used false names but all the other information they supplied was accurate
- All but one admitted with diagnosis of schizophrenia
- Once they were admitted they stopped displaying any symptoms of abnormality and started behaving normally
- Took notes on their experiences
- Collected data on the way that the hospital staff interacted with the patients

Results

- Length of time in hospital varied from 7 to 52 days
- Mean was 19 days
- No detection by staff (although some patients were suspicious)
- Discharged with diagnosis 'schizophrenia in remission' (rarely used)
- Behaviours interpreted within the context of schizophrenia. Examples:
  1. Normal account of a pseudo-patient's relationship was interpreted as dysfunctional within the psychiatric context.
  2. Queuing early for lunch was described as 'oral-acquisitive syndrome'.
  3. Taking notes was described as 'writing behaviour'.
- Very little contact with hospital staff

Interaction	Response rates
Responses to requests made to psychiatrists	13 responses to a total of 185 requests 7%
Responses to requests made to nurses and attendants	47 responses to a total of 1,283 requests 3.6%
Amount of time spent with psychologists, psychiatrists etc	Average was less than 7 minutes a day

- Feelings of powerlessness and depersonalisation

  '... the patient is deprived of many of his legal rights ... his freedom of movement is restricted, he cannot initiate contact with staff ... personal privacy is minimal, his personal history is available to any staff member (including volunteers) who chooses to read his file, and water closets [toilets] may have no doors'

Rosenhan (1973)

- Staff are making Type 2 errors (false positives)

Study two

- Large teaching and research hospital
- Knew about the first study
- Told to expect pseudo-patients over the next three months

Results

- 193 patients were rated – 41 suspected of being pseudo-patients by at least one member of staff (23 by at least one psychiatrist and 19 by a psychiatrist and one other staff member)
- No pseudo-patients were actually sent
- Staff are making Type 1 errors (false negatives) in attempt to avoid making Type 2 errors

Conclusions

The process of diagnosis is open to many errors. The hospital environment and the 'labels' given to the patients influence perceptions of behaviour making them more likely to be interpreted as insane.

What do you think?

What do you think it might have been like to be a pseudo-patient in this study? Discuss this with your teacher or with other students.

Test your knowledge

Answer the multiple choice questions below by ticking the correct answer(s) to test your knowledge of the study. You will find the answers at the bottom of the page.

1 *What is the advantage of classifying mental health problems into identifiable groups?*

a) ☐ so that people can be labelled
b) ☐ communication between doctors/psychiatrists is easier as they can be confident that they are talking about the same illness
c) ☐ so that we know who is mentally ill
d) ☐ so that we can research them

2 *Why is the diagnosis of mental health problems more problematic than the diagnosis of physical health problems?*

a) ☐ because the pseudo patients were not telling the truth
b) ☐ symptoms of mental health problems are more objective and less subjective than physical health problems
c) ☐ symptoms of mental health problems are more subjective and less objective than physical health problems
d) ☐ it is not more problematic

3 *What is a pseudo-patient?*

a) ☐ a schizophrenic patient
b) ☐ a depressive patient
c) ☐ a cured patient
d) ☐ a researcher posing as a patient

4 *A Type 2 error is a false positive. Which of the following is an example of a Type 2 error from the study?*

a) ☐ admitting an insane person to the hospital
b) ☐ admitting a sane person to the hospital
c) ☐ not admitting an insane person
d) ☐ not admitting a sane person

5 *Which one of the following is not a finding from the study?*

a) ☐ normal behaviours interpreted as abnormal within the hospital environment
b) ☐ patient records kept safely under lock and key
c) ☐ patient records available for anyone to see
d) ☐ staff spent hardly any time with patients

6 *What was the average length of time that the pseudo-patients spent in the hospitals?*

a) ☐ 7 days
b) ☐ 19 days
c) ☐ 45 days
d) ☐ 52 days

7 *Rosenhan conducted his research using the participant observation method. Which of the following statements best describes this method?*

a) ☐ a method of observation where the researcher is also a participant in the activity or environment being studied
b) ☐ a method of observation where participants observe themselves
c) ☐ a method of observation where participants know they are being observed
d) ☐ a method of observation which uses a detailed coding scheme

8 *Which of the following best describes the findings of the second study conducted by Rosenhan?*

a) ☐ psychiatrists thought that everyone was a pseudo-patient
b) ☐ no one was thought to be a pseudo-patient
c) ☐ 41 out of 193 patients were suspected of being pseudo-patients
d) ☐ 141 out of 193 patients were suspected of being pseudo-patients

Answers: 1 b; 2 c; 3 d; 4 b; 5 b; 6 b; 7 a; 8 c

Test your understanding

Use the questions below to evaluate the study. Suggested answers can be found at the back of the book.

1 This research can be described as using the participant observation method.

a Outline one advantage of this method

b Outline one disadvantage of this method

2 This research has been criticised for being unethical.

a Outline the ethical issues raised by this study

b Suggest how this research could be conducted without breaking ethical guidelines

c What effect do you think that this would have on the findings?

3 Do you think that this research should have been conducted? Give reasons for your answer.

Mind mapping

Using the mind map below make brief notes on the issues that can be used to evaluate this study. Some of the bubbles have been started for you and you should use the list below to select two further evaluation issues for this study. These issues are covered in detail on pages 176–187 of your textbook.

Ecological validity	Application to everyday life	Representativeness/generalisability
Ethics	Nature–nurture	Individual–situational explanations
Reliability	Validity	Qualitative and quantitative data
Control	Reductionism	Determinism

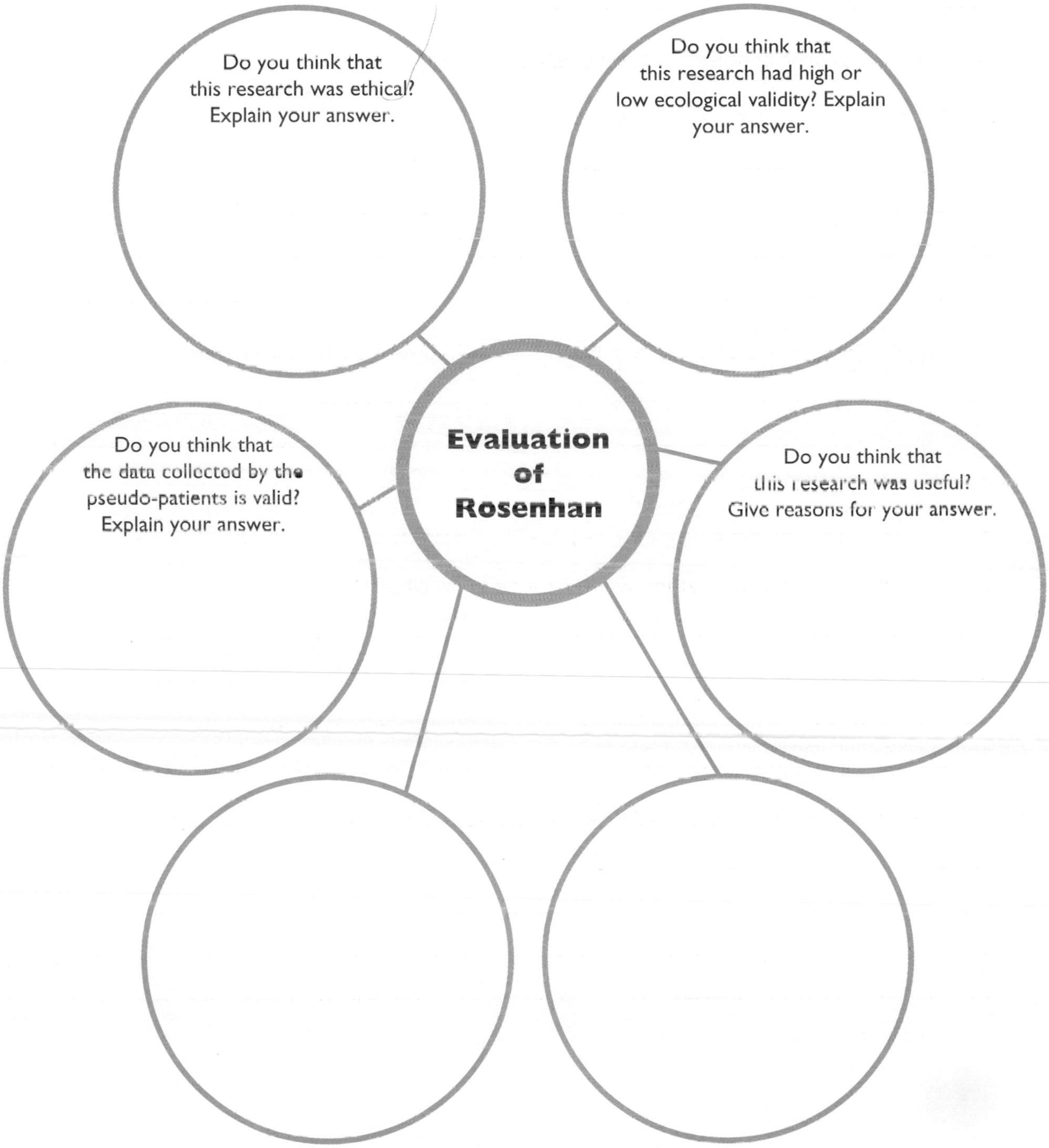

Evaluation of Rosenhan

Do you think that this research was ethical? Explain your answer.

Do you think that this research had high or low ecological validity? Explain your answer.

Do you think that the data collected by the pseudo-patients is valid? Explain your answer.

Do you think that this research was useful? Give reasons for your answer.

This study is covered on pages 132–139 of your textbook

Thigpen and Cleckley (1957) A case of multiple personality

What do I need to know?

Aim

To report on the diagnosis and therapy of a single case of Multiple Personality Disorder.

Participant

- Eve White (real name Christine Sizemore)
- 25 years old

Method

- Case study
- Originally referred to therapist for severe headaches and memory loss of a recent trip
- Treatment involved therapeutic interviews and occasional hypnosis
- Family members interviewed for background and to corroborate information
- Variety of tests used including:
  1. Psychometric testing
     - Weschler-Bellevue Intelligence test
     - Weschler Memory test
  2. Projective testing
     - Rorschach
     - Personality
  3. EEG
     - Therapy lasted 14 months
     - Approx 100 hours of sessions

Results

- Initially the therapists felt that this was an ordinary case with common symptoms mainly brought on by marital problems
- Memory loss restored by hypnosis
- Letter received a few days later finished in a different handwriting and which EW claimed to have no memory of posting
- EW asked if hearing voices meant she was insane
- Dramatic change of personality described by therapists
- Therapists gradually discover existence of second personality (Eve Black)
- Eve Black has had independent existence since EW's childhood
- EB conscious at all times
- EW no awareness of existence of EB and no conscious awareness when EB is 'out'
- EW described as quiet, feminine and dignified
- EB as lacking compassion, shallow, hedonistic and irresponsible
- Testing revealed:
  1. Differences in IQ (Eve White 110 and Eve Black 104)
  2. Eve White superior score on Memory test
  3. Projective tests suggest that Eve White had a repressive personality and Eve Black had a regressive personality
- A third personality (Jane) appeared later in the therapy
- Jane described as more mature, more vivid, more capable and more interesting than Eve White and without the faults and inadequacies of Eve Black
- EEG results showed Eve Black to be the most different, and Eve White and Jane difficult to distinguish from each other

Conclusions

This is a report of a single case and concludes only that Eve was suffering from MPD probably brought on by childhood trauma, that Jane may offer a partial resolution to the problem of integrating the personalities and that more research is needed into this disorder.

Test your knowledge

Answer the multiple choice questions below by ticking the correct answer(s) to test your knowledge of the study. You will find the answers at the bottom of the page.

1 *Multiple Personality Disorder is now referred to as Dissociative Identity Disorder (DID). Which of the following statements is the best description of DID?*

a) ☐ someone with a split brain
b) ☐ a type of schizophrenia
c) ☐ the existence of more than one personality which are totally separate and may be unaware of each other
d) ☐ an anxiety disorder

2 *Which of the following is the correct definition of a case study?*

a) ☐ an in-depth study of a single case
b) ☐ a study using hypnosis
c) ☐ a study of large numbers of people
d) ☐ a study conducted outside of a laboratory

3 *Which of the following is a strength of a case study?*

a) ☐ there are lots of participants
b) ☐ it enables an in depth examination of an individual
c) ☐ it is easily generalisable to others
d) ☐ it is quick and easy to conduct

4 *Which of the following is a weakness of a case study?*

a) ☐ there are too many participants
b) ☐ it is difficult to generalise the results to others
c) ☐ there is too much control
d) ☐ it produces in-depth data

5 *What was unusual about the letter sent to Thigpen and Cleckley by Eve?*

a) ☐ they didn't understand it
b) ☐ the handwriting changed at the end
c) ☐ Eve had no memory of posting the letter
d) ☐ both b and c

6 *Which of the following statements best describes the results from the IQ testing?*

a) ☐ Eve White had an IQ of 110 and Eve Black had an IQ of 104
b) ☐ Eve White had an IQ of 104 and Eve Black had an IQ of 110
c) ☐ Eve White had an IQ of 100 and Eve Black had an IQ of 101
d) ☐ they both had the same scores

7 *Which of the following best describes the results from the projective testing?*

a) ☐ Eve White was described as regressive and Eve Black as repressive
b) ☐ Eve White was described as repressive and Eve Black as regressive
c) ☐ Eve White had a higher IQ than Eve Black
d) ☐ Eve Black had a higher IQ than Eve White

8 *Which of the following statements best describes the resolution of the therapy conducted by Thigpen and Cleckley?*

a) ☐ to get rid of Eve Black
b) ☐ to get rid of Eve White
c) ☐ to get rid of Jane
d) ☐ to integrate the personalities

What do you think?

Do you believe that Eve had Multiple Personality Disorder? What other explanations might there be? Discuss this with your teacher or with other students.

Answers: 1 c; 2 a; 3 b; 4 b; 5 d; 6 a; 7 b; 8 d

Test your understanding

Use the questions below to evaluate the study. Suggested answers can be found at the back of the book.

1 This study was a case study as there was a single participant.

a Outline one advantage of using a case study for this research.

b Outline one disadvantage of using a case study for this research.

2 a Suggest one improvement that could be made to this study.

b Outline the effect that this improvement might have on the results of the study.

3 a Explain what is meant by the term 'researcher bias'.

b Give one example of possible researcher bias in this study.

4 Do you think that this research was useful? Give reasons for your answer.

Mind mapping

Using the mind map below make brief notes on the issues that can be used to evaluate this study. Some of the bubbles have been started for you and you should use the list below to select two further evaluation issues for this study. These issues are covered in detail on pages 176–187 of your textbook.

Ecological validity	Application to everyday life	Representativeness/generalisability
Ethics	Nature–nurture	Individual–situational explanations
Reliability	Validity	Qualitative and quantitative data
Control	Reductionism	Determinism

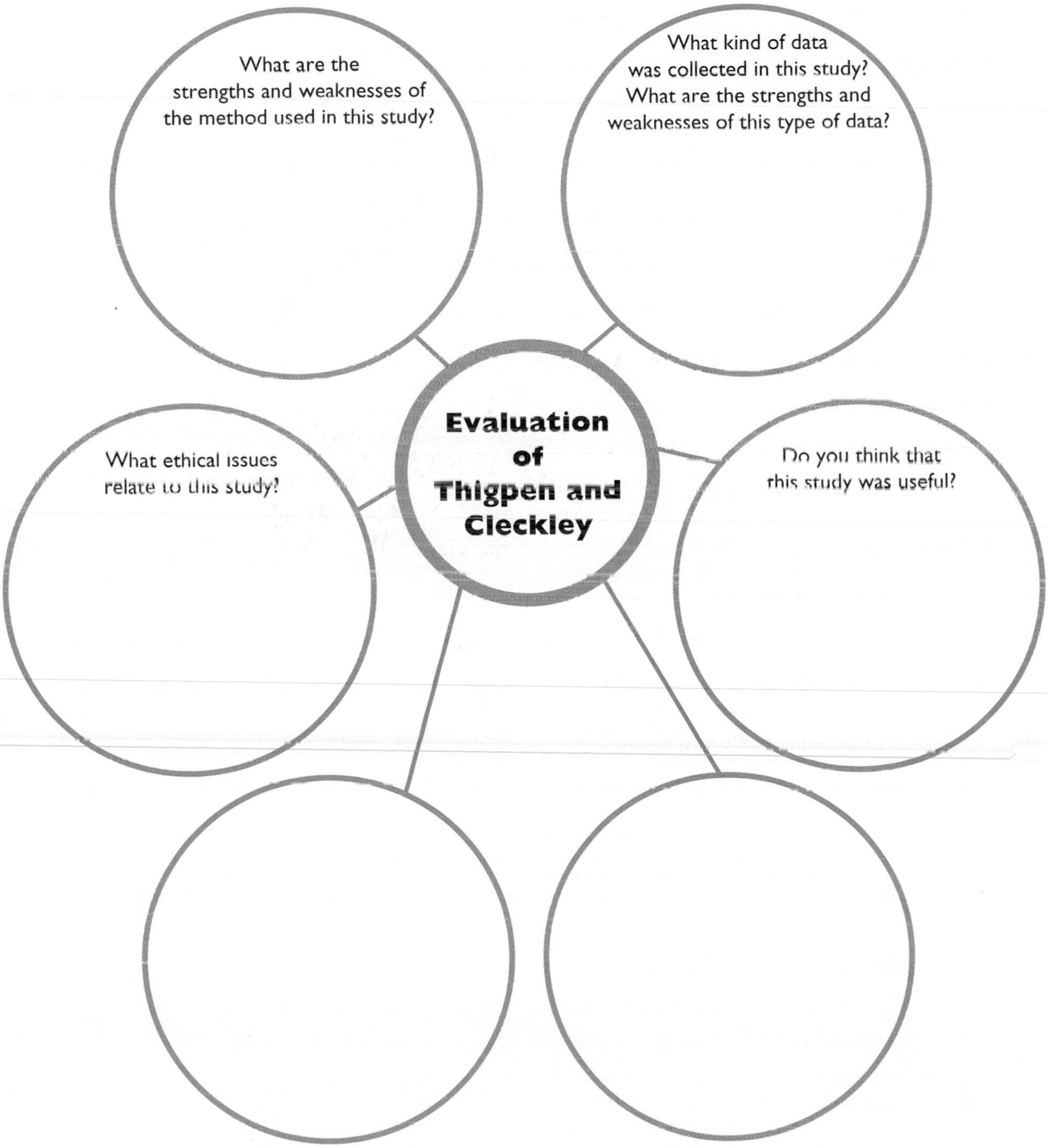

Evaluation of Thigpen and Cleckley

What are the strengths and weaknesses of the method used in this study?

What kind of data was collected in this study? What are the strengths and weaknesses of this type of data?

What ethical issues relate to this study?

Do you think that this study was useful?

This study is covered on pages 140–147 in your textbook

Griffiths (1994) the role of cognitive bias and skill in fruit machine gambling

What do I need to know?

Aim

To examine the thought processes and behaviours of regular and non-regular gamblers.

Two hypotheses:

1. There will be significant differences in the thought processes of regular and non-regular gamblers.
2. There will be no significant differences in the behaviours (skills) of regular and non-regular gamblers.

Participants

- 60 participants
- Mean age 23 years and four months
- 30 regular gamblers (29 male and one female)
- 30 non-regular gamblers (15 male and 15 female)
- Volunteer sample
- Recruited mainly via poster
- Fully informed consent

Method

- Quasi-experiment
- IV – regular/non-regular gamblers
- Variety of DVs
- 'Subjective' (qualitative) DVs – cognitive ability (measured by thinking aloud technique) and perception of skills (measured by post-experiment interview)
- 'Objective' (quantitative) DVs:
  1. total number of plays
  2. total minutes of play
  3. play rate (plays per minute)
  4. end stake – total winnings
  5. total number of wins in session
  6. win rate (time) – time between wins
  7. win rate (plays) number of plays between wins
- Each participant given £3
- Objective to stay on machine for 60 gambles
- Could keep winnings or carry on gambling if they achieved this
- Same machine (FRUITSKILL)
- Random allocation to thinking aloud/non-thinking aloud condition
- Recordings all transcribed within 24 hours

Results

- Regular gamblers:
  1. stayed on machine longer
  2. had a significantly higher play rate
  3. thinking aloud group of regular gamblers had a lower win rate than any other group
  4. produced significantly more irrational verbalisations than non-regular gamblers
  5. use a variety of heuristics e.g. illusion of control, flexible attributions
- Non-regular gamblers
  1. thinking aloud group of non-regular gamblers had slightly more wins than other groups

Conclusions

- Regular gamblers are slightly more skilful.
- Regular gamblers believe they are more skilful than they are.
- Regular gamblers know that they will lose but play with money rather than for money – staying on machine for longest time is their objective.
- Regular gamblers make more irrational verbalisations demonstrating cognitive bias.
- The study may be useful to help problem gamblers recognise and change their cognitive biases.

What do you think?

Which other forms of addictive behaviour could the results of this study be applied to? Are there any examples of addictive behaviour that can't be explained by this study? Discuss this with your teacher or with other students.

Test your knowledge

Answer the multiple choice questions below by ticking the correct answer(s) to test your knowledge of the study. You will find the answers at the bottom of the page.

1 *Which of the following is a prediction made by Griffiths?*

a) ☐ regular gamblers will have the same thought processes as non-regular gamblers
b) ☐ regular gamblers will be more skilled than non-regular gamblers
c) ☐ regular gamblers will have significantly different thought processes to non-regular gamblers.
d) ☐ non-regular gamblers will be more skilled than regular gamblers

2 *Which method was used by Griffiths?*

a) ☐ lab experiment
b) ☐ case study
c) ☐ observation
d) ☐ quasi-experiment

3 *How many participants took part in the study?*

a) ☐ 30
b) ☐ 60
c) ☐ 29
d) ☐ 100

4 *Which of the following is the correct outline of the procedure?*

a) ☐ the participants were given £6 and had to try and stay on the machine for 60 gambles
b) ☐ the participants were given £3 and had to try and stay on the machine for 30 gambles
c) ☐ the participants were given £3 and had to try and stay on the machine for 60 gambles
d) ☐ the participants were given £3 and had to try and stay on the machine as long as they could

5 *Which of the following is the best description of the thinking aloud technique?*

a) ☐ saying whatever is going through your head while you are playing
b) ☐ explaining to the experimenter what you are doing
c) ☐ shouting at the machine
d) ☐ blaming the machine when you lose

6 *Which one of the following variables was measured by the thinking aloud technique?*

a) ☐ total number of plays
b) ☐ end stake
c) ☐ cognitive ability
d) ☐ perception of skills

7 *Which of the following does not describe the findings for the regular gambler group?*

a) ☐ regular gamblers stayed on the machine longer than non-regular gamblers
b) ☐ regular gamblers had a significantly higher play rate
c) ☐ regular gamblers had a significantly lower play rate
d) ☐ regular gamblers who thought aloud had lower win rates than the other groups

8 *Which of the following is a correct finding from the study?*

a) ☐ regular gamblers believe that they are more skilful than they are
b) ☐ non-regular gamblers believe that they are more skilful than they are
c) ☐ regular gamblers do not believe that skill has anything to do with winning
d) ☐ regular gamblers believe that winning is all due to luck

Answers: 1 c; 2 d; 3 b; 4 c; 5 a; 6 c; 7 c; 8 a

Test your understanding

Use the questions below to evaluate the study. Suggested answers can be found at the back of the book.

1 This experiment was conducted in an amusement arcade.

a Outline one advantage of conducting this research in an amusement arcade.

b Outline one disadvantage of conducting this research in an amusement arcade.

2 The thinking aloud technique was used to try and find out how the participants were thinking as they were playing. Their verbalisations were transcribed and analysed using content analysis.

a Suggest one problem with the validity of the thinking aloud technique.

b Suggest one problem with the reliability of the thinking aloud technique.

3 All psychological research should conform to ethical guidelines.

Does this research conform to ethical guidelines? Give reasons for your answer.

4 a Suggest one improvement that could be made to the way that this research was conducted.

b Explain how you think this improvement might affect the results of the research.

Mind mapping

Using the mind map below make brief notes on the issues that can be used to evaluate this study. Some of the bubbles have been started for you and you should use the list below to select two further evaluation issues for this study. These issues are covered in detail on pages 176–187 of your textbook.

Ecological validity	Application to everyday life	Representativeness/generalisability
Ethics	Nature–nurture	Individual–situational explanations
Reliability	Validity	Qualitative and quantitative data
Control	Reductionism	Determinism

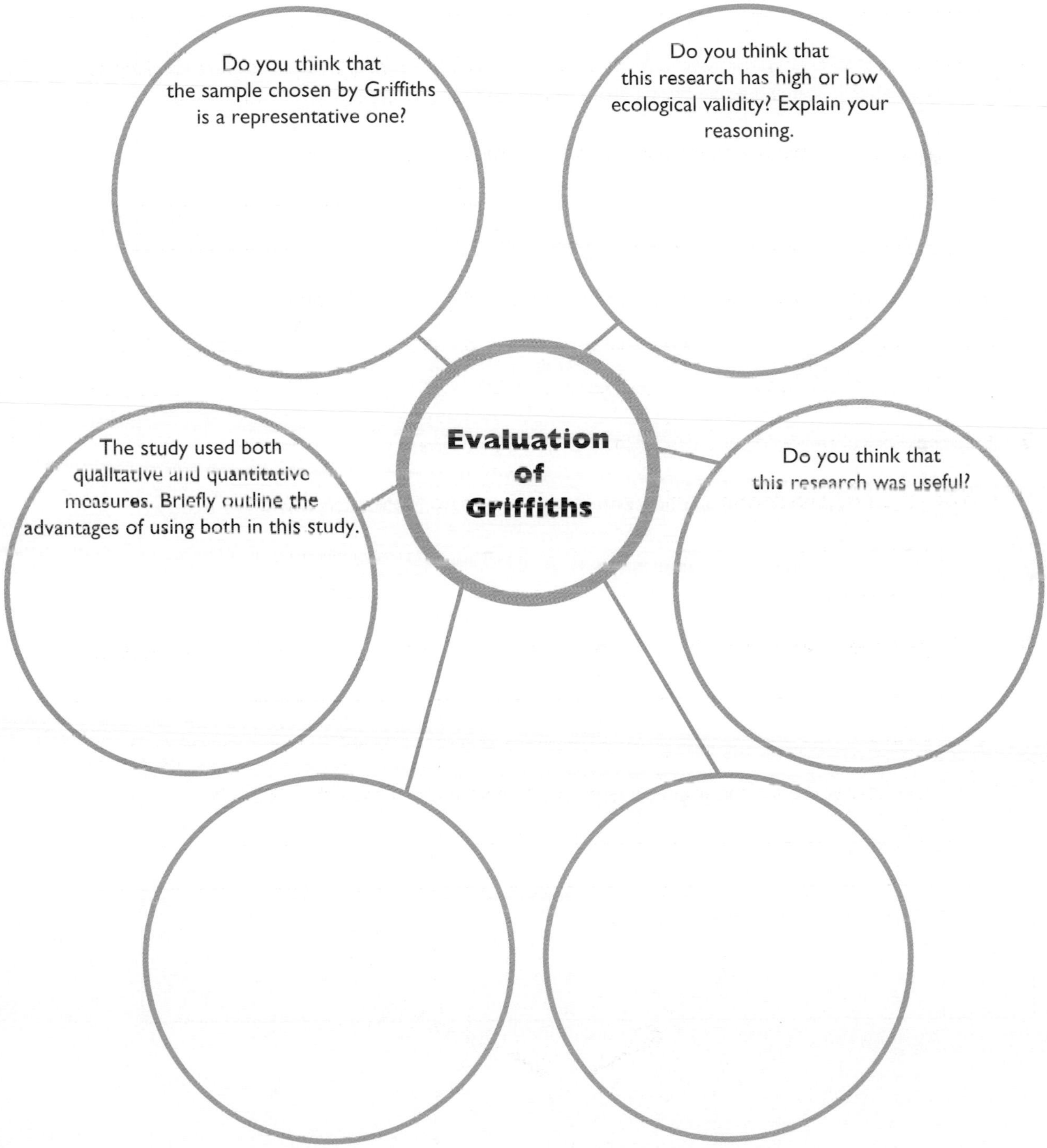

Evaluation of Griffiths

Do you think that the sample chosen by Griffiths is a representative one?

Do you think that this research has high or low ecological validity? Explain your reasoning.

The study used both qualitative and quantitative measures. Briefly outline the advantages of using both in this study.

Do you think that this research was useful?

Strengths and weaknesses of approach

The following tables suggest some strengths and weaknesses of the Individual Differences Approach in psychology. Using the three studies from this section try to complete the 'examples' column with one or more example to illustrate the strength or weakness. The first one has been done for you.

Strengths of INDIVIDUAL DIFFERENCES approach		Example from Core Study
1	Case studies are useful in therapy	Thigpen and Cleckley
2	Psychometric testing can allow comparisons between individuals	
3	Qualitative research is rich and detailed	
4	Research has many practical applications	
5	Can you think of any other strengths?	

Weaknesses of INDIVIDUAL DIFFERENCES approach		Example from Core Study
1	May be subjective	Griffiths – analysis of thinking aloud results
2	Tests may have problems of reliability and validity	
3	Case studies are difficult to generalise	
4	Can you think of any other weaknesses?	

Individual Differences Approach crossword

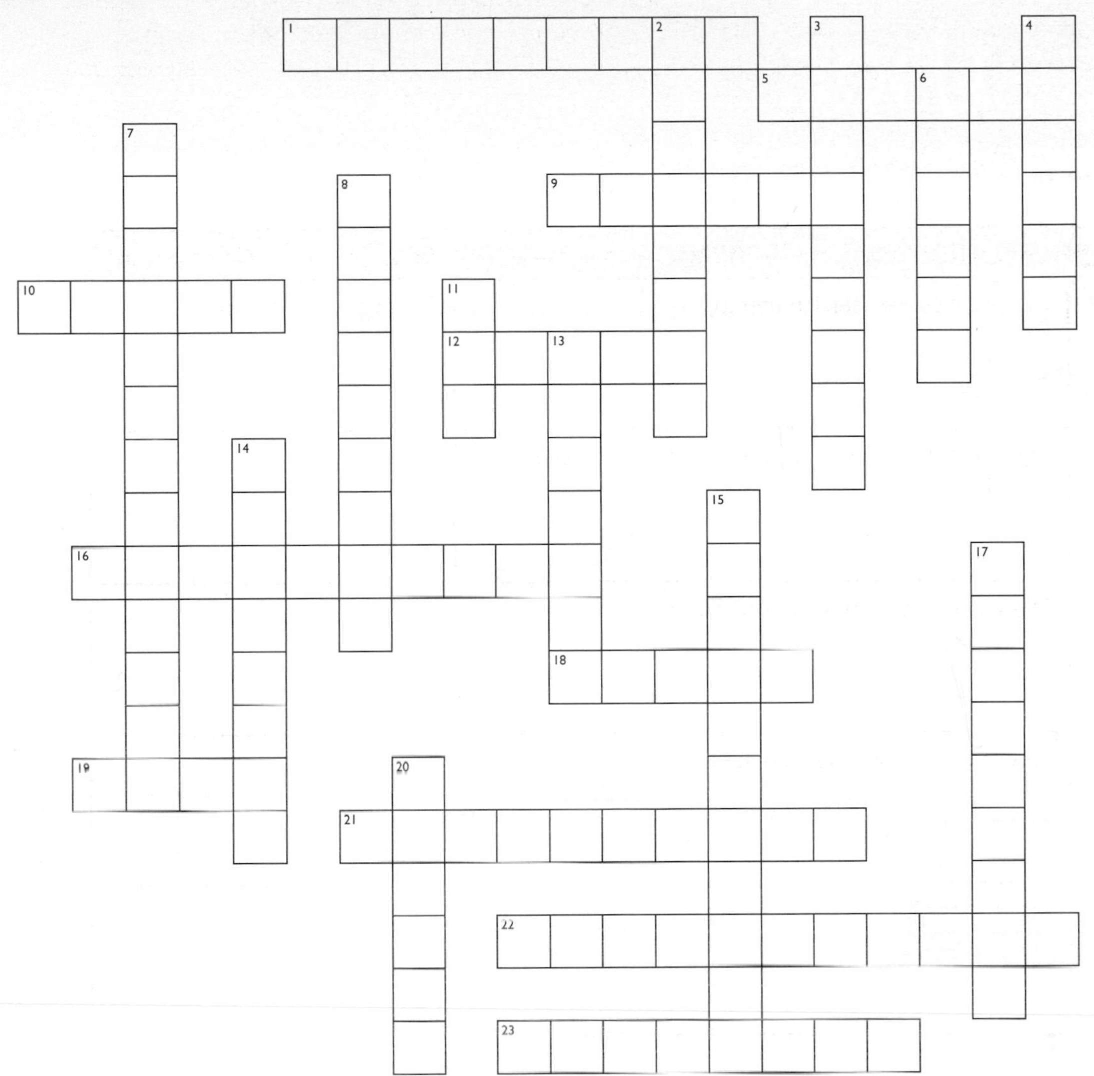

Clues

Across

1. this ability was tested using the thinking aloud technique (9)
5. one of the words that the pseudo patients claimed to be hearing (6)
9. the pseudo-patients in the Rosenhan study claimed to be hearing these (6)
10. the regular gamblers in the Griffiths study thought they had more of this than the non-regular gamblers (5)
12. the number of patients in the Rosenhan study (5)
16. the name of the fruit machine used in the study by Griffiths (10)
18. the total number of participants used in the study by Griffiths (5)
19. the third personality to emerge in the Thigpen and Cleckley study (4)
21. regular gamblers use a variety of these (10)
22. the consistency of a measurement (11)
23. the average number of days spent in hospital by the pseudo-patients in the Rosenhan study (8)

Down

2. the accuracy of a measurement (8)
3. a projective test using inkblots (9)
4. the number of hospitals used in the first part of the Rosenhan study (6)
6. Rosenhan said that these 'stick' (6)
7. all but one of the pseudo-patients were diagnosed with this disorder (13)
8. someone who treats patients with psychological disorders (9)
11. all three personalities in the Thigpen and Cleckley study were tested with this (3)
13. the participants in the study by Griffiths had to try and stay on the machine for sixty of these (7)
14. the number of responses received when the pseudo-patients made a request to a psychiatrist (8)
15. a type of observation used by Rosenhan (11)
17. Eve White experienced these (9)
20. Eve White's was superior (6)

Answers:
Across: 1. cognitive; 5. hollow; 9. voices; 10. skill; 12. eight; 16. fruitskill; 18. sixty 19. Jane; 21. heuristics; 22. reliability; 23. nineteen. **Down:** 2. validity; 3. Rorschach; 4. twelve; 6. labels; 7. schizophrenia; 8. therapist; 11. EEG; 13. gambles; 14. thirteen; 15. participant; 17. blackouts; 20. memory

Core Studies - bringing it all together

Which study does the image represent?

Each of these images represents a study. Identify which one and write your answer underneath the image. The answers are at the bottom of the page.

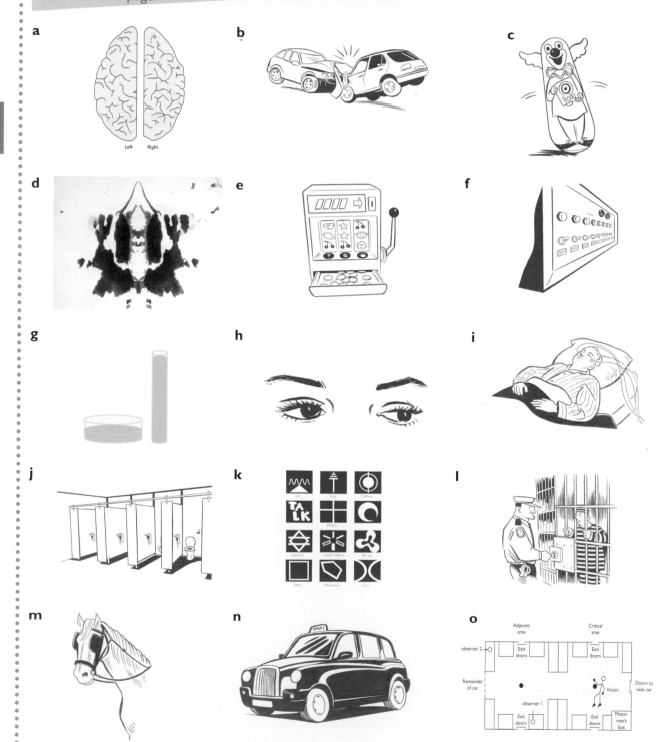

a

Left Right

b

c

d

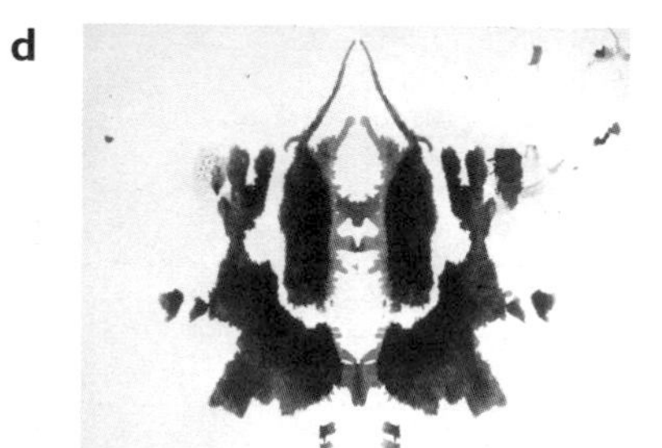

e

f

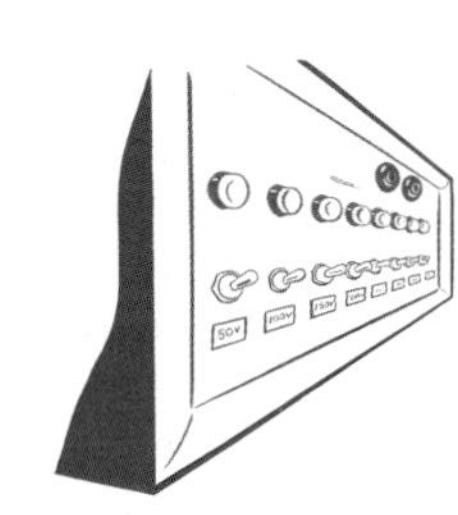

g

h

i

j

k

l

m

n

o

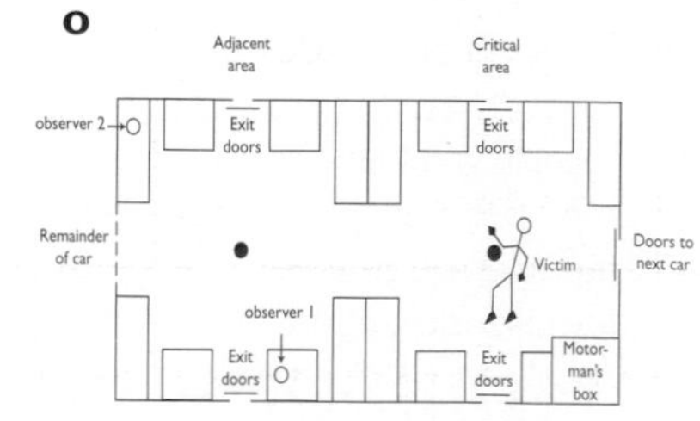

Answers: a. Sperry; b. Loftus and Palmer; c. Bandura; d. Thigpen and Cleckley; e. Griffiths; f. Milgram; g. Samuel and Bryant; h. Baron-Cohen et al; i. Dement and Kleitman; j. Rosenhan; k. Savage-Rumbaugh; l. Reicher and Haslam; m. Freud; n. Maguire; o. Piliavin et al

Match the topic to the study

Write the topics supplied next to the correct researcher in the table below. The answers are at the bottom of the page.

Sleep and dreaming	Obedience	Hemisphere function
Fruit machine gambling	Eyewitness testimony	Animal communication
Multiple Personality Disorder	Autism	Hippocampal volume in taxi drivers
Conservation	Accuracy of psychiatric diagnosis	Imitation of aggression
Bystander behaviour	Psychosexual development	Tyranny

a Loftus and Palmer	Eye Witness testimony
b Baron-Cohen	Autism
c Savage-Rumbaugh	Animal communication
d Samuel and Bryant	
e Bandura	Imitation of aggression
f Freud	Psychosexual development
g Maguire	
h Dement and Kleitman	
i Sperry	Hemisphere function
j Milgram	
k Haslam and Reicher	
l Piliavin	
m Rosenhan	
n Thigpen and Cleckley	
o Griffiths	

Answers: a. Eyewitness testimony; b. Autism; c. Animal communication; d. Conservation; e. Imitation of aggression; f. Psychosexual development; g. Hippocampal volume in taxi drivers; h. Sleep and dreaming; i. Hemisphere function; j. Obedience; k. Tyranny; l. Bystander behaviour; m. Accuracy of psychiatric diagnosis; n. Multiple Personality Disorder; o. Fruit machine gambling

Guess the psychologist

Test your knowledge of the psychologists featured in the Core Studies. You will find the answers at the bottom of the page.

1 Whose research took place in the New York subway?

____

2 Who found that adults with autism or Asperger's Syndrome, despite being of normal or above average IQ, performed poorly on the Eyes Test?

____

3 Who said, 'Obedience is a deeply ingrained behaviour tendency, indeed a potent impulse overriding training in ethics, sympathy and moral conduct'?

____

4 Whose participants were called Kanzi and Mulika?

____

5 Who claimed that Type 2 errors were occurring in psychiatric diagnosis?

____

6 Who found that observing adult models acting aggressively has the effect of weakening aggressive inhibitors in children, therefore making aggressive behaviour more likely?

____

7 Who said, 'Over time, the information from the two sources may be integrated in such a way that we are unable to tell from which source some specific detail is recalled. All we have is one memory'?

____

8 Who asked the following question: Is the direction of eye movement during REM sleep related to dream content?

____

9 Who used plasticine, counters and glasses in their study?

____

10 Who used the terms psychosexual development and Oedipus complex?

____

11 Who described their patient as 'a circumspect, matter-of-fact person, meticulously truthful and consistently sober and serious about her grave troubles'?

____

12 Who said, 'Professional dependence on navigational skills in licensed London taxi drivers is associated with a relative redistribution of grey matter in the hippocampus'?

____

13 Who gave participants £3 each at the start of the study?

____

14 Who said, 'Instead of the normally unified single stream of consciousness, these patients behave as if they have two independent streams of conscious awareness'?

____

15 Whose research took place in a BBC TV studio?

____

Answers: 1. Piliavin; 2. Baron-Cohen; 3. Milgram; 4. Savage-Rumbaugh; 5. Rosenhan; 6. Bandura; 7. Loftus and Palmer; 8. Dement and Kleitman; 9. Samuel and Bryant; 10. Freud; 11. Thigpen and Cleckley; 12. Maguire et al; 13. Griffiths; 14. Sperry; 15. Reicher and Haslam

Can you solve the following anagrams?

The following anagrams are all psychologists' names. Untangle the letters and write the correct name in the space provided. The answers can be found at the bottom of the page.

1 sflout ______

2 cnarnheoob ______

3 saesulm ______

4 rbuadna ______

5 fdreu ______

6 naktilme ______

7 giuearm ______

8 irerche ______

9 naiiivlp ______

10 sohrnena ______

11 yceklelc ______

12 mrelap ______

13 rvmhasbguuaaeg ______

14 nratby ______

15 orss ______

16 denmet ______

17 yrrsep ______

18 mmirgla ______

19 lasmha ______

20 iordn ______

21 gnetphi ______

22 isftfhigr ______

Answers: 1. Loftus; 2. Baron-Cohen; 3. Samuel; 4. Bandura; 5. Freud; 6. Kleitman; 7. Maguire; 8. Reicher; 9. Piliavin; 10. Rosenhan; 11. Cleckley; 12. Plamer; 13. Savage-Rumbaugh; 14. Bryant; 15. Ross; 16. Dement; 17. Sperry; 18. Milgram; 19. Haslam; 20. Rodin; 21. Thigpen; 22. Griffiths

Anagrams

These anagrams are a variety of psychology-related words. They will be useful for conducting the research activity outlined on page 111. Untangle the letters and write the correct word in the space provided. The answers can be found at the bottom of the page.

1 ooshlygcp	**2** uiiivladnd	**3** lsicao	**4** taiusm	**5** neihmpceza
______	______	______	______	______
6 ieassrgogn	**7** syhnipacslyosa	**8** llaipch	**9** rmeda	**10** rbooalaytr
______	______	______	______	______
11 lispepey	**12** eeeicnbod	**13** eenepxrremit	**14** skcoh	**15** gdrau
______	______	______	______	______
16 uswbay	**17** ieapptsetdnuo	**18** iiosnsdga	**19** gainlmbg	**20** lnepevldoamet
______	______	______	______	______
21 iivgceont	**22** aloiigchyopls	**23** seyetnwesi	**24** rxelgiam	**25** eorannctsovi
______	______	______	______	______
26 vhrimoaebsui	**27** pshpoimaucp	**28** nasc	**29** epmeehsirh	**30** eoeecrtdl
______	______	______	______	______
31 ytanmy	**32** eroectednaf	**33** mpiesro	**34** ydstaemb	**35** nhzaehrsiiocp
______	______	______	______	______
36 msomtpy	**37** inapyslteor	**38** cidtdonai		
______	______	______		

Answers: 1. Psychology; 2. Individual; 3. Social; 4. Autism; 5. Chimpanzee; 6. Aggression; 7. Psychoanalysis; 8. Phallic; 9. Dream; 10. Laboratory; 11. Epilepsy; 12. Obedience; 13. Experimenter; 14. Shock; 15. Guard; 16. Subway; 17. Pseudo-patient; 18. Diagnosis; 19. Gambling; 20. Developmental; 21. Cognitive; 22. Physiological; 23. Eyewitness; 24. Lexigram; 25. Conservation; 26. Behaviourism; 27. Hippocampus; 28. Scan; 29. Hemisphere; 30. Electrode; 31. Tyranny; 32. Confederate; 33. Prisoner; 34. Bystander; 35. Schizophrenia; 36. Symptom; 37. Personality; 38. Addiction

Core Studies crossword

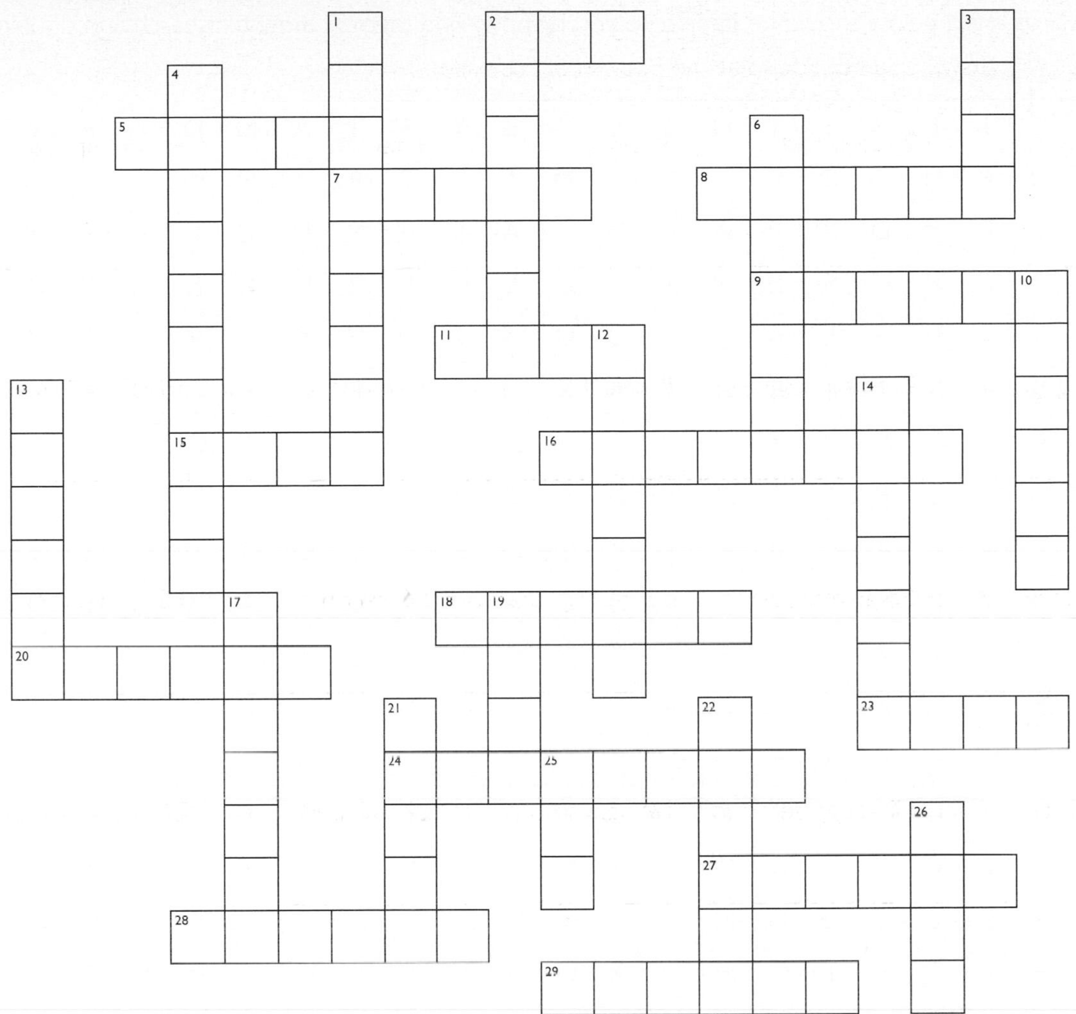

Clues

Across

2. a type of brain scan (3)
5. a chimpanzee (5)
7. he studied Little Hans (5)
8. what people do on fruit machines (6)
9. occur when we are asleep (6)
11. the hemisphere related to language (4)
15. the little boy Freud studied (4)
16. conducted research on the New York subway (8)
18. worked in a sleep laboratory (6)
20. first author of the conservation study (6)
23. plasticine is used to test for conservation of this (4)
24. conducted research as pseudo-patient (8)
27. where 'The Knowledge' is about (6)
28. second author of the conservation study (6)
29. the second author of the eyewitness testimony experiment (6)

Down

1. conducted research in an amusement arcade (9)
2. studied taxi drivers (7)
3. the third personality to emerge in the case study of Thigpen and Cleckley (4)
4. studied autism (10)
6. used a Bobo doll in his research (7)
10. won a Nobel Prize for his work (6)
12. one of Eve's therapists (7)
13. the first author of the eyewitness testimony experiment (6)
14. the author of a very unethical piece of research (7)
17. the first author of the prison study (7)
19. the test used by Baron-Cohen et al (4)
21. it's in your head! (5)
22. the second author of the prison study (6)
25. used to measure brain activity (3)
26. used in the study of the imitation of aggression (4)

Answers:

Across: 2. MRI; 5. Kanzi; 7. Freud; 8. gamble; 9. dreams; 11. left; 15. Hans; 16. Piliavin; 18. Dement; 20. Samuel; 23. mass; 24. Rosenhan; 27. London; 28. Bryant; 29. Palmer

Down: 1. Griffiths; 2. Maguire; 3. Jane; 4. Baron-Cohen; 6. Bandura; 10. Sperry; 12. Thigpen; 13. Loftus; 14. Milgram; 17. Reicher; 19. Eyes; 21. brain; 22. Haslam; 25. EEG; 26. Bobo

Wordsearch

All the words listed below should be familiar to you by now. Find them in the wordsearch and double-check any that you are not sure of.

G	R	I	F	F	I	T	H	S	S	C	B	Y	S	T	A	N	D	E	R	V
R	U	P	U	O	Q	S	L	X	I	M	I	L	G	R	A	M	N	B	U	G
N	S	F	M	D	X	P	A	R	D	F	A	S	A	M	U	E	L	R	E	A
S	B	X	X	C	S	E	M	X	G	U	L	M	S	B	K	K	K	A	P	M
H	R	J	N	H	L	R	J	L	D	U	W	T	O	V	P	L	R	I	I	B
O	Y	B	X	I	K	R	O	I	A	X	N	R	C	P	S	E	A	N	L	L
C	A	E	H	M	X	Y	V	U	S	A	D	D	I	C	T	I	O	N	E	E
K	N	H	O	P	A	I	P	Y	C	R	O	P	A	W	O	T	T	J	P	R
F	T	A	S	A	D	B	C	S	P	Q	D	F	L	V	Q	M	N	Q	S	V
C	U	V	P	N	H	I	P	P	O	C	A	M	P	U	S	A	W	S	Y	D
O	M	I	I	Z	B	P	S	Y	C	H	O	L	O	G	Y	N	N	F	A	E
N	A	O	T	E	I	T	P	H	Y	S	I	O	L	O	G	I	C	A	L	M
F	G	U	A	E	B	P	M	W	P	F	S	X	E	M	A	R	V	L	O	E
E	U	R	L	Q	Z	Z	P	N	C	L	E	C	K	L	E	Y	G	D	F	N
D	I	I	V	E	L	A	Q	V	P	H	A	L	L	I	C	Z	U	M	T	T
E	R	S	T	C	O	G	N	I	T	I	V	E	H	A	S	L	A	M	U	Q
R	E	M	P	S	Y	C	H	O	A	N	A	L	Y	S	I	S	R	S	S	J
A	K	R	D	E	V	E	L	O	P	M	E	N	T	A	L	Z	D	X	F	O
T	P	R	I	S	O	N	E	R	W	C	O	W	F	B	S	M	F	W	J	V
E	V	L	F	U	E	X	P	E	R	I	M	E	N	T	E	R	J	E	E	G
V	A	T	Y	R	A	N	N	Y	R	O	S	E	N	H	A	N	D	H	Q	O

Addiction
Behaviourism
Brain
Bryant
Bystander
Chimpanzee
Cleckley
Cognitive
Confederate
Dement
Developmental
EEG
Epilepsy
Experimenter
Gambler
Griffiths
Guard
Haslam
Hippocampus
Hospital
Individual
Kleitman
Loftus
Maguire
Milgram
MRI
Phallic
Physiological
Prisoner
Psychoanalysis
Psychology
Rosenhan
Samuel
Scan
Shock
Social
Sperry
Tyranny

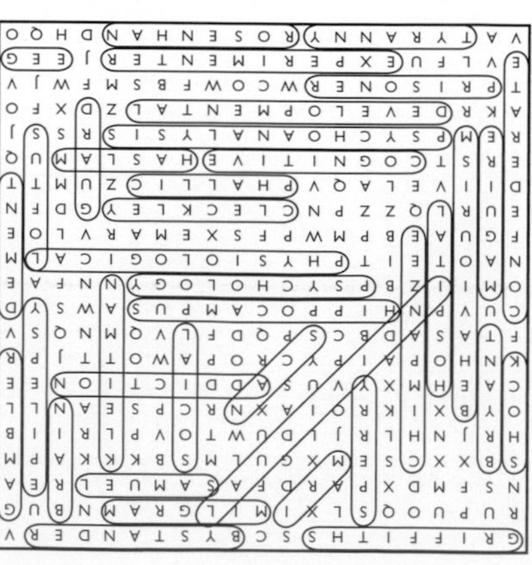

Answer:

Exam**Café**

Assumptions of each approach

Use the following tables to make notes on the assumption of each approach/perspective. As well as the five approaches covered so far, you should also be familiar with the Behaviourist and Psychodynamic perspectives, and these have also been included. Each table has been started for you!

Assumptions of the COGNITIVE approach	
1.	The brain is like a computer processing information
2.	
3.	

Assumptions of the DEVELOPMENTAL approach	
1.	Both maturation and experience influence behaviour
2.	
3.	

ptions of the **PHYSIOLOGICAL** approach	
	All behaviour has biological causes
2.	
3.	

Assumptions of the **SOCIAL** approach	
1.	All behaviour occurs within a social context
2.	
3.	

Assumptions of the **INDIVIDUAL DIFFERENCES** approach	
1.	People are unique
2.	
3.	

Assumptions of the **BEHAVIOURIST** perspective	
1.	All behaviour is learned
2.	
3.	

Assumptions of the **PSYCHODYNAMIC** approach	
1.	Behaviour has unconscious causes
2.	
3.	

Similarities and differences between studies

Use the following tables to make notes on similarities and differences between the studies – think about the methods, samples, findings, usefulness and ethics. A few boxes have filled in to get you started.

The Cognitive approach

Studies	Similarity	Difference
Loftus and Palmer and Savage-Rumbaugh		Loftus and Palmer used human participants and Savage-Rumbaugh used animal participants
Loftus and Palmer and Baron-Cohen et al	Both collected quantitative data	
Savage-Rumbaugh and Baron-Cohen et al		

The Developmental approach

Studies	Similarity	Difference
Bandura et al and Samuel and Bryant	Both laboratory experiments	Greater ethical concerns in Bandura regarding long term effects of study
Bandura et al and Freud		
Samuel and Bryant and Freud		

The Physiological approach

Studies	Similarity	Difference
Dement and Kleitman and Sperry		Dement and Kleitman manipulated the IV (lab experiment). Sperry used a naturally occurring IV (quasi-experiment)
Dement and Kleitman and Maguire et al	Both used highly specialised laboratory equipment (Dement and Kleitman – EEG, Maguire et al – MRI scans)	
Maguire et al and Sperry		

The Social approach

Studies	Similarity	Difference
Milgram and Reicher and Haslam	Both raise ethical concerns	
Milgram and Piliavin		Milgram used a laboratory environment and Piliavin et al used a real-life setting, so ecological validity may be higher in Piliavin's research
Piliavin and Reicher and Haslam		

The Individual Differences approach

Studies	Similarity	Difference
Rosenhan and Thigpen and Cleckley		Rosenhan used a participant observation study and Thigpen and Cleckley a case study
Rosenhan and Griffiths	Both conducted in real-life environments (Rosenhan – psychiatric hospital, Griffiths – amusement arcade)	
Griffiths and Thigpen and Cleckley		

The usefulness of each approach

Use the following table to make notes on the usefulness of each approach. Usefulness could include significant findings from the study which have added to our knowledge of human behaviour or practical applications from the research. Try to give as many examples as you can. Once again, this has been started for you.

Approach	Examples of 'usefulness' from each approach
Cognitive	Practical applications of Loftus and Palmer's research – better questioning techniques for interviewing witnesses
Developmental	Samuel and Bryant's research has practical applications for primary school teachers
Physiological	Maguire's research shows us that the brain has 'plasticity' and this may be useful for treating people who have suffered structural brain damage
Social	Reicher and Haslam's research has demonstrated the powerful effect of social roles
Individual Differences	Griffiths' research has practical applications for therapy with addictive gamblers

Section C questions

These questions will focus on the various approaches, perspectives and issues that are listed in the specification. These will include:

Approaches

- The Cognitive approach
- The Developmental approach
- The Physiological approach
- The Social approach
- The Individual Differences approach

Perspectives

- The Behaviourist perspective
- The Psychodynamic perspective

Issues

- Ethics
- Ecological validity
- Longitudinal and snapshot
- Qualitative and quantitative data

The following questions are taken from the OCR Specimen Paper.

Exam questions

a. Outline one assumption of the Social approach in psychology. (2)

b. Describe how the Social approach could explain obedience. (4)

c. Describe one similarity and one difference between the Milgram study and any other Social approach study. (6)

d. Discuss the strengths and weaknesses of the Social approach using examples from the Milgram study. (12)

The exam is two hours long and there are 120 marks in total. This means that you are working to the 'mark a minute' rule and you should bear this in mind when you are planning and writing your answers. There is no need to spend ten minutes on a two mark question and you should try to spend at least 12 minutes on a 12 mark question.

Exam question

a. Outline one assumption of the Social approach in psychology. (2)

Student answer

The Social approach assumes that human behaviour can be explained through an understanding of the social processes that operate in social contexts.

Exam question

b. Describe how the Social approach could explain obedience. (4)

Student answer

The Social approach would take a situational perspective when explaining obedience. Milgram concluded that obedience was the result of powerful social forces operating on the individual – the agentic state. From the Social approach, obedience would not be seen as an individual characteristic but as a result of the situation that the person found themselves in.

Exam question

c. Describe one similarity and one difference between the Milgram study and any other Social approach study. (6)

You can choose any focus here – perhaps the most obvious is to consider the methods used by the researchers, although you could also think about the ethics, the participants, the conclusions, the applications and so on. The other Social approach studies are Reicher and Haslam and Piliavin et al. For this example we will use Piliavin et al.

Student answer

One difference between the Milgram study and the Piliavin study is the location of the research. Milgram based his research in a highly artificial laboratory environment at Yale University whereas Piliavin et al based their research in a real-life setting – the New York subway. This arguably gives Piliavin et al's research higher ecological validity than Milgram's. Milgram's participants knew that they were taking part in research whereas Piliavin et al's participants had no idea that they were participants in research.

However, the two studies are similar in that they both raise ethical issues. Milgram's participants were deceived as to the real nature of the study and Piliavin et al's participants were deceived as they were not even aware that they were taking part in a study. Both studies could have distressed participants and neither study had the fully informed consent of the participants.

Exam question

d. Discuss the strengths and weaknesses of the Social approach using examples from the Milgram study. (12)

The mark scheme for this question requires that you discuss at least two strengths and two weaknesses in order to access the top band. For revision purposes you should attempt to learn three strengths and three weaknesses for each approach, and in the examination you should discuss the example that you use rather than just refer to it.

Student answer

One strength of the Social approach in psychology is the use of controlled laboratory environments to study social behaviour. For example, Milgram was able to construct a convincing and highly controlled environment for the research into obedience. Another strength is that the Social approach is able to explain many social phenomena, for example, Milgram's research has been applied to the behaviour of Nazi soldiers in WWII.

The final strength is that it illustrates the importance of studying the effects of situations on behaviour rather then assuming that all behaviour can be explained in terms of individual or personality characteristics. For example, Milgram's work demonstrates that people obey due to the powerful social forces acting on them rather than because they have particular personality characteristics.

One weakness of the social approach is that it may focus too much on social factors and ignore individual factors, for example, Milgram concluded that obedience was due to the social forces operating within the environment he had constructed but there may have been significant individual differences in the reactions of the participants which were not explored. For example, were there differences between the participants that stopped at 300 volts and those who continued to the end?

Research within the Social approach may also raise significant ethical concerns. As we are attempting to understand the behaviour of people it may be necessary to deceive and even distress them in order to be able to find out anything of any use. For example, if Milgram had used a different 'punishment' for the learner would the findings have been as useful? Finally, if social research occurs within a laboratory environment, participants are aware that they are being studied and therefore may respond to demand characteristics. For example, Milgram's participants may have continued to obey because they thought that was what the experimenter wanted them to do – they may have behaved differently in a different situation.

Have a go at an exam question

Now have a go at this question (also from the OCR Specimen Paper).

Exam question

a. Outline one assumption of the Behaviourist approach. (2)

b. Describe how the Behaviourist approach would explain aggression. (4)

c. Describe one similarity and one difference between the Bandura, Ross and Ross study and any other developmental study. (6)

d. Discuss the strengths and limitations of the Behaviourist approach using examples from any study involving behaviourism. (12) (Use a separate sheet to continue your answer.)

Psychological Investigations

What you need to know

There are a number of key terms that you should know.

Hypotheses

Hypothesis	A testable statement
Alternate hypothesis	A statement predicting that one variable will affect another
Null hypothesis	The 'no effect' hypothesis
One-tailed hypothesis	A hypothesis predicting the direction of the effect
Two-tailed hypothesis	A hypotheses with no prediction of the direction of the effect
Independent variable	The variable manipulated by the experimenter
Dependent variable	The variable measured by the experimenter

Sampling

Target population	The whole group of people in whom the researcher is interested
Sample	The group of participants selected to take part in the research
Random sample	A sample selected so that everyone in the target population has an equal chance of being selected
Opportunity sample	A sample selected by simply using the people who are available at the time the research takes place
Self-selected sample	A sample where people volunteer themselves to take part in a study

Methods

Laboratory experiment	An experiment conducted in a controlled situation and involving the manipulation of the independent variable
Independent measures design	Using different participants in each condition
Repeated measures design	Using the same participants in each condition
Field experiment	An experiment conducted in a natural environment where the independent variable is manipulated by the experimenter
Quasi-experiment	Where the effects of a naturally occurring independent variable are examined
Observation	A non-experimental design where the researchers observe and record behaviour
Inter-rater reliability	The extent to which observers agree on the way that behaviours should be categorised
Correlation	A method of statistical analysis showing a relationship between two variables
Self-reports	Techniques for asking people directly for information
Open questions	Questions that ask the participant to respond in their own words
Closed questions	Questions that ask the participant to choose from a range of predetermined answers
Case study	An in-depth study of a single individual or event

Fill in the blanks

Psychologists begin their research by making predictions about what is likely to happen. These predictions are called ______________. The______________ ______________predicts that one variable will affect another and the ______________ ______________ predicts that there will be no effect.

A _______ tailed hypothesis predicts the direction of the effect and a ______________tailed hypothesis simply predicts an effect without predicting the direction.

The variable that is manipulated by the experimenter is called the ______________variable and the variable that is measured is called the ______________variable.

Psychologists select a ______________of people to take part in their research. If they ensure that each member of the target population has an equal chance of being selected this is called a ______________ sample. Sometimes, psychologists simply use the people that are around at the time they wish to conduct their experiment and this is called an ______________ sample.

Psychologists can use a variety of different methods to conduct their research. Laboratory experiments are conducted in ______________conditions and involve the ______________of the _________ variable. Field experiments are conducted in ______________environments but still involve the manipulation of the ______________ variable. If the effects of a naturally occurring variable are examined this is termed a ______________ experiment. Experiments use different designs. An independent measures design uses ______________people in each ______________of the experiment and a __________measures design uses the ______________people in each condition.

Psychologists can also use non-experimental methods. One of these involves attempts to record behaviour as it occurs and this is called ______________. Techniques for asking people directly for information are called ______________ techniques. Finally correlation is a method of ______________ analysis showing the strength of the ______________ between two variables.

Answers:
hypotheses/alternate hypothesis/null hypothesis/one/two/independent/dependent/sample/random/opportunity/controlled/manipulation/independent/natural/independent/quasi/different/condition/repeated/same/observation/self-report/statistical/relationship

Strengths and weaknesses of the different methods

Experimental methods

The table below suggests some strengths and weaknesses of different types of experiments.

Strengths of laboratory experiments	Weaknesses of laboratory experiments
Cause and effect conclusions can be drawn as the independent variable has been manipulated High levels of control Accurate measurement Can be replicated if standardised procedures are used	May be low in ecological validity if conditions are very artificial Total control over all variables is never possible May be ethical problems of deception etc. High risk of demand characteristics as participants know they are part of experiment May be experimenter bias
Strengths of field experiments	**Weaknesses of field experiments**
Less likelihood of demand characteristics if the participants are unaware of being part of a study High ecological validity	Lower levels of control than in laboratory conditions Harder to replicate Ethical issues
Strengths of quasi-experiments	**Weaknesses of quasi-experiments**
Useful when it would be impossible/unethical to manipulate the independent variable Increased application to real life as change in independent variable is a natural one	Lack of control over extraneous variables Difficult to replicate May be subject to demand characteristics if the participants know they are being studied May be difficult to obtain sufficient participants

Laboratory experiments

Think of a Core Study which used a laboratory experiment. Which of the strengths and weaknesses listed above apply to that study? What improvements could you make to this study? Complete the table on page 98.

An example has been completed for you so you will need to choose a different laboratory experiment.

Core Study: Loftus and Palmer	
Strengths	**Weaknesses**
High levels of control Easily quantifiable measurements Easily replicated Consent gained	Low ecological validity Demand characteristics as participants knew they were in an experiment Restricted sample (all students of the experimenter) May have caused some distress
Improvements Larger sample? More varied sample? Investigate whether driving experience affects answers?	

Core Study:	
Strengths	**Weaknesses**
Improvements	

Field experiments

Think of a Core Study which used a field experiment. Which of the strengths and weaknesses listed on page 97 apply to that study? What improvements could you make to this study?

Core Study:	
Strengths	**Weaknesses**
Improvements	

Quasi-experiments

Think of a Core Study which used a quasi-experiment? Which of the strengths and weaknesses listed on page 97 apply to this study? What improvements could you make to this study?

Core Study:	
Strengths	**Weaknesses**
Improvements	

Self-report

The table below suggests some strengths and weaknesses of the self-report technique.

Strengths of self-report	Weaknesses of self-report
Gets information direct from participants rather than the researcher interpreting data	Closed questions may force people to give inaccurate responses
Closed questions very easy to score and analyse	Open questions are hard to analyse
Easy to replicate	Questions may be interpreted differently by different participants
Can collect large amounts of data easily and quickly	May be affected by social desirability, acquiescence and response set

Think of a Core Study which used self-report techniques. Which of the strengths and weaknesses listed above apply to this study? What improvements could you make to this study?

Core Study:	
Strengths	**Weaknesses**
Improvements	

Observation

The table below suggests some strengths and weaknesses of the observation technique.

Strengths of observation	Weaknesses of observation
Observations in natural environments where people are unaware of being observed have high ecological validity Observations in natural environments where people are unaware of being observed have low demand characteristics Useful where it is difficult/unethical to manipulate variables Can produce 'rich' data Can be used as starting point for research as experimental hypotheses may be generated	Can be subject to observer bias Can be difficult to ensure inter-rate reliability Very difficult to replicate Can be ethical issues if people are observed without their permission (although this is acceptable in public places) Lack of control Difficult to draw 'cause and effect' conclusions as no manipulation Could suffer from demand characteristics if people know they are being observed

Think of a Core Study which used observational methods. Which of the strengths and weaknesses listed above apply to this study? What improvements could you make to this study?

Core Study:	
Strengths	**Weaknesses**
Improvements	

Correlation

The table below suggests some strengths and weaknesses of the correlation technique.

Strengths of correlation	Weaknesses of correlation
Can give information about the strength and the direction of a relationship between two variables Useful where it is difficult/unethical to manipulate variables Can be used as starting point for further research as experimental hypotheses may be generated	No conclusions about 'cause and effect' can be drawn Other methods may have been used to measure variables (e.g. self-report or observation) and so the weaknesses associated with these methods would also apply

Think of a Core Study that used correlation methods. Which of the strengths and weaknesses listed above apply to this study? What improvements could you make to this study?

Core Study:	
Strengths	**Weaknesses**
Improvements	

Test your knowledge

Try the following multiple choice questions to test your knowledge of experimental methods. You will find the answers at the bottom of each page.

Experiments

1 *Which of the following is a definition of the experimental method?*

a) ☐ measuring two variables
b) ☐ manipulating one variable to see its effect on another variable
c) ☐ categorising behaviour
d) ☐ asking questions

2 *What is the name given to the variable manipulated by the experimenter?*

a) ☐ the dependent variable
b) ☐ confounding variable
c) ☐ independent variable
d) ☐ co-variable

3 *What is the name given to the variable measured by the experimenter?*

a) ☐ the dependent variable
b) ☐ confounding variable
c) ☐ independent variable
d) ☐ co-variable

4 *Which two of the following are strengths of laboratory experiments?*

a) ☐ high levels of control
b) ☐ low levels of control
c) ☐ high ecological validity
d) ☐ low ecological validity

5 *Which two of the following are weaknesses of laboratory experiments?*

a) ☐ high ecological validity
b) ☐ low ecological validity
c) ☐ high chance of demand characteristics
d) ☐ low chance of demand characteristics

6 *Which two of the following Core Studies used a laboratory experiment method?*

a) ☐ Loftus and Palmer
b) ☐ Bandura, Ross and Ross
c) ☐ Freud
d) ☐ Thigpen and Cleckley

7 *Which of the following Core Studies used a field experiment method?*

a) ☐ Loftus and Palmer
b) ☐ Bandura, Ross and Ross
c) ☐ Piliavin et al
d) ☐ Sperry

8 *Which of the following Core Studies can be described as using a quasi-experimental method?*

a) ☐ Sperry
b) ☐ Freud
c) ☐ Milgram
d) ☐ Piliavin et al

Answers: 1 b; 2 c; 3 a; 4 a and d; 5 b and c; 6 a and b; 7 c; 8 a

Observations

1 *Which of the following is a definition of the observational method?*

a) ☐ a non-experimental design where behaviour is observed and recorded
b) ☐ a study conducted in a natural environment
c) ☐ a study conducted in a laboratory
d) ☐ a study with lots of participants

2 *Which Core Study used observational techniques to collect data within a laboratory experiment?*

a) ☐ Freud
b) ☐ Griffiths
c) ☐ Bandura, Ross and Ross
d) ☐ Thigpen and Cleckley

3 *Which Core Study used observation within a field experiment?*

a) ☐ Bandura, Ross and Ross
b) ☐ Piliavin et al
c) ☐ Milgram
d) ☐ Rosenhan

4 *Which Core Study used a participant observation method?*

a) ☐ Rosenhan
b) ☐ Bandura, Ross and Ross
c) ☐ Milgram
d) ☐ Loftus and Palmer

5 *Why is observational research so difficult to replicate?*

a) ☐ because it is expensive
b) ☐ because it is almost impossible to find the same situation again
c) ☐ because it takes so much time
d) ☐ because it is not worth it

6 *What is meant by the term 'observer bias'?*

a) ☐ observers may interpret the behaviours to suit their aims
b) ☐ participants may not behave naturally
c) ☐ participants may find out they are being observed
d) ☐ observers acting unethically

7 *What is meant by the term 'inter-rater reliability'?*

a) ☐ the amount of agreement between observers
b) ☐ the accuracy of observers
c) ☐ a type of control
d) ☐ a type of variable

8 *How can inter-rater reliability be measured?*

a) ☐ by self-report
b) ☐ by correlating the ratings between observers
c) ☐ by a test of difference
d) ☐ by a test of significance

Answers: 1 a; 2 c; 3 b; 4 a; 5 b; 6 a; 7 a; 8 b

Self-reports

1 *Which of the following is not a type of self-report?*

a) ☐ a questionnaire
b) ☐ an interview
c) ☐ an observation
d) ☐ a survey

2 *Which of the following is an open question?*

a) ☐ how are you getting on with your psychology revision?
b) ☐ do you like psychology? Answer Yes or No
c) ☐ are you good at psychology? Answer Yes or No
d) ☐ what grade do you hope to get? A B C D E

3 *Which of the following is a closed question?*

a) ☐ how are you getting on with your psychology revision?
b) ☐ do you like psychology?
c) ☐ do you like psychology? Answer Yes or No
d) ☐ is this book helpful?

4 *Which of the following is a strength of self report measures?*

a) ☐ closed questions are difficult to analyse
b) ☐ closed questions are easy to analyse
c) ☐ participants may interpret questions differently
d) ☐ people may respond to demand characteristics

5 *Which of the following is a weakness of self-report measures?*

a) ☐ closed questions are difficult to analyse
b) ☐ closed questions are easy to analyse
c) ☐ they are hard to replicate
d) ☐ participants may interpret questions differently

6 *Which Core Study used self-report measures?*

a) ☐ Bandura, Ross and Ross
b) ☐ Griffiths
c) ☐ Thigpen and Cleckley
d) ☐ both b and c

7 *Which of the following topics could be tested using self reports?*

a) ☐ opinions on crime and punishment
b) ☐ actual helping behaviour
c) ☐ attitudes to helping
d) ☐ both a and c

8 *Which of the following topics could not be tested using self-reports?*

a) ☐ hippocampal size
b) ☐ attitudes to A level
c) ☐ opinions on crime and punishment
d) ☐ personality

Answers: 1 c; 2 a; 3 c; 4 b; 5 d; 6 d; 7 d; 8 a

Correlation

1 *Which of the following is a definition of correlation?*

a) ☐ a cause and effect relationship
b) ☐ the strength of the relationship between variables
c) ☐ the researcher's opinion
d) ☐ how closely people are related

2 *Correlation methods are particularly useful when…*

a) ☐ you are unable to manipulate variables
b) ☐ you are interested in the relationship between two variables
c) ☐ you want to find out how one variable affects another
d) ☐ both a and b

3 *Which of the following Core Studies used the correlation method?*

a) ☐ Loftus and Palmer
b) ☐ Freud
c) ☐ Maguire et al
d) ☐ Rosenhan

4 *Which of the following can be concluded from correlation research?*

a) ☐ how one variable affects another
b) ☐ how two variables are related
c) ☐ what participants think about a topic
d) ☐ none of the above

5 *Which of the following cannot be concluded from correlation research?*

a) ☐ how one variable affects another
b) ☐ the strength of the relationship between two variables
c) ☐ the direction of a relationship between two variables
d) ☐ the relationship between two variables

6 *Which of the following is a definition of a positive correlation?*

a) ☐ as one variable increases so does the other
b) ☐ as one variable increases, the other decreases
c) ☐ one variable causes a change in the other
d) ☐ a significant result

7 *Which of the following is a definition of a negative correlation?*

a) ☐ as one variable increases so does the other
b) ☐ as one variable increases, the other decreases
c) ☐ one variable causes a change in the other
d) ☐ a significant result

8 *Which of the following is a correlation hypothesis?*

a) ☐ time of day will affect scores on a psychology test
b) ☐ chewing gum will affect scores on a psychology test
c) ☐ there will be a relationship between students' self-assessment of ability in psychology and their scores on a psychology test
d) ☐ students who do three hours revision every night will do better than those who do no revision

Answers: 1 b; 2 d; 3 c; 4 b; 5 a; 6 a; 7 b; 8 c

Strengths and weaknesses of experimental methods

Using the information provided on pages 112–117, summarise the strengths and weaknesses of each method.

Experimental methods		Observational methods	
Strengths	**Weaknesses**	**Strengths**	**Weaknesses**

Self report methods		Correlation methods	
Strengths	**Weaknesses**	**Strengths**	**Weaknesses**

Which method?

Using the information in the Core Studies section, try to complete the table below by filling in the method used in each study. Remember that they may have used more than one. Why not check your answers with those of another student?

Name of Study	Type of method used
Loftus and Palmer	
Baron-Cohen et al	
Savage-Rumbaugh et al	
Samuel and Bryant	
Bandura, Ross and Ross	
Freud	
Maguire et al	
Dement and Kleitman	
Sperry	
Milgram	
Reicher and Haslam	
Piliavin, Rodin and Piliavin	
Rosenhan	
Thigpen and Cleckley	
Griffiths	

Method strengths and weaknesses

Using the information in this section, match the strength/weakness to the method by circling the appropriate method in the table. There may be more than one method to circle for each strength or weakness. Why not check your answers with those of another student?

Strengths

High ecological validity	lab experiment/field experiment/quasi-experiment/observation/self-report/correlation/ case study
Easy to replicate	lab experiment/field experiment/quasi-experiment/observation/self-report/correlation/ case study
Asking people directly rather than trying to infer something from their behaviour	lab experiment/field experiment/quasi-experiment/observation/self-report/correlation/ case study
Less chance of demand characteristics	lab experiment/field experiment/quasi-experiment/observation/self-report/correlation/ case study
Allows you to investigate relationships without manipulating data	lab experiment/field experiment/quasi-experiment/observation/self-report/correlation/ case study
Large amounts of data can be collected relatively quickly	lab experiment/field experiment/quasi-experiment/observation/self-report/correlation/ case study
High levels of control	lab experiment/field experiment/quasi-experiment/observation/self report/correlation/ case study
Allows for control of extraneous variables	lab experiment/field experiment/quasi experiment/observation/self report/correlation/ case study
Allows behaviours to be precisely coded or categorised	lab experiment/field experiment/quasi-experiment/observation/self-report/correlation/ case study
May be a useful starting point for research	lab experiment/field experiment/quasi-experiment/observation/self-report/correlation/ case study

Weaknesses

Low ecological validity	lab experiment/field experiment/quasi-experiment/observation/self-report/correlation/case study
Hard to replicate	lab experiment/field experiment/quasi-experiment/observation/self-report/correlation/case study
Participants may be subject to demand characteristics	lab experiment/field experiment/quasi-experiment/observation/self-report/correlation/case study
Participants may respond to social desirability bias	lab experiment/field experiment/quasi-experiment/observation/self-report/correlation/case study
Lack of control over variables	lab experiment/field experiment/quasi-experiment/observation/self-report/correlation/case study
Low generalisability	lab experiment/field experiment/quasi-experiment/observation/self-report/correlation/case study
Difficult to draw cause and effect conclusion	lab experiment/field experiment/quasi-experiment/observation/self-report/correlation/case study
May have problems with validity of questions	lab experiment/field experiment/quasi-experiment/observation/self-report/correlation/case study
May have problems with inter-rater reliability	lab experiment/field experiment/quasi-experiment/observation/self-report/correlation/case study
May be reductionist	lab experiment/field experiment/quasi-experiment/observation/self-report/correlation/case study

Ideas for research activities

You will gain a greater understanding of all these issues if you have a go at some research yourself. Although you will no doubt have done this already during your course, here are some mini activities to try.

Experiments

1. Design and conduct an experiment to see if psychology students are better at solving psychology-related anagrams than non-psychology students. You can find some anagrams on pages 81 and 82.
2. Write an alternate hypothesis for this experiment.
3. Write a null hypothesis for this experiment.
4. Identify the independent and dependent variables.
5. Which design have you used for this experiment?
6. Are there any ethical issues you should consider?
7. Calculate the mean scores for each condition.
8. Display these scores in a bar graph.
9. What conclusions can you reach?

If you were going to repeat this experiment, what improvements would you make?

What effect do you think these improvements would have?

Observations

1. Design an observation to find out which are the most popular fashion accessories (scarves, earrings, bag charms etc.).
2. Outline the categories that you will use for this observation.
3. Who will you observe?
4. Where will you observe?
5. How long will you observe for?
6. Are there any ethical issues you should consider?
7. Display your results in a table.
8. What conclusions can you reach?

If you were going to repeat this observation, what improvements would you make?

What effect do you think these improvements would have?

Self-reports

1. Design an investigation to find out which subjects are the most popular in your school or college.
2. Write at least one closed question.
3. Write at least one open question.
4. Write at least one question that uses a rating scale.
5. How many people are you going to question?
6. How are you going to select your sample?
7. Are there any ethical issues that you need to consider?
8. Display your results in a table.
9. What conclusions can you reach?

If you were going to conduct this investigation again, what improvements would you make?

What effect do you think these improvements would have?

Correlation

1. Design a study to see if there is a correlation between how much paid work students do and how much homework they do.
2. Write a correlational hypothesis for this investigation.
3. Do you think that there will be a negative correlation or a positive correlation between these variables?
4. Write a null hypothesis for this investigation.
5. Explain how you will measure the first variable.
6. Explain how you will measure the second variable.
7. How many participants are you going to have?
8. How are you going to select your sample?
9. Display your results in a scattergraph.
10. What conclusions can you reach?

If you were going to conduct this investigation again, what improvements would you make?

What effect do you think these improvements would have?

Psychological Investigations crossword

Clues

Across

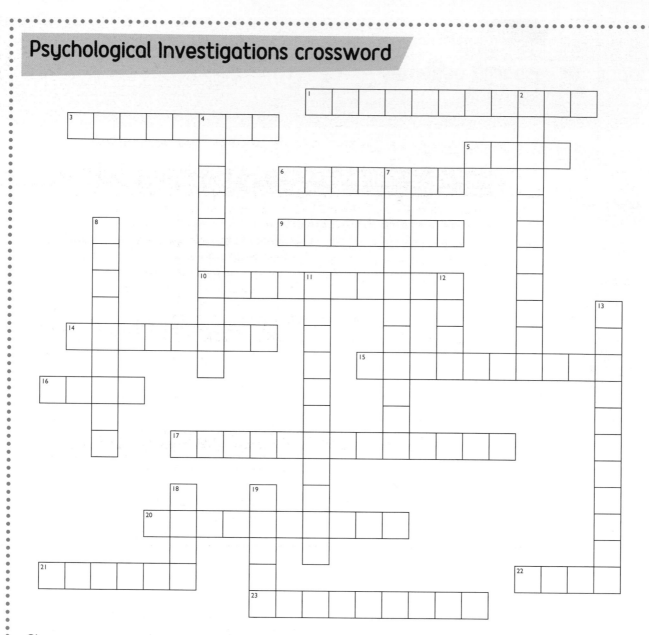

1. doing the research again (11)
3. this researcher used participant observation (8)
5. most common score (4)
6. all research should be this (7)
9. this researcher conducted his research in a laboratory (7)
10. the method that involves manipulation of variables (10)
14. accuracy of results (8)
15. techniques for analysing data (10)
16. the hypothesis that predicts no difference (4)
17. a self-report technique (13)
20. most experiments take place here (10)
21. the participants (6)
22. measure of central tendency (4)
23. the variable that is measured by the researcher (9)

Down

2. the variable that is manipulated by the researcher (11)
4. a prediction (10)
7. a relationship between two variables (11)
8. a hypothesis predicting the direction of the effect (3–6)
11. consistency of results (11)
12. you could measure IQ with one of these (4)
13. a method of research where researchers simply watch and record (11)
18. a study with a single participant (4)
19. this researcher conducted a case study (5)

Answers:

Across: 1. replication; 3. Rosenhan; 5. mode; 6. ethical; 9. Milgram; 10. experiment; 14. validity; 15. statistics; 16. null; 17. questionnaire; 20. laboratory; 21. sample; 22. mean; 23. dependent

Down: 2. independent; 4. hypothesis; 7. correlation; 8. one-tailed; 11. reliability; 12. test; 13. observation; 18. case; 19. Freud

Exam**Café**

Question (taken from OCR Specimen Paper)

A researcher has conducted an experiment to see if people recall more words from a list of ten words when they learn and recall in the same room rather than if they learn in one room and recall in a different room. This was an independent measures design.

The results were as follows:

Number of words recalled	Recall in same room	Recall in different room
	9	2
	8	6
	8	8
	7	6
	7	7
	8	9

1. a. Suggest an appropriate null hypothesis for this experiment. (4)

   b. Identify the independent variable and the dependent variable in this experiment. (2)

2. a. What is meant by an 'independent measures' design? (2)

   b. What is meant by a 'repeated measures' design? (2)

   c. Outline one strength and one weakness of using an independent measures design for this experiment. (6)

3. Outline two findings that might be drawn from this data (4)

Sample answer: Candidate 1

1a. People will recall more words when they recall in the same room as learning.

This is not a null hypothesis. Remember that a null hypothesis predicts that there will be no effect or no difference. A null hypothesis would be something like, 'There will be no difference between the number of words recalled from a list of ten where participants recall in the same room as learning compared to recalling in a different room from learning'.

This might seem quite complex but remember that there are four marks available for this and the examiner will be looking for a high level of detail and accuracy.

Sample answer: Candidate 1

1b. The room and the words.

First of all you need to state which variable is which. The correct answer is that the IV is whether people recall in the same room as learning or recall in a different room from learning, and the DV is the number of words recalled. 'The room' is partially correct but the examiner would probably not award any marks here as the answer is too vague.

Sample answer: Candidate 1

2a. Using different people.

The correct answer should explain that an independent measures design is where different people are used in each condition of the experiment. Simply saying 'using different people' is not giving the examiner enough information. However there is some indication that the candidate is on the right lines.

Sample answer: Candidate 1

2b. Using the same people.

The previous comment also applies to this answer.

Sample answer: Candidate 1

2c. The strength is that people won't get bored and the weakness is that they are different people.

There are six marks available here! This means that six minutes could be spent on this answer. To achieve full marks you need to fully explain the strength of the independent measures design and relate this to this experiment. You then need to do the same thing for the weakness. This answer would get some credit for identifying the strength but this needs to be described and explained in a lot more detail as well as clearly linking this to the study. The answer also needs to identify the weakness more clearly and then explain and link this to the study.

Sample answer: Candidate 1

3. People do better in the same room. The number of words recalled in the same room is higher than the number of words recalled in the different room.

The first sentence is vague – people do better at what? Compared to what? The second sentence is clear and really is a better worded version of the first sentence. The examiner would credit one clear finding here.

Overall this is a weak answer, although it is possible that the candidate left the exam feeling quite confident. Apart from their mistake in question one (giving an experimental hypothesis when a null was asked for) the rest of the answers suggest that this candidate may have been able to score more marks if they had explained their answers more fully. It is also likely that this candidate did not use the full 20 minutes for this answer.

Write some advice for this candidate here. This has been started for you.

Remember!

1 Read the question properly.

2 ____________________________________

3 ____________________________________

4 ____________________________________

Here are the answers given by two other candidates to the same examination question. Read their answers and comment on the strengths and weaknesses. Which answer do you think is the stronger one? Why? What might a candidate do to improve the quality of their answer? Write your comments in the box provided. Suggested answers can be found on page 124.

	Candidate 2	Candidate 3	Comments
Q1a (4 marks)	There will be no difference between the conditions.	There will be no difference between the number of words recalled by participants who learn and recall in the same room and participants who learn and recall in different rooms.	e.g. Candidate 3's answer is much stronger as it includes details of …
Q1b (2 marks)	The independent variable is the room and the dependent variable is the number of words recalled.	The independent variable is whether participants learn and recall in the same room or whether they learn and recall in different rooms. The dependent variable is the number of words recalled from a list of ten.	
Q2a (2 marks)	An independent measures design is where different people are used.	An independent measures design is where different people are used in each condition of the experiment.	e.g. Candidate 3 has given a clearer answer because …
Q2b (2 marks)	A repeated measures design is where the same people are used.	A repeated measures design is where the same people are used in each condition of the experiment.	

	Candidate 2	Candidate 3	Comments
Q2c (6 marks)	One strength of an independent measures design is that people are less likely to work out the aim of the experiment as they do not take part in the other condition and are less likely to work out what the experimenter is testing. One weakness of an independent measures design is that you are using different people in each condition and there might be differences between them that cause your results rather than your independent variable.	One strength of an independent measures design is that people only take part in one condition. In this study participants only took part in the 'same room' condition or the 'different room' condition and should not have been able to work out the aim of the experiment. This means that they are less likely to respond to demand characteristics such as trying harder in the 'same room' condition as that is what they think the experimenter expects. One weakness of an independent measures design is that you are using different people in each condition and there might be differences between them that cause your results rather than your independent variable. For example, the people in the 'same room' condition may have much better memories naturally than the people in the other condition and this may be the reason for the differences in scores rather than the manipulation of the independent variable.	
Q3. (4 marks)	One finding is that the participants who learned and recalled in the same room recalled more words than those participants who learned and recalled in different rooms. A second finding is that the range of the scores is much greater in the second condition.	One finding is that the participants who learned and recalled in the same room recalled more words than those participants who learned and recalled in different rooms. A second finding is that the range of the scores is much greater in the 'different room' condition as the scores range from 2–9. In the 'same room' condition the scores range from 7–9.	

Have a go at an exam question

This question was taken from the OCR Specimen Paper.

Exam question

A researcher wishes to conduct an observation of student's use of free time in college.

1. Describe and evaluate a suitable procedure for this observation. (10)
2. Describe one ethical issue that the researcher needs to consider when conducting this observation and suggest how this could be dealt with. (4)
3. a. Explain what is meant by inter-rater reliability. (2)
   b. Suggest how the researcher could ensure that this observation has inter-rater reliability. (4)

You are still working to the 'mark a minute' rule here so you have 20 minutes for this whole question and you should spend ten minutes on the first question.

Exam question

1. Describe and evaluate a suitable procedure for this observation.

Examiner hint – there are two parts to this question as you have to describe the procedure that you would use and then evaluate it.

First you need to describe the procedure that you would use. Try to write an answer to this part of the question using the following prompts.

- Say where the observation would take place.
- Say where the observer(s) would be located.
- Say how long the observation would last or how many people would be observed.
- Explain the behaviour categories that you would use (you could sketch out your coding sheet if that is easier).
- Outline any instructions that observers would need, any definitions of behaviour categories if they are not self-evident and any other information that you think someone would need to replicate this observation.

Now you need to evaluate your procedure (you could look back at the section on strengths and weaknesses of observations to help you). Try to write an answer to this part of the question using the following prompts.

- What strengths does this procedure have?
- What weaknesses does this procedure have?
- Look back at all the decisions that you have made in the first part of the study and try to justify them. For example, you could say that your choice of location is good because there will be a range of students there, that the place you choose to observe from is appropriate because people won't be aware of what you are doing or that the categories you have chosen will be easy to record. You could also consider whether there might be weaknesses with the location as the results will only generalise to a certain group or that the categories are too simplistic and won't allow you to draw conclusions about certain things.

You could give your answer to another psychology student and ask them to read it. Do they think it makes sense? Could they carry out this observation or would they need any other information?

Exam question

2. Describe an ethical issue that the researcher needs to consider when conducting this observation and suggest how this could be dealt with. (4)

This is a four mark question so you don't need to spend as long on this or write as much as you did for the previous question.

Hint – ethical issues include informed consent, confidentiality, deception, distress and right to withdraw. For example, you could discuss the issue of confidentiality and explain that you would not record students' names or anything that might allow them to be identified in order to make sure that this guideline was not broken. Choose one of the other issues and briefly explain how it relates to your observation and say how you would deal with it.

Exam question

3a. Explain what is meant by inter-rater reliability (2)

You should know the answer to this, but if not you can find it on page 95.

Exam question

3b. Suggest how the researcher could ensure that this observation has inter-rater reliability. (4)

In other words, how would you ensure that two or more observers used the coding scheme in exactly the same way? This might involve the instructions that you give them, training them or conducting a pilot (or practice) study, or keeping the categories simple so that observers are not faced with difficult or subjective decisions.

Remember that this question is not asking you about *measuring* the amount of agreement that there is between observers but about how to ensure that you *get* agreement between observers.

Another practice question

These questions have also been taken from the OCR Specimen Paper.

Exam question

A researcher has conducted a correlational study to investigate the relationship between how good people think their memory is and how well they do on a memory task. The first variable was 'self-rating of memory' and was measured by asking people to rate their memory on a 10 point scale (where 1 = very poor and 10 = excellent). The second variable was 'actual memory' and this was measured by showing them a video of a minor road accident and asking them a series of ten eyewitness questions.

Results were as follows:

Participant no	Self-rating of memory	Score on memory test
1	3	5
2	4	6
3	5	4
4	8	8
5	9	7
6	10	9
7	7	6
8	7	8
9	5	6
10	6	7

1. a. Sketch an appropriately labelled scattergraph displaying the results. (4)

   b. Outline one conclusion that can be drawn from this scattergraph. (3)

2. Suggest one problem with the way 'self-rating of memory' has been measured in this investigation. (3)

3. Describe and evaluate two other ways in which 'actual memory' might be measured. (10)

Total marks = 20

Suggested Answers

Loftus and Palmer (p 6)

1. One strength of using a sample like this could be the fact that the participants are readily available to the researcher (opportunity sample). Another strength could be the fact that they may be a group of relatively similar people, similar ages, experiences etc. This would reduce the amount of variability within and between the groups and may be seen as a type of control. A weakness of using this sample could be that a group of psychology students may have more knowledge of research methods than other groups and so might be more prone to demand characteristics. In other words they might be more likely to guess what the researchers are looking for and this is likely to affect the way that they behave. Another weakness may be that a group of students are likely to be a relatively young group and therefore may have limited driving experience. This might make them less able to estimate speed than other groups and perhaps more prone to the effects of the leading questions. They may also be more used to learning and remembering information compared to non-students.

2. There are many different groups that you could suggest here. You could suggest a group with driving experience such as taxi drivers or a group who may have more experience in estimating speed such as police officers. You could also suggest a group representing a wider range of ages and experiences.

   If you chose taxi drivers or police officers, one possible effect might be that their speed estimates would be more accurate and they might be less influenced by the leading verbs.

3. The obvious strength to mention would be the high levels of control that are possible in a laboratory experiment. Here the experimenters were able to ensure that everyone saw the same film and were asked the same questions at the same time. The major weakness would be the unrealistic nature of viewing a film of a car crash. It is difficult to know whether people would respond in the same way in a real-life situation. Another weakness is that people know that they are taking part in an experiment and this will have an effect on their behaviour.

4. There are many ways that EWT could be investigated outside the laboratory and the most likely answer here would be to suggest a 'staged' incident in a public place. This would have the opposite strengths and weaknesses to a laboratory experiment. It would be 'real', have high ecological validity and the participants would be unlikely to demonstrate demand characteristics. On the other hand, it would be very difficult to control the situation and there are likely to be a number of confounding variables making the results more difficult to interpret. This type of research may also raise ethical issues.

Baron-Cohen et al (p 10)

1. There are a number of improvements actually suggested in the article. The authors comment on the fact that judging emotion from a section of the face (showing just the eyes) is not the way that these judgements would be made normally. So one suggestion you could make is that whole faces might be shown rather than just the eye area. You could give as a reason for this the fact that it would be more like real-life and that the results would therefore be more applicable to real-life situations. You could also suggest that giving people only two choices of emotion for each photo may be a problem as they have a 50:50 chance of getting this right by guessing. So an improvement might be to give more than two emotion 'labels' to choose from. This would reduce the possibility of participants simply guessing correctly and would make the results more valid. You could also suggest increasing the size of the sample, although in general the more specific your suggestion is to the study the more likely you are to gain full marks.

2. The strengths of collecting quantitative data in this study are that the results are simple and easy to measure. There is little risk of researcher bias as there is no interpretation of the results required. The participant has simply got the answer right or wrong. However it could be argued that a weakness of this is that the answers are lacking detail and it might have been interesting to explore the answers in more depth. There are several ways in which this might have been done. Asking people 'why' they chose one word rather than another would allow the researchers to explore the processes by which this decision was reached. However this would be difficult to analyse and subject to bias. It would also be an extremely difficult thing to ask participants to do (think about the problems associated with the 'thinking-aloud' technique in the Griffiths study) especially those with autism or Asperger's Syndrome who may well struggle with communicating this kind of information.

Savage-Rumbaugh (p 14)

1. Longitudinal studies allow the collection of huge amounts of data and they also allow the researcher to study development in the same person/animal over time. This is advantageous as the differences between subjects which might occur in cross-sectional designs have been eliminated. It is also highly advantageous when studying any form of development. One weakness in the way that this study has been conducted could be the fact that there are large differences between the rearing environments of the two species. Any example of this would be appropriate and then you can suggest how the learning environments could be controlled in order to make them more similar. This would make the results easier to compare. It would allow us to establish whether any difference in performance between the two species is due to their innate abilities or to the environment in which they were taught. This would allow us to consider issues such as the nature–nurture debate.

2. There are several ethical issues that you could consider here. For example, the chimps were not in their natural habitat, were not given their natural diet and may have become distressed or frustrated by their experiences. You could also consider the wider ethical issue of whether we have the right to use animals in this kind of research. The answer to the final question is up to you. You may think that the study contributes greatly to our knowledge about language, communication, animal abilities etc. and that any ethical 'costs' are outweighed by the benefits. On the other hand you may feel strongly that the ethical costs outweigh any benefits gained from this research. Whichever view you hold, you need to explain your reasoning. Of course, it is also acceptable to present both sides of the argument in an answer like this.

Samuel and Bryant (p 20)

1. The main problem with this sample is that all the children came from the same part of the country. It is possible that all these children have been educated in particular ways that differ from other parts of the country (this study was conducted pre-National Curriculum). If this was the case, it would be very difficult to generalise these results to other areas. An appropriate alternative sample would therefore be one that was more representative of the whole of the UK for example. This would allow us to generalise from our results with more confidence.
2. The quantitative data collected in this study is simple and easy to collect. It is also easy to analyse and unlikely to be subject to researcher bias as there is no subjective analysis taking place. However it lacks detail, specifically of the reasons why the children made the choices that they did. You could suggest that the researchers asked the children to explain the reasoning behind their choices which would generate qualitative data, although this may be difficult to analyse and interpret.
3. You could suggest any kind of improvement here. One suggestion might be that you could make the task more realistic, perhaps by asking children to choose drinks or cakes of different shapes (but the same volume or mass). It would be hard to conduct the transformation in quite the same way with a cake but it would provide more realistic results. There might be marketing applications here too – why do manufacturers choose the bottle shape that they do for their soft drinks? You could also suggest that a longitudinal approach might have been more appropriate than a cross-sectional one. This would involve taking a group of children at around the age of four and testing them every year. This would obviously take a much longer time than using groups of children of different ages but would allow you to monitor development in the same individuals thus reducing the possibility of differences between the groups confounding the results.

Bandura (p 25)

1. The strength of conducting research in a laboratory is the high level of control that it gives the experimenter. This is particularly important when a large number of participants are tested one at a time as happened in this study. It is crucial that every participant in the same condition experiences the events in exactly the same way, otherwise there are confounding variables which make the results very difficult to interpret. The weakness is the artificial nature of the laboratory and the difficulty of knowing whether this is how participants would behave in 'real-life' situations. You could also consider the ethical implications of laboratory experiments, especially where children are concerned. You could suggest a variety of ways in which this research could have been conducted outside the laboratory. You could design a study involving a 'staged' incident of violence or you could conduct observational research of children before and after watching their normal choice of television programmes. The strengths and weaknesses will vary depending on what you suggest but the likely strengths are higher ecological validity, lower demand characteristics and possibly fewer ethical issues. The weaknesses are likely to be lower levels of control (more confounding variables).
2. There are a number of ethical issues raised by this study. You could discuss the issue of informed consent which should be given by parents when children are to take part in psychological research. Were the parents given a full account of what was going to happen to their child? You could also consider the possible distress caused to the child and also the potential for long term harm. Is it ethical to deliberately set out to make a child act violently? One way of improving the ethics might be to suggest far more information was given to parents – the effect of this might be that you would have no participants. Another suggestion might be to call a halt to the experiment if a child shows any sign of distress – again the possible effect might be that you would end up with very little data. You could also consider changing the experiment so that less distress/harm is likely – making the violence less extreme for example.

Freud (p 29)

1. The strengths of case studies are the amount of rich, detailed data that can be collected and the fact that they often have specific therapeutic aims. The weaknesses are their lack of generalisability to other people and the fact that researchers can often get over involved and hence prone to bias.
2. One strength of the way that data was collected in this study could be the amount of detail that was recorded by Hans' father and sent to Freud. A weakness is that these reports are likely to be biased in some form, either through selection of what to send (and what not to send), the use of leading questions when questioning Hans or the fact that his father was a great fan of Freud's work and would no doubt have attempted his own analysis of the data before he sent it to Freud. Of course, another weakness is that Freud only met Hans on one occasion and conducted his analysis 'second-hand'.
3. Improvements could include more direct contact with Hans, the removal of the father's interpretation of the data, the study of more children as comparisons or the involvement of another more objective researcher or therapist. These improvements would reduce bias and allow more reliable and generalisable conclusions to be drawn.

Maguire (p 35)

1. One strength of this study could be the use of both quasi-experimental and correlational techniques. Taken together the results provide much stronger evidence for a relationship between navigational experience and hippocampal size than would be possible if only a quasi-experiment or a correlation had been conducted. The weaknesses of quasi-experiments include the fact that there might be other differences between the groups and so it is harder to conclude that the IV directly affected the DV. In correlational research it is not possible to draw cause and effect conclusions at all as there has been no manipulation of the IV.
2. The major strengths of MRI scans is the precise nature of the measurement. It is unlikely that there could be any bias in this form of measurement and almost impossible for participants to be responding to any form of demand characteristics. They are also very safe.
3. One advantage of using a highly discrete sample of this kind is that you are able to explore the effects of highly specific experiences. This is of more use in this kind of research than selecting a highly representative sample of participants with a wide variety of navigational experiences. You could suggest alternative samples with navigation – related careers, such as flight navigators, pilots, other professional drivers etc. You could also suggest the inclusion of female participants or left-handed participants.
4. Any improvement/change to the sample would be appropriate here. You could also suggest the use of a more longitudinal approach, perhaps scanning the brain of the same individuals at regular intervals during training and at regular intervals after qualifying would allow you to see change in the hippocampal size, rather than inferring that the growth must have taken place (the correlational results strongly suggest this).

5. The practical applications are all based on the fact that the results strongly support the notion that the brain has 'plasticity'. This has significant implications for those who have experienced brain damage or disease as they suggest that the grey matter of the brain can in some way 'mend itself'.

Dement and Kleitman (p 39)

1. The sample used in this study is a relatively small one. Although this might lead to some concerns about the extent to which the results can be generalised, it does mean that the participants can be studied in a great deal of depth. You could also consider whether sample sizes in physiological research need to be as large as they do for social psychological research.
2. One example of quantitative data is the number of people who could or could not recall their dreams in REM or NREM sleep. One example of qualitative data is the descriptions people gave of the contents of their dreams. You should be familiar with the strengths and weaknesses of different types of data by now but if you are not, the strengths of quantitative data include the ease with which it can be collected and analysed and the weaknesses include its lack of depth/detail and the fact that it may be reductionist. The strengths of qualitative data are its richness (depth and detail) but it is harder to compare and much harder to analyse.
3. Sleeping in a laboratory is probably not much like sleeping in your own bed at home. Many people sleep poorly in hotel rooms so it is reasonable to suggest that someone sleeping in a laboratory with electrodes attached to them and with the knowledge that their sleep is going to be both observed and disturbed will not sleep well. This means that the results may be difficult to generalise to 'normal' sleep. You could suggest conducting this study in the participant's home although this would have a number of practical implications. Large pieces of equipment would need to be moved, experimenters would need some space and it would not be possible to have the same level of control over the environment.

Sperry (p 43)

1. Quasi-experimental research allows you to study variables that you can't manipulate experimentally. This could be for either practical or ethical reasons. For example, people would not consent to have their corpus callosum severed just because Sperry asked them to and so he took advantage of cases where this had happened for medical reasons. The disadvantages of quasi-experimental research include the lack of control over other variables and the lack of experimental manipulation means that it harder to draw cause and effect conclusions.
2. In some ways this can be considered as a representative sample as it was a large proportion of the people that had had this operation. So it would allow you to generalise the results with some confidence to other people who have had the same operation. On the other hand, it is more difficult to know if these people can represent 'normal' people who have not had this operation. It is possible that these 11 people may have had other differences or damage to their brain which might make them a non-representative sample.
3. There is no right or wrong answer here. Perhaps you could suggest seeing what everyday tasks they struggle with or asking them (or someone else) to keep a diary of these problems. This would obviously give you very useful data about the practical problems experienced by such patients but would be lacking in control and might be very difficult to analyse.
4. His contributions were considered significant enough to award him a Nobel Prize so clearly a lot of people in the scientific community would regard his work as useful. He revealed a great deal about the functioning of the two hemispheres and his experimental techniques were groundbreaking at the time. His work has been supported and extended by others although more recent research suggests that the degree of separation between the hemispheres is perhaps not as great as once thought.

Milgram (p 49)

1. There are obviously a number of ethical concerns raised by this study. These include the lack of informed consent, the lack of the right to withdraw, deception and distress. In an examination answer you should briefly outline why the study raises these concerns rather than simply identifying them. For example participants were told not the full details of the study; they were deceived about the drawing of lots, the shocks, the fact that the learner was a confederate and the real of aim of the study. They were 'prodded' to continue rather than being told that they could stop at any time and they were seriously distressed by the situation that they found themselves in.
   To conduct this study without breaking ethical guidelines is something of a challenge but if you take one issue at a time you can explore the effects of removing this concern. For example, if participants were told the full details of the study what effect do you think this would have on their behaviour? Would they continue because they knew that no one was getting hurt or would they refuse to administer any shocks at all? Perhaps you could also suggest that the results would have less application to real life but also that participants would not suffer the same level of distress. The question of whether there would be any point in conducting the research in this way also needs to be considered.
2. You could suggest a number of things as improvements. Using female participants might allow you to explore whether males or females are more obedient and using a female experimenter would allow you to explore which sex has the most authority. Taking the experiment out of the prestigious environment of Yale University would allow you to explore the extent to which this contributed to the high levels of obedience. Bringing the learner closer to the teacher would also allow us to explore the extent to which obedience is increased when the victim cannot be seen. All of these variables have been explored by Milgram and it might be interesting to research some of these as part of your exam preparation.

Reicher and Haslam (p 53)

1. This study collected both qualitative and quantitative measures. Examples of the quantitative measures include the daily physiological measures that were taken and the psychometric tests. The qualitative measures include the observation and recording of the participants at all times. This allows the researchers to illustrate their conclusions with examples and quotations from the participants. You should be familiar with the strengths and weaknesses of both types of data by now but briefly, the strengths of quantitative measures are the ease with which they can be collected, compared and analysed and the weaknesses are their lack of detail and their tendency to reductionism. The strengths and weaknesses of qualitative data are the reverse. They allow for detailed and in-depth analysis of a subject although they can be difficult to interpret and analyse.
2. One weakness could be the fact that this study was conducted in a BBC studio and four one-hour programmes were made. This means that the participants knew that some of their behaviour would be on television and this might have influenced their behaviour in a number of ways. Participants may have been reluctant to behave in certain negative ways due to this knowledge. One suggestion might be to remove the televised aspect of this study and to consider what effect this might have on the results.

Piliavin, Rodin and Piliavin (p 57)

1. The sample used was a large and varied group of people who happened to be on the train and did not know that they were part of an experiment. Alternative samples could include conducting the experiments at specific times of day, perhaps before 9am in order to see if a group of mainly working people behave any differently, or on different trains going to different places, or with more or less time between stops to see if there are differences. You could also suggest using a sample of volunteers to see what difference this would make. This last suggestion would not raise the same ethical issues as the original, although their knowledge of the study would no doubt influence their behaviour.

2. An obvious alternative to a field experiment would be a laboratory experiment. This would involve creating a similar emergency in a more controlled setting (strength) but perhaps losing something in terms of ecological validity (weakness). Another alternative would be to conduct a piece of questionnaire research. This might involve a number of written scenarios and participants would have to rate how likely they would be to help in each situation. The strengths would include the large numbers of variables that could be explored and the large number of participants who could be quickly and easily questioned. However the obvious weakness would be that of social desirability – participants might feel that they have to give certain answers in order to 'look good' and this might tell you nothing at all about how they would really behave if faced with that situation.

3. One of the ethical concerns with this study is the lack of informed consent. Although guidelines say that people can be observed in public places without their consent, this is an experiment rather than an observation as it involves the manipulation of variables. One way of dealing with this issue might be to put posters on the carriage doors explaining that an experiment is going to take place. This would have the effect of reducing any distress caused by viewing the emergency situation although it might raise another problem. If there was a real emergency people might assume that it was part of the experiment and not respond as quickly or take the situation as seriously.

Rosenhan (p 63)

1. The participant observation method has many strengths. The observer often becomes totally immersed in the situation. The observer is unknown to the participants who are not even aware that research is taking place. This means that their behaviour will be totally natural as they will not be responding to the demand characteristics that would exist if they knew that they were taking part in research. Most participant research takes places over a relatively long time span as opposed to being a 'snapshot' view taken over a very short time span. However, as with any observational research, the data that is recorded can be dependent upon the interpretations of the observer and may also be influenced by their existing opinions and expectations. Participant observation also raises ethical issues of consent and confidentiality.

2. There are several ethical issues raised by this study. First, the participants were not asked for their consent before the study began as they were unaware that the research was taking place. They were clearly also being deceived and there is the potential for distress once the study is made public. The study could have been conducted without breaking ethical guidelines by making it an overt observation, that is, an observation that all the participants were aware of. However, this is likely to have such dramatic effects on the behaviour of those being observed that it worth considering whether anything useful could be learned through this method.

3. This could be answered either way. If you think that yes, the research should have been conducted you would need to back up your answer with arguments. You could include the argument that no other method would have allowed the researchers to collect such accurate data and you could also argue that the research was extremely useful. On the other hand, you could argue that for ethical reasons the research is unacceptable. You could also consider the arguments of Spitzer (see page 129 of your textbook) who claims that many of Rosenhan's conclusions are flawed and that his criticisms of the diagnostic process are unjustified.

Thigpen and Cleckley (p 68)

1. Case studies are extremely useful in therapeutic situations when the focus is on dealing with an individual case. They allow a large amount of detailed data to be collected which will help the therapeutic process for that individual as well as contribute to a body of knowledge that may be useful to other therapists dealing with similar cases. The disadvantage is that as only one participant is being studied it is very difficult to generalise findings to other people and there is the potential for the researchers (therapists) to become over involved with the individual and lose their objectivity.

2. An obvious improvement would be suggesting that more cases of MPD are considered to increase the generalisability of the results. However you should remember that this is a report of a therapeutic process conducted with a single patient and the aims of this research were to help this patient. You could also suggest that more objective researchers or therapists could be involved who were unaware of Thigpen and Cleckley's diagnosis of MPD. This may reduce the effects of over involvement in the case. You could also suggest that the tests conducted on the three personalities be repeated several times. This would increase the reliability of these measures. For example, although the IQ scores of Eve White and Eve Black were different, they were not dramatically different and perhaps the same person could show this difference if tested on different days.

3. Researcher bias refers to the researcher's ideas, opinions and expectations about the research. It is possible that researchers can influence the outcome of even the most controlled laboratory research and this is the reason that 'double-blind' research is sometimes conducted. In case studies, the potential for researcher bias is even greater. There are several examples of this in this study. The researchers believed that they were dealing with a case of MPD and therefore may be more inclined to interpret behavioural change within the context of this diagnosis.

4. There are several aspects that you could put forward to argue that the research was useful. It contributes to our knowledge of a still controversial diagnosis and this is valuable. You could also argue that the treatment Eve received was useful to her. However there is still a debate over whether or not Eve was simply a very good actress and whether Thigpen and Cleckley were fooled into believing her.

Griffiths (p 72)

1. The main advantage of conducting the research in an amusement arcade is that it gives the research high levels of ecological validity. The study was examining fruit machine gamblers and so they were being studied in their normal gambling environment. However there is little control over extraneous variables in this environment and conditions may have been different for different participants.

2. Griffiths reports that the 'thinking aloud' technique proved very difficult for participants and it could be argued that the data

collected is largely descriptive rather than explanatory. The coding of the data collected also had low inter-rater reliability.

3. There are no major ethical concerns with this study. The participants gave their informed consent, were not deceived and there was little if any potential to cause distress. It could perhaps be argued that the research encourages gambling but this would be a very minor point.

4. Perhaps the research could look at female gamblers to see if there are any significant differences, although the majority of fruit machine gamblers are male. Perhaps it would be interesting to compare regular and occasional gamblers or even regular gamblers who had serious financial or other problems stemming from their gambling with regular gamblers without these problems. This would perhaps increase the usefulness of the research in terms of helping to understand problem gambling.

Suggested answers for comparison task (p 115-16)

Q1a. Candidate 3 has given more detail than Candidate 2. Candidate 2 has provided a correct but very general null hypothesis which is not specific to this study. Candidate 3 has provided details of both independent and dependent variables and this is an example of a very strong answer.

Q1b. Candidate 2 has identified 'the room' as the independent variable, which is not quite correct. The independent variable is, as Candidate 3 rightly says, whether someone is asked to learn and recall in the same room or learn in one room and recall in another room. It would be good practice to give this level of detail so that the examiner can be absolutely sure that you understand. There is not a huge difference in the answer given regarding the dependent variable, but Candidate 3 has given a more specific answer and this level of detail is worth including.

Q2a. Once again, Candidate 3 has provided a clearer explanation. Although Candidate 2 is partially right, as an independent measures design does use different people, it is necessary to explain that this means that different people are used in each condition of the experiment.

Q2b. Exactly the same comment as provided for Q2a. Candidate 3 has provided a clear explanation whereas Candidate 2 has simply hinted at the answer.

Q2c. Both candidates have provided good explanations of the strength and weakness of independent measures design but Candidate 3 has gone further and related their answer to the study described in the question. Candidate 2's answer is interesting as it shows that they have a good understanding of the independent measures design which was not clear in the answer they gave to Q2a. This shows how important it is to explain yourself fully. It is also important to read the question carefully. In this question you are asked to give a strength and a weakness of using an independent measures design *for this experiment*. Candidate 3 has done this very well whereas Candidate 2 has given a general description of a strength and weakness of an independent measures design.

Q3. Both candidates have given a strong first finding but Candidate 3 has given a much clearer account of the second finding. Candidate 2 has simply referred to 'the second condition' rather than saying which condition this was, and there is a lack of detail in this answer.

Revision Card Template

The sample study card below can be used as a template to help with your revision.

Front:

Study:	
Aim:	
Participants	**Results**
Method	**Conclusions**

Back:

Study:	
Evaluation Issue 1	**Evaluation Issue 2**
Evaluation Issue 3	**Evaluation Issue 4**
Evaluation Issue 5	**Evaluation Issue 6**